Lecture Notes in Artificial Intelligence 10257

Subseries of Lecture Notes in Computer Science

LNAI Series Editors

Randy Goebel
  University of Alberta, Edmonton, Canada
Yuzuru Tanaka
  Hokkaido University, Sapporo, Japan
Wolfgang Wahlster
  DFKI and Saarland University, Saarbrücken, Germany

LNAI Founding Series Editor

Joerg Siekmann
  DFKI and Saarland University, Saarbrücken, Germany

More information about this series at http://www.springer.com/series/1244

Patrick Brézillon · Roy Turner
Carlo Penco (Eds.)

Modeling and Using Context

10th International and Interdisciplinary Conference, CONTEXT 2017
Paris, France, June 20–23, 2017
Proceedings

 Springer

Editors
Patrick Brézillon (iD)
Pierre and Marie Curie University
Paris
France

Carlo Penco (iD)
University of Genoa
Genoa
Italy

Roy Turner
University of Maine
Orono, ME
USA

ISSN 0302-9743   ISSN 1611-3349 (electronic)
Lecture Notes in Artificial Intelligence
ISBN 978-3-319-57836-1   ISBN 978-3-319-57837-8 (eBook)
DOI 10.1007/978-3-319-57837-8

Library of Congress Control Number: 2017938324

LNCS Sublibrary: SL7 – Artificial Intelligence

Printed on acid-free paper

This Springer imprint is published by Springer Nature
The registered company is Springer International Publishing AG
The registered company address is: Gewerbestrasse 11, 6330 Cham, Switzerland

Preface

Context affects virtually all aspects of behavior in animals, humans, and computer systems. It affects how we understand the world, communicate with others, and plan and carry out our actions. It affects how computer systems should behave so that they act appropriately for their situation and their users.

Contextual effects have been studied in many different disciplines over the years, but usually without too much interaction between the researchers in the different fields. This began to change in the mid-1990s, beginning in a small way with a 1993 International Joint Conference on AI workshop in on modeling context in knowledge representation and reasoning, which sought to bring together some of the various threads of context-related research. The interdisciplinary focus on context as a subject of research truly began in 1997, when the First International and Interdisciplinary Conference on Modeling and Using Context, CONTEXT 1997, was held in Rio de Janeiro.

Conferences since the original have been held in Trento, Italy (1999), Dundee, UK (2001), Stanford, California, USA (2003), Paris, France (2005), Roskilde, Denmark (2007), Karlsruhe, Germany (2011), Annecy, France (2013), and Larnaca, Cyprus (2015).

This volume contains the proceedings of the 10th CONTEXT Conference, held in Paris, France, during June 20–23, 2017. CONTEXT 2017 was a very special conference in the series: not only was it the 10th CONTEXT conference, it marked the 20th anniversary of the start of the series and the start of the interdisciplinary community focusing on context-related research.

CONTEXT conferences over the years have showcased papers from some of the leading thinkers on the subject as well as newcomers from fields as diverse as artificial intelligence, philosophy, linguistics, neuroscience, management, and computer applications, and have included world-renowned invited speakers. This year's conference included invited talks from Robert Stalnaker ("Conversational Strategy"), Fausto Giunchiglia ("Personal Context Modelling and Annotations"), and François Récanati ("Indexical Thought").

CONTEXT 2017 included several workshops that took place on the day prior to the main conference. These were: Context and Philosophy (C. Penco and M. Vignolo, chairs), Context in Management (F. Santoro, K. Revoredo, M. Borges, and J. Canos, chairs), Context in Learning (J. Bourdeau and T. Forissier, chairs), Quality Awareness in Modeling and Using Context in Applications (QAMUCA, S. Chabridon and P. Marie, chairs), and Context in the Explanation of Human Reasoning (M. Sbisand P. Labinaz, chairs).

We took an unusual approach to organization for this conference in which the boundary between workshop papers and main conference (plenary) papers was considerably more fluid than usual. This was done to get the best work presented to the community, even if that work was not initially considered by the authors to have broad appeal. All submitted papers, including those submitted to the workshops, were reviewed the same way, with the final disposition of the papers decided by the conference chairs in consultation with the workshop chairs. Some papers submitted to workshops, for example, were considered of sufficient merit and broad enough interest to be included in the plenary sessions. A special session of topic tracks included high-quality papers from the workshops that, while perhaps not of broad appeal, were still likely to interest a segment of the general attendees. This also encouraged the workshops to focus less on paper presentation and more on substantive discussions and work.

There were 88 papers submitted to the conference. Of these, 26 were accepted as plenary papers for an acceptance rate of 29%. Additionally, 15 papers were presented as part of the topic tracks sessions, and 15 were presented as posters at a special session in the evening of the first day of the main conference. All plenary, topic track, and poster papers appear in these proceedings.

Many people and organizations contributed to the success of CONTEXT 2017. We would like to thank the invited keynote speakers, the workshop chairs, and the Program Committee members for their efforts, as well the local student-workers at the conference venue. We would also like to thank the Pierre et Marie Curie University for being the setting for the conference, the EasyChair conference management system, and the editors at Springer (and Springer itself) for their help with myriad questions and issues. We would also like to thank the Northwestern Italian Philosophy Consortium (FINO) for their financial support for some of the conference attendees.

This conference was held at a time when other fields had begun to recognize context as a subject of study in its own right, but CONTEXT still remains the premier venue for bringing together researchers from many different fields to share ideas and discuss commonalities. We foresee a need for this kind of forum going forward, and we feel that the future is very promising for many more CONTEXT conferences.

March 2017   Patrick Brézillon
                                                                    Roy Turner
                                                                    Carlo Penco

Organization

Program Chairs

Patrick Brézillon   University Pierre and Marie Curie, France
Roy Turner   University of Maine, USA
Carlo Penco   University of Genoa, Italy

Doctoral Consortium Chair

Peter Edklund   University of Copenhagen, Denmark

Technical Committee

Conference Chairs, Workshop Chairs, and Doctoral Consortium Chair

Scientific Committee

Varol Akman   Bilkent University, Turkey
Larry Barsalou   University of Glasgow, UK
Carla Bazzanella   Università degli Studi di Torino, Italy
Marcos Borges   Universidade Federal do Rio de Janeiro, Brazil
Fergal Carton   University of Cork College, Ireland
Sophie Chabridon   Telecom SudParis, France
Alan Colman   Swinburne University of Technology, Australia
Joelle Coutaz   IMAG, France
Klaus David   University of Kassel, Germany
Peter Eklund   IT University of Copenhagen, Denmark
Xiaoliang Fan   Lanzhou University, China
Anita Fetzer   University of Stuttgart, Germany
Thomas Forissier   University of Antilles and Guyane, France
Christian Freksa   University of Bremen, Germany
Kimberly Garcia   University Pierre and Marie Curie, France
Fausto Giunchiglia   University of Trento, Italy
Avelino Gonzalez   University of Central Florida, USA
Debra Hollister   Valencia College, USA
Patrick Humphreys   London School of Economics, UK
Kepa Korta   University of Basque Country
David Leake   University of Indiana, USA
Pierrick Marie   IRIT, France

Joël Martin	National Council Research, Canada
Alain Mille	University of Lyon 1, France
Andreas Nuernberger	Otto-von-Guericke-Universität Magdeburg, Germany
George Angelos Papadopoulos	University of Cyprus, Cyprus
François Récanati	EHESS, France
Ana Carolina Salgado	UFPE, Brazil
Marina Sbisà	University of Trieste, Italy
Luciano Serafini	FBK, Italy
Hassane Tahir	SOPRA STERIA
Ken Turner	University of Brighton, UK
Massimiliano Vignolo	University of Genoa, Italy
Larry Whitsel	University of Maine Augusta, USA
Arkady Zaslavsky	CSIRO, Australia

Organizing Committee

Patrick Brézillon	UPMC
Christophe Bouder	UPMC
Kimberly Garcia	Siemens, USA
Michel Hu	Master student, UPMC
Louis-Alexandre Jego	Master student, UPMC
Daphné Keller	France
Pauline Lee	Master student, UPMC
Christine Leproux	University of Paris 8
Olivier Levelt	Master student, UPMC

Additional Reviewers

Bianca Cepollaro	Marco Mazzone
Francesca Ervas	Andrea Parravicini
Andrea Iacona	Ines Skelac
Fabrizio Macagno	Danilo Suster
Diana Mazzarella	

Sponsors

Invited Speakers

Conversational Strategy

Robert Stalnaker

MIT, Cambridge, USA

The common ground framework represents a discourse context as a body of information that is presumed to be shared by the participants in a conversation. In this talk, I will sketch the general lines of this pragmatic framework, starting with the simple cases where cooperation predominates, but then emphasizing the way contexts evolve in situations in which conflict and disagreement play a central role, particularly in public discourse. The kind of strategic reasoning that game-theoretic concepts are designed to clarify is particularly interesting when common interest mixes with conflict of interest, and I will consider some patterns of strategic reasoning in contentious communicative situations.

Personal Context Modeling and Annotations

Fausto Giunchiglia

University of Trento, Trento, Italy

Current context modelling approaches mostly focus on a priori defined environments, while the majority of human life is in open, and hence complex and unpredictable, environments. We propose a context model where the context is organized according to the different dimensions of the user environment. In addition, we propose the notions of endurants and perdurants as a way to describe how humans aggregate their context depending either on space or time, respectively. To ground our modelling approach in the reality of users, we collaborate with sociology experts in an internal university project aiming at understanding how behavioral patterns of university students in their everyday life affect their academic performance. Our contribution is a methodology for developing annotations general enough to account for human life in open domains and to be consistent with both sensor data and sociological approaches.

Indexical Thought

François Récanati

Centre National de la Recherche Scientifique – CNRS, Paris, France

I will analyse indexical thoughts (e.g. first person thoughts, or demonstrative thoughts) in terms of functional properties of the vehicles through which we think such thoughts. These vehicles I will describe as 'mental files', whose role is to store information derived through certain types of contextual relation to objects in the environment. I will argue that mental files are typed by the type of contextual relation they exploit, and in this respect they are like indexicals. In the last part of the talk, if time permits, I will discuss various attempts to account for indexical thinking purely at the level of content, without bringing the vehicles into the picture.

Contents

Context in Communication

Context Awareness

Specific Topics: Context in Management

Specific Topics: Context in Learning

**Specific Topics: Quality Awareness in Modeling
and Using Context in Applications-QAMUCA**

Keynote-Related Papers

Assertion *De Re*

Gregory Bochner[(⊠)] [iD]

Université Libre de Bruxelles (ULB), Brussels, Belgium
gbochner@ulb.ac.be

Abstract. In this paper I sketch an alternative to Stalnaker's view of referential uses of descriptions. Stalnaker has long promoted a pragmatic account of assertions, presuppositions, and informativeness. He is also a fervent advocate of propositionalism, the doctrine that the contents of assertions, presuppositions, and attitudes, (are or) determine sets of possible worlds. I argue that the combination of a pragmatic account and propositionalism creates several problems. (i) It does not predict the right truth-conditions for some assertions. (ii) It cannot duly separate facts of reference from presuppositions about facts of reference. (iii) It reproduces, at the level of what is presupposed, the cognitive significance problems that pragmatic presuppositions were meant to solve at the level of what is asserted. I argue that the solution to these problems involves giving up propositionalism. While Stalnaker analyses assertions and presuppositions in terms of singular propositions and possible worlds, I propose to analyse them in terms of properties and centred worlds. But unlike other centred world accounts inspired by Lewis, the view I advertise is not egocentric: the circumstance of evaluation of an assertion need not be centred on the subject, it can be centred on an object. When the assertion involves a referential use of a description, the object at the centre is the one that the speaker "has in mind." Unlike its egocentric counterparts, this view can maintain that referential communication is direct: speakers and hearers can grasp the same truth-conditions.

Keywords: Referential uses of descriptions · Assertion · Keith Donnellan · Robert Stalnaker · David Lewis · Pragmatics · Context · Communication · Propositions · Centred worlds · Rigidity

1 Stalnaker on Referential Uses of Descriptions

Stalnaker [1, 2] combines a pragmatic account of assertion with a propositionalist analysis of content. The content and the context of an assertion are both represented by sets of possible worlds. An assertion made in a context c is a proposal to reduce in some particular way the set of possible worlds that are compatible with what is pragmatically presupposed by the conversational participants in c. The assertion is informative with respect to c if the truth of the proposition p it expresses in c rules out some possible world in c relative to which p is false – i.e. if the effect of locating the actual world @ in the set of possible worlds determined by p is to eliminate at least one possible world at which p is false from the set of possible worlds compatible with what will be presupposed about @ at the next stage of the conversation.

© Springer International Publishing AG 2017
P. Brézillon et al. (Eds.): CONTEXT 2017, LNAI 10257, pp. 3–14, 2017.
DOI: 10.1007/978-3-319-57837-8_1

How does Stalnaker's account capture the difference between attributive and referential uses of descriptions? He considers the following assertions:

1. Charles Daniels is bald. [said at time t1 in world w1 about a philosopher named Charles Daniels by one of his friends]
2. I am bald. [said at t1 in w1 by Charles Daniels]
3. The man in a purple turtleneck shirt is bald. [said at t1 in w1 by someone in a room containing one and only one turtleneck shirt, that man being Charles Daniels][1]

As Stalnaker had been one of the first to note, proper names and indexicals are commonly used as "rigid designators." In quite neutral terms, a designator can be said to be rigid if it is used to designate the same thing with respect to all the possibilities at which the statement in which it occurs is either true or false.[2] In propositionalist and less neutral terms, a designator will be rigid if it is used to designate the same thing with respect to all the possible worlds at which the statement in which it occurs is true or false. Given his propositionalist stance, Stalnaker takes the utterances in (1) and (2) to express the same singular proposition, that Daniels is bald at t1. That proposition determines (and even is, according to Stalnaker) the set of possible worlds in which Daniels himself is bald at t1. The proposition is true with respect to an arbitrary world w just in case w belongs to that set of possible worlds. Assuming that in the actual world @, Daniels is bald at t1, the proposition is true.

In the case of (3), Stalnaker says, echoing Donnellan [3], that there is a pragmatic ambiguity. Depending on how the description is used, the assertions will have different contents, sustained by different presuppositions. If it is used attributively, what is asserted is a general proposition: that the unique individual x who is a man in a purple turtleneck shirt (in that room at t1) is bald. Here, what is presupposed is also a general (and existential) proposition, that there is (in that room at t1) a unique individual x who is a man in a purple turtleneck shirt. If, instead, the description is used referentially, what is asserted is – as in the cases of (1) and (2) – the singular proposition that Daniels is bald at t1. And there, what is presupposed is also a singular proposition, that Daniels is (at t1) the unique individual (in that room) who is a man in a purple turtleneck shirt.

Stalnaker follows Strawson [4] and Donnellan [3] in (the common part of) their critique of Russell [5]. When a description of the form 'the F' is used referentially, the descriptive condition being the unique F plays only a presuppositional role. Nevertheless, Strawson, Donnellan and Stalnaker have different views about what is presupposed. Russell claimed that what is asserted in a statement of the form 'The F is G' includes the affirmation that there is a unique x who is F, which has general and existential truth-conditions. For Strawson, in referential uses, the satisfaction of this same general and existential truth-condition is not asserted but presupposed. For Donnellan, what is presupposed is rather the satisfaction of a singular truth-condition. Thus what is presupposed above is true just in case Daniels is the unique man in a

---

[1] See [1, pp. 40–41]. I am adding world and time coordinates w_1 and t_1 in the context of utterance.

[2] The characterisation is neutral in that it does not settle whether it is the designator or its use that is rigid; it is silent about possibilities at which the corresponding statement would be neither true nor false; and it does not say whether the domain of possibilities at which this dated statement is either true or false is contextually restricted or not.

purple turtleneck shirt in the room. Donnellan does not (further) claim that what is presupposed is a "singular proposition." In [3], he characterises the statements containing referential uses of descriptions only in terms of their truth-values and truth-conditions, without using the notions of "contents" or "propositions," and so without committing himself to the (additional) claim that such statements express or convey singular propositions.

Donnellan's neutral formulation remained compatible with two modal accounts of the singular truth-condition of what is presupposed (and of what is asserted). This might, as Stalnaker holds, amount to a singular proposition, evaluated as true or false with respect to entire possible worlds. Given his pragmatic view of assertion, then, the singular proposition will be true at all the possible worlds compatible with what is contextually presupposed about the actual world by the participants in the conversation. In the case above, it will be true with respect to all possible worlds compatible with what is presupposed about the actual world that Daniels is the unique man in a purple turtleneck shirt in the room. But there is also another option. The singular truth-condition might also correspond to a property as evaluated at a world centred on Daniels at t1. On that view, the property is true at all the centred worlds compatible with what is presupposed de re of that man, Daniels, considered at t1 in w1. Thus it is true with respect to all centred worlds compatible with what is presupposed of Daniels (at t1 in w1) that he is the unique man in a purple turtleneck shirt in the room.[3]

In the next sections, I will present arguments which seem to me to favour this centred world account over the propositionalist version of the pragmatic-modal account.

2   Semantic Arguments Against Stalnaker's Propositionalism

Consider the assertion of (3) when the description is used referentially. According to Stalnaker, what determines which (singular) proposition is expressed by the assertion of (3) is the context, construed as a background of presuppositions. The referent, Daniels, is determined not causally, via an empirical relation of acquaintance between the speaker and Daniels in the *actual* world, but descriptively: the referent is Daniels because he is the individual who satisfies, in each possible world of the context, the condition of being the unique x who is a man in a purple turtleneck shirt. Once Daniels has thus been determined to be the referent and a singular proposition is expressed about him, the truth-value of that proposition does not depend on the truth of the reference-fixing description. As Stalnaker writes, "[t]he presupposition helps to determine the

---

[3] This centred world view of asserted content is not entirely new. It is suggested by Recanati [6, 7] when he deals with examples like 'Very handsome!' (said concerning someone's appearance) or 'The carburettor is in good condition but there is a problem with the front wheels' (said concerning a certain car), in which no word stands for the relevant referent. Stojanovic [8] argues that, even when there is a word standing for the referent in the corresponding sentence, the referent may be part of the circumstance of evaluation rather than part of the content. She defends a similar account of assertions involving referential uses of descriptions [8, Chapter 3]. However, neither Recanati nor Stojanovic uses this centred world account to deal with Frege's puzzle and cognitive significance phenomena.

proposition expressed, but once that proposition is determined, it can stand alone. The fact that Daniels is bald in no way depends on the color of his shirt."

Stalnaker's view predicts the right truth-conditions in this case: the assertion is true if and only if Daniels is bald (at that time in the actual world). However, it seems to me that this success is only relative. It hangs on a contingent feature of the example. We get the right truth-conditions only because, as the case was described, the presuppositions happen to exclude all the possible worlds in which someone *other than Daniels* is the man in a purple turtleneck shirt.

Suppose that the speaker asserted (3) with the evident intention to refer to Daniels, whom she is observing from a distance, while it is mutually manifest that neither the speaker nor the hearer knows whether that man is Daniels or O'Leary. Given propositionalism, what is presupposed will not decide between two candidates for the role of the singular proposition asserted: *that Daniels is bald*, and *that O'Leary is bald*. Stalnaker's view predicts that the speaker has failed to say something about Daniels in particular. But this seems incorrect. There is a strong intuition that she has said something that is true if and only if Daniels is bald (at that time in that world).

Stalnaker may have foreseen this sort of worry. In discussing the referential use in (3), he suggests at some point that the referent will not *always* be fixed by what is presupposed about it:

> "As with the term *I*, there are relatively systematic rules for matching up definite descriptions with their denotations in a context: the referent is the one and only one member of the appropriate domain who is *presupposed* to have the property expressed in the description. **The rule cannot always be applied, but in the case described, it can be**." [1, p. 41; bold emphases added]

And the same tension surfaces further when he claims that proper names have attributive uses:

> "Proper names [...] are normally used to refer, but can be used in a way resembling the attributive use of definite descriptions. When you ask, "Which one is Daniels?" you are not *referring* to Daniels, since you do not presuppose of any one person that he is Daniels. When I answer "Daniels is the bald one" I am using "the bald one" referentially and the name Daniels attributively. I am telling you not that Daniels is bald, but that he is Daniels. Using this distinction, we can explain how identity statements can be informative, even when two proper names flank the identity sign." [1, p. 44]

But it seems incorrect to say that in asking this, the speaker is not referring to Daniels but only denoting whoever he might be amongst several individuals. After all, the only appropriate kind of answer is to tell who *Daniels* is. To be sure, in some cognitively significant sense, the speaker does not *know* who Daniels is: there are several candidates compatible with what he knows – that is why he is asking. But this does not mean that he is not *referring* to Daniels. Even if Daniels and O'Leary are the only candidates in that context, the answer 'Daniels is the bald one' will mean not that *either Daniels or O'Leary* is the bald one, but simply that *Daniels* is the bald one.

It seems to me that two lessons ought to be drawn here. The first concerns the relationships between cognitive significance and truth-conditional import: the actual referent of an assertion need not be identical with the referent as it is represented in the possibilities compatible with what is presupposed. *What* I in fact refer to is not always what my audience and I take me to be referring to. Thus I can be referring to Daniels even if all the conversational participants take me to be referring to someone who might, for all we are presupposing, be either Daniels or O'Leary. So the truth-conditions of my assertion can rigidly involve Daniels even if no unique individual is presupposed to be the referent. Likewise, they could rigidly involve Daniels even if it were falsely presupposed that I am referring to O'Leary (and to no one else).

The second lesson concerns the relationships between cognitive significance and the reference-fixing mechanism: the way in which reference is actually determined need not coincide with the way in which it is determined in the possibilities compatible with what is presupposed. *How* I in fact get to refer to what I am referring to and how my audience and I take me to have referred are different matters. Thus I could be referring to Daniels even if the conversational participants wrongly take me to be referring to O'Leary, who is (falsely) presupposed to be the man wearing a purple turtleneck shirt. On the one hand, O'Leary will be the putative referent of my assertion considered from the cognitive point of view of the context, because it will be *true* in each of the possibilities compatible with what is presupposed in that context that he is the man in a purple turtleneck shirt. On the other hand, Daniels will be the actual, objective referent of my assertion, in virtue of the fact that I bear a *causal* relation to him, independently of any presupposition regarding that fact.

As it stands, Stalnaker's account does not allow us to make these two dissociations. I submit that what precludes them is the propositionalist tenet of his account. Given propositionalism, assertions and presuppositions can have singular truth-conditions only if their contents are singular propositions. Given the pragmatic account of assertion, the content of a referential assertion must be some (unique) singular proposition that is expressed in all the possible worlds compatible with what is presupposed in the context. *This means that the determination of the singular proposition expressed by an assertion depends on the way in which the presuppositions represent the reference.* But then, whenever cognitive representation of reference and objective reference do not converge on the same object, the account predicts the wrong truth-conditions.

The alternative account I submit can secure the two dissociations. On that account, a referential assertion of (3) neither expresses nor presupposes singular propositions. The referent is not part of the contents at all. Instead, it is part of the *circumstance of evaluation* against which both the presupposition and the assertion must be evaluated: the world centred on Daniels (at that time). Intuitively, a "centred world" is a portion of a world. Formally, it is a pair $<w, c>$ consisting of a world w and some designated centre c in that world. On the version I submit, a referential assertion of (3) refers to a specific circumstance, one that is centred on the intended referent at a particular time.

This account involves the following claims. Assume that the referential assertion in (3) took place at a time t_1 in the world w_1. First, the presupposition is *de re*: it is presupposed *of that man*, Daniels, that he is the unique man in a purple turtleneck shirt in the room at the time. (The same context might also involve descriptions of the room and of the time. Let us assume that it does. We can abbreviate the descriptions as follows: it is presupposed *of that room* that it is F and it is presupposed *of the time* t_1 that it is G.) The *de re* presupposition concerning Daniels is true if and only if $<w_1, t_1,$ Daniels$>$ belongs to the set of centred worlds $\{<w, t, x>: x$ is the unique man in a purple turtleneck shirt in a room which is F at a time t which is G in w}. Second, the assertion is also *de re*: it is asserted of Daniels that he is bald. This assertion is true just in case $<w_1, t_1,$ Daniels$>$ belongs to the set of centred worlds {$<w, t, x>$: x is bald at t in w} — even if all conversational participants presuppose that the referent is O'Leary. Third, the assertion is informative in that context because it draws a contrast, within the set of centred worlds compatible with what is presupposed of $<w_1, t_1,$ Daniels$>$, between two subsets of centred worlds – viz., {$<w, t, x>$: x is bald at t in w} and {$<w, t, x>$: x is not bald at t in w} – and as, if it is accepted, its effect on the context is to rule out the centred worlds in the latter subset from what is subsequently presupposed of $<w_1, t_1,$ Daniels$>$.

Unlike Stalnaker's propositionalist account, this view can duly separate issues of reference and issues of cognitive significance. For Daniels (at t_1 in w_1) *remains* the objective referent of the assertion even if the conversational participants presuppose false descriptions of him, or even if they mistake him for someone else. This is because what determines Daniels as the referent is the *objective fact* that a causal relation holds between the speaker and Daniels in the actual world, independently of any presuppositions that might further represent that fact. The presupposition and the assertion both rigidly concern Daniels: their truth-values essentially depend on the way Daniels himself is (at t_1 in w_1). We get rigidity not by holding that the content involves the referent or that the intension of the description used referentially is a constant function from circumstances of evaluation into the same extension. We get rigidity by holding that the referent is part of the specific circumstance of evaluation that the assertion targets, and so by letting the referent stay all along where it was in the first place: in the external environment. This form of rigidity is pragmatic: it depends on causal interactions between users and things. The *uses* of descriptions are pragmatically rigid when the speakers have the referential intention to describe a specific portion of the world to which they are related independently of the words and the language that they use to describe it.

3   Cognitive Arguments Against Stalnaker's Propositionalism

Consider an instance of Frege's puzzle involving assertions and referential uses of descriptions. Two philosophy students, Sven and Enzo, are attending an official ceremony at their university. For some reason, they decide to draw a list of all the mathematicians who are present in the room. Sven recognises Professor Manfred, a renowned mathematician, who is the unique man wearing a bow tie in the room. With the manifest intention to refer to this man (Manfred), Sven says:

(4) The man wearing a bow tie is a mathematician.

Enzo understands his assertion and accepts it. In the meantime, Enzo glimpses a man in a mirror of the crowded room and mistakes him for Professor Robinson, an anthropologist. In fact, the man in question is Manfred. Seen from that angle, Manfred looks a lot like Robinson. While his bow tie is no longer visible, he can now be seen to hold a glass of sparkling white wine – in fact, of Prosecco. Then, with the manifest intention to refer to that man (Manfred), Enzo says:

(5) The man drinking champagne is not a mathematician.

Sven understands his assertion and accepts it. We now have a version of Frege's puzzle. Participants in the same conversation ascribe contradictory properties to the same referent.

But now, given Donnellan's crucial observations about referential uses of descriptions, the puzzle cannot be solved in a Fregean manner. We cannot conclude that the two assertions have different descriptive truth-conditions. Instead, they have referential truth-conditions. And we cannot conclude that the definite descriptions fix the referent (even relative to some contextual domain). For the intuitive referent in (5), Manfred, is not even drinking champagne. Donnellan's observations force us to acknowledge that the assertion in (4) is true just in case Manfred (at that time in that world) is a mathematician, while the assertion in (5) is true just in case Manfred (at the same time in the same world) is not a mathematician. So we cannot escape the problematic result that these two assertions are contradictory. Sven and Enzo, who are rational and understand each other, accept two contradictory assertions at the same time.

On the propositionalist version of the pragmatic account, the differing cognitive values of these assertions will have to be explained in terms of different propositions which would be presupposed about the referent. In all the possible worlds compatible with what Sven and Enzo presuppose in that context, there are *two* individuals in the room at the time: one individual x is the man wearing a bow tie and another individual y is the man drinking champagne. Given this, the proposition expressed by the first assertion should be a singular proposition about x (*that x is a mathematician*), and the proposition expressed by the second assertion should be a singular proposition about y (*that y is not a mathematician*). The reason why Sven and Enzo fail to realise that the asserted propositions are contradictory should then be that they presuppose a proposition that is false: *that x is not y*. They should not count as irrational: they are just presupposing some empirical falsehoods.

Now several difficulties arise. First, to overcome the problems raised in the last section, we should disentangle the (singular) propositions expressed by their assertions from the (singular) propositions that Sven and Enzo take themselves to have expressed. But there is no way to do this, provided that the propositions expressed by their assertions *are* the propositions that are expressed in the possible worlds compatible with what they presuppose. (This is a very general problem.) Second, we also face the problem of telling whether, in those possible worlds, Manfred, x, and y, are the same or different individuals. It seems that x and y should be different persons. But then, if we said that x is Manfred, we could not also say that y is Manfred. Either only one of x and y, or none of them, is Manfred himself.[4] Until we specify further the identities and differences between Manfred, x, and y, it remains unclear which propositions the propositions *that x is a mathematician* and *that y is not a mathematician* are, and so what logical relations hold between them. Third, Stalnaker claims that the

---

[4] One might want to argue that the three are only suitable counterparts of one another. But this is not what Stalnaker would want to say, given his own metaphysical preference for haecceitism over counterpart theories.

presuppositions attached to referential uses of descriptions are singular propositions. So the propositions *that x is a mathematician* and *that y is not a mathematician* should be different singular propositions. Hence, if the singular proposition *that x is not y* is true, it is *necessarily* true. But then, there is no possible world that a subsequent discovery of the identity of *x* and *y* could exclude. So the claim that the presuppositions determining what is asserted are singular propositions, which should have helped us to identify the possibilities excluded by such (contradictory) assertions, ultimately runs us into the same problems at the level of what is presupposed.

These three difficulties cast doubt on the capacity of a propositionalist account to secure the simple result that the assertions in (4) and (5) have *referential* truth-conditions at all. To secure that result, a propositionalist account of the pragmatic variety will have to find further ways of guaranteeing that, relative to that context, these assertions can express determinate singular propositions.

Now assume that the propositionalist managed to find ways of overcoming those three difficulties and secured the result that the two assertions target Manfred in particular. Then, what is asserted in (4) is the singular proposition *that Manfred is a mathematician at t_1* and what is asserted in (5) is the singular proposition *that Manfred is not a mathematician at t_1*. The next problem is this. There is no possible world *w* such that Manfred at the same time is and is not a mathematician in *w*. The intersection of the set of worlds {*w*: Manfred is a mathematician at t_1 in *w*} and the set of worlds {*w*: Manfred is not a mathematician at t_1 in *w*} yields the empty set of worlds. Given the propositionalist account, conversational participants can always only be talking about *one* possibility: the actual world. But then, *however the actual world turns out to be*, the two singular propositions could never both be true relative to it.[5] So that acquiring more empirical information *in the form of new propositions could not possibly help* Sven and Enzo to notice the contradiction.

4   Frege's Puzzle and *De Re* Presuppositions

The centred world account I favour avoids those difficulties by recognising a difference between contents and (absolute) truth-conditions.[6] Suppose that the assertions in (4) and (5) are both made at a time t_1 in the world w_1 and that the referential uses of the descriptions both target Manfred (at t_1 in w_1). Then, as Donnellan would insist, the two assertions must have referential truth-conditions involving Manfred. The referent is Manfred (at t_1 in w_1), not because he satisfies certain descriptive conditions, but because he happens to bear appropriate causal relations to the mental states underlying the assertions. So the assertions have contradictory truth-conditions: if the one is true,

---

[5] Note that Stalnaker's [2, 9] pragmatic version of the two-dimensionalist strategy to explain the informativeness of identity statements involving proper names and indexicals cannot be invoked here. First, it applies only to identity assertions, and we have only (negative) identity presuppositions here. Second, on that account, the diagonal proposition cannot become the proposition asserted unless there is a manifestly intentional violation of some Gricean maxim or conversational principle. But there is no such violation here.

[6] On that distinction, see Recanati [6, 7, 11].

the other false; and vice versa. The *de re* assertion in (4) is true just in case $<w_1, t_1,$ Manfred> belongs to the set of centred worlds $\{<w, t, x>: x$ is a mathematician at t in $w\}$, whereas the *de re* assertion in (5) is true just in case $<w_1, t_1,$ Manfred> belongs to the set of centred worlds $\{<w, t, x>: x$ is not a mathematician at t in $w\}$. But although, thus analysed, the assertions are still contradictory, they are so in a cognitively harmless sense. They are contradictory because the centred world $<w_1, t_1,$ Manfred> which they *both* target cannot belong to both sets. If it belongs to one, it does not belong to the other; and vice versa. Nevertheless, on this view, different assertions could in principle target *different* circumstances of evaluation. The assertions in (4) and (5) only *happen to* have contradictory truth-conditions, because their contents are *in fact* completed by the *same* circumstance. Had the contents not been evaluated at the same circumstance, the assertions would not have been contradictory. So, in order to notice the contradiction, it is not sufficient to compare the contents that are asserted. It will also be necessary to know that, *as a matter of (contingent) fact*, the contents are evaluated at the same centred world. And that additional knowledge will be empirical and *a posteriori*.

On the one hand, Sven and Enzo *take* the assertion in (4) to concern a man who is wearing a bow tie and is not drinking champagne. From this first contextual perspective, this assertion draws a contrast between two subsets of individuals *within the set of individuals (at a time in a world) wearing a bow tie and not drinking champagne*: the subset of individuals who are mathematicians and the subset of individuals who are not mathematicians. The cognitive effect of this assertion, if it is accepted, is to reduce the set of individuals compatible with what they presuppose of the man wearing a bow tie by eliminating, *in it*, the individuals who are not mathematicians. On the other hand, Sven and Enzo *take* the assertion in (5) to concern a man who is drinking champagne and is not wearing a bow tie. Hence, from that second contextual perspective, that assertion will draw a contrast between two subsets of individuals *within the set of individuals (at a time in a world) drinking champagne and not wearing a bow tie*: the subset of individuals who are mathematicians and the subset of individuals who are not mathematicians. The cognitive effect of that assertion, if it is accepted, is to reduce the set of individuals compatible with what they presuppose of the man drinking champagne by eliminating, *in it*, the individuals who are mathematicians. So, as desired, we predict that the assertions in (4) and (5) have different effects, or cognitive values, relative to that context.

Given their pragmatic presuppositions, the assertions in (4) and (5) target *different* referents. When we analyse these presuppositions in terms of properties, their conjunction is still contradictory (at the level of absolute truth-conditions), because together they describe in contradictory terms what turns out to be one and the same centred world. But here too, to notice the contradiction, it is not enough to compare the contents of the presuppositions. In addition, Sven and Enzo will have to realise that their presuppositions *happen to* describe the same individual (or centred world). And in order to realise that, they will need to gain more empirical information. They will need to ascribe further properties to Manfred. When they come to presuppose of the referent of (4) that he is drinking champagne and/or when they come to presuppose of the referent of (5) that he is wearing a bow tie, they can merge their information about these referents within what becomes one cluster of presuppositions for what is now taken to be one unique referent. Then, they are ready to accept that it was false of the referent of (4) that he was not drinking champagne (which is actually also false, as since he was drinking Prosecco), and they are ready to accept that it was false of the referent of (5) that he was not wearing a bow tie. So we can explain why they were not being irrational: they needed more empirical information to revise their presuppositions and to rule out some centred worlds — those whose centre is not wearing a bow tie *and* drinking champagne — from the (now unique) set of centred worlds compatible with what they now consider to be a unique centred world.

5   Conclusions: Context and Communication

Let me conclude with two brief remarks indicating how the view I have sketched, if it were fleshed out, might become part of a broader account of context and communication.

First, such a view will require to amend Stalnaker's pragmatic account in further ways. As alluded to, a context will not generally be represented by *one* set of possibilities (such as the set of possible worlds compatible with what is presupposed about the actual world at a given point of an exchange). Depending on the conversation, a context may and most often will involve a *multitude* of different circumstances of evaluation, each corresponding to a concrete (portion of the) environment. These external circumstances will be described via separate clusters of pragmatic presuppositions. Cognitive significance puzzles will tend to arise when the number of descriptive clusters forming a cognitive perspective on the circumstances in a given context does not correspond to the number of actual circumstances.

Second, this view will not be vulnerable to common objections against *egocentric* accounts invoking centred worlds. On Lewis's [10] view, any speaker making an assertion is *self*-ascribing a property. On the present view, by contrast, the speaker (and the hearer understanding the speaker's assertion) may ascribe a property directly to some other object. An advantage of this move is that referential communication can remain as direct as it could be. Suppose that (at t_1 in w_1) Giulia says:

(6) I am hungry.

Flaminia understands Giulia's assertion and accepts it. On Lewis's view, the belief expressed by Giulia is true just in case the centred world $<w_1, t_1,$ Giulia$>$ belongs to the set of centred worlds $\{<w, t, x>: x$ is hungry at t in $w\}$. But Flaminia must acquire *a different belief, endowed with other truth-conditions*. She does not come to ascribe the property of being hungry to Flaminia. She rather acquires a belief which is true just in case the centred world $<w_1, t_1,$ Flaminia$>$ belongs to the set of centred worlds $\{<w, t, x>: x$ is acquainted with an individual y who is hungry at t in $w\}$. So this simple assertion does not have the same truth-conditions for Giulia and Flaminia. In effect, Lewis's egocentric account makes *all* communication indirect. It thereby also makes it difficult to theorise about the interpersonal cognitive effects of assertions. How could Giulia's assertion reduce the set of centred worlds compatible with what Giulia and Flaminia *both* believed or presupposed? Various strategies have been proposed by Lewis's followers, which bite the bullet of indirect communication and seek a reasonable degree of similarity between the beliefs of the speaker, what is asserted, and the beliefs of the hearer.[7] But the view I have sketched points to a much simpler account of communication. Just as on a singular proposition account, Giulia's assertion has exactly the same referential truth-conditions for Giulia and for Flaminia: it is true just in case Giulia is hungry at t_1 in w_1. Of course, the two accounts distribute the truth-ingredients in different ways over content and circumstance. The former says that the assertion is true just in case the world w_1 belongs to the set of possible worlds $\{w$: Giulia is hungry at t_1 in $w\}$. The latter will say that the assertion is true just in case the centred world $<w_1, t_1$, Giulia$>$ belongs to the set of centred worlds $\{<w, t, x>: x$ is hungry at t in $w\}$. But the different distribution does not alter the *absolute* truth-conditions. On the present view, the effect of the assertion on the common context is also straightforward: if the assertion is accepted, it eliminates all the centred worlds whose centre is not hungry from the set of centred worlds compatible with what is presupposed *of Giulia at that time*. Then, Giulia and Flaminia both end up having a belief which is true (absolutely) just in case Giulia at t_1 in w_1 is hungry.

Acknowledgments. I am currently *Chargé de Recherches* by the *Fonds National de la Recherche Scientifique*, Communauté française de Belgique (F.R.S.-FNRS), at the *Université Libre de Bruxelles* (ULB), in the Centre of Research in Linguistics *LaDisco*. I am grateful to the F.R.S.-FNRS for its support. I thank my colleagues from ULB and from the Université de Liège, Philippe De Brabanter, Mikhail Kissine, Philippe Kreutz, Bruno Leclercq, Sébastien Richard, and Antonin Thuns, for helpful discussions on the ideas of this paper in a joint seminar in September 2016.

References

1. Stalnaker, R.: Pragmatics. Synthese **22**, 272–289 (1970). Reprinted in [12, pp. 31–46]; page references to the latter
2. Stalnaker, R.: Assertion. In: Cole, P. (ed.) Syntax and Semantics, vol. 9, pp. 315–332. Academic Press, New York (1978). Reprinted in [12, pp. 78–95]; page references to the latter
3. Donnellan, K.: Reference and definite descriptions. Philos. Rev. **75**(3), 281–304 (1966)
4. Strawson, P.: On referring. Mind **59**(235), 320–344 (1950)
5. Russell, B.: On denoting. Mind **14**, 479–493 (1905)
6. Recanati, F.: Perspectival Thought: A Plea for (Moderate) Relativism. Oxford University Press, Oxford (2007a)
7. Recanati, F.: Relativized propositions. In: O'Rourke, M., Washington, C. (eds.) Situating Semantics: Essays on the Work of John Perry 2007, pp. 119–154. The MIT Press, Cambridge (2007b)
8. Stojanovic, I.: What is Said: An Inquiry into Reference, Meaning and Content. VDM: Verlag Dr. Müller, Saarbrücken (2008)

---

[7] For a recent overview of this "communication problem" for Lewis, see [11] and references therein.

9. Stalnaker, R.: Assertion revisited. In: García-Carpintero, M., Macià, J. (eds.) Two-Dimensional Semantics: Foundation and Applications 2006, pp. 293–309. Oxford University Press, Oxford (2006)
10. Lewis, D.: Attitudes *de dicto* and *de se*. Philos. Rev. **88**(4), 513–543 (1979)
11. Recanati, F.: Indexical thought, communication, and mental files. In: Torre, S., Garcia-Carpintero, M. (eds.) About Oneself 2016. Oxford University Press, Oxford (2016)
12. Stalnaker, R.: Context and Content. Oxford University Press, Oxford (1999)

Pejoratives, Contexts and Presuppositions

Manuel García-Carpintero[✉]

LOGOS-Departament de Lògica, Història i Filosofia de la Ciència,
Universitat de Barcelona, Barcelona, Spain
m.garciacarpintero@ub.edu

Abstract. Kaplan started a fruitful debate on the meaning of pejoratives. He suggests that a dimension of *expressive meaning* is required, separated from the straightforward "at issue" content. To account for this, writers have elaborated on this suggestion, by arguing that the separated expressive meaning of pejoratives and slurs is instead either a *conventional or conversational implicatures*, or a *presupposition*. I myself prefer a presuppositional account; however, in order to deflate a very serious objection that has been raised against accounts of that kind, it is on the one hand essential that we take what is presupposed to be genuinely expressive, and, related, it is also essential that we adopt a more complex view than the one usually assumed on the nature of the context relative to which speech acts make their contributions.

Keywords: Pejoratives · Slurs · Expressive meaning · Presuppositions

Kaplan [21] started a fruitful debate on the meaning of pejoratives – as in 'that bastard Kresge is famous' – including slurs and racial epithets as in 'there are many chinks in our neighborhood'. Kaplan suggests that a dimension of *expressive meaning* is required, separated from the straightforward "at issue", asserted or truth-conditional content, which would just be in the latter case that there are too many Chinese people in the neighborhood. Hom [15] makes a case for a straightforward account, which avoids separated expressive dimension. Thus, according to him 'chink' makes a truth-conditional contribution akin to that of other predicates such as 'Chinese'. This would be a property determining an on his view necessarily empty extension, which can be roughly expressed as: *ought to be subject to higher college admissions standards, and ought to be subject to exclusion from advancement to managerial positions, and ..., because of being slanty-eyed, and devious, and good-at-laundering, and ..., all because of being Chinese* (Hom [15], 431). A serious problem for this view ([19], 316–319) lies in the *projection behavior* of these terms: when sentences such as those mentioned above are negated ('there are not many chinks in our neighborhood'), are antecedents of conditionals ('if there are many chinks in our neighborhood, it will be easy to find a good restaurant'), or embedded under modal operators ('there might be

Financial support for my work was provided by the DGI, Spanish Government, research project FFI2016-80588-R; and through the award *ICREA Academia* for excellence in research, 2013, funded by the Generalitat de Catalunya, and from the European Union's Horizon 2020 Research and Innovation programme under Grant Agreement no. 675415, *Diaphora*. Thanks to three reviewers for this journal for their comments, which led to several improvements, and to Michael Maudsley for his grammatical revision.

© Springer International Publishing AG 2017
P. Brézillon et al. (Eds.): CONTEXT 2017, LNAI 10257, pp. 15–24, 2017.
DOI: 10.1007/978-3-319-57837-8_2

many chinks in our neighborhood') or non-declarative mood ('are there are many chinks in our neighborhood?'), they still derogate the relevant targets.

To account for this, writers have elaborated on Kaplan's suggestion, by arguing that the separated expressive meaning of pejoratives and slurs is instead either a *conventional implicature* [32] or a *presupposition* [27, 28, 37].[1] In defense of his account, Hom ([17], 398–401) appeals to generalized conversational implicatures to explain the projection data. Now, in my view a presuppositional account is preferable; however, in order to deflate a very serious objection that has been raised against accounts of that kind, it is on the one hand essential that we take what is presupposed to be genuinely expressive, and, related, it is also essential that we adopt a more complex view than the one usually assumed on the nature of the context relative to which speech acts make their contributions. Moreover, the other two proposals – the conventional implicature account, and even Hom's generalized conversational implicature view – would also need to assume the extra complexity in contexts I will show we need, so their proponents might also benefit from the proposal that I'll argue for in this paper.

It is not easy to tell apart presuppositions (*that someone broke the computer*, for the cleft-construction in 'it was John who broke the computer') and conventional implicatures (*that somehow being poor contrasts with being honest*, for 'but' in 'he is poor but honest'; *that John is married*, for the non-restrictive wh-clause in 'John, who is married, will come to the party'). Both are *semantic*, by two counts: first, they are conventionally associated with some lexical items or constructions; second, grasping them is required for full competent understanding.[2] Both are ways of conventionally indicating "non-at-issue" content. This is the reason why they both project: thus, the negation in both 'he is not poor but honest' and 'it was not John who broke the computer' negates the "at issue" content, and as a result the same conventional implicature and presupposition indicated above are expressed. Neither can therefore be rejected by means of straightforward denials, and as a result speakers must resort to oblique means such as Saddock's "hey, wait a minute" objection ([33], 2521–2522; [3], 341–342).

Some researchers appeal to subtle projection differences [31, 43], but there is no agreement on this among linguists. In particular, the behavior of conventional implicatures and presuppositions when they occur in ascriptions of beliefs or acts of saying does not neatly distinguish between them. Presuppositions do not typically project in such cases, but conventional implicatures might behave like them in some (Bach [1],

---

[1] Williamson [45] argues for a similar view. He classifies the expressive contents he proposes as conventional implicatures, but he understands that category in a traditional way, wider than the one I assume following Potts's work (*ibid.*, 151, 153). I take his view to be compatible with the presuppositional account assumed here as much as with Potts's view. All these proposals can be viewer as different ways to elaborate on Kaplan's view that pejoratives should be account for by adding a "use-conditional" layer of meaning.

[2] In the case of presuppositions, Stalnaker and other writers dispute this; [11] defends it, for constructions such as the one just given for illustration.

338–343).[3] Conventional implicatures typically project in such environments, but presuppositions might also project in some cases ([37], 244).[4]

Presuppositions and conventional implicatures have different natures ([32], 2012). Conventional implicatures have the job of providing new information, exactly like assertions, except that it is information which (even if relevant) has a relatively background character. Felicitous presuppositions articulate (for some relevant purpose) part of what is already commonly known. Unfortunately, this fails to offer either a straightforward distinction, because speakers exploit the fact that a sentence carries a presupposition to provide uncontroversial background information, by inviting the process called *accommodation* [25]. Nonetheless, I am convinced by the arguments by Macià and Schlenker that the data of projection and rejection, given clear-headed assumptions about the respective nature of the two phenomena, show that the best way of classifying the expressive meanings of pejoratives and slurs counts them as presuppositions, understood as differing from conventional implicatures in the just described way: they impose requirements on the common ground, as opposed to providing potentially new but background information.

However, perhaps guided by simple-minded assumptions about context that I want to expose here, both Macià and Schlenker give an inadequate characterization of the expressive presuppositions of pejoratives, which opens their view to spurious criticism. Schlenker ([37], 238) offers this characterization for the slur 'honky': *the agent of the context believes in the world of the context that white people are despicable.* This is a clear-cut condition on a context as understood on the classical Stalnakerian account, "a body of information that is available, or presumed to be available, as a resource for

---

[3] As I have pointed out elsewhere ([10], 45–47), in spite of its title [1] in fact does not show that conventional implicatures (or presuppositions, for that matter), as understood here following Potts, are a "myth". Bach only shows that they are not part of "what is said" in his "illocutionary" sense, which is just to say that they are not part of the "at issue" content of declaratives. Rather they are, according to him, part of "what is said" in his "locutionary" sense. But this just means that they are conventional, semantic in the sense that they need to be grasped for full competent understanding. This is part of current standard views on conventional implicatures, such as Potts's. Hom ([15], 424–426; [17], 391–392) appears to have been misled by Bach's suggestions in his criticisms of the conventional implicature view. Similarly, in his defense of a Conventional Implicature account Whiting ([44], 274–275) fails to properly take this point into consideration.

[4] Ascriptions of propositional attitudes and speech acts are notoriously context-dependent; this explains the existential quantifications. In his interesting discussion of hybrid theories of evaluative terms, modeled on the views on pejoratives I am discussing, Schroeder [38, 39] places a strong emphasis on a distinction between hybrid expressions whose expressive content project even in attitude ascriptions, and those that do not. But, as [14] points out, these are not properties of expressions themselves: we can only trace tendencies here. Slurs tend to project in ascriptions, but, as the examples by Schlenker and others show, they do not always do so. Such tendencies are orthogonal to the divide between conventional implicatures and presuppositions. Quoting [1] (a work that he, unlike Hom – see previous fn. –appraises properly, cf. *op. cit.*, 287–288, fn. 19), Schroeder shows that 'but' might well not project in some ascriptions; but, following [31], I am taking non-restrictive wh-clauses as paradigm cases of conventional implicatures, and they do typically project in attitude ascriptions: *John said that Peter, who will be coming soon, is welcome to the party.*

communication" ([41], 24).[5] But, as Williamson points out ([45], 151–152), it cannot be right, because it does not capture the normative status of slurs. Confronted with slurring utterances like the above, we would challenge the speaker (using perhaps some variation of the "hey, wait a minute" strategy) to retract the derogation of Kresge or Chinese people; but we would hardly challenge her to retract the suggestion that she believes that Kresge or Chinese people are despicable. For all we care, she might well believe it. We do not need to question this; we do not need to dissociate ourselves from the assumption that they hold such beliefs when our interlocutors utter slurs we find objectionable. As Camp ([3], 333) points out, Potts's conventional implicature account has the same problem, for he just posits a condition on the subjective emotional state of the speaker – something to the effect that s/he actually is in a heightened emotional state ([32], 171; [33], 2532).[6]

How, then, should expressive meanings, and the contexts to which they contribute, be understood? This depends on what emotions, and the speech acts conveying them, are. What pejoratives and slurs express, in my view, is that a certain emotional state (which can contextually vary along different parameters, cf. [3, 15, 32], among others) is *fitting* or *appropriate*. Some philosophers argue that emotions are a particular kind of judgment, to the effect that an object or situation instantiates their "formal objects", say, that Chinese people are worthy of contempt, in our example (cf. [8, 42], and references there). If this is right, then we do not need to go beyond the Stalnakerian context. That a speaker of 'there are too many chinks in our neighborhood' takes it to be common knowledge that Chinese people are worthy of contempt explains the appropriate reaction to the utterance by non-prejudiced participants in the same conversation. [45] seems to assume something like this.[7]

This would be a way of dealing with pejoratives analogous to the one offered by a certain *flattening* strategy that was popular for a while for non-declaratives. Let me digress for a moment in order to elaborate on this. It is relatively uncontroversial that, while questions make contributions to context, their contributions differ from those that declaratives make. To account for this, elaborating on previous work by Carlson [4]

---

[5] This is formally modeled as the "context set" – the set of possible worlds compatible with the presumed common knowledge of the participants. For present purposes, I take Lewis' [25] model as a variant of the Stalnakerian model.

[6] [2] provides a hybrid account of pejoratives and evaluative terms in the framework of "success" semantics, along the lines of the Davidsonian proposals in [22, 26]. This is compatible with the main claims I am making here. However, like Schlenker and Potts, Boisvert assumes a psychological expressivist, non-normative account of the non-declarative additional speech acts that his account posits, which make it in my view similarly inadequate. To illustrate: there clearly is a semantic tension between uttering 'thank you for *p*!' together with 'shame on you for *p*!', but this cannot be adequately captured by an account on which the sentences merely indicate that the utterer actually feels grateful and disappointed regarding *p*; for, of course, there is no inconsistency in having such feelings regarding the same situation ([2], 34). In contrast, an account on which the sentences indicate acts subject to norms such that for them to be correct the same situation is to be both worthy of gratitude and of indignation does capture the tension.

[7] Likewise, [28] poses as the expressive presupposition of 'chink' *that speakers in the context are willing to treat Chinese people with a certain kind of contempt, on account of being Chinese*. This is better than Schlenker's and Potts' subjectivist proposals, but is still objectionable along the lines that I develop in the main text.

and others, [35] suggests that contexts are structured by a "question under discussion" (QUD) for which discussants try to provide adequate answers.[8] The QUD might have been explicitly asked, but it can also be merely implicit; in some cases, it may be very general, including the "Big Question", *what is the way things are?*

If this is so, contexts should be thought of as structured by including contents taken with different illocutionary forces: at the very least, a QUD, in addition to the Stalnakerian context of commonly accepted propositions updated by ordinary utterances of declarative sentences. Contexts thus include the Stalnakerian set of propositions to which speakers are committed in the way they are committed to their beliefs, updated by accepted assertions; but they include also a separate class of propositions to which speakers are committed in the way they are to the questions that direct their inquiry, updated by new questions and by the assertions that partially answer them. Both components are mutually known, in felicitous cases.

Now, as [23] suggests, questions can be taken as a particular kind of directive (what literal utterances of imperative sentences signify); and directives in general independently help to establish the same point about the complex illocutionary structure of contexts. Several writers have advanced semantic accounts on which these are semantically distinctive objects, distinct from assertions (what declarative sentences literally signify), just as questions (what interrogative sentences signify) are; [13, 18, 30] provide good overviews. Along the lines of [40], researchers such as Han, Portner and Jary & Kissine suggest that strong directives also have a content to be added (when successful) to a collection of propositions. However, these are not those constituting the Stalnakerian common ground, but rather a "To Do List" or "Plan Set" representing something like the active projects of the addressee.

In sum, contexts are illocutionarily structured in complex ways, including different classes of propositions to which speakers are committed in different modes: in the way we are committed to our beliefs, but also in the way we are committed to our intentions, and to the questions guiding our inquiries. And, as we pointed out above, in felicitous contexts it is all these different commitments that are matters of mutual knowledge. As Stalnaker's [40] account of assertion emphasizes, an accepted assertion comes to be presupposed afterwards, allowing for the satisfaction of presuppositional requirements later on in the discourse. Similarly, an accepted directive is taken for granted afterwards, constraining the legitimate moves that can be made in the discourse game, and the same applies to the QUD.

Now, we could avoid all that complexity if we adopted a well-known suggestion to deal with non-declaratives by taking them to be synonymous with explicit performatives, and then taking the latter to have, from a semantic standpoint, the truth-conditions they appear to do compositionally [5, 24]. Thus, 'take bus 44!' would just mean, from a semantic point of view, the proposition *that the speaker thereby requests the audience to take bus 44*. Cannot we just adopt this line and avoid having to ascribe to contexts the complex structure we have so far posited? By taking questions and

---

[8] [36] offers a clear, short presentation of the idea.

directives to express the propositions self-ascribing speech-acts that these views envisage, we could just stick to the Stalnakerian view of context as a set of propositions. This is what I am calling the *flattening scheme*, or simply *flattening*. In previous work [9, 11] I have argued that these views are unmotivated.

Like the flattening suggestion for directives and questions, however, the corresponding view of emotions and their expression outlined aboves is controversial, and is rejected by many researchers ([6], 67; [7], 18–21). If emotions are instead, as I believe, *sui generis* normative states [6, 7, 29], and their expressions speech acts defined by distinctive norms, then in order to properly incorporate the presuppositional view of pejoratives we should add further illocutionary structure to the context set. This additional structure will be constituted by the intentional objects of the emotional states (say, Chinese people, with their (alleged) condition of generically having such-and-such features in the case of 'chink'), taken as subject to the normative condition that they are thereby worthy of contempt and hence adequate recipients of mistreatment. On this view, the "formal object" of the emotion – the property of being contemptible in this case – is not part of the represented content, but the normative condition that allegedly justifies addressing the emotional attitude towards it.

On the suggested view of emotions and the speech acts expressing them, the additional "emotive" structure of contexts should be assumed not only on a presuppositional account of pejoratives, but also on one on which they are conventional implicatures. For, even if the expressive content of pejoratives is background but novel "information", if unchallenged it would become part of the context set, licensing presuppositions down the line. The fact that we need to dissociate ourselves from such a prospect explains our normative reaction to utterances including slurs we disapprove of. This is why, even if Potts [32, 33] is right that such contents are conventional implicatures, his subjective characterization of the expressive implicatures should be revised to incorporate the present view of contexts.

Presuppositions are "filtered" in some contexts: they do not project when their triggers occur in the consequent of a conditional whose antecedent states them, or in the second conjunct of a conjunction whose first conjunct states them: *if someone broke the computer, it was John who broke it*; *someone broke the computer, and it was John who did it*. Schroeder ([39], 176) uses this point to dismiss the view that the expressive contents we are considering are presuppositions: "I cannot see how to construct a sentence of the form "if P, then Mark is a cheesehead" that does not implicate the speaker in disdain for people from Wisconsin".

This is right, but it is just as a straightforward consequence of the fact that the expressive contents we are discussing – be they presuppositions, or conventional implicatures – are not just forceless propositions, which is what antecedents of conditionals or conjuncts must be. It only follows that we cannot use the filtering behavior to discern whether the relevant contents are presupposed or conventionally implicated. The fact leaves open whether such contents are presented as requirements on the common ground (and hence have a presuppositional character), or as new background commitments (and hence are conventional implicatures). Schroeder's argument is one more example of the misleading consequences of ignoring the main claim about the nature of the expressive contents of pejoratives and slurs, and the contexts on which they make an impact, which I am making here.[9]

Some of Hom's ([16], 176–179; [17], 390–391) criticisms of the presuppositional and conventional implicature view have already been discussed, others have received adequate replies in the literature. The data about projection and "cancellation" are less clear than he assumes, and in any case can be accounted for by both proposals [28]. Intuitions about the truth-values of utterances are much less clear-cut than he and others take them to be (cf. [19], 317), and again can be accounted for by both the presuppositional and the conventional implicature proposals. Hom mentions "non-orthodox" cases that lack derogatory implications; but, again, defenders of alternative views have shown them to have enough resources to deal with them, as pragmatic effects or cases of polysemy ([20], 326–330). Last but not least, what Hom ([16], 177) thinks is the "more fundamental problem with the presupposition account" can be adequately resisted if expressive meanings and contexts are assumed to have the sort of illocutionary complexity I am arguing for. This is how he summarizes it:

> To focus on slurring as a means of efficiently entering information into the conversational record is to miss the fundamental point of slurs, namely, that they are typically used to verbally abuse their targets, with no regard to whether the negative content actually gets accommodated within a framework of rational, cooperative behavior.

He (ibid.) summarizes this by approvingly quoting Richard ([34], 21): rather than trying to enter something into the conversational record, "someone who is using these words is insulting and being hostile to their targets". Now, the reply that the present proposal allows should be obvious. The contrast that Hom and Richard presume between making a requirement on the conversational record (or making an attempt at smuggling it there) and insulting/being hostile to some target presupposes a view of expressive meanings and the contexts to which they contribute of the sort I have been rejecting here. The contrast vanishes if what is presumed to be in the context is a represented target taken as fitting the normative condition that it is contemptible and thereby poised for mistreatment: for this is precisely what the insult and the hostility amount to. It should be granted that Hom's and Richard's presumption that presuppositions merely concern "information" in the conversational record is shared by most of the theorists they oppose, but it is nonetheless wrong.

Actually, it is not at all obvious how Hom's own view properly captures the insulting character of utterances including slurs. His proposal is a form of the already mentioned flattening strategy for straightforward truth-conditional treatments of non-declaratives – the view that emotions are ordinary judgments, and their expression corresponding assertions. As we said, an immediate concern this raises has to do with the "projective" behavior of all such expressions under negation, conditionalization, etc.: as we have seen, intuitively expressive contents "escape" the operators under which they are embedded in such cases, while, if the expressive content is just

---

[9] It is a particularly revealing one, because it occurs in a paper that is otherwise admirably clear about the distinction between contents and forces; Schroeder's ([39], 278–280) toy formal model is as clear as [12] when it comes to the proper articulation of meanings that, like expressive contents in my view, are propositions-cum-illocutionary forces.

straightforward truth-conditional content, it should remain embedded. But in fact, the problem already affects simple positive sentences: in principle, an assertion that a command is given can occur without the command being given; and an assertion that an emotional state, or the occasion for it, obtains (that something is frightening or contemptible) can equally occur without the emotional state obtaining (without the fear or contempt occurring).[10]

As indicated above, Hom ([17], 398–401) purports to explain the generation of the expressive content (in embedded and simple constructions) as a Gricean generalized conversational implicature.[11] I have serious doubts that this proposal can work on its own terms, but this need not concern us here. I want to make a point about it related to the one made above regarding Potts' conventional implicatures account. In some cases, generalized conversational implicatures are not projected, but rather generated "locally", i.e. interacting with the compositional determination of contents, exactly as "impliciatures"/"expliciatures" are. The data suggest that, in some cases, expressive contents are thus generated locally ([37], 244). It remains to be investigated whether these should be truly handled locally by our best theories; but, if they are, a full theoretical account of the data will need to contemplate the structurally enriched contexts we have advanced, even if we classify the generation of expressive contents as a generalized conversational implicature.

In this paper I have assumed a broadly Stalnakerian view of contexts, the concrete situations relative to which linguistic exchanges take place; I have assumed, that is, that they are meanings shared by the speakers participating in the relevant linguistic exchange. I have rejected Stalnaker's "info-centric" view of such contexts: they cannot be just propositions, or more in general representational contents, but rather these contents together with commitments towards them by speakers in different modes. This should be clear just on the basis of the fact that conversations involve not just assertoric utterances, but also directives and questions. With respect to this familiar fact, I have rehearsed the familiar "flattening" strategy that attempts to reduce non-declaratives to declaratives, and the reasons that have been advanced against it. In this framework I have discussed the semantics of pejoratives and slurs. I have suggested that flattening will not work in that case either, and I have provided what I take to be a stronger form of a presuppositional account on which such constructions indicate as requirements on the content expressive meanings additional to "at issue" contents.

---

[10] The same can intuitively obtain in the opposite direction: the non-cognitive attitude/act (the command or the derogation) can occur, without the cognitive one (the belief/assertion that the command or the derogation takes place) taking place, because the thinker/speaker lacks the conceptual resources to describe the non-cognitive state/act. Hom deals with this apparent necessity-failure of his account by appealing to semantic externalism: semantically the equivalence obtains, even if ordinary speakers lack the resources to appreciate it.

[11] The semantic externalism to which Hom appeals to deal with the apparent necessity-failure (see previous fn.) puts a strain on his appeal to conversational implicature to deal with this sufficiency-failure, because implicatures are supposed to be *derivable*. It is difficult to understand how ordinary speakers intuiting the allegedly implicatured condition – in our cases, the derogation of Chinese people, which is what everybody perceives in utterances of 'there are too many Chinks in our neighborhood' – can make the inferences, if they themselves lack the resources to articulate the content of Hom's truth-conditional analysis.

References

1. Bach, K.: The myth of conventional implicatures. Linguist. Philos. **229**, 327–366 (1999)
2. Boisvert, D.: The truth in hybrid semantics. In: Fletcher, G., Ridge, M. (eds.) Having it Both Ways: Hybrid Theories and Modern Metaethics, pp. 22–50. OUP, Oxford (2014)
3. Camp, E.: Slurring perspectives. Anal. Philos. **54**(3), 330–349 (2013)
4. Carlson, L.: Dialogue Games: an Approach to Discourse Analysis. D. Reidel, Dordrecht (1982)
5. Davidson, D.: Moods and Performances. In: Margalit, A. (ed.) Meaning and Use, pp. 9–20. D. Reidel, Dordrecht (1979)
6. D'Arms, J., Jacobson, D.: The moralistic fallacy: on the 'appropriateness' of emotions. Philos. Phenomenol. Res. **61**(1), 65–90 (2000)
7. Deonna, J., Teroni, F.: In what sense are emotions evaluations? In: Roeser, S., Todd, C. (eds.) Emotion and Value, pp. 15–31. OUP, Oxford (2014)
8. de Sousa, R.: Emotion. In: Zalta, E.N. (ed.) The Stanford Encyclopedia of Philosophy (Spring 2014 Edition) (2014). http://plato.stanford.edu/archives/spr2014/entries/emotion/
9. García-Carpintero, M.: Assertion and the semantics of force-markers. In: Bianchi, C. (ed.) The Semantics/Pragmatics Distinction. CSLI Lecture Notes, pp. 133–166. The University of Chicago Press, Chicago (2004)
10. García-Carpintero, M.: Recanati on the semantics/pragmatics distinction. Crítica **38**, 35–68 (2006)
11. García-Carpintero, M.: Accommodating presupposition. Topoi (2015). doi:10.1007/s11245-014-9264-5
12. Green, M.: Illocutionary force and semantic content. Linguist. Philos. **23**, 435–473 (2000)
13. Han, C.-H.: Imperatives. In: Maienborn, C., von Heusinger, K., Portner, P. (eds.) Semantics: An International Handbook of Natural Language Meaning, pp. 1785–1804. Mouton de Gruyter, Berlin (2011)
14. Hay, R.J.: Hybrid expressivism and the analogy between pejoratives and moral language. Eur. J. Philos. **21**(3), 450–474 (2011)
15. Hom, C.: The semantics of racial epithets. J. Philos. **105**, 416–440 (2008)
16. Hom, C.: Pejoratives. Philos. Compass **5**(2), 164–185 (2010)
17. Hom, C.: The puzzle of pejoratives. Philos. Stud. **159**, 383–405 (2012)
18. Jary, M., Kissine, M.: Imperatives. Cambridge U.P., Cambridge (2014)
19. Jeshion, R.: Slurs and stereotypes. Anal. Philos. **54**, 314–329 (2013)
20. Jeshion, R.: Expressivism and the Offensiveness of Slurs. Philos. Perspect. **54**, 307–335 (2013)
21. Kaplan, D.: The Meaning of 'Ouch' and 'Oops' (Unpublished manuscript)
22. Lepore, E., Ludwig, K.: Donald Davidson's Truth-Theoretic Semantics. Oxford U.P., Oxford (2007)
23. Lewis, D.: Convention: A Philosophical Study. Harvard U.P., Cambridge (1969)
24. Lewis, D.: General semantics. Synthèse **22**, 18–67 (1970)
25. Lewis, D.: Scorekeeping in a language game. J. Philos. Logic **8**, 339–359 (1979)
26. Ludwig, K.: The truth about moods. Protosociology **10**, 19–66 (1997)
27. Macià, J.: Presuposición y significado expresivo. Theoria **3**(45), 499–513 (2002)
28. Macià, J.: Expressive meaning and presupposition. In: Handout for a Talk at the Names, Demonstratives, and Expressives Conference in Gargnano, Italy (2014)
29. Mulligan, K.: From appropriate emotions to values. Monist **81**(1), 161–188 (1998)
30. Portner, P.: Imperatives. In: Aloni, M., Dekker, P. (eds.) The Cambridge Handbook of Semantics, pp. 593–627. CUP, Cambridge (2016)

31. Potts, C.: The Logic of Conventional Implicatures. OUP, Oxford (2005)
32. Potts, C.: The expressive dimensions. Theor. Linguist. **33**(2), 165–198 (2007)
33. Potts, C.: Conventional implicature and expressive content. In: Maienborn, C., vov Heusinger, K., Portner, P. (eds.) Semantics: An International Handbook of Natural Language Meaning, Mouton de Gruyter, Berlin, vol. 3, pp. 2516–2535 (2012)
34. Richard, M.: When Truth Gives Out. Oxford University Press, Oxford (2008)
35. Roberts, C.: Information structure in discourse: towards an integrated formal theory of pragmatics. Seman. Pragmat. **5**, 1–69 (2012). Yoon, J., Kathol, A. (eds.) Originally Published in OSU Working Papers in Linguistics, vol. 49 (1998)
36. Schaffer, J.: Knowledge in the image of assertion. Philos. Issues **18**, 1–19 (2008)
37. Schlenker, P.: The expressive dimensions. Theor. Linguist. **33**(2), 237–245 (2007)
38. Schroeder, M.: Hybrid expressivism: virtues and vices. Ethics **119**, 257–309 (2009)
39. Schroeder, M.: The truth in hybrid semantics. In: Fletcher, G., Ridge, M. (eds.) Having it Both Ways: Hybrid Theories and Modern Metaethics, pp. 273–293. OUP, Oxford (2014)
40. Stalnaker, R.: Assertion. In: Cole, P. (ed.) Syntax and Semantics 9, pp. 315–332. Academic Press, New York (1978). Also in Stalnaker, R. (ed.) Context and Content, pp. 78–95. Oxford UP, Oxford (1999), to which I refer
41. Stalnaker, R.: Context. OUP, Oxford (2014)
42. Todd, C.: Emotion and value. Philos. Compass **9**(10), 702–712 (2014)
43. Tonhauser, J., Beaver, D., Roberts, C., Simons, M.: Towards a taxonomy of projective content. Language **89**, 66–109 (2013)
44. Whiting, D.: It is not what you said, it's the way you said it, slurs and conventional implicatures. Anal. Philos. **54**(3), 364–377 (2013)
45. Williamson, T.: Reference, inference, and the semantics of pejoratives. In: Almog, J., Leonardi, P. (eds.) The Philosophy of David Kaplan, pp. 137–158. Oxford University Press, Oxford (2009)

Context in Representation

From a Contextual Graph to a Tree Representation

Kimberly García[(⊠)] and Patrick Brézillon[iD]

University Pierre and Marie Curie (UPMC), Paris, France
{Kimberly.Garcia,Patrick.Brezillon}@lip6.fr

Abstract. Through successfully applying the Contextual-Graph formalism in many fields (e.g. medicine, transport, and military), the need for an alternative visualization was recurrently encountered. Decision makers require: (1) a visual representation that clusters all the contextual information needed to develop a practice, and (2) a representation that allows them to easily identify each practice output. Either if this output corresponds to a real object (e.g. a medical image), or an object of the reasoning (e.g. a strategy for highway driving). This paper presents the response to decision-makers needs: the Practice Tree view, which is the result of transforming a contextual graph into a tree that complies the described requirements.

Keywords: Context modeling · Contextual-Graphs formalism · Tree representation · Contextual information · Task modeling

1 Introduction

The concept of context has been widely defined in several fields of study. In 2005, Bazire and Brézillon [2] created a corpus of over 166 definitions of context proposed in several fields of study. In Computer Science, the most popular definitions are the ones from Brézillon and Dey. In [4] context is defined as "what does not intervene explicitly in a focus but constrains it", while in [8] "context is any information that can be used to characterize the situation of an entity. An entity is a person, place, or object that is considered relevant to the interaction between a user and an application, including the user and applications themselves". By analyzing these two popular definitions, it is not surprising that the research conducted in the context field can be divided into two categories [11]: (a) the one which aim is to create context-aware applications [10], and (b) the one focused on formalizing, modeling, and creating frameworks to apply the context concept to different fields.

Two of the main formalisms for representing context are Contextual Graphs [6], and Context-based Reasoning (CxBR) [9]. CxBR is a paradigm for human tactical behavior representation, which aims at creating models of missions for controlling the physical actions of an agent that is part of a simulation or the real world. It allows to following the development of a mission at a high level, in a sort of context stages, providing transitions rules to change from one context to another. On its side, the Contextual-Graphs formalism offers a uniform representation of elements of knowledge, reasoning and context. This formalism has been conceived to support

P. Brézillon et al. (Eds.): CONTEXT 2017, LNAI 10257, pp. 27–40, 2017.
DOI: 10.1007/978-3-319-57837-8_3

decision-making, and knowledge transfer by providing semantic items to represent task realizations, as they occur in real life. Each path in a graph corresponds to a practice developed by an actor in a particular context. The Contextual Graph formalism has been successfully used in many fields, such as transport, medicine and military. This has been possible through the CxG software, which first objective was to let users create and edit a contextual graph in a friendly way.

However, over the years, decision makers have expressed their need for an alternative representation of task realizations once they have incorporated CxGs to their daily work. Even though, a Contextual Graph is a graphic, and easy to follow representation, it has one major limitation: is not possible to immediately associate an output to a Contextual Graph practice; which would give decision makers an immediate hint of the possible outcome of their decisions. However, by definition a contextual graph has a unique input and a unique output, even when the conclusion of each practice might be different. Thus, another representation that allows the easy association of a practice to its conclusion, and helps identifying all the contextual information required in each practice would satisfactorily comply the decision-maker needs. In this paper, we propose the introduction of the Practice Tree view. This view consists in transforming a contextual graph into a tree, in which the contextual elements found are placed on the left side of such a tree, and the actions that should be followed to complete the task are placed on the right side of the tree.

This paper is organized in the following way, Sect. 2 presents a quick overview of the Contextual-Graphs formalism as well as an introduction to the Practice Tree view. Then, Sect. 3 explains the integration of the Practice Tree view to the CxG software, followed by the difficulties faced to create such a view, which had led us to a deeper understanding of the CxGs types of user. Section 4 concludes this paper with the lesson learned and the future work.

2   On the Contextual Graph Formalism

In [4] context is defined as "what does not intervene explicitly in a focus but constrains it". Based on this working definition, the implementation of the Contextual-Graphs (CxG) formalism leads to a uniform representation of elements of knowledge, reasoning and context that are needed in a task realization. Four types of items can be found in a CxG [5]: actions, contextual elements, activities and Executive Structures of Independent Activities (ESIA).

A contextual graph has a unique input, a unique output and an organization of nodes connected by edges, in which each node can be an action, an activity, a contextual node or a recombination node. A contextual graph is formally defined as a directed and acyclic graph with a series-parallel structure [7]. A contextual graph takes a series-parallel structure from sets of elements placed one after the other in a series fashion. Contextual elements provide the parallel structure of a graph, since they lead to several alternatives of completing a task realization.

We are interested in providing the tree view of Contextual Graphs to satisfy the decision-makers needs regarding: (a) the visualization of the individual practices that can be followed to complete a task, (b) the quick identification of the contextual information needed to follow each practice, and (c) the conclusion a practice produces.

2.1   The Practice Tree View

More often than not, decision makers need a quick way to evaluate a situation in order to take immediate action (e.g. handle an incident in the Parisian subway [3]). Thus, a CxG could become difficult to follow in task representations that involve many contextual elements spread along the graph. Some task could also benefit from a different representation that allows them to relate a graphical output to the practices represented in a CxG. This is particularly important when the task to perform relies on the analysis of an object product of reasoning. Such an object can be a physical object (e.g. a digital slide in medicine) or a cognitive object (e.g. a decision at the end of a practice development). Figure 1 shows a contextual graph used by an ana-cyto-pathologist to determine if a medical slide contains a mitosis [1]. A well-trained physician would be able to infer the content of the practice by just looking at the output. However, this immediate association of a practice to an output is not possible in a graph, since all the components are connected, leading to a unique output for all the branches.

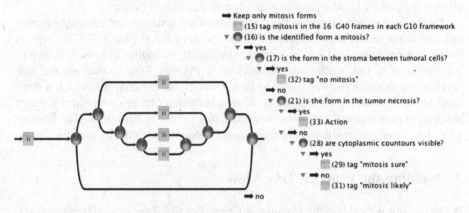

Fig. 1. CxG for mitosis identification

Thus, we incorporated a Practice Tree view to the CxG software. All the contextual elements contained in a CxG are orderly gathered in the left side of the tree (see Fig. 2) and the action, and activities are ordered in the right side of it. We have named it Practice Tree view, since each branch corresponds to a particular practice (i.e., a way to realize a task). Figure 2 shows the tree view of the contextual graph presented in Fig. 1. Here, a digital slide (physical object) is associated to each possible practice of the graph.

The Practice Tree view follows the decision-making definition since it allows easily the identification of the contextual information that experts need to know prior the task realization. Furthermore, this representation allows experienced users to build a

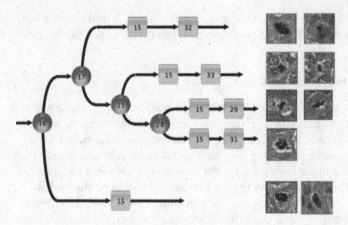

Fig. 2. A CxG and its practice tree view associated with the objects of the reasoning grouped according to the practices (i.e., each practice leads to a conclusion: "no mitosis", "mitosis sure", "mitosis likely").

proceduralized context of a situation, in order to identify the practice that should be followed by a less experienced user (e.g. an engineer is capable of quickly assessing the mission for identifying the practice that a technician should follow).

By incorporating the Practice Tree view to the CxG software, we are able to show a task realization model in two different formalisms: trees and graphs. A CxG focuses on the ways a problem is solved (i.e., practice structure), providing a chronological representation of a task realization. Meanwhile, a Practice Tree focuses on the link between the situation (e.g. an image to be classified) and the conclusion (e.g. a decision) by first presenting the rationality of the conclusion (the proceduralized context) obtained in each practice, and then the actions that should be performed. The Practice Tree view clearly shows that there are as many solutions as branches (see Fig. 2).

3   Building the Practice Tree View

In this section we explain the Contextual Graph Practice Tree view computation (cf. Sect. 3.1). Then, we propose a solution to the problem that arises when Contextual Graphs have a predominant series structure (cf. Sect. 3.2) and present its validation (cf. Sect. 3.3). Finally, we analyze further the graphs structures, and disclose some findings (cf. Sect. 3.4).

3.1   Computing the Practice Tree View

Since our objective is to gather all the contextual elements on the left side of the Practice Tree and the actions, and activities on the right side, we propose to perform two types of scans to the graph: from right to left, and from left to right. In a scan, the graph is traversed looking for a contextual element. When a scan from the right to the left of the graph is performed, the algorithm stops when a contextual element is found.

In case there are elements to the right of such a contextual element, they are replicated and placed at the end of each branch of the contextual element found. In a scan from left to right of the graph, the algorithm also stops when a contextual element is found. In case there are non-contextual elements placed to the left of such a contextual element, they are replicated at the beginning of each one of the contextual-element branches. The scan from the left is made just after several scans from right to left have been completed, so the algorithm ensures that there is not a contextual element with neighbors to the right that need to be duplicated on its branches. The algorithm is recursive. Every time a scan is performed, the CxG is verified, in order to determine if the Practice Tree view has been completed or more scans are required. A Practice Tree view is completed when each contextual element is either followed by another contextual element, or is the last element on the graph.

In Fig. 3 examples of both type of scans are presented. Figure 3(a) shows that the first contextual element has three neighbors to the right (two activities and a contextual element), which should be duplicated in each one of its branches. Thus, a scan from right is performed, copying the two actions and the contextual element (including all of its elements) to the end of each branch of the concerned contextual element, as shown in Fig. 3(b).

After verifying the CxG shown in Fig. 3(b), it is determined that there are contextual elements that have neighbors to the right. Thus, another scan from right to left is performed, resulting in the graph presented in Fig. 4(a). Then, the CxG is verified again, finding that there are not contextual elements with neighbors to the right, hence a scan to the left can take place now. In this scan the two actions at the very beginning of

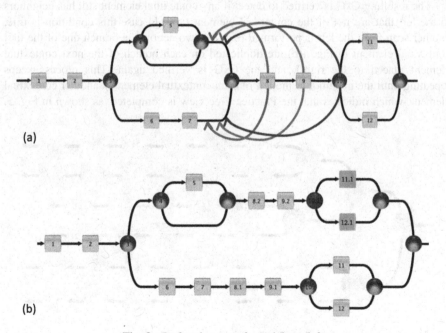

(a)

(b)

Fig. 3. Performing scan from right to left

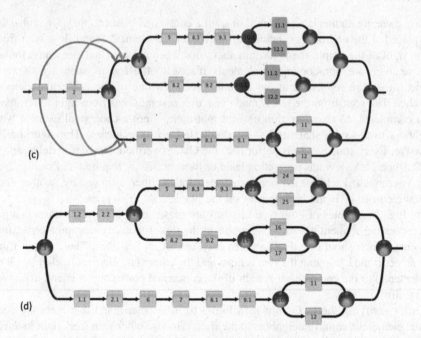

Fig. 4. Performing scan from the left

the graph are duplicated at the start of each branch of the first contextual element found, as the arrows in Fig. 4(a) indicate; the result is the graph shown in Fig. 4(b).

The resulting CxG is verified to detect if any contextual element still has neighbors to the left that are not of the contextual element type. In case this condition is true, another scan from the left is performed (e.g. the two actions on branch one of the first contextual element in Fig. 4(b) are duplicated on each branch of the next contextual element placed to the right), and the CxG is verified again. This process keeps repeating until the neighbor to the left of each contextual element is another contextual element, which indicates that the Practice Tree view is completed, as shown in Fig. 5.

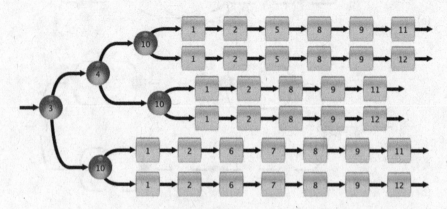

Fig. 5. The resulting practice tree

However, during the testing phase of the Practice Tree view, we found out that not all the models lead to manageable Practice Tree views, since depending on the structure of each graph, the number of duplicated elements can grow exponentially, making a Practice Tree overly bushy, and difficult to read, which is opposite to the objective of this view. In the following section we propose a way to detect and deal with these Practice Trees.

3.2 Bushy Practice Trees

In order to create the tree view of a graph, the recombination nodes of each contextual element are suppressed, and the neighbors to the right and to the left should be duplicated and ordered on each branch of the contextual element, as explained in the previous section (cf. Sect. 3.1). In case a graph has a predominant series structure, in which the neighbor to the right of a contextual element is another contextual element, the width of the practice tree increases proportionally to the number of branches of the current contextual element minus one time the number of branches of its neighbor.

However, in a graph with a predominant parallel structure, in which there are more contextual elements nested in other contextual elements, most of the items to duplicate would be of the action or activity type, thus the tree width will not increase as fast. Therefore, the Practice Tree of a Contextual Graph is more likely to be manageable if the number of possible practices (i.e. paths from the starting item to the last one) remains small, meaning the graph has a predominant parallel structure.

In order to assess the manageability of a graph, let us consider graph G1 in Fig. 6. It is integrated by five contextual elements and eleven actions. Thus, if we compute all the possible paths from contextual element 1 to the last recombination node, we obtain a set of 24 paths. Likewise, graph G2 in Fig. 7 has five contextual elements, and eleven actions. The number and type of items is exactly the same as in G1. However, the number of possible paths for G2 from the first action to the last recombination node is six (Fig. 8).

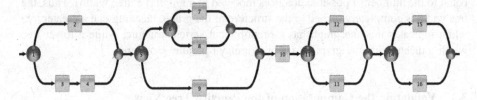

Fig. 6. G1 is a graph with a predominant series structure

When computing the Practice Tree views for G1 and G2, a significant difference was found on the tree width of each Practice Tree. Even though both graphs have the same number and type of items, the tree width of G1 Practice Tree is 24, four times the tree width of G2 Practice Tree, which is 6. Moreover, G1 and G2 width results ring a bell, since the number of possible paths from the first to the last item of the graph is

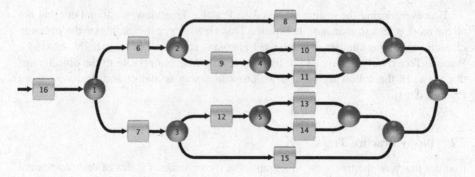

Fig. 7. G2 is a graph with a predominant parallel structure

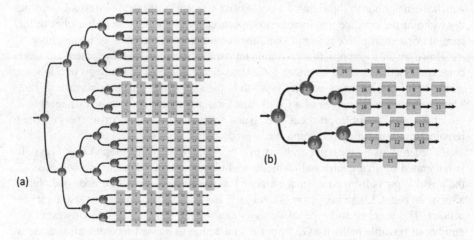

Fig. 8. G1 practice tree (a) and G2 practice tree (b)

equal to the number of possible practices modeled in a graph (i.e. tree width). Thus, the tree width is completely related to the structure of the graph, meaning that a greater tree width indicates that the graph has a predominant series structure, while a lower tree width indicates that the graph has a predominant parallel structure.

3.3 Validating the Computation of the Practice Tree View

During the testing phase of the Practice Tree view, it was observed that the resulting tree of a complex graph with a predominant series structure could be integrated by hundreds or even thousands of branches that can be almost identical; they typically differ from the neighbor practice by just few actions. An overly bushy tree is impractical for decision makers, since the purpose of providing a quick overview of the implications of each practice is defeated. A tree with these characteristics could become even harder to analyze than a CxG. Additionally, the actual image file of a bushy

Practice Tree becomes too big to be displayed in a normal size screen, forcing users to lose their focus on the overall task realization by requiring them to zoom-in in each practice. Thus, the analysis of the tree becomes weary and unfruitful. In order to maintain the advantages of the Practice Tree view, there is a validation step for estimating the total number of branches that a Practice Tree would have (i.e., tree width). By computing the tree width, it is possible to know if the resulting Practice Tree would be manageable or not. If the width is greater than a manageable threshold the view is not computed. Otherwise, the view is generated.

Algorithm 1 Compute tree width

---

1. Start traversing the graph
2. treeWidth = 0
3. if the current element is a CE then
4.   CE1 = current CE
5.   treeWidth = number of branches of the current CE
6.   for all branches do
7.   Traverse the branch
8.   if an element has not been visited yet then
9.   if the current element is a CE then
10.   CE2=current CE
11.   treeWidth=(treeWidth+number of CE2 branches-1)
12.   CE1=CE2
13.   Go to 6
14.   else
15.   Continue traversing the branch
16.   end if
17.   else
18.   Go to 7
19.   end if
20.   if CE1 has a neighbor to the right then
21.   Continue traversing the graph
22.   if the current element is a CE then
23.   CE1=current element
24.   treeWidth=(treeWidth_number of CE1 branches)
25.   Go to 6
26.   else
27.   Continue traversing the graph
28.   end if
29.   else
30.   Stop
31.   end if
32.   end for
33. else
34.   Continue traversing the graph
35. end if

The algorithm to compute the total number of branches Compute tree width (see Algorithm 1) consists in traversing the contextual graph until finding a contextual element, which would be the first level of the tree. As the algorithm is just starting, the total tree width is equal to the number of branches of the first contextual element. Then, the branches of the contextual element are visited in order to find nested contextual elements. In case a nested contextual element is found, the tree width increases by the number of branches in the nested contextual element −1. If there are not nested contextual elements, the neighbors to the right of the contextual element found are verified to determine if they are contextual elements. When a neighbor to the right is a contextual element, the tree width is multiplied by the number of branches of such a neighbor, and the neighbor is verified for nested contextual elements. The algorithm stops when there is not another contextual element neighbors to the right.

In order to establish an appropriate threshold for determining if a Practice Tree view should be computed or not, we performed several tests with complex contextual graphs with a series structure. According to our findings, a Practice Tree with 1440 branches creates a file image of size 55.7 MB, taking 1 min 3 s to compute. Meanwhile, a Practice Tree with 2736 branches takes around 4 min 44 s to compute, generating a huge image difficult to show on a common display. Based on such results, we have decided to set the threshold to 1800 branches. Even though it could be assumed that a tree wider than 1800 branches corresponds to a graph that is not often created, the reality is that task realizations expressed in a procedure-like way can easily lead to bushy practice trees. The selected threshold is safe in technical terms, since it ensures that: (a) the creation of a Practice Tree takes a reasonable amount of time (less than 1 min 10 s), (b) the created Practice Tree can be stored in an image _le that can be later displayed in a laptop or desktop screen, and (c) the software does not decrease its performance after computing the tree.

It is important to point out that although it is technically possible to create a Practice Tree with a thousand of branches width, the bushier a tree becomes; the less useful it is, as its simplification and explanation qualities decrease even just with a tree width larger than 100 branches. Thus, decision makers are encouraged to create CxGs with a parallel structure.

3.4 Understanding Overly Bushy Practice Trees

As explained in the previous section, a CxG with a series structure leads to a bushy Practice Tree. However, we wanted to discover why some people model task realizations in a parallel or in a series manner. Since the CxG formalism has been used in a diverse set of fields of application for several years now, we gathered a collection of graphs built over the years, and across different domains, by users with different levels of experience (i.e. novice, experts, and intermediate), in order to analyze their behaviors. Such an analysis leads us to believe that expert users tend to create CxGs with a predominant parallel structure, considering contextually dependent situations. Meanwhile, novices are more prone to create graphs with a series structure. In order to exemplify this finding let us revise the CxGs presented in Fig. 9.

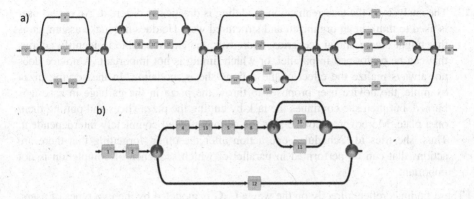

Fig. 9. The serving pizza task modeled by a novice (a), and by an expert (b) user

For clarity of the paper, we focus on the "serving a pizza" subtask of the more complex task: "eating pizza for dinner", since we asked two opposite users to model the general task, and the outcome was two totally different points of view. The graph presented in Fig. 9(a) was created by a young student who has just recently moved out from her parents' house. Thus, she knows the theory of making a pizza. The graph presented in Fig. 9(b) was created by a master student who has lived alone for several years. Therefore, his reasoning is more pragmatic. Through this experience, and the analysis conducted in the mentioned set of graphs, we highlight three clear findings concerning the users:

1. The amount of knowledge on the task realization reflects directly on the quality of the task realization model. A novice user has a narrower understanding of the problem since he might not be aware of information that for an expert user is evident. This was clear on the serving pizza example, the expert relies on the oven timer to know when the pizza should be taken out. Meanwhile, the novice suggests opening the oven repeatedly, until noticing that the pizza is ready.

2. The granularity of the reasoning differs according to the type of user. An expert has a holistic view of the task realization at a detailed but useful level, he is able to discriminate the relevant from the useless pieces of knowledge. Moreover, the expert is capable of integrating the task realization in a larger context, by making a "cognitive simulation" consisting in asking himself questions that determine the practices he models. Since a novice user is just discovering the task realization, he goes up and down in his reasoning, by sometimes omitting details, and some others considering irrelevant aspects, or relying on outsiders. In the pizza for dinner example, the expert user suggests a frozen pizza, and he considers, early on, the number of people invited to the dinner. Meanwhile, the novice proposes to make the pizza from scratch, considering making a list of ingredients, looking for a shop, trying to borrow a car, and several other actions that might not even belong to a realistic scenario. She also considers the number of people after she has already made the pizza, and it is time to serve it.

3. The analysis of the task-realization modeling is drastically different. An expert user is used to think in an organized and structured way. He does not make assumptions that might create unreal scenarios. Moreover, the expert is able to identify actions that can be performed in parallel, or which timing is not important. A novice does not always realize the effect of the actions she is modeling. In the serving pizza example, the novice user proposes to throw the pizza in the garbage in case it is burned, but then she continues the task by cutting the pizza slices and putting them on a plate. Moreover, a novice sees the actions needed completely interdependent. Thus, she tries to "schedule" one action after the other, forgetting that there are actions that can be performed in parallel or which sequence of completion is not important.

These findings reflect directly on the way a CxG is modeled by the two types of users. A novice user creates graph with a large series structure, which leads to bushy Practice Trees, because she tends to think that contextual elements are independent from each other, but that they should be analyzed one after the other. Novices forget that contextual elements that do not have an executing order could be represented in a parallel way, through an ESIA (which is a unit in a Practice Tree view). Moreover, they are unable to realize that many contextual elements are interdependent. Thus, instead of nesting them, they place such contextual elements in a series manner. On their side, CxGs created by expert users look cleaner, more compact, and have a predominant parallel structure. Since, through experience, these users have learned to organize their knowledge and their reasoning. As we have confirmed that a Practice Tree view is well adapted for representing experts' reasoning (i.e., resulting in few branches), it represents an important tool for novice training in several real-world applications.

4   Conclusions and Future Work

A CxG is integrated by all the possible practices existing to complete a task. However, sometimes a different view is required in order to quickly evaluate the contextual information a practice requires in order to follow it. Moreover, a view capable of associating a graphic output to each possible practice of a graph is useful in many applications (e.g., the analysis of medical images). Thus, we propose the Practice Tree view. To create it, we have implemented an algorithm consisting of two types of scans, which ensure that the elements are placed in the right order, and are duplicated when it is necessary.

However, when testing our solution, we found out that it was necessary to pay attention to the predominant structure of a CxG, since a series structure leads to a bushy Practice Tree that could be heavy to compute, and even useless for the user, since the image generated becomes too big and confusing to provide a proper analysis support. Thus, Practice Trees are valuable if they can be quickly computed and easily explored. Since we had to pay attention to the structure of the CxG, we introduce a validation step consisting in computing the total width of the CxG Practice Tree prior to its computation. In case the resulting width is smaller to a threshold established for technical reasons, the Practice Tree is computed. However, even if it is possible to compute a Practice Tree with a width larger than 100 branches, its actual usefulness is questionable. Thus, we were interested in discovering why some users create graphs with predominant series structures, and some others are able to model the same task realization in a parallel structure. From analyzing a set of graphs collected over the years, and conducting an experiment with an expert and a novice user modeling a trivial task, we found out that in fact novices tend to be the ones creating graphs with series structures. Since, due to the lack of experience, their knowledge on the task realization is limited, leading to constrained reasoning. Therefore, even when a bushy practice tree can be computed, it is not likely that the graph which was transformed into the tree becomes part of a real decision making process, since such a graph will for sure have to be refined by more advanced users.

The future of this work concerns the analysis and implementation of simulation capabilities to the Practice Tree view. This feature will provide full support to decision makers, since they will be able to see the evolution of the chosen practice, and the impact each decision has on the output. Furthermore, we have opened the door to a new challenging way of representing human reasoning, in which a practice is associated to an object of the reasoning (i.e., either a strategy or an actual object). Thus, we want to explore and analyze thoroughly the relationship among similar practices that lead to different outputs in crucial task realizations; such as the analysis of medical images to determine if a patient has cancer or not. This is a task realization that has not been automatized, since it has not been possible to fully capture the knowledge and experience of a specialized physician, in order to integrate it to a computational support. We expect that through such a deep analysis, we could provide insight to incorporate automatized reasoning features to the CxG software.

Acknowledgements. We thank the CONACyT (Consejo Nacional de Ciencia y Tecnología) for funding Kimberly García's post-doctoral fellowship at LIP6, UPMC. Proposal number: 238920.

References

1. Attieh, E., Capron, F., Brézillon, P.: Context-based modeling of an anatomo-cyto-pathology department workflow for quality control. In: Brézillon, P., Blackburn, P., Dapoigny, R. (eds.) CONTEXT 2013. LNCS (LNAI), vol. 8175, pp. 235–247. Springer, Heidelberg (2013). doi:10.1007/978-3-642-40972-1_18
2. Bazire, M., Brézillon, P.: Understanding context before using it. In: Dey, A., Kokinov, B., Leake, D., Turner, R. (eds.) CONTEXT 2005. LNCS (LNAI), vol. 3554, pp. 29–40. Springer, Heidelberg (2005). doi:10.1007/11508373_3
3. Brézillon, P., Pomerol, J.C.: Contextual knowledge and proceduralized context. In: Proceedings of the AAAI-99 Workshop on Modeling Context in AI Applications, Orlando, Florida, USA, July. AAAI Technical Report (1999)
4. Brézillon, P.: Context-based intelligent assistant systems: a discussion based on the analysis of two projects. In: Proceedings of the 36th Annual Hawaii International Conference on System Sciences. IEEE (2003)

5. Brézillon, P.: Task-realization models in contextual graphs. In: Dey, A., Kokinov, B., Leake, D., Turner, R. (eds.) CONTEXT 2005. LNCS (LNAI), vol. 3554, pp. 55–68. Springer, Heidelberg (2005). doi:10.1007/11508373_5

6. Brézillon, P.: Context modeling: task model and practice model. In: Kokinov, B., Richardson, D.C., Roth-Berghofer, T.R., Vieu, L. (eds.) CONTEXT 2007. LNCS (LNAI), vol. 4635, pp. 122–135. Springer, Heidelberg (2007). doi:10.1007/978-3-540-74255-5_10

7. Brézillon, P., Attieh, E., Capron, F.: Modeling glocal search in a decision-making process. In: DSS, pp. 80–91 (2014)

8. Dey, A.K., Abowd, G.D., Salber, D.: A conceptual framework and a toolkit for supporting the rapid prototyping of context-aware applications. Hum.-Comput. Interact. 16(2), 97–166 (2001)

9. Gonzalez, A., Brian, J., Stensrud, B., Barrett, G.: Formalizing context-based reasoning: a modeling paradigm for representing tactical human behavior. Int. J. Intell. Syst. 23(7), 822–847 (2008)

10. Perera, C., Zaslavsky, A., Christen, P., Georgakopoulos, D.: Context -aware computing for the internet of things: a survey. IEEE Commun. Surv. Tutor. 16(1), 414–454 (2014)

11. Vieira, V., Tedesco, P., Salgado, A.C.: Designing context-sensitive systems: an integrated approach. Expert Syst. Appl. 38(2), 1119–1138 (2011)

Enriching a Situation Awareness Framework for IoT with Knowledge Base and Reasoning Components

Niklas Kolbe[1]($\boxtimes$), Arkady Zaslavsky[2,3], Sylvain Kubler[1], Jérémy Robert[1], and Yves Le Traon[1]

[1] Interdisciplinary Center for Security, Reliability and Trust, University of Luxembourg, 4 Rue Alphonse Weicker, 2721 Luxembourg, Luxembourg
{niklas.kolbe,sylvain.kubler,jeremy.robert,yves.letraon}@uni.lu
[2] Commonwealth Scientific and Industrial Research Organisation, Data61, Clayton, VIC 3168, Australia
arkady.zaslavsky@csiro.au
[3] Saint Petersburg National Research University of ITMO, 49 Kronverksky Pr., St. Petersburg 197101, Russia
arkady.zaslavsky@acm.org

Abstract. The importance of system-level context- and situation awareness increases with the growth of the Internet of Things (IoT). This paper proposes an integrated approach to situation awareness by providing a semantically rich situation model together with reliable situation inference based on Context Spaces Theory (CST) and Situation Theory (ST). The paper discusses benefits of integrating the proposed situation awareness framework with knowledge base and efficient reasoning techniques taking into account uncertainty and incomplete knowledge about situations. The paper discusses advantages and impact of proposed context adaptation in dynamic IoT environments. Practical issues of two-way mapping between IoT messaging standards and CST are also discussed.

Keywords: Context space theory · Situation awareness · Situation theory · Ontology · O-MI/O-DF · Context adaptation

1 Introduction

With the growth of the Internet of Things (IoT) more and more devices publish sensed information, promoting the development of smart services and pervasive computing systems. The key feature of such systems is called context awareness; i.e. computing systems become aware of their state and environment in which they run, and provide services of higher value to humans [1]. Existing implementations of pervasive computing systems include for example home automation, smart energy systems, decision support systems for emergency cases, environmental impact monitoring, improved efficiency of transportation systems and

© Springer International Publishing AG 2017
P. Brézillon et al. (Eds.): CONTEXT 2017, LNAI 10257, pp. 41–54, 2017.
DOI: 10.1007/978-3-319-57837-8_4

many more. Furthermore, the IoT is considered as a key technology that could potentially enable the transition to a more sustainable society by providing the necessary information for a fundamental change in the way societies produce goods, use products, and consume resources as well as services. The advances towards sustainability are driven by large-scale problems and global challenges like resource depletion, food security, and climate change, as for instance stated by the Ellen MacArthur Foundation[1]. Still, several research challenges in various disciplines remain unsolved to deploy IoT-based systems more vastly and in a bigger scope, particularly regarding its pervasive feature.

A pervasive computing system needs to interpret acquired sensor data to fully understand the environment. Whereas *context* refers to features of entities [1], *situations* are of a more complex structure, e.g. involving relations between entities, temporal aspects, and requiring additional semantic interpretation. Situation aware applications thus rely on the integration of external knowledge to achieve an understanding of the environment on a higher level of abstraction than context [23]. This paper is concerned with challenges in knowledge representation and reasoning to achieve situation awareness in a general way, and discusses several issues that need to be considered when developing the knowledge base. The paper is built upon prior work: A domain-independent approach combining various concepts, e.g. ontologies, Context Space Theory (CST), Situation Theory and IoT messaging standards to provide a holistic framework for situation awareness [14]. Based on this framework, the following discussions cover the knowledge base integration, issues that are caused by incomplete knowledge about situations, and the implications of adaptation to current context for the knowledge base.

Section 2 presents related work and background in the domain of ontologies as knowledge base for situation aware systems. Section 3 introduces the framework that is considered in this paper to achieve situation awareness. It forms the foundation for discussions in the subsequent sections. Section 4 is concerned with defining and handling the knowledge base and preprocessing it for run-time reasoning. Sections 5 and 6 deal with incomplete knowledge and context adaptation related to the knowledge base respectively; the conclusion follows.

2   Ontology-Based Situation Awareness

Ontologies are defined as an *"explicit specification of a conceptualization"* [12] and have often been applied to develop a general model for situation awareness. The advantages of ontologies as a technique for situation modelling over other techniques – like graph models, object-role modeling, markup schemes, and spatial logic – are the eligibility of handling the heterogeneity of sensor data, capturing relationships and dependencies between context information and the native support for reasoning [3]. Moreover, *"being understandable, shareable, and reusable by both humans and machines"* [23] is another important

---

[1] Ellen MacArthur Foundation, Report on Intelligent Assets: https://www. ellenmacarthurfoundation.org/publications/intelligent-assets.

characteristic of ontologies, because it supports the complex and error-prone process of gathering and maintaining required domain knowledge. Ontologies can also be integrated into the existing infrastructures of relevant computing environments [20].

The presented features of ontologies reduce the knowledge engineering efforts, which motivates the incorporation of ontologies into a general situation awareness framework. However, ontologies have known limitations in the native reasoning support and performance issues during run-time in large-scale systems. Thus, the consideration of ontologies is restricted to the modelling and initialization phase of the system.

2.1   Situation Models and Upper Ontologies

Semantic web technologies like RDF, RDFS, OWL, and ontology reasoners, provide tools to share and reuse defined knowledge and are thus a feasible technology to develop a knowledge base for situation aware systems in IoT settings. The design of ontologies for this purpose needs to comply with semantic requirements regarding the capabilities of representing contexts and situations in a general way. In the following, a brief overview of existing approaches to define such situation models in the form of domain-independent, so-called *upper* ontologies, is presented.

Upper ontologies that were developed to provide a context or situation model have already been surveyed, for example in [2]. The authors developed an evaluation framework with context- and situation-related criteria and compared the design of four ontologies, namely SAWA [15], Situation Ontology [22], SOUPA [7] and CONON [21]. It is concluded that ontologies which are primarily targeted for context awareness (SOUPA and CONON) do not comply with the criteria for a general situation model. Most of the defined criteria are met by the SAWA ontology, however, even this approach lacks the support for situation types, roles and representation of space and time.

Other related approaches include the Situational Context Ontology [3]. The model combines contextual information (spatial and temporal) with related situations of an individual. Situation definitions are not entities of the ontology definition itself, but formulated externally with rules based on the Semantic Web Rule Language (SWRL).

The Situation Theory Ontology [13] is based on the semantics of the Situation Theory [10]. In Situation Theory, facts about the world are denoted as *infons*. An infon is defined as a *relation* among *objects* (e.g. individuals, attributes or other situations) with a *polarity* that defines whether this relation is true or false. A situation is characterized by the set of infons that this situation *supports*. Moreover, the Situation Theory supports logical operators and parameters representing types of objects and situations for more complex statements which can also be formulated in the Situation Theory Ontology.

2.2 Requirements for Situation Models to Support Reasoning

Further considerations for the situation model have to be taken into account to allow for reliable reasoning results and practical applicability of the approach. These include for example mobility, timeliness as well as uncertainty (imperfection and ambiguity) [3] in the model. Furthermore, incompleteness of knowledge, distributed composition of the system [20] – e.g. incorporation of sensor data from various sources and interoperability aspects – and the ability of the system to adapt current context may have implications on the requirements of the situation model. In this paper, the discussion is limited to aspects of uncertainty, incompleteness, sensor data integration, and dynamic context adaptation, related to ontology-based situation models.

Uncertainty aspects of a pervasive computing system, i.e. imperfect sensor data (e.g. missing values, imprecision) and incomplete knowledge about situations, are often approached with fuzzy logic. In fuzzy logic, membership functions can be defined, which map a set of numerical values to a fuzzy shape. The rule-based reasoning calculates a membership degree (between 0 and 1) for each fuzzy set, since the conditions for the sets may overlap. One approach that combines fuzzy logic and ontologies for situation awareness is the Fuzzy Situation Theory Ontology (FSTO) [11]. It extends the polarity of the infons of Situation Theory. Instead of assigning boolean values to the relation among objects, vagueness can be added through expressions like *quite true*. Situation occurrence is inferred through a model which considers the membership functions for infons and situations.

From a holistic viewpoint of a situation aware approach, the integration of sensor data also plays an important role; both from a modelling perspective (i.e., linking sensor data from physical data to modelled context) as well as an interoperability perspective (i.e., acquiring sensor data in an IoT setting). An example and W3C standard to model a sensor setup in an ontology is the Semantic Sensor Network (SSN) ontology [8]. SSN defines the relation between the network setup, sensing devices, and their observations (i.e. sensor data readings). In an effort to provide a similar model for actuators, the SAN ontology[2] was developed. Both ontologies were applied for example in [19] to provide a complete *IoT ontology*.

Smart, situation aware services in the IoT are based on the access to contextual information and other services that often reside in domain-specific platforms (also referred to as *vertical silos* in the IoT), where interoperability for cross-domain and -platform services is difficult to achieve. In the framework of this research, the IoT messaging standards of the bIoTope H2020 project[3] are considered to achieve cross-platform interoperability, namely the O-MI (Open-Messaging Interface[4]) and O-DF (Open-Data Format[5]) standards. These provide a generic and standardized way to expose and describe contextual data on top of

---

[2] SAN ontology: https://www.irit.fr/recherches/MELODI/ontologies/SAN.owl.

[3] bIoTope project: http://www.biotope-project.eu/.

[4] Open-Messaging Interface: https://www2.opengroup.org/ogsys/catalog/C14B.

[5] Open-Data Format: https://www2.opengroup.org/ogsys/catalog/C14A.

the techniques used by different platforms, which makes the access to contextual data and thus the situation aware component domain-independent.

3 Framework Based on Context Space Theory

This section introduces the framework on which the work of this paper is based on (originally presented in [14]). The combination of different techniques is necessary to meet the aforementioned requirements for a situation aware system, as the exclusive use of ontologies is not sufficient to provide reliable reasoning. The presented approach is based on ontologies for modelling and merged with the Context Space Theory for reasoning and O-MI/O-DF for sensor data acquisition.

The Context Space Theory [17] was developed for reasoning about context based on a multidimensional spatial metaphor. Figure 1 visualizes the main concepts of this theory. Context attributes, which are measurable properties usually provided by sensors, form the dimensions of the context or application space. Real-life situations are represented as subspaces (illustrated as multi-dimensional *bubbles*) of the application space, named situation spaces. The context state describes a point that moves through the application space depending on the current values of a corresponding set of context attribute values over time (as represented by the dashed line). If the context state lies in the subspace of a situation, this situation is occurring. This inference is based on a place-holder function that allows the usage of different techniques to reason about situation occurrence.

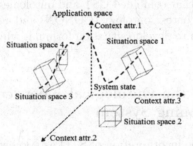

Fig. 1. Illustration of the context space theory [6]

The overall architecture of the framework and underlying building blocks (based on ECSTRA [4]) are displayed in Fig. 2. The upper ontology designed for this framework is based on STO and SSN. The concepts of these different ontologies were mapped and specific CST-related aspects were added to the ontology (presented in [14]). The upper ontology is used to capture domain- and application-specific knowledge about situations, individuals, attributes, sensors, actuators, and their relations. The combined usage of these upper ontologies provides a complete specification of all relevant knowledge assets relevant for a situation aware system.

The information provided by this knowledge base is used for the initialization of the system, i.e. to generate the situation spaces in the context space based on the situation definitions in the ontology. Furthermore, the situation definitions

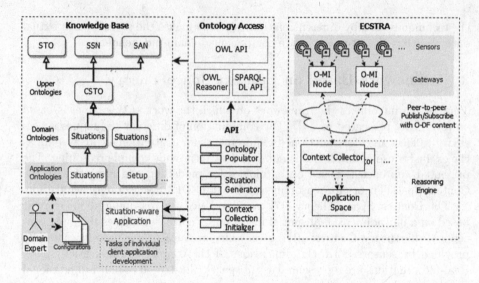

Fig. 2. Framework architecture for situation awareness

from the ontology can be used to assign sensor data to relevant context attributes and involved individuals in situations, which extends the concepts defined in CST.

A related approach that combined CST and ontologies is presented in paper [5]. In this approach, a context ontology (CONON) and a sensor ontology (SSN) are used as a foundation to develop situation formulas which are then translated to Context Space.

4 Integration of the Ontological Knowledge Base into the Reasoning System

This section presents the incorporation of STO as a knowledge base for a CST-based reasoning approach. Firstly, the situation representations of STO and CST are mapped, in order to extract the knowledge from the ontology and to create the situation spaces in the context space. Secondly, issues are discussed that occur when the situation definitions are translated to the CST model, and how additional processing allows for situation space generation with reduced knowledge engineering effort.

4.1 Mapping of Situation Representations in ST and CST

In the following, both the formal representation of situations in CST and in ST are presented in order to develop a formal mapping of these concepts. Both theories and their formal denotations are summarized in Table 1, moreover, it also shows the mapping of the individual representations by assigning corresponding, general concepts.

In CST, a situation space S_j is formally defined by an acceptable region $A_{a_i}^{S_j}$ for each corresponding context attribute a_i, which form the dimensions of this situation space in the overall context space. An acceptable region $A_{a_i}^{S_j}$ contains the elements that satisfy a predicate $P(V)$ and thus, defines the shape of the multidimensional bubble.

Inferring whether a situation is occurring is based on the context state, which is the set of current values of all context attributes. The inference function μ_{S_j} uses a Dempster-Shafer approach to calculate a confidence level for situation is occurrence. For this, the inference function takes the general relevance and the contribution of the current value of each context attribute into account. The relevance function $w_{S_j}(a_i)$ formally assigns a weight $w \in [0, 1]$ to each context attribute a_i of a situation space S_j. This weight defines the relative importance of a particular context attribute to infer a situation occurrence. To allow more refined specifications, the contribution function $\eta_{a_i}^{S_j}(x_{a_i})$ assigns a contribution degree c for each value x_{a_i} in an acceptable region for a situation space. If, for example, the value of a context attribute is at the border of a situation space, it might be uncertain whether this value contributes to the occurrence of the situation, thus, this value within the acceptable region can be assigned with a lower contribution degree. The calculated confidence value for situation occurrence by μ_{S_j} is compared to a confidence threshold ε_i to get a boolean output.

In Situation Theory [10], on the other hand, situations are defined by specifying which infons they support, denoted as $s \models \sigma$. Infons represent facts about the world and are defined as a relation r among n objects, with the polarity i whether this relation is true or false: $\sigma = \ll r, a_1, ..., a_n, i \gg$. Objects that stand in a relation can be individuals, attributes and situations. Moreover, ST considers the definition of types and parameters to make statements about a group of objects, which were extended for STO. *ATTR*, *SIT* and *VAL* for example represent the types of attributes, situations and values correspondingly.

As already mentioned, Table 1 not only summarizes these definitions presented before but also shows how these concepts of the two theories correspond to each other. Consequently, it can be inferred that the basic composition of a situation space can be extracted from the situation definition in ST. Information assets that are required for CST-based reasoning, however, cannot be extracted from native ST definitions. Thus, the situation specification in STO requires extensions to allow the integration of all required assets in the knowledge base. On the other hand, ST comes with concepts that are not considered in CST that can enhance the reasoning capabilities, as presented in the following subsection.

4.2   On Involved Individuals and Type Definitions

Situation reasoning is not only dependent on the context attributes, but also on *individuals* – items, persons, objects, etc. – that are involved in the situation. In CST, multiple involved individuals for one situation definition can be handled in two different ways. The first approach is to maintain multiple context states

Table 1. Mapping of CST and ST concepts for situation representation

Concept	CST representation	ST representation
Situation	Situation space S_j	Situation s
Attribute	Context attribute a_i	Attribute a_n type $ATTR$
Values & ranges	Acceptable region $A_{a_i}^{S_j} = \{V|P(V)\}$	Values a_n type VAL in σ
Situation composition	Set of acceptable regions $S_j = (A_1^j, A_2^j, ..., A_n^j)$	Set of supported infons $s \models \sigma$ $\sigma = \ll r, a_1, ..., a_n, i \gg$
State	Context state $x = (x_{a_1}, x_{a_2}, ..., x_{a_n})$ x_{a_i}: value of a_i	-
Attribute weight	Relevance $w_{S_j}(a_i) = w;$ $w \in [0,1]; \sum_{i=1}^{n} w_{S_j}(a_i) = 1$	-
State weight	Contribution $\eta_{a_i}^{S_j}(x_{a_i}) = c; c \in [0,1]$	-
Inference	Inference function $\mu_{S_j} = \sum_{i=1}^{n} w_{S_j}(a_i) * \eta_{a_i}^{S}(x_{a_i})$ Confidence threshold ε_i	-
Type abstraction	-	Situation types, object types $[\dot{s}|\dot{s} \models \sigma], \dot{a_n}$
Involved individuals	-	Involved individuals a_n type IND

simultaneously and to reason about a general situation space, whereas in the second approach a single context state is maintained and reasoning is performed over dedicated situation spaces for each involved individual. For example, the second case needs to be considered if situation spaces of a type definition differ depending on the involved individual, and if the situation space moves over time depending on reasoning results. As discussed before, the context values from external sources are linked to attributes, individuals, and situation definitions by extending the model with the SSN ontology.

The support of type abstraction is an important feature to keep the complexity of the modelling process low. ST facilitates such general specifications through the use of (abstraction) parameters in situation type definitions. As defined in [10], situation types are formally denoted as $[\dot{s}|\dot{s} \models \sigma]$. The transformation from a situation definition to a situation space depends on whether the situation definition is based on objects or types, as explained in the following.

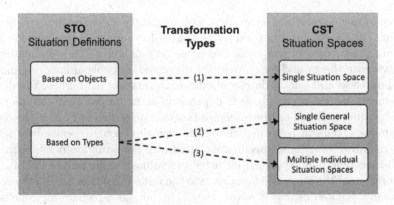

Fig. 3. Transformation from situation definition to situation space

The situation space generation has to be handled in different ways based on the situation definition in ontology. Figure 3 shows a classification of the transformation types from situation representation in ST to CST.

If a situation definition is solely based on objects it can be transformed to a corresponding single situation space in a straight-forward manner. The transformation is formally denoted in Eq. (1).

$$s \models \sigma \Rightarrow S_j \tag{1}$$

If a situation definition in STO includes type abstraction two approaches for situation generation can be differentiated, based on the considerations in the beginning of this section. The first option, denoted in Eq. (2), represents the generation of a general situation space for a set of involved individuals.

$$[\dot{s}|\dot{s} \models \sigma] \Rightarrow S_j \tag{2}$$

The second option for a type-based transformation, formally given in Eq. (3), generates multiple situation spaces. In the first step, all possible situations based on objects are derived from the type definition by calculating the n-fold Cartesian product over the objects of the n type definitions involved in the situation definition. In the second step, the resulting definitions based on objects are transformed to corresponding situation spaces.

$$[\dot{s}|\dot{s} \models \sigma] \Rightarrow \{s \models \sigma\} \Rightarrow \{S_j\} \tag{3}$$

The decision on how situations should be defined and how the application space should be initialized are application-specific. The framework presented in Sect. 3 thus allows corresponding configurations.

5   Incompleteness and Ambiguity in the Situation Model

The previously presented inference function of CST is based on the evidential Dempster-Shafer approach [18] to calculate confidence levels, which has also been used in ECSTRA [4]. The inference function in CST is defined as a place-holder function that can be substituted by other approaches which can apply other well-known reasoning techniques, as for example shown with the Bayesian approach [16]. Techniques applied for reasoning have different strengths in covering uncertain aspects like incompleteness or ambiguity. The application of both, evidence theory and fuzzy logic, for example is capable of handling incomplete, imprecise and out of date contextual information [23]. Thus, the design requirements for knowledge base is dependent on the input that the inference function requires. Based on the inference function presented in Sect. 4, the ontology requires extension regarding the confidence thresholds (specified for situations), relevance functions (specified for attributes per situation definition), and contribution functions (specified for attribute values), as presented in [14]. The incorporation of the relevance function into the infon definition, for example, can be formally denoted as $\sigma = \ll r, (a_1, w_1), ..., (a_n, w_n), i \gg$, where w_n represents the weight for the attribute a_n.

The availability of knowledge is a major concern for specification-based approaches. Domain experts are required to describe the relevant situations beforehand. The contribution function and the relevance function in the presented approach already allow modelling of situations with imprecise knowledge. With STO as an underlying situation model, this aspect can be even further improved. The integration of the earlier introduced related approach of Fuzzy STO [11], for example, proposes a non-numerical specification in case of vague knowledge about a situation. In FSTO, the polarity i of infons is replaced with τ which is element of a grammar that allows statements like *quite, less, really* true or false.

Even though both approaches, adding the weight w_n assigned to attributes from CST and extending the polarity with τ in FSTO, extend the infon definition to handle uncertain aspects due to incompleteness of knowledge, they are semantically not equal. Whereas the weight assigns a relative importance to the attributes, τ makes a statement about the truth of the overall infon, which could affect a combination of objects. Integrating both approaches would increase the imprecise modelling capabilities for domain experts. The corresponding extended inference function for CST is shown in Eq. (4) in which $\tau_\sigma(a_i)$ represents the confidence in the infon truth of the supported infon in which the attribute a_i is involved.

$$\mu_{S_j} = \sum_{i=1}^{n} w_{S_j}(a_i) * \eta_{a_i}^{S}(x_{a_i}) * \tau_\sigma(a_i) \tag{4}$$

Another issue of situation aware systems is the absence of knowledge during the modelling process. This is a major concern for any specification- or learning-based approach, either in the form of missing situation definitions or incompleteness in the training data. It is a difficult challenge to react properly to an unknown situation, i.e. when the contextual circumstances cannot be interpreted with the provided knowledge. In CST, this occurs when the context state reaches a point in the context space which is not in any of the known situation spaces. The following measures can be considered to address these issues.

Verifying completeness. The knowledge base could be analyzed before the deployment of the system to identify gaps. For the presented framework, this could be done by looking for gaps in acceptable regions for context attributes.

Reasoning-supported completion. Previous and following situations, situations with same context attributes, and situations close to the context state can give a semantic indication to the domain expert when a gap in the context space is encountered during run-time.

Accessing remote repositories. The possibility to look up situation definitions stored in remote, standardized repositories, e.g. with semantic web technologies, might allow to automatically close the gaps for undefined situations.

To summarize, handling uncertainty in the knowledge base of a situation aware system is a necessary step to enable reliable reasoning and to provide a practical approach to represent domain knowledge. Identifying and resolving gaps in the knowledge base is important to avoid malfunctions of the overall situation aware system.

6 IoT Interoperability and Context Adaptation

Situation aware systems rely on the access to contextual information of the environment. IoT interoperability aims to integrate data from various sources (like sensor networks, files, APIs and so on) across different platforms. Thus, the integration of relevant standards in the overall situation aware system is investigated. Furthermore, the dynamic aspect of the environment has also an impact on the situation model. In particular, adapting to current context will be discussed.

6.1 IoT Interoperability with O-MI/O-DF Integration

Interoperability across heterogeneous platforms is a major concern for the IoT. *Vertical silos* prevent communication between different platforms on several levels, limiting the access to contextual information [9]. As previously mentioned, several H2020 projects (as part of the IoT-European Platforms Initiative) are working on this challenge by developing protocols, tools, and platforms that provide communication interfaces on top of well-established IoT communication protocols (such as MQTT, CoAP, HTTP, etc.). The framework presented in this paper relies on the open standards O-MI and O-DF, which are developed in the H2020 bIoTope project. O-MI provides a messaging interface that can be used on top of session protocols, which includes operations like *read, write* and *subscribe*. O-DF, on the other hand, provides a generic service description model for IoT services, in which the message payload is structured as a tree of *objects* and their *infoitems* with corresponding *values* and *metadata*.

The integration of this standardized API and the upper ontology allows for automation of processes and thus reduces the implementation effort for context collection of the reasoning engine. Furthermore, the final situation awareness framework can be applied independent of the platforms and technologies that are used on site. Solely configuration files are required to map the O-DF data stream to objects that are defined in the ontology (sensors, attributes, etc.). The situation spaces and the context collectors are both automatically generated upon initialization of the system. Context collectors start to subscribe (event-based) to the sensor data streams using the O-MI subscription mechanisms. During runtime, the O-DF payload is resolved with the semantic model of the ontology, which allows to update the context state without the development of custom modules. This enables automated reasoning with minimal implementation effort for client applications, considering a standardized IoT embedment.

6.2 Adaptation of the Knowledge Base to Current Context in a Dynamic Environment

Situation aware systems are often deployed in dynamic environments, which requires the knowledge base to adapt to current context. The following two dynamic aspects that have a direct impact on the knowledge base are considered, (i) involved individuals entering or leaving the system's scope, and (ii) sensors entering or leaving the system's scope

Adapting to these changes does not only imply maintaining the knowledge base (e.g. adding and removing involved individuals and sensors) but also maintaining the application space (e.g. adding and removing situation spaces). Since the framework already provides situation awareness, the adaptation mechanism can be i ntegrated on top of the existing functionalities in a straight-forward manner. Individuals or sensors that are entering or leaving the system can be perceived as a contextual information that is provided by sensors.

Recognizing and clearly identifying involved individuals in situations might require additional sensing, e.g. sensed smartphone locations and gathered user profiles could be used to track the presence of persons (which can be also exposed and described through O-MI/O-DF gateways). The different events of tracking individuals and sensors can be modelled as situations. Upon the occurrence of such a situation the framework automatically takes all necessary steps (regarding knowledge base and application space) to adapt the system to the new circumstances.

7   Conclusion and Future Work

This paper discussed the incorporation of an ontology as a knowledge base for a situation aware framework. Detailed explanation of the mapping of Situation Theory and CST demonstrated the enrichment of a reasoning framework with a situation model based on STO. The discussions related to a knowledge base for situation aware systems further included the required knowledge assets that must be provided to allow reasoning, modelling incomplete knowledge, handling unknown situations, cross-domain and -platform interoperability issues in the IoT, and adaptation to current context.

In conclusion, the situation model could be extended to accommodate all relevant assets and to enhance the run-time reasoning. Moreover, the knowledge base allows modelling with imprecise knowledge and allows the tracking of semantic changes of the system's environment and to provide situation awareness in a dynamic environment.

Future work includes the development of use cases to compare different approaches to uncertainty modelling and resolving unknown situations. Furthermore, the framework could be enhanced by integrating learning-based techniques. The challenge of meeting run-time reasoning requirements, performance and scalability expectations is as well an important part of future work.

Acknowledgment. Part of this work has been carried out in the scope of the project bIoTope which is co-funded by the European Commission under Horizon-2020 program, contract number H2020-ICT-2015/688203 – bIoTope. The research has been carried out with the financial support of the Ministry of Education and Science of the Russian Federation under grant agreement RFMEFI58716X0031.

References

1. Abowd, G.D., Dey, A.K., Brown, P.J., Davies, N., Smith, M., Steggles, P.: Towards a better understanding of context and context-awareness. In: Gellersen, H.-W. (ed.) HUC 1999. LNCS, vol. 1707, pp. 304–307. Springer, Heidelberg (1999). doi:10. 1007/3-540-48157-5_29
2. Baumgartner, N., Retschitzegger, W.: A survey of upper ontologies for situation awareness. In: Proceedings of the 4th IASTED International Conference on Knowledge Sharing and Collaborative Engineering, St. Thomas, US VI, pp. 1–9 (2006)
3. Bettini, C., Brdiczka, O., Henricksen, K., Indulska, J., Nicklas, D., Ranganathan, A., Riboni, D.: A survey of context modelling and reasoning techniques. Pervasive Mob. Comput. **6**(2), 161–180 (2010)
4. Boytsov, A., Zaslavsky, A.: ECSTRA–distributed context reasoning framework for pervasive computing systems. In: Balandin, S., Koucheryavy, Y., Hu, H. (eds.) NEW2AN/ruSMART -2011. LNCS, vol. 6869, pp. 1–13. Springer, Heidelberg (2011). doi:10.1007/978-3-642-22875-9_1
5. Boytsov, A., Zaslavsky, A., Eryilmaz, E., Albayrak, S.: Situation awareness meets ontologies: a context spaces case study. In: Christiansen, H., Stojanovic, I., Papadopoulos, G.A. (eds.) CONTEXT 2015. LNCS (LNAI), vol. 9405, pp. 3–17. Springer, Cham (2015). doi:10.1007/978-3-319-25591-0_1
6. Boytsov, A., Zaslavsky, A., Synnes, K.: Extending context spaces theory by predicting run-time context. In: Balandin, S., Moltchanov, D., Koucheryavy, Y. (eds.) NEW2AN/ruSMART -2009. LNCS, vol. 5764, pp. 8–21. Springer, Heidelberg (2009). doi:10.1007/978-3-642-04190-7_2
7. Chen, H., Finin, T., Joshi, A.: The SOUPA ontology for pervasive computing. In: Tamma, V., Cranefield, S., Finin, T.W., Willmott, S. (eds.) Ontologies for Agents: Theory and Experiences, pp. 233–258. Springer, Heidelberg (2005)
8. Compton, M., Barnaghi, P., Bermudez, L., García-Castro, R., Corcho, O., Cox, S., Graybeal, J., Hauswirth, M., Henson, C., Herzog, A., et al.: The SSN ontology of the W3C semantic sensor network incubator group. Web Semant.: Sci. Serv. Agents World Wide Web **17**, 25–32 (2012)

9. Desai, P., Sheth, A., Anantharam, P.: Semantic gateway as a service architecture for IoT interoperability. In: 2015 IEEE International Conference on Mobile Services, pp. 313–319. IEEE (2015)

10. Devlin, K.: Situation theory and situation semantics. Handb. Hist. Log. **7**, 601–664 (2006)

11. Furno, D., Loia, V., Veniero, M.: A fuzzy cognitive situation awareness for airport security. Control Cybern. **39**(4), 959–982 (2010)

12. Gruber, T.R.: Toward principles for the design of ontologies used for knowledge sharing? Int. J. Hum Comput Stud. **43**(5), 907–928 (1995)

13. Kokar, M.M., Matheus, C.J., Baclawski, K.: Ontology-based situation awareness. Inf. Fusion **10**(1), 83–98 (2009)

14. Kolbe, N., Zaslavsky, A., Kubler, S., Robert, J.: Reasoning over knowledge-based generation of situations in context spaces to reduce food waste. In: Galinina, O., Balandin, S., Koucheryavy, Y. (eds.) NEW2AN/ruSMART -2016. LNCS, vol. 9870, pp. 101–114. Springer, Cham (2016). doi:10.1007/978-3-319-46301-8_9

15. Matheus, C.J., Kokar, M.M., Baclawski, K., Letkowski, J.A., Call, C., Hinman, M.L., Salerno, J.J., Boulware, D.M.: SAWA: an assistant for higher-level fusion and situation awareness. In: Defense and Security, pp. 75–85. International Society for Optics and Photonics (2005)

16. Padovitz, A.: Context Management and Reasoning About Situations in Pervasive Computing. Monash University, Melbourne (2006)

17. Padovitz, A., Loke, S.W., Zaslavsky, A.: Towards a theory of context spaces. In: Proceedings of the Second IEEE Annual Conference on Pervasive Computing and Communications Workshops, pp. 38–42. IEEE (2004)

18. Shafer, G.: A Mathematical Theory of Evidence, vol. 1. Princeton University Press, Princeton (1976)

19. Spalazzi, L., Taccari, G., Bernardini, A.: An internet of things ontology for earthquake emergency evaluation and response. In: 2014 International Conference on Collaboration Technologies and Systems (CTS), pp. 528–534. IEEE (2014)

20. Strang, T., Linnhoff-Popien, C.: A context modeling survey. In: Workshop on Advanced Context Modelling, Reasoning and Management, UbiComp 2004 (2004)

21. Wang, X.H., Zhang, D.Q., Gu, T., Pung, H.K.: Ontology based context modeling and reasoning using owl. In: Proceedings of the Second IEEE Annual Conference on Pervasive Computing and Communications Workshops, pp. 18–22. IEEE (2004)

22. Yau, S.S., Liu, J.: Hierarchical situation modeling and reasoning for pervasive computing. In: The Fourth IEEE Workshop on Software Technologies for Future Embedded and Ubiquitous Systems, 2006 and the 2006 Second International Workshop on Collaborative Computing, Integration, and Assurance, SEUS 2006/WCCIA 2006, p. 6. IEEE (2006)

23. Ye, J., Dobson, S., McKeever, S.: Situation identification techniques in pervasive computing: a review. Pervasive Mob. Comput. **8**(1), 36–66 (2012)

When Do the Truth-Conditions of *S Knows that p* Change?

An Inquiry in the Conversational and Epistemic Mechanisms Involved in the Variations of Contexts

Stefano Leardi[1(✉)] and Nicla Vassallo[2]

[1] FINO Consortium, Department of Philosophy and Education,
University of Torino, via Sant'Ottavio 20, 10124 Torino, Italy
stefano.leardi@unito.it
[2] DAFIST, School of Humanities, University of Genova,
via Balbi 4, 16126 Genova, Italy
nicla.vassallo@unige.it

Abstract. The debate on epistemic contextualism has been mainly focused on the contextualist solutions to sceptical paradoxes, neglecting many questions that arise from the contextualist understanding of the semantic behaviour of knowledge ascriptions. One of those questions concerns the dynamics of contexts changes: it is not clear when contexts change and which conversational and epistemic mechanisms determine these variations. Here we will scrutinize four accounts of these mechanisms (Lewis' view, the veto power view, the gap view, and the intentionalist view) identifying the virtues and the lacks of each position. We will conclude that Lewis' view and the veto power view are both inadequate, and that the gap view provides the better account of the dynamics of contexts changes for it vindicates our intuition that in those cases where the conversational partners do not agree on which epistemic standard should be applied in their context they are contradicting one another.

Keywords: Contextualism · Knowledge ascriptions · Gap view · Context · Rule of attention · Scoreboard semantics · Conversational dynamics

1 Introduction

Epistemic contextualism (hereafter just "contextualism") has become one of the most prominent positions in contemporary epistemology. According to this theory a proper analysis of our ordinary linguistic practices would establish a viewpoint on the semantic behaviour of knowledge ascriptions that can improve our understanding of some remarkable epistemological questions, such as the sceptical problem or the lottery paradox. In the last years the debate on contextualism especially focused on these aspects of the theory, neglecting some other relevant issues that arise from its internal structure. In this paper we will concentrate our attention precisely on one of those issues: we will try to single out which conversational and epistemic mechanisms are involved in the variation of the truth-conditions of knowledge ascriptions. After a brief

© Springer International Publishing AG 2017
P. Brézillon et al. (Eds.): CONTEXT 2017, LNAI 10257, pp. 55–68, 2017.
DOI: 10.1007/978-3-319-57837-8_5

introduction of contextualism and of some useful contextualist terminology, in Sect. 3 we will analyse different accounts of the mechanisms involved in a context's change - Lewis's view, the veto power view, the gap view, and the intentionalist view, - with the purpose of identifying the virtues and the lacks of each proposal. In the end we will conclude that both Lewis' view and the veto power view are inadequate, and we will maintain that the gap view seems to be superior to the intentionalist view since it vindicates our intuition that, in that cases where the conversational partners do not agree on which epistemic standard should be in place in their conversational context, the speakers are, at least under a certain respect, contradicting one another.

2 Contextualism

Contextualism is the semantic thesis that the truth-conditions of knowledge-ascribing and knowledge-denying sentences of the form "S knows that p" and "S doesn't know that p" depend upon certain features of the context of the knowledge attributor - $i.e.$ the context of the person making the assertion. Therefore, accordingly, a sentence as:

(1) Christian knows that he's looking at a dandelion

can be true if uttered in a certain context C_1 at the time t and false if uttered in another context C_2 at the same time t without contradiction since the two utterances of the same sentence would express two different propositions (Cohen 1987: 1; Lewis 1996: 550; DeRose 2009: 2; Rysiew 2016). Contextualists usually account for this peculiar idea about the semantics of knowledge ascriptions resorting to the so-called "argument of the ordinary language". According to this argument the analysis of our ordinary usage of knowledge ascriptions would prove that what we will deem as "knowledge" in certain contexts we will not recognise as such in others (DeRose 2009: 47). Consider, as an example, the sentence (1) and assume that Christian is in an ordinary epistemic position with respect to the proposition that he's looking at a dandelion (the proposition q). As the contextualists predict, it seems that we will probably judge an utterance of (1) as true if we are in the context of an ordinary conversation, but as false if we are in the context of a botanical symposium. Indeed, the circumstances of an ordinary conversation would presumably establish a set of conditions at which a subject can count as knowing that q that are less strict than that defined in the context of a botanical symposium. In the context of an ordinary conversation, in fact, we can imagine that to Christian it will be simply requested to be able to tell the difference between a dandelion and oxeye daisy in order to make true a sentence as (1), while in the more demanding context of the botanical symposium he will probably have to be able to list all the relevant botanical characteristics of a dandelion in order to count as knowing that he's looking precisely at that flower. Thus, for Christian is an ordinary epistemic position with respect to q - and therefore he's able to tell the difference between a dandelion and oxeye daisy, but he can't list all the relevant botanical characteristics of a dandelion, - an utterance of (1) will be evaluated as true in the first context but false in the latter.

It should be noted that, traditionally, knowledge-ascribing sentences are not held to be context-sensitive expressions. According to the classical "invariantist" view there is one and only one set of truth-conditions for knowledge ascriptions.[1] Some clarification about the contextualist main claim are thus in order. To illustrate the contextualist stance it's useful to resort to a compelling analogy often employed by the advocates of the theory (Cohen 1986: 580, 1999: 60; DeRose 2009: 166). Consider gradable adjectives as "tall" or "flat". The truth-conditions of this kind of adjectives almost certainly vary in different contexts since it is the context of utterance that establishes the parameter that defines how those terms apply - *e.g.* a context can determine the maximum height in order for a person to count as "short". Therefore, since knowledge ascriptions seem to vary in degree of "strength" or "goodness", each context can define the strength or the goodness of the epistemic position of a subject *S* such that *S* can count as a knower in that context. Another way to illustrate the context-sensitivity of "know" is to regard this term as an indexical like "I" or "here" (Cohen 1999: 61; DeRose 1992: 925). To this kind of expressions are connected the well-known notions introduced by Kaplan (1989) of "character" (the rule associated by convention to an expression that sets the contextual parameters to locate the reference of the occurrences of the expression in contexts) and "content" (the intension, or the semantic value of the expression). Making use of this distinction, we can thus associate to a knowledge ascription of the form "*S* knows that *p*" a character such as "*S* has a true belief that *p* and she is in a strong (or good) enough epistemic position with respect to *p*". Clearly, this element of the meaning of "*S* knows that *p*" will be stable among contexts, while how much strong or good an epistemic position must be in order to make true a knowledge ascription will change from context to context (DeRose 2009: 3).[2]

2.1 The Strength of the Epistemic Position and the Epistemic Standard

In the previous paragraph we have spoken of contexts resorting to a popular terminology among contextualists that involves expressions as "strength of epistemic position" and "epistemic standard". From a very general point of view, being in a strong epistemic position with respect to a certain proposition one believes is for one's belief in that proposition to have an adequate amount of the properties the having enough of which is what's needed for a true believe to constitute a piece of knowledge. The epistemic standard set in the context is, instead, "the standard for how strong a position a subject must be in with respect to a proposition … for a sentence attributing knowledge to her in the context in question to be true" (DeRose 2009: 7).

Contextualists have proposed different hypotheses to clarify and specify how those notions should be understood. According to an influential interpretation proposed by Keith DeRose, the strength of the epistemic position of a subject *S* with respect to a

---

[1] The term "invariantism" is used to label the position of those who deny contextualism with respect to a certain class of statements - see Unger (1984). The invariantist about knowledge ascriptions maintains that the truth-conditions of these expressions do not change across contexts.

[2] The adequacy of both analogies has been contested. For the debate about which linguistic model better captures the context-sensitivity of knowledge ascriptions see Capellen and Lepore (2003), Stanley (2004, 2005), Hawthorne (2004), Bianchi and Vassallo (2005), Kompa (2005), Ludlow (2005), DeRose (2009), Stainton (2010), Jaster (2013).

proposition p should be understood in terms of truth-tracking or of "sensitivity": S's true belief that p tracks the truth or is sensitive to the truth value of p if S would not have believed that p if p had been false (DeRose 1995).[3] Consider Christian's true belief that he's looking at a dandelion: he certainly believes this both in the actual world and in some other nearby possible worlds where he is, in effect, looking at a dandelion. Consider, however, other nearby possible worlds where it is not the case that Christian is looking at this flower for he's looking at a rose or at a storksbill: in these worlds where it is not the case that Christian is looking at a dandelion he is perfectly aware of this fact - using DeRose's own words, Christian's belief "matches the fact of the matter" (1995: 34), - hence, in these worlds Christian does not believe that he's looking at a dandelion. There are, however, other possible worlds in which notwith-standing it is not the case that Christian is looking at a dandelion he will believe this anyway - think, for example, to a sceptical scenario in which Christian is deceived by an evil demon. Nevertheless, for these worlds are really *far* from the actual world, we could consider Christian's belief sensitive and conclude that he's in a pretty strong epistemic position with regard to the proposition that he's looking at a dandelion (DeRose 1995: 35). Therefore, according to this model, the strength of the epistemic position of a subject S depends upon the possible worlds which are considered "fairly near" in the context: the epistemic standard defines the set I of possible worlds which in its turn determines the sensitivity of S's belief that p, and if S's belief can track the truth in all the possible worlds considered fairly near (*i.e.* all the possible worlds which belong to I) then S's epistemic position with respect to p is strong enough - and hence a knowledge ascription as "S knows that p" can be judge as true in the context.

Yet, the notions of epistemic standard and of strength of epistemic position can be considered differently. Another popular way of defining standards consists in making use of the theory of relevant alternatives. According to this theory, knowledge is strictly tied to our ability of discriminating between epistemic alternatives; indeed, it seems that we would probably not say that Christian knows who Marian is if we would know that he cannot tell apart Marian from her monozygotic twin Vivian, even if he would say - precisely pointing at Marian, - "I know that she is Marian". Therefore, accord-ingly, in order to count as knowing a certain proposition p a subject S should rule out all the *relevant alternatives* to p (Goldman 1976; Schaffer 2005). We can thus regard each context as a certain set - or as a "segmentation" using Antonia Barke's words (2004: 354), - of alternatives that are considered to be relevant in that context.[4] If we consider again our example involving (1), we can outline the two contexts in the following way: in the first case - the one sets in an ordinary context, - to Christian it will be asked to rule out certain ordinary alternatives, while in the latter - the botanical symposium context, - he could have to rule out much extreme alternatives: for example, in the more demanding context also the remote possibility that the flower in front of Christian is a dandelion* (an extremely rare flower which is quite identical to the dandelion and is distinguishable from it only by a very skilled botanist) could be

---

[3] The notion of sensitivity of a belief is due to Nozick (1981).

[4] A remarkable example of this reading of contextualism is Stine (1976).

included in the set of alternatives that Christian must rule out to count as knowing that he's looking at a dandelion.

Clearly, the sensitivity approach can be understood in a way that it's rather similar to the relevant alternative approach: the fairly near possible worlds can be interpreted as the worlds in which are located the alternatives that are considered relevant. However, opting for the sensitivity approach could be a dangerous step. Indeed, Ron Wilburn maintains that this approach presupposes a metric to evaluate the modal distance (the amount of metaphysical differences between possible worlds) that is "implicitly calibrated" by a metric for judging epistemic distance. According to him:

> this implicit calibration threatens circularity by effectively presupposing the truth of the very claim for which the contextualist must argue, *i.e.*, that various skeptical scenario worlds (in which truth-tracking is sabotaged) stand at a greater distance from actuality than do more prosaic worlds (in which truth-tracking remains in order) (Wilburn 2010: 260).

Evaluating Wilburn's objections goes beyond the aims of this paper, but for the relevant alternative approach is not certainly saddled with these kind of worries, here we will resort to this reading of the notions of epistemic standard and strength of epistemic position to characterise contextualism.

3 Context Changes

3.1 The Rule of Accommodation and the Rule of Attention

Now that we have a clearer understanding of some relevant contextualist notions, we can begin to examine the dynamics of contexts changes. Consider two speakers involved in a conversation: in which manner each conversational partner can manipulate the epistemic standard in place in the context? A first answer to this question has been developed by David Lewis. The American philosopher maintains that the variations of the truth-conditions of knowledge ascriptions are induced by certain conversational manoeuvres; in particular, according to Lewis the mere mention of an epistemic alternative would be sufficient to install a certain epistemic standard in a context (1996: 559). For a better understanding of this proposal we should consider it in the light of Lewis' claim that at any stage of a well-run conversation is associated a "conversational score":

> Sentences depend for their truth value, or for their acceptability in other respects, on the components of conversational score at the stage of conversation when they are uttered. Not only aspects of acceptability of an uttered sentence may depend on score. So may other semantic properties that play a role in determining aspects of acceptability. For instance, the constituents of an uttered sentence - subsentences, names, predicates, *etc.* - may depend on the score for their intension or extension (Lewis 1979: 345).

According to Lewis, the conversational manoeuvres of the speakers can manipulate and change the values of the score during the conversation. Conversational contexts are in fact governed by a "rule of accommodation" which posits that:

> If at time t something is said that requires component s_n of conversational score to have a value in the range r if what is said is to be true, or otherwise acceptable; and if s_n does not have a

value in the range *r* just before *t*; and if such-and-such further conditions hold; then at *t* the score-component s_n takes some value in the range *r* (1979: 347).

Therefore, if during a conversation a speaker utters the sentence "Smith's Ford is in the parking lot" this utterance will immediately manipulate the conversational score posing the presupposition that Smith owns a Ford and, consequently, making rather odd a caveat as "… and he owns a Ford". The rule of accommodation, thus, seems to be responsible for the set of the epistemic standards. Consider again the case where Christian is looking at a dandelion. If someone says that:

(2)   Christian doesn't know that he's looking at a dandelion

claiming, for instance, that the flower at which Christian is looking could be not a dandelion, but rather a very similar flower, the mention of (2) - according to the rule of accommodation, - will manipulate the conversational score changing the epistemic standard in place in the context so that (2) can be true.

If it is in virtue of the rule of accommodation that the standards can change, we could expect that in the same way in which the standards can be raised they can also be lowered. However, if according to Lewis the standards for many terms can be both raised and lowered in many occasions (1979: 339), the same manoeuvre cannot be employed when it concerns the epistemic standards. Lewis maintains that, in order to count as knowing a certain proposition *p*, a subject *S* must rule out any epistemic alternative that he is not properly ignoring. However, according to the "rule of attention" (1996: 559) an epistemic alternative is properly ignored only when it is, in fact, ignored *simpliciter* - that is, if the subject is attending to it then the alternative is not properly ignored. Therefore, since the statement of an epistemic alternative entails the fact that this very alternative has been attended by the subject, it follows that when the epistemic standard has been raised it cannot be lowered anymore.

From the conjunction of the rule of accommodation and the rule of attention it follows an extremely prudent characterisation of our epistemic rationality: indeed, according to this view any epistemic alternative - even the most farfetched as, for instance, the brain-in-a-vat hypothesis, - should be considered and ruled out by the epistemic subject. Lewis' view can thus be labelled as a very "sceptical-friendly" view since it implies that when sceptical hypotheses are put in place sceptical standards are automatically installed.

It should be noted that Lewis' proposal did not obtain a positive outcome among contextualists: Michael Ashfield, for instance, has defined it as depicting "a worst-case-scenario for the contextualist" (2013: 122), while in many passages of his works DeRose denies his support to the rule: "… actually I have a lot of sympathy for the thought that the mere mention of the alternative is not sufficient for making it relevant …" (DeRose 2000); "Nor do either of us [DeRose and Cohen] accept the view that is the next most commonly ascribed to the contextualist: that, in the situations under consideration, the sceptic's extraordinarily high standards prevail" (DeRose 2004). An in-depth analysis of Lewis' position is developed by Barke. According to her (2004: 214) a first problem of Lewis' viewpoint lies in its characterization of the dynamics that rules the set of the epistemic standard as a conversational one, since it would not be able to account for the cases in which no conversational context is involved - as the one of a solitary reflection. As Barke notices, it could be replied that solitary considerations are cases of "conversation with oneself," but nevertheless, according to her this "does not seem to be a very attractive solution". Yet, Barke does not propose any argument for the rejection of a response that, at least to us, seems to be perfectly adequate; indeed, just as a conversation between two speakers, also a monologue - or an interior monologue in the case of a solitary consideration, - can be governed by a conversational score: if speaking with himself *S* thinks to a certain parameter for the predicate "being tall" and then, later, he changes this parameter for he's thinking to basketball players, this change can be perfectly described in terms of variations in the values of a conversational score. Another remark posed by Barke concerns the ease that characterised the conversational move of rising the standard. Indeed, for many other context-sensitive terms we can manipulate the score in both ways: we can tighten the standard for tallness speaking about basketball players and then we can broad it driving the conversation to eight years old children; in the case of knowledge ascriptions, instead, a return to a loose standard cannot be achieved by mentioning a low-standard knowledge ascription. Clearly, this difference between the conversational mechanics of terms as "tall" or "flat" and knowledge ascriptions depends upon the assumption of the epistemic rule of attention. As Lewis claims, "speaking of knowledge despite uneliminated possibilities of error just sounds contradictory" (1996: 549) and the statement of a not ruled out epistemic alternative seems to prevent an effective ascription of knowledge; as an example, it seems that we would not say that Christian is looking at a barn if we would know that the countryside in which Christian is it's full of fake barns that are indistinguishable from real barns. Yet, according to Barke this explanation of the asymmetry between the manoeuvres of rising and lowering the standards is not promising for she considers the rule of attention highly implausible. Indeed, according to Barke "discussing our presuppositions and agreeing on the question of which ones are reasonable … and which ones are not it's an integral part of our epistemic practices" (2004: 358), and clearly Lewis' position does not vindicate this part of our epistemic custom.

Since contextualists generally aim to construe a theory that it's in consonance with our ordinary knowledge-attributing practices (Kompa 2014: 59; Rysiew 2016), the asymmetry between the manoeuvres of rising and lowering the standards that results from Lewis' view seems to suggests that an alternative account of these mechanisms should be preferred.

3.2 The Veto Power

As Barke rightly points out, our ordinary epistemic practice seems to grant to us the possibility to stop that conversational manoeuvres that attempt to rise the epistemic standard. Appealing to this intuitions, many contextualists have contested the rule of attention maintaining that, just as in the case of other context-sensitive terms, the attempt of raising the standards can be resisted also when knowledge ascriptions are involved. According to this view, to the speakers is conferred a "veto power" over the changing of the conversational score (DeRose 2009: 140). Stewart Cohen describes this plausible conversational manoeuvre in these terms:

The pressure toward higher standards can sometimes be resisted. One device for doing this is adopting a certain tone of voice. So in response to the sceptic, one might say, "C'mon, you've got to be kidding - I know I am not a brain-in-a-vat!". If this is the dominant response among the conversational participants, then everyday standards may remain in effect. In such a case, the speaker unmoved by skeptical doubt is not failing to adjust his ascriptions to contextually determined standards. Rather, such a speaker is managing to keep the standards from rising (Cohen 2001: 93).

The veto power view seems to perfectly conform to our ordinary epistemic custom. Moreover, it vindicates the contextualist's claim according to which the standards are determined not by a rule as the rule of attention, but by the presuppositions, the purposes and the practical interests of the speakers (Cohen 2001; Kompa 2014). Michael Blome-Tillmann posits an interesting distinction among these lines. According to him the rule of attention should be restated for simply attending to a certain epistemic alternative it's not enough for making it impossible to ignore in a "epistemologically relevant sense" (Blome-Tillmann 2009: 247). In order to prove that, Blome-Tillman proposes this case:

Imagine you saw your teenage son sneaking away through the window of his room late at night. When you confront him the next morning he replies somewhat desperately: 'How do you know I left the house? I mean, for all you know you might have dreamt it. It was late at night, wasn't it?' (Blome-Tillmann 2009).

Now, according to the rule of attention the objection of the son would have the automatic consequence of raising the epistemic standard to a sceptical level; this consequence, however, seems to be extremely implausible to Blome-Tillmann since he maintains that in order to make a certain epistemic alternative relevant we should *take it seriously*. Yet, Blome-Tillmann example appears to be rather ambiguous since, as Daniele Sgaravatti rightly observes, the son's response sounds so odd that it is even dubious if it could be considered as a proper contribution to the conversation. However, if the son's objection would be sincere then the veto power view would grant to the father the possibility to overlook the son's objection. Note that according to Sgaravatti a better contextualist response would be "You might be right that I do not know in an absolute sense what happened: we hardly know anything in that way. But this is just not relevant now!" (Sgaravatti 2013: 7). Yet, it seems that Sgaravatti's remark is missing the point, since according to the advocates of the veto power this manoeuvre is effective also in that cases where the epistemic alternatives are sincerely affirmed by their proponents.

This veto power view seems to be really promising because it efficaciously prevents the standards to raise automatically. Unfortunately, this view has an highly undesirable consequence for it seems unable to account for cases of radical disagreement concerning the application of the epistemic standards. Imagine a dispute between a common-sense epistemologist and a sceptic: when the sceptic will try to raise the standard the common-sense epistemologist will immediately employ the veto power. Now, can the sceptic employs the veto power too preventing the lowering of the standard? Who wins? The one who *first* employed the conversational manoeuvre? But in such a situation it seems extremely implausible to tie the efficacy of the veto power to the temporal sequence of its employment in the conversational context. Thus, the result of this peculiar case of disagreement seems to be an opaque impasse since it's not clear which value should assume the conversational score according to the veto power view (DeRose 2009: 141). Hence, also the adequacy of this view seems to be questionable.[5]

3.3 The Gap View and the Intentionalist View: Single vs. Multiple Scoreboard Semantics

In order to give to the speakers the possibility to freely manipulate the truth-conditions of knowledge ascriptions we should thus opt for an account able to explain the outcomes of the cases of disagreement about the epistemic standard. DeRose proposes an account along these lines (the "gap view") according to which in the cases where two speakers - as, for instance, a sceptic and a common-sense epistemologist, - do not agree on which standard should be applied in their conversational context an utterance of "*S* knows that *p*" assumes the following truth-conditions: the sentence is true if *S* meets the extremely high standard of the sceptic, false if *S* doesn't meet the common-sense epistemologist ordinary standard and neither true or false if *S* does not meet the sceptic standard and meets the common-sense epistemologist standard.

As DeRose observes, this view has the remarkable virtue of respecting two strong intuitions that we have about the cases of disagreement in question: the first, according to which the two speakers are contradicting each other, and the latter that posits that the truth-conditions of each speaker's assertion should match his personally indicated content (DeRose 2009: 144–148). On the other hand, however, the gap view seems to be saddled with some thorny problems. First of all, DeRose's proposal could be considered a rather sceptical-friendly approach: in a dispute between a sceptic and a common-sense epistemologist, even if the sceptic does not manage to install his extremely high standard in the conversational context, at least he is able to prevent the knowledge ascription of the common-sense epistemologist. Furthermore, according to Montminy (2013) the gap view would entail another serious problem related to those subjects (that Montminy labels as "dogmatic Mooreans") who impose low epistemic standards and refute any raising of them. "A dogmatic Moorean" Montminy writes "… insists that he 'knows,' even though he cannot rule out salient alternatives" (2013: 2348). In order to explain why those subjects would represent a problem for the contextualist who endorse the gap view, Montminy resorts to the well-known airport case developed by Cohen (1999: 58). Suppose then that John and Mary are at the Los Angeles airport and that they want to know whether their flight has a layover in Chicago. They ask to another passenger, Smith, who replies that he knows that the flight stops in Chicago for he has just checked his flight itinerary. Since Mary and John have a very important business contact who's waiting for them at the Chicago Airport, Mary points out that Smith's itinerary may be

---

[5] Notice that the use of the veto power does not prevent the speakers from negotiating the epistemic standard that should be in place in their conversational context. Suppose that Tom and Louis are involved in a conversation where is in place the loose epistemic standard C_1; when Tom employs the veto power to prevent his conversational partner Louis to install the more demanding standard C_3 it can happen that after a discussion the two agree that in this case the more reasonable choice is to adopt the average standard C_2.

misprinted and concludes that Smith doesn't know that the plane will stop in Chicago. In the original case John agrees with her. In Cohen's intention, this fact should suggest to us, the readers, that the sentence "Smith knows that the flight will stop in Chicago" can assume different truth-conditions depending upon its context of utterance. However, according to Montminy, assuming that John is a dogmatic Moorean can cause serious troubles to the contextualist who endorses the gap view since this stance entails that if John does not agree with Mary, then she cannot succeed in establishing high epistemic standard in their context. Therefore, the case cannot be used anymore to illustrated and to support the contextualist position. Since examples as the airport case represent the main argument in favour of contextualism (Rysiew 2016), it seems that the gap view has the undesirable consequence of jeopardizing "the chief motivations" for the theory (Montminy 2013: 2348).

For the abovementioned reasons Montminy claims that the gap view should be abandoned. Montminy proposes an alternative position, the "intentionalist view" (2013: 2351–64), according to which the epistemic standard involved in the content of an utterance of "*S* knows that *p*" is defined only by the speaker's intention. Clearly, contrary to DeRose's position, Montminy's proposal is a multi-scoreboard view for every speaker has his own conversational scoreboard.

An important virtue of the intentionalist view is that it isn't a sceptical-friendly approach: indeed, even if the sceptic affirms truly that "*S* does not know that *p*" (for he is intending very high epistemic standard) also the common-sense epistemologist is speaking truly when he says that "*S* knows that *p*" (for he has in mind ordinary epistemic standard). Moreover, this view does not affect the contextualist cases since the objection of the dogmatic Moorean John cannot prevent Mary to adopt high epistemic standards.

Yet, also the intentionalist view faces some problems. Indeed, the distinction that Montminy draws between his intentionalist view and the classical contextualist stance it's not perfectly clear. Cohen and DeRose - the two main proponents of contextualism, - generally describe their position as one according to which the truth-conditions of a knowledge ascription are determined by certain features of the ascriber's context, as the ascriber's purposes and practical interests. Think, for example, to DeRose's bank cases (2009: 1–3): in the first scenario of his famous example DeRose ascribes knowledge to himself with regard to the proposition "The bank will be open on Saturday morning" despite his wife has pointed out that the bank could be closed on that day. DeRose considers this error possibility, yet he does not "take it seriously" or, better, he judges his own contrary evidence strong enough to rule out it. However, in the second scenario of the example DeRose's practical interests raise the standard (if the bank will be closed on Saturday morning he won't be able to deposit a very important check) and he prefers to admit that he doesn't know whether the bank will be open on Saturday morning. Therefore, it seems that the "purposes" and the "practical interests" of DeRose's contextualism are not so different from the "intentions" of Montminy's view. Furthermore, Cohen explicitly says that the epistemic standards are defined by "the intentions, the expectations, and the presuppositions of the members of the conversational context" (Cohen 2001: 92). Nevertheless, one could object, as Montminy does (2013: 2352), that according to the classical contextualist view others factors than the practical interests, the intentions, and the purposes of the knowledge ascriber can define the truth-conditions of his knowledge attributions. For instance, one could say that, according to the classical contextualist view, the fact that a certain region R is full of fake barns should affect the truth-conditions of Henry's knowledge ascription that "Tom (who is in R) knows that he's looking at a barn" even if Henry does not know that R is full of fake barns. However, it seems that the classical contextualist view does not posit anything like this: according to DeRose and Cohen if a certain epistemic alternative is ignored by the ascriber this possibility cannot affect the truth-conditions of his knowledge ascriptions. Furthermore, even if the ascriber is aware of a certain epistemic alternative it's up to him to decide if taking it seriously or not. Yet, if so, it seems that the truth-conditions of the knowledge ascriptions of the ascriber strongly depend by his conscious intentions.[6] After this important clarification, it appears that we can conclude that the true characterizing element of Montminy's proposal is the fact of being a multi-scoreboard view. However, it's by no means certain that a multi-scoreboard view is preferable to a single-scoreboard view.

Has we have seen Montminy claims that the intentionalist view should be preferred to the gap view since the latter would be too sceptical-friendly. Could we consider this as a real problem for DeRose's multi-scoreboard position? The answer seems to be negative. The contextualist anti-sceptical argument simply claims that from the fact that we do not know ordinary propositions according to the sceptical standard it cannot be inferred that we do not know that very propositions according to ordinary standards.[7] Thus, what it is important for the contextualist is to preserve the legitimacy of our knowledge ascriptions made in ordinary contexts, a legitimacy that the gap view does not prevent.

On the contrary of the gap view Montminy's single-scoreboard position doesn't jeopardize the chief motivation for contextualism. However, it seems that contextualism could peacefully survive to this consequence. After all, as DeRose rightly points out (2009: 53–59), only certain properly construed cases are able to represent a compelling argument for contextualism. Hence, putting aside cases as the one where the speakers do not agree on the epistemic standard does not seem to restrict too much the contextualist's motivations.

A more debatable aspect is tied instead with the intuition that when two speakers do not agree on which standard should apply to their context they are, in effect, contradicting one another. According to DeRose this intuition is confirmed by the fact that, in a case as the one that sees a sceptic opposing to a common-sense epistemologist, each speaker is *explicitly* indicating that he's contradicting what his opponent is claiming. The gap view seems to do a nice work in accounting for the contradiction that we intuitively recognise in such cases, what about the intentionalist view? Montminy's position involves an error theory for it maintains that the two conversational partners are mistaken in believing that they are contradicting one another (Montminy 2013: 2361). As Montminy rightly points out, an error theory is posed also by the classical

---

[6] It should be noted, however, that according to the classical contextualist view the truth-conditions of a knowledge ascription *strongly* depend by the intentions of the ascriber, but do not *totally* depend on it, for the epistemic standard operative in a conversational context depends upon the intentions of all the conversational partners.

[7] For the contextualist anti-sceptical argument see DeRose (1995) and Cohen (1998, 1999).

contextualist view since even according to this position the knowledge ascriptions assessed in different contexts express different propositions, with the only difference that:

> proponents of the [classical] view need to explain away only the intuition of contradiction across contexts, whereas intentionalists have to account for why we are mistaken about there being both inter- and intra-contextual contradiction (Montminy 2013, p. 2361).

Therefore, the intentionalist view has to deny our intuition that in that cases where the speakers do not agree on which epistemic standard should be in place in their context they are, in effect, involved in a genuine dispute. However, it's difficult to imagine how such a denial could be efficaciously supported. As we have seen before our intuitions strongly suggest that the two speakers, the sceptic and the common-sense epistemologist, are contradicting one another. Furthermore, it is quite clear that the sceptic and the common-sense epistemologist are intending to do so: in fact, they do not simply argue, respectively, that their personal assertion of "S knows that p" is false or true according to their personal epistemic standard, but that in the conversational context in which they are - and that includes also their conversational partner, - it should be applied a certain epistemic standard instead of another. The purpose of each speaker is clearly to impose his epistemic standard to his conversational partner. In order to illustrate the strength of these intuition we will resort to an example. Consider the sentence "Louis is tall". If it seems extremely plausible to assume that there isn't a real contradiction between two utterances of this sentence made in two contexts in which are in place different standards for "tall", it seems much less plausible to maintain that, when two speakers are debating on which standard for tallness should be adopted in their conversational context, they are not involved in a genuine dispute.

4   Concluding Remarks

In the previous paragraphs we have analysed the different dynamics that have been proposed to explain how the epistemic standards can be changed. Our aim was to scrutinize each position in order to find the better mechanisms of contexts changes, from both a conversational and an epistemic point of view. We have argued that the account proposed by Lewis reveals its undesirable limits for it sacrifices its consonance with some of our plausible epistemic customs: speakers can, after all, employ conversational manoeuvres in order to prevent the raise of the epistemic standards in the conversational contexts. We have seen that *prima facie* the veto power view efficaciously vindicates this intuition, but also that it faces a serious problem that consists in its inability to handle those cases in which the speakers do not agree on which standard should prevail in their contexts. Two proposals appear able to deal with this problem, the gap view and the intentionalist view. The two approaches conform to the contextualist anti-sceptical argument and, contrary to Montminy opinion, they both seems to not seriously undermine the main arguments for contextualism. The pivotal difference between these two view seems to concern their treatment of our intuition regarding that case where the speakers do not agree on which epistemic standard should be in place in their contexts. We have maintained that the main virtue of the gap view's single scoreboard semantics strategy consists in its ability to account for the intuition that in the abovementioned cases the conversational partners are, in effect, contradicting one another. The intentionalist view clearly cannot obtain this results and this seems to be its main limit: indeed, the intuition that in the cases in question the speakers are contradicting one another seems very difficult to be explained away. Therefore, we conclude that, at least under this respect, the gap view appears to be superior to the intentionalist view. Yet, for this superiority depends upon a minute and not definitely decisive aspect, the problem surely deserves additional attention and further inquiry.

References

Ashfield, M.D.: Against the minimalistic reading of epistemic contextualism: a reply to Wolfgang Freitag. Acta Anal. **28**(1), 111–125 (2013)

Barke, A.: Epistemic contextualism. Erkenntnis **61**(2–3), 353–373 (2004)

Bianchi, C., Vassallo, N.: Epistemological contextualism: a semantic perspective. In: Dey, A., Kokinov, B., Leake, D., Turner, R. (eds.) CONTEXT 2005. LNCS (LNAI), vol. 3554, pp. 41–54. Springer, Heidelberg (2005). doi:10.1007/11508373_4

Blome-Tillmann, M.: Knowledge and presupposition. Mind **118**(470), 241–291 (2009)

Cappelen, H., Lepore, E.: Context shifting arguments. Philos. Perspect. **17**(1), 25–50 (2003)

Cohen, S.: Knowledge and context. J. Philos. **83**(10), 574–583 (1986)

Cohen, S.: Knowledge, context, and social standards. Synthese **73**(1), 3–26 (1987)

Cohen, S.: Contextualist solutions to epistemological problems: skepticism, gettier, and the lottery. Australas. J. Philos. **76**(2), 289–306 (1998)

Cohen, S.: Contextualism, skepticism, and the structure of reasons. Philos. Perspect. **13**(s13), 57–89 (1999)

Cohen, S.: Contextualism defended: comments on Richard Feldman's 'skeptical problems contextualist solutions'. Philos. Stud. **103**(1), 87–98 (2001)

DeRose, K.: Contextualism and knowledge attributions. Philos. Phenomenol. Res. **52**(4), 913–929 (1992)

DeRose, K.: Solving the skeptical problem. Philos. Rev. **104**(1), 1–52 (1995)

DeRose, K.: Now you know it, now you don't. In: Proceedings of the Twentieth World Congress of Philosophy, Epistemology, vol. V, pp. 91–106 (2000)

DeRose, K.: Single scoreboard semantics. Philos. Stud. **119**(1–2), 1–21 (2004)

DeRose, K.: The Case for Contextualism: Knowledge, Skepticism, and Context, vol. 1. Oxford University Press, Oxford (2009)

Goldman, A.: Discrimination and perceptual knowledge. J. Philos. **73**(20), 771–791 (1976)

Hawthorne, J.: Knowledge and Lotteries. Oxford University Press, New York and Oxford (2004)

Jaster, R.: Contextualism and gradability. In: Spitzley, T., Hoeltje, M., Spohn, W. (eds.) GAP.8 Proceedings, pp. 318–323 (2013)

Kaplan, D.: Demonstratives. In: Almog, J., Perry, J., Wettstein, H. (eds.) Themes from Kaplan, pp. 481–563. Oxford University Press, Oxford (1989)

Kompa, N.: The semantics of knowledge attributions. Acta Anal. **20**(1), 16–28 (2005)

Kompa, N.: Knowledge in context. Riv. Int. Filos. Psicol. **5**(1), 58–71 (2014)

Lewis, D.: Scorekeeping in a language game. J. Philos. Log. **8**(1), 339–359 (1979)

Lewis, D.: Elusive knowledge. Australas. J. Philos. **74**(4), 549–567 (1996)

Ludlow, P.: Contextualism and the new linguistic turn in epistemology. In: Preyer, G., Peter, G. (eds.) Contextualism in Philosophy: Knowledge, Meaning, and Truth, pp. 11–49. Oxford University Press, Oxford (2005)

Montminy, M.: The role of context in contextualism. Synthese **190**(12), 2341–2366 (2013)

Nozick, R.: Philosophical Explanations. Harvard University Press, Harvard (1981)

Rysiew, P.: Epistemic contextualism. In: Zalta, E.N. (ed.) The Stanford Encyclopedia of Philosophy (2016). http://plato.stanford.edu/archives/sum2016/entries/contextualism-epistemology/

Schaffer, J.: What shifts? Thresholds, standards, or alternatives? In: Preyer, G., Peter, G. (eds.) Contextualism in Philosophy: Knowledge, Meaning, and Truth, pp. 115–130. Oxford University Press, Oxford (2005)

Sgaravatti, D.: In conversation with the skeptic: contextualism and the raising of standards. Int. J. Study Skept. **3**(2), 97–118 (2013)

Stainton, R.: Contextualism in epistemology and the context-sensitivity of 'knows'. In: Campbell, J.K., O'Rourke, M., Silverstein, S. (eds.) Knowledge and Skepticism, pp. 137–163 (2010)

Stanley, J.: On the linguistic basis for contextualism. Philos. Stud. **119**(1–2), 119–146 (2004)

Stanley, J.: Knowledge and Practical Interests. Oxford University Press, Oxford (2005)

Stine, G.C.: Skepticism, relevant alternatives, and deductive closure. Philos. Stud. **29**(4), 249–261 (1976)

Unger, P.: Philosophical Relativity. University of Minnesota Press, Minneapolis (1984)

Wilburn, R.: Possible world of doubt. Acta Anal. **25**(2), 259–277 (2010)

Derived Contexts: A New Argument for Their Usefulness

Josep Macià[(✉)]

Departament de Filosofia, Universitat de Barcelona,
Montalegre 6, 08001 Barcelona, Spain
josep.macia@ub.edu

Abstract. This paper aims to vindicate the adequacy and usefulness of the notion of *derived context* (Stalnaker 1988), by showing how it helps to successfully account for phenomena that lay beyond the data that motivated Stalnaker to first introduce the notion. We will focus on phenomena related to Binding Theory (BT) principles (B) and (C) (Chomsky 1981, 1993). These principles account for an impressive array of data. They are subject, though, to well known counterexamples. As part of a more general attempt to defend standard BT, this paper will focus on one specific kind of counterexamples to the BT (some of which have not yet been considered in the literature), and will show how they can be successfully accounted for without any substantive departure from standard BT. All is needed is (1) to take the semantic restriction placed by the Binding Principles to be not that of *co-reference* (or *co-valuation*) but rather that of *presupposed co-reference* (or *presupposed co-valuation*) (as in Heim 1993), and (2) to appeal in the appropriate way to the existence of derived contexts.

Keywords: Context · Derived context · Anaphora · Binding principles · Presupposition · Co-reference

1 Binding Principles (B) and (C)

Structural relations among NPs (Noun Phrases) place constraints on the possible anaphoric dependencies among those NPs. So, for instance, (1a) cannot be interpreted as meaning that Núria admires herself or (1b) as meaning that everybody loves oneself; (1c) can, though, be interpreted as meaning that everybody loves his own mother, and (1d) can be interpreted as meaning that every man thinks of himself that he is smart. In (1e) but not in (1f) we can be asking about who the person is that said that she herself should be invited.

1.
  (a) She admires Núria
  (b) Everybody loves him
  (c) Every man loves his mother
  (d) Every man thinks that he is smart
  (e) Who said we should invite her?
  (f) Who did she say we should invite?

© Springer International Publishing AG 2017
P. Brézillon et al. (Eds.): CONTEXT 2017, LNAI 10257, pp. 69–80, 2017.
DOI: 10.1007/978-3-319-57837-8_6

Binding Theory Principles (B) and (C) account for an impressive array of data, including that in (1). In Chomsky (1993), (B) and (C) are formulated as

(B) If α is a pronominal, interpret it as distinct in reference from every c-commanding phrase in its Governing Category.

(C) If α is an r-expression, interpret it as distinct in reference from every c-commanding phrase.

For the purposes of this paper it will be enough to keep in mind that, according to Binding Theory, when two NPs are in the sort of structural relation that *She* and *Núria* exhibit in (1a) then they cannot be interpreted as being co-referential.

. Notice that, as stated, (B) and (C) would seem to cover only the examples that involve expressions that refer to an individual but not quantificational expressions (i.e., (1a) but not (1b)). They should, therefore, be re-formulated so that the relation that is constrained includes both co-reference and the sort of relation that exists between a quantifier and the NPs which are bound by it (as we do in Sect. 3).

2 Some Counter-Examples

There are different kinds of well known counterexamples to Principles (B) and (C). Here we will focus on one significant type of such counterexamples. They are illustrated in (2) and (3)[1]:

2. I think that woman talking on TV is Zelda. *She* says the same things that *Zelda* says in her book
3. I believe that the man with the devil costume at the Halloween party is Joe. It is suspicious that *he* knows *him* so well

Both sentences can be interpreted so that the two italicized NPs have the same referent, even if they are in the kind of syntactic configuration that, according to principle (B) (in the case of (3)) and Principle (C) (in the case of (2)), should not allow a co-referential interpretation.

3 An Alternative Proposal

I propose that (B) and (C) are modified as in (B)* and (C)*:

(B)* If a sentence whose LF representation is of the form ...α...β... (where β is a pronominal, and α is a NP that c-commands β in its GC) is used in a context C, it is not *presupposed* in C that α and β are *co-valued*.

---

[1] See, for instance, Evans (1980), Reinhart (1983) and Heim (1993) for other kinds of counterexamples. I discussed and tried to account for all the different kinds of counterexamples to BT in Macià (1996, 1997). The general proposal in Macià (1997) was based on the same version of principles (B) and (C) that I present in Sect. 4 of this paper. The account of other kinds of counterexamples not considered in the present paper was based on additional considerations. Here I focus on that part of my proposal that is directly relevant to vindicate the usefulness of the notion of *derived context*.

(C)* If a sentence whose LF representation is of the form ...α...β... (where β is an r-expression, and α is an NP that c-commands β) is used in a context C, it is not *presupposed* in C that α and β are *co-valued*[*2].

Again, for the purposes of this paper it will be enough to keep in mind that, according to (B)* and (C)*, when two NPs are in the sort of structural relation that *She* and *Núria* exhibit in (1a) then they cannot be interpreted in such a way that it is *presupposed* in the *context* C that they are *co-valued*.

The sense of 'being presupposed', 'context' and 'being co-valued*', as we use them in stating these principles, is the following:

The notions of 'context' and 'presupposition' that we use in stating (B)* and (C)* are the same as in Stalnaker (1973, 1974): linguistic communication always takes place on the basis of a background of common beliefs and assumptions, or *context*. Using the possible worlds framework we can identify a context in which some instance of linguistic communication takes place with a set of possible worlds: those worlds that are open possibilities (could be the actual world) according to what the participants in the conversation believe, and believe that the others believe, and believe that the others believe that they believe, and so on. (If we wanted to make this characterization more precise we should take into consideration that what is relevant is not really what the participants believe but rather what they pretend to believe; that is, p is part of context C if, and only if, all the participants in the conversation are disposed to behave, for the purposes of the conversation, as if they believe that p, and believe that the others believe that p, etc.). A proposition p is *presupposed* in a context C if p is true in each world in C. That is, a presupposition of a conversation is whatever the participants in the conversation take to be part of their common assumptions.

For the purposes of the present paper the difference between being co-referent and being co-valued will not be important. Still, let's mention that we take the relation of being co-valued* to be the transitive closure of the relation *to bind or to be bound to or to be covalued with* (we understand here *bound* and *co-valued* in the sense of Reinhart (2000)). This means, for instance that if α is co-valued with β, and β is bound to χ, then α is covalued* with χ.

Having provided some clarification of the notions of *context, presupposition* and *being co-valued** we can now explain the central notion in our principles (B)* and (C)*: What does it mean to say that two NPs are presupposed to be co-valued* in a certain context C?

As we said, we can identify a context with a set of possible worlds: those worlds that are compatible with what the participants in the conversation take to be their shared assumptions. Sometimes a conversation may take place in a context where someone's identity is in question. For instance, it might be an open question whether the person we are looking at is, say, Angela Merkel. That it is an open question whether she is

---

[2] I take the idea of appealing to what is *presupposed* rather than to what is actually the case in trying to deal with the phenomena related to principles (B) and (C) from Heim (1982, 1993). Heim, in turn, credits Postal (1970) for this idea. The main difference between Heim's formulation of the binding principles and mine is that she states her conditions as purely syntactic principles that rule out certain co-indexations among NPs.

Merkel or not means that there are two kinds of worlds that are both compatible with what the speakers are assuming: worlds where Merkel is the person we are looking at, and worlds where we are looking at someone other than Merkel.

Some terminology: we say that a referential NP *picks up* an individual I at a world W in the context C, if I is the individual that the NP would refer to if W were the actual world.

Let's consider now one example. Suppose I utter the sentence *She is a smart person* while pointing to a woman who is in front of us. Since all the participants in the conversation will believe (and believe that the others believe, etc.) that the woman is in front of us and that I uttered *She* while pointing at her, it will be part of the context that the woman is in front of us and that she is the one I am referring to with my use of *She*. That is, for each world in the context W *She* will pick up the woman that is in front of us in W. Let's suppose further that we are unsure whether the woman is Angela Merkel. That means that there will be some worlds in the context where the woman in front of us is Angela Merkel, but there will also be some worlds in the context where Angela Merkel is someone other than the woman in front of us. *She* will pick up Angela Merkel in those worlds where Merkel is the woman in front of us, but will not pick up Angela Merkel in those worlds where someone other than Angela Merkel is in front of us. This agrees with the intuitive idea that, if we do not know whether the woman is or not Angela Merkel, then we are unsure as well as to whether my use of *She* refers to Angela Merkel or to someone else.

If NP_1 and NP_2 are referential NPs, then NP_1 and NP_2 are presupposed to be co-valued* when used in a context C when NP_1 and NP_2 pick up the same individual in each world in C.

In our example *She* and *Angela Merkel* are not presupposed to be co-valued* since in some worlds in the context they pick up different individuals. As we saw, there are worlds in the context where the person in front of us is not Merkel, and in those worlds *She* and *Angela Merkel* will pick up different individuals.

Even if it is not directly relevant for the purposes of the present paper, that focuses just on counterexamples to BT such as (2) and (3), it might be worth pointing out the following regarding sentences that might contain quantificational NPs: if NP_1 is interpreted as bound to NP_2 then it follows that NP_1 and NP_2 are not just co-valued* but presupposed to be co-valued*: if one NP is interpreted as bound by the other then it is not possible that a situation of the kind we just described for *she* and *Merkel* arises. If we interpret, for instance, *her* as bound to *Every girl* in *Every girl loves her father* then there is no room for the two NPs to be co-valued in some worlds in the context and not in others (since being bound implies being co-valued).

With our formulation of (B)* and (C)* it is easy to explain why the last clause of (2) and of (3) are completely acceptable sentences. Consider again, for instance, (3):

3. At the Halloween party: I think that the man with the devil costume is Joe. It is suspicious that *he* knows *him* so well.

The reason why (3) is completely good even if *he* and *him* in the last clause actually refer both to Joe is this: when uttering the last part of (3) it is still an open question whether the man in the devil costume (who is the one *he* refers to) is or is not Joe (who is the one *him* refers to). Whether they are the same or not is precisely what is being discussed. Putting it in terms of the two-dimensional possible worlds framework: in some worlds in the context, Joe is the man that is wearing the devil costume at the Halloween party, but in some other worlds in the context someone other than Joe is the one who is wearing the devil costume. That means that we interpret *he* and *him* so that they pick up the same individual in those worlds in the context where Joe is the one wearing the devil costume, but they pick up different individuals in those worlds where someone else is wearing the costume. So, we interpret the two NPs so that it is not presupposed that they pick up the same individual (and so it is not presupposed that they are co-valued*). There is no problem, then, in interpreting the last part of (3) in accordance to (B)*.

An analogous explanation could be given for the acceptability of (2).

Notice, finally, that we could not interpret "He knows him so well" in (3) with *He* referring to whoever is the man in the devil costume, and *him* referring to Joe if it were not an open question whether the two individuals are the same or not. We can see this in (4), where the previous discourse has been modified so as to try to make clear that when the utterance of the last clause takes place it is presupposed that Joe is the man with the devil costume.

4. A: Do you have the list of who is each person in the party?
   B: I certainly do.
   A: Could you tell me who is the man with the devil costume?
   B: The man with the devil costume is Joe.
   A: Oh, I see. It is suspicious that he knows him so well.

We cannot understand the last clause so that *he* and *him* both refer to the individual that we have already established that is both Joe and the man with the devil costume[3].

---

[3] We can make the sentence good, or at least much better, by changing the tense of the discourse to past, and by replacing "It's suspicious that" in the last clause by an expression such as "This is why", "This explains that" or "No wonder then that". I do not think this poses a problem for the claim that what makes the last part of (3) good is that we are not presupposing that the individuals that *he* and *him* refer to are the same. The use of past tense and of expressions like "This is the reason why..." facilitates interpreting the sentence with respect to the context *as it was* before the previous sentence had been uttered. We can also see this in a text like (i):

(i) A: I wonder why Tom did not come to the party with his wife.
    B: Tom has never been married.
    A: This explains why he did not come with his wife.

The use of *his wife* in the last clause requires that it is not presupposed that Tom is not married. This, though, is exactly the information that has been introduced in the context by B. Nevertheless, the use of "this explains why" makes easier to understand that what follows does not take for granted the information that *this* (in "this explains why") refers to.

4 Relevant Contexts

4.1 New Problematic Examples

In this section we are going to consider new data that will show the necessity of modifying our formulation of the Binding Principles so that the context that is relevant for the application of (B)* and (C)* is identified in a more accurate way. Our discussion will provide, I believe, some clear evidence in support of the usefulness of the notion of *derived context*. Consider the following texts:

5. A: That man over there who is talking to Delia is Miguel.
   B: Right. But Delia does not know that he is Miguel. Actually, she thinks that he hates Miguel.
6. A and B are talking about their mutual friend David, who is an amnesiac:
   A: Has David already realized that he is David?
   B: No, this very morning he told me that he saw him in a video.
7. A: I would like to know certain thing about Tim.
   B: Tim is that man over there. Ask him.
   A: I see.
   B: Even if he were not Tim, you should ask him, because he would be someone playing in the same band (he is wearing the band's suit) and he would know him well.

These texts pose a problem for the proposal I have been defending (as well as, of course, for Standard Binding Theory). In (5) when *She thinks that he hates Miguel* is uttered A and B are assuming that Miguel is the man they are looking at (B's saying "Right" helps to indicate that what A has said has been accepted and can be taken as being part of the context). So both *he* and *Miguel* pick up Miguel in each world in the context. So the two NPs are presupposed to be co-valued. So according to (C)* the sentence could not have the interpretation that it actually has. Similar considerations can be made with respect to (B)* and the clauses *he saw him* in (6), and *he would know him well* in (7).

4.2 Derived Contexts

I think that the right way to try to approach this problem is by appealing to the notion of *derived context* as introduced in Stalnaker (1988).

The point of a speech act is generally to distinguish among different possibilities that at a given moment in a conversation are regarded as open. That is, to distinguish among the possible worlds in the context. Certain parts of the discourse do not primarily distinguish between the possibilities that the participants in the conversation regard as live options but rather between some other set of possibilities.

In a belief attribution, for instance, the clause that expresses what the belief being attributed is does not primarily distinguish among the possibilities that the participants in the conversation regard as open but rather among the possibilities that are open according to what the participants in the conversation take *the subject of the belief attribution* to believe[4].

The set of possibilities among which the embedded clause in a belief attribution sentence distinguishes plays a role in regard to the embedded clause similar to the role that the context set plays in regard to the main sentence. Stalnaker calls this set of possibilities a *derived context*. It will contain all the possible worlds compatible with what it is presupposed in the main context that the subject of the belief attribution believes. We will say that it is the derived context *for* some particular clause in a sentence, *relative to* some particular *main context*.

In the same way that the main context has to satisfy any presupposition carried by a sentence which is uttered in that context, the derived context for an embedded clause has to satisfy the presuppositions carried by that embedded clause: the sentence "John believes that Spei stopped beating her brother" carries the presupposition that John believes that Spei was beating her brother, and so, requires that it be presupposed *in the derived context* that Spei was beating her brother (it is not necessary that the main context has that presupposition).

In the same way that a referential expression is felicitously used only if there is a suitable individual in each possible world in the context that it can pick up, a referential expression in the embedded clause of a belief attribution must pick up a suitable individual in each world in the derived context. I will not try here to give any specific semantics for belief attribution sentences. For our present purposes it will suffice to notice that referential expressions in an embedded clause expressing a belief pick up an individual in each world *in the derived context* and so the question can arise if two expressions are presupposed to refer to the same individual in the derived context (i.e. whether they pick up the same individual in each world in the derived context).

We have seen, focusing on the particular case of the derived context for the interpretation of a belief attributions, three characteristics that help identify derived contexts in general: first, the derived context for the interpretation of a certain clause is the set of possibilities that that clause distinguishes among; second, a derived context must satisfy the presuppositions of the corresponding clause; third, in each world in the derived context there must be a referent for each referential expression in the corresponding clause.

Subjunctive conditionals (as well as indicative conditionals) are also evaluated in part with respect to a derived context: the consequent of the conditional is evaluated with respect to a set of possibilities similar in some relevant sense to the possibilities which are open in the main context, but such that what the antecedent says is true. The presuppositions of the consequent clause must be satisfied in the derived context (as it happens in "If Spei had been beating her brother, she would have stopped beating him by the time he was 33"). A referential expression in the consequent of a subjunctive

---

[4] Of course by distinguishing among the possibilities that are open according to what the participants on the conversation assume that the subject of the belief attribution believes, the embedded clause will indirectly distinguish among the possibilities that are open according to what the participants in the conversation believe (what *they* assume as open regarding what the subject believes). This is why I say the embedded clause does not *primarily* distinguish among those possibilities.

conditional will pick up an individual in each world in its derived context (as it happens in "If there were a thief on the roof, he would be very cold").

4.3   Binding Principles and Derived Contexts

I think we will be able to account for sentences like (5)–(7) by modifying Binding Principles (B)* and (C)* so that they take into consideration the possible existence of different contexts in the evaluation of certain parts of a sentence. They could be modified in the following way:

(B)**   If a sentence whose LF representation is of the form ...α...β... (where β is a pronominal, and α is an NP that c-commands β in its GC) is used in a context C, and C' is the *relevant context* relative to C for a clause containing α and β, then it is not *presupposed* in C' that α and β are *co-valued*.

(C)**   If a sentence whose LF representation is of the form ...α...β... (where β is an r-expression, and α is an NP that c-commands β) is used in a context C, and C' is the *relevant context* relative to C for a clause containing α and β, then it is not *presupposed* in C' that α and β are *co-valued*.

Similarly to what we did when introducing the previous versions of (B) and (C), we should point out here that, for the purposes of this paper, it will be enough to keep in mind that, according to (B)** and (C)**, when two NPs are in the sort of structural relation that *She* and *Núria* exhibit in (1a) then they cannot be interpreted in such a way that it is presupposed in the *relevant context for the interpretation of the clause that contains the two NPs* that they are co-valued.

Regarding the notion of *relevant context* we stipulate that if C' is the derived context for a clause s' of a sentence s uttered in C, then C' is the relevant context relative to C for s'. For a clause with no special context other than the main context, the relevant context is the main context.

Using (B)** and (C)** we can see that (5) and (7) do no longer present a counter-example to our version of the Binding Principles. (We will comment on (6) in the next section).

The clause *He hates Miguel* in (5) is part of a belief attribution sentence. The two NPs would pick up the same individual in each world in the main context, but they pick up different individuals in the derived context for this clause. According to what A and B suppose that Delia believes, Miguel and the man that Delia is talking to are two different people (or at least it is not determined that they are the same–i.e. at least for some world in the derived context, they are not the same). So the two NPs in *He hates Miguel* are not presupposed to pick up the same individual in each world in the relevant context, namely, the derived context for the embedded clause of the belief attribution sentence.

An analogous explanation applies to the clause *he would know him well* in (7): in the relevant context, i.e., in the derived context for the consequent of the subjunctive conditional, the man A and B are looking at is not Tim, since in all the worlds in the derived context for a subjunctive conditional what the antecedent says is true, and the antecedent of the subjunctive conditional in (7) says that the man A and B are looking at is not Tim. So, if for each world in the derived context *he* picks up the man A and B are looking at, and *him* picks up Tim, the two NPs are not presupposed to be co-valued (actually they are presupposed not to be co-valued, i.e., they pick up a different individual in each world in the derived context).

4.4 'Saying Attributions'

In the case of sentences containing what we might call a *saying attribution* it does not seem possible to specify a 'derived context' that plays all the roles that we have seen a derived context plays for belief attribution sentences and subjunctive conditionals.

One important difference between belief attributions and saying attributions is that the former are related to a state whereas the latter are related to an event: saying attributions describe the content of some particular utterance that the subject of the saying-attribution performed. Even when we use several saying attribution sentences about the same subject, there might not be one single set of possibilities which each saying attribution makes a contribution in trying to specify. Each saying attribution might be about a different utterance, and it will be concerned with specifying which worlds are compatible with the content of that particular utterance. This is not the same as specifying the possibilities left open by all what the subject said. I might report that John said that he is from Cambridge, and that he said that he is from Newport. The two saying attributions do not attempt to describe a single set of possibilities–the one compatible with what John 'said', but rather they report two different utterances of John, each with its own content.

We could still say that the derived context for a saying attribution is the set of possible worlds compatible with what we believe is the content of the utterance we are attributing to the subject when we say that he said so and so. If this were the derived context then it would be unlike the derived context for belief attributions or conditionals, since it does not have to contain the presuppositions that the words used in the saying attribution might carry: as it is well known, sentences with 'verbs of saying' (*say*, *tell*, *announce*, *ask*) are such that the sentence containing them does not require any presupposition that might usually be carried by some of the expressions in the embedded clause[5]. So, for instance, I can felicitously and even truly say of my bachelor friend Ambròs that he said that his wife had stopped beating the king of France.

It seems that referential expressions in the embedded clause of a saying attribution sentence must have a suitable referent in the following set of possible worlds: those worlds that according to the main context are compatible with what the subject of the saying attribution was assuming when making his utterance. So, for instance, I can utter (8).

8. Gemma believed that some moonlight reflected on the room wall was a ghost. She said that he probably was friendly.

---

[5] See, for instance, Karttunen (1974).

When making the saying attribution we are assuming that in all the worlds compatible with what Gemma was assuming when she made her utterance there was a ghost in the room. *He* in the embedded clause will pick up, for each world in the set of worlds compatible with what Gemma was assuming when she made her utterance, the ghost that Gemma thought was in the room[6]. I propose that we take the set of worlds that in the main context are regarded as compatible with what the subject of the saying attribution was assuming when he made the utterance we are attributing to him as the relevant context for the embedded clause of a saying attribution sentence.

Then we can account for (6): the relevant context for the embedded clause in *he told me that he saw him in a video* is the set of worlds compatible with what A and B assume that David was assuming when he made the utterance we are attributing to him. From what is said in the first part of (6) it is clear that in each possible world compatible with what A and B know that David believed and that he believed that people who were listening to him believed and, so, in each world compatible with what they know that David assumed when he uttered a sentence there are two different people: himself and David. So the pronouns *he* and *him* do not pick up the same individual in the relevant context for the embedded clause, and so the interpretation of this clause in not in conflict with our new version of the Binding Principles[7].

4.5   Checking Our Examples

In order to make sure that what explains (5)–(7) is what we claimed that explains them (i.e. that certain parts of the sentences must be evaluated with respect to a context which is not the main context) and not something else, we could do the following: we should check that the relevant clauses can not be interpreted as in (5)–(7) when we make just the minimal changes necessary to prevent evaluating the clause with respect to a derived or special context (i.e. different from the main context).

Consider (9), (10) and (11), which are the analogues of, respectively, (5), (6) and (7).

9. A: That man over there who is talking to Delia is Miguel.
    *B: Right. But Delia does not know that he is Miguel. Actually he hates Miguel.
10. A and B are talking about their mutual friend David who is amnesiac:
    A: Has David already realized that he is David?
    *B: No, this very morning he saw him in a video.

---

[6] Notice that for most utterances of this sentence, *he* would not have a referent in each world in the main context, and this is why usually we could not say: "Gemma believed that some moonlight on the room's wall was a ghost. He probably was friendly" (we could say this only in a context where we were willing to share Gemma's special belief in a ghost).

[7] See Stalnaker (1988: 165) for a brief discussion of the question of how to understand the idea that a world has two individuals whose properties are sensitive to facts about a single actual individual.

11. A: I would like to know certain thing about Tim.

    B: Tim is that man over there. Ask him.

    A: I see.

    *B: You should ask him, because he is someone playing in the same band (he is wearing the band's suit) and he knows him well.

The clause *He admires Miguel* in (9) is no longer acceptable if we intend *He* to pick up, for each world in the context, the man that A and B are looking at and for *Miguel* to pick up the man A and B call "Miguel". Similarly for *he saw him in a video* in (10), and *he knows him well* in (11).

5 Conclusion

In this paper I have presented an argument in favour of the adequacy and usefulness of the notion of *derived context*, as first introduced in Stalnaker (1988). We have shown that this notion can successfully be employed to account for a kind of phenomena quite different from that that first motivated introducing it: the phenomena regarding the structural constraints on anaphora that the Binding Principles try to account for.

We have first shown that if we reformulate Binding Principles (B) and (C) in the appropriate way, they can successfully account for sentences such as (2) and (3) that have been regarded as seriously problematic for Standard Binding Theory. I have then introduced texts (5), (6) and (7) which pose a new, enhanced difficulty for both the standard formulation of Binding Theory and for my first reformulation of it. I have then shown how a new version of the Binding Principles (B) and (C) that appeals to the notion of "relevant context" (which, in turn is characterized in terms of the Stalnakerian notion of "derived context"), can successfully account for this new problem posed by texts such as (5), (6) and (7).

References

Chomsky, N.: Lectures on Government and Binding. Foris, Dordrecht (1981)

Chomsky, N.: A minimalist program for linguistic theory. In: Hale, K., Keyser, S. (eds.) The View From Building 20: Essays in Linguistics in Honor of Sylvain Bromberger. MIT Press, Cambridge (1993). (Reprinted in: Chomsky, N.: The Minimalist Program. MIT Press, Cambridge (1995))

Evans, G.: Pronouns. Linguist. Inq. **11**, 337–362 (1980). (Reprinted in: Evans: Collected Papers. Clarendon Press, Oxford (1985))

Heim, I.: Anaphora and semantic interpretation: a reinterpretation of Reinhart's approach. SfS-Report-07-93, University of Tubingen (1993). (Reprinted in: Sauerland, U., Percus, O. (eds.) The Interpretative Tract, MIT Working Papers in Linguistics, vol. 25. MITWPL, Cambridge (1998))

Higginbotham, J.: Anaphoric reference and common reference (1992, unpublished manuscript)

Karttunen, L.: Presupposition and linguistic context. Theor. Linguist. **1**, 181–194 (1974)

Macià, J.: Binding theory, semantic interpretation and context. Catalan Work. Papers Linguist. **5** (1), 81–112 (1996)

Macià, J.: Natural language and formal languages. MIT, Doctoral dissertation (1997)

Postal, P.: On coreferential complement subject deletion. Linguist. Inq. **1**, 439–500 (1970)

Reinhart, T.: Anaphora and Semantic Interpretation. Croom Helm, London (1983)

Reinhart, T.: Strategies of anaphora resolution. In: Bennis, H., Evaraert, M., Reuland, E. (eds.) Interface Strategies. North Holland, Amsterdam (2000)

Stalnaker, R.: Presupposition. J. Philos. Log. **2**, 77–96 (1973). (Reprinted in: Stalnaker, pp. 31–46 (1999))

Stalnaker, R.: Pragmatic presuppositions. In: Munitz, M., Unger, P. (eds.) Semantics and Philosophy, New York (1974). (Reprinted in: Stalnaker, pp. 47–62 (1999))

Stalnaker, R.: Belief attribution and context. In: Grimm, M. (ed.) Contents of Thoughts. University of Arizona Press, Tucson (1988). (Reprinted in: Stalnåker, pp. 117–129 (1999). Page numbers refer to the reprinted version)

Stalnaker, R.: Context and Content. Oxford University Press, Oxford (1999)

Discovering Context to Prune Large and Complex Search Spaces

Arjun Satish[1]([✉]), Ramesh Jain[2], and Amarnath Gupta[3]

[1] Turn Inc., Redwood City, CA, USA
arjun.satish@turn.com
[2] University of California, Irvine, USA
[3] SDSC, University of California, San Diego, USA

Abstract. Specifying the search space is an important step in designing multimedia annotation systems. With the large amount of data available from sensors and web services, context-aware approaches for pruning search spaces are becoming increasingly common. In these approaches, the search space is limited by the contextual information obtained from a fixed set of sources. For example, a system for tagging faces in photos might rely on a static list of candidates obtained from the photo owner's Facebook profile. These contextual sources can get extremely large, which leads to lower accuracy in the annotation problem.

We present our novel **Context Discovery Algorithm**, a technique to progressively *discover* the most relevant search space from a dynamic set of context sources. This allows us to reap the benefits of context, while keeping the size of the search space within bounds.

As a concrete application for our approach, we present a simple photo management application, which tags faces of people in a user's personal photos. We empirically study the role of CueNet in the face tagging application to tag photos taken at real world events, such as conferences, weddings or social gatherings. Our results show that the availability of event context, and its dynamic discovery, can produce 80% smaller search spaces with nearly 100% correct tags.

1 Introduction

With the popularity of global social networks and proliferation of mobile phones, information about people, their social connections and day-to-day activities are becoming available at a very large scale. The web provides an open platform for documenting many real world events such as conferences, weather events and sports games. With such context sources, multimedia annotation algorithms [1–3] are being designed where the search space of tags is obtained from one or more sources (Fig. 1(b)). These approaches rely on a single *type* of context. For example, using social network information from Facebook to solve the face recognition problem. We refer to such a direct dependency between the search space and a data source as **static linking**. Although these systems are meritorious in their own right, they suffer from the following drawbacks: they do not employ

© Springer International Publishing AG 2017
P. Brézillon et al. (Eds.): CONTEXT 2017, LNAI 10257, pp. 81–95, 2017.
DOI: 10.1007/978-3-319-57837-8_7

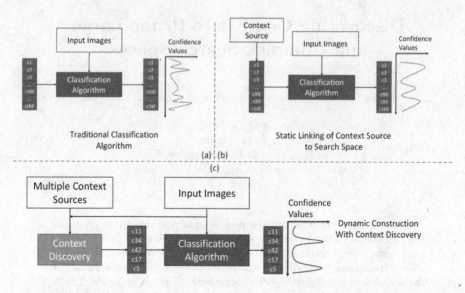

Fig. 1. The different approaches in search space construction for a multimedia annotation problem. A traditional setup (a), where the search space candidates are manually specified. Context is used (b) to generate large static search spaces. The CueNet framework (c), aims to produce small relevant search spaces.

multiple sources, and therefore the **relations** between them. By realizing that these sources are interconnected in their own way, we are able to treat the entire source topology as a network. Our intuition in this work is to navigate this network to progressively discover the search space for a given media annotation problem. Figure 1(c) shows how context discovery can provide substantially smaller search spaces for a set of images, which contain a large number of correct tags. A small search space with large number of true positives provides the ideal ground for an annotation algorithm to exhibit superior performance.

We present the CueNet framework, which provides access to multiple data sources containing event, social, and geographical information through a unified query interface to extract information from them. CueNet encapsulates our **Context Discovery Algorithm**, which utilizes the query interface to discover the most relevant search space for a media annotation problem. To facilitate a hands-on discussion, we show the use of context discovery in a real world application: face tagging in personal photos. As a case study, we will attempt to tag photos taken at conference events, weddings and social gatherings (birthday parties, for example) by different users. These photos could contain friends, colleagues, relatives or friends-of-friends or newly found acquaintances (who are not yet connected to the user through any social network). Real world event photos are particularly interesting because no single source can provide all the necessary information. It emphasizes the need to utilize multiple sources in a meaningful way (Fig. 2).

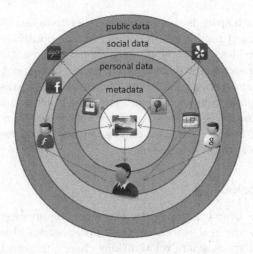

Fig. 2. Navigation of various data sources by the discovery algorithm.

Here is an **example** to illustrate CueNet's discovery process. Let's suppose that Joe takes a photo with a camera that records time and GPS in the photo's EXIF header. Additionally, Joe has two friends. One with whom he interacts on Google+, and the other using Facebook. The framework checks if either of them has any interesting event information pertaining to this time and location. We find that the friend on Google+ left a calendar entry describing an event (a title, time interval and name of the place). The entry also marks Joe as a participant. In order to determine the category of the place, the framework uses Yelp.com with the name and GPS location to find whether it is a restaurant, sports stadium or an apartment complex. If the location of the event was a sports stadium, it navigates to upcoming.com to check what event was occurring here at this time. If a football game or a music concert was taking place at the stadium, we look at Facebook to see if the friend "Likes" the sports team or music band. By traversing the different data sources in this fashion, the number of people, who could potentially appear in Joe's photograph, was incrementally built up, rather than simply reverting to everyone on his social network or people who could be in the area where the photograph was taken. We refer to such navigation between different data sources to identify relevant contextual information as **progressive discovery**. The salient feature of CueNet is to be able to progressively discover events, and their associated properties, from the different data sources and relate them to the photo capture event. We argue that given this structure and relations between the various events, CueNet can make assertions about the presence of a person in the photograph. Once candidates have been identified by CueNet, they are passed to the face tagging algorithm ([4], for example), which can perform very well as their search space is limited to two candidates.

Contributions: Real-world search spaces are large and complex (owing to their time varying relationships). Our contribution in this paper is a technique to discover the search spaces for multimedia annotation problems by using contextual information (events and their interrelations) from multiple data sources. We claim that this search space is significantly smaller than one obtained by static linking approaches, but retains a high number of true positives. We describe our findings when these ideas are applied to a personal photo annotation problem.

In the following sections, we develop our notion of context, and identify its properties which make discoveries like the above possible. We discuss the CueNet framework, its different components, and the conditions it creates which allow for progressive discovery. We present a context discovery algorithm to use these properties and tag faces in personal photos. Finally, we present an empirical evaluation to support our above claims.

1.1   Related Work

Our work has been deeply informed by the modeling strategy used by Karen Henricksen [10]. In the real world, relationships between objects change continuously. A search space where relationships change frequently is a **complex search space**. Our context discovery is built to handle such situations. In terms of tagging photos using context, Naaman et al. have exploited GPS attributes to extract place and person information [1]. Rattenbury and Naaman [5] devised techniques to find tags which describe events or places by analyzing their spatiotemporal usage patterns. Time alone is used for organizing photos by Graham et al. [6]. Context information and image features are used in conjunction by O'Hare and Smeaton in [2] and Cao et al. in [7] to identify event tags. The biggest difference in our work is the ability of our discovery algorithm to add personal, geographical or event tags to a given photo.

2   Context

Our justification for the use of context begins with the statement: *For a given user, the correctness of face tags for a photograph containing people she has never met is undefined.* This observation prepares us to understand what context is, and how contextual reasoning assists in tagging photos. The description of any problem domain requires a set of abstract data types, and a model of how these types are related to each other. We **define** contextual types as those which are semantically different from these data types, but can be directly or indirectly related to them via an extended model which encapsulates the original one. Contextual reasoning assists in the following two ways. **First**, contextual data restricts the number of people who might appear in the photographs. We can also argue that all the personal data of a user (her profile on Facebook, LinkedIn, email exchanges, phone call logs) provides a reasonable estimate of all these people who might appear in her photos. **Second**, by reasoning on abstractions in the contextual domain, we can infer conclusions on the original problem. We exploit this property to develop our algorithm in the later sections. Though CueNet can be applied to a variety of recognition problems, we focus on tagging people in personal photos for concreteness, where, the image and person tag form the abstractions in the problem domain. The types used in the contextual domain, but not limited to, are **Events:** includes description of events like conferences, and their structure (for example, what kind of sessions, talks and keynotes occur within the conference); **Social Relationships:** information about a user's social graph and **Geographical Proximity:** various tools like Facebook Places, Google Latitude or Foursquare provide information about where people are at a given time.

The above classes of contextual data can be obtained from a variety of data sources. Examples of data sources range from mobile phone call logs and email conversations to Facebook messages to a listing of public events at upcoming.com. Sources can be classified into **Personal Data Sources:** include all sources which provide details about the particular user whose photo is to be tagged (for example, email and Google Calendar); **Social Data Sources:** sources such as Facebook, DBLP or LinkedIn which provide contextual information about a user's friends and colleagues, or **Public Data Sources** which provide information about public events.

Social and public data sources are enormous in size, containing information about billions of events and entities. Trying to use them directly will lead to scalability problems faced by face recognition and verification techniques. But, by using personal data, we can discover which parts of social and public sources are more relevant. For example, if a photo was taken at San Francisco, CA (where the user lives) his family in China is less relevant. Thus, the role of personal information is twofold. **Firstly**, it provides contextual information regarding the photo. **Secondly**, it acts as a bridge to connect to social and public data sources to discover interesting people connected to the user who might be present in the event and therefore, the photo.

We must note the **temporal relevance** property of a data source. Given a stream of photos taken during a time interval, the source which contributed interesting context for a photo might not be equally useful for the one appearing next. This is because sources tend to focus on a specific set of event types or relationship types, and the two photos might be captured in different events or contains persons with whom the user maintains relations through different sources. For example, two photos taken at a conference might contain a user's friends in the first, but with advisers of these friends in the next. The friends might interact with the user through a social network, but their advisers might not. By using a source like DBLP, the relations between the adviser and friends can be discovered. We say that the temporal relevance of these context sources is *low*. This requirement will play an important role in the design of our framework.

3   The CueNet Framework

Figure 3 shows the different components of the CueNet framework. The Ontological **Event Models** specify various event and entity classes, and the different relations between them. These declared types are used to define the **Data Sources** which provides access to different types of contextual data. The **Person Verification Tools** consist of a database of people, their profile information and photos containing these people. When this module is presented with

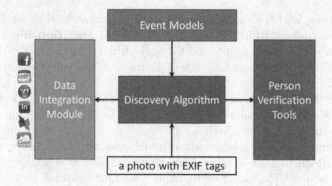

Fig. 3. The conceptual architecture of CueNet.

a candidate and the input photograph, it compares the features extracted from the candidate's photos and the input photo to find the confidence threshold. In this section, we describe each module, and how the context discovery algorithm utilizes them to accomplish its task.

3.1 Event Model

Our ontologies extend the E* model [8] to specify relationships between events and entities. Specifically, we utilize the relationships "**subevent-of**", which specifies event containment. An event $e1$ is a subevent-of of another event $e2$, if $e1$ occurs completely within the spatiotemporal bounds of $e2$. Additionally, we utilize the relations **occurs-during** and **occurs-at**, which specify the space and time properties of an event. Also, another important relation between entities and events is the "**participant**" property, which allows us to describe which entity is participating in which event. It must be noted that participants of a subevent are also participants of the parent event. A participation relationship between an event and person instance asserts the presence of the person within the spatiotemporal region of the event. We argue that the reverse is also true, i.e., if a participant P is present in $\mathcal{L}_P$ during the time T_P and an event E occurs within the spatiotemporal region $(\mathcal{L}_E, T_E)$, we say P is a participant of E if the event's spatiotemporal span contained that of the participant.

$$\texttt{participant}(E, P) \iff (\mathcal{L}_P \sqsubset_L \mathcal{L}_E) \wedge (T_P \sqsubset_T T_E) \tag{1}$$

The symbols $\sqsubset_L$ and $\sqsubset_T$ indicate spatial and temporal containment respectively [8]. In later sections, we refer to the location and time of the event, $\mathcal{L}_E$ and T_E as $E.$**occurs-at** and $E.$**occurs-during** respectively.

3.2 Data Sources

The ontology makes available a vocabulary of classes and properties. Using this vocabulary, we can now declaratively specify the schema of each source. With these schema descriptions, CueNet can infer what data source can provide what type of data instances. For example, the framework can distinguish between a source which describes conferences and another which is a social network. We use a LISP like syntax to allow developers of the system to specify these declarations. The example below describes a source containing conference information.

```
(:source conferences
(:attributes name time title)
(:relation conf type-of conference)
(:relation t type-of time-interval)
(:relation attendee type-of person)
(:relation attendee participant-in conf)
(:relation conf occurs-during t)
(:mappings [ [t time] [conf.title title] [attendee.name name] ] )
```

The above source declaration consists of a s-expression, where the source keyword indicates a unique name for the source. The attributes keyword is used to list the attributes of this source. The relation keyword constructs the instances conf, time, loc, attendee which are of conference, time-interval, location and person class types respectively, and relates them with relations specified in the ontology. Finally, the mappings are used to map nodes in the relationship graph constructed above to attributes of the data source. For example, the first mapping (specified using the map keyword) maps the conference's time-interval object (t) to the (time) attribute of the source.

3.3   Conditions for Discovery

CueNet is entirely based on reasoning in the event and entity (i.e., person) domain, and the relationships between them. These relationships include participation (event-entity relation), social relations (entity-entity relation) and subevent relation (event-event). For the sake of simplicity, we restrict our discussions to events whose spatiotemporal spans either completely overlap or do not intersect at all. We do not consider events which partially overlap. In order to develop the necessary conditions for context discovery, we consider the following two axioms:

Entity Existence Axiom: Entities can be present in one place at a time only. The entity cannot exist outside a spatiotemporal boundary containing it.

Participation Semantics Axiom: If an entity is participating in two events at the same time, then one is the subevent of the other.

Given, the ontology O, we can construct event instance graph $G^I(V^I, E^I)$, whose nodes are instances of classes in C^O and edges are instances of the properties in P^O. The context discovery algorithm relies on the notion that given an instance graph, *queries* to the different sources can be automatically constructed. A query is a set of predicates, with one or more unknown variables. For the instance graph $G^I(V^I, E^I)$, we construct a query $Q(D, U)$ where D is a set of predicates, and U is a set of unknown variables.

Query Construction Condition: Given an instance graph $G^I(V^I, E^I)$ and ontology $O(C^O, P^O)$, a query $Q(D, U)$ can be constructed, such that D is a set of predicates which represent a subset of relationships specified in G^I. In other words, D is a subgraph induced by G^I. U is a class, which has a relationship $r \in P^O$, with a node $n \in D$. Essentially, the ontology must prescribe a relation between some node n through the relationship r. In our case, the relation r will be either a **participant** or **subevent** relation. If the relationship with the instances does not violate any object property assertions specified in the ontology, we can create the query $Q(D, U)$.

Identity Condition: Given an instance graph $G^I(V^I, E^I)$, and a result graph $G^R(V^R, E^R)$ obtained from querying a source, we can merge two events only if they are identical. Two nodes $v_i^I \in V^I$ and $v_r^R \in V^R$ are identical if they meet the following two conditions. **(i)** Both v_i^I and v_r^R are of the same class type, and **(ii)** Both v_i^I and v_r^R have exactly overlapping spatiotemporal spans, indicated by the $=_L$ and $=_T$. Mathematically, we write:

$$v_i^I = v_r^R \iff (v_i^I.\textbf{type-of} = v_r^R.\textbf{type-of}) \wedge$$
$$(v_i^I.\textbf{occurs-at} =_L v_r^R.\textbf{occurs-at}) \wedge \qquad (2)$$
$$(v_i^I.\textbf{occurs-during} =_T v_r^R.\textbf{occurs-during})$$

Subevent Condition: Given an instance graph $G^I(V^I, E^I)$, and a result graph $G^R(V^R, E^R)$ obtained from querying a source, we can construct a subevent edge between two nodes $v_i^I \in V^I$ and $v_r^R \in V^R$, if one is spatiotemporally contained within the other, and has at least one common **Endurant**.

$$v_i^I \sqsubseteq_L v_r^R,$$
$$v_i^I \sqsubseteq_T v_r^R \qquad (3)$$
$$v_i^I.\textbf{Endurants} \cap v_r^R.\textbf{Endurants} \neq \{\phi\} \qquad (4)$$

Here $v_i^I.\textbf{Endurants}$ is defined as a set $\{w | w \in V_i^I \wedge w.\text{type-of} = \text{Endurant}\}$. If Eq. (4) does not hold, we say that v_i^I and v_r^R co-occur.

Merging Event Graphs: Given the above conditions, we can now describe an important building block for the context discovery algorithm: the steps needed to merge two event graphs. An example for this is shown in Fig. 4(b–d). Given the event graph consisting of the photo capture event on the left of (b) and a meeting event m and conference event c, containing their respective participants. In this example, the meeting event graph, m is semantically equivalent to the original graph. But the conference event, c is telling that the person AG is also participating in a conference at the time the photo was taken. The result of merging is shown in (d). An event graph merge consists of two steps. The first is a `subevent hierarchy join`, and the second is a `prune-up` step.

Given an original graph, O_m, and a new graph N_m, the join function works as follows: All nodes in N_m are checked against all nodes in O_m to find identical counterparts. For entities, the identity is verified through an identifier, and for

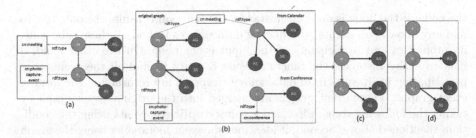

Fig. 4. The various stages in an iteration of algorithm in Sect. 3.4. (a) shows an example event graph describing a photo taken at a meeting. The meeting consists of three participants AG, SR and AS. The photo contains SR and AS. (b) shows two events returned from the data sources. One is a meeting event which is semantically identical to the input. The other is a conference event with AG. (c) shows the result of merging these graphs. (d) The **prune-up** function removes the duplicate reference to AG.

events, Eq. (2) is used. Because of the entity existence and participation semantics axioms, all events which contain a common participant are connected to their respective super event using the subevent relation (Eqs. (3) and (4) must be satisfied by the events). Also, if two events have no common participant, then they can be still be related with the subevent edge, if the event model says it is possible. For example, if in a conference event model, keynotes, lunches and banquets are declared as known subevents of an event. Then every keynote event, or banquet event to be merged into an event graph is made a subevent of the conference event, if the Eq. (3) holds between the respective events. It must be noted that node AG occurs twice in graph (c). In order to correct this, we use the participation semantics axiom. We traverse the final event graph from the leaves to the root events, and remove every person node if it appears in a subevent. This is the **prune-up** step. Using these formalisms, we now look at the working of the context discovery algorithm.

3.4 Context Discovery Algorithm

The input to the algorithm is a photo (with EXIF tags) and an associated owner (the user). By seeding the graph with owner information, we bias the discovery towards his/her personal information. An event instance graph is created where each photo is modeled as a photo capture event. Each event and entity is a node in the instance graph. Each event is associated with time and space attributes. All relationships are edges in this graph. All EXIF tags are literals, related to the photo with data property edges. Figure 4 graphically shows the main stages in a single iteration of the algorithm.

The event graph is traversed to produce a queue of entity and event nodes, which we shall refer to as DQ (discovery queue). The algorithm consists of two primary functions: **discover** and **merge**. The discover function is tail recursive, invoking itself until a termination condition is reached (when at most k tags are obtained for all faces or no new data is obtained from all data sources for all generated queries). The behavior of the query function depends on the type of the node. If the node is an event instance, the function consults the ontology to find any known sub-events, and queries data sources to find all these subevents, its properties and participants of the input event node. On the other hand, if it is an entity instance, the function issues a query to find all the events it is participating in. Results from data source wrappers are returned in the form of event graphs. These event graphs are merged into the original event graph by taking the following steps. First, it identifies **duplicate** events using the conditions mentioned above. Second, it identifies subevent hierarchies using the graph merge conditions described above, and performs a **subevent hierarchy join**. Third, the function **prune-up** removes entities from an event when its subevent also lists it as a participant node. Fourth, **push-down** is the face verification step if the number of entities in the parents of the photo-capture events is small (less than T). Push down will try to verify if any of the newly discovered entities are present in the photo and if they are (if the tagging confidence is higher than the given threshold), the entities are removed from the super event, and linked to the photo capture event as its participant. On the other hand, if this number is larger than T, the algorithm initiates the **vote-and-verify** method, which ranks all the candidates based on social relationships with people already identified in the photo. For example, if a candidate is related to two persons present in the photo through some social networks, then its score is 2. Ranking is done by simply sorting the candidate list by descending order of score. The face verification runs only on the top ranked T candidates. If there are still untagged faces after the termination of the algorithm, we vote over all the remaining people, and return the ranked list for each untagged face.

4　Experiments

In this section, we analyze how CueNet drives a real world face tagging application. The application contains a set of photos, and a database of people, and its goal is to associate the right persons for each photo, with high accuracy. The goal of CueNet, and the focus of our analysis, is to provide small search spaces so that the application can exhibit high accuracy in all datasets. In the following evaluation, we investigate three questions. **First**, what sources provide the most interesting context? **Second**, how small are the candidates lists constructed by the discovery algorithm, which are provided to the classification algorithm as a "pruned" version of the search space? And **third**, what percentage of true positives does this pruned search space contain?

4.1　Setup

We collected 2000 photos taken at 17 different real-world events by 6 different people in our face tagging experiment. The total number of candidates obtained from all the social, personal and public sources in our experiment is 7736. Each photo contains one or more persons from this database. The owner of the photos was asked to provide access to their professional Google Calendar to access personal events. Information from social networks was gathered. Specifically, events, social graph, photos of user and their friends from Facebook. In order to obtain information of the conference event, we used the Stanford NER [9] to extract names of people from the conference web pages. Descriptions of the keynote, session and banquet events were manually entered into the database. Our sources also included personal emails, access to public events website upcoming.com (Yahoo! Upcoming) and used Yahoo! PlaceFinder for geocoding addresses. The ground truth was annotated by the user with our annotation interface. For each photo, this essentially consisted of the ID of the persons in it. We will denote each dataset as 'Di' (where $1 \leq i \leq 17$ for each dataset). Table 1 describes each dataset in terms of number of photos, unique annotations in ground truth and the year they were captured. The total number of unique people who could have appeared in any photo in our experiments is 7736.

Table 1. Profile of datasets used in the experiments.

Dataset	Unique people	No. of photos	Year
D1	43	78	2012
D2	24	108	2012
D3	6	16	2010
D4	7	10	2010
D5	36	80	2009
D6	18	65	2013
D7	7	11	2013

We divide the sources into different categories to facilitate a more general discussion. The categories are "Personal Information" (same as Owner Information in Sect. 3.4), "Event sources", and "Social Networks". Event sources include Facebook events, Yahoo Upcoming web service, our conference events database among other sources. Social networks include Facebook's social graph. Personal information contained information about the user, and a link to their personal calendars. An annotation is considered "Out of Context Network" if it is not in any of these sources.

Figure 5 shows the distribution of the ground truth annotations across various sources, for each conference dataset. For example, the bar corresponding to D2 says that 87.5% of ground truth annotations were found in event sources, 41.67% in social networks, 4.17% in personal information and 12.5% were not found in any source, and therefore marked as "Out of Context Network". From this graph it is clear that event sources contain a large portion of ground truth annotations. Besides D4, a minimum of 70% of our annotations are found in event sources for all datasets, and for some datasets (D3, D7) all annotations are found in event sources. The sum total of contributions will add up to values more than 100% because they share some annotations among each other. For example, a friend on Facebook might show up at a conference to give the keynote talk.

Context Discovery: Now, lets look at the reduction obtained in state space with the discovery algorithm. The total number of people in our experiment

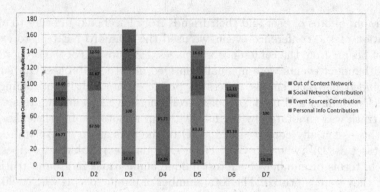

Fig. 5. The distribution of annotations in the ground truth for the conference data sets across various sources.

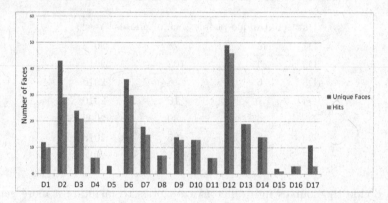

Fig. 6. Hit counts for all datasets using context discovery algorithm.

universe is 660. By statically linking the sources, we would expect the search space to contain 660 candidates for tagging any of the datasets. However, the context discovery algorithm reduced the size of the search space as shown in Fig. 6. The search space varies from 7 people in D7 (1%) to 338 people in D2 (51%). We denote the term hit rate as the percentage of true positives in the search space. Even if our search space is small, it might contain no annotations from the ground truth, leading to poor classifier performance. The hit rates are also summarized in Fig. 6. For D4, the algorithm found no event sources (as seen in Fig. 5), and therefore constructed a search space which was too small, thereby containing none of the ground truth. With the exception for D4, the hit rate is always above 83%. **We observe an overall reduction in the search space size, with a high hit rate for majority of the datasets.**

We now investigate the role of different context sources in the discovery algorithm. If an entity in the search space was merged into the event graph by an event source, they are said to be "contributed" from it. Figure 8 shows the contribution from various sources for all datasets. For example, D1 obtained 69.77% of true positives in its search space from event sources, 2.33% from

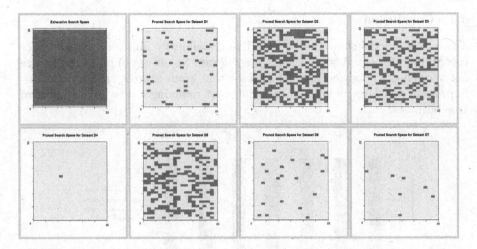

Fig. 7. Grid plots showing the exhaustive search space and pruning in search space for different datasets. (Color figure online)

personal information and 11.63% from social networks. 16.28% of true positives for D1 were obtained from no source, and were therefore marked as "Out of Context Network". This graph brings to light our argument that most of the true positives, for all datasets, were obtained as a result of navigating the event sources. It will also be noted that the role of social networks is minimal. It was found useful for only one dataset. Relying on social sources alone would have led to a large number of false positives in the classifier performance. Even though the direct impact of personal information is negligible, it is critical in linking in photos to the owner, and from there to different events. Without the availability of personal information, the algorithm would not have reached the context rich event sources.

Finally, we compare the various search spaces constructed by discovery algorithm. We represent all people in our experiment universe in a color grid (with 33×20 cells for 660 people). Each cell represents the presence or absence of a person in the search space. If a person was present in the candidate list provided to the tagging algorithm, we color the corresponding cell green, otherwise it is colored white. Figure 7 shows the color grids describing search spaces for all datasets, and an exhaustive search space (top-right grid). The positioning of people along the grid is arbitrary, but consistent across grids. Our aim here is to see the diversity in search spaces created by the algorithm. It can be seen that CueNet prunes the search space very differently for different datasets. As we move from dataset to dataset, the data sources present different items of information, and therefore CueNet constructs very search spaces. Dataset D2, D4 and D5 are very large conferences hosting hundreds of people in the same field. This explains why a large portion of the grid is covered. Also, this was the same conference held in three different years, and therefore, had a lot of common attendees resulting in overlap.

4.2   Conclusion

These experiments show that we need to dynamically link sources to extract context out of them. A source which was relevant for one set of photographs was not very effective for another. We also see that event sources are very effective in pruning very large number of candidates yet retaining a very large number of true positives.

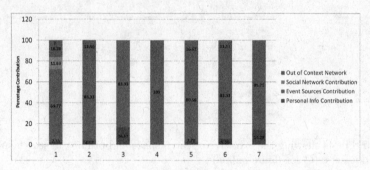

Fig. 8. Graph showing the contribution of each source type in context discovery.

5   Summary

We presented a innovative context based technique to prune complex search spaces for the entity identification problem in multimedia objects, specifically personal photos. We model context as a time varying relationship of entities and events to architect a novel context discovery framework CueNet, and designed its discovery algorithms to progressively query various heterogeneous data sources and merge context relevant to a given photo. We empirically analyzed the ability of context discovery to remove a large number of irrelevant candidates.

References

1. Naaman, M., Yeh, R.B., Paepcke, A., Garcia-Molina, H.: Leveraging context to resolve identity in photo albums. In: Proceedings of the 5th ACM/IEEE-CS Joint Conference on Digital Libraries (2005)
2. O'Hare, N., Smeaton, A.F.: Context-aware person identification in personal photo collections. IEEE Trans. Multimed. **11**(2), 220–228 (2009)
3. Stone, Z., Zickler, T., Darrell, T.: Autotagging facebook: social network context improves photo annotation. In: Computer Vision and Pattern Recognition (2008)
4. Kumar, N., Berg, A., Belhumeur, P.N., Nayar, S.: Describable visual attributes for face verification and image search. IEEE Trans. Pattern Anal. Mach. Intell. **33**, 1962–1977 (2011)
5. Rattenbury, T., Naaman, M.: Methods for extracting place semantics from Flickr tags. ACM Trans. Web (TWEB) **3**, 1 (2009)

6. Graham, A., Garcia-Molina, H., Paepcke, A., Winograd, T.: Time as essence for photo browsing through personal digital libraries. In: Proceedings of the 2nd ACM/IEEE-CS Joint Conference on Digital Libraries (2002)

7. Cao, L., Luo, J., Kautz, H., Huang, T.S.: Annotating collections of photos using hierarchical event and scene models. In: Computer Vision and Pattern Recognition (2008)

8. Gupta, A., Jain, R.M.: Managing Event Information: Modeling, Retrieval, and Applications. Morgan & Claypool Publishers, San Rafael (2011)

9. Finkel, J.R., Grenager, T., Manning, C.: Incorporating non-local information into information extraction systems by Gibbs sampling. In: The 43rd Annual Meeting on Association for Computational Linguistics (2005)

10. Henricksen, K., Indulska, J., Rakotonirainy, A.: Modeling context information in pervasive computing systems. In: Mattern, F., Naghshineh, M. (eds.) Pervasive 2002. LNCS, vol. 2414, pp. 167–180. Springer, Heidelberg (2002). doi:10.1007/3-540-45866-2_14

Context Modeling of Human Activities

Reasoning in Epistemic Contexts

Yves Bouchard[✉]

Université de Sherbrooke, Sherbrooke, QC J1K2R1, Canada
`yves.bouchard@usherbrooke.ca`

Abstract. In this paper, I develop a framework for representing knowledge, that aims at exploiting logically epistemological objects, namely epistemic contexts. Even though this framework is mostly logical and epistemological in character, it takes advantage of many works in artificial intelligence, in particular the ones of McCarthy and Buvač (1997). In Sect. 1, I characterize the notion of epistemic contexts. In Sect. 2, I present a natural deduction system that allows for the introduction and the elimination of knowledge operators. Such a system enables classical reasoning among contexts governed by different concepts of knowledge. Finally, in Sect. 3, I discuss some corollaries of the proposed framework (knowledge transfer, introspection, and closure).

1 Introduction

When representing knowledge either for logical or computational purposes, one has to consider two importants aspects (among others). The first aspect has to do with the choice of the type of representation to model knowledge. In artificial intelligence, for example, knowledge is commonly represented as an assertion in a knowledge base.[1] What makes a specific assertion an instance of knowledge is *the fact* that this piece of information constitutes an entry in a knowledge base. Such a view offers the advantage of making knowledge directly exploitable both logically and computationally, while expressing a homogeneous conception of knowledge.[2] But, on the other hand, this choice of representation has for consequence that an important aspect of knowledge is inhibited, and that is the *epistemic process* in virtue of which a given epistemic item can be *qualified* as an instance of knowledge. In other words, epistemic normativity is implicit in this sort of knowledge representation.

The second aspect is a semantic one: should the working concept of knowledge (K-concept) allow the expression "*x* knows that ϕ" to have different meanings?

I want to thank three anonymous referees for helpful comments on a previous version of the paper.

[1] Description logics [1], which are used as knowledge-based representation systems, are particularly illustrative of this point. A description logic is defined by two entities, namely a terminological box (TBox) and an assertion box (ABox), that are respectively a set of declarations and a set of assertions.

[2] For a thorough review of knowledge representation systems, see [24].

P. Brézillon et al. (Eds.): CONTEXT 2017, LNAI 10257, pp. 99–112, 2017.
DOI: 10.1007/978-3-319-57837-8_8

If it does not, and this is the usual choice, then the K-concept is conceived *univocally*. But such a view, as desirable as it might be under some conditions, seems to conflict with our ordinary epistemic practices, which make sense, in general, of different types of knowledge. If the working K-concept is conceived so as to express various types of knowledge, then the possibility of variations in meaning must be granted. In this view, different types of knowledge have different properties. Some are more robust, others are more defeasible. As *types* of knowledge, logical knowledge, mathematical knowledge, scientific knowledge, empirical knowledge, testimonial knowledge, ordinary knowledge all exhibit significant differences in their epistemic qualification processes that involve different epistemic standards. The need for a pluralist view on knowledge stems precisely from the variety of epistemic standards used to qualify knowledge.

In this paper, I develop a natural deduction system in which these two aspects are made explicit. Epistemic standards will have an explicit representation in the system by means of epistemic contexts, each of which will be defined by a unique K-concept. This framework will be compatible with a pluralist view on knowledge, so, in the end, this is a contextualist proposal. Concepts from artificial intelligence will be here put at work in an epistemological setting. The main goal is to devise a system in which epistemic normativity can be logically investigated. In the first section, I characterize the notion of epistemic context. In the second section, I define the set of introduction and elimination rules for the K-operator in a natural deduction system. In the third section, I discuss some corollaries of the proposed framework.

2   Logic and Context

2.1   Contexts in AI

Since the seminal work of McCarthy [21, 22] on contexts, there has been many theories of context, as Brêzillon [8] showed in his comprehensive survey. This is not the place to discuss all of these conceptions. I just want to point at three salient conceptions of context in order to contrast the present proposal.

A context may be conceived as an abstract object encoded in a formal language by means of an operator. More specifically, in McCarthy [21], Buvač et al. [10,11], and Buvač [9], the ist modality is interpreted as truth in a model (or validity).[3] In that view, $ist(c, \phi)$ means that a formula ϕ is true (or valid, after some generalization) in context c, i.e. ϕ is true in all truth assignments of context c. Buvač and Mason [9–11] have extended McCarthy's intuitions to modal logic.[4] Under another interpretation, centered around meaning in natural languages, a context can be envisaged as a situation, i.e. a formal representation

---

[3] It may be interpreted more weakly as truth depending on the kind of constraints imposed on the model.

[4] In [5], I presented a treatment of the notion of epistemic context in terms of McCarthy's ist operator.

of factual dimensions [2]. One interesting feature of these two views on context is that they both provide means for lexical disambiguation. According to a third view, a context is a *"subset of the complete state* of an *individual* that is used for reasoning about a given goal" [18]. These states are belief states, hence a context is a set of an agent's beliefs. From a broader perspective, several semantics have been used to model contextual reasoning, for instance dynamic semantics [3,4] and local models semantics [15].[5]

In the proposed framework, the notion of context will be defined in epistemological terms, but I will approach the characterization of this notion from a proof-theoretic perspective, namely a natural deduction system. McCarthy [21] was well aware of this possible connection between the notion of context and the notion of derivation (or deduction), as he wrote

> "Suppose we have the sentence $\mathtt{ist}(c,p)$. We can then enter the context c and infer the sentence p. We can regard $\mathtt{ist}(c,p)$ as analogous to $c \supset p$, and the operation of entering c as analogous to assuming c in a system of natural deduction as invented by Gentzen and described in many logic texts."

The development of a natural deduction system for contextual reasoning has been undertaken by Giunchiglia [18,19] in the perspective of avoiding recourse to modal logic. This resulted in a system described as *multilanguage hierarchical logics*, or multilanguage systems (ML), not only capable of embedding modal system K for instance, but also richer that standard modal systems. Compared to such a project, my goal is very modest. I want to make logically explicit the qualification process of epistemic items. This requires that I define (1) the conditions under which knowledge operators are introduced in the first place, and (2) how knowledge instances can be propagated through contexts.

2.2   Epistemic Contexts

I will use the notion of epistemic context to capture the idea behind the requisite (1), and the notion of epistemological theory to capture the requisite (2). An epistemic context will be defined by an epistemic *standard*. According to this view, a K-context is an abstract entity that associates a K-operator to an epistemic standard. Generally, a K-context is totally defined by the set of all the formulas prefixed with the corresponding K-operator. The semantic rule for K is given by

$$[\![K_i\phi]\!] = \text{true iff } \vdash_i \phi,$$

where $\vdash_i \phi$ means any wff ϕ derivable in K-context i. This provides for an *indexical* interpretation of the K-operator which makes possible in turn the representa-

---

[5] For clarifying comparisons of formal theories of context, see [6,7,23].

tion of a plurality of K-concepts.[6] The epistemic differences between K-operators are explicit in the representation as they are indexed to their associated epistemic context. Another consequence of this reading is that truth is synonymous with satisfaction of a standard.

An epistemological theory Θ is defined by a pair $\langle \kappa, \tau \rangle$, where κ is a family of K-contexts and τ is a set of transfer rules between K-contexts. Transfer rules are here conceived as axioms rather than inferential schemas in order to make epistemic qualification through contexts variable in the system. In this way, an epistemological theory specifies the epistemic relations among a set of K-contexts. The difficulties pertaining to the characterization of these relations have been clearly underlined by Guha and McCarthy [20]:

"If the statements ϕ and $\phi \Rightarrow \beta$ have different contextual dependencies, the program [inference engine] can't always combine them to conclude β. Before combining two sentences with different contextual dependencies, the program needs to reconcile relative contextual dependencies. [...] To cope with the contextuality, it [the program] needs to be able to factor out the relative contextuality so that it can use knowledge gathered in one context in another." (166)

So, in the formal representation, not only the contextual dependencies of assertions should be made explicit, but the relations between contexts should also be explicit. The proposed framework satisfies these demands.

3   Natural Deduction Rules

For the purpose of simplicity, I will restrict the deductive resources to classical propositional logic. I want to center the attention around the particular behavior of the K-operator.[7] I will follow a Fitch-style presentation for the natural deduction system to emphasize graphically the relation of conditionality between epistemic contexts (or derivations).

3.1   Reiteration

Two rules of reiteration are distinguished for formulas prefixed and not prefixed with a K-operator:

---

[6] An indexical term is a term whose meaning is twofold: the first part of the meaning, the *character*, is an invariant part, and the second part, the *content*, varies in accordance with the context of use (Kaplan). Such a reading of the K-operator is typical of indexical contextualism in epistemology.

[7] For a generalized approach allowing for differents sets of deductive schemas, see [15, 17, 19].

$$
\begin{array}{c|l}
\vdots & \vdots \\
m & \phi \\
\vdots & \vdots \\
\hline
\vdots & \vdots \\
n & \phi \quad \text{R, } m
\end{array}
\qquad\qquad
\begin{array}{c|l}
\vdots & \vdots \\
m & K_i\phi \\
\vdots & \vdots \\
\hline
\vdots & \vdots \\
n & i \;\; \vdots \\
o & \quad K_i\phi \quad \text{KR, } m
\end{array}
$$

Any hypothesis can be reiterated in the same context (R). This is a restricted form of the usual natural deduction rule. As for the other rule (KR), it states that a hypothesis of type $K_i\phi$, and only a hypothesis of this type, can be reiterated in a K-context i (KR).

3.2 K-Operator

Introduction (KI) and elimination (KE) of the K-operator satisfy the constraint (and the conception) that a derivation is associated with a K-context:

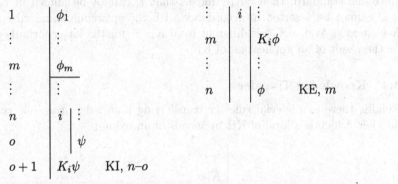

provided ψ is not a formula
prefixed with K_i

KI expresses the idea that the formula ψ satisfies the epistemic standard which defines the K-context i (provided ψ is not prefixed with K_i). The rule prohibits the construction of formulas of type $K_iK_i\psi$, because it is incoherent to apply directly any standard to itself.[8] The rule KE conforms with the principle of factivity of knowledge, as long as truth is understood as assertability in a K-context.

3.3 Negation

There is also a rule for the negation of the K-operator ($\neg$KI), which behaves like the usual negation:

---

[8] It is incoherent in the sense that, for example, the length of the *standard meter* cannot be used to measure the length of the standard meter itself.

$$
\begin{array}{c|c}
1 & \phi_1 \\
\vdots & \vdots \\
m & \phi_m \\
\vdots & \vdots \\
n & i \;\; \psi \\
 & \quad \vdots \\
o & \quad \omega \\
 & \quad \vdots \\
p & \quad \neg\omega \\
p+1 & \neg K_i\psi \quad\quad \neg\mathrm{KI},\, n\text{-}p
\end{array}
$$

$\neg K_i\psi$ does not mean to be *ignorant* with respect to ψ. Ignorance is a property of an agent. Since a K-operator refers to a K-context, which is defined by a unique epistemic standard, then $\neg K_i\psi$ means that ψ cannot be known in K-context i; ψ cannot be asserted in accordance with the epistemic standard specific to K-context i. And, $\neg K_i\psi$ is different from $K_i\neg\psi$, for the latter formula can only be the result of an application of KI.

3.4   Knowledge Transfer

Finally, there is a special rule for transferring knowledge from one context to another, which is a kind of KR by means of an axiom:

$$
\begin{array}{c|c}
\vdots & \vdots \\
m & K_i\phi \\
\vdots & \vdots \\
n & j \;\; \vdots \\
o & \quad K_j\phi \quad\quad \mathrm{KT}_{i-j},\, m
\end{array}
$$

A formula of type $K_i\phi$ can be transferred in a K-context j, where $i \neq j$, by means of a transfer rule $i-j$ such that $KT_{i-j}: K_i\phi \supset K_j\phi$. The KT rule acts as a kind of reiteration rule through epistemic contexts on the basis of a conditional epistemic qualification. Transfer rules, when available, are provided by the epistemological theory, and they determine the configuration of K-contexts.

4   Discussion

In order to stress a few peculiarities of the proposed framework, I will address some epistemological issues. In this section, I (1) highlight the importance of transfer rules, (2) examine the KK-thesis (introspection), and (3) analyze the closure principle (under known entailment).

4.1 Transfer Rules

In the proposed perspective, an epistemological theory is fundamentally specified by a set of transfer rules. For instance, if one compares the following epistemological theories $\Theta_1 - \Theta_3$, two of which are determined by one single different transfer rule τ with respect to the main context K_0 (implicit) and an arbitrary context i, then one gets deductions in Table 1. In the epistemological theory Θ_1, for which no transfer rule is defined ($\tau = \varnothing$), none of the five deductions are valid. Such an epistemological theory is strongly restrictive, since all K-contexts are isolated one from the other. At the opposite end of the spectrum, a theory Θ_4 defined as being equal to $\Theta_2 \cup \Theta_3$ would trivialize the notion of epistemic context, since all K-contexts would be equivalent to each other.[9] This shows clearly the impact of transfer rules on the way information is accessed and exploited throughout epistemic contexts.

Table 1. Comparison of three epistemological theories

Θ_1	Θ_2	Θ_3
$\tau = \varnothing$	$\tau = KT_{i-0}$	$\tau = KT_{0-i}$
$K_i p \nvdash p$	$K_i p \vdash p$	$K_i p \nvdash p$
$p \nvdash K_i p$	$p \nvdash K_i p$	$p \vdash K_i p$
$\nvdash K_i p \supset p$	$\vdash K_i p \supset p$	$\nvdash K_i p \supset p$
$\nvdash p \supset K_i p$	$\nvdash p \supset K_i p$	$\vdash p \supset K_i p$
$\{K_i p, (p \supset q)\} \nvdash K_i q$	$\{K_i p, (p \supset q)\} \vdash K_i q$	$\{K_i p, (p \supset q)\} \nvdash K_i q$

The present framework exhibits some similarities with ML, but there are also differences. One of these differences pertains to transfer rules. According to Giunchiglia [18], a context encapsulates an agent's (subjective) perspective about the world, a kind of *point of view*. The relations that take place between contexts, as point of views, are conceived in a multiagent perspective, and the propagation of knowledge is made possible by means of what Giunchiglia calls *bridge rules*. One such rule is the *multicontextual* version of modus ponens (MMP):

$$\text{MMP:} \quad \frac{\langle \phi \supset \psi, i \rangle \qquad \langle \phi, j \rangle}{\langle \psi, k \rangle}$$

---

[9] The difference between Θ_1 and Θ_4 echoes the distinction between modal systems K and $S5$ with respect to the accessibility relation.

The MMP rule allows an agent k to believe a propositional formula ψ, given the beliefs that $\phi \supset \psi$ and that ϕ of agents i and j respectively. This bridge rule permits a fusion between contexts, i.e. between sets of agents' beliefs. In ML, a bridge rule is an inference schema, and it requires, as such, a logical account. But, in the proposed framework, logic alone is not sufficient to warrant this kind of intercontextual relations. The epistemological notion of transfer rule conveys precisely the idea that there is a change in *epistemic qualification* involved in the process, as opposed to sheer reiteration for instance. So, epistemic qualification rules are properly understood as constituents of an epistemological theory, and they demand an epistemological account. Of course, this is a matter of theoretical choice. But the rationale for the present framework is the focus put on epistemic qualification, i.e. on epistemic normativity. In that view, this framework is more of a norm-based framework than an agent-based framework.

One virtue of MMP is that it warrants the propagation of knowledge among agents considered as epistemic peers (knowledge bases, for instance). But when a group of epistemic agents is rather heterogeneous and the modalities of knowledge acquisition (or K-contexts) in the group are numerous and not equivalent, then variation in the epistemic qualification processes must be allowed.

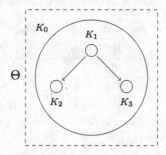

Fig. 1. Example of an epistemological theory

For instance, consider an epistemological theory Θ comprised of four K-contexts, where K_0 is the main logical context (tacit), K_1 is an expert context, and K_2 and K_3 are two sorts of mundane contexts, equipped with a single transfer rule $KT_{1-i} : K_1\phi \supset K_i\phi$, as in Fig. 1. In such an epistemic situation, Θ would permit theses instances of MMP,

$$\frac{\langle \phi \supset \psi, 1 \rangle \qquad \langle \phi, 2 \rangle}{\langle \psi, 2 \rangle} \text{ MMP} \qquad\qquad \frac{\langle \phi \supset \psi, 1 \rangle \qquad \langle \phi, 3 \rangle}{\langle \psi, 3 \rangle} \text{ MMP}$$

but it would not allow neither of the following deductions:

$$\frac{\langle \phi \supset \psi, 1 \rangle \qquad \langle \phi, 2 \rangle}{\langle \psi, 3 \rangle} \qquad\qquad \frac{\langle \phi \supset \psi, 1 \rangle \qquad \langle \phi, 3 \rangle}{\langle \psi, 2 \rangle}$$

In general, if an epistemological theory does not assume a homogeneous process of epistemic qualification (i.e. a unique epistemic standard), then the contingency of MMP is no surprise. So, this is one way to represent the heterogeneity and richness of an epistemology theory. Such a pluralism in the representation of epistemic normativity not only provides an adequate model for epistemic situations involving expert and profane modes of knowledge acquisition, but it also amounts to make room for *testimonial* knowledge in the representation. And, sure enough, the representation of testimonial knowledge is a major challenge for a formal system.

The proposed framework differs from Giunchiglia's ML in that a K-context cannot be assimilated to the set of an agent's beliefs, unless the agent is an idealization of a unique epistemic standard. MMP, as an inference schema, embodies some kind of an idealized relation between epistemic agents; it requires a univocal reading of the knowledge operator. But, from an epistemological point of view, an agent's knowledge base is the result of the application of many epistemic standards, which have different epistemic strength. The preference to use axioms rather than inference rules, that would impact on the structure of the system from a proof-theoretic perspective, becomes manifest in that an inference schema expresses a metaproperty of the whole deduction system, but an axiom is rather an object-language property particular to an epistemological theory.

Ghidini and Serafini [17] have proposed a significant extension of bridge rules that provides more generality.[10] In their system, i.e. distributed first-order logic (DFOL), bridge rules are enriched with cross-domain variables. And one important property of DFOL consists in the understanding of a bridge rule as a distributed relation of logical consequence.[11] But, here again, some differences between transfer rules and bridge rules lie in the fact that knowledge is a modality (iterable) and that transfer rules are not strictly assimilable to logical consequence. A transfer rule defines a relation of epistemic qualification between two epistemic standards, which is expressed as an axiom in terms of material implication, not in terms of logical consequence. Transfer rules are stipulated in the object-language; they are not part of the metalinguistic machinery *stricto sensu*, as opposed to bridge rules. So, one can see a difference between transfer rules and DFOL bridge rules not so much in the results of their application, but rather in the *level* according to which they are imposing their constraints on the deductive system.[12]

---

[10] I am indebted to an anonymous referee for drawing my attention to this paper.

[11] In that regard, DFOL shares some properties with labeled deduction systems (LDS) [14]. Differences between DFOL and LDS are presented in [16].

[12] There might be some way to capture transfer rules by means of bridge rules that I am overlooking, but at this point in time it is not clear to me at all how to encode the former into the latter. A difficulty is particularly apparent in the case of second-order knowledge. For instance, assume a transfer rule such as $KT_{1-2} : K_1\phi \supset K_2\phi$ for which $\phi := K_3(p)$ in K_1. Then, in K_2, one would get $K_3(p)$. How would this translate in terms of a bridge rule?

4.2   Introspection

Now let us put the proposed framework at work and appreciate how it can deal with some epistemological issues. Among the derivable formulas of an epistemological theory that includes three K-contexts, without transfer rules (like Θ_1), one has

$$K_1(p \supset q) \vdash K_1 p \supset K_1 q \qquad\qquad (D)$$

$$\{K_1 p, K_1(p \supset q)\} \vdash K_1 q \qquad\qquad (C)$$

$$K_1 p \vdash K_2 K_1 p \qquad\qquad (I)$$

These formulas express some properties of K-operators with respect to material implication and to iteration. Formula (D) is analogous to axiom K in modal logic, i.e. the K-operator distributes over material implication. In the epistemological literature, some of these formulas are litigious from an epistemological point of view, namely the formulas expressing *closure* (C) and *introspection* (I).

Consider introspection (I) first. Introspection means that knowledge iterates, i.e. if one knows that ϕ then one knows that one knows that ϕ, or formally $K\phi \supset KK\phi$. Usually, introspection is understood as being an analogue of axiom 4 in modal logic, i.e. $\Box \phi \supset \Box\Box \phi$. The main difficulty with such a reading, from a strict epistemological standpoint, lies in the fact that no distinction is made between iterated K-operators. In other words, iterations of K-operators are conceived *univocally*. This interpretation is typical of epistemological theories that rely on a concept of knowledge expounded in representational terms (cognition). But, a univocal interpretation conceals some epistemic discrepancies. In the case of perception, for example, a univocal interpretation of the introspection principle implies a perceptual impossibility, as long as an agent a cannot see herself seeing a book, in a univocal sense i: $See_i^a(book) \supset See_i^a(See_i^a(book))$. On the other hand, there is no a priori difficulty in conceiving that $See_i^a(book) \supset See_j^a(See_i^a(book))$ when $i \neq j$. One can see in a *cognitive* sense that one sees in a *perceptual* sense. From an epistemological standpoint, a univocal reading of the K-operator also jeopardizes the idea that an epistemic agent must be in a position to assess her own epistemic process. But, if an agent cannot discriminate between a situation where she does satisfy an epistemic standard from a situation where she does not, then this agent does not exhibit epistemic agency. The capability of assessing epistemic processes (or satisfaction of standards) is a necessary condition for epistemic agency. When a theory conflates knowledge and cognition, the KK-thesis, just like a univocal reading of the K-operator, faces the very same difficulty as in the perceptual case. In the present view, it is possible to escape this difficulty insofar knowledge is conceived as a *qualified* form of cognition, in that it is the result of the satisfaction of an epistemic standard, and applicability of epistemic standards is assessable.

In this framework, prefixed formulas of the form $K_i K_i \phi$ are prohibited by the KI rule. But formulas of the form $K_i \phi \supset K_j \phi K_i \phi$, when $j \neq i$, are straightforwardly deducible:

$$
\begin{array}{ll}
1 \quad & K_1 p \\
2 \quad & \quad 2 \mid 1 \mid K_1 p \qquad \text{KR, 1} \\
3 \quad & \qquad\qquad p \qquad\quad \text{KE, 2} \\
4 \quad & \quad\; K_1 p \qquad\qquad \text{KI, 2–3} \\
5 \quad & K_2 K_1 p \qquad\qquad \text{KI, 2–4} \\
6 \quad & K_1 p \supset K_2 K_1 p \qquad \supset\text{I, 1–5}
\end{array}
$$

So, *heterogeneous* forms ($j \neq i$) of the KK-principle are vindicated, but *homogeneous* forms ($j = i$) are invalidated. This is in line with the idea that in order to be able to apply an epistemic standard, an epistemic agent needs to be able to evaluate *epistemologically* the result of its application; when one knows something, *one knows that she has satisfied some epistemic standard.* More generally, and this is what the framework expresses, any K-context can be part of a broader K-context.[13]

4.3 Closure

Another bone of contention is the principle of closure under known entailment (C). The property of epistemic closure expresses a form of contextual distributivity over material implication. In addition to that, the closure principle served, and continues to serve, as a basis for numerous skeptical arguments.[14] Here again, part of the problem stems from a lack of explicit specification of the K-operators involved in the principle. As stated in (C), the closure principle requires that the K-operators in the premises and in the conclusion are the same:

$$
\begin{array}{ll}
1 \quad & K_1 p \\
2 \quad & K_1 (p \supset q) \\
3 \quad & \quad 1 \mid K_1 p \qquad\qquad\; \text{KR, 1} \\
4 \quad & \qquad\; p \qquad\qquad\qquad \text{KE, 3} \\
5 \quad & \qquad K_1 (p \supset q) \qquad \text{KR, 2} \\
6 \quad & \qquad p \supset q \qquad\qquad\; \text{KE, 5} \\
7 \quad & \qquad q \qquad\qquad\qquad \supset\text{E, 4, 6} \\
8 \quad & K_1 q \qquad\qquad\qquad\; \text{KI, 3–7}
\end{array}
$$

In such a case, closure holds, as the current epistemological theory shows. Let us call this form of closure, *intracontextual* closure. In the case where several K-operators are involved in the reasoning, then the situation is quite different, and

---

[13] There is a connection in that regard with what McCarthy [21] referred to in terms of *transcending contexts* by means of lifting.

[14] Among many others, see Dretske [13] (zebra argument) and DeRose [12] (argument from ignorance).

this form of closure is an *intercontextual* one. For instance, consider a typical argument against closure formulated by Dretske [13]. An agent might accept that she knows that p, and that she knows that p is incompatible with q, *while denying* that she knows that $\neg q$; an agent might accept that she knows that *the animals in the pen are zebras*, and that she knows that *being a zebra is incompatible with being a cleverly disguised mule*, while denying that she knows that *the animals in the pen are not cleverly disguised mules*. The crux of the problem in this sort of argument is the difference between types of knowledge: there is a difference between knowledge resulting from perceiving the animals in the pen, and knowledge resulting from conceiving the incompatibility between two properties (being a zebra, and being a cleverly disguised mule). In this view, the principle that is challenged by the argument, in this particular instance, is not intracontextual closure, but rather intercontextual closure. Consequently, the problem should be reframed accordingly, and the two K-operators K_1 and K_2 could be interpreted, for illustrative purpose, as referring respectively to perceptual knowledge and to reflective (or some kind of abstract) knowledge. In the present framework, the deduction would be represented this way:

1		$K_1 p$	
2		$K_2(p \supset \neg q)$	
3	1	$K_1 p$	KR, 1
4		p	KE, 3
5		$K_1(p \supset \neg q)$	? (requires KT_{2-1})
6		$p \supset \neg q$	KE, 5
7		$\neg q$	$\supset$E, 4, 6
8		$K_1 \neg q$	KI, 3–7

Without a transfer rule between the different epistemic contexts involved in the reasoning (line 5), there is no way to preserve closure between contexts.[15] So, intercontextual closure is not a valid principle in an epistemological theory that does not contain a transfer rule like KT_{2-1}. But, this fact does in no way alter the validity of intracontextual closure. So, it is possible, in the same epistemological theory (like the one under consideration) to have intracontextual closure without intercontextual closure. It is worth stressing that a total rejection of closure has the devastating consequence of compromising the expansion of knowledge, not only between different K-contexts (inter), but also within the same K-contexts (intra). And, one lesson we can draw for this difficulty is that an adequate analysis of the closure principle, both from a logical point of view and an epistemological point of view, demands an epistemological framework capable of differentiating between K-operators (or epistemic standards).

---

[15] In that perspective, Dretske's argument, which amounts to deny intracontextual closure by means of a failure of intercontextual closure, does not hold and the problematic fragment of the reasoning is made explicit in the framework.

5 Conclusion

The proposed framework is based on the idea that knowledge can be conceived as the satisfaction of an epistemic standard; thus knowledge is a success term. Such a characterization, in terms of a successful application of rules (epistemic norms), can be adequately captured by a proof-theoretic approach, and this is the motivation behind the development of a natural deduction system in which knowledge is expressed by means of K-operators and K-contexts. It provides a logical framework for the investigation of epistemological theories (in the above sense) and their respective properties. Hence, this framework enables a pluralist view on knowledge.

This kind of epistemological pluralism might appear to some as an untenable stand. I agree that this conception of an epistemological theory as being a structure of K-contexts augmented by some relations is quite an abstraction. But, in my view, the chief interest of such an abstraction lies in its expressive power with respect to the (observable) variety of epistemic norms which are characteristic not only of our most robust scientific endeavors, but also of our most ordinary epistemic practices. In a laboratory situation, experimenters articulate several knowledge acquisition means, such as perception, measurements, statistics, logic, and so on. In an ordinary situation, epistemic agents articulate knowledge acquisition means like personal experience, history, reflection, testimony, and so on. It is my main claim that these complex epistemic situations reflect various epistemological theories, and that an epistemic logic capable of expressing variations in epistemic normativity is interestingly informative about knowledge, and how we, as a species, use it to cope with our environment.

References

1. Baader, F., McGuinness, D.L., Nardi, D., Patel-Schneider, P.F. (eds.): The Description Logic Handbook: Theory, Implementation, and Applications. Cambridge University Press, Cambridge (2003)
2. Barwise, J.: The Situation in Logic. CSLI, Stanford (1989)
3. van Benthem, J.: Changing contexts and shifting assertions. In: Aliseda, A., van Glabbeek, R., Westerståhl, D. (eds.) Computing Natural Language, pp. 51–65. CSLI Publications, Stanford (1998)
4. van Benthem, J.: McCarthy variations in a modal key. Artif. Intell. **175**, 428–439 (2011)
5. Bouchard, Y.: Epistemic contexts and indexicality. In: Lihoreau, F., Rebuschi, M. (eds.) Epistemology, Context, and Formalism, Synthese Library, vol. 369, pp. 59–79. Springer International Publishing, Cham (2014)
6. Bouquet, P., Ghidini, C., Giunchiglia, F., Blanzieri, E.: Theories and uses of context in knowledge representation and reasoning. J. Pragmat. **35**, 455–484 (2003)
7. Bouquet, P., Serafini, L.: Two formalizations of context: a comparison. In: Akman, V., Bouquet, P., Thomason, R., Young, R. (eds.) CONTEXT 2001. LNCS (LNAI), vol. 2116, pp. 87–101. Springer, Heidelberg (2001). doi:10.1007/3-540-44607-9_7

8. Brézillon, P.: Context in problem solving: a survey. Knowl. Eng. Rev. **14**, 47–80 (1999)
9. Buvač, S.: Resolving lexical ambiguity using a formal theory of context. In: van Deemter, K., Peters, S. (eds.) Semantic Ambiguity and Underspecification, pp. 101–124. CSLI Publications, Stanford (1996)
10. Buvač, S., Buvač, V., Mason, I.A.: The semantics of propositional contexts. In: Raś, Z.W., Zemankova, M. (eds.) ISMIS 1994. LNCS, vol. 869, pp. 468–477. Springer, Heidelberg (1994). doi:10.1007/3-540-58495-1_47
11. Buvač, S., Buvač, V., Mason, I.A.: Metamathematics of contexts. Fundam. Informaticae **23**, 263–301 (1995)
12. DeRose, K.: Solving the skeptical problem. Philos. Rev. **104**, 1–52 (1995)
13. Dretske, F.I.: Epistemic operators. J. Philos. **67**, 1007–1023 (1970)
14. Gabbay, D.M.: Labelled Deductive Systems, vol. 1. Clarendon Press, Oxford (1996)
15. Ghidini, C., Giunchiglia, F.: Local models semantics, or contextual reasoning=locality+compatibility. Artif. Intell. **127**, 221–259 (2001)
16. Ghidini, C., Serafini, L.: A context-based logic for distributed knowledge representation and reasoning. In: Bouquet, P., Benerecetti, M., Serafini, L., Brézillon, P., Castellani, F. (eds.) CONTEXT 1999. LNCS (LNAI), vol. 1688, pp. 159–172. Springer, Heidelberg (1999). doi:10.1007/3-540-48315-2_13
17. Ghidini, C., Serafini, L.: Distributed first order logic. Computing Research Repository (CoRR) [cs.LO], pp. 1–89 (2015). arXiv:1507.07755
18. Giunchiglia, F.: Contextual reasoning. Epistemologia **16**, 341–364 (1993)
19. Giunchiglia, F., Serafini, L.: Multilanguage hierarchical logics, or: how we can do without modal logics. Artif. Intell. **65**, 29–70 (1994)
20. Guha, R., McCarthy, J.: Varieties of contexts. In: Blackburn, P., Ghidini, C., Turner, R.M., Giunchiglia, F. (eds.) CONTEXT 2003. LNCS (LNAI), vol. 2680, pp. 164–177. Springer, Heidelberg (2003). doi:10.1007/3-540-44958-2_14
21. McCarthy, J.: Notes on formalizing context. In: Bajcsy, R. (ed.) Proceedings of the 13th International Joint Conference on Artificial Intelligence (IJCAI), pp. 555–560. Morgan Kaufmann, Chambéry (1993)
22. McCarthy, J., Buvač, S.: Formalizing context (expanded notes). In: Aliseda, A., van Glabbeek, R., Westerståhl, D. (eds.) Computing Natural Language, pp. 13–50. CSLI Publications, Stanford (1997)
23. Serafini, L., Bouquet, P.: Comparing formal theories of context in AI. Artif. Intell. **155**, 41–67 (2004)
24. Sowa, J.F.: Knowledge Representation. Logical, Philosophical, and Computational Foundations. Brooks/Cole, Pacific Grove (2000)

Contextual Modeling of Group Activity

Patrick Brézillon[✉] [iD]

University Pierre and Marie Curie (UPMC), Paris, France
Patrick.Brezillon@lip6.fr

Abstract. We extend the Contextual-Graphs formalism for modeling interaction in a group activity. Group activity is modeled as the cyclic traversing of a contextual meta-graph representing the group activity in terms of member activities, and of the shared context as a hub for interaction management. We propose a model of group-member interaction at the level of the transitions between turns. The model relies on the representation of members' activities in terms of independent tasks that are structured by simulation parameters in the shared context.

Keywords: Group activity · Interaction model · Task realization · Turn · Contextual graphs · Contextual element · Context-based simulation

1 Introduction

The term "group" is used when the completion of some works requires crossing the organizations frontiers, enabling the creation of groups involving actors from different organizations (i.e. different hierarchies). The notion of activity takes into account contextual aspects of the task realization in addition to its theoretical definition: the activity is the (physical and mental) behavior that the actor exhibits for realizing the task [9]. Complementary to the engineering approach, the cognitive approach provides a computational support for effectively representing, analyzing and simulating activities in real-world applications. However, this supposes the integration of the contextual dimension in the representation of the activity.

Brézillon and Pomerol [5] propose the following operational definition of context: "Context is what constrains the focus without intervening in it explicitly." It results a conceptual framework that supposes a uniform representation of elements of knowledge, reasoning and context that are needed in a task realization [2].

Initially, a contextual graph (CxG) represented the model of a task realization, each path is a practice developed by an actor in a particular context for realizing the task. Formally, contextual graphs are acyclic and series-parallel due to the time-directed representation that ensures algorithm termination. A contextual graph contains four items: actions, contextual elements, activities and Executive Structures of Independent Activities (ESIA). An action is the building block of the model at the given representation granularity. A contextual element is a pair of a contextual node and a recombination node. The former has one input and N outputs (branches) corresponding to N known values of the contextual element leading to N different methods for realizing a subtask. The latter is a [N, 1] relationship that represents the moment at which the instantiation of the contextual element does not matter anymore. An activity—a

© Springer International Publishing AG 2017
P. Brézillon et al. (Eds.): CONTEXT 2017, LNAI 10257, pp. 113–126, 2017.
DOI: 10.1007/978-3-319-57837-8_9

complex action described as a contextual graph by itself—is identified by actors in different task realizations as a work unit. Finally, an ESIA expresses the execution of different independent (sub-) activities in a parallel or sequential way, regardless of their order. In some sense, an ESIA is a kind of complex contextual element.

This paper is organized as follows. Section 2 presents what must be taken into account for extending the Contextual-Graphs formalism from a user's task realization to a group activity. Section 3 introduces the elements for extending the formalism for modeling group activity. Section 4 then discusses the modeling of interaction between an operator and a simulator in an application. Finally we conclude with the possibilities offered by this modeling of group activity.

2 From User Task Realization to Group Activity

2.1 Modeling of Task Realization

Actors use knowledge and experience (their mental representation) to interpret and to realize their tasks [3]. An actor selects a particular method to realize the task according to different contextual elements and their instantiations depending on actor's preferences, the task, the situation at hand and the available resources in the local environment.

An actor develops a practice jointly with the building of a proceduralized context, i.e. a context-specific model represented by an ordered series of instantiated contextual elements [2]. Because the structure of a contextual graph is structured by contextual elements, practices can be organized by the contextual elements in a tree representation [6].

The use of the Contextual-Graphs formalism for modeling a group activity requires some extensions for managing the way in which the different members participate in the group activity (e.g. ordered or concurrent subtasks, negotiation process, etc.). Generally, the viewpoint of the activity processing is chosen for having a homogeneous presentation of the process. The choice of the member's viewpoint on a group activity implies that the contribution of each actor in the group activity is clearly identified as a specific activity, and, second, the modeling of a group activity as a contextual graph must make these members' activities explicit. As a consequence, the context in which the group activity is performed must be enriched with specific contextual elements for modeling group-member interaction during the practice development that is generally followed by simulation.

2.2 Modeling Group Activity

Benitez-Guerrero et al. [1] present effective activity as an instance of an activity model that describes the family of actors that can participate in the activity, how the activity can be carried out, the family of objects that can be manipulated or produced, and which roles actors and objects will play in the activity. The notion of effective activity is similar to our notion of practice and leads to define the realization of a group activity as the development of a group practice.

A group practice implies the building of a shared base of contextual elements. Brézillon et al. [4] present the results of an experiment for modeling verbal exchanges between two participants for building collaboratively an answer to a question. The two participants begin the development of a shared context by gathering a maximum of contextual elements. Each actor finds a way to integrate the contextual elements provided by the other participant in his own mental representation of the question. When participants think that their shared context is sufficient for building the answer, they enter the second phase of the process by organizing, assembling and structuring these shared contextual elements in a proceduralized context that will lead then to build the answer.

The shared context contains in addition specific contextual elements for the management of the group activity (turn, acceptance, etc.). Thus, the shared context is a crucial place for managing member interactions during the group-practice development as well as the management of the tasks in each member's activity.

3 Extension of the CxG Formalism for Group-Activity Modeling

Based on what happens in enterprises, we use the notions of roles and tasks for representing a group activity in terms of members' activities. Interaction between group members corresponds to a movement of the group leadership from one member to another one, and, concretely, from one subtask inside a member activity to another subtask in another member activity. The natural extension of the CxG formalism for group activity then is to represent the group activity as a contextual meta-graph where member activities are represented on the exclusive branches of a contextual element for deciding who is the manager for the turn. This implies that:

- There is a special contextual element that controls which group member is the manager of the current turn;
- The activity of each group member must be modeled as a set of independent tasks structured by another special contextual element corresponding to the management of the independent tasks in the manager activity;
- The traversing of the contextual meta-graph corresponds to the realization of a specific independent task in the manager's activity;
- The development of the group practice then corresponds to a sequence of turns taken in different members' activities, a turn corresponding to the realization of an independent task and the management of special contextual elements controlling, on the one hand, transitions between turns and, on the other hand, the task status of the group practice development;
- The shared context is composed of contextual elements specific to (i) each member activity, (ii) information that is transferred between member activities, and (iii) interaction management between members during the group-activity development.

The special contextual elements will be called hereafter "simulation parameters" (SPs). Let us first introduce a running example.

3.1   A Context-Based Model of Group Activity

Garcia and Brézillon [6] use the example of a paper submission to a journal for illustrating their purposes on their CxG-based simulator. The paper-submission processing (i.e. the group activity) requires interaction among actors, which have with different roles: author, editor, reviewers and publisher. Figure 1 shows the contextual meta-graph for managing all members' activities at the same level, and thus facilitating their coordination based on the role of manager of the group activity holds by a group member during the traversing of the contextual meta-graph.

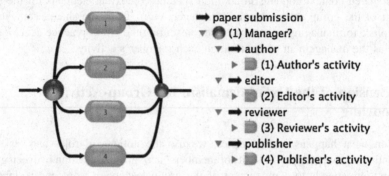

Fig. 1. The contextual meta-graph of the submission example [6]

Each branch corresponds to the activity linked to a role (i.e. the tasks associated with the role). The active role during a traversing of the contextual meta-graph is selected by the instantiation of the contextual element "Manager" to one of the values "author", "editor", "reviewer" or "publisher".

The cyclic traversing of the contextual meta-graph represents the group-practice development across member's activities through the role of manager successively played by group members. This allows a given member to play different roles, such as the editor being a third reviewer. By entering in a member activity, then an independent task is selected and realized in that member activity. Thus, the member is the temporary manager (a simulation parameter) of the group-practice development, and the specific independent task to realize is managed by another simulation parameter for controlling the status of the group-practice development.

The challenge here is to monitor the group-practice development when different members held successively the role of manager during the cyclic traversing of the contextual meta-graph. This supposes the organization of members' activities in terms of specific subtasks, each subtask corresponding to the traversing of the contextual meta-graph. Thus, there are two simulation parameters that allow, on the one hand, the management of role—the "manager"—and, on the other hand, of the group activity—the "task status", the latter simulation parameter orients the group-practice development towards the specific task inside the manager's activity.

3.2   Simulation Parameters

The simulation parameters discussed in previous section have a general interest in collaborative work. In the following we call them "MANAGER" and "TASK_ STATUS". Such simulation parameters have a different nature of those of the contextual elements intervening in the task realization. They impose a hierarchical organization on each member activity in terms of independent task. This organization is dynamical because "MANAGER" and "TASK_STATUS" for the next turn are instantiated just before exiting the independent task at hand. For example, MANAGER may be "editor" or "reviewer" in the submission problem, and "Head of the Department" and "Secretary" in another problem. This shows that simulation parameters and subtasks are intertwined.

Indeed, four simulation parameters manage a group-practice development, namely the MANAGER, the RECIPIENT, the SENDER, and TASK_STATUS. RECIPIENT is the member that will become manager at the next turn. MANAGER is the group member that is concerned by the traversing of the contextual meta-graph (this is implemented by an action "MANAGER = RECIPIENT" at the beginning of the contextual meta-graph, which represents the group activity. SENDER is the previous manager who just solicits the MANAGER for executing the turn at hand (this is implemented by an action "SENDER = MANAGER" at the end of the contextual meta-graph for the next turn). TASK_STATUS specifies the independent task in the next manager's activity to consider. At the end of the independent-task realization, the instantiations of RECIPIENT and TASK_STATUS are modified according to the result of the independent task realized. Thus the interaction pattern is managed at the end of turns through the simulation parameter RECIPIENT. This shows that interaction sequence is related to the notions of roles and tasks in a strategy of "moment-to-moment interactions" [10], which is a simple mechanism to model group-activity realization but its simplicity provides, thanks to the Contextual-Graphs formalism, insights that inform on more complex interactions.

For example, the editor (the RECIPIENT that becomes MANAGER) receives a submission (TASK_STATUS = "Submitted") from an author (SENDER). At the end of the independent task, the editor's decision is made (say, accept the submission for the journal) and the submission will be sent to a reviewer (RECIPIENT) with TASK_STATUS modified for "to be reviewed" and SENDER instantiated to "editor" for the next turn.

The notions of simulation parameter, independent task and turn are domain-independent but their values have a semantic depending on the domain and thus are domain-dependent.

3.3   The Model of a Turn

Now it is possible to give a definition of a turn. A turn corresponds to the traversing of the contextual meta-graph, entering the manager's activity, realizing an independent task, managing key contextual elements for the next turn, and exiting the contextual meta-graph for going back in the shared context.

Figure 2 represents the model of a turn where the independent task is represented by a proceduralized context and a sequence of actions, and the shared context is composed (among others) of the simulation parameters RECIPIENT, SENDER and TASK_STATUS and contextual elements transferring information between two successive turns. The simulation parameters play the role of activation conditions and post-conditions of the turn. The turn model is the building block of the modeling of a member's activity in terms of independent tasks and, as a consequence, of the group activity. The turn model is domain-independent but the internal description of the independent task at a finer granularity is domain-dependent (like a kind of instantiation of the turn model in a domain).

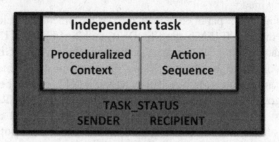

Fig. 2. Model of a turn

The turn processing is defined by: (1) select the member to be manager; (2) select the independent task in the manager's activity to realize; (3) compute the proceduralized context and make the decision (i.e. the sequence of actions to execute); and (4) manage the instantiations of the simulation parameters RECIPIENT (i.e. the next MANAGER) and TASK_STATUS (the next independent task in the MANAGER activity). It is the basic principle of the CxG-based simulation that is discussed in another paper [7]. However, for modeling an activity, the turn mechanism requires to:

- Identify turns, i.e. decompose each member's activity in independent tasks that encapsulate the operational knowledge, the reasoning and the actions that the manager has to perform for addressing the sender's request and the transmission of the relevant results to the next group member (i.e. the interaction management).
- Organize the turns during a group-activity development with a mechanism ensuring the flexibility of the interaction management among group members.

Once the representation of member activities in terms of turns made, the next step is to represent the assembling of the turns taken in different member activities in a sequence during the group-practice development in a given context.

3.4   A Model of Turn Mechanism for Interaction Simulation

The turn mechanism plays a role of synchronizer (coordinator) of the group activity. A group-practice development corresponds to a sequence of turns taken in different roles (we do not discuss here about the possibility of parallel turns such as the review process that concerns the same role holds by two or more actors in the submission example). The group activity is developed jointly with the incremental building of a turn sequence. Interaction is described as a sequence of transitions from one turn in the activity of one member to a turn in the activity of another member. The turn sequence and the on-going interaction process are progressively builds along the cyclic traversing of the contextual meta-graph in different shared contexts.

At a lower level, this corresponds to the assembling of independent tasks coming from different members' activities. The dynamical aspect of the turn assembling come from the fact that an independent task may lead to different conclusions and, thus, a turn may have different recipients for the next turn according to the specific working context associated with the manager activity. Thus, a group practice is not a linear extrapolation of an actor's practice where practices have a fixed structure given by contextual elements.

The turn mechanism can be implemented by a system of production rules. For example, the following rule will move the focus on the next actor:

IF   RECIPIENT is <NIL>,
THEN   stop the simulation
ELSE   MANAGER = RECIPIENT,
            go into MANAGER's activity.

The rule corresponds to the first simulation parameter ("Manager?") in Fig. 1.

Figure 3 illustrates the conceptual representation of the turn management for the paper-submission example. (This part of the work will be developed in the paper on CxG-based simulation [7].)

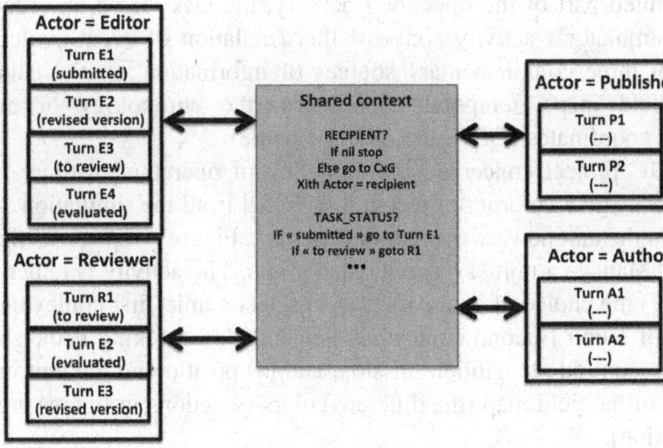

Fig. 3. A conceptual representation in term of turns of the submission example

The implementation of the turn mechanism is a simple extension of the CxG formalism that, indeed, can be applied to a task realized by a unique actor. The explicit consideration of the shared context with the contextual meta-graph opens the door to more options than before like:

- To stop the simulation (with an action "RECIPIENT = <nil>" at the end of a turn),
- To introduce loops for managing a negotiation between two actors, and for realizing several times a sub task,
- The possibility for an actor to change his goal when an unexpected event occurs (e.g. the actor select an object and discovers that finally the object is not adapted to his objective),
- To allow an actor (or a group) to backtrack in his reasoning, and
- To allocate several actors to a same role (e.g. reviewers in the paper submission example).

4 Modeling Interaction

The mechanism for going from one turn to the next one is the inference engine in a CxG-based simulation of the movement of the focus during group-member interaction. The interaction modeling is introduced in the framework of a real-world application.

4.1 Brief Presentation of the TACTIC Project

In the TACTIC project [8], the group activity is the monitoring of a (small part of) a battlefield through simulation, and the group leading this activity is composed of two actors, namely the operator and the simulator, which interact through an interface. The model of the operator's activity for the simulation task is a contextual graph (we use here only a limited part of the operator's activity, the task "Give an order of recognition"). The simulator's activity concerns the simulation of event evolution on the battlefield from three complementary sources of information: spatial coordinates of objects (the field map), temporal coordinates (the chronology of events) and socio-technical coordinates (ODB, the order of battle).

The TACTIC project concerned the modeling of operators' activity in the realization of the task "give an order of recognition", that is all the simulation activity was considered from the unique viewpoint of the operator. Figure 4 represents the modeling of the activity "Manage a unit" as a contextual graph. The activity is rather sequential, beginning by (1) the choice of an area where to select a unit (first contextual element), (2) the choice of a unit (second contextual element), (3) checking if the selected unit may realize the required recognition mission, and (4) positioning the unit in the center of the window of the field map (the different colors of actions in figures are explained in the next section).

This modeling is made according to the operator's viewpoint. As a consequence, a part of the operator's reasoning (in yellow on Fig. 4) expresses a compilation of elementary actions realized by the operator and the simulator through the interface. For example, "Show mission orders" implies to (a) select the unit, (b) ask for opening the order window, and (c) show the list of the mission orders. The lessons learned here

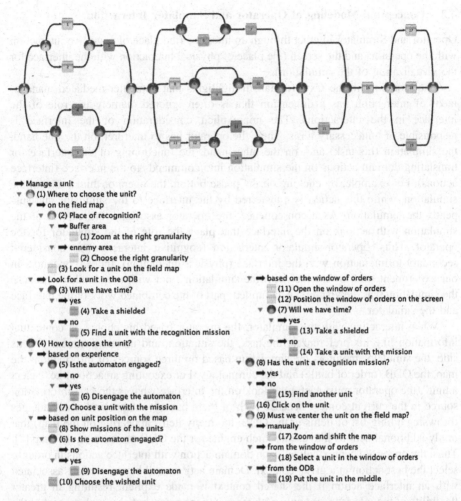

Manage a unit
▾ ◐ (1) Where to choose the unit?
  ▾ ➡ on the field map
    ▾ ◐ (2) Place of recognition?
      ▾ ➡ Buffer area
          ▨ (1) Zoom at the right granularity
      ▾ ➡ ennemy area
          ▨ (2) Choose the right granularity
          ▨ (3) Look for a unit on the field map
  ▾ ➡ Look for a unit in the ODB
    ▾ ◐ (3) Will we have time?
      ▾ ➡ yes
          ▨ (4) Take a shielded
      ▾ ➡ no
          ▨ (5) Find a unit with the recognition mission
▾ ◐ (4) How to choose the unit?
  ▾ ➡ based on experience
    ▾ ◐ (5) Isthe automaton engaged?
        ➡ no
      ▾ ➡ yes
          ▨ (6) Disengage the automaton
          ▨ (7) Choose a unit with the mission
  ▾ ➡ based on unit position on the map
      ▨ (8) Show missions of the units
    ▾ ◐ (6) Is the automaton engaged?
        ➡ no
      ▾ ➡ yes
          ▨ (9) Disengage the automaton
          ▨ (10) Choose the wished unit

▾ ➡ based on the window of orders
    ▨ (11) Open the window of orders
    ▨ (12) Position the window of orders on the screen
  ▾ ◐ (7) Will we have time?
    ▾ ➡ yes
        ▨ (13) Take a shielded
    ▾ ➡ no
        ▨ (14) Take a unit with the mission
  ▾ ◐ (8) Has the unit a recognition mission?
      ➡ yes
    ▾ ➡ no
        ▨ (15) Find another unit
        ▨ (16) Click on the unit
  ▾ ◐ (9) Must we center the unit on the field map?
    ▾ ➡ manually
        ▨ (17) Zoom and shift the map
    ▾ ➡ from the window of orders
        ▨ (18) Select a unit in the window of orders
    ▾ ➡ from the ODB
        ▨ (19) Put the unit in the middle

Fig. 4. The contextual graph of the activity «Manage a unit» from the operator's viewpoint (Color figure online)

point out that some actions depend on the simulator (e.g. show mission orders of the unit) but others concern the interaction of the operator and the simulator with the interface (e.g. open the mission-order window).

Another lesson is that the simulator had to be considered as a group member in this activity. Items in yellow on Fig. 4 are places where the role of the simulator has been interpreted according to the operator's viewpoint, like "Where to choose the unit?" (The first contextual element on Fig. 4) and letting in green actions that are specific of the operator, like "Find a unit with the recognition mission" (lower actions on the left on Fig. 4). This mixing of roles in a task realization leads to a representation that is difficult to interpret.

4.2   Conceptual Modeling of Operator and Simulator Interaction

Operator and Simulator interact through an interface (the place of cognitive interaction with the operator) and the screen (the place of physical interaction with the interface for the visualization of the simulation).

The modeling in the CxG formalism highlights that computer-mediated management of interaction has a dimension that is often ignored, namely the role of the interface in the interactions. The non-explicit consideration of the interface is responsible of unnecessary turns. Thus, the operator has to interpret, on the one hand, the simulation (his task) and, on the other hand, the functioning of the interface for translating domain actions on the simulation into commands to the interface (interface actions). For example, by clicking on the pause button, the operator thinks to stop the simulation, while this action is transferred by the interface to the simulator that suspends the simulation. As a consequence, the operator associates the control of the simulation with actions on the interface that plays the role of the simulator for the operator. Thus, operator-simulator interaction (cognitive interaction) is considered secondary to interaction with the interface (physical interaction). Indeed, operators in our experiment said to "interact with the simulation", not with the simulator because the simulation was the visible (i.e. compiled) part of the combined work of the interface and the simulator.

When interacting with the simulator, the operator based his choice on contextual information like his preferences, the task, the situation, and the environment. On its side, the simulator monitors the simulation based on three sources of information: the map, the ODB (order of battle) and the chronology. For executing an action like "Select a unit", the operator must each time look on the interface what is the best information source in the current context because each of them has advantages and disadvantages (browsing a long list of items in the ODB, too many items appearing on the map) that imply additional actions like use a search engine for the ODB or zoom on the map [8]. Thus, the operator "contextualize" each domain action with interface actions in order to select the best action in a given context. Domain actions will be more easily associated with an interface action if the shared context is made explicit, resulting in greater flexibility of the interface, not only with respect to the actor, but also with respect of the task realization.

Figure 5 shows a conceptual view of the previous discussion in order to simplify operator's activity during interaction with a simulator. A first observation concerns the need to distinguish the interface interaction and operator-simulator interaction. This supposes the separation of "domain_actions" and "interface_actions" [3]. The second observation concerns the cognitive interaction, i.e. to make compatible the mental map of the operator with the "mental map" of the simulator (i.e. the three sources of information). Clarifying the fact that a simulation results of the interaction of the operator with a simulator gives the interface the role of a flexible communication medium included in the shared context of the simulation through which the operator (with domain_actions in his reasoning) and the simulator (with domain_actions in its model of the battlefield) communicate with a simple translation in interface_actions.

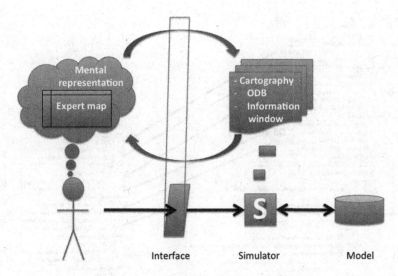

Fig. 5. A model of user-simulator interaction

4.3 Implementation of the Interaction Model

The contextual meta-graph of this particular group activity contains two branches only, one for the operator and the other for the simulator (but a more precise model would have the interface as a third group member). Figure 6 shows the result of a partial re-writing of the initial operator's activity described in Fig. 4 by separating the independent tasks specific of the operator from those specific of the simulator (i.e. the two columns), often by "decompiling" operator's actions in Fig. 4. The rectangles with a label Oi or Sj in Fig. 6 represent the independent tasks and key contextual elements management respectively of the operator and of the simulator. Arrows symbolize the transitions between turns. Rectangles represent the part of the turn corresponding to the independent tasks like in Fig. 2 and arrows correspond to the conceptual representation of interaction mechanism on Fig. 3.

Most of the independent tasks in Fig. 6 are not detailed (i.e. the branches of contextual elements are not visible) to facilitate a focus on the study of the turn mechanism symbolized by arrows. Items concerning the domain keep their initial colors (i.e. green square boxes for actions and blue circles for contextual elements). Simulation parameters for the shared-context management appear in the figure as yellow items. Actions in pink (both in operator and simulator activities) are interface actions (e.g. the action 19 "Click on the chosen unit" is an operator's action on the interface).

Such an interaction model presents several interesting features. First, the use of the simulation parameters introduces, in a natural way, the notion of loop (e.g. independent task O4), thanks to the association of the contextual graph and the shared context. Secondly, a turn starts in the shared context by checking the instantiation of MAN-AGER, and then of TASK_STATUS that directs the focus on an independent task in MANAGER's activity. For instance, the first turn in the operator's activity corresponds

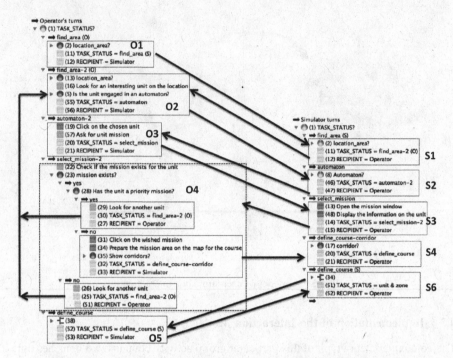

Fig. 6. Partial model of the operator and simulator interaction (Color figure online)

to Value (TASK_STATUS) = "find_area (O)" that moves the focus on the independent task O1 and yellow actions at the end of the rectangles on Fig. 6 modify the instantiation of the simulation parameters TASK_STATUS and RECIPIENT for the next turn. Thirdly, the turn with the independent task O4 is particular in the sense that there are three possible outputs, two towards another operator's turn (arrows on the left) and one towards the turn S4 in the simulator's activity. The two arrows on the left correspond to a loop in the operator's activity for changing of unit. Fourthly, in addition to the simulation parameters discussed previously for managing the turn mechanism, there are other yellow contextual elements that are also instantiated in one member's activity and use in another one and thus are shared by the group members. For example, the contextual elements "local area" and "automaton" in Fig. 6 are instantiated by the operator and guide the choice of the next independent task in the simulator's activity (contextual elements 2 and 8). However, such contextual elements are domain-dependent and only ensure an information transfer between members.

In addition to what is presented in Fig. 6, the explicit association of the shared context with the contextual meta-graph solves the main weaknesses of the contextual graph used alone, namely: (1) the turn O4 allows the operator to change his reasoning when encountered an unexpected event (e.g. the unit do not have the required mission) and thus compensates the acyclic nature of contextual graphs; and (2) the simulation parameter "RECIPIENT" = <nil> allows to "stop" the turn mechanism and to exit the group activity (and stops the CxG-based simulation).

The lessons learned from the TACTIC project are threefold. The first lesson concerns, at the physical interaction level, the differentiation of the actions of the operator and those of the simulator for the control of the simulation, and finally the identification of the actions that are related to the interface. The second lesson is to make compatible, at the level of the cognitive interaction, the operator's mental representation and the three sources of information of the simulator, say the "simulator's mental representation". The third lesson is the interest to consider the interface as a real group member in a computer-mediated group activity (but not modeled in this study) with the operator and the simulator.

5   Conclusion

The paper proposes an approach for a contextual modeling of group activity at two levels. At a conceptual level, group activity is modeled as a sequence of interactions between the group members. In our model, a turn is the building block of the group-activity representation, and the shared context is the place where are managed interactions between group members. At the implementation level, a group activity is represented as a contextual meta-graph composed of members' activities that are built as independent tasks. The contextual meta-graph is structured by simulation parameters that manage member interactions through the turn mechanism in the shared context. Thus, a group activity is simultaneously built and developed by combining task realization and interaction management.

The set of changes in our initial conceptual framework ensures a logical shift of our paradigm of Contextual Graphs from the representation of a task realization by an actor to a group activity. Indeed, a group activity is expressed as the cyclic traversing of the contextual meta-graph in different contexts, while a task realization corresponds to a unique traversing of the contextual graph.

We discussed all these points in reference to different real-world applications, namely, (1) the paper submission modeling, which proposes a modeling of a group activity as a contextual meta-graph; (2) the building of the answer to a question, which points out the need to build a shared context from contextual elements specific to each actor, contextual elements ensuring exchanges between members' activities during interaction, and contextual elements for managing interaction (simulation parameters) as a prerequisite to a group activity; (3) the battlefield simulation, which introduces in the group-activity modeling the importance to separate cognitive interaction (mental representations and thus context) and physical interaction (at the interface level) in order to model interactions in a group activity. Interaction is modeled in relation to the mental maps of the group members. The interface must be considered as a full member in the group activity.

The notions of turn mechanism, independent task, key contextual elements open the door to a new type of simulation of interaction in a group activity such as the CxG-based simulation that is the topic of a companion paper [7]. A tool for exploiting this new version of the CxG formalism, the CxG Simulator is under study.

References

1. Benitez-Guerrero, E., Mezura-Godoy, C., Montané-Jimenez, L.G.: Context-aware mobile collaborative systems: conceptual modeling and case study. Sensors **12**, 13491–13507 (2012)
2. Brézillon, P.: Task-realization models in contextual graphs. In: Dey, A., Kokinov, B., Leake, D., Turner, R. (eds.) CONTEXT 2005. LNCS (LNAI), vol. 3554, pp. 55–68. Springer, Heidelberg (2005). doi:10.1007/11508373_5
3. Brézillon, P.: Modeling expert knowledge and reasoning in context. In: Christiansen, H., Stojanovic, I., Papadopoulos, G.A. (eds.) CONTEXT 2015. LNCS (LNAI), vol. 9405, pp. 18–31. Springer, Cham (2015). doi:10.1007/978-3-319-25591-0_2
4. Brézillon, P., Drai-Zerbib, V., Baccino, T., Therouanne, T.: Modeling collaborative construction of an answer by contextual graphs. In: Bouchon-Meunier, B., Yager, R.R. (eds.) Proceedings of IPMU-2006, pp. 11–26. Editions EDK, Paris (2006)
5. Brézillon, P., Pomerol, J.-Ch.: Contextual knowledge sharing and cooperation in intelligent assistant systems. Le Trav. Hum. **62**(3), 223–246 (1999)
6. García, K., Brézillon, P.: A contextual model of turns for group work. In: Christiansen, H., Stojanovic, I., Papadopoulos, G.A. (eds.) CONTEXT 2015. LNCS (LNAI), vol. 9405, pp. 243–256. Springer, Cham (2015). doi:10.1007/978-3-319-25591-0_18
7. Garcia, K., Brézillon, P.: Contextual graphs for modeling group interaction. In: Brézillon, P., Turner, R., Penco, C. (eds.) CONTEXT-2017. LNAI, vol. 10257, pp. 151–164. Springer, Cham (2017)
8. Kabil, A., Brézillon, P., Kubicki, S.: Contextual interfaces for operator-simulator interaction. In: Christiansen, H., Stojanovic, I., Papadopoulos, G.A. (eds.) CONTEXT 2015. LNCS (LNAI), vol. 9405, pp. 483–488. Springer, Cham (2015). doi:10.1007/978-3-319-25591-0_36
9. Sarrazin, P., Biddle, S., Famose, J.-P., Curry, F., Fox, K., Durand, M.: Goal orientations and conceptions of the nature of sport ability in children: a social cognitive approach. Br. J. Soc. Psychol. **35**(1996), 399–414 (1996)
10. Hackmans, J.R., Morris, C.G.: Group tasks, group interaction process, and group performance effectiveness: a review and proposed integration. Adv. Exp. Soc. Psychol. **8** (45), 1–55 (1982)

Accountability Breeds Response-Ability: Contextual Debiasing and Accountability in Argumentation

Vasco Correia[✉]

ArgLab, Nova Institute of Philosophy (IFILNOVA), FCSH,
Universidade Nova de Lisboa, Lisbon, Portugal
vasco.correia75@gmail.com

Abstract. While there is growing consensus over the need to counteract biases in contexts of argumentation and decision-making, researchers disagree over which debiasing techniques are likely to be most effective. I attempt to show that *contextual debiasing* is more effective than *cognitive debiasing* in preventing biases, although I challenge the claim that critical thinking is utterly ineffective. In addition, a distinction is introduced between two types of contextual debiasing: *situational correction*, and *dispositional correction*. Drawing on empirical work on accountability, I argue that the later type of correction is more likely to prove effective against biases in everyday contexts. Holding arguers accountable is a contextual constraint that has the virtue of also enhancing cognitive skills and virtues.

Keywords: Accountability · Biases · Critical thinking · Debiasing · Rationality

1 Introduction

Research on cognitive and motivational biases has attracted bourgeoning interest over recent decades, not least since cognitive illusions purportedly bring about maladaptive effects, such as risk mismanagement, group polarization, discrimination, procrastination, overconfidence, social conflict, and so forth [2, 17, 24, 30]. In parallel to this research, some authors have focused their work on the correlative issue of *debiasing*, i.e. the problem of how to suppress, or at least reduce people's biases and their unwanted effects [4, 8, 10, 18, 21].

Although most authors agree that biases should be counteracted, there is controversy as to what type of debiasing strategies are the most likely to prove effective. Traditionally, the hypothesis that critical thinking and other forms of *cognitive debiasing* can effectively mitigate cognitive illusions has appealed to many philosophers and argumentation theorists [5, 7, 9, 16, 23, 29, 35]. Nevertheless, a growing number of authors now question the effectiveness of critical thinking against biases, and even the assumption that people can learn how to debias themselves [18, 24, 26, 38]. Some researchers cautiously warn that critical thinking "is not as effective as one might hope" [18, p. 343], or that it can only "claim modest success" [38, p. 8], while others go as far

© Springer International Publishing AG 2017
P. Brézillon et al. (Eds.): CONTEXT 2017, LNAI 10257, pp. 127–136, 2017.
DOI: 10.1007/978-3-319-57837-8_10

as to suggest that critical thinking "does not seem to yield very good results" [24, p. 65], or even that it "has proven to be absolutely worthless" [3, p. 326].

In this paper, I argue that *contextual debiasing* methods, and particularly accountability, more effectively enhance people's ability to overcome biases. By contextual debiasing, I mean to refer to strategies that are designed to mitigate biases by using environmental and social constraints, rather than critical thinking and other forms of cognitive change. I begin by showing that the traditional approach to debiasing (critical thinking) is insufficient to enhance people's ability to counteract their own biases, and that it needs to be supplemented by strategies of contextual debiasing (Sect. 2). In Sect. 3, I distinguish between two types of contextual debiasing—(a) situational correction, and (b) dispositional correction, and suggest that the latter is overall more fruitful than the former. Although strategies of *situational correction*, such as selective exposure, prove very effective within restricted contexts, I show that such devices have intrinsic limitations and that strategies of *dispositional correction*, such as accountability, are more likely to promote rational thinking in real-life contexts. Finally, in Sect. 4, I draw on empirical research to substantiate the claim that accountability is probably the most effective tool to counteract biases in everyday debates, particularly with regard to argumentation skills. As Koch and Wüstemann [20, p. 128] point out in their recent review of research on accountability, "[b]eing accountable to someone else is predicted to influence judgment and decision-making because people seek the social approval of others and will unconsciously apply strategies to ensure this approval". Although accountability also has its own limitations, it appears to combine both the benefits of contextual debiasing (environmental constraint) and the advantage of indirectly fostering critical thinking skills and virtues.

2 The Shortcomings of Cognitive Debiasing

Cognitive debiasing may be described as a strategy (or set of strategies) designed to reduce or suppress biases by reforming people's way of thinking. While some authors seem to reduce cognitive debiasing to critical thinking, it is worth noting that it may also include other methods, such as training in logic and argumentation, training in statistics, raising awareness of biases, "considering the opposite", and the use of heuristics as cognitive repair. The proponents of cognitive debiasing rely on three main arguments to justify the claim that lone individuals can correct their own biases.

First, it is argued that the very awareness of the existence of biases renders individuals more vigilant against their own propensity to be biased, thereby facilitating the detection and correction of systematic errors of judgment [22, 23, 35]. Mele [23, p. 99] gives an example of this: "Consider the biasing effect of the *vividness* of information ... People aware of that effect may resolve to be vigilant against it in important matters, and they may occasionally issue relevant, salutary reminders to themselves at critical junctures". The point to be made here is that people who recognize their own cognitive illusions are presumably less prone to perpetuate them.

Second, there is evidence that at least some strategies of cognitive debiasing seem to work effectively. The most remarkable example of this is the "consider the opposite" strategy, in which subjects are urged to consider a range of hypotheses at odds with their own standpoint. This strategy has been proven effective in reducing the over-confidence effect, the confirmation bias, the hindsight bias, and anchoring effects [12, 13, 39]. In addition, empirical research shows that the study of logic, statistics, and more generally some degree of training in abstract thinking can also contribute to reduce a certain number of cognitive illusions [15, 21, 37].

And third, it is argued that cognitive debiasing methods can be incorporated into people's intuitive (or "automatic") thinking processes through the teaching of epistemic and argumentative virtues, i.e. good habits of thinking [1, 7, 14, 40]. The hope here is that by reinforcing the so-called "virtues of the mind" individuals will be able to reason and decide rationally almost effortlessly, without a permanent effort to debias them-selves. As Hogarth [14, p. 24] explains, "[o]ver time, and with practice, these new habits will become more automatic and less costly to implement. In other words, they should migrate from the deliberate to the tacit system". In the best-case scenario, the virtues of one's "analytical thinking" (or System 2) would be progressively incorpo-rated into one's "intuitive thinking" (or System 1) and lead more reliably to rational judgments and decisions.

The critics of this model challenge each of the former arguments. First, the hypothesis that simply teaching people about biases will significantly enhance their ability to debias themselves hinges on the assumption that people are generally moti-vated to correct their own biases. However, as Lilienfeld et al. [22, p. 394] point out, "many individuals may be unreceptive to debiasing efforts because they do not perceive these efforts as relevant to their personal welfare". And even when arguers are motivated to counteract their irrational tendencies, it is worth noting that the mere awareness of biases as a phenomenon does not necessarily make them more aware of their own specific biases. This problem is partly explained by what Pronin et al. [27] call the "bias blind spot", which is the tendency to believe that other people are more biased than we are. Ironically, most people seem to be biased even with respect to how biased they are, which presumably affects their ability to detect and correct their own biases.

Second, the evidence on the effectiveness of cognitive debiasing is in fact mixed. While some debiasing strategies appear to reduce certain biases, others seem to have either no effect or the effect of amplifying the subjects' biases [3, 8, 11, 12, 28]. Furthermore, the fact that some strategies seem to work in the laboratory does not mean that they can be easily applied in real-life contexts. Regarding the "consider the opposite" strategy, for example, Kenyon and Beaulac [18, p. 347] observe that "there is little reason to expect it will be employed with regularity by individual agents in normal contexts". What is worse, several studies indicate that biases can be amplified by certain debiasing attempts. For example, Sanna et al. [28] found that the hindsight bias is attenuated when the subjects have to come up with a few alternative hypotheses, but increased when they try to come up with many alternative hypotheses. Likewise, when subjects are instructed to avoid stereotypes about a given group, such instructions appear to remind them of those stereotypes and paradoxically increase their implicit biases [12]. Cognitive debiasing can therefore backfire and increase people's biases, either because the wrong strategy is applied or because the appropriate strategy is wrongly applied.

And finally, there is no evidence that cognitive debiasing can be accomplished through the incorporation of epistemic or argumentative virtues. This is not to say that cultivating such virtues does nothing to enhance one's ability to think rationally, but simply that it is difficult to measure their benefits in the laboratory. After all, most empirical studies are one-shot interventions that fail to examine the effects of repeated and systematic debiasing training over long periods of time [22, 38]. Lilienfeld et al. [22, p. 394] observe, in particular, that "repeated training may be needed to shift the habit of considering alternative viewpoints from a controlled to an automatic processing mode". Therefore, it seems plausible that the long-lasting acquisition of at least some cognitive skills and epistemic virtues may pass unnoticed in these evaluations.

Based on this diagnosis, the proponents of *contextual debiasing* contend that critical thinking programs should be replaced, or at least supplemented by debiasing strategies that rely instead on extra-psychic devices, environmental constraints and social structures. This model is partly inspired by Thaler and Sunstein's [36] notion of "choice architecture", which seeks to promote rationality, not by reforming people's way of reasoning, but by imposing constraints on the contexts in which people reason. As Larrick [21, p. 318] also points out, "[d]ebates about rationality have focused on purely cognitive strategies, obscuring the possibility that the ultimate standard of rationality might be the decision to make use of superior tools". Contextual debiasing thus draw on the notion that critical thinking can be developed beyond the individual's natural capacities via the use of external devices (or "tools") such as group interaction, decision aids, incentives, formal decision analysis, statistic models, accountability, and so forth.

Having said that, contextual debiasing need not exclude cognitive debiasing. Contrary to other advocates of contextual debiasing, and particularly Kenyon and Beaulac [18], I maintain that cognitive debiasing can also significantly enhance rational thinking (albeit less effectively), and that there must be a complementarity between cognitive and contextual debiasing strategies. In the next section, I show that there are in fact two types of contextual debiasing and argue that accountability has better chances of counteracting biases in everyday contexts than other extra-psychic strategies.

3   Two Types of Contextual Debiasing

The interest of contextual debiasing strategies is that they allow us to overcome the main shortcomings of critical thinking, namely (a) unawareness of biases, (b) lack of motivation to debias, and (c) inadequate correction of biases. Whereas cognitive debiasing needs to rely on optimistic assumptions regarding people's ability to counteract their own biases, contextual debiasing takes into account people's cognitive and motivational limitations and relies instead on environmental constraints to enforce rational standards.

There are fundamentally two types of contextual debiasing strategies. The first operates by suppressing or reducing a given bias, i.e. by counteracting the subject's cognitive illusion (dispositional correction). The second, by contrast, operates by suppressing or reducing merely *the effects* of a given bias, leaving intact the bias itself (situational correction). According to Kenyon and Beaulac [18], the latter type of contextual debiasing (Level 4 in their taxonomy) is the most effective tool to prevent biased outcomes. To illustrate this, the authors consider an example of "selective exposure" (or *blinding*), which typically involves omitting information susceptible to trigger a potential bias:

A hiring committee member has an uncorrected bias of judgment against women in the profession; but anonymized applications hide candidates' gender information, and the committee member ultimately (unknowingly) votes to hire a superior woman candidate [18, pp. 351–352].

The advantage of this type of device is that it minimizes the impact of biases on the task at hand, without requiring a correction of the subject's judgment. However misogynous (or racist, etc.) the committee member might be, his or her prejudices will not have an impact on the evaluation of the candidates, since the latter remain anonymous. The blind-review system is another good example of selective exposure: by anonymizing works that are submitted, editors prevent the reviewer's potential biases from affecting his or her evaluations. Thus, for example, when the journal *Behavioural Ecology* decided to adopt a peer review process, they found that it led to a 33 per cent increase of representation of female authors [6]. Granted, reviewers do not become less biased in virtue of this debiasing method, but at least their implicit biases do not have an impact on their assessments.

Although this type of strategy is remarkably effective in certain cases, my suggestion is that it is neither sufficient nor the most effective way of promoting rational thinking from a broader perspective. First and foremost, it is difficult to apply this approach in everyday contexts. As Wilson et al. [39, p. 195] point out, it is often difficult to control exposure to biasing information: "[w]hen deciding which employees should be promoted, for example, we already know their gender, age, and race". In most real-life contexts, we simply do not know in advance whether the available information is likely to be biasing. Moreover, selective exposure can also end up amplifying certain biases. Research shows, in particular, that people's selective exposure to mass media tends to increase the confirmation bias and the "group polarization" effect. Knobloch-Westerwick [19, p. 3] suggest that this may stem from the fact that "media users often select media messages to instigate desired media effects upon themselves".

But above all, this type of debiasing does nothing to suppress the unwanted bias, but only its immediate repercussions. Although this is not neglectable when it comes to fairness of opportunities and social change, it does not bring about a significant improvement when it comes to critical thinking. Thus, for example, the fact that groups traditionally discriminated increasingly succeed in getting published can lead, at best, to an indirect reduction of the stereotype, and thereby to fairer assessments of the quality of their work. But selective exposure does nothing to eliminate the bias itself or to prevent it from resurfacing in a less controllable situation. As Kenyon and Beaulac [18, p. 358] acknowledge, this type of debiasing process "can be entirely arational from the perspective of the agents in the situation".

In light of these considerations, I argue that the second type of contextual debiasing (dispositional correction), and particularly accountability, is more likely to produce overall improvements with regard to rational thinking than the former one (situational correction). Similarly to cognitive debasing (and unlike situational correction), accountability involves a correction of people's biases, rather than a mere suppression of their repercussions. And similarly to situational correction (and unlike cognitive debiasing), accountability seeks to achieve this by using environmental and social constraints, rather than simply relying on critical thinking and epistemic vigilance.

4 Accountability Breeds Response-Ability

Accountability is generally defined as the expectation that one will have to justify one's judgment or action to others [21, 32, 33]. Why would holding arguers accountable contribute to making them less biased or better critical thinkers? The hypothesis is that people's motivation to think rationally may be enhanced by the social costs/gains inherent to accountability. As Larrick [21, p. 322] explains, individuals tend to be think more thoroughly and judiciously when they believe that they will have to answer for it, particularly if this expectation is linked to some type of social sanction or reward:

> The logic of accountability is similar to the logic of incentives, except that it depends on the motivational effects of social benefits (such as making a favorable impression and avoiding embarrassment).

Research seems to confirm this hypothesis to a large extent. Tetlock [32, p. 590], who has conducted a series of empirical studies on accountability, contends that holding people accountable for their judgment effectively mitigates a range of cognitive biases: "There is indeed a substantial list of biases that are attenuated, if not eliminated, by certain forms of accountability". This list includes the biases of overconfidence, primacy, overattribution, illusory correlation, and the fundamental attribution error, among others.

The most notable empirical finding, in that respect, is that accountability leads subjects to be more self-critical and analytical in their reasoning when they ignore the views of the audience. To test this hypothesis, Tetlock and Boettger [34] designed an experiment in which they asked participants to write down their thoughts and feelings on controversial policy issues (e.g. capital punishment, defense spending, affirmative action). The subjects were assigned randomly to four distinct groups. (1) The first group was told that their responses would remain *confidential*. (2) The second group was instructed that they would have to justify their opinions to a person with *unknown* views. (3) The third group expected to justify their opinions to a person with *liberal* views. (4) And the fourth group expected to justify their opinions to a person with *conservative views*. The answers were then subjected to a structural analysis designed to assess the complexity of the subjects' argumentation on the issues at stake (how many dimensions of a problem are taken into account, connections between differentiated aspects, etc.). The results revealed that subjects in the second group—who did not know the views of the audience—appeared to engage in preemptive self-criticism and to develop more complex analyses than their peers. More specifically, accountability seems to be an effective debiasing tool inasmuch as it prompts individuals to (a) consider a wider range of alternative hypotheses, (b) pay more attention to relevant information, and (c) take into account potential counter-arguments.

In a later article, Tetlock [32, p. 586] suggests that this enhanced critical thinking is probably motivated by the subjects' fear that the audience might detect flaws in their reasoning and challenge their standpoint:

This can be viewed as an adaptive strategy to protect both one's self-image and social image. Expecting to justify one's views to an unknown audience raised the prospect of failure: the other person might find serious flaws in one's position. To minimize potential embarrassment, subjects demonstrated their awareness of alternative perspectives: 'You can see that I am no fool. I may believe X, but I understand the arguments for Y'.

The other important result of this experiment, however, is that subjects in the third and fourth group—who were accountable to an audience with known liberal or conservative views—tended to shift their views toward the views of the audience. In other words, subjects accountable to a liberal person tended to express more liberal views, and those accountable to a conservative person tended to express more conservative views. Consequently, accountability to an audience with *known* views tends to exacerbate certain biases (group polarization, ambiguity aversion, compromise effect, etc.), rather than reduce biases, presumably because of people's propensity to seek approval from the audience. These results are also consistent with what the research on the "group polarization effect" seems to indicate. For example, a group of feminist women became even more feminist after discussion [25], and a group of federal judges appointed by Republican presidents tended to show even more conservative voting patterns when sitting only with fellow Republican appointees [31].

Despite these limitations, accountability is arguably the most effective debiasing tool, particularly in contexts of argumentation. I base this claim on three different arguments. The first is empirical and directly anchored in the aforementioned results: accountable arguers tend to be better critical thinkers, and thereby less prone to biases, provided that they ignore the views of the audience. To avoid backfiring effects, accountability devices simply need to ensure that arguers know as little as possible about their audience's viewpoint regarding the topic at hand. But this constraint leaves plenty of room for conceiving debiasing strategies in which accountability can plausibly foster rational thinking without undesirable effects.

In fact, some of the structures in place within important argumentative contexts already exploit the benefits of accountability, whether intentionally or not. For example, although the peer-review system was initially designed to neutralize the reviewers' biases by ensuring the anonymity of authors (selective exposure), it also seems to work as a debiasing tool with regard to the author's argumentation: Given that the author utterly ignores the views of the reviewers, he or she needs to take into account alternative hypotheses, avoid focusing exclusively on confirming evidence, develop sound arguments, and so forth—or run the risk of not being accepted for publication. Similarly, journalists are also accountable to an audience whose views they ignore and generally follow an "ideal of objectivity" that includes taking into account two sides of an issue, considering all available relevant evidence, avoiding the use of loaded terms, and maintaining an impartial stance. More generally speaking, any argumentative context in which the arguer is accountable to an unknown audience should in principle contribute to promote the rationality of argumentation (televised parliamentary debates, conferences and workshops, blogs, teaching, etc.).

The second argument in support of the effectiveness of accountability is that it demonstrably enhances people's motivation to debias. Unlike traditional critical thinking methods, accountability strategies make use of the individual's desire to achieve certain goals (seek the audience's approval, publish a work, maintain the newspaper's credibility, avoid social embarrassment, etc.) as an indirect means to boost his or her willingness to reason in fair and impartial terms, rather than merely relying on well-intended efforts to think critically. For example, the author who submits an article or the political analyst are generally motivated to make sure that their arguments are two-sided and impartial, not (just) because of their dispassionate pursuit of the truth, but (also) because they seek the audience's approval and dread that their reasoning might be flawed. To paraphrase Thaler and Sunstein's [36] leitmotif, it seems reasonable to suggest that accountability devices "nudge" individuals into wanting to abide by the standards of rationality.

And this brings us to the third argument; namely, that accountability devices arguably tend to reinforce the individual's epistemic/argumentative skills and virtues. By systematically having to submit their argumentation efforts to contexts of audiences with unknown views (classrooms, peer reviewers, journalist critics, conferences, blogs, etc.), arguers tend to *internalize* good habits of thinking required to win the audience's approval (two-sidedness, attention to all relevant evidence, open-mindedness, deductive skills, thoroughness, etc.). In other words, arguers used to being held accountable to unknown audiences are presumably more likely to incorporate the standards, the methods and the skills that are generally associated with critical thinking. The advantage of acquiring such argumentative virtues is that they tend to become a sort of "second nature" which leads people to think fairly and rationally *even when they are no longer accountable to someone else.*

Accountability thus helps bolstering cognitive debiasing and critical thinking skills from a long-term perspective. While selective exposure merely suppresses the immediate repercussions of a given bias, but does nothing to eliminate the bias itself (or to prevent it from resurfacing in a less controllable situation), accountability fosters the development of argumentative skills and virtues that enhance rational thinking even when the external constraint is no longer in place. It is in this sense that it makes sense to claim that "accountability breeds response-ability".

5   Conclusion

There is growing consensus that critical thinking and other methods of cognitive change are by and large insufficient to mitigate biases. Although, in my view, the present state of research does not justify the claim that critical thinking is utterly ineffective, we have seen that contextual debiasing is both more reliable and more effective, insofar as it relies on external constraints that "coerce" individuals into overcoming their own biases. However, there are different kinds of contextual debiasing and I have attempted to show that accountability is the most effective tool to promote rationality in everyday contexts. This is not to say that other methods of contextual debiasing, such as selective exposure, incentives or group interaction, are useless tools. On the contrary, debiasing methods should be used complementarily depending on the context at hand. But unlike other contextual strategies, accountability demonstrably enhances (1) people's self-criticism, (2) people's motivation to debias themselves, and (3) people's argumentative virtues. In other words, accountability is a contextual strategy that simultaneously fosters cognitive change at the level of the individual. Granted, these improvements only make sense when arguers address audiences with unknown views, but there are many contexts in which this condition is fulfilled, particularly in the argumentation arena.

Acknowledgments. I would like to thank the editor and three anonymous reviewers for their constructive comments. Work on this article was conducted under the grant SFRH/BPD/ 101744/2014 by the "Portuguese Foundation for Science and Technology" (FCT).

References

1. Aberdein, A.: Virtue in argument. Argumentation **24**(2), 165–179 (2010)
2. Adler, J., Rips, L. (eds.): Reasoning. Cambridge University Press, Cambridge (2008)
3. Arkes, H.: Impediments to accurate clinical judgment and possible ways to minimize their impact. J. Consult. Clin. Psychol. **49**, 323–330 (1981)
4. Arkes, H.: Costs and benefits of judgment errors. Psychol. Bull. **110**(13), 486–498 (1991)
5. Audi, R.: The ethics of belief. Synthese **161**, 403–418 (2008)
6. Budden, A., Tregenza, T., Aarssen, L., Koricheva, J., Leimu, R., Lortie, C.J.: Double-blind review favors increased representation of female authors. Trends Ecol. Evol. **23**(1), 4–6 (2008)
7. Cohen, D.: Keeping an open mind and having a sense of proportion as virtues in argumentation. Cogency **1**(2), 49–64 (2009)
8. Croskerry, P., Singhal, G., Mamede, S.: Cognitive debiasing 1. Qual. Saf. **22**(2), 58–64 (2013)
9. Engel, P. (ed.): Believing and Accepting. Kluwer, Dordrecht (2000)
10. Fischhoff, B.: Debiasing. In: Kahneman, D., Slovic, P., Tversky, A. (eds.) Judgment Under Uncertainty, pp. 422–444. Cambridge University Press, Cambridge (1982)
11. Fischhoff, B.: Heuristics and biases in application. In: Gilovich, T., Griffin, D., Kahneman, D. (eds.) Heuristics and Biases. Cambridge University Press, Cambridge (2002)
12. Galinsky, A., Moskowitz, G., Gordon, B.: Perspective taking. J. Pers. Soc. Psychol. **784**, 708–724 (2000)
13. Hirt, E., Markman, K.: Multiple explanation. J. Pers. Soc. Psychol. **69**, 1069–1086 (1995)
14. Hogarth, R.: Educating Intuition. University of Chicago Press, Chicago (2001)
15. Holland, J., Holyoak, K., Nisbett, R., Thagard, T.: Induction. MIT Press, Cambridge, London (1986)
16. Johnson, R., Blair, A.: Logical Self-defense. International Debate Association, New York (2006)
17. Kahneman, D.: Thinking, Fast and Slow. Farrar, Straus and Giroux, New York (2011)
18. Kenyon, T., Beaulac, G.: Critical thinking education and debiasing. Informal Logic **34**(4), 341–363 (2014)
19. Knobloch-Westerwick, S.: Choice and Preference in Media Use. Routledge, London (2015)
20. Koch, C., Wüstemann, J.: Experimental analysis. In: Bovens, M., Goodin, R., Schillemans, T. (eds.) The Oxford Handbook of Public Accountability, pp. 127–142. Oxford University Press, Oxford (2014)
21. Larrick, R.: Debiasing. In: Koehler, D., Harvey, N. (eds.) The Blackwell Handbook of Judgment and Decision Making, pp. 316–337. Blackwell Publishing, Oxford (2004)
22. Lilienfeld, S., Ammirati, R., Landfield, K.: Giving debiasing away. Perspect. Psychol. Sci. **4**(4), 390–398 (2009)

23. Mele, A.: Autonomous Agents. Oxford University Press, Oxford (2001)
24. Mercier, H., Sperber, D.: Why do humans reason? Behav. Brain Sci. **34**, 57–111 (2011)
25. Myers, D.: Discussion-induced attitude-polarization. Hum. Relat. **28**, 699–714 (1975)
26. Paluk, E., Green, D.: Prejudice reduction: what works? Annu. Rev. Psychol. **60**, 339–367 (2009)
27. Pronin, E., Lin, D., Ross, L.: The bias blind spot. Pers. Soc. Psychol. Bull. **28**, 369–381 (2002)
28. Sanna, L., Schwarz, N., Stocker, S.: When debiasing backfires. J. Exp. Psychol. **28**, 497–502 (2002)
29. Siegel, H.: Educating Reason. Routledge, New York, London (1988)
30. Stanovich, K.: Rationality and the Reflective Mind. Oxford University Press, New York (2011)
31. Sunstein, C.R., Schkade, D., Ellman, L.: Ideological voting on federal courts of appeal. Va. Law Rev. **90**(1), 301–354 (2004)
32. Tetlock, P.: Intuitive politicians, theologians, and prosecutors. In: Gilovich, T., Griffin, D., Kahneman, D. (eds.) Heuristics and Biases, pp. 582–600. Cambridge University Press, Cambridge (2002)
33. Tetlock, P.: Expert Political Judgment. Princeton University Press, Princeton (2005)
34. Tetlock, P., Boettger, R.: Accountability. J. Pers. Soc. Psychol. **57**, 388–398 (1989)
35. Thagard, P.: Critical thinking and informal logic. Informal Logic **31**(3), 152–170 (2011)
36. Thaler, R., Sunstein, C.: Nudge. Yale University Press, New Haven, London (2008)
37. Tversky, A., Kahneman, D.: Extensional versus intuitive reasoning. In: Adler, J., Rips, L. (eds.) Reasoning, pp. 114–135. Cambridge University Press, Cambridge (2008)
38. Willingham, D.: Critical thinking: why is it so hard to teach? Am. Educ. **31**(2), 8–19 (2007)
39. Wilson, T., Centerbar, D., Brekke, N.: Mental contamination and the debiasing problem. In: Gilovich, T., Griffin, D., Kahneman, D. (eds.) Heuristics and Biases, pp. 185–200. Cambridge University Press, Cambridge (2002)
40. Zagzebski, L.: Virtues of the Mind. Cambridge University Press, Cambridge (1996)

Human Activity Recognition Using Place-Based Decision Fusion in Smart Homes

Julien Cumin[1,2(✉)], Grégoire Lefebvre[1], Fano Ramparany[1],
and James L. Crowley[2]

[1] Orange Labs, Meylan, France
{julien1.cumin,gregoire.lefebvre,fano.ramparany}@orange.com
[2] Laboratoire d'Informatique de Grenoble, Université Grenoble Alpes & Inria,
Grenoble, France
james.crowley@inria.fr

Abstract. This paper describes the results of experiments where information about places is used in the recognition of activities in the home. We explore the use of place-specific activity recognition trained with supervised learning, coupled with a decision fusion step, for recognition of activities in the *Opportunity* dataset. Our experiments show that using place information to control recognition can substantially improve both the error rates and the computation cost of activity recognition compared to classical approaches where all sensors are used and all activities are possible. The use of place information for controlling recognition gives an F1 classification score of 92.70% ± 1.26%, requiring on average only 73 ms of computing time per instance of activity. These experiments demonstrate that organizing activity recognition with place-based context models can provide a scalable approach for building context-aware services based on activity recognition in smart home environments.

1   Introduction

The arrival of low-cost computing and wireless communications has provided the potential for a technological rupture in home technologies. In theory, it has became possible to provide "smart" home services for applications such as environmental control, energy efficiency, security, entertainment, active healthy ageing and assisted living. Activity recognition from environmental sensors is generally recognised as a key enabling technology for such services. However, to date, this vision of the "smart" home remains a technology of the future. The complexity and scalability of activity recognition from environmental sensors has emerged as an important barrier to the emergence of practical systems and services [5].

A scalable approach for smart-home services requires the use of context [2], where context can be defined as any information that can be used to characterise situation [7]. For smart home services, time-of-day, place, identity of inhabitants and activity are key elements of context information for providing appropriate services.

© Springer International Publishing AG 2017
P. Brézillon et al. (Eds.): CONTEXT 2017, LNAI 10257, pp. 137–150, 2017.
DOI: 10.1007/978-3-319-57837-8_11

Time-of-day, place, identity and activity are abstract semantic concepts. Each of these provides key information that can condition the suitability or appropriateness of smart home services. Time-of-day refers to periods such as morning, evening or night, as well as day of the week and summer vacation or Christmas holidays. Time-of-day is strongly correlated with local time and date, with only minor variations in sequence and boundary that can be inferred from activities of inhabitants. Places are generally defined as region of space where specific classes of activities occur and can be easily inferred from location information. In a home, identity refers not only to the identity of the inhabitant but also to their position within the family for each other person (Father, mother, child, family-friend, etc.). Social role is a static property that is easily determined from the identity of an inhabitant.

Activity in the home is the most difficult to determine. Activity refers to the collections of actions that are performed in order to accomplish a task. Activity recognition is challenging both because the number of activity classes can be very large, and because the manner in which an activity occurs can vary from one individual to the next. Even for a single individual, an activity may be highly variable. In addition, it is not unusual for individuals to perform several activities in parallel, interleaving the actions of the individual activities.

Human activity recognition is currently a hot topic in computer vision. Certainly, image sequences can be a rich source of information about activity. However, the use of cameras for activity recognition is generally not well accepted by inhabitants, because of privacy concerns [12]. An alternative is to recognise activities based on a large number of environmental sensors. In particular, instrumenting an electrical system to monitor electrical use converts every electrical switch into a sensor. This information can be enriched by infrared presence detectors, switches on doors, wearable sensors, or even smartphones carried by the inhabitant as in [10]. The result is a large number of simple data elements that can be used to construct systems to monitor activity.

Many authors have speculated that context information, such as time-of-day, identity and place can be used to organize smart services. In this paper we report on experiments that show the extent to which context can improve error rates and execution time of recognition of activity. In particular, we focus on place as an organizational element for activity recognition. We note that activity is highly dependent on place. For example, the activity "*Cooking*" is very likely to happen in the place "*Kitchen*". Therefore, place information would appear valuable to improve activity recognition.

In this paper we investigate a place-based approach to activity recognition, which relies on multiple supervised classification models, one for each place in the home, as well as a decision fusion step. In Sect. 2 we present a summary of the state of the art of activity recognition in the home, and discuss differences that exist between those works and our approach. In Sect. 3 we present details of our approach. The experiments we lead to evaluate this approach are presented in Sect. 4, after which we conclude in Sect. 5 on the suitability of our approach for human activity recognition in smart homes.

2   State of the Art

Activity recognition in smart homes is a very active research subject. Here, we are particularly interested in approaches which use low level data, as opposed to image-based techniques. Approaches based on machine learning are naturally very popular in this field, most of which are supervised learning approaches. We are however starting to see some works emerge that are based on unsupervised techniques, as in [4]. Although they are simpler to use than unsupervised approaches, supervised approaches are still not, to this day, sufficiently accurate to provide an information of activity that is reliable enough in order to generate context-based services which are useful to inhabitants [2]. More efforts are thus still needed on this research topic.

Some recent supervised activity recognition approaches are based on *deep learning*. We find for example the work of Ordóñez and Roggen [9] which seek to exploit, on low level data of smart homes, the capabilities of Convolutional Neural Networks (CNN) and Long Short-Term Memory (LSTM) neural networks, CNNs being very effective on signals such as images, and LSTMs being capable of modeling the temporal dimension of data. This work is very convincing, in particular because they are applied on a dataset that is more limited in its number of instances than typical datasets used for deep learning. The number of labeled instances is still substantial, which makes the acquisition, training and tuning processes very hard tasks. It is indeed very difficult to obtain labeled data of inhabitants of homes for a commercial application. Providing sufficient information is very uncompelling for users, and activities that they perform in their home will probably evolve frequently too. The necessity of having a large number of labeled data and long training times are thus definitive drawbacks for such applications.

On the other hand, the literature proposes approaches that are based on *ontologies*, as in [1] or [3]. In the latter, activity recognition is based on expert knowledge of smart home environments: sensors, rooms of the home, inhabitants, activities and sub-activities, etc. Expert knowledge is more reliable and not annoying to obtain for users, compared to labeled data provided by inhabitants. This approach also allows to have a logical and formal view of the home, which can be used in other applications than activity recognition (e.g. energy management), whereas a machine learning approach is limited to the application for which it was trained. However, those ontology-based approaches also have drawbacks: they rely on expert knowledge, which ought to be as exhaustive as possible (which is very expensive) in order for the system to work properly for a random home. Consequently, we can expect those approaches to be somewhat efficient in general but way too rigid to perfectly adapt to the specificities of each possible inhabitant, which greatly impacts the capability of the system to provide services that correspond to inhabitants' needs.

Lastly, there are hybrid approaches which are based on machine learning, but that attempt to exploit expert information in order to improve the performances of the recognition algorithm. This is for example the case in the work of Wu et al. [14], where the localization of the person is estimated so as to reduce the set of possible activities that can correspond to the current instance. Here, the only expert information needed are the positions of sensors throughout the home, as well as the sets of activities possible in each room. Reducing the set of possible activities based on the localization of the person performing the activity is a technique that we also use in the work presented in this paper. However, we believe that reducing the set of sensors used as well, based on their location, can simplify the classification task. Lastly, instead of relying on an estimation of the localization of the person, we believe that it is simpler and more robust to classify the instance with all local models simultaneously, and then let a decision fusion step decide which of the classes corresponds to the instance. This allows to alleviate the need for localization estimation (which can add errors if not accurate enough), while allowing the possibility of recognizing simultaneous activities which would happen in different places of the home (not covered in this paper).

3   A Place-Based Approach to Activity Recognition

3.1   Places and Motivations for the Approach

Inhabitants of a home have *routines*, that is, sequences of activities that they perform in repeated fashion during their time in the home. Those activities are performed in what we can call *places*, such as a bedroom or a bathroom, which reciprocally get associated to a set of activities by the inhabitant: for example, the activity *"Brushing your teeth"* will be unique to the place *"Bathroom"*. Moreover, every place very often corresponds to exactly one room of the home; a finer granularity does not seem very useful for anything but large rooms where activities would be very diverse in different parts of the room.

It is obvious that, by proposing an activity recognition approach based on places, we need to have *a priori* knowledge of the existing places in the home (the correspondence between rooms and places making this step relatively simple), as well as both the distribution of sensors in the places and the activity classes that can happen in each place. If those information seem difficult to obtain in current smart homes, we can conceive that, for all but the activity classes, those information will be readily available: indeed, the constructor of proper smart homes could directly fill in the distribution of sensors that they installed in the rooms, as well as a set of places based on those rooms. As for the distribution of activity classes, this information seems to go in pair with the knowledge itself of the activity classes, which is typically assumed to be given by the user in supervised approaches, such as the one we present in this work.

As presented in Sect. 2, supervised activity recognition approaches are typically "global" approaches: in order to classify a new instance of activity, a classifier trained in advance will try to decide the correct class, among all possible activity classes of the home, based on all sensors available. Here, we propose a "local" approach which exploits the information available on places, by building a different classifier for each place; this classifier of a place will only use the sensors in that place as inputs, and will only have to model activity classes which can happen in that place. An additional step of decision fusion (presented in Sect. 3.3) allows to take a final decision for the entire home.

That way, a classifier specific to one place has a simpler model to learn, because of the reduced number of available sensors and decidable classes, as opposed to a global approach where the model can become so complex that learning is too difficult. Consequently, parametrization of classifiers is greatly simplified, and computing times during the learning step ought to be shortened. Besides, every classifier being independent from place to place, it is possible to parallelize the learning step between all places. Thus, one can retrain a subset of classifiers instead of the entire global model, if some changes happened in the home (e.g. a new activity class exists, or a new sensor was installed).

3.2   Place-Based Activity Recognition

Suppose that there are three places in a home (see Fig. 1). We can identify, for each place P_i, the data sources (i.e. sensors) $S_j^{(i)}$ that are in that place. Note that some sensors can appear in more than one place (e.g. bodily-worn sensors); it is thus possible that for two places P_i and $P_{i'}$, we have $S_j^{(i)} = S_{j'}^{(i')}$.

We can then associate a classifier C_i to each place, which will classify an activity instance using only the $S_j^{(i)}$ sources as inputs. Moreover, C_i can only decide the classes that can happen in P_i; thus, if the current activity instance does not happen in P_i, then C_i should ideally decide the dummy class *None*.

Therefore, to classify a new activity instance, we use all classifiers of each place simultaneously, and then fuse the resulting decisions $\{D_i\}$ into a final decision D_F, using a decision fusion method C_F (see Sect. 3.3). The classifiers of each place are trained in a supervised fashion such that, for a training instance, the classifiers of places in which the activity class of that instance cannot happen are trained to decide the class *None*, and the classifiers of places (usually only one) where that instance really takes place are trained to decide the class label of the training instance. In the test phase, classifiers of places only use the sensors and classes of their respective place, like in the training phase.

The *None* class is a source of difficulty during the training and testing phases. It indeed represents in our approach three different situations: no activity is happening, an unknown activity is happening, or an activity from another place is happening. The instances' data of the *None* class for a place will thus be much more varied than for other activity classes.

We assume here that only one activity can happen at a time in the home. It would be possible, with our place-based approach, to recognize activities that happen simultaneously in two different places by simply removing the decision fusion step; this would not be feasible as straightforwardly using the classical global approach.

3.3   Decision Fusion

In order to combine the decisions taken by the classifiers of each place, we can use multiple approaches of decision fusion that can be found in the literature [6].

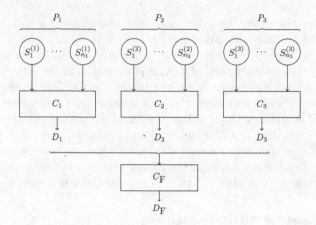

Fig. 1. Data flow of place-based decision fusion.

We only retain the two best decision fusion methods that we tested, both based on the principles of *Stacking* [13], which are that the problem of decision fusion is completely equivalent to a classification problem. Therefore, it is possible to fuse the decisions taken in all places by using the confidence of each classifier as *inputs to the stacking classifier*. The two stacking classifiers that we have retained, after preliminary experiments, to perform the decision fusion step are the MultiLayer Perceptron (MLP) and the Support Vector Machine (SVM).

Since we propose to use a fusion step to get a global decision, for the entire home, on which activity class the current instance belongs to, it seems natural to exploit even more this fusion step by using multiple classifiers in each place. Therefore, looking back at the example of Fig. 1, we can imagine that we have three classifiers per place, instead of just one, and thus fuse nine decisions instead of three (three decisions would be taken per place). This can lead to better performances of the system, by ensuring that more than one classifier give their opinions on the class of the current instance, and thus combine the strengths of different kinds of classifiers. Decision fusion is also directly usable in the standard global approach, where we would this time for example have three classifiers which would classify the current instance using all available data sources (which is the classical use of decision fusion).

4   Experiments

4.1   The Opportunity Dataset

Opportunity is proposed by Roggen et al. [11] to be a reference dataset for the evaluation of algorithms related to human activity recognition in the home, such as classification or automatic segmentation of activities. In this dataset, each of the four inhabitants has performed by themselves five sessions of activities of daily living (see Fig. 3), during which they performed the activities by following

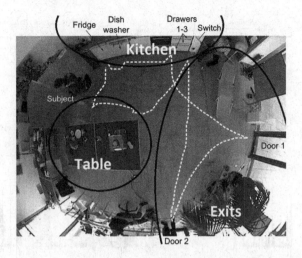

Fig. 2. *Opportunity's* environment, annotated with instrumented objects and places.

a brief description of the session, with no specific restrictions. Each inhabitant also performed a "Drill" session, during which they perform 20 times a precise sequence of 17 activities.

The activities of *Opportunity* are performed in a unique room (see Fig. 2), in which both its elements (drawers, forks and knives, doors, etc.) and the inhabitant themselves are instrumented, with 39 inertial sensors (19 on the inhabitant, 20 in the environment) and 13 state-change sensors (all in the environment). *Opportunity* offers multiple levels of labeling of activities; we are only interested here in the 17 mid-level activities, namely *Clean Table*, *Drink from Cup*, *Open Dishwasher*, *Close Dishwasher*, *Open Drawer 1*, *Close Drawer 1*, *Open Drawer 2*, *Close Drawer 2*, *Open Drawer 3*, *Close Drawer 3*, *Open Fridge*, *Close Fridge*, *Toggle Switch*, *Open Door 1*, *Close Door 1*, *Open Door 2* and *Close Door 2*. A dummy activity *None* is used when there is no activity or when no other activity fits. This class also corresponds to the *None* class mentioned in Sect. 3.2, used for activities that do not happen in a certain place.

4.2 Experimental Protocol and Data Preprocessing Strategy

To experimentally evaluate our approach on the *Opportunity* dataset, we assume the segmentation of each activity instance to be known. Therefore, the beginning and the end of each instance are marked by the transition between two labels of different activities, at two successive timesteps. We use a 10-fold random cross-validation where each fold contains, for each of the 18 classes (including *None*), 72 training instances, 22 test instances and 18 validation instances (used to optimize the parameters of classifiers). Those instances are randomly selected for each fold among the four inhabitants. After preliminary experiments, we decided not to use the localization data and quaternion data, for all following experiments.

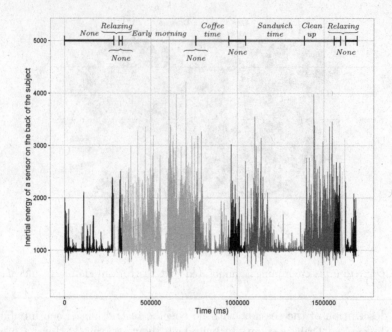

Fig. 3. High level activities during a session of activities of daily living.

Data are preprocessed such that missing values are interpolated using cubic splines. A low-pass filter is applied on the data and they are normalized so that the average value of each sensors is 0 and its standard deviation is 1. For classifiers that require a feature vector of fixed size as input, we construct that vector by resampling the data into 20 samples, and then concatenating each sample one after the other. The information of duration of the instance as well as its start timestamp are prepended to the vector.

We evaluate our approach using three standard classification models: the MultiLayer Perceptron (MLP), the Support Vector Machine (SVM) and the Bayesian Network (BN). Those classifiers use feature vectors of fixed size as input, and their implementations are taken from the Weka library [8]. We had also used Hidden Markov Models (HMM) and Dynamic Time Warping (DTW) during our experiments, but they proved to be respectively not accurate enough and too slow; we will thus not report the results of those two methods in the rest of the paper.

We define three places in the *Opportunity* experiment (see Fig. 2):

- *Table:* represents the table in the center-left part of the room; contains the 12 sensors placed on the objects that are on the table, as well as the 19 sensors on the inhabitant. Activities *Clean Table*, *Drink from Cup* and *None* can happen in this place.
- *Kitchen:* represents the kitchen counter; contains the 18 sensors on the fridge, drawers, dishwasher, light switch, and the 19 sensors on the inhabitant.

Table 1. F1 scores of classifiers for each place.

Place	Classifier		
	MLP	SVM	BN
Table	**98.97% ± 0.48%**	98.77% ± 0.54%	98.70% ± 0.48%
Kitchen	**94.06% ± 1.58%**	93.78% ± 1.32%	91.79% ± 1.27%
Exits	99.15% ± 0.39%	**99.24% ± 0.34%**	98.34% ± 0.62%

Parameters :

- **MLP** 80 hidden neurons, 100 epochs, 0.2 learning rate, 0.1 momentum.
- **SVM** $C = 1000$, $\gamma = 0.01$.
- **BN** K2 search, *SimpleEstimator* estimator.

Activities *Open/Close Dishwasher/Fridge/Drawer1/Drawer2/Drawer3, Toggle Switch* and *None* can happen in this place.
- *Exits:* represents the two doors in the room; contains the two sensors on those doors, the sensor placed on the lazy chair next to one of the doors, and the 19 sensors on the inhabitant. Activities *Open/Close Door1/Door2* and *None* can happen in this place.

We will also use the *Home* configuration for comparison's sake, which corresponds to the classical approach where all sensors are used and all activities that can happen in the home are decidable.

Our protocol is quite different from the usual protocol that is used on the *Opportunity* dataset [9], which comes from a challenge. The protocol of this challenge only uses the sensors on the inhabitant, which would not allow us to validate the benefits of a significant part of our approach, which is that each place's model only uses the sensors of the place they are in. Moreover, this protocol does not cross-validate its results and requires an additional segmentation step (which might skew the results); it is thus not well-adapted to validate an activity recognition approach, which should not be optimized for a specific dataset.

4.3 Results

We present in Table 1 the F1 scores of classifiers for each place. We can observe that activity recognition in the places *Table* and *Exits* is relatively "easy", since all classifiers manage to reach scores above 98%. The task seems more difficult in the place *Kitchen*, which can be explained by the fact that 12 classes can happen in this place (including *None*), whereas only 5 and 3 respectively can happen in *Table* and *Exits*. Moreover, some classes of *Kitchen* are very similar (e.g. *Open Drawer 1* and *Open Drawer 2*), which makes it difficult to distinguish them from the available data.

We present in Table 2 the F1 scores of classifiers on the *Home* configuration and the F1 scores of the fusion of decisions taken on the 3 places, when all

Table 2. F1 scores of classifiers on the *Home* configuration or of decision fusion of classifiers of the same type in all places.

Approach	Classifier MLP	SVM	BN
Table ⎫ Kitchen ⎬ Fusion Exits ⎭	**92.52% ± 1.25%**[1]	**91.78% ± 1.37%**[2]	89.14% ± 1.27%[3]
Home	90.21% ± 1.62%	90.05% ± 1.64%	**90.61% ± 1.37%**

Parameters on *Home*:

- **MLP** 500 hidden neurons, 200 epochs, 0.2 learning rate, 0.1 momentum.
- **SVM** $C = 100$, $\gamma = 0.0005$.
- **BN** K2 search, *SimpleEstimator* estimator.

Decision fusion in places :

- [1] **SVM stacking** $C = 100$, $\gamma = 0.01$.
- [2] **MLP stacking** 100 hidden neurons, 100 epochs, 0.2 learning rate, 0.1 momentum.
- [3] **MLP stacking** 20 hidden neurons, 100 epochs, 0.2 learning rate, 0.1 momentum.

places uses the same type of classifier. Those results allow us to see that the place-based approach we propose, fusing decisions taken on each place, attains significantly better scores than the classical global approach (e.g. for the MLP, 92.52%±1.25% versus 90.21%±1.62%), for all tested classifiers but the Bayesian Network (BN), for which the *Home* configuration attains slightly better scores (89.14%±1.27% versus 90.61%±1.37%). We can also observe that our approach produces more stable results: the standard deviations recorded are smaller for all tested classifiers.

Finally, we present in Table 3 the F1 scores of decision fusion of multiple classifiers for each place and for *Home*. SVM stacking fusion on the set of decisions taken by the three types of classifiers used previously in each place (9 decisions) reaches an F1 score of 92.70% ± 1.26%, which is slightly better than decision fusion using only the MLP in the three places (92.52%±1.25%, see Table 2). SVM stacking fusion on the three classifiers in the *Home* configuration only reaches an F1 score of 91.62% ± 1.59%. We present in Fig. 4 the confusion matrix of one fold of test of the place-based three classifiers decision fusion approach. We find as expected that most confusions happen for very similar activities (e.g. *Open Drawer 1* and *Close Drawer 1*), and for the class *None*.

4.4 Computing Times

Besides an improvement of performances in classification, the approach we propose also allows, thanks to the reduction of the number of sensors used and activity classes per model, to reduce computing times. We present in Table 4 the training and testing computing times for the three classifiers in the three places

Table 3. F1 scores of decision fusion for local and global approaches.

	Classifier		
	MLP	SVM	BN
Approach		Fusion	
Table + Kitchen + Exits		**92.70% ± 1.26%**[1]	
Home		91.62% ± 1.59%[1]	

Classifiers' parameters : see Table 2.
Fusion : [1] **SVM stacking** $C = 1, \gamma = 0.1$.

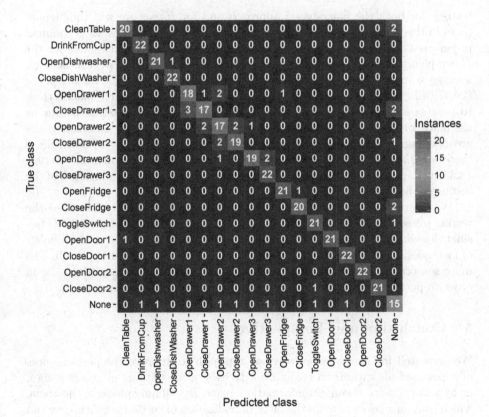

Fig. 4. Confusion matrix of one fold of test of our best configuration.

and the global model *Home*. Those computing times were evaluated on a 4-cores Intel i7 2.8 GHz processor with 16 GB of RAM. The computing times of the final decision fusion step are very stable and less than 1 s for one fold of training or

Table 4. Average computing times in seconds of classifiers in training and testing phase for each model, for an entire fold of cross-validation.

Classifier	Phase	Model			
		Table	Kitchen	Exits	Home
MLP	Training	947.65 ± 160.77	732.83 ± 60.04	561.71 ± 30.78	11250.06 ± 1593.57
	Testing	12.64 ± 1.56	9.84 ± 1.22	8.49 ± 1.99	20.70 ± 1.19
SVM	Training	24.42 ± 0.23	19.11 ± 0.16	12.75 ± 0.23	35.37 ± 0.48
	Testing	6.56 ± 0.06	12.49 ± 0.13	4.21 ± 0.03	29.47 ± 0.96
BN	Training	19.06 ± 0.34	13.87 ± 0.28	11.34 ± 0.25	26.49 ± 0.37
	Testing	8.75 ± 0.06	6.71 ± 0.13	5.49 ± 0.07	11.73 ± 0.10

Classifiers' parameters : see Table 1 and Table 2.

testing, for both the place-based approach and for *Home*; we will thus ignore them in this analysis. If we assume to have four computing cores, as is common in personal computers nowadays, we can parallelize the three classifiers for the *Home* configuration; thus, to process all instances of one fold, we will need on average as much time as the slowest classifier, e.g. the SVM in the testing phase (29.47 s). In our place-based approach, we can parallelize the three places; thus, to process all instances of one fold, we will need on average as much time as the place for which the sum of the computing times of its three classifiers is the greatest, e.g. *Kitchen* in the testing phase $(9.84 + 12.49 + 6.71 = 29.04 \text{ s})$. Since there are $22 \times 18 = 396$ instances per fold, our approach requires on average 73.33 ms to process one instance, which is much shorter than the duration of the instances themselves.

We clearly see, on this dataset, that our approach is slightly faster for the testing phase. For the training phase, it is much faster because of the MLP; classifiers for which their training complexity grows quickly compared to the number of instances, inputs and classes will thus greatly benefit from our approach. The more sensors and activities, the more complex a global model needs to be in order to perform well, and thus the more our approach is appropriate.

5   Conclusion and Perspectives

We presented in this paper an original approach to improve the performances of supervised algorithms to recognize activities of inhabitants of smart homes, using another piece of context information: place. By defining places in the home, which contain sensors and are the place of realization of certain activities, we can greatly reduce the size of the input data and the number of decidable classes for a classifier, instead of building a classifier which uses all sensors of the home and that ought to recognize all possible activity classes. A decision fusion step allows to combine the decisions taken in each different place in order to attain a global decision. Our approach does not require the knowledge or an estimation of the localization of inhabitants in the home. In fact, our approach can actually help estimate that localization by observing in which places activities are recognized.

We have evaluated our approach on the *Opportunity* dataset, by comparing it to the classical global approach where all sensors are used to recognize all possible activities. On this dataset, our approach reaches better classification scores while being faster, whether it be in the training or testing phase.

We have applied our approach on places. But we could also imagine to apply it on qualitative time periods (*Morning, Afternoon*, etc.) or on the identity of inhabitants. The usefulness of such granularities for activity recognition remains unknown. The approach we propose requires *a priori* knowledge of places, the sensors and the activities they contain. Even though those information could be obtained through smart home contractors and inhabitants, we can hope to discover those information automatically based on data, in an unsupervised fashion. Advances on that subject seem essential to improve the acceptability of smart home solutions for the average user.

References

1. Allègre, W., Burger, T., Berruet, P., Antoine, J.Y., et al.: Modèle de supervision d'interactions non-intrusif basé sur les ontologies. In: EGC, pp. 285–290 (2012)
2. Brdiczka, O., Crowley, J.L., Reignier, P.: Learning situation models in a smart home. IEEE Trans. Syst. Man Cybern. Part B (Cybern.) **39**(1), 56–63 (2009)
3. Chen, L., Nugent, C.D., Wang, H.: A knowledge-driven approach to activity recognition in smart homes. IEEE Trans. Knowl. Data Eng. **24**(6), 961–974 (2012)
4. Cook, D.J., Krishnan, N.C., Rashidi, P.: Activity discovery and activity recognition: a new partnership. IEEE Trans. Cybern. **43**(3), 820–828 (2013)
5. Crowley, J.L., Coutaz, J.: An ecological view of smart home technologies. In: Ruyter, B., Kameas, A., Chatzimisios, P., Mavrommati, I. (eds.) AmI 2015. LNCS, vol. 9425, pp. 1–16. Springer, Cham (2015). doi:10.1007/978-3-319-26005-1_1
6. Cumin, J., Lefebvre, G.: A priori data and a posteriori decision fusions for human action recognition. In: 11th International Joint Conference on Computer Vision, Imaging and Computer Graphics Theory and Applications (VISAPP) (2016)
7. Dey, A.K.: Understanding and using context. Pers. Ubiquit. Comput. **5**(1), 4–7 (2001)
8. Hall, M., Frank, E., Holmes, G., Pfahringer, B., Reutemann, P., Witten, I.H.: The Weka data mining software: an update. ACM SIGKDD Explor. Newslett. **11**(1), 10–18 (2009)
9. Ordóñez, F.J., Roggen, D.: Deep convolutional and LSTM recurrent neural networks for multimodal wearable activity recognition. Sensors **16**(1), 115 (2016)
10. Ouchi, K., Doi, M.: A real-time living activity recognition system using off-the-shelf sensors on a mobile phone. In: Beigl, M., Christiansen, H., Roth-Berghofer, T.R., Kofod-Petersen, A., Coventry, K.R., Schmidtke, H.R. (eds.) CONTEXT 2011. LNCS (LNAI), vol. 6967, pp. 226–232. Springer, Heidelberg (2011). doi:10.1007/978-3-642-24279-3_24
11. Roggen, D., Calatroni, A., Rossi, M., Holleczek, T., Forster, K., Troster, G., Lukowicz, P., Bannach, D., Pirkl, G., Ferscha, A., Doppler, J., Holzmann, C., Kurz, M., Holl, G., Chavarriaga, R., Sagha, H., Bayati, H., Creatura, M., Millan, J.d.R.: Collecting complex activity datasets in highly rich networked sensor environments. In: 2010 7th International Conference on Networked Sensing Systems (INSS), pp. 233–240, June 2010

12. Townsend, D., Knoefel, F., Goubran, R.: Privacy versus autonomy: a tradeoff model for smart home monitoring technologies. In: 2011 Annual International Conference of IEEE Engineering in Medicine and Biology Society, pp. 4749–4752. IEEE (2011)
13. Wolpert, D.H.: Stacked generalization. Neural Netw. **5**(2), 241–259 (1992)
14. Wu, C., Khalili, A.H., Aghajan, H.: Multiview activity recognition in smart homes with spatio-temporal features. In: Proceedings of 4th ACM/IEEE International Conference on Distributed Smart Cameras, pp. 142–149. ACM (2010)

Contextual Graphs for Modeling Group Interaction

Kimberly García$^{(\boxtimes)}$ and Patrick Brézillon

University Pierre and Marie Curie (UPMC), Paris, France
{Kimberly.Garcia,Patrick.Brezillon}@lip6.fr

Abstract. In a vast range of domains, decision makers have taken advantages of the benefits of the Contextual-Graph (CxG) formalism for representing the way(s) an actor(s) executes a real-world task. For this purpose, the CxG software formalism provides actors with edition tools that help them create and explore contextual graphs in an intuitive manner. However, the modeling of group interaction requires the introduction of new elements for managing each actor's intervention. In this paper, we incorporate simulation functionalities to the CxG software. The simulation of a task execution relies heavily on the concept of working context, which corresponds to the contextual elements existing in a CxG, their value, and their instantiations taken during the simulation, as well as the instantiation of the simulation parameters for managing the turn mechanism.

Keywords: Contextual model · Turns mechanism · Simulation · Group task · Collaborative work

1 Introduction

Several ways of modeling tasks have been proposed [8, 10] over the years to fulfill different modeling requirements (e.g., software designing, procedures representation). These modeling paradigms provide means to represent the theoretical ways in which a task or a procedure should be completed. However, relating such paradigms to reality often becomes difficult since they do not consider many dynamic elements that affect the current conditions of a situation (e.g., weather, actor preferences', time, etc.). The Contextual-Graph formalism has proven to be a good response to the lack of specialization of such paradigms. It provides means to incorporate contextual variables for representing the actual state of affairs of a situation. Such variables can change completely the way a task is carried out from one actor to another, from one moment to another, or from one setting to another.

Brézillon [3] introduced the Contextual-Graphs (CxG) formalism for obtaining a uniform representation of elements of knowledge, reasoning and context. A contextual graph represents the accomplishment of a task, in which each path represents a practice developed by an actor in a particular context. Thus, a contextual graph contains the accumulated experience of one or several actors, i.e. the practices developed for executing the same task.

The Contextual-Graph formalism has been successfully incorporated in multiple decision-making applications [1, 5] through the CxG software, which allows users to

© Springer International Publishing AG 2017
P. Brézillon et al. (Eds.): CONTEXT 2017, LNAI 10257, pp. 151–164, 2017.
DOI: 10.1007/978-3-319-57837-8_12

create, edit and explore their own contextual graph for representing the development of a task executed by an actor. However, we wanted to exploit the potential of this paradigm further for several actors working collaboratively by incorporating means to model group task, and we have added simulation capabilities to the software that supports the creation of Contextual Graphs. Our aim is to provide actors with a comprehensive formalism that allows them to represent all the aspects of a group task realization, and to easily visualize the evolution of the modeled task.

This paper is organized as follows. Section 2 presents the related work concerning the modeling of group tasks realization. Section 3 describes the Contextual-Graph formalism and the paper submission example, which is our case of study. Section 4 presents an effort to create a clear representation of a group task. Section 5 introduces the turn mechanism and the simulation parameters that are essential to model group tasks. Section 6 describes the actual implementation of the CxG simulation capabilities by simulating our use case and such capabilities are validated through a real world application. Finally, the conclusions and future work are presented in Sect. 7.

2 Related Work

We have explored the areas of Business and Work Process Modeling, as well as Human Computer Interaction (HCI) in search for a frame that would provide support for decision-making and knowledge transferring in group tasks. In the field of Business and Work Process Modeling, the Action Port Model (APM) [7] is a modeling language based on the speech act theory from linguistics [14]. APM provides support for: (a) resource modeling, including actors, roles, available information, and software resource involved, (b) interaction modeling, concerning the way the actors and/or roles communicate, (c) a unified approach of actors and their actions, (d) shared workspaces, which are made available when tasks share information, (e) templates, which represent commonly used interaction patterns found across several work processes.

In the HCI and Computer Supported Cooperative Work (CSCW) fields, the Contextual Design paradigm [2] is a user centered and well-structured methodology that provides guidelines for understanding, and modeling a task. It is "contextual" because it highlights the importance of considering the users' motivations and strategies when preforming a job. This methodology is integrated by five perspectives reflected in different diagrams, which in some cases is a customized version of a UML diagram. The DUTCH method (Designing for Users and Tasks from Concepts to Handles) [15] proposes a conceptual framework for modeling tasks for complex situations from three different points of view: agents, work, and situation. This method proposes a piece of software that provides support for creating a series of diagrams that looks like the Contextual Design ones. ConcurTaskTrees (CTT) [12] goal is to provide meaningful task modeling for application design, but also to provide users with support to understand a system.

In CTT each task is associated to a goal. A CTT diagram has a hierarchical structure, in which a tasks is decomposed in smaller parts, which allows identifying reusable part of the task, as well as understanding the task in different granularities. For multi-user applications, there is a model for each role, plus a task model for the cooperative part of the full task. The Collaborative Interactive Application Notation (CIAN) [11] is a visual language for designing collaborative applications. CIAN provides a series of views to cover the most important elements of design: organizational view, process view, data view, and the interaction view. The Collaborative Interactive Application Tool (CIAT) is the software support for the CIAN language.

As described above, many works have been developed to provide modeling languages for understanding the way(s) a group task is performed. Their objective varies, from understanding the task to the building of a useful and responsive user interface, to model a piece of software for supporting a group task. However, none of these works provides a simple, clean, and comprehensive model that can be used at any granularity level.

The APM modeling language gives a general overview of the modeled process; it provides a useful way to determine the input and output of a task, as well as the flow of the process. Nonetheless, the diagram can quickly become unreadable. On their side, the Contextual Design model and the DUTCH method are based in a series of diagrams, each one covering one aspect of the task modeling. Unlike APM, these approaches are good in providing different granularity levels for understanding the group task. However, as the modeling is divided in several diagrams, it is difficult to have a quick overview and understanding of the task. Each representation is built separately. Moreover, the diagrams for representing the interaction among actors are just a small tweak from either UML Activity diagrams or Workflow diagrams, which incorporate legends denoting the passing of parameters. Finally, the CTT model and a view of the CIAN notation are based on a diagram with a hierarchical structure that divides a task into smaller pieces of work, until arriving to a single unit performed by an actor. CTT provides a wide range of operators to specify the sequence, input and output, choices, parallelism of actions, etc. However, this view is difficult to follow, as there are many graphic details in a single tree-like structure. Moreover, when modeling a complex task that includes several actors, and actions, the tree like structure fails at showing the sequence of the task performance and the interaction among actors in an easy manner. CIAN tries to overcome this problem by adding a sociogram, a data, and an interaction view. However, it also requires several diagrams to represent a task completion.

3   The CxG and the Paper Submission Example

Pomerol and Brézillon [13] define context as the sum of: (1) the contextual knowledge, corresponding to all the knowledge relevant for a person in a given decision problem, (2) the external knowledge, considering the rest of the knowledge that is not important for the current situation, and (3) the proceduralized context, which is a part of the contextual knowledge that becomes important at a specific step of the decision problem. From this context definition, Brézillon [3] introduces the Contextual-Graphs (CxG) formalism for obtaining a uniform representation of elements of knowledge, reasoning and context. A contextual graph represents the realization of an individual task. Each path in such a graph corresponds to a practice developed by an actor in a particular context for realizing the task. Thus, a contextual graph represents the accumulated experience of one or several actors performing the same individual task.

We aimed at going one step further from the traditional CxG, by exploring the ways group tasks could be modeled.

We have chosen a well-known task in the research community: the submission of a scientific paper to a journal. To summarize this example, just remember that an author submits a paper to a journal, the editor receives it. He may either accept the paper for reviewing, or reject it in case the topics covered in the paper mismatch the journal scope. In the latter case, the author is notified about the editor's decision. An accepted paper is sent for evaluation to (at least) two reviewers. The reviewers read and provide their feedback on the paper before the deadline assigned by the editor arrives. Once the editor receives all the reviews, he makes his decision by comparing the reviewers' evaluations. This process can be long if the reviews are really different, or if the editor considers that a third review is needed. Thus, the editor must assess his options and time constraints, in order to choose the best alternative. If the paper is not rejected, the editor could: (a) conditionally accept the paper by requesting the authors for an improved version, which is verified by the editor or the reviewers, or (b) accept the paper with minimal suggested changes. If the final editor's decision is to reject the paper, the author is notified and receives the reviewers' comments. Otherwise, after receiving the new version, the editor sends the paper for publication.

The paper submission process requires interaction among different actors playing different roles: author, editor, reviewers and publisher. We decided to explore different ways for representing the interaction among actors involve in a group tasks, since the graphic representations found in the literature for modeling this type of tasks, and specifically for showing the interaction among actors often rely on a series of diagrams that quickly become over complicated to follow (c.f. Sect. 2). In the following section, we briefly present our better attempt for creating a clear visual representation of this group task.

4 Modeling Interaction Through a Series of Turns

In this representation, we identified the turns taken by each actor. We have grouped such turns, and named them with the first letter of each type of actor (A for author, E for editor, R for reviewer, and P for publisher) plus a subsequent number corresponding to the moment in which the turn is activated. However, some turns are more complex than others, since they have multiple outcomes. Thus, we added sub-turns represented by a lower case letter (see Fig. 1, turn E1a). In order to follow the task evolution, we introduced the TASK_STATUS parameter (cf. Sect. 5) to each arrow depicting a change of turns. Therefore, we create a representation that involves all the actors interacting in a task. This model is easy to understand, since we just have to identify the actor in turn, and follow the arrow that lands in the next actor, at the corresponding turn.

In Fig. 1 the task starts at turn A1 (highlighted with a ticker circle), and ends at either turn P1 (final version to be published) or A4 (paper rejection). In turns E2b and E4f waiting is necessary. That is why those turns are distinguished with a different background color. The arrows and legends shown in Fig. 1 correspond to the task execution in which a paper is conditionally accepted with minor revisions, and it is finally accepted for publication after a revised version is submitted. The turns that are not connected

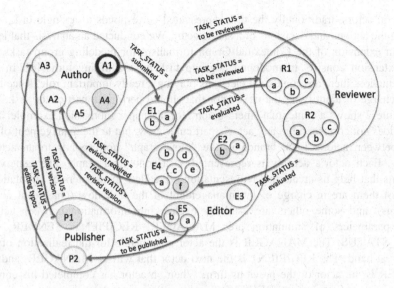

Fig. 1. Turns and sub-turns representation (Color figure online)

through arrows in Fig. 1 (e.g., turn A5, E2 and E3) correspond to turns that are activated in other scenarios (e.g., when a paper is rejected). In Fig. 1, the author submits the paper (turn A1). Then, the editor decides to accept the paper for review (turn E1a) and send it to at least two reviewers (turns R1 and R2). Reviewers evaluate the paper (turns R1a and R2a). Since the reviews match, the editor accepts the paper with minor changes (turn E4). Then, the author creates a revised version of the paper, and he submits it (turn A2). The editor evaluates the new version (turn E5), and decides to send the paper to the publisher (turn E5a). The publisher revises the paper, and asks the author to correct some typos (turn P2). The author corrects the typos and sends the final version to the publisher (turn A3). Finally, the publisher concludes the process (turn P1).

In Fig. 1, we are able to include the four types of actors involved in the group task. The Figure is cleaner and easier to read than some other attempts we tried (which turned out to be irrelevant for this paper), and the partial outcome of each turn is clearly identified. However, this representation takes a long time to build, since we have to identify the turns, sub-turns, and then construct the figure. Moreover, the lack of expressiveness of this diagram is a big drawback, since a deep knowledge of the group task is required to fully understand the interaction. Finally, the names of the turns, by themselves, do not provide any information regarding the actions that take place inside them.

5 The Turns Mechanism and Simulation Parameters

The Contextual-Graphs formalism was conceived to represent the ways a task can be performed. Thus, several actors can enrich a contextual graph by adding their own experiences to the model. Even though a contextual graph could contain the experience of several actors, traditionally the task represented corresponds to a single task, concerning the actions and decisions of a single actor. We conducted an analysis that leads us to an extension of the Contextual-Graph formalism for modeling group tasks [9]. This extension consists in modeling a group task by identifying turns [6]. In this representation, there are contextual elements playing a really important role, since they are in charge of identifying the next actor that should perform a part of the task.

Figure 2 shows a contextual "meta-graph" for the paper submission example. This graph does not correspond to any actor's particular view, but to the management of the turns between actors. Each branch in the "meta graph" corresponds to an actor's activity. Each actor's activity is represented as a contextual graph. The contextual elements that help us create this representation are called "parameters of simulation". Some of them are in charge of the management of the task flow (change of actors on focus), and some others are used for exchanging information between actors. These parameters of simulation are: MANAGER, RECIPIENT, SENDER, and TASK_STATUS. The MANAGER is the actor responsible for the realization of the subtask at hand. The RECIPIENT is the next actor that will be MANAGER, and the SENDER is the actor of the previous turn. When an actor has completed his current task, he informs to the correct RECIPIENT, who will perform the task corresponding to the SENDER and the shared context. The traversing of the graph is cyclic because at the start of the current turn, the MANAGER takes the value of the RECIPIENT assigned in the previous turn, and the corresponding branch is selected. Thus, at the end of a turn, the SENDER holds the value of the current MANAGER because the next actor needs to know who sent the focus. The cycle is created through MANAGER = RECIPIENT, making the initial working context of the current turn the final working context of the previous turn. The TASK_STATUS is a contextual element shared among the actors. In the paper submission example, TASK STATUS corresponds to the status of the document (e.g., submitted, reviewed, etc.). TASK STATUS is instantiated in the current turn and used (in a contextual element) in the next turn to identify the subtask to consider. This turns representation preserves and enhances the use of shared contextual elements, since a contextual element is instantiated by one actor and used by another.

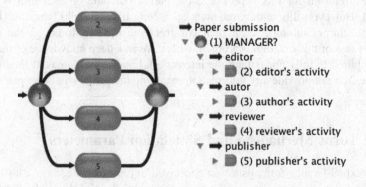

Fig. 2. The turns mechanism

6   Simulating Group Tasks in the CxG Software

The CxG software has been extended to provide the actor with a simulation component to follow the development of a practice. The concept of working context is vital for a task execution simulation as it concerns the contextual elements and their instantiations. These instantiations define the practice that should be followed to complete the simulated task. Specifically, the working context is composed of two parts [4]: (1) a static one containing the list of all the contextual elements present in a contextual graph and their known values; and (2) a dynamic one, corresponding to the list of contextual element instances that are known at simulation time.

The instantiation of a contextual element can be: (a) done prior to the practice development, (b) provided by the user during simulation, or (c) found by the simulator along the followed practice (e.g., the change of instantiation of a simulation parameter in an action). During a CxG simulation, a different instantiation of a simulation parameter implies a change of practice at the next turn. An instantiation may be altered by either an internal or an external event. The former event concerns a change in the instantiation of a contextual value triggered by an action found in the followed practice. The external event corresponds to an unpredicted event that has not yet been represented in the contextual graph yet.

The CxG software has been enriched with simulation capabilities. Figure 3 shows the start of the submission example. In this simulation, the first selected actor is the author and the TASK_STATUS is ready for submitting.

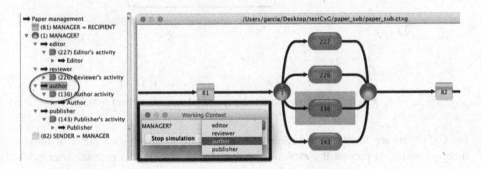

Fig. 3. Simulation of the first author turn

Figure 4 shows the simulation at the meta model granularity; in it, the activity corresponding to the author's turns is visited, and a new turn is found. Figure 5 presents the detailed evolution of the task. The simulation provided by the software is visually represented as a timed sequential change on the color of the components, from a gradient pattern to a solid darker color, and the arrows connecting such elements are colored in red instead of black.

Once the author has submitted the paper to the journal, the simulator identifies a new turn. The next MANAGER is the editor, who knows that the SENDER is the author, and the TASK_STATUS instantiation received is equal to "submitted". Since

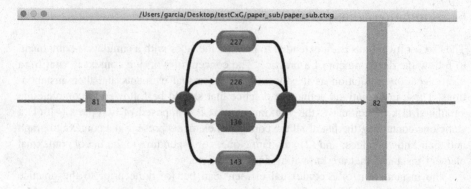

Fig. 4. General view of an author's paper submission (Color figure online)

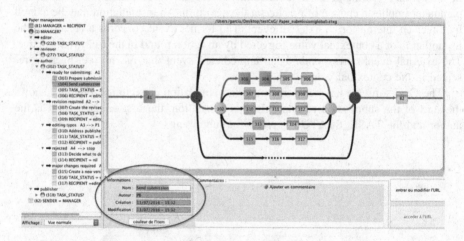

Fig. 5. An author submits a paper (Color figure online)

the CxG software knows already this information, there is only one piece of information missing to present the evolution of the second turn. In this case the user is in charge of selecting in a dialog box the value of the contextual element "suitable paper for journal?"

For this demonstration, the selected value is "yes". With this value the simulation of the second turn can start. As the dialog box in Fig. 6 shows, all the contextual elements corresponding to the current turn are presented, the ones already known from the previous turn are prefilled, and the actor is in charge of providing the missing information. However, the prefilled information can be changed at any time, providing a flexible experience to the actor. He can decide to skip the simulation of a turn or change the actor in turn at any time.

Figure 7 shows the completion of the editor's turn. Since the CxG software finds a new turn, a dialog box presents the values of the simulation parameters. The actor then decides if he wants to simulate the next turn with reviewer as MANAGER, editor as

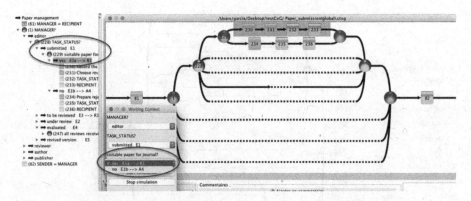

Fig. 6. The editor receives and accepts the paper for revision

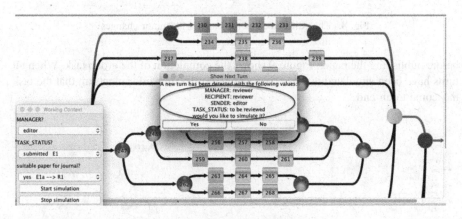

Fig. 7. The reviewers' turn is found

SENDER, and TASK_STATUS to "be reviewed". In such a turn, the reviewer accepts to evaluate the paper, and sends his comments to the editor.

Once the editor has received both reviews, he should make a decision on whether to accept the paper, but asking for major or minor changes, or to reject the paper. Figure 8 shows this editor's turn where the "fit to screen view" is enabled, allowing the actor to see the complete contextual graph. One also can note the visual support that the CxG software offers. When a new value for a contextual element is selected in the dialog box, the branch that is going to be traversed at simulation time is highlighted with a gray shade. In the next turn, the author is required to submit a revised version of his paper. In the dialog box, the user has to decide if he is interested in seeing the simulation of the next turn or not.

After the author has sent the revised version of his paper, the editor verifies it and decides if the process should continue or not. In case the author decides that the new paper version is satisfactory, he sends the paper to the publisher, which in turn communicate briefly with the author in case there are typos to correct, or any small issue

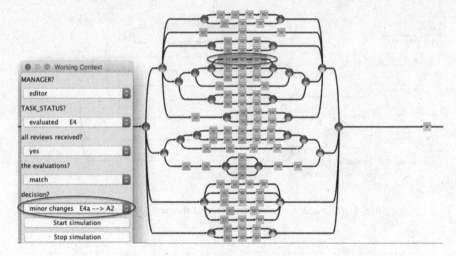

Fig. 8. The editor accepts the paper with minor changes

before publishing the paper. Figure 9 shows the completion of the group task. When all turns have been simulated, a message is shown to the user informing him that the task has come to an end.

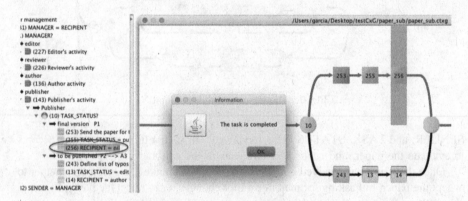

Fig. 9. The group task simulation has ended

The TACTIC project [6] used the tool in order to validate the simulation capabilities of the CxG software in a real world application. In such a project, the group task consists in monitoring the simulation of a small part of a battle field. There are two actors involved: the operator, and the simulator.

The operator is the team performing the task. In this case the task concerns "a recognition order". The simulator is in charge of tracking the evolution of the task from three different sources of information: spatial coordinates of objects (the field map), temporal coordinates (the chronology of events), and socio-technical coordinates

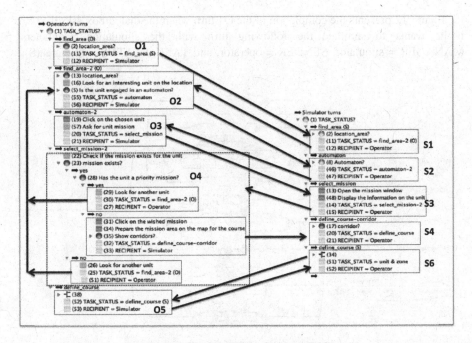

Fig. 10. The TACTIC project turns [6]

(ODB, the order of battle). Figure 10 presents the turn movement between actors. On the left side the operator's turns are identified by an O plus a number, and on the right side, the simulator turns are marked with an S plus a number.

Figure 11 presents the meta-graph of the TACTIC simulation; the two branches corresponding to the actors are clearly identified in this Figure. To start the O1 turn, the simulation parameters are set as following: MANAGER = operator, TASK_STATUS = find area(O).

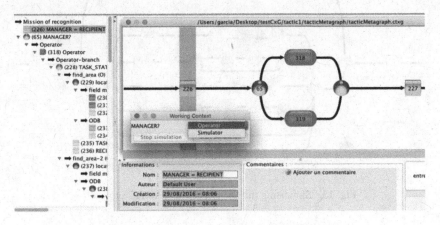

Fig. 11. Simulating the O1 turn of the TACTIC project

Figure 12 presents the completion of the O1 turn when the dialog box asks the user if he wants to simulate the following turn with the simulation parameters: MANAGER = simulator, SENDER = operator, and TASK_STATUS = find area(S).

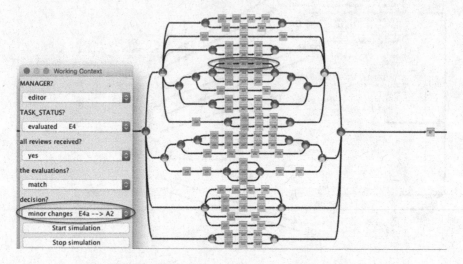

Fig. 12. S1 turn of the TACTIC project is found

Finally, in Fig. 13, it can be seen that the simulator asks the user to provide the value missing to start the simulation of the S1 turn. When the simulation of a turn has finished, and a new turn is found, the user has the choice to simulate it or not.

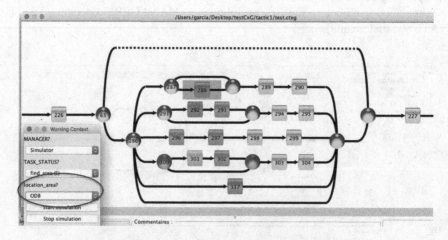

Fig. 13. Simulating the S1 turn of the TACTIC project

7   Conclusions and Future Work

The CxG software has provided decision makers with functionalities to explore contextual graphs, in order to learn new practices and/or assess their options by analyzing the effects that choosing one path could bring. Such functionalities have been of great use in multiple applications and fields. However, in order to provide actors with a better and more helpful experience, we have incorporated simulation capabilities to the software, through the introduction of the working-context concept. Moreover, by paying attention to the proposed works for modeling group tasks, we found out that they always fall in an over complicated visual representation that includes several diagrams. Thus, we accepted the challenge of exploring the Contextual-Graphs formalism potentialities to incorporate group tasks modeling in an easy and comprehensive way. We refined the turns mechanism proposed in [9], and added simulation capabilities to the CxG software to match such a proposal.

The current version of the software provides a practical and a cognitive interface for manipulating the working context, which allows actors to instantiate contextual elements that are dependent of the task. Simulation parameters were identified to determine: (a) the change of turns among actors involved in the group task, and (b) the shared context corresponding to important information on the current state of the task. Such simulation parameters are automatically identified by the software in order to show the development of the corresponding turn and practice. Each time a turn has been simulated, the software informs the actor of the current state of the simulation parameters, and ask him if he wants to simulate the next turn (in case there is one). The simulation of the task stops when the actor decides so, or when by comparing the initial and final working context, the software is not able to detect any other turn.

Although, the current implementation of the software proposes many visual advantages in modeling and understanding group tasks, the software could provide a more interactive experience. Moreover, we aim at incorporating a "recording functionality", in which the user could generate an animated GIF of the simulation he has just completed. This would be useful for training purposes. Regarding the turn mechanism, we are exploring ways to efficiently represent more complex interactions among actors (e.g., conflict resolution, consensus, and negotiations).

Acknowledgements.   We thank the CONACyT (Consejo Nacional de Ciencia y Tecnología) for funding Kimberly García's post-doctoral fellowship at LIP6, UPMC.

References

1. Attieh, E., Capron, F., Brézillon, P.: Context-based modeling of an anatomo-cyto-pathology department workflow for quality control. In: Brézillon, P., Blackburn, P., Dapoigny, R. (eds.) CONTEXT 2013. LNCS (LNAI), vol. 8175, pp. 235–247. Springer, Heidelberg (2013). doi:10.1007/978-3-642-40972-1_18
2. Beyer H., Holtzblatt, K.: Contextual Design: A Customer-Centered Approach to Systems Designs. Morgan Kaufmann Series in Interactive Technologies (1997)

3. Brézillon, P.: Context modeling: task model and practice model. In: Kokinov, B., Richardson, D.C., Roth-Berghofer, T.R., Vieu, L. (eds.) CONTEXT 2007. LNCS (LNAI), vol. 4635, pp. 122–135. Springer, Heidelberg (2007). doi:10.1007/978-3-540-74255-5_10

4. Brézillon, P.: Context-centered tools for intelligent assistant systems. In: Brézillon, P., Gonzalez, A.J. (eds.) Context in Computing, pp. 97–110. Springer, New York (2014)

5. Brézillon, P., Attieh, E., Capron, F.: Modeling glocal search in a decision-making process. In: DSS 2.0 Supporting Decision Making with New Technologies, Frontiers in Artificial Intelligence and Applications, pp. 80–91. IOS Press, Amsterdam (2014)

6. Brézillon, P.: Contextual modeling of group activities. In: Brézillon, P., et al. (eds.) CONTEXT 2017, The International Conference in Modeling and Using Context (CONTEXT-2017), LNAI, vol. 10257, pp. 113–126. Springer, Cham (2017)

7. Carlsen, S.: Action port model: a mixed paradigm conceptual workflow modeling language. In: Proceedings of the 3rd IFCIS International Conference on Cooperative Information Systems. IEEE (1998)

8. Fan, X., Zhang, R., Li, L., Brézillon, P.: Contextualizing workflow in cooperative design. In: Proceedings of the 15th International Conference on Computer Supported Cooperative Work in Design (CSCWD-11), pp. 17–22. IEEE, Lausanne (2011)

9. García, K., Brézillon, P.: A contextual model of turns for group work. In: Christiansen, H., Stojanovic, I., Papadopoulos, G.A. (eds.) CONTEXT 2015. LNCS (LNAI), vol. 9405, pp. 243–256. Springer, Cham (2015). doi:10.1007/978-3-319-25591-0_18

10. Larman, C.: Applying UML and Patterns: An Introduction to Object-Oriented Analysis and Design and Iterative Development, 3rd edn. Prentice Hall, Upper Saddle River (2004)

11. Molina, A.I., Gallardo, J., Redondo, M.A., Ortega, M., Giraldo, W.J.: Metamodel-driven definition of a visual modeling language for specifying interactive groupware applications: an empirical study. J. Syst. Softw. **86**(7), 1772–1789 (2013). Elsevier

12. Paternó, F.: ConcurTaskTrees: an engineered notation for task models. In: The Hand-Book of Task Analysis for Human-Computer Interaction, pp. 483–503. Lawrence Erlbaum Associates (2004)

13. Pomerol, J.-Ch., Brezillon, P.: Dynamics between contextual knowledge and proceduralized context. In: Bouquet, P., Benerecetti, M., Serafini, L., Brézillon, P., Castellani, F. (eds.) CONTEXT 1999. LNCS (LNAI), vol. 1688, pp. 284–295. Springer, Heidelberg (1999). doi:10.1007/3-540-48315-2_22

14. Searle, J.R., Vanderveken, D.: Foundations of Illocutionary Logic. Cambridge University Press, Cambridge (1985)

15. Van Welie, M., Van Der Veer, G.: Groupware task analysis. In: Handbook of Cognitive Task Design. Human Factors and Ergonomics, pp. 447–476 (2003)

Constraint-Based Context Model for Business Process Integration in a Higher Education Domain

Jorge E. Giraldo[1,2][✉], Demetrio Arturo Ovalle[1],
and Flavia Maria Santoro[3]

[1] Facultad de Minas, Universidad Nacional de Colombia, Medellín, Colombia
{jegiraldp,dovalle}@unal.edu.co,
jegiraldo@elpoli.edu.co
[2] Politécnico Colombiano Jaime Isaza Cadavid, Medellín, Colombia
[3] Universidad Federal del Estado de Rio de Janeiro, Rio de Janeiro, Brazil
flavia.santoro@uniriotec.br

Abstract. The Business Process integration focuses on consolidation of process models in order to changes propagation. The aim of this paper is to propose a constraint-based contextual approach for business process integration. The context model description is through contextual situations represented by a constraint set as well as an inference mechanism. In order to validate the proposed model a case study regarding an admission process of postgraduate careers is perform. The main conclusion of this research is that the contextual variables used in the model directly depend on the process's execution domain and in consequence affect the possible updates on process models.

Keywords: Business process integration · Context model · Contextual situations · Constraints · Academic management

1 Introduction

The business process integration (BPI) is considered as the consolidation of several processes in order to implement updating procedures on them. The updating goal is either to generate new processes from a process merge or to update changes on processes using propagation mechanisms [1].

In this way, the propagation of changes consists in updating changes from a reference model to its associated variants but guaranteeing its performance and information regarding the functionality of the business involved [2]. Thus, it is necessary to analyze the consistency of the changes propagated to the variants considering aspects of the domain as well as the associated context [3].

Based on the above, we propose a context model depicted through situations being formalize by means of constraints [4]. The constraint representation considers not only the domain organizational information but also the kind of structural change that has generated the creation of a new variant. The changes can be addition or deletion of elements of the structure of the process; therefore, some contextual elements in the domain are labeled when in such situations they affect the performance of the variant.

P. Brézillon et al. (Eds.): CONTEXT 2017, LNAI 10257, pp. 165–174, 2017.
DOI: 10.1007/978-3-319-57837-8_13

For the model validation, a academic process was taken as the application domain, specifically the Postgraduate Program Admission at the *Universidad Nacional de Colombia* [5]. It is important to highlight that this process is characterized by its dynamism and dependence along with own actors (aspirants) attributes such as research experience, geographical location, student scholarships, among others.

The rest of the paper is as following. Section 2 presents the related works on BPI and context-based process modeling. Section 3 details the context model for process integration, the constraint based domain contextual situations definition and its application in the academic domain. Section 4 presents the validation of the proposed model through the design of a case study concerning the admission process to postgraduate careers; likewise a reflexion of its application in others domain as "coffee production" and "academic self-assessment". Finally, an analysis and discussion of the results obtained, as well as conclusions are presented.

2 Related Works

This section presents the most representative works in the area of business process integration, as well as the approaches concerning the context modeling for the analysis and reasoning of processes and their execution.

Weidlich et al. [6] propose process integration from the processes data so that from a database schema the semantic relationships among the elements are validate in order to construct a new process model. Schubert and Legner [7] demonstrate that through the data representation at several abstraction levels a better control of their consistency regarding the execution domain is achieved.

Mendling et al. [8] use the role description involved in the process execution in order to determine their conformity among them. Sebu and Ciocarlie [9] propose an integration mechanism based on similarity measures among processes to select the processes with greater degree of similarity and based on this proceeds to perform the change update.

La Rosa et al. [10] propose a model to align the process resulting from integration with integrated processes. Based on this, a method is defined for the construction of process models from model collections. From the point of view of context modeling and business process Weidlich et al. [11] focus their work in propagating model changes through previously aligned processes. Pretzel et al. [12] propose a mechanism to provide flexibility to process models through a rule-based representational analysis. On the other hand, Milanovic et al. [13] present a method to identify the patterns of changes in processes.

Saidani and Nurcan [14] develop a strategy for the use of meta-models that allows the identification of the context which is useful to business requirements elicitation. Ploesser et al. [15] expose the importance of handling the context to business process management and how companies should be prepared to deal with it. They propose possible applications for discovery, analysis, and automation of business processes.

Having variant repositories becomes important due to their direct relationship with the creation domain, therefore, the same process can generate different behaviors, depending on the execution context. Bucchiarone et al. [16] present a verification mechanism using a domain context based on semantic metrics. Lassoued et al. [17] propose a solution involving the grouping of process collection based on attributes in common for which the algorithm K-Means is used.

Taking into consideration the above we can establish that contextual information in the execution of business processes plays an important role in the definition of contextual dependencies. In consequence it is necessary to look into the design of reasoning mechanisms through a context model as well as the contextual entities related to the specific process application domain.

3 Context Model Proposed

The context model definition is from contextual considerations expressed through constraints at each level of information. The contextual considerations are formalized by associated situations domain's values. Based on the above, a representation based on functional layers is proposed and then to allowing the identification of levels and thus to associate contextual information to the stages of the integration process, promoting the reasoning about it [18].

It is important to highlight, that the context model should consider the information concerning the following elements of the process: the organization or institution where it executes, the data flow, the data types, and the process structure given in terms of activities and control structures.

3.1 Contextual Considerations in Process Integration

Considering that the business processes integration constitutes a flow of data related to its domain of execution organization where it is executed and other variables a systemic approach is proposed in which information can be located at different levels of abstraction.

Physical Contextual Considerations: These considerations take into account the type and information of source data. It also considers the process structure in terms of activities.

Consideration-1: Process actors: The description of the actors should be associated to a domain of execution represented by conceptual roles in order to facilitate the validation of competences and previous knowledge.

Consideration-2: Process domain. The geographic location of the domain represents different instances of the business rules and associated institutions. Both the variants and the reference model must include it in its representation.

Consideration-3: Variant event creation: It includes the events that gave rise to the variants. From previous event logs it is possible to analyze integration logs based on events in order to avoid inconsistencies.

Consideration-4: Domain representation: The representation mechanism must allow making inferences about the variants in order to apply a matching and retrieval reasoning.

Logical Contextual Considerations: These considerations take into account the organization and competencies of the actors in the process. It also controls information associated with the execution domain.

> *Consideration-5: Similarity based Reasoning.* For selection and retrieval of variants a comparison should be performed based on the degree of similarity. Grouping techniques can be used for comparison. Similarity techniques focus their operation on information related to activities.
>
> *Consideration-6: Variant Prioritization:* Once the variants are selected they must be sorted according to the degree of dependency to the identified domain and contextual alerts. In this case the domain will include information concerning the data sources and resources employed.
>
> *Consideration-7: Process Integration Regression:* The regression refers to the optimization of the integration process results and can begot by comparing obtained versus expected results.
>
> *Consideration-8: Integration Report:* Consideration should be given through the design of a recommendation interface which allows decision-making during the propagation of changes stage.

Therefore, constraints can be defined from ranges of values associated with the information of the logical or physical levels. Each contextual consideration includes the ranges of values at each level to determine the validity of the presence of a contextual situation. Finally the process model is labeled with a contextual alert and thus allow the support to the decision making.

3.2 Formalization of Contextual Situations

The constraints definitions use the approach of constraint satisfaction problems in order to reduce the search space. The ranges of domain's values are related with the domain concepts.

Based on Carvalho [19] we propose the representation of the following constraint-based situations which define the context model for process integration.

Situation 1 - Given an addition event – Event(add) – this situation occurs when a contextual element $-CtxE$-is affected by an Organizational Rule $-OR_r$-hover a domain element; since this situation is true so a contextual priority $-CtxP$-is activated.

$$St(Event(add), CtxE) \wedge Org_R(domainE) \equiv CtxP(active < -ok) \qquad (1)$$

Situation 2 - Unlike Situation 1, this one is based on a delete structural event – Ev(delete). In addition, it includes a priority contextual activation.

$$St(Event(delete), CtxE) \wedge Org_R(domainE) \equiv CtxP(active < -ok) \qquad (2)$$

Situation 3 - Given an addition event – Ev(add) – on a contextual element –*eCtx*- and a restriction –R_{Og}-is satisfied hover a domain element then a contextual priority –*pCtx*-is activated.

$$St(Event(add), CtxE) \wedge Op_R(domainE) \equiv CtxP(active < - ok) \qquad (3)$$

Situation 4 - Unlike Situation 3, this one is based on a deletion event – Ev(del) and its outcome also involves a priority contextual activation.

$$St(Event(delete), CtxE) \wedge Op_R(domainE) \equiv CtxP(active < - ok) \qquad (4)$$

3.3   Change Propagation Module Proposed

A reasoning mechanism is proposed to implement the context model of process integration focus on change propagation. This reasoning is based on the development of a propagation algorithm considering structural changes among process variants (see Fig. 1).

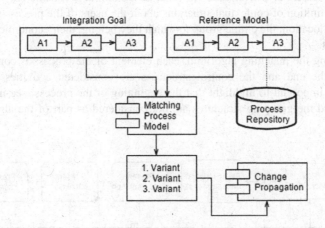

Fig. 1. Change propagation module for BPI.

The algorithm starts from the application of similarity metrics using complementary process mining techniques such as decision trees and clustering [20]. The process takes as input the definition of an integration goal (represented as a process model) that describes the structural changes that must be propagated from the reference model to its variants.

For the variants retrieval it was used a classification and grouping algorithm which considers as selection variables the contextual attributes being formalized through situations that are dependent on structural changes events.

The change propagation mechanism has as main component a ranking based on defined contextual situations. This is the way it could be demonstrated that the actor context of the process can affect the performance of the process after propagations.

Subsequently a merger among the recovered variants is performed in order to carry out the propagation and then processes will be separated again in order to assess the effects produced by changes.

4   Model Validation

The validation of the context model is composed of three elements: the case study description, a log of executions, and an inference algorithm. From the situations already identified by the algorithm a contextual filter is applied that allows improving the selection of processes to integrate.

4.1   Case Study Description

In order to validate the proposed model a case study regarding the admission process of postgraduate careers at Universidad Nacional de Colombia is considered. The process allows the definition of contextual situations about the users of the process such as the geographical location, the ethnic group to which they belong, their economic condition, among others.

Concerning the matching algorithm, each element of the process is considered an activity, so the end and the control structures are considered activities within the process. It is important to highlight that the beginning of the process (see initial circle on Fig. 2) and the grouping structures are not considered as part of the algorithm.

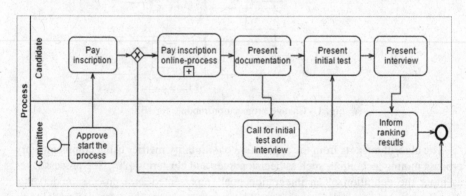

Fig. 2. Admission postgraduate process at the Universidad Nacional de Colombia. Based on UNAL, 2015

Based on the above, from a total of 11 activities only 2 of them are susceptible to contextual situations considering that there will be context labels within the domain, which allow the analysis of possible situations that arise.

Activity 3 – Pay admission fees: this activity depends on the geographic location of the applicant. A related situation may be that the student is located in a region of the country where it is necessary to pay for other means, because the disbursement of resources is done directly through a state scholarship.

Activity 6 – Call for initial test and interview: Due to the importance of this activity, this can only be executed by the admissions committee, however, there may be a situation where such a role lacks its work and needs to be replaced. In this case, the process considers the competencies of other positions to suggest a replacement, omitting in some cases the most obvious response within the organizational chart of the organization.

4.2 Logs Execution Processes

To analyze the process behavior we proceed to generate 100 logs of executions taking as main element the execution probability of a determined flow. The flow is given in terms of the transitions between each of the activities (control structures included). Each of the executions varies the execution probability of each of the flows.

Figure 3 presents an example of the probability to execute the flows of a process. Thus by making the probability dependent by using context variables it is possible to identify situations that generate different executions for the process. According to A3 in Fig. 3, for instance, this activity gets a probability of 80% since its control structure and data allow it.

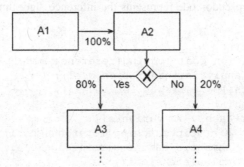

Fig. 3. Structure of log execution process.

Based on the proposed structure, the executions vary according to manipulated variables from the domain that affect the context through contextual situations.

Table 1 presents the first 15 of 100 executions performed for the case study. It is observed that in some executions the Activity 12 (End of the process) is reached and in others only until Activity 3 (System is not enabled). However, if domain values are modified then some situations are generated which vary the executions.

Table 1. Log executions

Log	Control 1	Control 2	Path
1	True	False	[A1, A2, A3, A4, A5, A6, A7, A8, A9, A10]
2	True	False	[A1, A2, A3, A4, A5, A6, A7, A8, A9, A10]
3	True	True	[A1, A2, A3, A4, A5, A6, A7, A8, A9, A10, A11, A12]
4	True	False	[A1, A2, A3, A4, A5, A6, A7, A8, A9, A10]
5	True	False	[A1, A2, A3, A4, A5, A6, A7, A8, A9, A10]
6	False	False	[A1, A2, A3]
7	False	True	[A1, A2, A3]
8	True	True	[A1, A2, A3, A4, A5, A6, A7, A8, A9, A10, A11, A12]
9	False	False	[A1, A2, A3]
10	True	False	[A1, A2, A3, A4, A5, A6, A7, A8, A9, A10]
11	True	True	[A1, A2, A3, A4, A5, A6, A7, A8, A9, A10, A11, A12]
12	False	True	[A1, A2, A3]
13	True	True	[A1, A2, A3, A4, A5, A6, A7, A8, A9, A10, A11, A12]
14	False	True	[A1, A2, A3]
15	True	True	[A1, A2, A3, A4, A5, A6, A7, A8, A9, A10, A11, A12]

4.3 Context Reasoning

Once the execution logs are generated an inference algorithm is applied based on the comparison performed among the variants concerning structure and semantic. This algorithm is designed in order to select and identify contextual labels from declared situations. The next pseudo-code represents the inference algorithm we propose.

```
inference():
  integration_goal_loading(reference_model);
  change_analysis(integration_goal);
  variants[] = variants_retrieval();
  matching():
      for-each v in variants[]:
          sintatic_matching(referenceModel, v[i]);
          semantic_matching(referenceModel, v[i]);
          calculate_simil();
          groups=clustering();
      end-for-each
  end-matching

contextFiltering(identifiedSituations(), groups);
if(analysis_data()<-ok):
  generate_report(groups);
else:matching();

end_inference
```

The algorithm allows the execution of iterations by modifying the context-dependent values that affect the situations. In this way, external data associated with the domain can be used which represent specific attributes within the process context.

5 Conclusions and Future Work

The business process integration focuses on the generation of a new process in order to propagate changes from a reference model. However, it is necessary to consider variables associated to the domain that can affect the process execution, this is due to the presence of contextual situations associated.

Due to the above, it is necessary to define a context model, which is represented by information constraints associated with abstraction levels. Thus, through the formalization of contextual situations gives way to the realization of inferences in order to identify and select contextual elements susceptible to get variations on values according to the process domain.

The use of matching techniques offers precision in the search and retrieval of variants; therefore, it is necessary to explore those kinds of techniques in order to define the most appropriate solutions oriented to the context management.

As future work, the modeling of contextual situations in formal logics is proposed in order to implement such artificial intelligence techniques that allow the execution of clustering algorithms and the reasoning mechanism.

References

1. Morrison, E.D., Menzies, A., Koliadis, G., Ghose, A.K.: Business process integration: method and analysis. In: Proceedings of the Sixth Asia-Pacific Conference on Conceptual Modeling-Volume 96, pp. 29–38. Australian Computer Society, Inc., January 2009
2. La Rosa, M., Dumas, M., Uba, R., Dijkman, R.: Business process model merging: an approach to business process consolidation. ACM Trans. Softw. Eng. Methodol. (TOSEM) 22(2), Article No. 11 (2013)
3. Gerth, C., Küster, J.M., Engels, G.: Language-independent change management of process models. In: Schürr, A., Selic, B. (eds.) MODELS 2009. LNCS, vol. 5795, pp. 152–166. Springer, Heidelberg (2009). doi:10.1007/978-3-642-04425-0_12
4. Kumar, A., Yao, W.: Design and management of flexible process variants using templates and rules. Comput. Ind. 63(2), 112–130 (2012)
5. UNAL-Universidad Nacional de Colombia. Manual del Sistema Integrado de Gestión (2008). http://www.simegebogota.unal.edu.co/. Accessed November 2016
6. Weidlich, M., Polyvyanyy, A., Desai, N., Mendling, J., Weske, M.: Process compliance analysis based on behavioural profiles. Inf. Syst. (IS) 36(7), 1009–1025 (2011). Elsevier B.V.
7. Schubert, P., Legner, C.: B2B integration in global supply chains: an identification of technical integration scenarios. J. Strateg. Inf. Syst. (2011)
8. Mendling, J., Strembeck, M., Recker, J.: Factors of process model comprehension – findings from a series of experiments. Decis. Support Syst. 53(1), 195–206 (2012)

9. Sebu, L., Ciocarlie, H.: Merging business processes for a common workflow in an organizational collaborative scenario. In: 2015 19th International Conference on System Theory, Control and Computing (ICSTCC), pp. 134–139 (2015)

10. La Rosa, M., Dumas, M., Uba, R., Dijkman, R.: Business process model merging: an approach to business process consolidation. ACM Trans. Softw. Eng. Methodol. (2012)

11. Weidlich, M., Mendling, J., Weske, M.: Propagating changes between aligned process models. J. Syst. Softw. (JSS) (2012)

12. Prezel, V., Gaševic, D., Milanovic, M.: Representational analysis of business process and business rule languages. In: 1st International Workshop on Business Models, Business Rules and Ontologies (BuRO 2010), September 2010

13. Milanovic, M., Gaševic, D., Rocha, L.: Modeling flexible business processes with business rule patterns. In: The Fifteenth IEEE International EDOC Conference (EDOC 2011), Helsinki, Finland, 29 August–2 September 2011

14. Saidani, O., Nurcan, S.: Context-awareness for adequate business process modelling. In: RCIS 2009, pp. 177–186 (2009)

15. Ploesser, K., Recker, J., Rosemann, M.: Challenges in the context-aware management of business processes: a multiple case study. In: ECIS 2011 (2011)

16. Bucchiarone, A., Mezzina, C., Pistore, M., Raik, H., Valetto, G.: Collective adaptation in process-based systems. In: SASO 2014, pp. 151–156 (2014)

17. Lassoued, Y., Bouzguenda, L., Mahmoud, T.: Context-aware business process versions management. Int. J. e-Collab. (IJeC) **12**(3), 7–33 (2016)

18. Berente, N., Vandenbosch, B., Aubert, B.: Information flows and business process integration. Bus. Process Manag. J. **15**(1), 119–141 (2009)

19. Carvalho, J., Santoro, F., Revoredo, K.: A method to infer the need to update situations in business process adaptation. Comput. Ind. **71**, 128–143 (2015). ISSN 0166-3615

20. van der Aalst, W.M.P.: Process Mining: Discovery, Conformance and Enhancement of Business Processes. Springer, Heidelberg (2011)

The ContextAct@A4H Real-Life Dataset of Daily-Living Activities

Activity Recognition Using Model Checking

Paula Lago[1]([✉]), Fréderic Lang[2,3], Claudia Roncancio[2],
Claudia Jiménez-Guarín[1], Radu Mateescu[2,3], and Nicolas Bonnefond[3]

[1] Systems and Computing Engineering Department, Universidad de Los Andes,
Bogotá, Colombia
{pa.lago52,cjimenez}@uniandes.edu.co
[2] Univ. Grenoble Alpes, CNRS, Grenoble, France
Claudia.Roncancio@imag.fr
[3] Inria, Grenoble, France
{Frederic.Lang,Radu.Mateescu,Nicolas.Bonnefond}@inria.fr

Abstract. Research on context management and activity recognition
in smart environments is essential in the development of innovative well
adapted services. This paper presents two main contributions. First, we
present *ContextAct@A4H*, a new real-life dataset of daily living activities
with rich context data (This research is supported by the Amiqual4Home
Innovation Factory, http://amiqual4home.inria.fr funded by the ANR
(ANR-11-EQPX-0002)). It is a high quality dataset collected in a smart
apartment with a dense but non intrusive sensor infrastructure. Second,
we present the experience of using temporal logic and model checking
for activity recognition. Temporal logic allows specifying activities as
complex events of object usage which can be described at different granularity. It also expresses temporal ordering between events thus palliating
a limitation of ontology based activity recognition. The results on using
the CADP toolbox for activity recognition in the real life collected data
are very good.

Keywords: Smart home · Context · Activity recognition ·
Temporal logic

1 Introduction

Activity recognition in smart environments is a necessary step for the development of innovative services. In the health-care domain, recognizing activities
of daily living (ADL) enables health status monitoring, functional assessments
and smart assistance. Despite the broad efforts made in recent years to improve
activity recognition, ADL recognition (e.g. cooking, washing dishes, showering)
is still not commercially available as is physical activity recognition (e.g. running, cycling). ADL recognition is complex and some barriers have hindered its

© Springer International Publishing AG 2017
P. Brézillon et al. (Eds.): CONTEXT 2017, LNAI 10257, pp. 175–188, 2017.
DOI: 10.1007/978-3-319-57837-8_14

passage from laboratory settings to real-life. One of these barriers is the difficulty of evaluating methods in real-life scenarios, which differ widely from the scripted scenarios that are usually used for testing activity recognition algorithms. Real-life scenarios are inherently imbalanced, not only because some activities are more frequent than others but also because of the different durations of the activities. Learning from imbalanced data poses new challenges and can impact the performance of traditional algorithms [9]. Moreover, in real-life there are, often several ongoing activities, making it challenging to recognize the "interesting" ones [12]. More real-life datasets and shared activity labels are needed to allow researchers evaluating their proposals and comparing the results of their recognition methods [3].

Activity recognition methods are broadly classified into data-based and knowledge-based [4]. Data based methods use machine learning or data mining algorithms to learn a model of activities. However, supervised methods require labeled data which is often hard to acquire. On the other hand, knowledge based methods specify the semantics of activities to be inferred from sensor measurements. Ontologies that specify both objects used and other characteristics of an activity (e.g. actor, location, duration) is one of the most used knowledge-based method for their ability to specify concepts at different granularity and their reasoning capabilities on uncertain knowledge. Nevertheless, ontologies lack support for the temporal characterization of activities [19] which is an important aspect of activity recognition as they take place during a span of time. For ADL recognition it is important to consider context information such as environmental conditions, visitor presence, current location and part of day [14]. Nonetheless, the usefulness of different context variables has not been proven in real-life scenarios due to the lack of available data in the same dataset.

In this paper we present two main contributions. First, we present a real-life dataset of daily living activities. This new dataset, named *ContextAct@A4H*, will be publicly available with reference to this paper. *ContextAct@A4H* includes sensor raw data reflecting the context as well as standard daily living annotated activities. Context information can help study how contextual changes affect user behavior and preferences [14]. To the best of our knowledge it will be the first public available dataset including such rich real-life data. *ContextAct@A4H* was gathered at the Amiqual4Home flat using a large variety of sensors to improve the potential reuse of the data. Researchers can choose the desired "configuration" according to their evaluation requirements. We highlight the experience of collecting the dataset and some lessons learned in the process. The second contribution of this paper, is the experience of using temporal logic for activity recognition. Using temporal logic allows specifying activities as complex events of object usage which can be described at different granularity. It also expresses temporal order between events thus palliating a limitation of ontology based activity recognition. The results on using the CADP toolbox [7] for ADL recognition in the real life collected data are very good.

The rest of this paper is organized as follows: Sect. 2 presents the experience and the setting up of our experience to collect *ContextAct@A4H*, a real life dataset of ADL and context data. Section 3 presents the formalism of temporal logic used for ADL recognition in real life settings. Section 4 presents the results of using temporal logic in the recognition of ADL in the *ContextAct@A4H* dataset. In Sect. 5 we present a summary of related work in activity recognition methods and real-life datasets. Finally, in Sect. 6 we present the conclusions of this work and research perspectives.

2   Amiqual4Home System Architecture and Experience Setup

Amiqual4Home is an experimental platform consisting of a smart apartment, a rapid prototyping platform and tools for observing human activity. For collecting the *ContextAct@A4H* dataset of activities of daily living, a 28 years old woman lived in the apartment during one week in July 2016 and three weeks in November 2016. The woman is a part of the research group designing the experiment.

In the following we first describe the sensing infrastructure at the apartment and then present the activity annotation process and the dataset itself.

2.1   Sensing Infrastructure at the Smart Home

The Amiqual4Home apartment is equipped with 219 sensors and actuators. To make activity monitoring non-intrusive, in our experience all sensors are ambient sensors. No wearable sensors nor cameras were used for this experiment. Sensors allow observing both object usage and context conditions of each room and the exterior. Measuring context conditions is one of the new contributions of the *ContextAct@A4H* dataset with respect to other publicly available datasets.

We measured the following context variables: temperature, CO2, noise, humidity, presence and music information for each room and weather information for the exterior. Appliance and object usage are measured through electric/water consumption sensors, contact sensors and state change sensors (for lamps, curtains and switches). These measurements are precise indicators of object usage. Other sensors are indirect measures of object usage such as pressure sensor in the bed. The main advantage of the sensing methods we used is that sensors do not interfere with the normal use of objects (no RFID tags that need to be taken care of for example). Table 1 presents a summary of the sensing infrastructure. Some sensors, as those related with energy consumption, are integrated in a single device.

Amiqual4Home uses the OpenHab[1] integration platform for all the sensors and actuators installed. Sensors use different communication protocols such as KNX, MQQT or UPnP to send measurements to the central server. To preserve privacy, only local network access is permitted to the sensing infrastructure, no cloud platforms are used. The general architecture of the platform is shown in Fig. 1.

---

[1] http://www.openhab.org/.

Table 1. Sensing devices deployed at the Amiqual4Home apartment

Sensing devices (# variables)	Measured property	Locations
Interaction sensors		
Water consumption meters (15)	Hot or Cold water faucet usage	Handwasher, Shower, Toilet, Sink
Power consumption meters (11)	Appliance usage (direct measure)	Stove, fridge, exhaust fan, washing machine, electric dishwasher and heating systems (5)
Voltage consumption meters (11)	Appliance usage (direct measure)	Stove, fridge, exhaust fan, washing machine, electric dishwasher and heating systems (5)
Current consumption meters (11)	Appliance usage (direct measure)	Stove, fridge, exhaust fan, washing machine, electric dishwasher and heating systems (5)
Other electric-related meters (Energy, frequency, power factor, counter status) (44)	Appliance usage (direct measure)	Stove, fridge, exhaust fan, washing machine, electric dishwasher and heating systems (5)
Pressure Sensors (1)	Presence on furniture	Bed
Contact sensor (21)	Door/window state (open—closed)	Kitchen gabinets (5), fridge, drawers (2), Bedroom door, Studio door, Bathroom door, Main entrance door, Closet door, Terrace door, All windows (8)
Curtain aperture sensor (8)	Curtain state (open—close and aperture percentage)	All curtains
Lamp state sensor (17)	Lamp state (on—off and luminosity percentage)	Living room (4), Bedroom (4), Studio (1), Kitchen (2), Floor hall (2), Main entrance hall (2), Bathroom (2)
Smart electric outlet (3)	Appliance on—off status	TV, Coffee machine, blender
Hue lamp state (5)	Hue lamp state (on—off), color, intensity	Living room (3), Bedroom, Studio
Switches (54)	Change of lamp/curtain/music state	Throughout the apartment
Thermostat (5)	Thermostat temperature	Living room, Dining room, Bedroom, Studio, Bathroom
Context feature sensors		
Microphone (7)	Noise levels	Kitchen, Living room, Dining room, Floor hall, Main entrance hall, Bedroom, Studio
Infrared sensor (6)	Movement in room	Kitchen, Living room, Dining room, Bedroom, Studio, Bathroom
Luminosity sensor (6)	Luminosity level in room	Kitchen, Living room, Dining room, Bedroom, Studio, Bathroom
CHT device (12)	CO_2, Temperature and relative humidity of room	Kitchen, Living room, Bedroom, Bathroom
OpenWeather information (14)	Exterior weather variables	Exterior
Music information (25)	Speaker status, Music volume, Song title, Song artist, Song genre	Kitchen, Bedroom, Studio, Living room, Bathroom
Indoor positioning system (1)[a]	Inhabitant position	Wearable device

[a] Used only during the fall period of the experiment

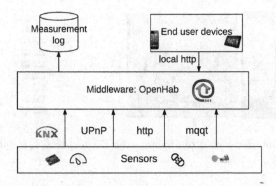

Fig. 1. General architecture of the data collection system

2.2   Activity Annotation

The choice of activities to be annotated was motivated by two main concerns: being in concordance with available datasets and with the classification of basic and instrumental ADL that can be measured at home. Some activities can be measured at different granularity levels. For example eating is annotated as eating breakfast in the ARAS dataset [2]. We chose high level labels to reduce the number of different activities preserving the desired semantics while considering time of day as part of context. Some activities were not annotated (like doing laundry) but the event using washing machine fully corresponds with this activity (same for watching tv). The following is the list of annotated and measured activities.

Activities of Daily Living

– Bathing/Showering (Annotated)
– Toileting (Annotated)
– Feeding/Eating (Annotated)
– Mobility (Unannotated but measured by bspoon sensor)
– Dressing (Unannotated but recognized by opening of dressing drawers)

Instrumental Activities of Daily Living

– Preparing meals (Annotated as Cook)
– Housework. Two finer activities are found: wash dishes (Annotated) and do laundry (Unannotated but measured through washing machine use).
– Other instrumental activities not included

Other Annotated Activities (for correspondence with other datasets)

– Sleeping
– Going out

Other Unannotated but Measurable Activities

– Watching TV
– Use of handwasher (for handwashing, brushing teeth and general grooming)

Fig. 2. Interfaces used to annotate the *ContextAct@A4H* dataset.

Activities were annotated by self-reporting in place at the moment of starting and ending each activity. For this, three different interfaces were available: a web and mobile app, a remote control and a button interface placed strategically (see Fig. 2). The combination of annotation methods allowed the inhabitant to remember easily to do the annotations and minimized interruptions of the activities. The inhabitant annotated the beginning and end of each activity. The inhabitant reported missing some annotations, specially at the end of the second period when there was more familiarity with the environment. This confirms the fact that sensing technology "dissapears" when it truly blends with our environments.

2.3 *ContextAct@A4H* Dataset

We collected a dataset for one week during summer and three weeks during fall in the same apartment configuration. Having data of different months of the year enables both the analysis of the generalization of a model of activities and the analysis of changing behavior throughout the year. As mentioned before, 219 properties were measured during the whole experiment. For the duration of the experiment, all sensors logged their measurements successfully. The accuracy of the measurements was not verified and filtering methods were not used. The properties represent either object interactions or context features. Most object interactions are measured redundantly. For example, opening the fridge is measured by the electric consumption and the door state of the fridge. In this way, the dataset enables many different forms of detecting activities. Context features are measured per room. They include: temperature, carbon dioxide level, noise level, relative humidity, luminosity level and presence in the room. Each context feature is measured at a constant rate, but a change point representation is available. A change is considered when the value varies more than 2% with respect to the last measurement. Additionally, weather information from OpenWeathe[2] is logged every hour and visitor presence is self-reported by the user.

The dataset with changepoint representation of features contains a total of 1 473 011 tuples (364394 in july and 1108617 in november) of sensor measurements. A tuple consists of a timestamp, a sensor id and a measurement value. Of those

---

[2] https://openweathermap.org/.

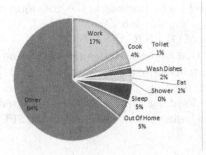
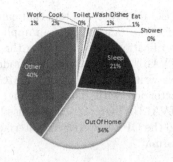

Fig. 3. Distribution of activities during summer (left) and fall (right).

397 correspond to activity records (157 in july and 240 in november). Figure 3 shows the distribution of time in each activity.

Other data logged that can be exploited for different applications is the music information (title, artist, genre and timestamp) corresponding to the music the inhabitant listened while in the apartment.

3   Using the MCL Temporal Logic to Monitor Activities in Logs of Events

An alternative to self-reporting of activity annotations is automatic detection of activities by analysing the sensor raw data present in the dataset. In this section, we report on our use of model checking techniques to do so.

Model checking [5] is a formal verification technique that consists in exploring a user-written *formal model* of a system in order to check the satisfaction of properties describing its proper functioning. The formal model generally has the form of an automaton obtained from a description in a language with mathematically defined semantics. The most general way of defining properties is to use *temporal logics* [17], which combine the standard connectors of logic with modalities and fixpoint operators that enable to reason about the necessity or possibility to reach certain states of the model.

In this work, we consider so-called *action-based* temporal logics, which are appropriate to reason about the actions which involve a state change in the model (e.g., the communication actions in a distributed/concurrent system), rather than the contents of states (e.g., the state variables).

In cases where there is no formal model of a system, it turns out that action-based temporal logics can also be used to analyse sequences of actions generated by a concrete, running system (e.g., logs of events). Indeed, such sequences can be (trivially) seen as particular cases of automata. The model can be simply replaced by the log, which becomes the object on which checks are performed. In this work, we thus naturally consider *ContextAct@A4H* as log of events.

In practice, we use the CADP toolbox [7], which is equipped for such a task. Among the (more than) 50 tools and code libraries present in CADP, we use in particular the following ones:

– SEQ.OPEN [8] is a tool that can parse a sequence of actions in the SEQ format of CADP and provide an application programming interface with the CADP verification tools, following the principles of OPEN/CAESAR [6].

– EVALUATOR 4.0 [16] is a model checker that evaluates temporal logic formulas written in the language MCL, an alternation-free modal mu-calculus [11] extended with data handling, regular expressions, and fairness operators. EVALUATOR 4.0 can be used to verify formulas on any system connected to the OPEN/CAESAR interface, thus including action sequences in the SEQ format.

In the framework our experiment, each event constitutes a line in the log, in CSV format. Each line contains first the event occurrence date (including day time), the sensor id, and the sensor value, separated by semicolons. The first step is to translate this log into the SEQ textual format of CADP, which is done using a simple Unix sed script. The transformation principally consists in turning lines of the form "date; sensor_id; sensor_value" into the form "A !date !sensor_id !sensor_value" accepted as input by SEQ.OPEN, where A is a dummy symbol added here for technical (and unimportant) reasons, and where "!" is the symbol used to delimit action fields in CADP.

MCL macro definitions can then be defined to interpret log lines as more abstract events. Each macro definition can be understood as an action pattern that recognizes certain fields in log lines. For instance, the following macro definition recognizes that the light of the office is on, sensor L14 corresponding to a light dimmer located in the office of the Smart apartment:

```
macro Office_Light_On () =
  { A ... !"L14" ?value:Nat where value > 0 }
end_macro
```

Note how the "..." symbol (wildcard) allows the date field to be ignored and how the "?" symbol allows some typed field to be captured in a variable, whose value can be constrained by a Boolean condition (guard) specified by the "where" clause.

Macro definitions can be parameterized as the following one, which matches log lines indicating that a light button in the bathroom (whose sensor_id starts with I7_ or I11_) has the value SWITCH passed as parameter:

```
macro Bathroom_Button (SWITCH) =
  { A ... ?snsr:String SWITCH where
    (prefix (snsr, 3) ="I7_") or (prefix (snsr, 4) = "I11_") }
end_macro
```

Other, more complex macro definitions can be defined by combining simpler ones using Boolean connectors. For instance, the macro definition below detects the fact that either the oven or the cooktop is switched on, where Cooktop_On and Oven_On are already defined macro definitions:

```
macro Cooking_Appliance_On () = (Cooktop_On or Oven_On) end_macro
```

In our experiment, we wrote 125 macro definitions.

Once macros have been defined to give simple meanings to complex log events, thus facilitating the log analysis, they can be used in temporal logic formulas to detect activities in the log. We give two examples.

The first example below is a formula that detects the beginning of a shower activity, which is defined as follows: the door of the shower is open then closed, and then the water flows. Angles denote the existence of a sequence of events, defined by a regular expression. The symbol ".". denotes sequential composition, "*" denotes repetition (0 or more times), true matches any log event, and not and or have their usual meaning. This formula evaluates to true if their exists a sequence in the log that matches this regular expression.

```
< true* . Shower_Door (!"OPEN") .
  (not Shower_Door (!"CLOSED"))* . Shower_Door (!"CLOSED") .
  (not Shower_Door (!"OPEN"))* . Shower_Water_On > true
```

Note how the "!" symbol allows a field to be matched against the value of a data expression (here, a character string constant).

The second example, defined in Fig. 4, is slightly more complex. It detects the start of a cooking activity, defined as follows: a food container (the fridge or a drawer) was opened and at least one cooking appliance is on.

This formula is defined as a least fixpoint (mu) which, evaluated on a sequence (as opposed to a general automaton), can be seen as a recursive function on the events of the log. It has two parameters, namely a Boolean Fd_Cntnr_Opn, which is initially false and becomes true once an event corresponding to the opening of a food container is detected, and a natural number N_Ckng_Appl_On, which counts the number of cooking appliances that are currently on (initially 0). When Fd_Cntnr_Opn is true and N_Ckng_Appl_On is greater than 0, then the start of a cooking activity was detected. Otherwise, the property is applied recursively depending on the next event that is found in the sequence, parameters being updated accordingly.

CADP detects the time the activity starts as the time when all conditions defined by the model are met. It creates a file with all sensor measurements up to this time as an output. To detect all occurrences of an activity we find the difference between the original dataset and the output file using the *grep* utility on Linux, and then use this new file as the input log file. This process is repeated until the output file is empty.

4   Experimental Evaluation

We evaluated the model checking approach for activity start and/or end recognition using *ContextAct@A4H* taking annotation as ground truth. We defined models to recognize the start of the sleeping, cooking and washing dishes activities and the end of the showering and using toilet activities. When the model infers the start or end of the same activity within 3 min, we take the smaller time (greater time) as the start time of the activity (end time of the activity). We

```
mu Ckng_Act (
   Fd_Cntnr_Opn: Bool := false, (* true if fridge or drawer was opened *)
   N_Ckng_Appl_On: Nat := 0 (* nb of cooking appliances that are on *)
) .
   if Fd_Cntnr_Opn and (N_Ckng_Appl_On > 0) then
      true (* cooking activity detected *)
   else
      < Food_Container_Door (!"OPEN") > Ckng_Act (true, N_Ckng_Appl_On)
      or
      < Cooking_Appliance_On > Ckng_Act (Fd_Cntnr_Opn, N_Ckng_Appl_On+1)
      or
      < Cooking_Appliance_Off >
         if N_Ckng_Appl_On > 1 then
            Ckng_Act (Fd_Cntnr_Opn, N_Ckng_Appl_On-1)
         else (* was not a cooking activity *)
            Ckng_Act (Fd_Cntnr_Opn, 0)
         end if
      or
      < not Food_Container_Door (!"OPEN") and
        not Cooking_Appliance_On and not Cooking_Appliance_Off >
         Ckng_Act (Fd_Cntnr_Opn, N_Ckng_Appl_On)
   end if
```

Fig. 4. MCL formula for detecting the start of a cooking activity

calculate the difference between the inferred time and the actual time annotated by the inhabitant. Table 2 shows the results obtained.

Table 2. Activity recognition results with model checking approach

Activity	Precision	Recall	Avg. time diff (minutes)
Sleep (start)	78 %	95 %	4,42
Toilet use (end)	98 %	78 %	0,71
Cooking (start)	81 %	88 %	1,5
Taking a shower (end)	70 %	89 %	3
Washing dishes (start)	14 %	97 %	12,45

To evaluate the performance of the activity recognition approach we calculate its *precision* and *recall* considering that the annotated activities are the relevant ones that should be recognized. A recognized activity is considered "relevant" if it corresponds effectively to an annotated activity. *Precision* is the fraction of the recognized activities that are relevant wrt the number of recognized activities. *Recall* is the fraction of annotated activities that are successfully recognized wrt the number of annotated activities.

Most of the activities have high precision and recall measures, similar to results reported with hidden markov models or support vector machines in other datasets. To provide a comparison, the highest average f-measure (a weighted average of the precision and recall) reported by Krishnan et al. [12] was 0.61 while our average f-measure is 0.72. This depends on many factors such as sensors used, features selected and the number of activities making the comparison non-depending on just the recognition method. In our case, the high precision is due to the precise object usage measurements that we gathered thanks to the sensing devices installed. We can see that the average time difference between the inferred start or end of the activity and the time the inhabitant annotated is rather small. The activity washing dishes has a low precision due to a high number of false positives. The false positives are due to the fact that the only detectable event corresponding to this activity is the sink faucet being opened. Yet, the sink faucet can also be opened for many other activities including washing fruits and vegetables, washing hands, and washing few pieces of tableware while cooking, which were not annotated as washing dishes. Possible ways to increase precision could be to take into account both a minimal proportion of hot water flowing through the sink faucet (taking into account that vegetables and fruits are usually washed with cold water whereas dish washing requires hotter water) and the time during which the sink faucet has been opened (thus requiring to define a minimum time that dish washing usually takes and that hand washing or tableware washing usually do not exceed).

5   Related Work

In this section we briefly discuss related work on activity recognition and current available datasets of daily living in smart homes.

5.1   Daily Living Activity Recognition in Real Life Scenarios

Activity recognition refers to inferring an activity label from observations made through sensing devices. These sensing devices can be either vision-based, wearable sensing or ambient sensing. Vision based sensing is often seen as a privacy invasion and its use is not accepted by many elders. Wearable sensing is better for physical activity such as running or walking and is now commercially available for this. For daily living activities however, wearables can be forgotten by the user and have been used for fined-grained activities such as grabbing a glass or turning the lights on [15]. Ambient sensing allows inferring object use and coarsed-grained activities. Since activities are often performed with the same objects this is better for daily living monitoring. Also, it is less intrusive as sensing capabilities merge with the environment and do not interfere with normal activity performance.

Sensor-based activity recognition in smart homes methods can be classified in knowledge based and data based [4]. Knowledge based methods use semantic descriptions of activities based on object usage and context features such as location or time of day. The most common methods include ontologies [20], situational models and event calculus. Data-based methods, on the other hand, use sensor features to build machine-learned models. The models can be learned with supervised or unsupervised methods. Supervised methods, such as Hidden Markov Models [22], Bayes Networks and Support Vector Machines [12] have shown promising results but need ground truth data to be learned. Unsupervised methods such as clustering, topic models and frequent sequences do not need ground truth data and have been used as methods for activity discovery [18].

Most proposed activity recognition methods have been tested in scripted datasets showing promising results. Nevertheless, passing from laboratory settings to real life settings is not as transparent since there are crucial differences in both settings. Activity recognition in real-life datasets differs in the following aspects from activity recognition in scripted datasets:

- Class imbalance: real-life scenarios are inherently imbalanced due to the different frequencies and durations of each activity [15].
- Intra-class variability: the same activity can be performed in different ways, using different objects, at different locations, etc. [14,15].
- The *Other* activity: scripted datasets only represent activities of interest, while in real-life scenarios most of the time it is other activity is being performed [12]. This 'other' activity is a highly variable class since it represents many activities.

5.2   Datasets of Daily Living in Smart Homes

Testing activity recognition and behavior modeling algorithms in real life is difficult due to the lack of real data. Real-life scenarios are difficult to gather both for the costs of equipping a real home and the availability of subjects willing to live in such homes. Therefore, making these datasets public helps advance research and is of great interest for the community. Some equipped apartments over the world, notably: The Aware Home [10] at Georgia Tech, Domus at France, Van Kasteren [22], CASAS at Washington University [1], PlaceLab [21] at MIT, ARAS [2] at Istanbul, Turkey. Most publicly available datasets feature scripted and acted daily life activities, lack ground truth annotations or feature office or other scenario activities that do not correspond to daily living activities.

Nonetheless, the Placelab, CASAS and ARAS projects have publicly available datasets of real life daily activities with ground truth annotations. Common activities in these datasets include sleeping, toilet use, taking a shower or bath, eating, leaving home, cooking or preparing meals, washing dishes, working or using computer and leisure activities (relax, watching tv, reading). These are daily living activities that can be measured through available sensors. Eating and fine-grained activities are usually the most complex to recognize [12,21]. Context features are often not measured, being the ones measured temperature at some locations and presence in rooms. Nonetheless, rich context information can not only improve activity recognition but also it can help to better understand behavior patterns and user triggers (for example, loud noises may trigger anxiety) [13].

6   Conclusions and Research Perspectives

In this paper we have detailed our approach of using temporal logic for ADL recognition in real-life settings showing promising results. We use the CADP tool to describe each activity as a temporal logic property that is checked repeatedly in the log of sensor measurements until all occurrences of the activity have been found. The property is described based on object usage by an expert (in our case the inhabitant). One of the main advantages of this approach over other techniques is the ability to recognize start and end of the activity, thus not requiring to segment sensor data. The model checking approach using CADP also enables to specify durations and gaps between events, by capturing the date fields present in events and storing them as parameters of fixpoint operators. We plan to exploit this feature in the future for carrying out timed analyses of activities. We believe model checking is an interesting alternative for activity recognition in real life settings.

We have also presented the *ContextAct@A4H* dataset, an annotated real-life dataset of activities and context of daily living covering four weeks of data. One drawback in public datasets for ADL recognition is that there is no correspondence between the activities nor the sensors used, which makes it difficult to compare results from one dataset to the other. This is since available sensors change through time. Data in terms of semantic measured properties can be more stable and we propose to focus on these to compare results and for future datasets. Still, the need of creating shared knowledge and agree on a taxonomy of activities [3] continues, although some common activities emerge. Most datasets include other activities so more data is available but these are not common with other datasets. We have presented a dataset with these common activities and some others as well. The dataset is described with both the sensor measurements and with semantic measured properties.

ContextAct@A4H is the first daily living dataset featuring rich context information. It features six context variables per room in the apartment plus weather, music and number of visitor information. This information is of high interest for applications such as content recommendation, domotics and behavior analysis among others.

References

1. Cook, D.J., Crandall, A.S., Thomas, B.L., Krishnan, N.C.: CASAS: a smart home in a box. IEEE Comput. **46**(7), 62–69 (2013)
2. Alemdar, H., Ertan, H., Incelt, O.D., Ersoy, C.: ARAS human activity datasets in multiple homes with multiple residents, pp. 232–235 (2013)
3. Brush, A., Krumm, J., Scott, J.: Activity recognition research: the good, the bad, and the future. In: Pervasive 2010 Workshop: How to Do Good Research in Activity Recognition, pp. 1–3 (2010)
4. Chen, L., Hoey, J., Nugent, C.D., Cook, D.J., Yu, Z., Member, S.: Sensor-based activity recognition. IEEE Trans. Syst. Man Cybern. Part C (Appl. Rev.) **42**(6), 790–808 (2012)

5. Christel Baier, J.P.K.: Principles of Model Checking. MIT Press, Cambridge (2008)
6. Garavel, H.: OPEN/CÆSAR: an open software architecture for verification, simulation, and testing. In: Steffen, B. (ed.) TACAS 1998. LNCS, vol. 1384, pp. 68–84. Springer, Heidelberg (1998). doi:10.1007/BFb0054165
7. Garavel, H., Lang, F., Mateescu, R., Serwe, W.: CADP 2011: a toolbox for the construction and analysis of distributed processes. Springer Int. J. Softw. Tools Technol. Transf. (STTT) **15**(2), 89–107 (2013)
8. Garavel, H., Mateescu, R.: SEQ.OPEN: a tool for efficient trace-based verification. In: Graf, S., Mounier, L. (eds.) SPIN 2004. LNCS, vol. 2989, pp. 151–157. Springer, Heidelberg (2004). doi:10.1007/978-3-540-24732-6_11
9. Garcia, E.: Learning from imbalanced data. IEEE Trans. Knowl. Data Eng. **21**(9), 1263–1284 (2009)
10. Helal, S., Mann, W., El-Zabadani, H., King, J., Kaddoura, Y., Jansen, E.: The Gator tech smart house: a programmable pervasive space. Computer **38**(3), 50–60 (2005)
11. Kozen, D.: Results on the propositional μ-calculus. Theoret. Comput. Sci. **27**, 333–354 (1983)
12. Krishnan, N.C., Cook, D.J.: Activity recognition on streaming sensor data. Pervasive Mob. Comput. **10**, 138–154 (2014)
13. Lago, P., Jiménez-Guarín, C., Roncancio, C.: Contextualized behavior patterns for change reasoning in ambient assisted living: a formal model. Expert Systems (to appear)
14. Lago, P., Jiménez-Guarín, C., Roncancio, C.: A case study on the analysis of behavior patterns and pattern changes in smart environments. In: Pecchia, L., Chen, L.L., Nugent, C., Bravo, J. (eds.) IWAAL 2014. LNCS, vol. 8868, pp. 296–303. Springer, Cham (2014). doi:10.1007/978-3-319-13105-4_43
15. Logan, B., Healey, J., Philipose, M., Tapia, E.M., Intille, S.: A long-term evaluation of sensing modalities for activity recognition. In: Krumm, J., Abowd, G.D., Seneviratne, A., Strang, T. (eds.) UbiComp 2007. LNCS, vol. 4717, pp. 483–500. Springer, Heidelberg (2007). doi:10.1007/978-3-540-74853-3_28
16. Mateescu, R., Thivolle, D.: A model checking language for concurrent value-passing systems. In: Cuellar, J., Maibaum, T., Sere, K. (eds.) FM 2008. LNCS, vol. 5014, pp. 148–164. Springer, Heidelberg (2008). doi:10.1007/978-3-540-68237-0_12
17. Pnueli, A.: The temporal logic of programs. In: Proceedings of Foundations of Computer Science, pp. 46–57. IEEE (1977)
18. Rashidi, P.: Stream sequence mining for human activity discovery. In: Plan, Activity, and Intent Recognition, pp. 123–148. Elsevier (2014)
19. Riboni, D., Pareschi, L., Radaelli, L., Bettini, C.: Is ontology-based activity recognition really effective? In: 2011 PERCOM Workshops, pp. 427–431, March 2011
20. Rodríguez, N.D., Cuéllar, M.P., Lilius, J., Calvo-Flores, M.D.: A survey on ontologies for human behavior recognition. ACM Comput. Surv. **46**(4), 43:1–43:33 (2014)
21. Tapia, E.M., Intille, S.S., Larson, K.: Activity recognition in the home using simple and ubiquitous sensors. In: Ferscha, A., Mattern, F. (eds.) Pervasive 2004. LNCS, vol. 3001, pp. 158–175. Springer, Heidelberg (2004). doi:10.1007/978-3-540-24646-6_10
22. Kasteren, T.L.M., Englebienne, G., Kröse, B.J.A.: Transferring knowledge of activity recognition across sensor networks. In: Floréen, P., Krüger, A., Spasojevic, M. (eds.) Pervasive 2010. LNCS, vol. 6030, pp. 283–300. Springer, Heidelberg (2010). doi:10.1007/978-3-642-12654-3_17

Smart Is a Matter of Context

Julien Nigon[✉], Nicolas Verstaevel, Jérémy Boes, Frédéric Migeon,
and Marie-Pierre Gleizes

University of Toulouse/IRIT-Team SMAC, 118 Route de Narbonne,
31062 Toulouse Cedex 9, France
{julien.nigon,nicolas.verstaevel,jeremy.boes,
frederic.migeon,marrie-pierre}@irit.fr

Abstract. Smart cities involve, in a large scale, a wide array of interconnected components and agents, giving birth to large and heterogeneous data flows. They are inherently cross-disciplinary, provide interesting challenges, and constitute a very promising field for future urban
developments, such as smart grids, eco-feedback, intelligent traffic control, and so on. We advocate that the key to these challenges is the
proper modelling and exploitation of context. However, said context is
highly dynamic and mainly unpredictable. Improved AI and machine
learning techniques are required. Starting from some of the main smart
cities features, this paper highlights the key challenges, explains why
handling context is crucial to them, and gives some insights to address
them, notably with multi-agent systems.

Keywords: Smart cities · Multi-agent systems · Complexity

1 Introduction

The term "Smart City" regroups various problematics and features stemming
from the use of new information and communication technologies (ICTs) in order
to build a better living for every citizen. This includes many different fields such
as governance, city planning, health, mobility, housing, energy, and so forth,
making smart cities an active cross-disciplinary research ground.

The various features of smart cities share a common trait, that may seem
trivial: they are all context-dependent. Accessing or forecasting contextual data,
and extracting relevant information from it, is always the key to push forward the
efficiency of smart cities features. However, context in smart cities is complex.
The wide array of interconnected components, their dynamics, their heterogeneity, and reliability issues of real-world problems make smart cities' contextual
data very difficult to handle, even for automated systems. This often requires
advanced artificial intelligence and machine learning techniques. Such complexity
can only be dealt with bottom-up approaches. Thanks to their self-* properties
and their "built-in" notion of environment, Multi-Agent Systems (MASs) are a
good candidate for designing context handlers for smart cities features.

© Springer International Publishing AG 2017
P. Brézillon et al. (Eds.): CONTEXT 2017, LNAI 10257, pp. 189–202, 2017.
DOI: 10.1007/978-3-319-57837-8_15

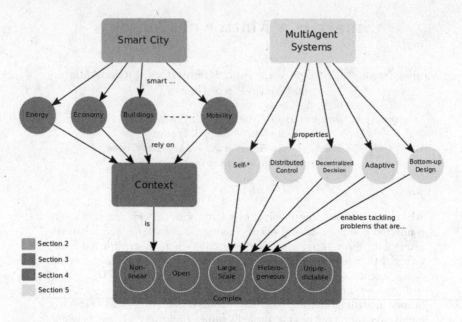

Fig. 1. Graphical abstract

Figure 1 proposes a graphical abstract of this paper. Section 2 presents definitions of smart cities from litterature, while Sect. 3 goes deeper with common features of smart cities. Section 4 explains the main challenges that arises when dealing with context in smart cities. Finally, Sect. 5 presents multi-agent systems and explains why they are suitable for these challenges, before we conclude with perspectives in Sect. 6.

2   Smart Cities

Being a transdisciplinary subject, it is difficult to have an accurate and consensual definition of what a smart city is. Depending on its focus, each author proposes a different definition, and sometimes relative words are used to emphasise a specific dimension of smart city (like "Intelligent City", "Creative City", etc.) [22]. However, most of the time, the use of information and communication technologies is an important part of the design of a smart city. In this paper, we consider that three characteristics (proposed by Harrison et al. [12]) are common to all smart cities: instrumented, interconnected and intelligent. *Instrumented* means that the city can use a large set of data-acquisition systems in order to produce data from the real world. *Interconnected* means that these data can be used across different services and users in the city, and finally *intelligent* emphasises the ability to analyse and use efficiently these data.

3   Smart Cities Features

It is almost impossible to provide an exhaustive list of all possible features of a smart city, due to the large number of way to think smart cities. In this section are presented various features selected to illustrate the importance of taking into account the context in the management of the smart city. The different application areas are inspired by Neirotti et al. [23].

3.1   Natural Resources and Energy

With the growing threat of resource scarcity, the improvement of resource and energy management in cities becomes a major issue.

Smart Grids. In the classic way to distribute energy, electricity is in a centralised way, then it is distributed to all the customers. The energy flow is unidirectional, from the producer to the customer. In a smart-grid, the energy flow is bidirectional, allowing greater flexibility in the management of energy [11]. This kind of technology is very interesting for smart cities, because it allows to easily add decentralised energy production units in the energy grid, like wind turbine or solar panel. These green power sources are a promising way to make smart cities self-sufficient in energy and to reduce their natural resources consumption. But, these energy sources are intermittent. So, currently, energy grids can't rely only on these energy sources. If energy demand reaches a peak, or if energy coming for intermittent sources decreases, thermal power plants must provide energy to meet the demand in order to avoid a blackout. But thermal power plants can't be activated instantaneously. In order to efficiently use smart grids in smart cities, we must be able to anticipate the need for additional power sources.

It is in this anticipation requirement that lies the need for proper context understanding. Indeed, the variation of production and the variation of consumption must be taken into account. The first one depends on the weather, but also on the facilities conditions, and the second one is affected by pretty much all the events that affect the city (season, hour, weather, events, etc.). All this contextual information must be efficiently used in order to provide good forecasting.

3.2   Transport and Mobility

Smart cities, by concentrating a large number of people, must deal with traffic congestion. The presence of numerous sensors offer interesting opportunities for transport management [30].

Traffic Control. One of the most significant use case is about automatic control of traffic lights. Indeed, an efficient management of these traffic lights can have a great impact on traffic congestion. In a smart city, sensors (cameras) could be used to measure the number of cars at many points in the city, and so traffic congestion could be measured in real time. But these data are not the only thing that affect the traffic in the city. To efficiently manage traffic lights, contextual data must be considered. For instance, these data could be considered: current day and hour, people and car localisation, weather, price of fuel, etc. In fact, because of the complexity of an urban network, a huge array of data could be interesting to consider. It's at this point that efficient context management become essential. Choosing the most relevant data in a large sensor panel, and using them to determine the best behaviour for traffic control is a complex task.

3.3   Buildings

At a more local scale, smart cities rely on smart buildings to improve quality of life and optimise energy consumption. Smart buildings are designed for energy efficiency. Equipped with ICT, they can monitor and control their own devices while also communicating with other buildings [19].

Anomaly Detection. Smart buildings, using a large array of sensors, are able to provide an overview of energy consumption and production of a building. It's an useful tool to improve management of energy. But it should be possible to get even more interesting results. In fact, using these data, it is possible to identify anomalies [31] (by analysing the behavior of sensors data). The automated detection of such situations opens up many possibilities in terms of predictive maintenance: identifying flawed sensors, broken effectors, leaks, mechanical failures, and so on. It becomes possible to improve the time reaction to repair, thus improving the management of the building, and optimising energy consumption.

Eco-Feedback. The human aspect is an important concern in many definitions of the smart city. So the mechanisms which allow to influence the behavior of citizens naturally have a role to play in smart cities. An example of such mechanism is *eco-feedback*. The goal of eco-feedback technology is to provide feedback to people on their behaviour in order to optimise environmental impact [9]. Making such eco-feedback is complex, because each individual potentially reacts differently to a specific feedback in a specific context. So, an automatic system trying to produce an eco-feedback must take in account who is the recipient [26], which medium is used, where the action takes place, in order to deliver a meaningful information. Once again, context is a key to this problem.

3.4   Governance

In a smart city, institutions interact dynamically with multiple stakeholders (communities, citizens and businesses) [22]. In such a system, a decision maker can't rely on data specific to its own department. Data coming from other stakeholders are essential to efficiently manage the city. For instance, the construction of a new shopping mall is affected by many different contextual data coming from different stakeholders: cadastre from the public administration, different services offered from close providers, habits from citizens. Each stakeholder is involved. This is also true for "classic" cities, but the need for efficiency of smarts cities combined with an increased access to data makes it both necessary and possible to optimise decision making thanks to contextual data.

3.5 Economy and People

Cultural Heritage. The development and valorization of the cultural heritage of a smart city are an important issue, either from an economic perspective (tourism) or from a societal perspective [1]. One of the tracks laid down by smart cities is that of augmented reality [28]. Here, augmented reality is designed to provide additional background information to allow the user to benefit the most from the wealth of monuments, art, and more generally speaking culture of the city. To this end, it is necessary to use at best all available data, in order to provide information that is relevant to the user. This data can be: the position of the user, what he has seen, the time of day, his current attendance, and so on.

3.6 Contextual Features

In all of these features, the intelligent management of the environment is of primary importance. Given the complexity of a system such as a smart city, it becomes mostly impossible for human operators to effectively use and understand the flow of dynamic data produced by the smart city. In fact, today the majority of methods focus on computational approaches to manage these data effectively, with the goals of controlling, monitoring, and providing decision support. However, the particularities of complex systems in general, and smart city in particular, create some problems which need to be addressed in order to successfully manage context in such approaches.

4   Challenges for Context Management in Smart Cities

The previous section stated that a proper context handling is crucial for many smart city applications. Here, context handling means extracting relevant information from data and being able to forecast and anticipate their occurrence (learning predictive relationships).

However, cities are complex systems [2, 23]. Hence, applications in smart cities are plunged into a complex context. Along with the social challenges that go with new technologies, such as acceptability or ethical dilemma, the complexity of context adds (among others) non-linearity, openness, heterogeneity, and large-scale data to the challenges that context management systems have to face.

4.1 Non-linearity

When a small change on the input of a system may result in a big change on its output, the system is said non-linear. Controlling such a system is a difficult task. Unfortunately, voltage in smart grids, heating in buildings and housing, traffic, and many smart cities systems we seek to control are non-linear.

In a linear system, the distribution of data is such that it can be exactly abstracted using only simple mathematical functions. On the contrary, machine learning algorithms have to be sophisticated and fine-tuned to be able to learn non-linear patterns and perform with contextual data from smart cities [34].

4.2   Openness

A system is said open when parts may dynamically enter and exit the system. With the Internet of Things, smart cities are inherently open [13]. New devices, new sources of contextual data, are continually added, and some old ones are deleted, or suffer fatal failures. An intelligent algorithm designed to handle contextual data in a smart city should be able to easily incorporate new sources and delete old ones. For instance, a new room is built in a smart building and equipped with various sensors and effectors that add their data to the contextual data flows of the energy management system. This system had learnt the optimal behaviours to balance energy consumption and comfort. Now, it has to seamlessly incorporate these new data sources to its decision making process. Otherwise, administrators would have to reset and restart the whole learning process. It would be very time costly. Such openness can prove really difficult to achieve for many types of machine learning algorithms, particularly artificial neural networks and evolutionary algorithms.

4.3   Large-Scale

Smart city are deemed to generate huge masses of data. For instance, a traffic light control system managing all the crossroads of a city would have to deal with all the various sensors of all the roads and crossroads to take simultaneously multiple decisions about which light to turn on and off. All these decisions are so interdependent that distributed control should be favoured over a central decision making process [7]. The solution has to rely on autonomous unit taking local decisions.

4.4   Heterogeneity

Contextual data in smart cities include a large variety of data types, whether they are numerical or not, continuous or discrete, multidimensional or not. Not all algorithms are able to deal with such heterogeneity. While numerical data are usually easily handled by current algorithms, modelling and treating ontologies and abstract concepts is a whole field of research. If some algorithms work very well with continuous numerical data, they are utterly unable to deal with data like the colour of an object, the smell of an animal, or more abstract concepts like the emotion of people. Sophisticated methods have to be employed to process together heterogeneous data in a single algorithm. For instance, Lewis et al.

use kernel methods, but it does not answer the problem of modelling abstract concepts [15]. Moreover, heterogeneity also appears in time scales. Fore some data and tasks, it is relevant to make measurements every millisecond. For other it is days, weeks, or months. Algorithms are usually suited for a given timescale, but struggle to manage several at once.

4.5 Unpredictable Dynamics

Contextual data in smart cities are always dynamic. Weather changes, density of population changes, traffic changes, and so on. This is a quite obvious fact to state. There would be very little interest to gather constant data. Current algorithms can easily find predictive relationships in smooth linear and complete data set. However, in the real world, the way data change is difficult to handle, and often unpredictable. The dynamics you have learnt at a given moment may not be true some times later. This stems from several factors such as non-linearity, partial perception (there is not always a sensor for every relevant data), unreliable or missing data, failures, openness, and so on. This pressures the machine learning algorithms to perpetually self-adapt to the ever-changing data. Offline learning [25] is out of the question if we do not wish to regularly perform a new costly training.

4.6 Privacy

Smart cities are able to collect and gather large amounts of information, and this could harm the privacy of citizens [17]. But whatever the services brought by new connected technologies, nobody should have to give up its privacy. Data should not be used outside of what the considered services need. A good alternative to enforce this would be for the data to be processed physically close to its source, and not being transferred and stored when it is not necessary.

To answer these difficult challenges, the ideal context handler would have to be decentralised, adaptive, open, and modular. The next section describes the Multi-Agent Systems approach which, done right, could exhibit all of these properties.

5 Multi-agent Systems and Smart Cities

The challenges listed in the previous section are not restricted to Smart Cities. In fact, they are at the very heart of **complex systems**. Smart Cities are representative of complex systems, notably by merging problematics coming from several domains, like politics, urban planning, health or ecology, each domain coming with its own requirements. Thereby, the "Smart" component of tomorrow cities is not just deploying state-of-the-art information and communication technologies, but doing it intelligently. To play well its role, ICTs, and especially artificial intelligence, must adopt methodologies that enable to face the problematics of those complex systems but also ensure its massive deployment and sustainability. *Ad hoc* solutions, aiming to develop for each problematic its own new solution, are clearly not answering those needs. On the contrary, abstraction and re-usability of solutions must be taken into account. In this section, we argue that the Multi-Agent approach is not only suitable for the challenges of smart city, but that the agent paradigm includes *de facto* the notion of context.

5.1   The Multi-agent Paradigm

Multi-Agent Systems (MAS) are systems composed of multiple interacting and autonomous entities, the agents, within a common environment. MASs offer a methodological way to model and study complex systems with a bottom-up approach. In computer science, the MAS paradigm focus on the design of agents and their collective behaviours leading to the realisation of a particular task. However, the MAS paradigm is not restricted to computer science as it allows to express a large variety of problems focusing on the entities composing it and their interactions. Thus, it is used in areas such as sociology, cognitive science, geography, or ethology, each of those domains use the MAS paradigm to model, study or even simulate complex phenomenon. The natural distribution of tasks inside the different agents composing a MAS, and the possibility to decentralise control and decision, makes them highly suitable to overcome a greater complexity than conventional methods and tackle the Smart City challenges (see Sect. 4).

A classic definition of an agent given by Ferber is that *"an agent can be a physical or virtual entity that can act, perceive its environment (in a partial way) and communicate with others, is autonomous and has skills to achieve its goals and tendencies."* [8].

This definition highlights the fundamental properties of an agent:

- An agent is **autonomous**, which means the agent is the only one to control its own behaviour. This implies that the choice to act or not is only driven by the agent's own behaviour. The agent's capacity to say "no" (to choose not to act) makes a concrete differentiation between an agent and a sub-program.
- An agent evolves in an **environment** (physical or virtual) on which it is able to locally perceive information and locally act. This environment is everything that is external to the agent and which can be perceived by the agent, including the other agents. This environment acts as the interaction medium.
- An agent is able to **interact** and **communicate** with other agents either directly or through the environment. The other agents are then part of the social component of the agent's environment.
- An agent possesses a **partial** knowledge of this environment.
- An agent possesses its own **resources** and **skills**.

The notion of environment is crucial in MASs. Indeed, the environment is not only a source of information, but also the medium through which those agents act and interact. Agents are coupled with their environment, the activity of one constantly influencing the activity of the others. They are designed to extract information from their environment and to reason based on this information. In many aspects, the notion of environment is very similar to the notion of context.

The most common way to model the behaviour of an agent in its environment is to adopt a three steps looping lifecycle of *Perception-Decision-Action* (Fig. 2):

- 1: **Perception** is the process during which the agent acquires information from its environment and updates its internal representations.
- 2: **Decision** is the process during which the agent decides of actions to perform. This decision is based on its local perceptions, its internal knowledge and its own objectives.
- 3: **Action** is the process during which the agent applies the actions.

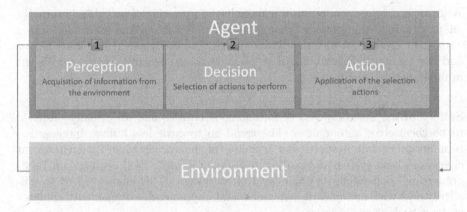

Fig. 2. The lifecycle of an agent [33].

5.2   Multi-agent Properties Addressing Complexity

Multi-Agent Software Engineering (also called Agent-Oriented Software Engineering) is gathering a rather long practice of systems development. It focuses on enabling designers to have precise ideas on which Multi-Agent System properties can address the features of complex systems.

Bottom-Up Design. Bottom-up design starts by adding interaction and decision skills to entities from the application domain in order to "transform" them into agents. Even if the application domain is a complex system with heterogeneous parts, it still can easily be represented in terms of agents. Focusing on the entities and their interactions at a local level makes it easier to deal with complexity.

Distributed Control. In almost every multi-agent system, there is no predefined hierarchical organisation. Combined with the autonomy of agent, this drives the designer towards architectures where control is distributed, with no

Master-Slaves nor Client-Server patterns. Hence, with every agent being aware of its environment, deciding on its own what to do when this environment changes, being able to adapt to these changes, multi-agent systems are naturally open and can easily handle the openness of a complex system to which it is coupled.

Decentralised Decision. Since every decision is made at the agent level, the structure of a multi-agent system decentralises the decision making process. This decentralisation eases the addition of new agents in the system (openness) and also eases the scaling of the whole system by avoiding unnecessary combinatory computing.

Adaptive. Multi-agent systems usually have interesting capabilities in terms of adaptivity. Indeed, agents can change their own behaviour and their relationship with other agents and with their environment, and the whole MAS can remove or add new agents. This flexibility of MASs make them efficient for solving problems in unpredictable environments.

Self-*. MASs are composed of autonomous entities and are usually designed to be themselves autonomous. The trend go towards less human intervention to maintain certain properties or activities of the system when its environment changes. These systems are called "self-maintaining", "self-healing", or "self-organizing" depending on their level of autonomy. This enables MAS to efficiently deal with non-linearity, openness and unpredictable dynamics of complex systems such as smart cities.

5.3   Multi-agents Usage in Smart Cities

As a matter of fact, the paradigm is more and more used in the context of Smart Cities [27]. Those usage can be categorised in three categories:

- **Modelling**: By focusing on the agents and their interactions, the MAS paradigm eases the design of complex systems. The design of a MAS take into account of the heterogeneity of the entities involved in the problem to model, their distributed nature (with may be physically distributed and/or logically distributed) and the openness. It is notably used to "*offer a decentralised and collaborative architecture with requirements of autonomy, pro-activity, decentralisation, inter-operability, easiness of deployment, and ability to seamlessly incorporate future evolutions*" [4]. But the benefits of agent based modelling may also be found in the fact that the egocentric approach to design an agent enables to model natural and social structures such as human organisations [29], and to "*allow solving problems in a distributed manner by taking advantage of social behaviours as well as the individual behaviour of the agents*" [6].
- **Simulation**: Another usage of the MAS paradigm in Smart Cities is the simulation of complex phenomenons. For example, Gueriau et al. [10] use a

multi-agent simulation to study the impact of cooperative traffic management strategies. Here, the MAS paradigm enables to address the problematic of traffic management both in a behavioural way, by modelling the cooperative strategies, and a topological way, with the characterisation of the environment on which the different car-agents drives. Another example of simulation with a MAS is the work of [20] who proposed a framework for the study of the impact of a specific natural disaster organisational structure and its related management policies on natural disaster response performance. Here, the MAS paradigm enables to study how the organisation of a set of agents may affect a decision process. Another example of MAS usage in the context of Smart City is the work of Vaubourg et al. [32] that shows how the multi-agent paradigm can be successfully applied for smart grids multi-model simulation.

- **Problem solving**: The MAS paradigm partly emerged from the community working on distributed problem solving. Its popularity is growing when it comes to face complex problem coming from real world, notably by using its natural distribution of tasks among the system. Scientific literature is filled with examples of problem solving with multi-agent systems [16]. We propose to illustrate these usages with some examples coming from Smart City challenges. One of these example, which is applied to Smart Cities, is the work of Cerquides et al. [5] who proposed a multi-agent approach for the design of marketplaces for the trading and distribution of energy in the Smart Grid. They face the challenge to design markets for producers and consumers in smart grids that consider distribution grid constraints. In their model, the local producers of electricity are modelled as agents, which can trade electricity within their neighbourhood. Through message-parsing, the agents manage to trade electricity while satisfying the constraints of the grid in a decentralised way. Another example is the work of Mazac et al. [18] which proposes to detect recurrent patterns at the interaction between a system and its environment. In this approach, inspired by the constructivist theory [21], three populations of agents interact with each other, guided by a feedback from the global system activity in order to construct relevant patterns and provide a model of the environment dynamic. This work is applied to ambient systems. The last example is the work of Nigon et al. [24], which designed a generic multi-agent system to model, by observation, the dynamics of a system. In this approach, the agents which are dynamically created by the system intend to model the consequences of the application of a particular action in a particular context. At the opposite of the approach from Mazac et al., the different agents cooperate to build a model of the system. This approach is deployed and tested with real world applications such as smart-building monitoring, energy efficiency and user satisfaction in ambient systems.

All these applications truly depend on their context: context of deployment when we focus on architectural design, topological or structural context when we focus on simulation, or decision context when we deal with problem solving. Each of these applications is designed, thanks to the focus set by the MAS approach on the locality of agents decisions, to model, simulate or take decisions based on the context of the entities involved in the problem to study. Moreover, MASs are naturally good to deal with context, and have been used to explicitly learn actions from contextual observations [3].

6   Conclusion

Smart city is a research field full of promises. From efficient natural resources management to transport and mobility, ICTs may be able to significantly improve the living conditions in cities. For many of smart cities applications, context is the cornerstone around which great progress can be made. However, the complex nature of smart cities raises challenges that have to be tackled, especially dealing with unpredictable dynamics, openness and heterogeneity in large-scale environments. The large amount of sensors is not by itself a sufficient answer to this complexity and, in a seemingly paradoxical way, the integration of additional technology to make the city smarter adds even more complexity to it [14]. An efficient way to automatically manage the complexity of the context is the next big step forward in many aspects of the smart city.

Furthermore, an interesting parallel can be drawn between the requirements expected to handle such complex systems and the properties of a well known paradigm in science: multi-agent systems. Indeed, the adaptive and self-* properties, the decentralised decisions, the ability to be easily distributed, and their bottom-up design philosophy offer interesting perspectives to handle complexity in smart cities. In this approach, the context (similar to the notion of environment in multi-agent systems) is a first-class citizen, and offers different ways to think about interactions between agents and environment. In the case of smart cities, MASs can be used to model, simulate and solve problems, and answer a lot of needs. This paper advocates for their usage for context handling in complex environments such as smart cities, and aims at triggering discussion among different fields in order to better understand their cross-disciplinary needs.

Acknowledgements. This work is partially funded by the Midi-Pyrénées region for the neOCampus initiative (www.irit.fr/neocampus/) and supported by the University of Toulouse.

References

1. Amato, F., Chianese, A., Moscato, V., Picariello, A., Sperli, G.: SNOPS: a smart environment for cultural heritage applications. In: Proceedings of the Twelfth International Workshop on Web Information and Data Management, pp. 49–56. ACM (2012)
2. Bai, X., McAllister, R.R.J., Beaty, R.M., Taylor, B.: Urban policy and governance in a global environment: complex systems, scale mismatches and public participation. Current Opin. Environ. Sustain. 2(3), 129–135 (2010)
3. Boes, J., Nigon, J., Verstaevel, N., Gleizes, M.-P., Migeon, F.: The self-adaptive context learning pattern: overview and proposal. In: Christiansen, H., Stojanovic, I., Papadopoulos, G.A. (eds.) Modeling and Using Context. LNCS (LNAI), vol. 9405, pp. 91–104. Springer, Cham (2015). doi:10.1007/978-3-319-25591-0_7

4. Briot, J.-P., de Nascimento, N.M., de Lucena, C.J.P.: A multi-agent architecture for quantified fruits: design and experience. In: 28th International Conference on Software Engineering & Knowledge Engineering (SEKE 2016). SEKE/Knowledge Systems Institute, PA, USA (2016)
5. Cerquides, J., Picard, G., Rodríguez-Aguilar, J.A.: Designing a marketplace for the trading and distribution of energy in the smart grid. In: Proceedings of the 2015 International Conference on Autonomous Agents and Multiagent Systems, International Foundation for Autonomous Agents and Multiagent Systems, pp. 1285–1293 (2015)
6. Chamoso, P., De la Prieta, F., Pérez, J.B., Rodríguez, J.M.C.: Conflict resolution with agents in smart cities. In: Interdisciplinary Perspectives on Contemporary Conflict Resolution, p. 244 (2016)
7. Choy, M.C., Srinivasan, D., Cheu, R.L.: Neural networks for continuous online learning and control. IEEE Trans. Neural Netw. 17(6), 1511–1531 (2006)
8. Ferber, J.: Multi-agent Systems: An Introduction to Distributed Artificial Intelligence, vol. 1. Addison-Wesley, Reading (1999)
9. Froehlich, J., Findlater, L., Landay, J.: The design of eco-feedback technology. In: Proceedings of the SIGCHI Conference on Human Factors in Computing Systems, pp. 1999–2008. ACM (2010)
10. Guériau, M., Billot, R., El Faouzi, N.-E., Monteil, J., Armetta, F., Hassas, S.: How to assess the benefits of connected vehicles? A simulation framework for the design of cooperative traffic management strategies. Transp. Res. Part C: Emerg. Technol. 67, 266–279 (2016)
11. Hancke, G.P., Hancke Jr., G.P., et al.: The role of advanced sensing in smart cities. Sensors 13(1), 393–425 (2012)
12. Harrison, C., Eckman, B., Hamilton, R., Hartswick, P., Kalagnanam, J., Paraszczak, J., Williams, P.: Foundations for smarter cities. IBM J. Res. Dev. 54(4), 1–16 (2010)
13. Jin, J., Gubbi, J., Marusic, S., Palaniswami, M.: An information framework for creating a smart city through Internet of Things. IEEE Internet Things J. 1(2), 112–121 (2014)
14. Kitchin, R.: The real-time city? Big data and smart urbanism. GeoJournal 79(1), 1–14 (2014)
15. Lewis, D.P., Jebara, T., Noble, W.S.: Support vector machine learning from heterogeneous data: an empirical analysis using protein sequence and structure. Bioinformatics 22(22), 2753–2760 (2006)
16. Lützenberger, M., Küster, T., Masuch, N., Fähndrich, J.: Multi-agent system in practice: when research meets reality. In: Proceedings of the 2016 International Conference on Autonomous Agents & Multiagent Systems, International Foundation for Autonomous Agents and Multiagent Systems, pp. 796–805 (2016)
17. Martínez-Ballesté, A., Pérez-Martínez, P.A., Solanas, A.: The pursuit of citizens' privacy: a privacy-aware smart city is possible. IEEE Commun. Mag. 51(6), 136–141 (2013)
18. Mazac, S., Armetta, F., Hassas, S.: On bootstrapping sensori-motor patterns for a constructivist learning system in continuous environments. In: Alife 14: Fourteenth International Conference on the Synthesis and Simulation of Living Systems (2014)
19. Morvaj, B., Lugaric, L., Krajcar, S.: Demonstrating smart buildings and smart grid features in a smart energy city. In: Proceedings of the 2011 3rd International Youth Conference on Energetics (IYCE), pp. 1–8. IEEE (2011)

20. Mustapha, K., Mcheick, H., Mellouli, S.: Smart cities and resilience plans: a multi-agent based simulation for extreme event rescuing. In: Gil-Garcia, J.R., Pardo, T.A., Nam, T. (eds.) Smarter as the New Urban Agenda: A Comprehensive View of the 21st Century City. PAIT, vol. 11, pp. 149–170. Springer, Cham (2016). doi:10.1007/978-3-319-17620-8_8

21. Najjar, A., Reignier, P.: Constructivist ambient intelligent agent for smart environments. In: 2013 IEEE International Conference on Pervasive Computing and Communications Workshops (PERCOM Workshops), pp. 356–359. IEEE (2013)

22. Nam, T., Pardo, A.T.: Conceptualizing smart city with dimensions of technology, people, and institutions. In: Proceedings of the 12th Annual International Digital Government Research Conference: Digital Government Innovation in Challenging Times, pp. 282–291. ACM (2011)

23. Neirotti, P., De Marco, A., Cagliano, A.C., Mangano, G., Scorrano, F.: Current trends in smart city initiatives: some stylised facts. Cities **38**, 25–36 (2014)

24. Nigon J., Glize, E., Dupas, D., Crasnier, F., Boes, J.: Use cases of pervasive artificial intelligence for smart cities challenges. In: IEEE Workshop on Smart and Sustainable City, Toulouse, juillet (2016)

25. Opper, M.: Online versus offline learning. Philos. Mag. B **77**(5), 1531–1537 (1998)

26. Pittarello, F., Pellegrini, T.: Designing and evaluating interfaces for domestic eco-feedback: a blended educational experience. In: Proceedings of the 11th Biannual Conference on Italian SIGCHI Chapter, pp. 18–25. ACM (2015)

27. Roscia, M., Longo, M., Lazaroiu, G.C.: Smart city by multi-agent systems. In: 2013 International Conference on Renewable Energy Research and Applications (ICRERA), pp. 371–376. IEEE (2013)

28. Schaffers, H., Komninos, N., Pallot, M., Trousse, B., Nilsson, M., Oliveira, A.: Smart cities and the future internet: towards cooperation frameworks for open innovation. In: Domingue, J., et al. (eds.) FIA 2011. LNCS, vol. 6656, pp. 431–446. Springer, Heidelberg (2011). doi:10.1007/978-3-642-20898-0_31

29. Singh, M., Duggirala, M., Hayatnagarkar, H., Balaraman, V.: A multi-agent model of workgroup behaviour in an enterprise using a compositional approach (2016)

30. Su, K., Li, J., Fu, H.: Smart city and the applications. In: 2011 International Conference on Electronics, Communications and Control (ICECC), pp. 1028–1031. IEEE (2011)

31. Szabó, R., Farkas, K., Ispány, M., Benczúr, A.A., Bátfai, N.; Jeszenszky, P., Laki, S., Vágner, A., Kollár, L., Sidló, C., et al.: Framework for smart city applications based on participatory sensing. In: 2013 IEEE 4th International Conference on Cognitive Infocommunications (CogInfoCom), pp. 295–300. IEEE (2013)

32. Vaubourg, J., Presse, Y., Camus, B., Bourjot, C., Ciarletta, L., Chevrier, V., Tavella, J.-P., Morais, H.: Multi-agent multi-model simulation of smart grids in the MS4SG project. In: Demazeau, Y., Decker, K.S., Bajo Pérez, J., de la Prieta, F. (eds.) PAAMS 2015. LNCS (LNAI), vol. 9086, pp. 240–251. Springer, Cham (2015). doi:10.1007/978-3-319-18944-4_20

33. Nicolas, V.: Self-organization of robotic devices through demonstrations. Thesis, Université de Toulouse, Toulouse, France, juin (2016)

34. Vlahogianni, E.I., Kepaptsoglou, K., Tsetsos, V., Karlaftis, M.G.: A real-time parking prediction system for smart cities. J. Intell. Transp. Syst. **20**(2), 192–204 (2016)

On Conceivability and Existence in Linguistic Interpretation

Salvatore Pistoia-Reda[✉]

Leibniz-Zentrum Allgemeine Sprachwissenschaft (ZAS), Berlin, Germany
pistoia.reda@zas.gwz-berlin.de

Abstract. This paper discusses the role of existence presuppositions and conceivability in linguistic interpretation. In particular, it is discussed evidence that the non-emptiness requirement on universally-quantified propositions might be satisfied through access to a background of knowledge concerning what might be the case in the actual world, as opposed to a background of knowledge concerning what is actually the case. The evidence discussed comes from empirical observations on the behavior of the scalar implicature mechanism. The crucial piece evidence amounts to the fact that the entailment pattern with existentially-quantified propositions, which is crucial to generate the desired inference, is established when quantifiers range over non-existing but conceivable entities, but it cannot be established when quantifiers range over non-exiting and inconceivable entities.

Keywords: Existence presupposition · Entailment · Implicatures · Conceivability

1 Introduction

In standard literature (see, e.g., [15] and reference cited therein), universally-quantified propositions, such as example (1) below, are taken to carry an *existence* presupposition, i.e. a presupposition to the effect that the quantifier's restrictor is not empty. In the example, the presupposed material attached to the proposition is that Greeks exist, i.e. that there are in fact individuals for the universal quantifier to range over. As follows from classic discussion in the philosophy of language, a similar existence presupposition is assumed to be carried by propositions containing definite descriptions, such as the example in (2). Also in this example, we seem to be invited to draw an inference to the existence of some individual, i.e. the individual who happens to be the author of the Organon.

(1) Every Greek is a philosopher.

(2) The author of the Organon lived in Athens.

© Springer International Publishing AG 2017
P. Brézillon et al. (Eds.): CONTEXT 2017, LNAI 10257, pp. 203–212, 2017.
DOI: 10.1007/978-3-319-57837-8_16

In semantic analysis, presuppositions are treated as definedness conditions on the propositions containing the presuppositional items. Accordingly, presupposition failures, i.e. the cases in which the requirement fails to be satisfied, are analyzed in terms of undefinedness, that is truth-valuelessness. As a consequence, a universally-quantified proposition cannot receive a semantically proper evaluation unless the presupposition to the effect that the quantifier's restrictor is not empty can be satisfied. In the example (1) above, the universally-quantified proposition cannot be properly evaluated unless we can safely assume, against the background of information that we possess, that the set of Greek people is not empty. In a similar fashion, the example in (2) cannot receive a proper interpretation unless the existence presupposition can be satisfied.

A crucial consequence of this analysis in terms of undefinedness is that entailment patterns between the propositions containing the presuppositional items and other related propositions are suspended in case of a presupposition failure. Recall that, according to a generalized definition of entailment, two propositions ϕ and ψ of the same entailing type are taken to stand in an entailment relation if and only if for any world in which ϕ is assigned True as semantic value, ψ must receive the same assignment. Let us consider the entailment relation between universally-quantified propositions and existentially-quantified variants, such as in the example (3) below. Assuming that the universally-quantified propositions carry an existence presupposition, the entailment relation will be established whenever the presupposition can be satisfied. However, this entailment relation will not be established in case a presupposition failure occurs, since in this case the universally-quantified proposition cannot be assigned a proper semantic value. So, the entailment relation between propositions (1) and (3) will not be established, following such an analysis, whenever *it is known* that Greek people do not exist.

(3)   Some Greeks are philosophers.

Let me now provide some specifications concerning the nature of the background of information that is standardly assumed to play a role in establishing whether presuppositions are satisfied. In standard analysis (see [5,17,18] and much subsequent work), presuppositions are computed with respect to a so-called presuppositional *common ground*. This is a set of assumptions which are mutually believed by speakers while engaging in a conversation, i.e. a set of propositions that such conversationalists take for granted while exchanging information. The presuppositional common ground essentially relates to a set of uniquely determined circumstances - the *context set* - which is defined as the intersection of all propositions included in it.

Presuppositions are described as entailments from the presuppositional common ground, i.e. as propositions that must follow from the set of shared assumptions or, equivalently, as propositions that must be true in every circumstance included in the context set, if the proposition carrying the presupposition has to be properly evaluated. To consider a classic example, a proposition like (4) below carries a presupposition to the effect that there was a time in the past in which Socrates used to drink wine during symposia. However, if it is contextually known that Socrates never indulged in drinking alcohol while engaging in philosophical disquisitions, the proposition will suffer from a presupposition failure and will consequently be unevaluable. Back to our examples with quantified propositions, the universally-quantified proposition will not be defined if conversationalists share the information that Greeks do not exist. So, a consequence of this assumption is that the entailment relation between quantified propositions will not be established in case contextual knowledge implies that the restrictor of the universal quantifier is empty.

(4)   Socrates has stopped drinking wine during symposia.

In this work, I will follow standard treatment in analyzing the existence presupposition of universally-quantified propositions as a definedness condition on such propositions. In particular, I will follow standard analysis in assuming that the entailment pattern between quantified propositions cannot be established unless the existence presupposition of universally-quantified propositions is satisfied. However, in my discussion I will show that such an entailment pattern does seem to be established even in cases in which the existence presupposition cannot be satisfied with respect to the presuppositional common ground. In such cases, the presuppositional common ground will actually entail the presupposed proposition to be false. This, I take it, is proof that in these cases the background of information with respect to which the existence presupposition is checked is different from the presuppositional common ground. In the end, I will propose that the entailment relation, while not being sensitive to what is actually the case in the real world, is sensitive to what might be the case in the real world.

2 Implicatures and Entailment

In order to make the empirical point that the entailment pattern between quantified propositions obtains without reference to the common ground I have to introduce the phenomenon of scalar implicatures. In Gricean accounts (see, among others, [4,6,7]), a scalar implicature is obtained as a result of a meaning strengthening procedure activated by the observation that the speaker has made a weaker statement than she could have made in principle. Under the assumption that the speaker is cooperative and rational (this conjunction is held to be redundant in some versions of the theory), the hearer is thus entitled to draw the conclusion that the speaker does not believe an alternative stronger proposition to be the case. Under the further assumption that the speaker is opinionated as to the truth-value of propositions, the hearer can conclude that the speaker believes the alternative stronger proposition to be false and subject to negation. Such a procedure is mainly based on the exploitation of the first conversational maxim of quantity, according to which alternative statements are ordered based on their informativeness, operationally treated in terms of contextual entailment, i.e. entailment given common knowledge. Classic examples of scalar implicatures involves the meaning strengthening of a disjunctive propositions like (5a), obtained by negating the alternative stronger conjunctive proposition (5b), and of an existentially-quantified proposition like (6a) derived via negation of the universally-quantified proposition (6b).

(5) a. Socrates was denounced by Anytus or Meletus.

    b. Socrates was denounced by Anytus and Meletus.

(6) a. Some philosophers read the Organon.

    b. Every philosopher reads the Organon.

In grammatical approaches (see, e.g., [1–3]), however, it is assumed that the meaning strengthening procedure is part of a computationally-oriented mechanism and obtains on account of the pure logical properties of the propositions involved. In particular, in such accounts propositions are taken to be compared based on pure logical, rather than contextual, entailment. Evidence in favor of this analysis seems to come from the following reasoning. Consider the existentially-quantified proposition (7a) below. Now, common knowledge entails that all Greeks come from the same country. Based on this piece of information, the base proposition and its universally-quantified alternative (7b) provide the exact same amount of information, which can be rendered as the information that Greece is a warm country. In other words, assuming contextual information, the two propositions stand in a relation of contextual equivalence rather than contextual entailment. However, if this is the case, we shouldn't expect a scalar implicature to arise, if we assume that the mechanism can access contextual information. [10] argued that the oddness effect produced by the base proposition in this case is proof that a scalar implicature has been generated (see also [11, 12] for discussion). Indeed, if generated, the scalar implicature is predicted to generate a contextual contradiction, since assuming what we know it cannot be the case that some Greeks come from a country which is warm and some other Greeks come from a country which is not warm. And contextual contradictions notoriously give rise to infelicity effects. Magri proposes that this oddness is thus proof that the scalar implicature mechanism is based on a computational principle of contextual blindness.

(7) a. Some Greeks come from a warm country.

    b. Every Greek comes from a warm country.

3 Entailment with Empty Sets

Despite Magri is quite explicit in this respect (see, e.g., [10, p. 258]), evidently the entailment pattern between quantified propositions cannot be established on account of the purely logical properties of quantifiers. The point here is that there are circumstances in which universally-quantified propositions are true while, at the same time, existentially-quantified propositions are false. Such circumstances typically obtain when the universal quantifier's restrictor is empty. Given the definition in (8a), whenever the restrictor is empty the whole universally-quantified proposition will have to be assigned True as semantic value, since a false antecedent cannot but produce a true proposition in an implication. However, in this case the existentially-quantified variant has to be assigned False as a semantic value given the definition in (8b), since there cannot be an non-empty intersection of two sets one of which is the empty set. To be sure, there are of course alternative possibilities to establish the entailment pattern between universally-quantified and existentially-quantified propositions *logically*, i.e. assuming that the entailment pattern follows on account of the pure meaning of quantifiers. To make an example, connexive logics (see, e.g., [13]) submit a different of existentially-quantified proposition, along the lines of (9). As it is clear, if we assume this modified definition, we aren't forced to derive an inference to the existence of P-individuals. But I will not pursue this direction here.

(8)   a. $\forall x \, (Px \rightarrow Gx)$
        b. $\exists x \, (Px \wedge Gx)$

(9) $\exists x \, (\neg \, (Px \rightarrow Gx))$

As suggested in [16], a possible response for grammatical accounts building on the principle of contextual blindness would involve imposing that universally-quantified propositions carry an existence presupposition, as discussed at the outset. However, there are reasons to suspect that the satisfaction of the existence presupposition is at the origin of the entailment pattern in this case, at least assuming standard presuppositional analysis discussed above. Consider for instance the existentially-quantified base proposition in (10a) below. Now, our common knowledge entails that Greece is currently a republic, which amounts to the assumption that Greek kings do not exist, once we have also made clear that we are not referring to past sovereigns of Greece. If we assume the presuppositional analysis of universally-quantified proposition, the universally-quantified alternative proposition in (10b) should be taken to be undefined, since the non-emptiness requirement on the restrictor of the universal quantifier cannot be satisfied with respect to the presuppositional common ground. In other words, the presuppositional common ground entails the presupposed proposition, i.e. the proposition that Greek kings exist, to be false. But, as we know, undefinedness of a universally-quantified proposition implies that the entailment pattern with existentially-quantified variants cannot be established. Now, a crucial consequence of the latter fact, i.e. of the fact that no entailment pattern can be established in this case, is that no scalar implicature should be attached to the existentially-quantified base proposition under analysis. However, as suggested in [14], this base proposition also produces an infelicity effect, and this new case of oddness could be explained by assuming a natural modification of the reasoning that we have discussed above in order to account for the infelicity of (7a). To be more precise, common knowledge entails that all Greeks come from the same country, *irrespective of their occupation or social status*. The crucial modification is italicized here. Consequently, negating that every Greeks come from a country which is warm (as it would be obtained by generating the scalar implicature), while asserting that some Greeks come from a country which is warm (which amounts to the so-called existential base meaning of the proposition), would contradict the above-mentioned piece of contextual information, and is then expected to generate a clear infelicity effect.

(10)   a.   Some Greek kings come from a warm country.
       b.   Every Greek king comes from a warm country.

But the generation of a contradictory scalar implicature is not the only possible explanation of the oddness effect produced in the case of existentially-quantified propositions such as (10a). One alternative explanation would capitalize on the fact that the existentially-quantified proposition is construed with a reference failure noun phrase. As a consequence, this reference failure might be the source of the oddness effect in this case. However, there are at least two reasons to reject this alternative explanation. To begin with, experimental analysis on speakers' judgments showed that existentially-quantified propositions with reference failure noun phrases, such as (10a), statistically correlate with existentially-quantified propositions construed without reference failure noun phrases, such as (7a), in case both would produce a contextual contradiction when enriched with the scalar implicature, i.e. in case both are construed by combining the reference failure with a verb phrase yielding a contextual contradiction. This would seem to demonstrate that the basis of this correlation is the contextual contradiction generated by the scalar implicatures attached to the two propositions. In addition, existentially-quantified propositions like (10a) have been demonstrated to elicit inappropriateness judgments. However, this observation contradicts the standard empirical pattern observed in, e.g., [9], according to which existentially-quantified propositions construed with reference failure noun phrases, such as (11) below, can be used naturally (as opposed to reference failures obtained with propositions containing strong quantifiers). In conclusion, assuming that a contradictory scalar implicature has been generated in the case of (10a) would seem to provide the best explanatory account of the observed oddness.

(11)   Some Greek kings enjoy hunting.

But if a scalar implicature has been generated in this case, an immediate conclusion would be that the entailment pattern between the two quantified propositions has been established even if this pattern was not established logically and the definedness of the universally-quantified proposition does not follow from the presuppositional common ground.

4   Entailment with Inconceivable Entities

A possible solution to account for the observed behavior would be imposing that the scalar implicature mechanism be sensitive to the notion of Strawson-entailment, as proposed and defended by [20] (see also [19,21] for earlier discussion). According to the definition, two propositions ϕ and ψ of the same entailing type stand in a Strawson-entailment relation if and only if they stand in a classic, generalized entailment pattern in the intersection of worlds in which presuppositions are satisfied. From a theoretical point of view, it is crucial to realize that Strawson-entailment is part of an *algorithmic* machinery, in that it simply depends on adding an additional, tacit premise to the argumentative scheme connecting the two propositions, i.e. the premise that presuppositions are satisfied. Once such an additional premise is put in place, and justified as part of our explanation, the argumentative scheme connecting universally-quantified and existentially-quantified propositions will be realized by simply assuming knowledge of the meaning of quantifiers. In other words, the definition does not require the existence presupposition attached to universally-quantified propositions to be satisfied in the actual world. This is the reason why this solution based on Strawson-entailment is generally held to be compatible with grammatically-oriented accounts building on notions such as blindness in the case of scalar implicatures. But, in addition, and crucially from our point of view, this solution does not require the existence presupposition to be satisfied in *any world*, as the entailment pattern is supposed to be established on account of purely logical relations between quantifiers, plus the enriching tacit premise to the effect that presuppositions are satisfied.

According to this solution based on Strawson-entailment, then, the scalar implicature mechanism does not assume (actual or constitutive) knowledge when establishing the entailment pattern between quantified propositions. As we have seen in the case of existentially-quantified propositions such as (10a) above, this solution generates a desired prediction. In such cases, the entailment pattern is shown to be obtained even if actual knowledge cannot play a role in establishing it, i.e. even if the presupposed presupposition does not follow from the presuppositional common ground. However, this solution would also wrongly predict an entailment pattern between existentially-quantified and universally-quantified propositions such as (12a) and (12b) below, featuring not merely non-existing but inconceivable entities, i.e. entities such that our constitutive knowledge of things entails that cannot exist in the actual world or in any conceivable world. Under the crucial assumption that alternative propositions which are part of a relevant entailing pair are obligatorily subject to negation, a consequence of this prediction would be the generation of a scalar implicature attached to the base proposition. It is immediate to realize that the scalar implicature possibly attached to this base proposition would generate a contradiction when conjoined with the piece of knowledge that the property of being equal to rectangles must hold for any instance of a given geometrical entity, including round squares. In other words, it cannot be the case that some round squares are equal to rectangles while some other round squares are distinct from rectangles. The proposition is thus expected to produce an infelicity effect; and it is not difficult to realize that the proposition does, in facts, generate a clear oddness effect. This would seem to demonstrate that a scalar implicature has been generated in this case, by virtue of a Strawson-entailment relation.

(12)   a. Some round squares are rectangles.

       b. Every round square is a rectangle.

There are reasons to doubt, however, that the source of the infelicity produced in the case of (12a) is the scalar implicature attached to the proposition. The main evidence against this explanation is the fact that the very same oddness effect seems to be replicated in the case of (13), where the reference failure noun phrase with inconceivable entities is combined with a verb phrase not yielding a contradiction. However, the proposition does not seem to correlate with the existentially-quantified proposition in (14), where the noun phrase, construed without reference failures of any kind, is combined with a verb phrase this time yielding a contextual contradiction. Experimental analysis is needed in this case to clarify what the judgments really are with respect to the different oddness effects generated in the distinct cases; but, if this intuition is correct, then the source of the oddness of propositions such as (12a) does not seem to be a contradictory scalar implicature.

(13)   Some round squares are green.

(14)   Some squares are rectangles.

Let us suppose, then, that a scalar implicature cannot be generated in the case of existentially-quantified propositions such as (12a) (and 13). This fact can be understood as a consequence of the impossibility of establishing a proper entailment pattern between the existentially-quantified proposition in (12a) and its universally-quantified alternative in (12b). And this has to be understood as a consequence of the undefinedness of the universally-quantified proposition. In other words, the reasoning to account for all of the data that we have considered up to this point, provided that our judgments are confirmed by experimental analysis, would be the following: Definedness of universally-quantified propositions through satisfaction of the existence presupposition is a necessary and sufficient condition for the entailment pattern with existentially-quantified propositions to be established. So, whenever the universally-quantified proposition is not satisfied, we can safely assume that the said entailment pattern is not established. And whenever the entailment pattern can be observed, we can safely assume the definedness of the universally-quantified proposition. Similarly, we assume that whenever the entailment pattern cannot be observed, we can conclude that the universally-quantified proposition is not defined. We observed the entailment pattern in cases such as (10a), where the existentially-quantified proposition is construed with a reference failure noun phrase. Since the definedness of the universally-quantified proposition is to be assumed in this case, this means that the existence presupposition has been satisfied but not through access to the presuppositional common ground. However, we do not observe the entailment pattern between quantified propositions in the case of (12a), where the existentially-quantified proposition is construed with non-existing and inconceivable entities. This means that the universally-quantified proposition is not defined. In other words, the existence presupposition has not been satisfied. So, satisfaction of the existence presupposition must depend on access to a background of knowledge which contains non-existing entities but excludes entities that we cannot possibly conceive of. This is why the tentative conclusion we can draw from this discussion is that the satisfaction of the existence presupposition, and thus the entailment pattern between quantified proposition, clearly does not depend on what is the case in the actual world; however, our discussion shows that existence presupposition and entailment pattern depend on what might actually be the case. That is to say, the existence presupposition is enriched with a modal flavor in this case, à la [8].

5 Conclusion

In this paper I have discussed the role of existence presuppositions in the interpretation of universally-quantified propositions. Satisfaction of the existence presupposition carried by such propositions is intended as a definedness condition. Definedness of universally-quantified propositions through satisfaction of the existence presupposition is interpreted as a necessary and sufficient condition for the entailment patterns with existentially-quantified propositions to be established. I have submitted evidence that the entailment pattern is established when universally-quantified propositions would not be satisfied with respect to the presuppositional common ground of conversationalists. Since the satisfaction of the existence is necessary for establishing the entailment pattern, this means that the existence presupposition has been satisfied though access to a background of knowledge which does not necessarily include existing entities, i.e. entities that we mutually believe to exist in the actual world. I have also discussed evidence that the entailment pattern cannot be observed in cases where universally-quantified propositions would not be satisfied if the relevant background contained inconceivable entities. The conclusion that we can tentatively draw from this discussion is that the existence presupposition must be understood as having a modal flavor in such cases, that is to say it is satisfied through access to a background of knowledge which does not depend on what is the case in the actual world but on what might actually be the case.

References

1. Chierchia, G.: Broaden your views: implicatures of domain widening and the 'logicality' of language. Linguist. Inq. **37**(4), 535–590 (2006)
2. Chierchia, G., Fox, D., Spector, B.: Scalar implicature as a grammatical phenomenon. In: Maienborn, C., von Heusinger, K., Portner, P. (eds.) Semantics: An International Handbook of Natural Language Meaning, vol. 3, pp. 2297–2331. Mouton de Gruyter, Berlin (2012)
3. Fox, D.: Free choice and the theory of scalar implicatures. In: Sauerland, U., Stateva, P. (eds.) Presuppositions and Implicatures in Compositional Semantics. Palgrave Studies in Pragmatics, Language and Cognition. Palgrave Macmillan, Basingstoke (2007)
4. Geurts, B.: Quantity Implicatures. Cambridge University Press, Cambridge (2010)
5. Heim, I.: On the projection problem for presuppositions. In: Barlow, M., Flickinger, D.P., Westcoat, M.T. (eds.) Proceedings of the West Coast Conference on Formal Linguistics, pp. 249–260. Stanford Linguistic Association, Stanford University (1983)

6. Hirschberg, J.L.B.: A Theory of Scalar Implicature. University of Pennsylvania, Philadelphia (1985)
7. Horn, L.: A Natural History of Negation. The University of Chicago Press, Chicago (1989)
8. Kratzer, A.: What 'must' and 'can' must and can mean. Linguist. Philos. **1**(3), 337–355 (1977)
9. Lappin, S., Reinhart, T.: Presuppositional effects of strong determiners: a processing account. Linguistics **26**(6), 1021–1038 (1988)
10. Magri, G.: A theory of individual-level predicates based on blind mandatory scalar implicatures. Nat. Lang. Semant. **17**(3), 245–297 (2009)
11. Magri, G.: Another argument for embedded scalar implicatures based on oddness in downward entailing environments. Semant. Pragmat. **4**, 1–51 (2011)
12. Magri, G.: Two puzzles raised by oddness in conjunction. J. Semant. **33**(1), 1–17 (2016)
13. McCall, S.: Connexive implication and the syllogism. Mind **76**(303), 346–356 (1967)
14. Pistoia-Reda, S.: Contextual blindness in implicature computation. Nat. Lang. Semant. (2017). doi:10.1007/s11050-016-9131-6
15. Sauerland, U.: Implicated presuppositions. In: Steube, A. (ed.) The Discourse Potential of Underspecified Structures. Language, Context and Cognition, vol. 8, pp. 581–600 (2008)
16. Schlenker, P.: Maximize presupposition and Gricean reasoning. Nat. Lang. Semant. **20**(4), 391–429 (2012)
17. Stalnaker, R.: Assertion. In: Cole, P. (ed.) Pragmatics, pp. 315–332. Academic Press, New York (1978)
18. Stalnaker, R.: Common ground. Linguist. Philos. **25**(5), 701–721 (2002)
19. Strawson, P.F.: Identifying reference and truth-values. Theoria **30**(2), 96–118 (1964)
20. Von Fintel, K.: NPI licensing, Strawson entailment, and context dependency. J. Semant. **16**(2), 97–148 (1999)
21. Von Fintel, K.: Counterfactuals in a dynamic context. Curr. Stud. Linguist. Ser. **36**, 123–152 (2001)

Multi-purpose Adaptation in the Web of Things

Mehdi Terdjimi[1]([✉]), Lionel Médini[1], Michael Mrissa[2], and Maria Maleshkova[3]

[1] Univ Lyon, LIRIS Université Lyon 1 - CNRS UMR5205,
69622 Villeurbanne, France
{mehdi.terdjimi,lionel.medini}@liris.cnrs.fr
[2] LIUPPA, Université de Pau et des Pays de l'Adour,
BP 1155, 64013 Pau Cedex, France
michael.mrissa@univ-pau.fr
[3] AIFB, Karlsruhe Institute of Technology (KIT), Karlsruhe, Germany
maria.maleshkova@kit.edu

Abstract. Web of Things applications require advanced solutions to provide adaptation to different purposes from common context models. While such models are application-specific, the adaptation itself is based on questions (i.e. concerns) that are orthogonal to application domains. In this paper, we present a generic solution to provide reusable and multi-purpose context-based adaptation for smart environments. We rely on semantic technologies and reason about contextual information to evaluate, at runtime, the pertinence of each adaptation possibility to adaptation questions covering various concerns. We evaluate our solution against a smart agriculture scenario using the ASAWoO platform, and discuss how to design context models and rules from "classical" information sources (e.g. domain experts, device QoS, user preferences).

Keywords: Web of Things · Multi-purpose adaptation · Semantic reasoning

1 Introduction

The Web of Things (WoT) relies on Web technologies and standards to build applications that make heterogeneous objects (i.e. things) interoperate in diverse situations. As WoT applications cover numerous domains such as healthcare, smart cities, smart factories and smart agriculture, their development has been substantially gaining interest in the past few years.

In the ASAWoO project, we have defined a virtual extension for a thing called *avatar*. Just like a servient [1], an avatar allows access to and control over a thing. An avatar is a component-based software artifact that relies on a semantic architecture to process and reason about semantically-annotated information. This way, in the ASAWoO platform, avatars can communicate with one another and expose high-level *functionalities* to form *WoT applications* involving several things that achieve a common goal. A WoT application consists of a hierarchy of functionalities: composed functionalities may require several devices to

© Springer International Publishing AG 2017
P. Brézillon et al. (Eds.): CONTEXT 2017, LNAI 10257, pp. 213–226, 2017.
DOI: 10.1007/978-3-319-57837-8_17

communicate and terminal ones are implemented using device *capabilities* (sensors, actuators, processing units). WoT application execution relies on several research fields [9], among which semantic web services and multi-agent systems. The functionality composition approach is not detailed here, but is precised in [11].

Avatars must also adapt their behaviors to comply with non-functional concerns such as quality of service (QoS), energy efficiency and security, with respect to several factors like environmental and natural conditions, computing resources and user preferences. To do so, they embed a generic, multi-purpose adaptation process designed to answer *adaptation questions*. Due to the set of concerns addressed in the ASAWoO project, we herein target the following adaptation questions [15]:

Q_1 *Which protocols should the application use to communicate with things?*
Q_2 *Where should the application code be executed?*
Q_3 *Which thing capability should be involved in a given terminal functionality?*
Q_4 *Which functionality should be involved in a given composed functionality?*
Q_5 *Which functionality should be exposed to clients and other avatars?*[1]

They may relate to concerns that are independent of the application domain, so that any application can be deployed on the ASAWoO WoT platform. And so must be the hardware and software architecture that provides adaptation facilities to the avatars. However, the actual data about sensors, domain concepts or users' preferences are application-dependent. As adaptation questions must be answered using these data, these questions need to be related to the application domain and actors.

In this paper, we provide a multi-purpose context adaptation process, able for any WoT application to simultaneously answer domain-independent adaptation questions with data originating from application-specific sources. To do so, we turn data into semantically-explicit contextual information, transform these information into *context model instances*, and infer all *adaptation possibilities*, along with their pertinence values. We detail the different types of rules involved in the adaptation process, and show how reifying RDF sets of triples that represent adaptation possibilities allows keeping the genericity of adaptation questions and preserving the domain-agnostic nature of avatar components.

Section 2 presents a smart agriculture scenario that illustrates our approach. Section 3 details our adaptation and question answering processes. Section 4 presents our implementation and evaluates it in terms of accuracy and performance. Section 5 presents related work in context description and management. Section 6 discusses our results and compares our solution to the state of the art. Section 7 provides a summary of our results and insights for future work.

2   Smart Agriculture Scenario

Throughout the paper, we use the following scenario derived from [9], from the sustainable agriculture domain. The considered WoT application aims at

---

[1] Functionalities must be exposed by avatars prior to be called by clients and executed.

watering a vineyard (aka *field*) according to its local water needs. The field is divided in several *parts*, each of which can be watered separately using an irrigation network. Even though each object has its own avatar, this scenario only focuses on *drones* that are in charge of taking photos of the field parts to detect which parts lack water. The application takes into account current weather conditions and forecast, in order not to water if precipitations are expected and to only provide each field part with the necessary quantity of water otherwise.

The application is designed as a hierarchy of functionalities, on top of which *ManageFieldWatering*, which is composed of several *ManagePartOfFieldWatering* functionalities, each of which requires *DetectWateringNeeds*, which implies *TakePicture*, *ProcessPicture*, *TransferPicture*, etc. Drones can collaborate to achieve a composed functionality such as DetectWateringNeeds. In this case, a drone "takes the lead" and selects its most appropriate collaborators to take pictures. In the same way, drones can serve as network relays to transmit information between drones over the field and a gateway connected to the cloud. Complex processing task can also be executed on the platform cloud.

The application is deployed in a WoT platform that comprises a cloud infrastructure and several wireless gateways around the field. The field is equiped with an anemometer and a pluviometer to sense actual weather conditions. However, it is not covered with a wide wireless network. 3 Drones can be used. They are equiped with a GPS sensor, a camera that can take photos of different qualities, two wireless network interfaces (Wifi and Bluetooth), and can sense their own current capabilities (battery, memory availability, CPU usage, storage space). Lastly, the application is connected to a weather forecast service.

As there are multiple ways to achieve these functionalities, the WoT application must adapt its behavior. To precise our scenario, we consider an example of situation in which an avatar has to answer the five adaptation questions described in Sect. 1. We hereafter instantiate each adaptation question and precise the elements that would allow a human operator to answer it in this situation.

Q_1 Choosing a network interface to transfer a picture depends on the distance between the drones and on the energy consumption of available interfaces.
Conditions: The drone has to transmit data to another drone located at 11 m and has 45% of battery left.
Deduction: The distance is too high for using Bluetooth and the battery level is sufficient for both.
Decision: Use Wifi to perform TransferPicture.

Q_2 The application module that processes pictures to determine water needs may be executed either on the drone or on the cloud. It requires high CPU availability and a minimum battery level. In addition, executing it on the cloud requires high bandwidth to transfer the picture in acceptable time.
Conditions: CPU availability is 80% and battery 45%.
Deduction: The CPU level is sufficient to do the processing on the drone and the battery level is sufficient for both.
Decision: Execute the ProcessPicture code on the drone.

Q_3 Taking HD pictures is preferable when implementing the functionality DetectWateringNeeds. However, this requires a high-resolution camera and sufficient storage capacity.
Conditions: The drone has the capability to take HD pictures and 2.5 Gb of free internal storage.
Deduction: The picture can be taken and stored in high definition.
Decision: Use the TakeHdPicture capability to realize the TakePicture functionality.

Q_4 Choosing the right drone to identify if part of field #1 needs to be watered depends on the remaining battery power and on distance from the part of the field of each drone.
Conditions: Drone1 (resp. drone2, resp. drone3) is at 120 (resp. 20, resp. 70) meters from part of field #1, and has 90 (resp. 45, resp. 70)% battery left.
Deduction: All drones can fulfill the functionality, but drone 2 is closer.
Decision: Choose drone 2 to perform DetetWateringNeeds on field part 1.

Q_5 Drones may deteriorate if they are exposed to strong wind or to the rain. They should not be able to go outside if the weather is inconvenient.
Conditions: No rain, but a 55 km/h wind.
Deduction: Drones 1, 2 and 3 have no risk to be deteriorated by rain, but have significant risk to be damaged by wind.
Decision: Do not expose the GoOutside functionality on drones 1, 2 and 3. Consequently, do not expose the TakePicture and DetectWaterNeeds either.

3   Multi-purpose Adaptation in WoT Applications

Multi-purpose context adaptation in WoT applications originates from several processes in which various actors take part. WoT platform designers create complex execution environments that need to handle several concerns to support a variety of use cases and applications; they document these concerns and the corresponding adaptation questions. Appliance manufacturers describe device characteristics (QoS) in their documentations. Domain experts identify application concepts and processes, along with all the environmental sensors and Web services able to provide useful contextual data. Users specify their preferences (e.g. working hours, preferred devices, privacy levels, etc.).

WoT application designers then need to interpret all those instances of contextual dimension and to integrate them in a comprehensive adaptation process. Their work consists in designing a context model and two sets of rules: *transformation* and *adaptation*. Then, they wire the model to the available data sources. The ASAWoO platform does the rest. At configuration time, static data (e.g. application context model, appliance configuration, user preferences) are stored in semantic repositories [11]. At runtime, an avatar receives raw data from various sources, including devices and Web services. These data are semantically annotated and transformed into instances of the context model, using transformation rules. Adaptation rules are then applied to the instantiated context model to infer each possible adaptation choice. When avatar components require adaptation decisions, they send adaptation questions to the avatar *context manager*, which retrieves the best candidate. The querying process is the same, regardless of whether the question relies on filtering (e.g. can I expose a given functionality) or on ranking (e.g. which communication protocol is the most suitable). The whole process is based on the management workflow described in [15], depicted in Fig. 1. In this section, we focus on the following activities: identifying semantic instances of the context model, building transformation and adaptation rules, and solving adaptation questions. We apply these processes on our scenario, which involves three drones in the ManageFieldWatering functionality.

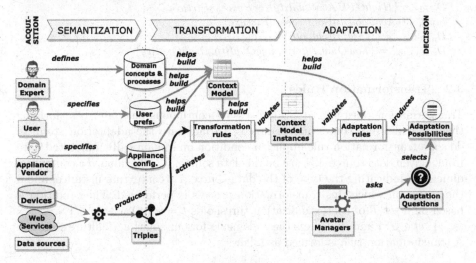

Fig. 1. The adaptation process and its actors.

3.1 Context Model Instantiation

We use hereafter the following formalization.

- The context model M is structured according to contextual *dimensions* D_j [15], that correspond to the conditions described in the example in Sect. 2. $M = \sqcup D_j, j \in \{1, ..., n\}$, where n is the number of dimensions.
- A contextual dimension D is a set of possible contextual *instances* i. $D_j = \{i_{jk}, k = 1, ..., Card(D_j)\}$, where $Card(D_j)$ depends on the transformation rules defined in Sect. 3.2.
- An instantiated context model is called a contextual *situation* ς. It denotes a semantized observation of all available contextual data at a given instant t, at which each dimension can be valued or empty.
$\varsigma_t = \{i_{tj}\}, i_{tj} \in D_j \cup \varnothing, j \in \{1, ..., n\}$

In our scenario, we identify the sets of contextual instances in our WoT infrastructure below:

$D_{wind} = \{NoWind, Breeze, StrongWindForGoOutside\}$
$D_{rain} = \{NoRain, Rainy\}$
$D_{distance} = \{CloseToFieldPart1, CloseToFieldPart2, CloseToFieldPart3,$
$FarFromFieldPart1, FarFromFieldPart2, FarFromFieldPart3\}$
$D_{bandwidth} = \{HighBandwidthForTransferPicture,$
$LowBandwidthForTransferPicture\}$
$D_{storage} = \{HighCapacityForStorePicture, LowCapacityForStorePicture\}$
$D_{battery} = \{HighBatteryForMoving, LowBatteryForMoving,$
$HighBatteryForTakePicture, LowBatteryForTakePicture,$
$HighBatteryForTransferPicture, LowBatteryForTransferPicture,$
$HighBatteryForProcessPicture, LowBatteryForProcessPicture\}$
$D_{CPU} = \{HighCPUAvailabilityForProcessPicture,$
$LowCPUAvailabilityForProcessPicture\}$
$D_{protocols} = \{Wifi, Bluetooth\}$
$D_{resolution} = \{LowQuality, AverageQuality, HighQuality\}$

3.2   Transformation Rules

Transformation rules aim at pre-processing continuous data and transforming them into discrete contextual instances, to facilitate the adaptation step. To do so, a transformation rule applies a condition on semantically annotated data from a given data source. Let src be the data source, v_{src} its value, d a contextual dimension indicating the type of the data source, i a contextual instance, and a the avatar on which this transformation process is performed. The condition is based on a set T of contextualization thresholds $t = (o, v_t)$ with $o \in \{>, <, >=, <=\}$, $v_t \in \mathbb{R}$. Figure 2 depicts these elements for our smart agriculture scenario. A transformation rule is formed as follows:

$$src \ \wedge \ v_{src} \ \wedge \ T \ \rightarrow \ [d :hasContextualInstance \ i] :hasContextualSource \ a$$

The inferred graph is composed of two triples. The subject of the first one is the URI of the contextual dimension, its predicate $hasContextualInstance$ and its object the URI of the contextual instance. The second one has the first as subject (by applying *triple reification* [8]), $hasContextualSource$ as predicate and the avatar URI as object. An example of transformation rule is the following:

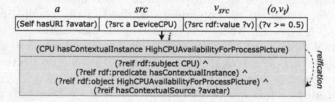

3.3   Adaptation Rules

Adaptation rules infer *adaptation possibilities* from contextual instances. An adaptation possibility is a triple that is a potential answer to an adaptation question. The head of an adaptation rule is a conjunction of reified graphs $G_i, i \in \mathbb{N}$ produced using transformation rules. Its body is a new reified graph with

Contextual Information	Data Source	Raw Value Type	Contextual Instance Thresholds
Wind	Anemometer	Integer (wind speed in km/h)	NoWind: x=0 Breeze: 20<x<50 StrongWindForGoOutside: x>=50
Rain	Web service, Pluviometer	Integer (precipitation rate in mm/s)	NoRain: x=0 Rainy: x>0
Distance	GPS	Integer (distance from a part of the field)	CloseFromFieldX: x <= 100 FarFromFieldX: x > 100
Bandwidth	Cloud Infrastructure	Integer (ping in milliseconds)	HighBandwidth ForTransferPicture: x<100 LowBandwidth ForTransferPicture: x>=100
Storage	(self) memory	Decimal (% of remaining capacity)	LowCapacity ForStorePicture: x<0.5 HighCapacity ForStorePicture: x>=0.5
Battery	(self) battery	Decimal (% of remaining power)	LowBatteryForMoving: x<0.6 LowBatteryFor(others): x<0.5 HighBatteryForMoving: x>=0.6 HighBatteryFor(others): x>=0.5
CPU	(self) CPU	Decimal (% of CPU load)	LowCPUAvailability ForProcessPicture: x<0.5 HighCPUAvailability ForProcessPicture: x>=0.5
Protocols	(self) network interfaces	Boolean (presence of the interface)	(Bluetooth/Wifi) x=1
Resolution	(self) camera	Integer (number of horizontal lines)	LowQuality: x<240 AverageQuality: 240<x<720 HighQuality: x>=720

Fig. 2. The relation between contextual dimensions, data sources, raw value types and contextual instance thresholds.

three triples, stating the adaptation candidate triple p, the source avatar a of this candidate triple, and its contextual ranking value r. Thus, an adaptation rule has the form: $\wedge \, G_i \, \rightarrow \, p, \, p :hasContextualSource \, a, \, p \, rdf:value \, r$

The form of an adaptation possibility triple varies according to adaptation questions. Its subject is the URI of either a preferred protocol (Q_1), a code location (Q_2), a local capability (Q_3), another avatar functionality (Q_4) or a local functionality (Q_5). Its predicate is the URI of the adaptation question itself, and the object is the URI of the functionality to adapt. The ranking value determines the accuracy of a candidate in the current contextual situation. An example of adaptation rule is the following:

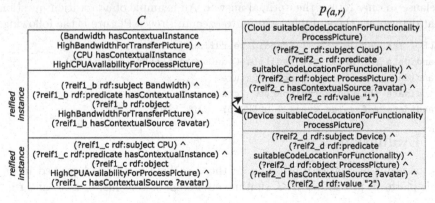

Figure 3 depicts the reifications in the semantized contextual data both on the transformation scope (i.e. ready-to-provide adaptation possibilities) and on the adaptation scope (i.e. ready-to-provide adaptation answers).

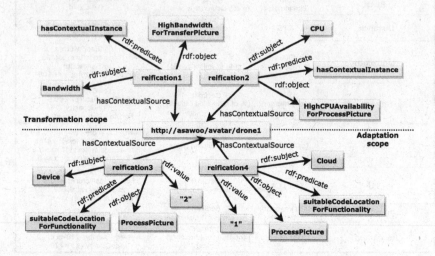

Fig. 3. Linked graph of reified results of transformation and adaptation rules.

3.4   Adaptation Question Answering

Answering an adaptation question aims at retrieving the subject of the best valued adaptation possibility triple (along with its avatar), for a given adaptation question and regarding a given functionality. The context manager converts such questions into SPARQL SELECT queries with two variables: the adaptation question answer ?answer and the contextual source ?ctxSrc. The adaptation decision either relies on filtering (e.g. the functionality can be exposed or not as in [10]) or on ranking (e.g. select the appropriate features as in [4]). While Q_5 acts as a filter, answering Q_1, Q_2, Q_3 and Q_4 require adaptation possibilities to be ranked. For ranking-based adaptation questions, the SPARQL query includes an ORDER BY clause depending on the rank value ?rank, along with a LIMIT 1 clause to only return the optimal answer. An example of adaptation question that determines the suitable location to execute ProcessPicture is the following:

```
SELECT ?answer ?ctxSrc { ?candidate rdf:subject ?answer .
?candidate rdf:predicate <suitableCodeLocationForFunctionality> .
?candidate rdf:object <ProcessPicture> .
?candidate <hasContextualSource> ?ctxSrc .
?candidate rdf:value ?rank } ORDER BY ?rank LIMIT 1
```

4   Evaluation

We base our evaluation prototype on the ASAWoO platform described in [9]. This platform provides a WoT runtime environment that instantiates and runs one avatar for each connected device, and provides facilities to store application and contextual data in semantic repositories. Avatars are implemented in Java and their components are OSGi bundles. Each avatar exposes its device functionalities and context data to the other platform elements using Web standards. Inside an avatar, components ask adaptation questions at runtime to the context manager, which delegates answering to a local semantic reasoner by interpreting them as SPARQL queries. At the same time, the context manager constantly acquires raw data from various sources and transmits them to the semantic reasoner as described in Sect. 3.

As, to the best of our knowledge, there exists no similar work that led to the design and implementation of a domain-agnostic, semantic-based and multi-purpose adaptation platform for the Web of Things, we could not compare our work to the state of the art. We then chose to evaluate our prototype according to two criteria based on the work of Bass [2]. First, we evaluate its accuracy, i.e. its ability to do the work for which it was intended. Second, we evaluate its performance for both the data integration and query answering tasks. All experiments were performed using the HyLAR semantic reasoner [14].

4.1 Qualitative Evaluation

We evaluate the accuracy of our solution by simulating the scenario from Sect. 2 by connecting three drones to our WoT platform, with the objective of realizing the ManageWatering functionality. For the sake of simplicity, we focused on the tasks that only required drones and did not consider other appliances such as the automatic irrigation system. The experimental setup was the following: our platform is the ASAWoO platform and runs in an Ubuntu 16.04 VM with 2 VCPUs and 4 Gb of RAM, in an OpenStack cloud infrastructure. We vary the contextual parameters identified in Sect. 3 in a 2-days time interval. In this interval, we ask our five adaptation questions to each drone avatars, at different times $t1$, $t2$, $t3$ and $t4$, as depicted in Fig. 4. We expect the answers to these questions to correspond to the adaptation rules described in Sect. 3.3.

Figure 5 shows the answers returned to the adaptation questions by the five managers. At $t2$, we see that the optimal protocol for the TransferPicture functionality between drone 1 and drone 2 is Wifi as they are in different parts of the field. At $t2$ and $t3$, executing ProcessPicture in devices is preferable due to ping timeouts or long delays caused by the weather conditions. At $t2$, drone 1 capabilities are preferred as drone 3 capacity is too low. We also see that drone 2 is not a good choice for detecting parts of field to water due to its insufficient resolution. At $t1$ and $t3$, drone 3 is the optimal choice to take pictures due to its proximity to part-of-field 1. However, drone 1 is preferred at $t2$ due to its high battery level. At $t2$ and $t3$, the functionality GoOutside is not exposed as either the wind is too strong or it rains.

In all cases, we verified that all avatar context managers provided the expected answers to all adaptation questions. The correctness of our system is enforced by the use of a standard semantic reasoner, which ensures that any other rule-based solution would have given the same answers. In addition, this

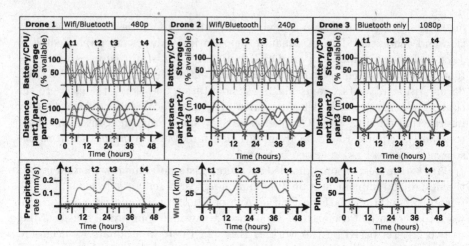

Fig. 4. Variation of contextual data during a simulated 2-days time interval.

Time	Q1 – Protocol for TransferPicture (Drones 1 & 2)	Q2 – Location of ProcessPicture	Q3 – Implementation of DetectWateringNeeds	Q4 – Composition with TakePicture (FieldPart1)	Q5 – Exposability of GoOutside
t1	Bluetooth	Cloud	Drone 3	Drone 3	Exposable
t2	Wifi	Device	Drone 1	Drone 2	Not exposable
t3	Bluetooth	Device	Drone 3	Drone 3	Not exposable
t4	Bluetooth	Cloud	Drone 3	Drone 1	Exposable

Fig. 5. Answers to five adaptation questions in four different times.

evaluation shows that our solution allows performing accurate multi-purpose adaptation from a common semantic contextual model.

4.2 Quantitative Evaluation

In this section, we evaluate the performance of our prototype in terms of processing times. These experiments were performed on a Dell OptiPlex 780 - Core 2 Duo E8400 @ 3 GHz. As the integration (semantization, transformation and application of adaptation rules) and adaptation question answering processes can run in parallel, we evaluate them in separate runs, and with different goals (i.e. maximum processing times). Contextual data integration runs as a background task, but must not monopolize all computing capabilities allocated to the avatar, especially if this avatar runs on a constraint device. Hence, it must be lightweight but does not need to be immediate. We then chose a threshold of 1 s as success for this experiment[2]. Adaptation question answering, however, is time-critical, as it is required for the current functioning of the avatar and of the WoT application. We then limit its acceptable response time to 100 ms.

---

[2] One second is the commonly admitted threshold upon which the user's attention stops focusing on the current task.

For both processes, we ran two experiments varying the number of rules and of triples in the knowledge base. The results of these experiments are depicted in Fig. 6. They show that we reach by far our two initial goals as the respective processing times for integration and answering do not exceed 650 ms and 30 ms.

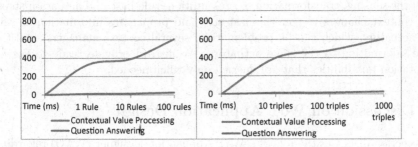

Fig. 6. Context processing and question answering times on different situtations.

5   Related Work

This section overviews related work on context identification, as well as on context management lifecycles in pervasive environments.

The definition of context depends on the domain concepts, the actors of the tasks, the application's infrastructure, etc. In [5], Brézillon describes the *focus* as the identification of context elements that are relevant for the current task. He separates the contextual knowledge (related to the current focus) and the external knowledge (which is not relevant to the current focus of the task operator). In [6], he identifies and represents the type of knowledge using expert maps, where the expert is the task operator. This differs from our work, where the task operator is actually the application user. Brézillon's context representation varies across operators and allows flexibility in terms of users, while our avatar-centered vision of context provides reusability of the context model amongst each object of the infrastructure and allows capitalizing on the reasoning process. In [13], Schaap et al. propose four steps that rely on stakeholders expertise and existing data about the domain. Their solution is based on specific climate risks that are linked to the adaptation process. This specificity and the lack of context representation both make their solution difficult to reuse in general cases. We instead provide a loose coupling between adaptation possibilities and contextual information, allowing applications from any domain to fit our infrastructure.

The management of contextual information also varies across context-aware adaptation solutions. Based on the literature, Perera et al. propose in [12] a context lifecycle in four steps: context acquisition, context modeling, context reasoning, and context dissemination to other devices. The context modeling step implies structuring the context as part of the lifecycle. Our solution separates context modeling from context instantiation, as the model is fixed throughout the lifecycle of the application, while the instances vary according to a given contextual situation. The workflow proposed by Bernardos et al. [3] (acquisition, processing, reasoning and decision) separates context processing from reasoning. We instead process reasoning tasks simultaneously at context instantiation time and at adaptation possibility generation time. Thus, we provide straightforward decision-making through generic adaptation questions. Ferscha et al. propose in [7] the sensing, transformation, representation, rule-base and actuation steps. The context changes trigger this last step and propagates information to several actuators, which can be problematic if several context managers send the same information to the same actuators. We instead provide ready-to-answer adaptation possibilities that are queried only when needed.

6   Discussion on WoT Application Design

This section discusses the role of a WoT Application Designer (WAD) regarding the definition of the contextual management cycle in an application. It complements Sect. 3, which deals with automated aspects of the management process, and defines the knowledge required for a WAD to bridge functional and non-functional concerns. It provides guidelines to link "classic" sources (i.e. appliance documentation, domain expert knowledge, user preferences, etc.) with other data sources (devices, Web services) to realize the adaptation.

The choice of contextual dimensions to build the context model requires knowledge of the main concepts and processes of the domain. At this stage, the WAD asks the domain expert which factors may change the behavior of the application (environmental occurrences, defects, etc.) to provide the appropriate solutions. The WAD then interprets these factors as contextual instances to build the context model. When designing transformation rules, the WAD confronts the expert's assessments to the appliance's technical constraints. The context meta-model we have presented in [15] can validate the choice of contextual dimensions and instances to ensure they fit the infrastructure needs. Designing transformation rules requires expressing thresholds using comparison operators and associate data sources to their value using two triple patterns, where the first pattern describes the carried value and the second pattern describes the nature of the data source. The WAD also identifies possible user preferences as triple patterns that link data sources to preferential characteristics, such as service fee, type of technology, brand, etc. Designing adaptation rules consists in interpreting expert answers as adaptation possibilities for a given contextual situation. Finally, the WAD determines the rank values, based on device properties and quality-of-service agreements.

As we aim to ease joint work between WADs and domain experts, the design of the adaptation solution itself can be adapted all along the application use. In addition to easing the WAD's work by mutualising contextual data collection for various adaptation purposes (which would anyway have been collected and processed separately otherwise), our adaptation solution design cycle is iterative and incremental, similarly to agile methods used in software development. It supports changes in domain knowledge, as well as in appliances and actors' description through the use of generic semantic methods. For instance, in our scenario, if the user buys new drones with different characteristics (in terms of battery, storage or computing capabilities), the platform will seamlessly integrate them and adapt the application to these new devices, to the cost of a simple configuration task.

7 Conclusion

We propose an adaptation solution for Web of Things platforms that simultaneously supports several adaptation concerns, ensures compatibility across devices, applications and domains, and relies on extensible sets of context dimensions. This solution is based on semantic reasoning and limits the reasoning extent to a closed world determined by semantization thresholds. After presenting the general framework of our proposition (i.e. the ASAWoO platform), we focus on the definition of the following elements: set of context model instances, transformation rules that turn semantized sensor data into actual contextual model instances, adaptation rules that infer adaptation possibilities from contextual situations, and multi-purpose adaptation questions answering to make adaptation decisions. We evaluate our solution in a smart agriculture scenario both in terms of accuracy and performance. Results validate adaptation answers and reach performance goals on context processing and adaptation question answering. We compare our approach to the literature regarding context identification and management. Finally, we describe the role of WoT application designers in the collection of contextual data and specification of application context management workflows, and open a discussion on the design of adaptive solutions that can in turn diachronically evolve while managing dynamic data that synchronically change.

Our perspectives include the automatic generation of domain-specific transformation and adaptation rules through meta-rules. We also aim at formalizing a method to rank adaptation possibilities using discretization techniques.

Acknowledgement. This work is supported by the French ANR (Agence Nationale de la Recherche) under the grant number <ANR-13-INFR-012>.

References

1. Web of Things Architecture, Unofficial Draft: General Description of WoT Servient. https://w3c.github.io/wot/architecture/wot-architecture.html#general-description-of-wot-servient. Accessed 09 Sept 2016
2. Bass, L.: Software Architecture in Practice. Pearson Education India, London (2007)
3. Bernardos, A.M., Tarrio, P., Casar, J.R.: A data fusion framework for context-aware mobile services. In: IEEE International Conference on Multisensor Fusion and Integration for Intelligent Systems, MFI 2008, pp. 606–613. IEEE (2008)

4. Blouin, A., Morin, B., Beaudoux, O., Nain, G., Albers, P., Jézéquel, J.M.: Combining aspect-oriented modeling with property-based reasoning to improve user interface adaptation. In: Proceedings of the 3rd ACM SIGCHI Symposium on Engineering Interactive Computing Systems, pp. 85–94. ACM (2011)

5. Brézillon, P.: Task-realization models in contextual graphs. In: Dey, A., Kokinov, B., Leake, D., Turner, R. (eds.) CONTEXT 2005. LNCS (LNAI), vol. 3554, pp. 55–68. Springer, Heidelberg (2005). doi:10.1007/11508373_5

6. Brézillon, P.: Modeling expert knowledge and reasoning in context. In: Christiansen, H., Stojanovic, I., Papadopoulos, G.A. (eds.) CONTEXT 2015. LNCS (LNAI), vol. 9405, pp. 18–31. Springer, Cham (2015). doi:10.1007/978-3-319-25591-0_2

7. Ferscha, A., Vogl, S., Beer, W.: Context sensing, aggregation, representation and exploitation in wireless networks. Scalable Comput.: Pract. Exp. **6**(2) (2001)

8. Hayes, P., McBride, B.: RDF semantics. W3C Recomm. **10** (2004)

9. Médini, L., Mrissa, M., Terdjimi, M., Khalfi, E.M., Le Sommer, N., Capdepuy, P., Jamont, J.P., Occello, M., Touseau, L.: Building a web of things with avatars. In: Sheng, M., Yongrui Qin, L.Y., Benatallah, B. (eds.) Managing the Web of Things: Linking the Real World to the Web. Morgan Kaufmann, Elsevier (2016). https://hal.archives-ouvertes.fr/hal-01373631, domains (unavailable categories): Internet of Things, Web of Things

10. Mizouni, R., Matar, M.A., Al Mahmoud, Z., Alzahmi, S., Salah, A.: A framework for context-aware self-adaptive mobile applications SPL. Expert Syst. Appl. **41**(16), 7549–7564 (2014)

11. Mrissa, M., Médini, L., Jamont, J.P., Le Sommer, N., Laplace, J.: An avatar architecture for the web of things. IEEE Internet Comput. **19**(2), 30–38 (2015)

12. Perera, C., Zaslavsky, A., Christen, P., Georgakopoulos, D.: Context aware computing for the internet of things: a survey. IEEE Commun. Surv. Tutor. **16**(1), 414–454 (2014)

13. Schaap, B.F., Reidsma, P., Verhagen, J., Wolf, J., van Ittersum, M.K.: Participatory design of farm level adaptation to climate risks in an arable region in the Netherlands. Eur. J. Agron. **48**, 30–42 (2013)

14. Terdjimi, M., Médini, L., Mrissa, M.: HyLAR+: improving hybrid location-agnostic reasoning with incremental rule-based update. In: 25th International World Wide Web Conference Companion WWW 2016, April 2016

15. Terdjimi, M., Médini, L., Mrissa, M., Le Sommer, N.: An avatar-based adaptation workflow for the web of things. In: 2016 IEEE 25th International Conference on Enabling Technologies: Infrastructure for Collaborative Enterprises (WETICE), pp. 62–67. IEEE (2016)

Context and the Virtual Human

Chris Wilson[(✉)] and Roy M. Turner

School of Computing and Information Science, University of Maine,
Orono, ME 04469, USA
{chris.wilson,rturner}@maine.edu

Abstract. Artificial agents that simulate aspects of human behavior
are expected to behave much like a real human in a similar situation
would. Human behavior however, is largely context-dependent. Ignoring
the effect context can have on an agent's behavior can hinder the quality
and plausibility of agent's behavior. In this paper, we present a context-
driven approach to modeling plausible aspects of human behavior which
focuses on endowing an agent with the ability to recognize and deal
effectively with anticipated contextual changes.

Keywords: Context-mediated behavior · Human behavior · Simulation

1 Introduction

There can be no serious objection to the statement that for humans in general,
behavior is context-dependent. For example, a person who hopes to become gain-
fully employed would not consider text messaging a friend to discuss weekend
plans while attending a job interview. Why not? Because most people know
(either through social inheritance or from prior experience) that this type of
behavior is not appropriate while they are in the context "attending an interview".

For artificial agents, context-appropriate behavior is just as important as it
is for humans. After all, an agent that is unable to behave appropriately for the
contexts it will operate in is essentially useless.

This is especially true for "virtual humans" (i.e., agents used to simulate
aspects of human behavior). Virtual humans can be found in a variety of applications ranging from military and social simulations to commercially available
video games. The quality of a simulation or the entertainment value of a video
game depends on the plausibility of a virtual human's observable actions. For
example, a virtual human that always performs its goals in the same order or an
enemy soldier that aims and fires at an opponent with 100% accuracy may not
be considered realistic.

Ignoring the effects of context can also cause a virtual human to exhibit unrealistic behaviors. For example, in the Fallout 3 video game, a village populated
with friendly townsfolk is attacked by mutants, whom the player must repel.
After the attack, surviving villagers still greet the player in the same friendly
fashion, even though they are surrounded by the corpses of their neighbors [3].

© Springer International Publishing AG 2017
P. Brézillon et al. (Eds.): CONTEXT 2017, LNAI 10257, pp. 227–239, 2017.
DOI: 10.1007/978-3-319-57837-8_18

In this paper, we propose an approach to improving the quality of virtual human behavior using context. Unlike our previous work on context-mediated behavior (CMB) [5], which uses knowledge of known contexts to mediate an agent's behavior while in them, our current approach couples knowledge of known contexts with knowledge of how contexts can change to *drive* an agent's behavior, thus allowing it to avoid situations where context-inappropriate behavior can occur.

Our approach is part of a larger body of work aimed at developing technologies to support people with various forms of cognitive impairment. Part of that work involves simulating behaviors (both "healthy" and erroneous) associated with cognitive impairment to conduct simulated tests of prototype technologies [7]. Consequently, the examples and discussion in this paper are tailored to the simulation of humans performing basic activities of daily living.

1.1 Overview of Our Approach

During plan execution, the actions performed by an agent can cause features of its situation to change. These situational changes can in turn lead to changes in the agent's context. As we will discuss below, an agent's context does not change as a whole, and some features of the current context may not be appropriate for the contexts that will arise. These features can be problematic and should be remedied before the agent enters those contexts.

In our approach, problematic features of an agent's current context are used to impose constraints on the contexts the agent can enter as long as those features exist. These constraints are then used to influence the agent's choice of plan for achieving its goals. Our approach incorporates a form of plan projection that helps an agent determine how features of its context will evolve during plan execution. The resulting features are then analyzed to determine if the chosen plan will cause the agent to exhibit behaviors that may be inappropriate for the contexts that will arise, then take steps to modify any problematic features so they are appropriate for accomplishing its goals.

The remainder of this paper is organized as follows. In Sect. 2, we present a summary of related work. Section 3 provides a discussion of context as it relates to our work and in Sect. 4, we provide a discussion of our approach to contextual reasoning. Finally, in Sect. 5 we provide a high-level summary of other applications that can benefit from our approach.

2 Related Work

All agents use some form of contextual knowledge, whether implicit or explicit. In rule-based agents, contextual knowledge is encoded in rule antecedents describing when a rule is applicable. For planners, contextual knowledge can be contained in preconditions or filter conditions that are part of the operator schema description.

A problem with contextual knowledge being local to rules or operators, however, is that unless care is taken, it can cause an agent to exhibit the same behavior regardless of the current context. For example, a precondition to performing the step (exit-house agent) might be (is-dressed agent). Alone, this rule will cause an agent to get dressed regardless if it is exiting the house to run errands or because the house is on fire. While this type of behavior could be remedied by adding additional constraints that indicate when a particular behavior is appropriate, this approach could lead to an explosion of such qualifiers.

As an alternative, some researchers have proposed the use of "smart objects" and situations to make an agent's behavior more context-appropriate [3]. For example, a smart object might, depending on the current context, inform an agent how to hold or gaze at it. These approaches do not, however, aid an agent in planning to achieve a specific goal and they may not lend themselves to applications where agents operate in uncontrolled or unstructured environments. In fact, since the agent cannot know a priori what the object will tell it, this may actually hinder an agent's ability to plan.

In our earlier work, we argued for the benefits of explicitly representing contexts and contextual knowledge with respect to acquiring, learning, reasoning about, and using such knowledge [5]. In our approach to context-mediated behavior (CMB), known contexts are represented as contextual schemas (c-schemas), which both describe the contexts as well as prescribe how to behave while in them. For the purpose of our current work, however, we are not only interested in using contextual knowledge to mediate aspects of an agent's current behavior, but also aspects of its future behavior. To this end, we treat an agent's context as a dynamic object that continuously evolves as an agent works to achieve its goals.

Similar to other approaches, we do not treat context as a monolithic object that evolves over time, but rather, as a collection of smaller contextual objects that evolve at different rates. For example, Brézillon and colleagues [1] propose three types of contextual knowledge, namely *contextualized, contextual* and *external* knowledge, that can be applied to a problem-solving step. Contextualized knowledge describes any knowledge that is used by an agent during a problem-solving step, whereas contextual knowledge is any knowledge that is not explicitly used during a step, but that constrains it. External knowledge is all other knowledge that has nothing to do with the problem-solving step.

This approach allows an agent's contextual knowledge to evolve during problem solving. For example, while pursuing a goal, a piece of contextualized knowledge might become either contextual or external knowledge. In our approach, the use of c-schemas allows us to explicitly represent both contextualized and contextual knowledge and also provides, in the current work, a way to reason about future contexts in order to help create plans.

3   Context

Nearly all AI research on contextual awareness provides its own definition of context. Some definitions are tailored to a specific application [2], whereas others are more general [4]. We too need a definition that is suitable for our current work. Because we are interested in using context to simulate plausible aspects of human behavior, our definition should allow us to represent context as it pertains to real-world situations. Our definition should also allow us to represent contextual changes.

Previously, we defined the term *context* to mean any identifiable configuration of situational (e.g., environmental, goal-related and agent-related) features that has predictive power for an agent's behavior [5]. This definition is very general, which makes it suitable for a variety of applications. We are able to exploit this generality for the purpose of our current work.

First, defining a context in terms of situational features allows us to define contextual changes in terms of changes to the features that make up those contexts. For example, the contexts "at home" and "away from home" can be defined in terms of a single spatial feature such as an agent's location. As a result, an agent's context can change from "at home" to "away from home" when the agent's location changes from (at-home) to (not(at-home)).

Second, our definition also allows an agent to be in multiple contexts simultaneously. This is highly desirable when simulating aspects of human behavior because real humans can find themselves in multiple contexts at any given moment. While running errands for example, a person might be in the contexts "dressed", "morning", "away from home", "hungry" and "at grocery store".

Being in multiple contexts can have implications for how an agent achieves its goals, because behaviors that are appropriate for one context may not be appropriate for the other contexts. Consider for example, a person who is in the context "hungry" and "at home". In this case, it is perfectly normal for the person to satisfy his or her hunger by preparing and eating a meal. This plan for achieving the goal satisfy hunger may not be appropriate if for example, the latter context were "at friend's house".

3.1   Types of Contexts

At a given moment, an agent can be in numerous contexts. These contexts define what we will refer to as an agent's *current* context. As it pursues its goals however, those contexts will change. For example, while pursuing the goal satisfy hunger, an agent's context might change from "preparing meal" to "cooking a meal" to "eating a meal". At the same time, its temporal context might change from "morning" to "afternoon". Given this, we do not treat an agent's current context as a monolithic object. Instead, we partition this context into dynamic collections of smaller contexts each having its own implications for an agent's behaviors. Our partitioning scheme is based on the manner in which the individual contexts change.

Existential Contexts. Some features of an agent's situation are always present but continuously changing. For example, the time of day, day of week and the weather outside are features of any person's situation as long as he or she is alive. We refer to contexts defined in terms of these features as *existential contexts* (ECs). Trivial examples of ECs include the temporal contexts "morning", "afternoon" and "night" as well as environmental contexts such as "sunny weather".

ECs are rigid in that there are generally no actions an agent can take that will affect these contexts. ECs place constraints on which goals an agent will pursue while it is in those contexts. For example, existential contexts can prevent erroneous behaviors such as visiting a store after closing time, cooking breakfast in the middle of the night or placing phone calls at 3 am.

Problem-Solving Contexts. Some features of an agent's situation exist as a result of the goal(s) currently being pursued. For example, a plan for cooking a grilled cheese sandwich can introduce into an agent's situation features such as the ingredients and cooking utensils required to cook the sandwich. The state of objects in the agent's environment can also be affected. For example, cooking the cheese sandwich requires that the agent turn the stove on and place the cheese sandwich in a pan on the stove. These features define what we will refer to as *problem-solving contexts* (PSCs). PSCs, are ephemeral and usually removed from the agent's current context by "cleanup" actions that are either part of the plan or specified by the agent's prior knowledge about the context (e.g., remove pan from stove, turn off stove).

PSCs can have implications for how an agent achieves goals while in those contexts. Unlike ECs, PSCs can be modified to allow for goal accomplishment. As a motivating example, suppose that while cooking a grilled cheese sandwich, an agent is presented with the goal `check the mail`. Suppose further that the agent's mailbox is next to a road and far from the agent's house. Due to the inherent risk of burning the sandwich or, worse, starting a fire, the sandwich being on the stove and the stove being powered on are not appropriate for the context "away from house". Therefore, the agent should avoid committing to the goal `check the mail` as long as those features exist. To allow for the achievement of the goal `check the mail`, the agent could remove the pan from the stove and turn the stove off temporarily.

Persistent Contexts. Other situational features are longer-lived and can persist across successive changes to an agent's context. These features define what we refer to as *persistent contexts* (PCs). In some cases, a PC is a direct consequence of achieving a goal. For example, by achieving the goal `get dressed`, an agent will be in the context "wearing clothes" or "dressed". PCs can also be a side-effect of achieving a goal. Suppose for example that while buying groceries, an agent spends all of its money. As a result it will be in the context "out of money" until it acquires more.

3.2   Representing and Using Contextual Knowledge

Explicitly representing contextual knowledge allows an agent to reason about the context itself, which is critical to assessing the context and behaving appropriately while in it. In our earlier work [5,6], we used contextual schemas (c-schemas) to explicitly represent an agent's a priori contextual knowledge. C-schemas are knowledge structures that contain descriptive and prescriptive knowledge about a particular context. This can include physical and temporal features of the context as well as information related to other agents and objects that are relevant during problem solving. We continue to use c-schemas in the current work. However, we have augmented them with additional knowledge to support reasoning about contextual changes.

Contextual Constraints. In some instances, features of an agent's current context can be considered problematic and may not be appropriate for subsequent contexts an agent can enter into. For example, due to the inherent risk of burning food or starting a fire, contextual features such the presence of food on the stove and the stove being powered on should be used to mediate an agent's behavior while it is in the context "cooking a meal". We are particularly interested in using problematic features to influence which goals (if any) an agent should commit to while it is in a particular context. For example, we would not want our agent checking the mail, running errands or committing to any other goal which distracts its attention from the food on the stove.

One way to achieve this type of behavior is to explicitly define the goals that an agent should avoid while it is in a particular context. Much like encoding contextual knowledge in rule antecedents, this approach can lead to an explosion of qualifiers, as there could be a significant number of goals that an agent should not pursue while in a particular context. We face a similar situation if we were to explicitly define which goals are appropriate for a particular context.

As an alternative, we use problematic features themselves to define which contexts an agent can enter into. This is accomplished by augmenting c-schemas with what we will refer to as *contextual constraints*. Contextual constraints specify contextual features that must be part of any context an agent will enter into while a problematic feature exists. Figure 1 shows a partial example of a c-schema for the context "cooking a meal". From this figure, we see that problematic features related to the cooking process are used to impose constraints on the agent's location (e.g., (at-home agent), (at-kitchen agent) and (at-stove agent)).

We also note that each contextual constraint carries a preference value. Preference values indicate whether a constraint should be strictly adhered to or if there are situations where it can be ignored. For example, constraints on the agent's location (e.g., (at-home agent) and (at-kitchen agent)) carry strong preference values, which means they should not be ignored and that any context the agent enters into should intersect the current context on the features of that constraint or "clean-up" actions will be required.

Weak preference values allow for greater flexibility in an agent's behavior by allowing an agent to pursue multiple goals simultaneously when appropriate.

```
Actors:
    self
    *others  ;;zero or more intelligent agents
Setting:
    Day: *
    Time: *
    Location: (and (at-home self)
                   (at-kitchen self)
                   (at-counter self))
    Environment: (and (is-on stove)
                      (in-pan food)
                      (on-stove food)
    Agent: (is-hungry self)
Contextual constraints:
    Constraint: (in-house self)
        Constrained-by: (and (is-on stove) (on-stove pan))
        Constraint preference: strong
    Constraint: (at-kitchen self)
        Constrained-by: (and (is-on stove) (on-stove pan))
        Constraint preference: strong
    Constraint: (at-stove self)
        Constrained-by: (and (is-on stove) (on-stove pan))
        Constraint preference: weak
```

Fig. 1. C-schema - *cooking a meal*

Suppose for example that while cooking a meal, the kitchen phone rings or that the agent wants to get a drink from the refrigerator. By allowing weak constraints (e.g., `(at-stove agent)`) to be violated, the agent could commit to these goals or any other goal that takes place in the kitchen while it is still in the context "cooking a meal". We might expect a real human to behave similarly when he or she is in a comparable situation.

4 Using Context to Drive Behavior

During plan execution, an agent can transition through a variety of contexts. For example, while pursuing the goal go to work, an agent's context might transition from "at home" to "driving a car" to "at coffee shop" and finally "at work". Our approach to contextual reasoning is focused on endowing an agent with the ability to identify context transitions related to plan execution as well as any inappropriate behaviors stemming from those transitions. More important, our approach also allows for an agent to modify its plan to allow appropriate goal accomplishment if inappropriate behavior is detected. As opposed to simply replanning, our approach allows an agent to make context-specific modifications to a plan, thus avoiding the need to completely replan.

4.1 Focusing Attention

Much like a real human, a virtual human does not have unlimited problem-solving resources, and must therefore decide which goals it should focus its attention on. In our approach, goals are assigned a numeric priority value, with the agent giving preference to goals with higher priority values. We note that a goal's priority does not indicate whether or not a goal is appropriate for a particular context, it simply informs the agent that the goal should be considered. For example, suppose an agent is presented with the goals `watch television` and `use bathroom` and that the priority assigned to these goals are 1 and 3 respectively. In this case, the agent would consider using the bathroom over watching television.

4.2 Predicting Inappropriate Behavior

Before an agent commits to a goal, it must construct or choose a plan for achieving that goal, then determine if the plan allows context-appropriate goal accomplishment.

Contextual constraints provide a simple heuristic for predicting when context-inappropriate behavior can occur. By comparing constrained features of its current context with features of a new goal's c-schema, an agent can determine if transitioning into that context will violate any constraints that are currently imposed.

In our approach, when a constraint violation is detected, the agent constructs a more detailed representation of its future context, because constraint violations alone do not account for contextual changes that might occur during plan execution. For example, it is possible for a plan's steps to remove problematic features and associated constraints from an agent's current context. At the same time, it is possible for a plan to introduce problematic features which may violate constraints imposed by future contexts.

To construct a future representation of an agent's context, we use a form of plan projection to determine how an agent's context will evolve during plan execution. For the purpose of our current work, this involves traversing a plan's steps and applying knowledge of each step's effects to existing knowledge about the agent's current context. This process is used to determine which features of the agent's current context will persist and which will be removed. Persistent features are then merged with features from a pending goal's c-schema to form what we will refer to as a *predicted context*.

Predicted contexts form a partial representation of an agent's future context and can be used to make decisions about the appropriateness of an agent's actions. A predicted context is a partial representation of a future context because a predicted context does not represent contextual changes such as those related to the agent's environment which are beyond the agent's control.

To demonstrate our approach, suppose that is 12:30 pm on Saturday. It is sunny outside and our agent has committed to the goal `satisfy hunger`. Assume that the agent's plan for achieving this goal consists of the subgoals `prepare cheese sandwich`, `cook cheese sandwich`, `eat sandwich`, `clean up`, and the agent is currently committed to the subgoal `cook sandwich`. A partial example of the agent's PSC is shown in Fig. 2.

```
Actors:
    self
    *others ;; zero or more intelligent agents
Setting:
    Day: Saturday
    Time: 12:30PM
    Location: (and (at-home self)
                   (at-kitchen self)
                   (at-counter self))
    Environment: (and (is-on stove)
                      (in-pan sandwich)
                      (on-stove pan))
    Agent: (is-hungry self)
Contextual constraints:
    Constraint - location: (at-home self)
        Constrained-by: (and (is-on stove) (on-stove pan))
        Constraint preference: strong
    Constraint - location: (at-kitchen self)
        Constrained-by: (and (is-on stove) (on-stove pan))
        Constraint preference: strong
    Constraint - location: (at-stove self)
        Constrained-by: (and (is-on stove) (on-stove pan))
        Constraint preference: weak
```

Fig. 2. Problem-solving context - *cook sandwich*

Suppose that while cooking the cheese sandwich, the agent is presented with the goal **check mail** and that its plan for achieving this goal consists of the high-level steps shown in Fig. 3. By comparing the constrained features of the PSC against the corresponding features of the new goal's c-schema (see Fig. 4) we see that by entering this context, the agent will violate the strong constraint (at-home self) which is imposed on its current location.

```
Step-1: (:action exit :parameters (house agent)
         :preconditions (in-house agent)
         :effect (not (in-house agent)))
Step-2: (:action goto :parameters (mailbox agent)
         :preconditions (not (in-house agent))
         :effect (at-mailbox agent))
Step-3: (:action open :parameters (mailbox agent)
         :preconditions (at-mailbox agent)
         :effect (is-open mailbox))
Step-4: (:action get :parameters (mail agent)
         :preconditions (and (is-open mailbox)
                             (have-mail mailbox))
         :effect (have-mail agent))
```

Fig. 3. Sample plan: check mail

Projecting the agent's plan and merging the resulting features with the c-schema for checking the mail (see Fig. 4) results in the predicted context shown

```
Actors:
    self
    *others ;;zero or more intelligent agents
Setting:
    Day: *
    Time: *
    Location: (and (not (in-house self))
                   (at-road self)
                   (at-mailbox self))
    Environment: *
    Agent: *
Contextual constraints:
    Constraint: (dressed self)
        Constrained-by: (not (in-house self))
        Constraint preference: strong
```

Fig. 4. C-schema - `check mail`

in Fig. 5. Analyzing this predicted context reveals that the agent's future location will violate the constraints imposed on the agent's current location. Therefore, to avoid inappropriate behaviors, the agent should not commit to the goal **check mail** given its current context and the plan for achieving this goal.

```
Actors:
    self
    *others ;;zero or more intelligent agents
Setting:
    Day: Saturday
    Time: 12:30PM
    Location: (and (not (in-house self))
                   (at-road self)
                   (at-mailbox self))
State:
    Environmental:
        (and (is-on stove)
             (on-stove pan)
             (is-sunny weather))
    Agent:
        (and (is-dressed self) (is-hungry self))
Constraints:
    Constraint: (is-dressed agent)
        Constrained-by: (not (in-house agent))
        Constraint preference: strong
```

Fig. 5. Predicted context - `check mail`

4.3   Choosing a Course of Action

When an agent predicts context-inappropriate behavior, it must decide how to proceed. One possible course of action is to simply defer the pending goal until the agent's context allows for appropriate goal accomplishment (e.g., when problematic features have been removed and contextual constraints have been lifted). While this solution is guaranteed to avoid any inappropriate behaviors, it can also lead to unwanted patterns behavior because the agent might always defer a pending goal (regardless of priority or urgency) if inappropriate behavior is predicted.

Modifying a Plan. Before deferring a goal, our agent attempts to modify its current context to allow for appropriate goal accomplishment. Contextual constraints provide insight on how to achieve this. For example, each constraint references two features, namely the problematic and constrained feature. To determine how to modify the chosen plan, an agent can reference its procedural knowledge to identify the actions required to remove a problematic feature from the current context if such an action exists, then augment the chosen plan with those actions.

Continuing our previous example, an agent might determine that clean-up actions (e.g., removing the pan from the stove and turning off the stove) associated with the subgoal cook sandwich will remove problematic features from its current context, thus lifting the imposed constraints. Adding these steps to the chosen plan results in the modified plan shown in Fig. 6.

```
Step-1: (:action remove :parameters (pan stove)
          :preconditions (on-stove pan)
          :effect (not (on-stove pan)))
Step-2: (:action turn-off :parameters (stove agent)
          :preconditions (is-on stove)
          :effect (not (powered-on stove))
Step-3: (:action exit :parameters (home agent)
          :preconditions (at-home agent)
          :effect (not (at-home agent)))
Step-4: (:action goto :parameters (mailbox agent)
          :preconditions (not (at-home agent))
          :effect (at-mailbox agent))
Step-5: (:action open :parameters (mailbox agent)
          :preconditions (at-mailbox agent)
          :effect (is-open mailbox))
Step-6: (:action get :parameters (mail agent)
          :preconditions (and (is-open mailbox)
                              (have-mail mailbox))
          :effect (have-mail agent))
```

Fig. 6. Modified plan: *check mail*

Choosing a Different Plan. In some instances, it may not be possible to modify a plan to allow appropriate goal accomplishment. For example, suppose that an agent is bedridden yet needs to achieve the goal check mail. In this context, the agent is unable to achieve this goal using the plan in Fig. 3 and there may not be any way to modify this plan to allow for goal accomplishment in this context. As a result, the agent might choose to satisfy this goal by invoking an alternative goal such as asking another agent to check the mail on its behalf.

Deferring the Pending Goal. If an agent is unable to formulate an appropriate course of action for achieving a goal, it might be forced to defer the goal until a later time. For example, suppose we are simulating a person who at 10 pm, recalls the goal `schedule doctor's appointment`. In this case, the agent should defer this goal because there is no way to modify a plan to allow for its accomplishment given the agent's current context (e.g., "night time").

5   Other Applications

Our approach to context-driven behavior will also be useful for real-world agents, such as robots and autonomous vehicles. In our prior work in the domain of autonomous underwater vehicles (AUVs), we have used c-schemas for understanding the agent's situation and selecting and modulating behavior appropriate for it. Missing from past work was any consideration on the agent's part of intentionally changing its context intelligently or of contexts themselves having primacy over goals in some instances. The current work addresses both of these gaps in CMB.

As an example of the need for a real-world agent to reason about and intentionally change its context, consider the example we have used elsewhere of an AUV entering a mined harbor. In previous work, we emphasized that the AUV would need to recognize the context, which would bring to mind a c-schema that tells it to modulate its behavior: e.g., go slowly, turn off obstacle avoidance sonar that could trigger a mine, etc.

This is reasonable if the AUV suddenly and unexpectedly encounters a minefield. However, in many cases, operating in a minefield is the primary purpose of the AUV (e.g., to map the mined harbor or to detect and destroy the mines). In such cases, the approach outlined in this paper makes much more sense. While en route to the work site, the AUV could reason about its *future* (i.e., predicted) context of being in a mined harbor and realize that *before* entering the harbor, it needs to slow down, turn off its sonar, etc. This allows the vehicle to cleanly enter the new context without risking catastrophe while it reasons about how to behave in it.

As an example of a context being the primary consideration rather than a goal, suppose a scientist wants to deploy an AUV to remain on station in an area, looking for interesting or anomalous events. It is somewhat artificial to give the AUV the nebulous goal of looking for such things: what actions would the goal entail? what predictions could be made about it? Instead, it would be much more reasonable for the agent to commit to (or be told to commit to) being in the *context* of looking for such events. The corresponding c-schema would provide guidance to the AUV about what constitutes "interesting" or "anomalous" event, perhaps in relation to other c-schemas having to do with the particular location, without the need for there to be a vague goal. For example, the c-schema might contain the knowledge that any sensor data that is two standard deviations from what is expected in the (locational) context is anomalous and should be reported.

6   Conclusions

In this paper, we have presented a brief discussion of our approach to improving the plausibility of virtual human behavior using a novel form of contextual reasoning. This approach allows an agent to predict inappropriate behavior that can occur during plan execution and take appropriate steps to avoid such behaviors. One advantage to this approach is that it highlights specific steps that may result in inappropriate behaviors. This allows an agent to make context-specific modifications to a plan when it predicts context-inappropriate behavior might occur, thus avoiding the need to completely replan. We intend to continue our work on the approach developed so far, using it to address limitations associated with our earlier approach to CMB. This includes using this approach both for virtual humans and for intelligent real-world agents.

References

1. Brézillon, P., Pomerol, J., Saker, I.: Contextual and contextualized knowledge: an application in subway control. Int. J. Hum.-Comput. Stud. **48**(3), 357–373 (1998)
2. Dey, A.K.: Understanding and using context. Pers. Ubiquit. Comput. **5**(1), 4–7 (2001)
3. Sloan, C., Kelleher, J.D., Namee, B.M.: Feeling the ambiance: using smart ambiance to increase contextual awareness in game agents. In: Proceedings of the 6th International Conference on Foundations of Digital Games, pp. 298–300. ACM (2011)
4. Stensrud, B.S., Barrett, G.C., Gonzalez, A.J.: Context-based reasoning: a revised specification. In: FLAIRS Conference, pp. 603–610 (2004)
5. Turner, R.M.: Adaptive Reasoning for Real-World Problems: A Schema-Based Approach. Psychology Press, Abingdon (1994)
6. Turner, R.M.: Context-mediated behavior. In: Brézillon, P., Gonzalez, A.J. (eds.) Context in Computing: A Cross-Disciplinary Approach for Modeling the Real World, pp. 523–539. Springer, New York (2014). doi:10.1007/978-1-4939-1887-4_32. chap. 32
7. Wilson, C., Turner, R.M.: Modeling erroneous human behavior: a context-driven approach. In: Christiansen, H., Stojanovic, I., Papadopoulos, G.A. (eds.) CONTEXT 2015. LNCS (LNAI), vol. 9405, pp. 538–543. Springer, Cham (2015). doi:10.1007/978-3-319-25591-0_45

Context in Communication

Is Flew's *No True Scotsman Fallacy* a True Fallacy? A Contextual Analysis

Robert Ian Anderson[✉]

School of Philosophy and Theology, University of Notre Dame Australia,
Sydney, NSW 2007, Australia
robert.anderson@nd.edu.au

Abstract. In this paper, I discuss ways where context can help to explain why the *No True Scotsman 'Fallacy'* may not always be fallacious. I discuss different focus areas of context from speaker's meaning, the syntactical position of the inserted term 'true', to dialectical contexts involving dialogues about classification and definition.

Keywords: Persuasive definition · Fallacy · Falsification · Context · Antony Flew · *The No True Scotsman Fallacy*

1 Introduction

Various authors have recently discussed the importance of context in determining the legitimacy of good argumentation over fallacious reasoning.[1] Moreover, there is a growing trend, if not, a "preoccupation" as Fabio Paglieri calls it, of "non-fallacious fallacies". These are arguments that resemble traditional fallacies, "but are actually respectable enough to be used in appropriate contexts".[2] My aim in this paper is to discuss how context can be applied to both *explain* and *evaluate* the reasoning contained in the *No-True-Scotsman Move* as a good and non-fallacious argument in appropriate contexts. The sense of fallacy here is broader than the traditional standard treatment since it is rare that the NTSM is deemed properly fallacious in the academic literature. Rather it thought fallacious through identification with persuasive definitions that are sometimes thought to be fallacious. The sense of fallacy here is closer to the Pragma-dialectic account of a fallacy as a violation of one or more rules of critical discussion.

Throughout this essay, I shall briefly name possible areas of contextualization. My aim is to defend the speaker (S) who has been charged for committing the No-True-Scotsman Move while my approach is to apply a heavy dose of the principle of charity in interpreting what S means against the respondent's R refutation by counterexample. Due to space limitations I cannot pay proper attention to actual cases of the No-True-Scotsman Move.

---

[1] For example, van Eemeren and Houtlosser (2007), pp. 59–67, and van Eemeren (2011), pp. 141–161.
[2] Paglieri (2016).

© Springer International Publishing AG 2017
P. Brézillon et al. (Eds.): CONTEXT 2017, LNAI 10257, pp. 243–253, 2017.
DOI: 10.1007/978-3-319-57837-8_19

2 Popper and Falsificationism

The 'No-True-Scotsman Move' was formulated by Anthony Flew in his monograph, *Thinking About Thinking,* Flew's own words explain best via his lucid writing,

> ...the No true-Scotsman Move is an attempt to evade falsification. Through it a piece of sleight of mind replaces a contingent by a logically necessary proposition.[3]

The primary way the No-True-Scotsman Move operates is through *redefinition*, either high or low,

> If we put things in terms of this fundamental distinction between the apriori and aposteriori, then the No-True-Scotsman Move consists in responding to the falsification of a contingent proposition by covertly reinterpreting the words in which it was originally formulated that these now become the expression of an arbitrarily constructed necessary truth. This maneuver always involved either a high or low redefinition of a crucial term. Where the qualifications for membership of the class are increased, we have high redefinition. Where they are reduced, we have a low redefinition. To rate as a true Scot you have to be mot merely a Scot but a Scot who is not a sex maniac.[4]

We should note that the label contains the term 'move' or better, 'maneuver' which demonstrates that the ploy is 'inconsistent with a forthright concern for truth.'[5] The idea of move or maneuver here suggests some kind of trickery or deceit, if intentional, reminiscent of Popper's complaints about Freudians and Marxists who offer *ad hoc* modifications to their claims to avoid refutation. The general Popperian moral taught by Flew in this present chapter and the previous chapter of 1975 is that, "whenever we are certain... then we ought to press home The Falsification Challenge: just what, please, would have to happen, or to have happened, to show that this statement is false, or that this theory is mistaken?"[6]

Flew gives a number of actual, real life cases that he thinks instantiates this fallacy while the most memorable story is his fictitious thought experiment about an imaginary Scot – a chauvinist – who upon reading his newspaper, learns of the headline, 'Sidcup Sex Maniac Strikes Again'. This Scottish chauvinist pauses to ponder then confidently asserts, (1). *No Scot would do such a thing.* Flew's story continues where the following week's edition of the same newspaper reports on "the even more scandalous ongoings of Mr. Angus MacSporran in Aberdeen", to the surprise of our Scottish reader. According to Flew, this news presents a counterexample that clearly falsifies the previously asserted universal proposition, (1). Instead of backing down and withdrawing the original assertion, something that a rational person should do in the face of counter-evidence, this imaginary Scot asserts the new proposition, (2). *No true Scot would do such a thing.*

Fabio Paglieri argues that fallacies are "gappy on all accounts" and this is not problematic. It is akin to an enthymeme argument requiring further work to articulate

---

[3] Flew (1975), p. 56.

[4] Flew (1975), p. 49.

[5] Flew (1975), p. 53.

[6] Flew (1975), pp. 55–56. This quote he cites from Flew and Macintyre (1955), pp. 96–100.

missing premises or inferences.[7] The term "non-fallacious fallacies" is of course oxymoronic as Paglieri remarks since it "refers to an error that is not an error".[8] What Paglieri has in mind by the terminology is a shorthand label for "non-fallacious arguments that structurally match the definition of a certain fallacy".[9] A loose characterization of this is to posit that particular fallacy *types* have forms that are *structurally* fallacious on paper, but their tokens, or instances in real life may be non-fallacious and plausible depending on contexts. Sometimes these contexts may prefer a *dialectical* understanding of the error involved over a structural analysis of the error though Paglieri sees problems in both approaches and prefers an evaluation in terms of errors of reasoning than poor communications as may be countenanced by pragma-dialectical methods.[10] What I aim to do is to contrast the structure of the NTSM (albeit, it is strictly informal) and consider whether various substitution-instances of it could render the result a non-fallacious process in an argument.

3   The Standard Analysis of the No-True-Scotsman Move – Outside of Contexts

The NTSM structure has this simplified dialectical structure where *Su* and *Ru* corresponds to the Speaker's utterance and Respondent's utterance respectively. In the NTSM, the Speaker is alleged to have committed the fallacy, broadly construed, or an elicit persuasive definition while the Respondent raises the counterexample.

1. Su_1: 'No S is P'; $\forall x(Sx \rightarrow \sim Px)$
2. Ru_1: 'There is an S that is P'; (counterexample) $\exists x(Sx \wedge Px)$
3. Su_2: 'No *true* S is P';   (redefinition) $\forall x((Sx \rightarrow \sim Px) \leftrightarrow (Px \rightarrow \sim Sx))$

Logically, Respondent's $\exists x(Sx \wedge Px)$ is the contradictory of Speaker's $\forall x(Sx \rightarrow \sim Px)$; both formulas cannot be true (or false) at the same time. As empirical evidence trumps a universally generalized proposition, in step (1) the NTSM directs as a normative principle that Speaker should give up his or her commitment to $\forall x(Sx \rightarrow \sim Px)$ over $\exists x(Sx \wedge Px)$. Moving from 'No S is P' (a contingent/synthetic claim) to 'No *true* S is P' in step (3), (a necessary/analytic claim) converts the former into the latter logical tautology. In 'No *true* S is P', the predicate is now contained in the (newly defined) subject as seen in the embedded parenthetical remark below:

> 3* 'No *true* S, (which is defined as an S that does not do P), is (or) does P'.
> More directly: '*True* S'$_{def}$ = an S that does not-P.

---

[7] Paglieri (2016), p. 1. Paglieri cites further evidence of the need for this strategy from Godden and Zenker (*Informal Logic* 2015, 35: 88–134), who have argued that "reinterpreting alleged fallacies as non-fallacious arguments requires supplementing the textual material with something else, e.g., probability distributions, pragmatic considerations, *dialogical context*." p. 1, *my emphasis*.

[8] Paglieri (2016), p. 4.

[9] Paglieri (2016).

[10] Paglieri (2016).

Table 1. Logical analysis of the No-True-Scotsman Move

Distinction	No S is P		No *true* S is P
'The maneuver'	*from*	→	*to*
Semantic	Synthetic		Analytic
Metaphysical	Contingent		Necessary
Epistemological	*a posteriori*		*a priori*
Falsifiable?	Yes		No

According to Flew, the Speaker changes his or her statement into an analytically and necessarily true claim where no evidence can be bought against it. It is no longer falsifiable and remains immune to counterexample. In this sense, Speaker has 'evaded' Respondent's counterexample. The maneuver allegedly also involves *equivocation,* if Speaker unconsciously reverts back to asserting the original claim; that is, the Speaker does not notice any difference between asserting 'No S is P' and 'No true S is P' and shifts attention from one to another. This, however, is not manifested in the above dialectical structure since it is an item about the pragmatics of an actual dialogue. Nevertheless, equivocation is a judgment that Flew makes about the Speaker. Not only has Speaker evaded falsification, but essentially ends up not making any assertion at all, according to Flew. Quoting from Ludwig Wittgenstein's *Tractatus Logico-Philosophicus,* Flew affirms the view that "The propositions of logic are tautologies. The propositions of logic therefore say nothing. (They are analytical propositions)."[11] Therefore, the Speaker as the perpetrator of the illicit move or fallacy asserts nothing of importance. Since the NTSM involves a move or maneuver, it will help to tabulate (see Table 1) the various ways Speaker's original assertion and the alleged redefinition conform to standard philosophical conceptions of semantic truth, metaphysical truth, and epistemological truth.

4 Fallaciousness and Persuasive Definitions

To be sure, the NTSM is standardly treated in the professional literature as *a persuasive definition* (PD) and not a fallacy. References to it as a fallacy tend to be found in domestic versions of books and fallacies as well. The NTSM is now almost always demoted by exaggeration to the status of a fallacy since becoming an internet meme.[12]

---

[11] Flew (1975), p. 54. The quote referred to by Flew comes from Propositions 6.1–6.11 from the *Tractatus.*

[12] For example, it is listed as a fallacy (of an 'Ad Hoc Rescue') in *The Internet Encyclopedia of Philosophy,* http://www.iep.utm.edu/fallacy/#NoTrueScotsman, accessed 26 February, 2017; the popular *The Fallacy Files* website lists is as the subfallacy of *Redefinition,* http://www.fallacyfiles.org/ redefine.html, accessed 26 February, 2017; it is listed as a *Fallacy of Presumption* and a circular argument at Logical Fallacies, http://www.logicalfallacies.info/presumption/no-true-scotsman/ accessed 26 February 2017, and the site Your Logical Fallacy Is calls it an appeal to purity, http:// www.logicalfallacies.info/presumption/no-true-scotsman/ accessed 26 February, 2017. The popular philosophy magazine *Philosophy Now* names it as an informal fallacy in a short article *Bad Arguments That Make You Smarter,* Henrik Schoeneberg, August/September edition (2016) pp. 26–27.

Research on Persuasive Definitions find their origins with Charles Leslie Stevenson.[13] Persuasive Definitions are sometimes taught in critical thinking textbooks as an item of the pathology of reasoning usually under sections concerning language and definitions. For example, Trudy Govier calls a persuasive definition,

> ...a stipulative definition disguised as a claim or as a reportive definition. In a persuasive definition there is an attempt to change attitudes by keeping the emotional connotations of a word while altering its applications. Persuasive definitions attempt to alter our attitudes and beliefs by redefining terms instead of stating reasons and arguments.[14]

It is easy to witness the comparability of persuasive definitions with the NTSM because of the inserted word *true*, etc.,

> Terms such as *real, true, authentic,* and *genuine* are often elements of persuasive definitions. If someone claims that modern abstract art is not true art because true art must depict objects realistically, he is using a premise based on a persuasive definition of "art."... But he offers no reasons to support that conception. Instead of reasons, he offers a disguised definition. Often, when persuasive definitions are used, important issues are a stake.[15]

I note the following points from this brief quotation from Govier:

- PDs contain locutions where the syntactical structure has a valuational term such as *true,* in the attributive adjective position.
- When PDs are used, important issues are at stake. These issues are items of controversy.
- Yet the controversial topics are not argued for but disguised beneath a PD.

4.1   In What Way is the NTSM a Persuasive Definition?

Given the above three bullet points, the NTSM is allegedly equivalent or at least similar to a PD. But there needs to be more to distinguish the former from the later. The NTSM is not *just* a persuasive definition, the speaker allegedly *redefines* the original assertion, Su_1: *No S is P*, to Su_2: *No true S is P*.

I propose there are three properties of the NTSM that act as rules to identify them. These three properties can be considered to be individually necessary and jointly sufficient to describe the nature of a NTSM:

P1. The NTSM is *persuasive definition* by virtue of utterance Su_2 alone.

P2. The NTSM involves a *redefinition* by moving from Su_1 to Su_2 where the redefinition is obtained by an insertion of an attributive adjective. (Call this the Attributive Adjective Insertion component, AAI).

P3. This redefinitional move is *evasive* where (S)peaker tries to avoid falsifiability from (R)espondent.

---

[13] Stevenson (1938, 1944). The subsequent literature on PD's is quite broad. Of note are papers by Macagno and Walton (2008a, 2008b), Walton and Macagno (2009), Zarefsky (2006) and Aberdein (2000, 2006).

[14] Govier (2009), p. 77.

[15] Govier (2009).

I note also that the redefinition (P2) can be elaborated into the following components:

i. The redefinition involves Dissociation, splitting the original concept into two concepts.[16]

ii. The move from Su_1 to Su_2 is a High Redefinition where the extension of the redefinition excludes R's counterexample.

iii. The dialectical context may involve equivocation if S slides back from Su_2 to Su_1.

iv. Su_2 is now tautologous; it is not an interesting assertion. Hence S "says nothing".[17]

Wherein, exactly, is the charge of fallacy or wrongdoing on the part of S contained in the above analysis? Is it in the persuasive redefinition, (P1); the redefinition, (P2); or the evasion, (P3)? I will briefly comment in relation to these three areas.

The NTSM as a Persuasive Definition

(P1): Persuasive definitions are not always problematic. Aberdein cites Stevenson, agreeing with him that, "many cases of PF are much less objectionable".[18] If this is the case, that PDs are prima facie neutral until identified as wrong, then we need a theory to distinguish "harmless and malign cases of PD."[19] However, as suggested earlier with my discussion of Govier, the persuasive definition as taught in logic textbooks is "usually treated as though it were invariably fallacious."[20] There is indeed, much discussion on how to demarcate neutral from harmful PDs in the literature cited in this paper. Moreover, there are variations in theory of what the nature of PDs actually are. Macagno and Walton explain some of the variation where, in distinction to Stevenson and Hallden's positions, "Burgess-Jackson, Aberdein and Schiappa defend the view that a word's meaning basically stem from theories. Supporting a definition becomes, in this view, supporting the thesis it is based on. The persuasiveness of words depend, in these cases, on a meaning which is already given in the term, or in the theory constituting the instrument of evaluation."[21] If this is so, and there is uncertainty that PDs are always, or mostly, problematic in dialogue, it follows the NTSM cannot be considered problematic, harmful, or fallacious by virtue of (P1) alone. This rules out that the NTSM is fallacious *qua* a persuasive definition. Something else is needed.

---

[16] Cf. Aberdein (2006), p. 8.

[17] Flew compares Wittgenstein's attribution that tautologies "say nothing" to the Speaker of the NTSM. Su_2 is "not really making any assertion at all about what is or is not supposed to happen in the universe around us," (1975), p. 54.

[18] Aberdein (2006), p. 4.

[19] Aberdein (2006).

[20] Aberdein (2006). About the alleged fallaciousness of PDs, Aberdein cites Walton (2005), p. 173.

[21] Macagno and Walton (2003) for example, lists Hallden's position that the author of a PD tries to find the real or true meaning, that is, *true X* seeks to find an "essence definition". For Schiappa, PD's have nothing to do with essences but reveal our perceptions of the world where defining imposes a theory on reality where every term and definition is persuasive because "they frame the situation in a particular way". Burgess-Jackson's theory pertain to the inherent vagueness of terms where PD's precisify and increase or decrease the extension of the term.

The Alleged Evasiveness of the Speaker

I shall discuss the properties (P2) and (P3) together for the act of moving from Su_1 to Su_2 is ostensibly a redefinition and an evasion. I argue however, that rather than redefining the first statement, S is clarifying it and actually rebutting R's counterexample, (see discussion below). If I succeed in demonstrating this, the charge that the Speaker commits an objectionable redefinition and evasion can be ameliorated. If there is any indictable offense in the NTSM, it is likely to be involving (P3) as an illicit dialogical move to evade falsification. Since this maneuver involves the pragmatics of dialogic exchange, this is where the element of context plays an important part in determining if the NTSM is always structurally fallacious in a wide meaning of fallacy. Within the discussion of strategic maneuvering which is the dual aim of resolving an issue in a *reasonable way* but resolving it in an interlocuter's *own way*, the alleged fallaciousness of the NTSM can be identified as violating the tenets of good strategic maneuvering by violating the first condition, of being reasonable, and of emphasizing the second, of performing an illicit move that is too motivated by the speaker's intention to win his or her case.[22]

4.2   Context of Object 1: Does the *Kind* of Object of Redefinition Matter?

In this section I look briefly at the issue of whether the objects referred to in NTSM are natural, artificial, or social kinds. We can well imagine situations where S and R are discussing natural kind term such as water, or gold, (to use familiar examples), where S is justified in exclaiming *This is not gold … this is not real gold*. The interpolated value-adjective dissociates the true from the false but does not change the extension of gold. There is no persuasive definition and no evasion, for the speaker, in this fictitious situation is right. The Respondent refers to a fake piece of gold. "Not real" is paraphrastic for *fake*, an *alienans* adjective which clearly dissociates the real from the fake. One reason why the NTSM does not succeed to operate fallaciously on natural kind terms can be explained by the Kripke-Putnam theory of the *necessary/a posteriori* where essences are empirically discovered with a subsequent linguistic label applied referentially. The object having certain properties is already a necessary truth, it cannot be transformed again into a necessary truth. And since the phenomenal properties of the natural kind are empirically testable it is much easier to identify and falsify incorrect claims about some natural kinds without committing a persuasive definition.

The same can be said about some instances of artificial kinds. For example, what constitutes Scotch Whiskey is determined by law and policy. It has the following necessary conditions, among others: it must be produced in Scotland, from only malted barley with yeast as the only fermentation additive, matured only in oak casts not exceeding 700 L, matured only in Scotland for not less than three years, and has a minimum alcohol strength of 40%.[23] Again we can image a fictitious conversation

---

[22] Van Rees describes strategic maneuvering as holding in tension two aims, of *dialectical reasonableness* and *rhetorical effectiveness* (2006). Cf. Zarefsky (2006).

[23] For the legislation see, 'The Scotch Whiskey Regulations 2009', http://www.legislation.gov.uk/uksi/2009/2890/regulation/3/made. Accessed 30 December, 2016.

between two people with fake Scotch Whiskey. For one to express, *this is not true Scotch Whiskey* is a clear and valid expression of *this is not true X,* for there are clearly specified necessary conditions. Again, no PD or NTSM is committed.

In real cases of alleged NTSM, the ontological kinds that are the items of controversy are rarely natural or artificial kinds, but *social kinds*, which because they are *social* kinds, are highly controversial. Francesco Guala mentions that social or human kinds "seem to be dependent on human classificatory practices"[24], and though rejecting it, discusses the Difference Thesis: "unlike natural kinds, social kinds depend crucially on our attitudes towards them."[25] Khalidi summarises further differences in understanding social kinds as follows, for John Searle they are "ontologically subjective since they depend on human mental attitudes..."[26] Ian Hacking distinguishes them from natural kinds because, "they are interactive and can change in response to our attitudes towards them"[27]. P. Griffiths sees them as, "fundamentally evaluative or normative in nature."[28] My point in referring to these characterizations of social kinds is to demonstrate that they are highly contestable so there is little wonder that there are disputes or differences of opinion in alleged NTSM dialogues. Speakers disagree, not because they avoid falsification, or evade, but because the subject matter of dialogue is controversial – what is a person's true national or cultural identity? What is it to be an English citizen? What is it to be a feminist? These are not questions about natural kinds, or "brute-facts" in Searle's parlance. There are social kinds, so there will be disagreement and disputes about definition.

4.3   Contexts of Object 2: What Counts as an Object of a Particular Kind and Who is to Say What It Is?

Schiappa understands definitional disputes to be less about "philosophical or scientific questions of 'is' and more as sociopolitical and pragmatic questions of 'ought'.[29] Schiappa's approach sees our shared social knowledge and rhetorical practices as integral to definition and it is not so easy to separate fact from value. Hence definitions are "largely persuasive, always political, serving interests and advancing values",[30] They are the consequences of the theories we have about the world. Borrowing from John Searle's idea that definitions are not brute facts but *institutional facts*, Schiappa uses Searle's theory that "every institutional fact is underlain by a (system of) rule(s) of the form 'X counts as Y in context C'.[31] Explicit and implicit rules are both descriptive

---

[24] Guala (2014), p. 57.

[25] Guala (2014).

[26] Khalidi (2013), p. 1 citing Searle (1995).

[27] Khalidi (2013), citing Hacking (1995, 1999).

[28] Khalidi (2013), citing Griffiths (2004).

[29] Schiappa (2003), p. 3 Schiappa here cites Searle (1969), pp. 51–52.

[30] Schiappa (2003), p. 177.

[31] Schiappa (2003), p. 50.

and prescriptive".[32] A country's laws about the institution of marriage detail what marriage "is" and what one must do to marry". Hence these laws both describe and prescribe what one must do to get married.[33]

From Schiappa, I suggest we can evaluate the NTSM in two more ways. First, we should not necessarily assume that Speaker's first assertion in Su₁: is descriptive, though the verb is in the indicative mood, the illocutionary force appears to be better understood as modal, if not prescriptive. What Speaker has in mind is this, *that is not how a Scotsman ought to behave*, or counterfactually, *He did that, but a true Scot would not have done so*. This sentiment is revealed in another common prefix 'un'. When a speaker calls another person or their behavior 'un-American', they are not calling them a fake-American, false-American, or even a non-American. There is no hint of dissociation or high-redefinition. The illocutionary force is more like, *yes, though that person is American, they are not acting as an American should*. Relating this to the NTSM, the first utterance in Su₁ embeds an expression of value. It would be puzzling, I claim, for the speaker to hear an attempted empirical falsification of his own values, (is that even possible), which is why he re-asserts the claim more emphatically as if to say, "though he is Scottish, that is not how a Scotsman should act", or, "a true Scotsman *would* not do such a thing". Dialogues between speakers and respondents in NTSM contexts tend to stop abruptly where an impasse is reached, much like Socratic aporia. Each is puzzled by what the other says, suggesting they are speaking from different perspectives, fact versus value, different contexts of illocutionary force – descriptive versus prescriptive. In other words they are not even on the same page.

A second point of departure from the Searle/Schiappa theme is that whatever counts as an instance of an object *x* depends on contexts of speakers attitudes as situations. This is a strong defeater to the theory of the NTSM as a persuasive definition. As already mentioned, Searle's notion of an institutional fact is borne out in the expression 'X counts as Y in Context C'. Returning to the logical form of each utterance in the basic structure of the NTSM, the speakers first utterance, 'No S is P' or $\forall x$ $(Sx \rightarrow \sim Px)$ is a statement of definition, definition by negation in this case. Macagno and Walton in their discussion on Argument from Verbal Classification[34] call this the,

Classification Premise: For all *x*, if *x* has property *F*, then *x* can be classified as having property *G*.

Along with the,

Individual Premise: *a* has property *F*,

We can infer the conclusion: *a* has property *G*.

All of this is straight forward, but what is assumed, or question-begged, is the Respondents presumption that *a* is an instance of *x*, whether the person identified in the counterexample *really* is a Scot. Utilizing the Searle/Schiappa approach, we ask what counts as an instance of a Scot? What, in Context C, makes X counts as a Y? This is the

---

[32] Schiappa (2003).

[33] Schiappa (2003).

[34] Macagno and Walton (2008b) p. 211.

hinge of the argument, if not, the stasis where the clash between the interlocuters reveal their fundamental disagreement, for simply, the Respondent counts the object or **Person** referred to as an instance of a Scot, $\exists x(Px \ \& \ Sx)$/*this person is Scottish*. In contrast, and in flat contradiction, the Speaker thinks otherwise, $\exists x(Px \ \& \sim Sx)$/*this person is not Scottish*. What we have here is the question of correct existential instantiation. Put in terms of the Argument from Verbal Classification schema, does *a* count as in instance of an *x*? The answer is *yes* according to Respondent, *no* according to Speaker. The critical questions supplied by Macagno and Walton for arguments from verbal classification are the following:

CQ1.   What evidence is there that *a* definitely has property *F* as opposed to evidence indicating room for doubt on whether it should be so classified?

CQ2.   Is the verbal classification in the classification premise based merely on an assumption about word usage that is subject to doubt?

Applying these critical questions to some instances of the NTSM is likely to reveal that the speaker is not committing an illicit No-True-Scotsman Move since the point of disagreement is what counts as an object of a social kind. Furthermore, I ask, "**who is to say**....what counts as an *x*?" It is not enough for the Respondent to rely on endoxa or presumption. Hence, I posit that the speaker is not committing a persuasive definition nor is evading falsification since the point of dispute is whether the alleged counterexample *is a Scot*, not whether *this Scot does so and so*. The scope of this paper does not allow for space to investigate actual cases of alleged NTSM though I speculate that in some instances, the Respondent is guilty of question-begging that their appeal to $\exists x (Px \ \& \ Sx)$ is assumed without proof.

5   Conclusion and Final Remarks

In this paper I analysed the structure of the NTSM and question wherein exactly is the failure of the Speaker in committing this 'fallacy', broadly understood. I argue that because persuasive definitions have differing theoretical explanations by philosophers, and that it is not always an indictment that persuasive definitions are problematic, then the NTSM *qua* PD is not necessarily fallacious or problematic in some instances. As Trudy Govier remarks when PDs arise, important issues are at stake. Furthermore, if the alleged crime in the NTSM is the evasive maneuver to avoid falsification to remain in one's prejudice, I have argued that there is a better explanation from the move from Su_1 to Su_2. I have pointed to various theories, some mutually exclusive, that could explain via differing contexts that there can be no redefinition, no high-redefinition, no tautology and no evasion on the Speaker's part. Obviously we can reach this conclusion only on a case by case basis by looking at particular instances of alleged No-True-Scotsman Moves.[35]

---

[35] I would like to thank two anonymous referees for their valuable insights and comments of a previous draft of this paper.

References

Aberdein, A.: Persuasive definition. In: Tindale, C.W., Hansen, H., Sveda, E. (eds.) Proceedings of Argumentation at the Century's Turn. Ontario Society for the Study of Argumentation (2000)

Aberdein, A.: Raising the tone: definition, bullshit, and the definition of bullshit. In: Reisch, G., Hardcastle, G. (eds.) Bullshit and Philosophy, pp. 151–169. Open Court, Chicago (2006)

Flew, A.: Thinking About Thinking. HarperCollins, New York (1975)

Gover, T.: A Practical Study of Argument. Wadsworth, Boston (2009)

Guala, F.: On the nature of social kinds. In: Gallotti, M., Michaels, J. (eds.) Perspectives on Social Ontology and Social Cognition, pp. 57–68. Springer, Dordrecht (2014)

Macagno, F., Walton, D.: The argumentative structure of persuasive definitions. Ethical Theory Moral Practice **11**, 525–549 (2008a)

Macagno, F., Walton, D.: Persuasive definitions: values, meanings and implicit disagreements. Informal Log. **28**(3), 203–228 (2008b)

Paglieri, F.: Don't Worry, Be Gappy! On the unproblematic gappiness of alleged fallacies. In: OSSA Conference Archive, vol. 119 (2016)

Schiappa, E.: Defining Reality: Definitions and the Politics of Meaning. Southern Illinois Press, Carbondale (2003)

Searle, J.R.: Speech Acts: An Essay in the Philosophy of Language. Cambridge University Press, Cambridge (1969)

Stevenson, C.L.: Persuasive definitions. Mind **47**, 331–350 (1938)

Stevenson, C.L.: Ethics and Language. Yale University Press, New Haven (1944)

van Eemeren, F.H., Houtlosser, P.: The contextuality of fallacies. Informal Log. **27**(1), 59–67 (2007)

van Eemeren, F.H.: In context: giving contextualisation its rightful place in the study of argumentation. Argumentation **25**, 141–161 (2011)

van Rees, M.A.: Strategic maneuvering with dissociation. Argumentation **20**, 473–487 (2006)

Walton, D., Macagno, F.: Reasoning from classifications and definitions. Argumentation **23**, 81–107 (2009)

Zarefsky, D.: Strategic maneuvering through persuasive definitions: implications for dialectic and rhetoric. Argumentation **20**, 399–416 (2006)

Occasion-Sensitive Semantics

Tamara Dobler[(✉)]

Institute for Logic, Language, and Computation,
University of Amsterdam, Amsterdam, Netherlands
t.dobler@uva.nl

Abstract. In this paper we provide a formal model for occasion-sensitive semantics motivated by so called 'Travis cases' (Travis 1978, 2000, 2008, 2009). We suggest that understanding of an utterance of φ (knowing its truth conditions) can be modelled as a twofold partitioning of worlds in logical space, where the initial partition is induced by the context-invariant meaning of the sentence uttered and the latter on the basis of context-dependent goals. Our model uses only a single parameter to capture occasion-sensitivity of sentences: *practical goals*.

1 Introducing Occasion-Sensitivity

Context-sensitivity is a phenomenon that affects natural language expressions. Frege already pointed out that some sentences express thoughts only when certain features of context are known, such as the time of an utterance or the speaker. The case in point are sentences containing context-sensitive terms such as indexicals or demonstratives (see Frege 1956: 296). For Frege, as for many others, context-sensitivity seemed a fairly isolated phenomenon, affecting only a small class of expressions. More recently, however, *radical contextualists* (e.g. Travis 2008, Recanati 2004, Carston 2002) have suggested that context-sensitivity is pervasive, that it affects all open class expressions (i.e. not just pure indexicals), and that it does so in a way that classical truth-conditional semantic theories may find difficult to track.

1.1 Motivation: Travis Cases

Radical contextualism is motivated by examples such as following:[1]

The leaves are green[2]
State of affairs: Pia's Japanese maple is full of russet leaves. Pia paints them green.

---

[1] In the literature these are known as *Travis cases* (sometimes referred to as context-shifting arguments, see Cappelen and Lepore (2008). For critical discussion see Hansen (2011), Hansen and Chemla (2013), Predelli (2005), Vicente (2012), Vicente (2015), Kennedy and McNally (2010), Rothschild and Segal (2009), MacFarlane (2009).

[2] Travis (2008): 111.

© Springer International Publishing AG 2017
P. Brézillon et al. (Eds.): CONTEXT 2017, LNAI 10257, pp. 254–266, 2017.
DOI: 10.1007/978-3-319-57837-8_20

Zoe needs some green leaves for her decoration:
Zoe: Do you have green leaves?
Pia: These leaves are green.

Pia's botanist friend seeks green leaves for a study of green-leaf chemistry:
Botanist: Do you have green leaves?
Pia: # These leaves are green.[3]

Sid has a desk[4]
State of affairs: Sid, an impoverished student, uses a door over two stacks of milk crates as a desk to write on.

Concerned if Sid has a desk to write on:
Pia: Does Sid have a desk?
Max: Sid has a desk.

On the look out for high end furniture:
Pia: Does Sid have a desk?
Max: # Sid has a desk

The shoes are under the bed[5]
State of affairs: Pia is looking for her shoes. Sid sees them, heels protruding from beneath the bed.

Retrieving shoes:
Pia: Are the shoes under the bed?
Sid: The shoes are under the bed.

Making sure the shoes are well hidden. Sid's response is meant to reassure Pia that the shoes are well hidden.
Pia: Are the shoes under the bed?
Sid: # The shoes are under the bed.

1.2   What Travis Cases are Taken to Show

Travis cases are taken as evidence for a number of claims. First, they demonstrate what we deem to be an uncontroversial fact that the interpretation and evaluation of utterances are somehow sensitive to contextual factors. However, the reason why Travis cases are particularly interesting is because the relevant sentences contain *no* pure indexicals (such as *I, you, here, today*) or other standard context-sensitive expressions (e.g. gradable adjectives, predicates of personal taste, modals, quantifier phrases), and yet their interpretation and evaluation varies across contexts of utterance. Second, in each example, the sentence

---

[3] We use the sign # to indicate that the response is in some sense inadequate or infelicitous, and that what is said is intuitively false.

[4] Travis (2000).

[5] Travis 2009: 119–120.

type used in both contexts is the same, and it is assumed that *its conventional meaning remains invariant*. One important consequence of the fact that the semantics of sentence types is invariant is that it would be impossible to avoid the denial of the law of non-contradiction, since the same sentence appears to be evaluated as true and false of the same state of the world, *if*, that is, the sentences used in these examples are taken at their face value (namely, as not being context-dependent in some sense). Third, the fact that the interpretation of utterances varies in this way is typically taken as evidence for the variability of intuitive *truth-conditions* or *truth-conditional content of utterances*.[6]

A number of analyses of Travis cases have been proposed, many whose primary concern is to preserve a compositional account of truth-conditions.[7] With the exception of semantic minimalists who reject that the intuitions about truth-value of utterances are good evidence for truth-conditions of sentences, almost all other solutions assume that at least some of the constituents in these sentences have context-dependent interpretations. Thus the appeal to context-dependence seems by far the most common way to avoid the attribution of contradictory beliefs to speakers or the denial of the law of non-contradiction, whilst also preserving truth-conditional compositional semantics.

1.3   Non-indexical Contextualism

In this paper we aim' to take a different approach because we believe that occasion-sensitivity is different from indexicality, and also that it is not a threat to compositional semantics. Thus, although we will propose what is, broadly speaking, a *contextualist* treatment of occasion-sensitivity, unlike Rothschild and Segal (2009) for instance, we won't treat individual lexical items (e.g. *green*) as (non-standard) full-blown *indexical* predicates. We fully agree with Kennedy and McNally (2010) that an indexical account which specifies no rule for determining the contextual value of an indexical (e.g. the speaker in context for *I*) places *no constraint* on its possible interpretations, and potentially creates the overgeneration problem (see Stanley 2005). Furthermore, unlike Szabó (2001), we will refrain from postulating hidden variables in the logical form of colour adjectives, mainly for the reasons already pointed out in Rothschild and Segal (2009) and Kennedy and McNally (2010), namely, because such an analysis lacks the required generality.

The approach defended in this paper is formally and conceptually closest (albeit not identical) to the position known as *non-indexical contextualism*

---

[6] See Recanati (2004) and Travis (2006) for a defense of this thesis; see Cappelen and Lepore (2008), Borg (2004) and Fodor (2003) for criticism.

[7] The phenomenon exhibited in Travis cases has thus far been analysed as a form of lexical ambiguity or polysemy (Fodor 2003; Vicente 2015; Carston 2010), structural ambiguity (Kennedy and McNally 2010), conversational implicature (Cappelen and Lepore 2008; Fodor 2003), circumstance of evaluation dependence (MacFarlane 2009; Predelli 2005), pragmatic modulation (Pagin 2005, Recanati 2012, Carston 2010) and (hidden) indexicality (Szabó 2001; Rothschild and Segal 2009.

developed in MacFarlane (2007, 2009). We agree with MacFarlane that context-sensitivity is a broader phenomenon than indexicality and it shouldn't be conflated with the latter. We also think that occasion-sensitivity is a good example of non-indexical context-sensitivity, where (i) semantic content of a predicate is invariant, (ii) the world of evaluation is invariant, and yet (iii) the extension of the predicate (and the truth-value of an utterance) varies. This is possible, MacFarlane argues, because the circumstance of evaluation includes *more parameters* than just a possible world (where these parameters are initiated by the context of use rather than the context of assessment).

With regards to Travis cases, MacFarlane's suggestion is that predicates such as *green* or *weighs 80 kilos* invariantly express a property of *being green* or *weighing 80 kilos* yet such a property has an intension which is a function from the circumstance of evaluation – consisting of a *pair* of parameters (counts-as parameter and world parameter) rather than one – to extension. A non-standard, all encompassing *count-as parameter* "settles what things have to be like to have various properties: e.g. the property of weighing 160 pounds, or of being tall" (MacFarlane 2009) such that the extension of a predicate varies when the value of the counts-as parameter varies, even when the world of evaluation remains the same.

We believe that this picture, generally speaking, adequately captures the phenomenon illustrated in Travis cases. However, we also contend that because of its generality it potentially suffers from similar problems as Rothschild and Segal (2009), in particular to do with lack of constraint and overgeneration. Our aim, therefore, is to further develop this approach, and revise it where necessary, in order to explain which features of occasions of use guide our judgements as to when something would count as having a certain property, and how these features constrain possible interpretations and evaluations of sentences.

Our proposal departs from MacFarlane's on several points (although the first two may be only terminological departures): first, we take it that properties that feed into the counts-as function can also be *zero-place properties* such as the property of *these leaves being green* or *Sid's having a desk*; second, we don't consider a zero-place property to be the same as the proposition expressed by an utterance on occasion (i.e. intuitive truth-conditions); we consider the proposition expressed by an utterance on occasion (i.e. the Austinian proposition)[8] to be an *output* of, rather than an input to, the counts-as function. Third, whereas MacFarlane leaves it open which feature of a context drives modifications of properties and why such modifications would ever take place, we suggest that a specific contextual feature mandates shifts in when things count as having certain properties.[9] By considering pragmatic processes as not linguistically

---

[8] See Recanati (2007).

[9] Reference is usually made to the speaker's intentions or the topic of conversation, without going into details of how or why these are able to determine correctness of selecting a certain function and not other. According to MacFarlane, "the counts-as parameter will be determined in complex ways by other features of the context, including the topic of conversation and the speaker's intentions" (Macfarlane 2007: 246).

mandated (rightly so), existing non-indexicalist approaches fail to put enough emphasis on why, in the course of communication, we nevertheless *do* systematically modify standing semantic contents of our expressions. We suggest that Travis cases point towards one specific contextual factor as playing part in fixing when things would count as having a certain property: relevance (of the information) for the *goals* that speakers pursue within particular practical projects. Even though objective predicates have their context-invariant semantic contents, these contents are *uninformative* unless they are restricted so that they become valuable for achieving contextually salient goals.

2   The Role of Standing Meaning

We will assume that each declarative[10] sentence φ has a context-invariant, compositional meaning in virtue of syntactic and lexical structure and linguistic conventions. On our view, standing meaning has a substantial role to play in the process of utterance interpretation. However, in the light of pervasive context-sensitivity of natural language, we believe it is crucial to capture the idea that the meaning of φ only *constrains* the intended interpretation, or the proposition(s) expressed, without fully determining it, i.e. the meaning of φ *underspecifies* the proposition that some utterance of φ expresses.

To capture this notion of semantic constraint on what is said, we suggest that the conventional meaning of an (atomic) declarative sentence can be viewed as the set of worlds which are *compatible* with its meaning, that is, those worlds where the sentence is true *on some of its uses* but false on others. For any atomic (NP+VP) sentence (used to state a piece of information) there will be: (i) some possible worlds or situations which are incompatible with what it means, and which can thus be eliminated purely with respect to its conventional meaning, and (ii) others which are compatible with the meaning of the sentence but in which an *utterance* of the sentence is not always true.

In standard truth-conditional frameworks, a world is considered to be compatible (incompatible) with the meaning of φ only when φ is true (or false) at that world. Accordingly, the set of worlds in $\mathcal{W}_\varphi$ would thus correspond to the proposition expressed by φ, modelled as the set of worlds in which φ is true. However, as evidenced in Travis cases, this common identification of meaning with truth is problematic insofar as the truth valuation of an utterance of φ may shift even when the world of evaluation and conventional meaning remain unchanged. So we believe it is crucial to resist the common assumption that conventional meaning is sufficient to determine when a sentence uttered in context would be true. Hence, on our view, the meaning function does not partition the worlds into those at which φ is true and those at which φ is false. Rather φ is considered to be truth-evaluable and worlds are considered to be truth-makers only after taking into account a further factor: an *occasion* on which φ is used.

---

[10] The model we are about to propose can be extended to interrogatives and imperatives, although this is beyond the scope of this paper.

Take **The shoes are under the bed** Travis case. The sentence *The shoes are under the bed* may be true if the shoes are well hidden under the bed, or if their heels are poking out. This sentence could also be true if the shoes are three floors down aligned with the bed. Or if they are buried in cement under the bed etcetera. However, an *utterance* of the sentence on an occasion won't necessarily be true at all these worlds: this is the lesson we learned from Travis cases. Even though all these very different conditions of the world are compatible with what the sentence means not all of them will make an utterance of the sentence on some occasion true since an occasion places some further constraints on success (i.e. truth) of the utterance.

Let us call this set generated by the meaning function *the compatibility set of φ, or $\mathcal{W}_\varphi$*. If a world is semantically *incompatible* with the meaning of φ, then there will be no possible understanding on which φ is true at that world (where an *understanding* of φ is a refinement of $\mathcal{W}_\varphi$). If a world is semantically compatible with φ then there will be some understanding on which an utterance of φ is true at that world, but also some understandings on which it is false at that world.

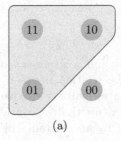

(a)

Fig. 1. Semantically compatible worlds, $\mathcal{W}_\varphi$

For simplicity's sake, let us assume there are only two possible ways of being green: *painted* green and *naturally* green. Figure 1 represents the set of all alternatives, where (11) is the world where the salient leaves are both painted and naturally green, (10) is the world where they are painted green but not naturally green, (01) is the world where they are only naturally green, and (00) is the world where they are neither painted nor naturally green. Since in our simplified model painted and naturally green exhaust the ways of being green, in the (00) world the leaves are *not* green. The set of worlds which are semantically compatible with the sentence *The leaves are green* is thus $\mathcal{W}_{green} : \{11, 10, 01\}$, whilst the set of semantically incompatible worlds is $\overline{\mathcal{W}}_{green} : \{00\}$.

Travis cases show that not all the worlds in $\mathcal{W}_{green}$ will make an utterance of *The leaves are green* on some occasion true: for instance, in the botanist context, the world (10) is ruled out as a truth-maker because it matters in this context that the leaves are naturally green (see Fig. 2). By contrast in the decorator context, it does not matter if the leaves are painted or natural, so the only world

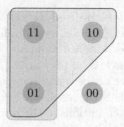

Fig. 2. Understanding of green in the botanist context. (Color figure online)

ruled out is {00}. Hence it depends on which understanding of green is relevant, which worlds will make an utterance of φ true. The resolution of the issue which understanding of φ is relevant for truth evaluation is here independent from its meaning. To fix which understanding of a predicate is correct we need to ask which information (about the world) would be relevant to an agent on some occasion. In the next section we suggest that the worlds in $\mathcal{W}_\varphi$ are kept or eliminated on the basis of how *conducive* they are to the *goal* that the agent aims to achieve on an occasion.[11]

3   Occasions and Goals

So far we used the term *occasion* and *occasion-sensitivity* without properly defining them, or showing what the relation between an occasion and a world is supposed to be. In this section we will try to give a more detailed account of these notions by identifying a feature that we consider necessary for determining which proposition is expressed by an utterance of a sentence on occasion. We shall suggest that a key feature of some occasion of using φ that gives rise to the phenomenon of occasion-sensitivity is a *practical goal* which is salient of that occasion and which agents strive to achieve. Recognising which goal is salient is necessary to determine which proposition someone expressed by an utterance of φ.

3.1   Communication Goals Understood Narrowly and Broadly

What does a practical goal have to do with determining when a sentence is true? In this section we try to motivate the connection between goal directed actions and correct understanding of utterances.

To get the idea that practical goals constrain interpretation off the ground, we take the following remark made by Robert Stalnaker (who cites Grice) as our guiding principle:

> "[W]e should see speech as action to be explained, like any other kind of action, in terms of the beliefs and purposes of the agent" (Stalnaker 1999: 2).

---

[11] In our diagram the world (01) is thus not fit for the botanist's goal.

To Stalnaker's principle we add the following observation about the success-conditions of actions: namely, that an action (including a speech action) is successful when it successfully achieves its goal. But what constitutes the goal of a speech act?

Ever since Frege (1956) it is common to distinguish two elements in a speech act: its *content* (truth-evaluable thought) and its *force*. The idea of (illocutionary) force is normally understood as capturing what a speech act aims at; an assertion characteristically aims at truth or saying something true, a question characteristically aims to raise an issue to be resolved by a (truthful) answer, and an order aims to issue an order to be successfully fulfilled. Saying something true, raising an issue, issuing an order etc. are thus *goals* that characterise different speech acts. Are *these* goals then sufficient to determine (together with the sentence meaning) when a particular speech act is successful?

Our answer to this question is negative because we believe that goals (and hence successes) that agents aim to achieve in the course of communication are typically *much broader* (and much more practical) than the characteristic goals of assertions, questions, or commands. That is, by virtue of performing an *assertive* speech act, an agent does aim to say something true and, if true, add the proposition to the common ground (see Stalnaker 1999). Nonetheless, as a rule, this is *not the only thing* that agents do whilst communicating: an issue raised and proposition asserted are always turned towards fulfilments of other *practical goals* such as hiding shoes from kleptomaniac friends, doing green leaf chemistry, decorating, putting kids to sleep, building houses and bridges, and so forth.[12] So, besides narrowly defined goals that characterise (conventional) illocutionary forces, there are various practical goals we aim to achieve on particular occasions. Our suggestion is that practical goals are another necessary factor in determining when a speech act (of assertion) is successful, and, in particular, when its content is true.

If communication, in general, is embedded in other goal-directed, practical activities, then we can also assume that what someone communicates on a particular occasion is directed at fulfilling some such goal. To take a Travis case again as our example, if I know that my friend is a botanist and is searching for green leaves for her experiment (assuming I am not totally ignorant about this topic) then I also should know that her request for green leaves bears on that particular goal and that so does my response. If I sincerely say to my friend, "Search no more, the leaves on my tree are green", then what I say is that the world is indeed such that her project can be successfully carried out. In other words, by asserting this, I suggested that the world is *conducive* to my friend's goal. If it turns out, however, that I have the leaves that are painted green but are naturally red, then her reasonable expectations as to the state of the world won't be satisfied and her project won't take off. That is, *this* state of the world is *not* conducive to the salient goal and so what I said to my friend was false (although it could have been true were her goal decorating rather than chemistry).

It is in this way that we take practical goals to be an important factor in interpreting and evaluating what someone has said.

---

[12] This idea of communication is based on Wittgenstein et al. (2009).

3.2   Goal-Conduciveness of a World

Agents communicate to exchange or gain the information about the world which helps them achieve their goals, which, it was argued, outstrip narrow goals that define illocutionary forces of particular speech acts. We also suggested that the state of the world can be such that it is more or less conducive to fulfilling some practical goal, and so, when we provide some information to someone about the state of the world, it goes without saying that this will have certain practical consequences, i.e., some positive or negative effect on salient plans and goals. For instance, the world where a room is such that the shadows of objects can be seen in it is *not* conducive to the goal of opening a camera and developing a film since such a project won't be successfully achieved in this state of the world. Consequently, if someone says that the room is dark, where this particular goal is salient in the conversation, then he said something false. If, however, he says this when the salient goal is to put a child to sleep, then he might well be saying something true.

Our main suggestion is that the worlds which are compatible with the meaning of a sentence (the members of $\mathcal{W}_\varphi$) may include those with very different potentials in terms of enabling a successful action (some very low, some high). For a particular goal g and world w we can take it that w will be more or less conducive to g (i.e. achieving g in w is more or less difficult). We will give a formal definition of this notion below.

We propose that, among the worlds that are semantically compatible with the sentence uttered (those belonging to the compatibility set), only those worlds that are conducive to the salient goal on an occasion constitute the proposition expressed by an utterance of the sentence on that occasion.

4   A Model

In order to determine which proposition is expressed by an utterance of the sentence on some occasion we propose to first evaluate all possible worlds in terms of how goal-conducive they are, and to assign each a numerical value, thus producing a ranking over worlds. The set of worlds with the highest rank that is also semantically compatible with the sentence will correspond to the proposition expressed by the utterance of that sentence on that occasion.

4.1   Language

Because we are take simple NP+VP sentences as our atom of analysis, we will use a language L for *propositional logic*, with its standard set of propositional letters and connectives. We assume the set of atomic sentences A and define formulas as follows:

$$\varphi := p, \varphi \vee \varphi, \neg\varphi, \varphi \wedge \varphi, \varphi \rightarrow \varphi$$

where $p \in A$, the set of atomic sentences.

4.2   Semantics

A *model M* for L is a tuple $M = \langle W, G, V, \mathcal{C}, \rangle$ in which W is a non-empty set of possible worlds, G is a non-empty set of goals, V is a valuation function which assigns to a sentence a numerical value 1 for semantically compatible or 0 for semantically incompatible, $\mathcal{C}$ is a goal-conduciveness function which maps a pair of worlds and goals to a value in the interval $[0, 1]$ ($\approx$ the c-value of the world w given the goal g).

Definition: conduciveness to goal

$$\mathcal{C} : G \times W \to [0, 1]$$

where $g \in G$ is a goal that agents are aiming to reach on occasion.

Definition: conduciveness ordering

$$\forall w, w' \in W, w' \preceq_g w \text{ iff } \mathcal{C}(w', g) \leq \mathcal{C}(w, g)$$

We can produce a ranking of all worlds in logical space with respect to how conducive they are to some goal. For any pair of possible worlds $\{w, w'\}$ the world with the lower conduciveness value will be ranked lower than the world with the higher conduciveness value. If they have the same value they will also have the same rank.

Definition: the top tier

$$w \in \text{MAX}_g \text{ iff } \forall w' \in W, w' \preceq_g w$$

The set of worlds with the highest ranking, MAX_g, will form the top tier of the worlds wrt to their goal-conduciveness. For any world w with a given ranking one can conceive of another world w' that has the same ranking despite differing in some way from w. So, in principle, there will also be more than one world with the MAX_g value.

We were able to order the worlds in terms of their conduciveness to a given goal quite independently of language. This is because a successful action that brings about some goal does not necessarily presuppose a use of language (i.e. a performance of a speech act). However, since our primary interest is in the interpretation and evaluation of sentences used in communication (i.e. speech acts), our model should capture how pragmatic constraints on interpretation we defined by means of contextual goals interact with semantic constraints we defined by means of the initial partition induced by conventional meaning.

Definition: valuation function

$$V : A \times W \to \{0, 1\}$$

where A is the set of atomic sentences, and values 1 and 0 designate *semantically compatible* and *semantically incompatible*, respectively (NOT: true and false).

Definition: valuation of formulas

$$M, w \models_g \varphi \text{ iff } w \in \text{MAX}_g \wedge V(\varphi, w) = 1$$
$$M, w \models_g \neg\varphi \text{ iff } M, w \nvDash_g \varphi$$
$$M, w \models_g (\varphi \wedge \Psi) \text{ iff } M, w \models_g \varphi \text{ iff } M, w \models_g \Psi$$

The proposition expressed by an utterance of an atomic sentence p is defined in model M as the intersection of $\mathcal{W}_\varphi$, the set of worlds that are semantically compatible with the sentence, and the set of worlds that have the MAX$_g$ value.

5   Examples

We can now analyse Travis cases using our present semantics in the form of the following conditional T-sentence:

(T) The utterance u of the sentence φ is true at world w relative to goal g iff w is conducive to g and w is semantically compatible with φ.

The leaves are green: In this example we have a shift of goals between the two occasions: on one occasion the salient goal is to decorate a table centrepiece, in which case the natural property of the leaves is not relevant; on another occasion the salient goal is to examine the green leaf chemistry, in which case the natural property is relevant. The stipulated world of evaluation is such that the leaves are only painted green (but are naturally red). This world is semantically compatible with the uttered sentence on both occasions, but is only conducive to the former goal and not to the latter. Therefore, the utterance is true at w only wrt to the goal of decorating and is false wrt the goal of doing chemistry.

(O1) u_{green} is true at w wrt $g_{decorate}$

(O2) u_{green} is false at w wrt $g_{chemistry}$

The shoes are under the bed: Again we have a shift of goals on the two occasions. On one occasion the goal is to retrieve the shoes and the extent to which they are visible is not relevant to a successful achievement of this goal. On another occasion the goal is to make sure the shoes are well hidden, so not visible at all. The world of evaluation is such that the heels of the shoes are visible from under the bed. Saying that the shoes are under the bed is conducive only to the former goal, whilst saying this on the second occasion would prevent the achievement of the latter goal. Therefore, the information conveyed by the sentence is true with respect to the former goal and false wrt to the latter.

(O1) u_{shoes} is true at w wrt $g_{retreive}$

(O2) u_{shoes} is false at w wrt g_{hide}

Sid has a desk: In this scenario, each occasion of utterance is paired with a different goal such that on one occasion the goal is to have something to sit and write on, and on another the goal is to find a piece of expensive office furniture. The world of evaluation is such that Sid has a door over two stacks of milk crates. Saying that Sid has a desk in the first case facilitates the fulfilment of the goal, whilst in the latter case it probably doesn't. Hence, the information conveyed by the utterance is true on the former occasion and false on the latter.

$$(\text{O1}) \ u_{desk} \text{ is true at } w \text{ wrt } g_{write}$$
$$(\text{O2}) \ u_{desk} \text{ is false at } w \text{ wrt } g_{office}$$

6   Conclusion

This completes our model for occasion-sensitive semantics. It is important to bear in mind that we do *not* claim that *all* meaning is occasion-sensitive insofar as we assumed that the conventional meaning of a sentence creates an initial partition which is not sensitive to any *particular* occasion. The outcome of the meaning partition corresponds to what is in the literature known as *minimal proposition*.[13] Unlike proponents of the notion of minimal proposition, we take intuitions behind Travis cases as evidence for the variability of intuitive truth-conditions across occasions. Although we decided to sidestep the terminological side of this debate by stipulating that occasion-sensitive utterances of φ are successful (an not merely true), the substantial point of Travis cases and occasion-sensitivity nonetheless remains: 'minimal proposition' is not only something with no 'psychological reality' (Recanati 2004) but moreover it plays no significant role in decision making, planning and action. And if we are interested to capture what propositions our utterances express in the course of communication, rather than in their structural semantic properties, then the analysis which stops at the initial meaning partition is incomplete, to say the least. We have shown that only once we take into account particular goals (and also agents' expectations) we are able to specify the subset of semantically appropriate worlds which corresponds to the proposition expressed on occasion.

References

Austin, J.L.: How to Do Things with Words. Oxford University Press, Oxford (1975)

Borg, E.: Minimal Semantics. Cambridge University Press, Cambridge (2004)

Borg, E.: Pursuing Meaning. Oxford University Press, Oxford (2012)

Cappelen, H., Lepore, E.: Insensitive Semantics: A Defense of Semantic Minimalism and Speech Act Pluralism. Wiley, Hoboken (2008)

Carston, R.: Thoughts and Utterances: The Pragmatics of Explicit Communication. Wiley, Hoboken (2002)

Carston, R.: Explicit communication and free pragmatic enrichment. In: Soria, B., Romero, E. (eds.) Explicit Communication, pp. 217–285. Springer, Heidelberg (2010)

Fodor, J.A.: Hume Variations. Cambridge University Press, Cambridge (2003)

---

[13] See Cappelen and Lepore 2008, Borg 2004, Recanati 2004, Pagin and Pelletier 2007, Travis 2006.

Frege, G.: The thought: a logical inquiry. Mind **65**, 289–311 (1956)

Hansen, N.: Color adjectives and radical contextualism. Linguist. Philos. **34**(3), 201–221 (2011)

Hansen, N., Chemla, E.: Experimenting on contextualism. Mind Lang. **28**(3), 286–321 (2013)

Kennedy, C., McNally, L.: Color, context, and compositionality. Synthese **174**(1), 79–98 (2010)

MacFarlane, J.: Semantic minimalism and nonindexical contextualism. In: Context-Sensitivity and Semantic Minimalism: New Essays on Semantics and Pragmatics, pp. 240–250 (2007)

MacFarlane, J.: Nonindexical contextualism. Synthese **166**(2), 231–250 (2009)

Pagin, P.: Compositionality and context. In: Contextualism in Philosophy, pp. 303–348 (2005)

Pagin, P., Pelletier, J.: Content, context and composition. In: Content and Context. Essays on Semantics and Pragmatics, pp. 25–62 (2007)

Pietroski, P.: Meaning before truth (2005)

Predelli, S.: Painted leaves, context, and semantic analysis. Linguist. Philos. **28**(3), 351–374 (2005)

Recanati, F.: Literal Meaning. Cambridge University Press, Cambridge (2004)

Recanati, F.: Perspectival Thought: A Plea for (Moderate) Relativism. Oxford University Press, Oxford (2007)

Recanati, F.: Compositionality, semantic flexibility, and context-dependence. Oxford Handbook of Compositionality, pp. 175–192 (2012)

Rothschild, D., Segal, G.: Indexical predicates. Mind Lang. **24**(4), 467–493 (2009)

Stalnaker, R.: Context and Content Essays on Intentionality in Speech and Thought. Oxford University Press, Oxford (1999)

Stanley, J.: Semantics in context. In: Contextualism in Philosophy: Knowledge, Meaning, and Truth, pp. 221–253 (2005)

Szabó, Z.G.: Adjectives in context. Pragmatics and Beyond New Series, pp. 119–146 (2001)

Travis, C.: Meaning versus truth. Dialogue **17**(03), 401–430 (1978)

Travis, C.: Unshadowed Thought: Representation in Thought and Language. Harvard University Press, Cambridge (2000)

Travis, C.: Insensitive semantics. Mind Lang. **21**(1), 39–49 (2006)

Travis, C.: Occasion-Sensitivity: Selected Essays. Oxford University Press, Oxford (2008)

Travis, C.: Thought's Footing: A Theme in Wittgenstein's Philosophical Investigations. Oxford University Press, Oxford (2009)

Vicente, A.: On travis cases. Linguist. Philos. **35**(1), 3–19 (2012)

Vicente, A.: The green leaves and the expert: polysemy and truth-conditional variability. Lingua **157**, 54–65 (2015)

Wittgenstein, L., Anscombe, G.E.M., Hacker, P.M.S., Schulte, J.: Philosophical Investigations. Wiley, Hoboken (2009)

Contextualism and Echolalia

Michal Gleitman[✉]

The Polonsky Academy, The van Leer Jerusalem Institute,
43 Jabotinsky Street, Jerusalem 9214116, Israel
michalg@vanleer.org.il

Abstract. This paper argues for the need to distinguish more clearly between the presence of a communicative intention (that a speaker is attempting to communicate something) and the content of the speaker's utterance (what that is that they are trying to communicate), and consider the role of contextual information in the recognition of the former, independently of the latter. The paper uses experimental and clinical evidence from studies on echolalia (a common symptom of autism spectrum disorder, in which a child repeats verbatim other people's utterances) to demonstrate the possibility of a speaker who utters conventional, supposedly meaningful sentences, in a seemingly automatic and noncommunicative manner. As a result, the listener is forced to rely on the wide context to determine the presence or absence of a communicative intention behind the speaker's utterance, as a condition for interpreting the content of the utterance.

Keywords: Contextualism · Communicative intention · Pragmatic interpretation · Wide context · Echolalia · Autism spectrum disorder · Language development

1 Introduction

There is a curious phenomenon in the literature on communicative intentions: on the one hand, it is generally acknowledged that the recognition of communicative intentions is a two-phase process that involves recognizing the presence of a communicative intention, in addition to identifying its content. However, while the first phase is occasionally mentioned, it is never actually discussed, since the common practice is to conflate the two phases, and concentrate on the second, which already presupposes the first. The underlying assumption seems to be that communicative attempts are instinctively recognized, so the preliminary phase of identifying the presence of a communicative intention requires no further elaboration. In contrast, this paper shows that the presence of a communicative intention isn't always evident, and could be difficult to recognize under certain circumstances. Drawing on experimental and clinical evidence on echolalia (the verbatim repetition of other people's speech), the paper discusses occasions of utterance where the presence of a communicative intention isn't clearly manifested, and is difficult to ascertain, because the speaker is uttering conventional sentences, but in a seemingly automatic and dysfunctional manner. Consequently, in echolalic episodes contextual information is necessary for determining the presence of a communicative intention, but the information needs to be

© Springer International Publishing AG 2017
P. Brézillon et al. (Eds.): CONTEXT 2017, LNAI 10257, pp. 267–276, 2017.
DOI: 10.1007/978-3-319-57837-8_21

examined carefully, because in some cases, most notably children on the autism spectrum, it can be misleading, and actually obscure the presence of communicative intent. By demonstrating the crucial and highly nuanced role of contextual information, and its potentially equivocal effect on the recognition of the presence of communicative intentions, the paper argues for the need to pay more theoretical attention to this phase, and consider it independently of the interpretation of the content of utterances.

The next section illustrates the insufficient discussion in the literature of the preliminary phase of recognizing the presence of communicative intentions. The third section presents the phenomenon of echolalia, highlighting the essential role of contextual information in identifying the presence of a communicative intention in echolalic episodes. The fourth section discusses the twofold effect of contextual information, which is necessary for revealing, but could also disguise, the presence of a communicative intention behind the echolalic behavior of children on the autism spectrum. The paper concludes with a brief discussion of the consequences of echolalia for contextualism.

2 Recognizing Communicative Intentions

"The central aim of pragmatic theory must be to explain how the speaker's communicative intentions are recognized."

(Sperber and Wilson, cited in: Recanati 1986, p. 215)

As pointed out by Sperber and Wilson, the founders of relevance theory, intentions and their recognition, particularly the recognition of communicative intentions, which are the foundation of communicative acts, are at the heart of any theory that seeks to explain how language is used in actual situations of utterance. Although Sperber and Wilson refer to the recognition of communicative intentions as a single stroke process, it is generally acknowledged that the process involves two distinct phases: recognizing the presence of a communicative intention, and identifying its content. The two phases are clearly distinguished in the following description by Searle: "if I am trying to tell someone something, then [...] as soon as he recognizes *that I am trying to tell him something* [phase 1] and exactly *what it is I am trying to tell him* [phase 2], I have succeeded in telling it to him" (1969, p. 47, my italics). Both phases are therefore alluded to in the literature, but for the most part, even when they are initially distinguished, the tendency is to subsequently conflate them and concentrate on the second phase, whose elaboration presumably poses more substantial challenges. For example, Bach puts forward a definition of communicative intentions that distinguishes between the two phases: "that a speaker is attempting to communicate something [phase 1], and what that is [phase 2], is a matter of his communicative intention (if indeed he has one)." He subsequently proceeds to consolidate the two phases for the sake of brevity, describing successful communication as a case in which "the listener succeeds in identifying the speaker's communicative intention" (2004, pp. 29–30, see also p. 31).

Such examples are common throughout the literature on communicative intentions, and they may seem inconsequential, since identifying what a speaker intends to communicate assumes already that they are trying to communicate something. However, neglecting to consider the recognition of the presence of a communicative intention on its own accord ignores occasions of utterance where such presence isn't clearly manifested, and cannot be instinctively recognized. By examining echolalic utterances in which the presence of a communicative intention is ambiguous, and not easily recognized, the following sections demonstrate the significance of distinguishing more clearly between the two phases and analyzing the first independently of the second. The ambiguous manifestation of communicative intent in echolalic episodes forces the listener to rely on the wide context, not only for interpreting the content of the utterance, but also for ascertaining whether such interpretation is required in the first place, i.e. whether the utterance was made with an underlying communicative intent. The phenomenon of echolalia therefore highlights the significance, as well as the breadth of scope of pragmatic interpretation, and suggests the need to consider the role of the wide context of an utterance in ascertaining not only its content, but its function as well.

3 Echolalia as a Context-Sensitive Phenomenon

Echolalia is a form of imitative behavior in which a person, typically a child, repeats linguistic expressions that are 'borrowed whole' from other people's speech. For example:

Mother:	Look sweetie, here's a dog!
Child:	here's a dog!
Mother:	That's right, a dog

Echolalic behavior is usually classified as immediate or delayed, to distinguish between repetitions that occur immediately after the original utterance (as in the above example), and repetitions that occur hours and even days later (e.g. a child who randomly repeats entire phrases they've previously heard on television). Echolalic behavior, both immediate and delayed, is a common phase in the course of normal language development, but it is mostly known for its pathological manifestations, primarily as a symptom of autism spectrum disorder (ASD) (see Schuler 1979 for a review). While in typically developing children imitation is viewed as facilitating language acquisition, in the context of ASD echolalic behaviors frequently appear dysfunctional, compulsive and noncommunicative, the product of a limited ability to comprehend language (Fay 1969; Fay and Butler 1968; Howlin 1982; Roberts 1989; Rutter 1978). Prizant and Rydell (1984) for example, describe a child who utters 'it's a piece of sponge' over 40 times in rapid succession, and speculate that since the child's behavior seems automatic and is not directed at another person it might be a form of self-stimulation (a common symptom of ASD that typically includes repetitive body movements or movement of objects for the purpose of sensory stimulation or relief) (p. 190). Another example of automatic, noncommunicative echolalia is a child who echoes parts of his teacher's utterances while she speaks in class; Wolf and Chess (1965), who cite this example, describe the child's speech as "not apparently directed at another person, conveying no obvious message and serving no evident purpose"

(p. 35). Another study describes this type of nonintentional, noncommunicative echolalic behavior as "a product of primitive, reflex-like mechanisms, not unlike parroting reflexes in birds. An automatic rudimentary ability to mimic" (Schuler and Prizant 2010, p. 177). Such examples, of dysfunctional echolalic behavior, have dominated the literature until a couple of decades ago, leading to the conclusion that echolalia in ASD is profoundly different from echolalia in normal language development, so while the latter was viewed as a sign of emerging language comprehension, the former was located "outside the realm of cognitive and linguistic growth" and viewed as interfering with the production of spontaneous language (see discussion in: Prizant 1983a, pp. 69–70).

More recently, the view that echolalic behavior in ASD is predominantly meaningless came under attack for being the result of "a focus on semantic-syntactic models of language," which are insufficient for determining the function and meaning of echolalic utterances that are conventional by definition. Drawing on the literature in pragmatics, several researchers argued that examining echolalic utterances as isolated behaviors, analyzing only their linguistic structure as compared to the model utterance with no regard to the "natural communicative interactions" in which they occur, obscures the range of functions that echolalia serves for children on the autism spectrum (Prizant 1983a, pp. 64–66; Prizant and Duchan 1981, pp. 241–242). For instance, echolalia frequently appears in response to questions, as in the following hypothetical exchange:

Father: do you want a cookie?
Child: want a cookie…

Here the echoing could be automatic, but it could also serve an interactive function by enabling the child to take her turn in the conversation, and maintain the social interaction despite her inability to understand what is being said. While still the product of lack of comprehension, Schuler (1979) argues that forms of echolalia that show "an element of turn-taking and social awareness" and "adherence to rules of conversation should be viewed differently from those that do not, because some communicative intent is demonstrated" (p. 425).[1] The difference between automatic and interactive echolalia reflects a significant difference in the child's underlying abilities, but since it is not coded in the syntax of the uttered sentence, its observable appearance could be very subtle and easily go unnoticed unless contextual information, such as paralinguistic features, the child's nonverbal behavior, and overall situational context, are taken into consideration.

The realization that echolalic behavior is context-sensitive inspired a series of studies that examined echolalic utterances within the broader context of the child's cognitive and linguistic functioning, and were subsequently able to identify various cognitive, interactional and communicative functions of echolalic behavior (Dyer and

---

[1] Schuler notes further that turn-taking echolalia is reminiscent of normal and common conversational behavior that reflects reciprocity and is instrumental in regulating joint action, thereby challenging the assumption that pathological echolalia can be strictly separated from other forms of imitative behavior that are not pathological (see next section for further discussion).

Hadden 1981; Prizant and Duchan 1981; Prizant and Rydell 1984; Wolff and Chess 1965. For a comprehensive survey see: Schuler and Prizant 2010). One study for example distinguished between turn-taking echolalia and automatic repetition by observing the participants' gaze and body orientation to determine if they are directing their echolalic utterances toward another person and attending to that person's reaction. The study found turn-taking to be the most common function of immediate echolalia (33% of all echolalic utterances), and concluded that by enabling the child to partake in verbal interaction, this type of echolalic behavior could be a step toward spontaneous language production (Prizant and Duchan 1981, p. 246). Other functions that were identified include the use of echolalic behavior to express affirmation and refusal, and make requests, as in the case of a child who uttered 'you don't want it' when refusing something offered to them and a child who asked his mother for ice cream by uttering 'you want some ice cream, Thomas? yes, you may' (Wolff and Chess 1965. For a detailed list of functions of echolalic behavior see: Prizant and Duchan 1981; Prizant and Rydell 1984).

However, even when contextual information is carefully considered, intentional and communicative echolalic behaviors of children with ASD can still be subject to considerable misinterpretation. Echolalic utterances, especially delayed ones in which the model utterance is not readily available to the interpreter, often have highly idiosyncratic meanings that render them noncommunicative to most listeners. Consequently, an echolalic utterance could be produced with a communicative purpose, but not be recognized as such by a listener, especially one who is not well acquainted with the speaker's behavior. Thomas' request for example, might not be easily understood if uttered when there is no ice cream present, but his mother, being well acquainted with her son's echolalic behavior, might still be able to figure out his intention based on their shared experience. Stiegler (2015) gives a similar example, of a child who repeatedly utters 'let's open the presents' in situations where there are no gifts. The child's behavior might seem acontextual to some listeners, who would consequently label it dysfunctional and meaningless, but other listeners might be able to recognize that the child is using this phrase to express happiness and excitement (the same feelings that were experienced when the model utterance was first encountered) (p. 755).

The echolalic behavior of children on the autism spectrum is therefore context-sensitive in a distinctive way that makes the listener's role especially crucial, not only in interpreting the meaning of the utterance but also in recognizing its communicative purpose, because the same utterance, produced under the same circumstances, may be rendered communicative by some listeners and noncommunicative by others. Prizant, a prominent figure in the field of echolalia and ASD, concludes:

> "*form cannot always be used as an indicator of the presence or absence of communicative intent*. It is possible that, due to specific linguistic deficits, autistic persons must often rely on utterances 'borrowed' from others in order to express their needs and intentions, even though the internal structure (i.e. semantic-syntactic relationships) of such utterances may not be analyzed or fully comprehended" (Prizant 1983b, p. 299, my italics. See also: Roberts 1989, p. 280; Stiegler 2015, p. 752).

Prizant rightly emphasizes the crucial role of contextual information in the identification of the presence of a communicative intention in the context of echolalia and

ASD. But even when contextual information is considered, the results aren't always conclusive, and the communicative attempts of children with ASD often go unrecognized because of their echolalic behavior, which makes the manifestation of communicative intent particularly ambiguous, and the identification of its presence especially nuanced. The next section describes some of the unique challenges involved in interpreting the echolalic behaviors of children with ASD, and demonstrates the equivocal effect of contextual information that makes these children particularly vulnerable to having their communicative efforts being overlooked and misrecognized by their listeners.

4   Recognizing the Presence of Communicative Intentions in Echolalic Episodes in ASD

It should be noted that repeating other people's utterances is not an uncommon discursive practice, so the mere fact that a speaker is repeating verbatim someone else's utterances is not, by itself, a reason for misinterpreting their intentions or questioning the presence of communicative intent (Tannen 2007. See also discussion of echoic utterances in Sperber and Wilson 1986, pp. 237–243). However, the efforts of children with ASD to mobilize their echolalic behavior to achieve interactive and communicative functions are frequently misconstrued even by their parents and caregivers. While echolalic behaviors in typically developing children are routinely regarded as intentional and communicative, and are usually encouraged by parents and caregivers, in children with ASD similar behaviors encounter a different reaction. Parents and caregivers are significantly less likely to encourage echolalic behavior, or regard it as intentional in the context of ASD, and researchers and clinicians often caution against the risk of attributing greater intent and meaning to it than is actually the case (c.f. discussion in Prizant and Rydell 1984, pp. 190–191). So while echolalic behavior is generally context-sensitive, in children on the autism spectrum it seems to make the manifestation of communicative intent particularly ambiguous, and the identification of its presence especially nuanced.

In a study comparing normal and pathological echolalia, Philips and Dyer (1977) observe that in the early stages of language development the echolalic behavior of children with ASD often appears very similar to that of typically developing children, but is treated significantly less favorably due to its late onset and prolonged duration.[2] Take for example the following typical exchange between a mother and a child who are looking at a book together:

---

[2] In fact, the heterogeneous nature of echolalic behavior drove some researchers to argue that pathological echolalia cannot be strictly separated from echolalic behavior in normal language development as well as other forms of normal imitative behavior. For example, Schuler (1979) submits that since "echolalia is not easy to define or distinguish from more normal forms of repetition," they "should not be viewed as separate, but rather as related entities; their difference being a matter of degree" (pp. 425, 427).

Mother: Look, that's a baby
Child: that's a baby
Mother: That's right and that's baby's nose
Child: baby's nose
Mother: Nose!   That's right!   Good boy!

In a two-year-old this kind of echolalic behavior would be considered perfectly normal, and therefore not only accepted but actively encouraged, as in the above exchange (p. 49). In contrast, children on the autism spectrum who exhibit this kind of imitative verbal behavior at a significantly later age (typically between the ages of five and ten years), are not encouraged in the same way, leading the authors to speculate that "autistic children, [...] being generally late in any speech onset [...] are possibly past the natural development point when a mother (or any adult) would spontaneously use the basic 'cuing for imitation' speech that would be the normal response to a baby from birth to about three years old" (p. 53). As a result, children with ASD "are further handicapped" because they don't receive the "spontaneous help" that a typically developing child at an equivalent point of development would receive, possibly perpetuating their echolalic behavior and inadvertently hindering their ability to move past this stage of development and acquire more productive forms of verbal behavior (p. 55).

Other features of the autism phenotype might contribute further to echolalic behavior being misclassified as nonintentional and noncommunicative. Since children with ASD often repeat utterances with an extreme degree of accuracy, their repetitions are more likely to be attributed to superior auditory memory and viewed as automatic and lacking comprehension, so even an echolalic utterance that occurs within an appropriate context could appear noncommunicative (Schuler 1979, p. 426). For instance, a child who sighs 'oh, it's too bad, bring it here to me, and let me see if I can fix it for you' when a toy breaks during group play is making a perfectly situation-appropriate utterance, but the author who cites it observes that since it's a literal repetition of a parent's utterance on a similar occasion, it could be the product of good associative memory skills rather than intentional linguistic behavior. Even repetitions that express affirmation, the most widely recognized form of intentional echolalic behavior in ASD, are treated with caution by some researchers, who point out that they could be the result of intermittent reinforcement (since the child rarely gets asked irrelevant questions, it's hard to tell if the echoing is discriminative) (Schuler 1979, p. 413).

In addition, the difficulties of conveying communicative intent could be symptomatic of more general communication difficulties that plague even high-functioning people with ASD, who are clearly capable of forming communicative intentions, but are strikingly worse communicators than expected considering their linguistic skills alone. The gap between linguistic skills and communication skills might contribute to the echolalic behavior of children with ASD appearing substantially different from other forms of repetition and echoing, thereby leading to it being labeled abnormal and to its communicative objective being underestimated (Schuler 1979, p. 426. See also: Prizant 1983b, p. 299). For example, the speech of individuals with ASD often sounds mechanical and monotonous due to difficulties with intonation; this is a general problem in ASD, but when combined with echolalic behavior it "might be attributable to a lack of communicative intent as evidenced by the absence of the facial, manual, and vocal expressions that normally accompany speech" (Schuler 1979, p. 426).

Contextual information is therefore an indispensable but problematic indicator of the presence or absence of communicative intent in the case of children on the autism spectrum, because while it is necessary for appreciating the functionality of their echolalic behavior, it can also make their echolalic utterances appear less intentional than they are. In light of these unique difficulties, some researchers have advocated adopting a more charitable approach to the echolalic behavior of children with ASD. Fay (1973) submits that "if a doubt remains as to whether echolalia reflects the last failure of human connections or a struggle to maintain them, *the child deserves the benefit of that doubt*. A return to mutism, either by choice or by well-meaning clinical intervention intent only upon echo abatement, marks the last failure" (p. 487, my italics). Following the same rationale, Stribling et al. (2006) advocate "the development of a new approach to the study of echolalia in which the child's actions [are] *seen more optimistically* as an adaptive response to the constraints of their learning difficulties rather than as an insurmountable barrier to accessing social interactions" (p. 5, my italics). These recommendations are remarkable in that they don't appeal to contextual information, but in a sense instruct the interpreter to ignore it, and adopt an optimistic approach regardless of how automatic and dysfunctional the behavior appears to be.

Nevertheless, from a developmental perspective such recommendations do make sense. Much of a child's early echolalic behavior (in both normal and delayed language development) is not produced with communicative intent, although intent might be, and often is, attributed to it. An utterance that is initially produced out of a pure imitative reflex, with no specific effect in mind, can take on a certain meaning as the child gradually begins to observe and realize its effects. Hence, in the early stages of language development the emergence of communicative intent relies heavily on the reactions that the child's behavior solicits from the surrounding adults. Because the early verbal behavior of children on the autism spectrum, which is often echolalic, frequently precludes the listener from attributing communicative intent to it, these children experience greater difficulty moving past the intermediate, borderline phase, and developing a stronger sense of communicative intent that can be more reliably recognized (Prizant and Rydell 1984, p. 190). Considering communicative intent from a developmental perspective, especially in the context of developmental disorders such as ASD, sheds new light on the relationship between the speaker's intention and the recognition of the hearer, and provides new avenues for examining the contribution of contextual information to the process of recognizing communicative intentions.

5   Conclusion

The complexity and diversity of echolalic behaviors in the context of ASD presents a confusing picture. Although the speaker is uttering conventional sentences, their literal meaning is divorced from their intended meaning in a way that not only makes them hard to interpret, it also raises doubts as to the speaker's comprehension of the linguistic message. Moreover, echolalia in ASD presents a combination of circumstances that makes the manifestation of communicative intent ambiguous, and puts the listener in a state of fundamental uncertainty, not only as to what is being communicated, but whether the utterance constitutes a communicative act in the first place. Echolalia is therefore a hybrid phenomenon: it presents a speaker who utters conventional linguistic expressions, sometime syntactically complex ones, while at the same time undermining the listener's ability to attribute intentions to the speaker. The ambiguous manifestation of communicative intent in echolalic episodes suggests the need to distinguish more clearly between the two phases of recognizing communicative intentions, in order to better account for the scope of pragmatic interpretation. The fact that it's not only the content of communicative intentions that is context-sensitive and needs to be pragmatically recognized, but also their presence suggests that pragmatic interpretation goes all the way down, infecting not only the interpretation of utterances, but also the decision whether to interpret at all. Ironically, this fact is concealed by the common tendency among contextualists to conflate the two interrelated, yet separated phases of recognizing communicative intentions.

References

Bach, K.: Minding the gap. In: Bianchi, C. (ed.) The Semantics/Pragmatics Distinction, pp. 27–43. CSLI Publications, Stanford (2004)

Dyer, C., Hadden, A.J.: Delayed echolalia in autism: some observations on differences within the term. Child Care Health Dev. 7, 331–345 (1981)

Fay, W.H.: On the basis of autistic echolalia. J. Commun. Disord. 2, 38–47 (1969)

Fay, W.H.: On the echolalia of the blind and of the autistic child. J. Speech Hear. Disord. 38(4), 478–489 (1973)

Fay, W.H., Butler, B.V.: Echolalia, IQ, and the developmental dichotomy of speech and language systems. J. Speech Hear. Res. 11, 365–371 (1968)

Howlin, P.: Echolalic and spontaneous phrase speech in autistic children. J. Child Psychol. Psychiatr. 23(3), 281–293 (1982)

Philips, G.M., Dyer, C.: Late onset echolalia in autism and allied disorders. Br. J. Disord. Commun. 12(1), 47–59 (1977)

Prizant, B.M.: Echolalia in autism: assessment and intervention. Semin. Speech Lang. 4(1), 63–77 (1983a)

Prizant, B.M.: Language acquisition and communicative behavior in autism: toward an understanding of the "whole" of it. J. Speech Hear. Disord. 48, 296–307 (1983b)

Prizant, B.M., Duchan, J.F.: The functions of immediate echolalia in autistic children. J. Speech Hear. Disord. 46, 241–249 (1981)

Prizant, B.M., Rydell, P.J.: Analysis of functions of delayed echolalia in autistic children. J. Speech Hear. Res. 27, 183–192 (1984)

Recanati, F.: On defining communicative intentions. Mind Lang. 1(3), 213–242 (1986)

Roberts, J.M.A.: Echolalia and comprehension in autistic children. J. Autism Dev. Disord. 19(2), 271–281 (1989)

Rutter, M.: Diagnosis and definition of childhood autism. J. Autism Child. Schizophr. 8(2), 139–161 (1978)

Schuler, A.L.: Echolalia: issues and clinical applications. J. Speech Hear. Disord. 44, 411–434 (1979)

Schuler, A.L., Prizant, B.M.: Echolalia. In: Schopler, E., Mesibov, G. (eds.) Communication Problems in Autism. Plenum Press, New York (2010)

Searle, J.: Speech Acts: An Essay in the Philosophy of Language. Cambridge University Press, Cambridge (1969)

Sperber, D., Wilson, D.: Relevance. Communication and Cognition, 2nd edn. Basil Blackwell, Oxford (1986)

Stiegler, L.N.: Examining the echolalia literature: where do speech-language pathologists stand? Am. J. Speech-Lang. Pathol. **24**, 750–762 (2015)

Stribling, P., Rae, J., Dickerson, P., Dautenhahn, K.: "Spelling it out": the design, delivery, and placement of delayed echolalic utterances by a child with an autistic spectrum disorder. Issues Appl. Linguist. **15**(1), 3–32 (2006)

Tannen, D.: Talking Voices. Cambridge University Press, Cambridge (2007)

Wolff, S., Chess, S.: An analysis of the language of fourteen schizophrenic children. J. Child Psychol. Psychiatr. **6**, 29–41 (1965)

Cooperating Context Method: A Contextual Approach to Story Generation and Telling

James Hollister[(⊠)] and Avelino Gonzalez

Intelligent Systems Lab (ISL), University of Central Florida, Orlando, FL, USA
JHollister@isl.ucf.edu, Avelino.Gonzalez@ucf.edu

Abstract. Oral story telling has become a lost art because social media and technology have come to dominate personal interactions. The concept of creating a computational system capable of creating, modifying and telling a story, all in real time, could be a compelling way to revive this lost art of oral storytelling. It could serve as a source of alternative entertainment for children. The stories could be decomposed into a series of end-to-end contexts faced by the characters in the story as they seek to attain their sometimes conflicting goals. Thus, contextualization of the story, and of the storytelling process, could become advantageous. With that in mind, this paper presents and evaluates a contextual approach called the Cooperating Context Method (CCM) that helps create and convey dynamic stories in real time. These stories can be easily customized by the listener, also in real time, even while the story is already being told. CCM was designed to overcome the limitations found in other contextual approaches during story generation, while still meeting the design criteria selected through an analysis of human storytellers. CCM begins by examining the current situation to create list of tasks. Through a series of algorithms, the list of tasks is narrowed down into two lists of high priority and low priority contexts while removing the irrelevant contexts. The set of context best suited to manage the tasks are selected and the contextual knowledge is utilized to solve the tasks defined. Testing of CCM revealed that it performs as it was intended.

Keywords: Context · Narrative generation · Story telling · Cooperating Context Method · CCM

1 Introduction

Story telling has long been a tradition for entertaining as well as for passing knowledge along to the younger generation. The ability to tell stories orally has been something that many families do every night to help their children fall asleep and help foster creativity and tradition in the next generation. With the advances in computing technology, it is understandable that one would look towards a computer to help in this by automatically generating a story and telling that story to a child at bedtime. As Cavazza and Charles have stated, user interaction with interactive storytelling is a neglected component area of research in story telling systems. [1] Our research has led to the creation of a contextual approach that can generate and tell narratives that can be changed in real time in the way requested by the listener. This approach is called the

© Springer International Publishing AG 2017
P. Brézillon et al. (Eds.): CONTEXT 2017, LNAI 10257, pp. 277–287, 2017.
DOI: 10.1007/978-3-319-57837-8_22

Cooperating Context Method (CCM). We begin with a discussion of the existing works in automated story generation and storytelling.

2 Background

Computer systems that can generate stories have been in existence since the late 1970's [2]. However, most systems fall within one of two categories: (1) *non-interactive* or (2) *full participation* by the participant. Because of page limitations, an extensive review of these systems is outside the scope of this paper. A more comprehensive review of these systems may be found in [3]. The non-interactive story generation systems such as STORYBOOK [4], MINSTREL REMIXED [5], and LOGTELL [6] can generate stories that are not alterable by the listener. Therefore, the listener can only listen to whatever story the system generates. The full participation category, such as MOE [7] and CRYSTAL ISLAND [8], on the other hand, places the listener into a virtual environment in which he/she becomes an active character in the story. Once portraying a character, the listener must continue portraying the character in order for the system to continue generating the story. For example in FAÇADE [9], the listener portrays a friend visiting a husband and wife. This leads to the problem of the level of interactivity within the story environment – the listener has to be totally involved in the story, or the system won't work. Unfortunately, there is nothing in-between the non-interactive and full interaction types of story generation systems. Our work overcomes this issue by creating a new context-based technique called the Cooperating Context Method (CCM) that serves as the foundation for a system that allows the listener to modify a story without having to constantly provide input into the system. None of the systems cited above appear to use context as the foundation of their operation. We find this to be rather surprising given the naturalness of context for composing a storyboard for a story. Storyboarding allows one to easily map out where a project is headed in detail by utilizing a cognitive map [10]. Storyboards can be found in many formats including pictures, words, and descriptions of the direction of how and where the project may be going.

   Our work is centered on finding a method to generate quest-type stories automatically, in real time and with the ability of the listener to make changes in the middle of the story (if desired). Quest-type stories involve a hero traveling long distances to seek an item, save a princess, or acquire knowledge that may be used to better his life and/or other lives in the future [11].

3 Cooperating Context Method (CCM)

The CCM was designed for story generation but could perform well in other application areas such as question-and-answer systems and virtual humans. Three design criteria were specified for the CCM process as it applies to story generation after examining how an oral storyteller tells a story: (1) creating a storyboard; (2) ability to create a narrative for a story that is entertaining to the listener; and (3) ability to modify the story to incorporate a listener's request for changes to the on-going story.

Storyboarding allows the story teller to incorporate a consistent theme throughout the story as well as uniform content that makes the story entertaining, understandable and where consequences are consistent with the rest of the story. CCM plans out a story, using a storyboard, to create that story outline. This outline contains the different elements that the hero will encounter at different stages in the quest story.

Another criterion is the ability to create a narrative that is entertaining to a listener. This is an important criterion because entertaining the listener is the main objective of a story. The generated story must be coherent, so that if an action occurs, it is deemed possible from prior events, allowing the entire story to make sense. For example, if the hero is climbing a mountain, the story should not be able to portray him digging up a buried treasure on a deserted beach in the next scene. The hero must climb down a mountain before he can go to the beach and acquire the tools prior to being able to dig for the treasure.

The ability to modify the current story and to incorporate the listener's request is the third criterion. This request is based on the current story being told and recognizes that the request can have repercussions on the rest of the story. It is important for the system to account for these modifications to the story line to make the change seamless. As an example, in the case of our mountain climbing hero, if the request is for him to be digging for treasure on a beach, the hero must transition from the mountain to the beach and acquire the necessary tools for the dig.

3.1 Justification for a New Contextual Approach

Stories can be thought of as characters going through several different contexts over time. Given the natural affinity of context and stories, it was decided that a contextual approach would be well-suited to this task of story generation and telling. Three common contextual models: Context Mediated Behaviors (CMB) [12], Contextual Graphs (CxG) [13], and Context-Based Reasoning (CxBR) [14] were examined for their ability to meet the stated design criteria and were found to be lacking in essential elements that would lead to an entertaining story. These limitations include the production of redundant stories and the extremely large model potentially generated because of similar contexts needed to create a meaningful story. A full discussion and analyses of the deficiencies of these contextual models for story telling is beyond the scope (and page limit) of this paper. This discussion can be found in [3].

The Cooperating Context Method (CCM) was developed to mimic human behavior and thought processes. This is accomplished by breaking down the current situation into a set of tasks that need to be completed during a cycle (a single execution of the CCM process), with the final goal of being able to use the contextual knowledge from a list of contexts that can address those stated tasks. These contexts are selected based upon how thoroughly they can complete a stated task, and are derived from internal contextual knowledge within the model itself. The main context or current situation is broken down into a set of tasks. The contextual knowledge from a set of contexts is then utilized/executed together to address the current situation as analyzed.

3.2   Contents of a Context

A single context in CCM contains three types of knowledge: *prescriptive, descriptive* and *contextual knowledge.*

Prescriptive Knowledge. The prescriptive knowledge allows an agent to perform whatever actions the context prescribes for the agent. For example, one action could be how to select a temptation and the location for the temptation that will best fit the story. Another example of prescriptive knowledge is which sentence template should be used at a given point of the story. This knowledge is important to the task(s) that the context is designed to perform. The action performed by the context might also include a recursive call to the CCM process that would allow the context to recognize a variation of the current situation. The recursive call is used to incorporate a listener's request into the story by calling the CCM process to generate a completely new story. While in the story generation and telling task, this system can adjust the story settings and generate a completely new and distinctive story.

Descriptive Knowledge. Descriptive knowledge describes to the system what knowledge is controlled within the context. Each context contains a summary of tasks that can be solved. However, there are two other functions within this knowledge that help describe the context to the system and help the system select the context that is best suited. The first function receives a list of tasks that was generated and returns a Boolean true if any of the context's tasks appears on this received list. The second function also receives a list of tasks but returns a numerical score on the given task list. The numerical score is calculated independently within each context and represents how well the context believes it is able solve the given task list. This calculation may be a simple fixed number or may be as complex as needed to describe the context. As an example, for most of the contexts the CCM prototype uses a scoring method that adds points for the items that the contexts can solve and subtracts points for tasks that it cannot solve.

Contextual Knowledge. The third type of knowledge is contextual knowledge. This knowledge contains information about other contexts and the relationships between these contexts. The two types of contextual knowledge are: *contextually relevant* and *contextually irrelevant*. This knowledge is provided by the developer and stored in two separate lists. The contextually relevant list (CRL) contains the names of contexts that should be examined as possible next contexts. While the contextually irrelevant list (CIL) contains the names of contexts that should not be examined at all as potential next contexts because they are inherently irrelevant. Both of these lists, are used by CCM to help focus the search process on contexts that are deemed to have a higher likelihood of success than those deemed more likely to fail.

4   Cooperating Context Method Process

The CCM process is described here in detail through one complete cycle. Figure 1 illustrates a CCM cycle.

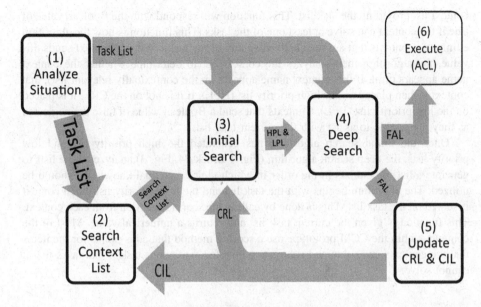

Fig. 1. The cooperating context method process

The CCM cycle begins by analyzing the situation (Fig. 1 Block #1). This is done by creating a list of tasks that need to be addressed. Creating this task list is accomplished by identifying which tasks are needed to properly manage the situation. This is done through a function that looks for key identifying features and adds the required tasks to the tasks list. Once the task list has been created, the search context list algorithm (Fig. 1 Block #2) begins with the entire set of contexts and removes the irrelevant contexts (those on the contextually irrelevant list).

The next step, the initial search algorithm (Fig. 1 Block #3, Fig. 2), begins by calling a function from the descriptive knowledge of every context on the search

> 1. Given Search Context List (SCL) from **Search Context List Algorithm**
> 2. Given Task List (TL) from Analyze Current Situation
> 3. Define High Priority List (HPL) created in this Algorithm
> 4. Define Low Priority List (LPL) created in this Algorithm
> 5. For each context C ∈ SCL
>   a. Analyze C with TL
>   b. If C returns True
>   i. If C exists in CRL
>   1. Add C to HPL
>   ii. Else
>   1. Add C to LPL

Fig. 2. Initial search algorithm

context list providing the task list. This function will respond with the Boolean value of true if the context can solve at least one of the tasks. This function is how the algorithm eliminates contexts that are unable to solve any of the tasks. When a context sends this value, the algorithm then analyzes the context list to determine whether the context name appears on it. If this context name appears on the contextually relevant list), that context is then placed on the high priority list (HPL). If it is not on the CRL, it is placed on the low priority list (LPL). Contexts that send a Boolean value of false are neglected as they are unable to assist with the current task list.

Once the initial search algorithm has generated the high priority list and low priority lists, the deep search algorithm (Fig. 1 Block #4, Fig. 3) analyzes these lists to generate a list of contexts in the order in which their contextual knowledge should be utilized. The algorithm begins with the task list and the high priority list. Each context is scored on the task list. This is done by calling the scoring function from each context. This function is given the current task list and returns a numerical value. Most of the contexts within the CCM prototype use a scoring method that adds points for the items that the contexts can solve and subtracts points for extraneous tasks - aka tasks that it cannot solve.

---

1. Given Task List (TL) from Analyze Current Situation
2. Given High Priority List (HPL) from **Initial Search Algorithm**
3. Given Low Priority List (LPL) from **Initial Search Algorithm**
4. Define Future Active List (FAL) created in this Algorithm
5. Main Loop
    a. For each context $C \in$ HPL
        i. Score C based upon TL
        ii. Highest scoring C is moved to FAL
        iii. C's tasks are removed from TL
    b. End Conditions: TL is empty or HPL is empty
    c. If TL is not empty
        i. For each context $C \in$ LPL
            1. Score C based upon TL
            2. Highest scoring C is moved to FAL
            3. C's tasks are removed from TL
6. End Conditions: TL is empty or LPL is empty

Fig. 3. Deep search algorithm

This numerical value is the score of how efficiently the context can solve the task list. The context with the highest score is then removed from the search (because it was selected), and placed on the future active context list (FAL); the context's knowledge will be utilized at the end of the cycle during the utilize/execute step.

The task list is also modified to reflect which tasks the selected contexts can solve. The HPL is analyzed until the task list is empty or when there are no more contexts on the list that can solve the problems. Once the algorithm has analyzed the entire HPL but there are tasks still left to be completed, the low priority list is then analyzed.

Each context is scored on the current task list. The tasks that the context can solve will be removed from the list. The LPL is analyzed until either all the tasks are completed or no more contexts can be added to the FAL. The system could create a solution that only partially completes the required tasks. If CCM is unable to locate an exact solution, it may apply a partial solution. This may help to create a situation that can be handled in the next cycle.

This allows the method to continue processing, even if an exact solution cannot be found, giving the system a chance to create a full solution the next time. The FAL contains a list of contexts in the order of priority in which they should be executed. The last step in the CCM process is to update the CRL and the CIL (Fig. 1 Block #5) for the next cycle using the like-named algorithm (Fig. 4). This algorithm begins by clearing the CRL and the CIL created during the previous cycle. This is done to ensure no context stays on any list longer than necessary.

1.	Given Future Active List (FAL) from **Deep Search Algorithm**
2.	Given Contextually Relevant List (CRL)
3.	Clear CRL
4.	Given Contextually Irrelevant List (CIL)
5.	Clear CIL
6.	For each context in the FAL C ∈ FAL
	a. If C is contextually-relevant then
	i. Add C's Contextually Relevant to CRL
	b. If C is contextually-irrelevant then
	i. Add C's Contextually Irrelevant to CIL
7.	For each context C ∈ CRL
	a. If C exists in CIL then
	i. Remove C from CRL and CIL
8.	Return

Fig. 4. Update contextually relevant list and contextually irrelevant list algorithm

The algorithm analyzes the contextual knowledge of the currently-active contexts and considers which contexts are relevant or irrelevant for the next execution cycle. This is done by examining the contextual knowledge within each context on the FAL. All the contextually relevant contexts that are listed in the active contexts list are placed in the relevant contexts list. Likewise, all the irrelevant contexts from the active list are placed in the irrelevant contexts list. The algorithm then analyzes both lists. If a context appears in both lists, it is removed from both lists. This is done to eliminate conflicting actions. The FAL becomes the active context list (ACL) and is executed in order. The system then starts the CCM process over again for the next cycle.

4.1   Planning Out a Story

Considering the design criteria for an oral story teller as stated above, a description of how CCM meets this requirement follows. The first design criteria of planning out a story are accomplished by CCM selecting contexts to make intelligent selections in the knowledge base. For CCM to function in a story generation and modification task, a story outline is needed.

CCM begins with an empty story outline, and then chooses the appropriate contexts, which selects items from a local knowledge base. The knowledge base contains the different characters, monsters, and locations that can appear within the story. Each item has multiple options in order to allow variations in the story. For example, the monster knowledge would contain various monsters that could be used within the story.

A story outline contains the basic stages of the type of story being told, as there are only a limited number of plots such as a quest plot [11]. A completed story outline for a quest story can be seen in Fig. 5. A well-known example of a quest story is the *Lord of the Rings* trilogy [15]. There are five elements in a quest story: the Call, the Journey, the Arrival-and-Frustration, the Final Ordeals, and the Goal [11].

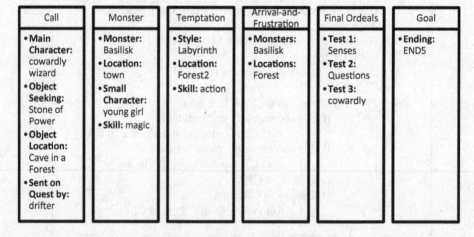

Fig. 5. Completed quest story outline

Quest stories begin with the Call, where the hero receives/finds his/her calling for the quest. This could be the result of the hero coming upon some significant item, person, or some type of unnatural vision. In general, the components of the Call are where the hero is to go, how he/she gets there and what to do when he/she arrives. After receiving the Call, the hero must travel somewhere to search for the item or person. The Journey portion of the plot is where the hero embarks on the quest, encountering diverse obstacles along the way, and facing various temptations that can distract, make captive, or even kill the hero at any time. These different obstacles may include facing some type of monster, or may test the morals and/or beliefs of the hero. The Arrival and Frustration element occurs as the hero arrives at the desired location and finds out that the quest is not yet over because of some unexpected obstacle. The Final Ordeal poses a series of tests that the hero must pass in order to attain the goal. These tests often follow the "Rule of Three" (i.e., there are three obstacles to overcome) and generally prove his value. The final element of a quest story is the Goal Achievement, where the hero finally attains the goal of the quest, thus ending the story. The hero finally discovered his treasure, love and/or fame, and lives "happily ever after".

4.2   Ability to Create a Narrative

After the outline has been completed, CCM is used to generate the text that relates the story orally. CCM selects the contexts for each element of the story outline and during the execution, these contexts contain pre-built sentences. Some of the information in the outline selected from the knowledge base is used to create the text of the story. For example, the pre-built sentence template "The #MONSTER# was spotted #MONSTERENTRANCE# and #MONSTERLANDED# in the #LOCATION#" would utilize information that was selected from the knowledge base. In our example, this pre-built sentence would be modified to read "The fire breathing dragon was spotted flying overhead and landed in the creepy forest." This pre-built sentence could also read "the alien was spotted flying overhead and landed in the canyon outside of town." The text generated is stored as a string in the outline, along with details about how the text was generated (i.e., the contexts used to create the text).

4.3   Modifying the Current Story to Incorporate a Listener's Request

In order to meet the design requirement for modifying the story, the CCM selects contexts designed to tell the system how to modify the story. The listener's changes are directly inserted into the story outline. These contexts contain the contextual knowledge of how to call CCM recursively to update the story outline and generate a completely new story based upon the listener's request.

Another context determines how the two stories should be merged together to form one cohesive story. This merge is accomplished by using the log of how the texts of both stories were created. The merge technique begins by determining what is the current part of the story being told. If the story has completed most of the current part, then the majority of changes will be rejected as the desired story length may be exceeded. Children often delay going to bed as long as possible and requesting story changes could be one way to delay bedtime [16].

Given the sample creation logs in Fig. 6, the merge technique first identifies where in the current stage the listener is.

In this example, the listener has heard text created by NLContextA, NLContextB, NLContextC, and NLContextD but not NLContextE, as this is where the listener decided to make a change to the story. NLContextE would be removed from that list. The merge technique begins with the last context still on the list (NLContextD) and looks for a shared context between the two lists. In the given example, NLContextB is

Original Story		New Story
NLContextA	1	NLContext1
NLContextB	2	NLContextB
NLContextC	3	NLContext3
NLContextD	4	NLContext4
NLContextE	5	NLContext5

Fig. 6. Sample creation logs of contexts

the shared context. The merge technique will identify this as the merge point and will begin telling the new story with the text created by the NLContext3 context. If no shared context can be found, the technique identifies the merge point at the start of the part and begins telling the new story from that point.

5 Summary and Discussion

This paper has introduced a new method of story generation utilizing a contextual approach that allows the listener to request changes and hear stories that incorporate those changes. This is a practical and innovative approach that can enhance the entertainment and novelty value of the story being generated. Because of page limitations, extensive testing of CCM cannot be displayed here. We refer the reader to [3] for a complete discussion of testing and the results obtained.

Although this method has only been applied in this paper to the generation and telling of stories, it could potentially be applicable to other areas. These areas could involve the use of virtual humans in a questioning and answer setting, intelligent tutoring systems. The CCM could provide virtual humans the ability to respond to questions without repetitious monologues while also allowing the virtual human to generate a response rather than using a scripted answer. The adaptability of CCM could allow an intelligent tutoring system to personalize and customize assistance when providing help to a student. Being able to adapt to the situation and generate different responses to the same question aids a virtual human in appearing more human-like attributes.

References

1. Cavazza, M., Charles, F.: User interaction for interactive storytelling. In: Nakatsu, R., Rauterberg, M., Ciancarini, P. (eds.) Handbook of Digital Games and Entertainment Technologies, pp. 1–14. Springer, Singapore (2016)
2. Meehan, J.: TALE-SPIN, an interactive program that writes stories. In: Proceedings of 5th IJCAI, pp. 91–98 (1977)

3. Hollister, J.: A contextual approach to real time interactive narrative generation. Doctoral dissertation, University of Central Florida, August 2016
4. Callaway, C.B.: Narrative prose generation. Doctoral dissertation, North Carolina State University (2000)
5. Tearse, B., Mateas, M., Wardrip-Fruin, N.: MINSTREL remixed: a rational reconstruction. In: Proceedings of Intelligent Narrative Technologies III Workshop. ACM, Monterey (2010)
6. Angelo, E.M.C., Cesar, T.P., Antonio, L.F., Bruno, F.: A logic-based tool for interactive generation and dramatization of stories. In: Proceedings of 2005 ACM SIGCHI ACE. ACM, Valencia (2005)
7. Weyhrauch, P.W.: Guiding interactive drama. Doctoral dissertation, Carnegie Mellon University (1997)
8. Rowe, J.P., Shores, L.R., Mott, B.W., Lester, J.C.: A framework for narrative adaptation in interactive story-based learning environments. In: Proceedings of Intelligent Narrative Technologies III Workshop. ACM, Monterey (2010)
9. Mateas, M.: Interactive drama, art and artificial intelligence. Doctoral dissertation, Carnegie Mellon University (2002)
10. Jantke, K.P., Knauf, R.: Didactic design through storyboarding: standard concepts for standard tools. In: Proceedings of 4th International Symposium on Information and Communication Technologies. Trinity College Dublin, Cape Town (2005)
11. Booker, C.: The Seven Basic Plots: Why We Tell Stories. Bloomsbury Academic, London (2004)
12. Turner, R.M.: Context-mediated behavior for AI applications. In: Mira, J., Pobil, A.P., Ali, M. (eds.) IEA/AIE 1998. LNCS, vol. 1415, pp. 538–545. Springer, Heidelberg (1998). doi:10.1007/3-540-64582-9_785
13. Brézillon, P.: Task-realization models in contextual graphs. In: Dey, A., Kokinov, B., Leake, D., Turner, R. (eds.) CONTEXT 2005. LNCS (LNAI), vol. 3554, pp. 55–68. Springer, Heidelberg (2005). doi:10.1007/11508373_5
14. Gonzalez, A.J., Stensrud, B.S., Barrett, G.: Formalizing context-based reasoning: a modeling paradigm for representing tactical human behavior. Int. J. Intell. Syst. 23, 822–847 (2008)
15. Tolkien, J.R.R.: The Fellowship of the Ring. Houghton Mifflin Company, Boston (1954)
16. Ginott, H.G., Ginott, A.: Between Parent and Child: The Bestselling Classic That Revolutionized Parent-Child Communication. Potter/TenSpeed/Harmony, Berkeley (2009)

Three Versions of Semantic Minimalism

Yang Hu[(✉)]

CNRS, UMR5304, Laboratoire sur le langage,
le cerveau et la cognition & Department of Philosophy, East China Normal
University & UMR 5317, ENS de Lyon, Lyon, France
yhu219@outlook.com

Abstract. All of the semantic minimalists come together in seeking to reduce contextual inputs in semantics to a minimum, but they disagree over what this quantity may be, and more specifically, the extent to which something can still be classed as "minimal". With this issue increasingly addressed, three versions of semantic minimalism can be identified: weak, strong, and radical. They are still gathered under the tag "Semantic Minimalism", yet what they share is in fact less than their divergences as regards the minimal role of context. By revealing their divergent answers to the Range Problem and the Intention Problem, we will clearly see within semantic minimalism the schism, which is preliminary to assessing it.

Keywords: Semantic minimalism · Context-sensitivity · The range problem · The intention problem

1 Introduction

A given sentence has its meaning, but beyond this meaning, there is what the speaker intended to communicate. Paul Grice distinguished between "sentence meaning" and "speaker meaning" – the latter being comprised of "what is said" and "what is communicated". A sentence meaning is determined by its lexical components and semantic compositionality. According to Grice, "what is said" corresponds to the propositional content of the utterance. Conversely, "what is communicated" corresponds to "what is said" plus the content inferred through contextual reasoning. Thus, the distinction between sentence meaning and speaker meaning corresponds to the distinction between semantics and pragmatics. In the wake of Grice's theories, there still lacks a clear division between semantics and pragmatics. It is here that the debate between semantic minimalism and contextualism comes in. A prominent issue in the debate concerns the quantity of contextual information needed for a sentence to have a truth value and to what extent the contribution (or influence) of context to (upon) semantics is acceptable. Minimalism proposes a formal sort of semantics, in which contextual contribution is limited to indexical reference assignment and disambiguation. Contextualism, by contrast, advocates that the contextual contribution to semantics is endemic. In this paper, what I shall focus on is the schism within semantic minimalism. Though all of the semantic minimalists come together in seeking to reduce contextual inputs in semantics to a minimum, they disagree over what this minimum is, and more specifically, the extent to which a specific semantic theory can still be classed as "minimal".

P. Brézillon et al. (Eds.): CONTEXT 2017, LNAI 10257, pp. 288–301, 2017.
DOI: 10.1007/978-3-319-57837-8_23

With this issue increasingly addressed by many minimalists, three versions of semantic minimalism can be identified: weak (Cappelen & Lepore), strong (Borg), and radical (Bach).[1] It is indeed not easy to uncover a shared argument between them. Nevertheless, there may be one such claim:

> **CT**: *Minimal Semantics only licenses the syntactically triggered contextual inputs to semantic content: such as the indexicals "I", "here", whose semantic contents syntactically require contextual information to get a semantic value.*

To say "grammar triggers contextual input in semantics" is actually to mean that the linguistic rules specify which contextual information is necessary for an expression to have a semantic content. "I", the first person singular pronoun, is explained as "used by the person speaking or writing to refer to himself or herself" in the dictionary, and therefore "I" is context-sensitive since context determines which user is the semantic content of "I". "She" or "that" seems less clear. Both do syntactically activate the contribution of contextual information to semantic content, and are context-sensitive in this regard. Nevertheless this seems not enough for them to be considered as getting semantic content through grammar and contextual information, because what "she", "he", "that", "there" (or etc.) are intended to refer to in any using of them may also be taken into consideration. When Peter says "she is so cute" to a friend as several girls are coming, "she" could refer to any one of the girls, and its referent accordingly depends on which girl Peter intends it to refer to. From this point of view, context-sensitivity, though indeed triggered by grammar, is also in need of speaker intention. So if the minimalists identify grammar as the trigger of context-sensitivity, it is however not the case that grammar, on its own, can limit context-sensitivity.

If context-sensitivity is exclusively justified by grammar and speaker intentions also admittedly play a necessary role in determining semantic contents of some context-sensitive expressions, there follow two key problems which any version of semantic minimalism must address:

(1) How many context-sensitive expressions can we have (the Range Problem)?
(2) What is exactly the role of speaker intention in determining a semantic content (the Intention Problem)?

2   The Range Problem

Semantic minimalists have to cope with the range problem. If they refute the contextualist view that context-sensitivity in semantics is endemic and argue for its minimal effects, it will be very naturally asked by the contextualists what the minimal effects are and how many expressions bring such effects. Likewise, seeking to reduce context-sensitivity in semantics to a minimum inevitably put the onus on semantic minimalists to specify to what extent context-sensitivity in semantics can be reduced. One of the possible ways to do this job is delimit the range of context-sensitive expressions in natural language.

---

[1] The distinction between weak minimalism and strong minimalism is borrowed from Robbins [17].

2.1   The Weak Answer

C&L contends that the pure indexicals and demonstratives listed in Kaplan [16] "plus and minor a bit"[2] constitute the full panoply of context-sensitive expressions and exhaust all contextual effects to semantic content. These expressions illustrated as follows ([14]: p. 1) comprise the so-called Basic Set:

Personal pronouns: "I", "you", "he", "she", "it" in their various cases and number (singular, plural, nominative, accusative, genitive forms); Demonstrative pronouns: "that" and "this" in their various cases and number; Adverbs: "here", "there", "now", "today", "yesterday", "tomorrow", "ago", "henceforth"; Adjectives: "actual" and "present"; Tense indicators; Some contextual elements: Common nouns ("enemy", "outsider", "foreigner", "alien", "friend" and "native"); Common adjectives ("foreign", "local", "domestic", "national", "imported", "exported").

The expressions enumerated above syntactically require context to get semantic contents, where context is construed as narrow, non-perspectival, and parameter-like. C&L uphold the Basic Set by suggesting two tests for context-sensitivity ([13]: pp. 7–8).

- *"Context Sensitive Expressions Block Inter-contextual Disquotational Indirect Reports"*: Louis (context1) says "I am going to the Chinese market", but when Sarah (context2) provides a disquotational indirect report with "Louis said I am going to the Chinese market", this report is false since "I" in the report does not refer to Louis but to the speaker of the report, Sarah.
- *"Context Sensitive Expressions Block Collective Descriptions"*: this is a test mainly for verbs. If in context 1 we said "Louis left", in context 2 we said "Sarah left", and we were capable to say in context 3 "Louis and Sarah left", "left" (ignoring the tense) would be context-insensitive. The reason why this is a case of context-sensitivity is that once the semantic content of "left" in the collective utterance is determined in one context, we could guarantee that this semantic content equals the semantic content of "left" in those contexts where "left" was used alone. In the Basic Set, there are no verbs, so C&L hold that verbs are not context-sensitive.

On C&L's view, all the expressions in the Basic Set pass the two tests, so they are context-sensitive and all others fall outside.

2.2   The Strong Answer

Prima facie, Borg's attitude to the Basic Set Assumption seems inconsistent. In Borg ([10], p. 350), she writes: "I think C&L are right to treat the Basic Set Assumption as a defining feature of minimalism, but we should be clear about exactly what this assumption commits us to." However, Borg ([11], p. 68) argues: "A first point of division among theorists in this are concerns the principle Cappelen and Lepore 2005

---

[2] Not precise enough as we see, "plus and minor a bit" blurs the scope of context-sensitive expressions, and in fact neither weak nor strong versions of semantic minimalism give a neat and definite scope.

use for defining their notion of minimalism: namely, allegiance to the 'Basic Set Assumption'… my variety of minimalism does not endorse this principle."

On the one side, Borg is clear that minimalists cannot bypass the range problem, otherwise she would not comment on the Basic Set Assumption. On the other, the superficial inconsistency we indicate above becomes unsurprising if we notice that what is stressed by her version of minimalism is not the number of context-sensitive expressions in a language but the mechanism a full-blown minimal semantics can accommodate. According to Borg [8, 11], this mechanism is the so-called "formal route to semantic content"[3]. To some extent, it is because of this very mechanism that she doubts whether C&L's allegiance to the Basic Set Assumption is prudent enough. One of her worries arises with respect to the demonstratives: they notoriously require the current speaker intentions to be involved in reference determination, which seemingly threatens the formal route to semantic content due to the nebulous nature of speaker intentions which are not formally traceable. Thus, given that Borg does not remove demonstratives from the Basic Set, she has to combine three things to defend the "formal route to semantic content": (1) the object referred to by this demonstrative in a context indeed exhausts its semantic content; (2) to fix this referent depends on speaker intentions; (3) the current speaker intentions are semantically irrelevant.[4]

Setting aside how and whether Borg can hang on all of them (which will be addressed in the next section), it is now necessary to explain why Borg's answer to the range problem is stronger than C&L's even if she does not identify fewer numbers of indexicals than the Kaplan's list. First, Borg is not tempted to regard a commitment to the range of context-sensitive expressions as the crux of semantic minimalism, and thus the range problem itself becomes of secondary importance, which, in fact, downplays the contextualist challenge arising in terms of this issue. In comparison with C&L's strategy of directly responding to such a challenge, Borg's downplaying it is obviously stronger. Second, she ([10], p. 358) claims, "…not only that every contextual contribution to semantic content must be grammatically marked but also that those features contributed by the context must themselves be formally tractable." Therefore, if the semantic content of an expression counts as context-sensitive, the context-sensitivity involved here must not only be grammatically marked but also be formally tractable. Clearly, Borg puts more constraints on acceptance of an expression as context-sensitive, and in other words, she is more austere in delimiting the range of context-sensitive expressions.

2.3 The Radical Answer

The Basic Set Assumption is refuted and shrunk in the radical minimalism argued by Bach [3, 6, 7]. Bach [6] distinguishes three kinds of indexicals: automatic indexicals, whose stable meanings (or character in Kaplan's sense) determine the semantic

---

[3] In this passage, Borg explains what the so-called formal route to semantics is: "According to minimalism, the only reasoning processes involved en route to recovery of semantic content are deductive, computationally tractable processes." ([11], p. 114).

[4] This point benefits from an anonymous reviewer.

contents relative to contexts, such as "I" and "today"; discretionary indexicals (or true demonstratives), whose references are determined by speaker's referential intention, the context in this case functioning as constraints on that intention and "on the hearer's inference as to what that intention is" ([6], p. 9), such as "now", "then", "here", "we", "you", "she", "this" and "that"; hidden indexicals, whose occurrences should be assumed for some particular sentences to express the truth-evaluable proposition, e.g. in "it is raining" a location and time where it rains seems required for the sentence to be a definite, truth-evaluable proposition like "it is raining in Lyon on 20 June 2015". The same thing is true of "John is ready" (ready for what?), "Louis is a fan" (a fan of what?), "the hospital is on the left" (on the left of what?).

On Bach's view, context-sensitive expressions are merely automatic indexicals. Discretionary indexicals get their references through speaker's referential intentions. Nevertheless, they are, though semantically incomplete, context-insensitive: context just plays a role in constraining speaker's referential intentions. Those reports and terms[5] above are also semantically incomplete, expressing propositional radicals, rather than propositions, and the hidden indexicals are thus not context-sensitive. It is crucial to note that semantic incompleteness and non-propositionalism are two grounds on which the number of context-sensitive expressions radically shrinks: discretionary and hidden indexicals make the sentence containing them semantically incomplete, yet the sentence does not need contexts to assign semantic values to these indexicals for expressing a proposition inasmuch as it can express a propositional radical rather than a proposition. Hence, these indexicals are context-insensitive.

2.4   Controversy on Non-propositionalism and Semantic Incompleteness

The greatest controversy here occurs over semantic incompleteness and non-propositionalism. C&L show no hesitation when they enumerate demonstrative pronouns (part of discretionary indexicals in Bach's term) in the Basic Set, and in addition, C&L advocates that the utterance of "John is ready" is true just in case John is ready, and the proposition semantically expressed here is complete: John is ready. It is the typical form of "minimal proposition" conceived in C&L's version of minimalism. There is no semantic incompleteness here in the proposition. As just noted, Borg may think that the Basic Set Assumption is dubious since the semantic contents of the demonstratives listed in the Basic Set could not be determined without speaker intentions (disruptive for the formal semantics she wants for minimalism). But what really matters for her is that how to get rid of the negative effect of speaker intentions on semantic contents of the demonstratives: she does not think of the demonstratives as semantically incomplete. Additionally, Borg regards propositionalism as an important feature of her minimalism. Even with regard to sentences in which hidden indexicals appear, Borg [8] formulates "liberal truth-conditions", for example: the utterance of

---

[5] These examples of hidden indexicals are tagged as "weather and other environmental reports ('it is raining')", "terms with missing complements('John is ready')", "relational terms ('Louis is a fan')" and "perspectival terms ('the hospital is on the left')".

"John is ready" is true in a context c iff John is ready for something in c.[6] By contrast, Bach defends semantic incompleteness and non-propositionalism by three arguments.

First, it is not enough for an expression to be context-sensitive that the speaker can mean something different when she uses the expression in different contexts. As Bach ([6], p. 178) argues, "it has to be the content of the expression itself that varies, and it has to be the context, in a way determined by the meaning of the expression, that makes the difference." When we explain the meaning of automatic indexicals by virtue of the "content-character" framework of Kaplan, we can show that they satisfy those requirements: the referent of "I" varies when different speakers say "I" because the character of "I" specifies that the content of "I" is a function of the context which is constituted by a set of parameters such as <the speaker, the time, the place>; as the name of this kind of indexicals hints, the process of explaining their meaning is automatic, and the recovery of their meaning has nothing to do with the intentional features of the context of utterance. But this is not the case for the discretionary indexicals due to the unavoidable involvement of speaker intentions in their semantic contents: different speakers at different times in different places could refer to the same object in using "that" since the speaker intentions, destroying that function mentioned above, can make this happen. Kaplan suggests adding a demonstration, such as "pointing at the object" the speaker intends to refer to, to the determinant elements of the semantic content of demonstratives, but it is sometimes unnecessary in the case, for instance, where someone says "that is terrible" after she has put a jackfruit in her mouth; there is no demonstration needed here for recovering the referent of "that". Stokke [18] proposes the inclusion of speaker intentions into context so that it will be feasible to make context determine the content of demonstratives. Bach rejects this inclusion by arguing that speaker intentions are not part of context (this point will be detailed later).

Second, we must distinguish two things: the intention, in using the discretionary indexicals, to refer to something and the intention for the discretionary indexicals to have a certain semantic value. [1][7] According to Bach, when we use a discretionary indexical, what is really happening is that the speaker is referring to something and directing the hearer to the thing she is referring to and the discretionary indexical is like the signal of what the speaker is doing; but no intention of endowing the discretionary indexical with a semantic content is involved here. So, if any utterance of a discretionary indexical lacks a determinate semantic content owing to the former kind of

---

[6] Prima facie, "liberal truth-conditions" seems to indicate that "John is ready" (relative to a context) alone cannot express a complete proposition since the complete proposition (truth-condition) is "John is ready for something in c" and it therefore seems that Borg stands in the same line with Bach in this regard. However, Borg construes a liberal truth-condition for the utterance of "John is ready" whereas Bach refutes that "John is ready" expresses any truth-evaluable proposition. As Bach ([7], p. 91) notes: "A great many sentences, such as 'Jerry is ready', 'Tom is tall', and 'Leaves are edible', do not express a proposition independently of context. It does not follow that such a sentence expresses a proposition relative to a context, for it may not express a proposition at all. Many supposed cases of context sensitivity are really instances of something else: *semantic incompleteness*."

[7] This distinction is from the unpublished work "Reference, Intention, Context: Do Demonstratives Really Refer" of Bach.

speaker intentions, it makes no sense to say the semantic content of a discretionary indexical itself varies in different contexts and it will then make no sense to say it is context-sensitive. Given that the semantic contents of discretionary indexicals are dependent on speaker intentions, they are semantically incomplete since the involvement of intentions means that those indexicals contribute to communication rather than have semantic contents.

Third, Bach thinks that propositionalism[8] overloads the minimalists with accounting for why a sentence including hidden indexicals, which intuitively seems not to express a complete proposition, actually does. "John is ready" seems not to express a complete proposition, for it cannot be truth-evaluable until what John is ready for is specified; that part can only be fulfilled by the context. While C&L and Borg conceive the "minimal" truth-evaluable propositions as the move to discard that semantic intuition, Bach propounds "a minimalism without propositionalism" which not only accommodates the ordinarily semantic intuition but also preserves minimalism. For Bach, the idea of non-propositionalism is not hard to accept if we think as follows:

"Since these [the propositions] are made up of building blocks assembled in a particular way, it makes sense to suppose that in some cases such an assemblage, put together compositionally from a sentence's constituents according to its syntactic structure, might fail to comprise a proposition" ([3], p. 436).

C&L doubt the assumption about semantic incompleteness and ask "what are the criteria by which one sentence is deemed semantically incomplete and another complete?" ([4], p. 3) Bach provides two such criteria:

α. "A (declarative, indexical-free) sentence is semantically incomplete if it fails to express a proposition." ([3], p. 440)
β. "A sentence is incomplete just in case what the speaker means has to go beyond the sentence meaning." ([3], p. 441)

Both are rejected by C&L. Regarding α, there is a vicious circle; whether or not a sentence is semantically incomplete depends on whether it fails to express a proposition, but if we want to know whether or not there is a well-formed proposition expressed by a sentence, it seems that we have to know whether or not the sentence is semantically complete. Regarding β, there seems to be a rule made here for what the speaker cannot mean, e.g., she can't mean a proposition radical and what she means should be a complete proposition. According to C&L,

"We are locked into a rather tight circle: draw the complete/incompleteness distinction by an appeal to what speakers can mean; characterize what speakers can mean by an appeal to the complete/incomplete distinction." ([15], p. 4).

Bach replies to the criticism:

"Such questions have to be settled on a case-by-case basis and what they're asking for is a general criterion. However, the lack of a general criterion does not show that the distinction is bogus. After all, there is no criterion, no principled basis, for distinguishing men who are bald from men who aren't. Would C&L argue, regarding men

---

[8] As Bach ([3], p. 435) claims, propositionalism is "the conservative dogma that every indexical-free declarative sentence expressed a proposition".

with at least one hair on their heads that either they're all bald or that none are? Would they proclaim that these are our sole options?" Bach ([4], p. 3).

To sum up, C&L's weak version accepts the Basic Set as the range of context-sensitive expressions in that all the expressions therein pass their two tests for context-sensitivity; Borg's strong version puts more constraints on accepting an expression as semantically context-sensitive in order to protect her formal route to semantics from the nebulous speaker intentions; Bach's radical version minimizes the Basic Set to automatic indexicals on grounds of semantic incompleteness and non-propositionalism.

3 The Intention Problem

If the demonstratives are assumed to be context-sensitive expressions, it is natural to ask how contexts and speaker intentions cooperate in determining the semantic contents of the demonstratives. The answers of the three versions diverge.

3.1 The Radical Answer

One important distinction should be kept in mind: narrow-context (NC) versus wide-context (WC). According to Bach [2], this distinction can be qualified as follows:

- NC: the identity of the speaker and the hearer, the time and place of an utterance
- WC: Narrow context + anything relevant for the hearer to arrive at the speaker's communicative (e.g. referential) intention

Bach holds that only NC contributes to the semantic contents of context-sensitive expressions; WC is taken into account for "whether the speech act is being performed successfully and feliciitously", it thus lies within pragmatics. Also, the speaker intention according to Bach is not counted as a parameter of either NC or WC. It mainly determines the content of semantically incomplete expressions like discretionary indexicals. He provides three arguments for separating speaker intentions from context.

First, speaker intentions are in effect the communicative content but not the context of communication. In ordinary communication, the speaker, in using "that", intends to refer to something and intends the hearer to get the thing she refers to, and she still intends the hearer to get her intentions. These intentions appear as part of communicative information, and communication is endowed with them, otherwise it would not be "communication". Hence, we say that speaker intentions are brought into play as the content exchanged between the speaker and the hearer in communication but not as the context which seems "behind" or "around" the communicative stage.

Second, WC involves the cognitive facet of the surroundings in communication such as "salient mutual knowledge" and "relevant common background knowledge" between interlocutors, and "the current state of conversation" (the information already delivered), the "physical settings" that the participants in conversation cognitively access. As Bach ([5], p. 1) argues, the role of WC is pragmatic, and it consists in constraining "what a hearer can reasonably take a speaker to mean in saying what he says" and "what the speaker could reasonably mean in saying what he says." But speaker intentions serve a different role: they determine what the speaker actually mean.

Third, for context to explain how expressions used in communication are interpreted, there has to be a symmetry between the access the speaker and the hearer respectively have to the effect of context. ([5], p. 2) Namely, they mutually acknowledge which items in context are contributing to the communicated meaning. In ordinary conversation, this is a necessary condition which allows the talk to proceed successfully. In this sense, speaker intentions should not be included in context, because apparently speaker intentions are not directly accessible to the hearer while they are to the speaker, and accordingly there is not the necessary symmetry between the speaker and the hearer.

With the arguments Bach provides in mind, we can now sum up Bach's general position on the relationship between semantic contents of indexicals, contexts, and speaker intentions:

– NC determines the semantic contents of context-sensitive expressions: automatic indexicals;
– Speaker intention determines the reference of semantically incomplete expressions (e.g. discretionary indexicals);
– WC is pragmatically but not semantically relevant (e.g. identifying speaker intentions, providing the conditions of the successful and fecilitious speech act).

3.2   The Strong Answer

Borg ([8], pp. 29–33) identifies two exclusive kinds of features of context: objective and perspectival (intentional). She advocates that full-blooded formal semantists should have no hesitation to appeal to the objective features of context for figuring out semantic values of all context-sensitive expressions; so-called objective features of context here are to be understood as narrow context in Bach. She argues: "specifically, though 'objective' features of the context of utterance, like who is speaking, when they are speaking and where they are located, are admissible, richer features, which require access to the speaker's mental state, are not similarly admissible." ([8], p. 39) And she continues to insist that "allowing current speaker intentions to be semantically relevant runs counter to the ethos of formal semantics". ([11], p. 113),

Borg's version of minimalism pursues all the way the formal approach to semantics whose aim is only to specify the formal features of linguistic expressions. One point should be noted however: so called "formal features" means the "repeatable, code-like and normative aspects of linguistic meaning" ([8], p. 21), and identifying these features are deductive, computationally, tractable processes. But, as is said above, Borg's formal semantics is jeopardized by the intention-sensitive terms like demonstratives. How to characterize their semantic content is therefore a necessary work for her.

First of all, Borg strictly distinguishes "semantic content" from "reference fixing (determination)". According to her, the latter presumes epistemic constraints on the object referred to by a referential expression. Obviously, identifying the referent of "that" is a process constrained by some epistemic state, and in other words, reference fixing process is intention-dependent. This is unacceptable in Borg's semantic picture. However, without reference fixing in semantics, where can we eventually find or know which object is referred to by the term "that"? This problem necessitates Borg's characterization of "semantic content" itself. Borg [8] defines this semantic content as a syntactically generated singular concept. Understanding a sentence in which a demonstrative occupies the subject position is tantamount to entertaining a singular thought which is merely syntactically driven:

"Entertaining a singular thought, where this is individuated syntactically, becomes entertaining a thought which relates in a specific, intimate way to an object, a thought whose truth depends on how things stand with a particular object, but which does not require that the agent is currently in a position to (non-descriptively) identify the object her thought is about." ([8], pp. 187–188).

She explicitly admits that this contention borrows from, and is even based on Fodor's notion of "language of thought". For Fodor, thought is syntactically driven, and all that happens in thought is a syntactical computation; in other words, thought reflect the syntax of language. Thus, the semantic content of a demonstrative involves no more than a singular concept in Fodor' language of thought and knowing how to single out the reference of a demonstrative from all other things becomes a post-semantic notion. In this way, the effect of speaker intentions is wiped off the semantic contents of demonstratives.

Another problem arises then. If the semantic content of a given demonstrative is just a singular concept which is extraneous to the external world, how is it possible to get the truth condition (proposition) of the sentence containing the demonstrative in subject position? Borg comes up with an extremely weak notion of "truth condition" for answering to this question. As she argues, for the utterance "that is mine", minimal semantics just simply produces its truth condition as follows: "If t is a token of 'that is mine' uttered by β, and the token of 'that' therein refers to α then t is true iff α is β's." ([8], p. 206) That is to say, what is specified by this weak notion of "truth condition" is nothing more than the concept of α belongs to β, and also, this sort of truth condition merely represents the knowledge about what would be the case not about what is the case for the utterance to be true. Thus, the actual object and speaker to which α and β respectively refer are not contained as constituents in the truth condition in that identifying that object and speaker is semantically irrelevant. In short, Borg's "truth condition" no longer denotes ways the world is (or might be) but just represents ways the world would be for a sentence to be true.

It is now clear that Borg wipes off the speaker intention from her minimal semantics generally by the three steps: (1) distinguish semantic content from reference fixing, (2) redefine the concept of "semantic content", and (3) provide a weak semantic notion of truth condition. Nonetheless, as we have indicated, Borg insists that the object referred to by a referential expression exhausts its semantic content, and it seems a thorny problem to keep consistent between the semantic content defined as a singular concept and the semantic content exhausted by the object. Finally, we may outline her general positions on the relationship between semantic contents of indexicals, contexts, and speaker intentions, as follows:

- Objective context determines the semantic contents of all context-sensitive expressions: pure indexicals and true demonstratives.
- Perspectival context (i.e. speaker intentions) is semantically irrelevant.

3.3 The Weak Answer

It is widely but not universally acknowledged that we would be closer to pragmatics if we allow more space to speaker intentions in determining semantic contents. Concerning the Intention Problem, C&L's semantic minimalism is a weak version in that they take for granted the role of speaker intentions in semantic contents. In their view, the content of a context-sensitive expression, fixed by speaker intention, still stays at the "semantic" level, and it is consistent with semantic minimalism that wide context, or particularly, speaker's referential intention is semantically relevant. On their view of determining the proposition semantically expressed, there are five steps:

a. Specify the meaning (or semantic value) of every expression in the sentence;
b. Specify all the relevant compositional meaning rules for English;
c. Disambiguate every ambiguous/polysemous expression in the sentence;
d. Precisify every vague expression in the sentence;
e. Fix the semantic value of every content sensitive expression in the sentence.

From this specification of the proposition semantically expressed, it is clear that C&L are not concerned at all with what may be relevant in the determination of the proposition in question or how semantic content is fixed or how context is employed for reference determination. As they claim, "the exact nature of the reference fixing mechanism" is out of their consideration. And another argument echoing their accommodating stance on the role of speaker intentions is given in Cappelen's [12] criticism of the semantic/pragmatic distinction. He argues that the distinction is not theoretically worthwhile.

"There is no such thing as the semantics-pragmatics distinction and looking for it is a waste of time. No such distinction will do any important explanatory work. You can… label some level of content 'semantic content', but in so doing no interesting problem is solved and no puzzling data illuminated." ([12], p. 3).

As Bach and Borg hold, the NC/WC distinction corresponds to one aspect of the semantics-pragmatics distinction. Given that Cappelen thinks of the semantics/pragmatics distinction as a matter of terminology, the NC/WC distinction therefore loses all its interest for Cappelen. Hence, when Cappelen confirms that speaker intentions (a key element of the NC/WC distinction) are involved in the semantic contents of context-sensitive expressions, the general idea seems to be that speaker intentions are a prerequisite of meaning for languages. Imagine a possible world where there are tokens similar to those of our languages, but where there are no agents: in such a world, those tokens would be meaningless. It is of course a trivial idea, and that's why C&L decidedly thinks that it would be cheating if someone claimed that the semantic content didn't depend in any way on speaker intentions. ([14], p. 149).

3.4   Real Divergence on *Speaker Intentions*

Prima facie, Bach and Borg differ in terms of the relationship between semantic contents of indexicals, contexts and speaker intentions, while C&L, taking the determinants of semantic contents for granted, only specify the steps in which a proposition is semantically expressed. However, the real divergence actually lies in what kinds of speaker intentions play the determinant role and how that role plays out for each side.

Borg [9] describes two options. First, there are "conventional speaker intentions" as constitutive of meaning (semantic content). Borg identifies this kind of speaker intentions in the Gricean explanation of utterer's meaning; as Borg reformulates it, "An agent means something by a given act only if she intends that act to produce some effect in an audience, at least partly by means of the audience's recognition of that intention." Furthermore, in the Gricean model analyzed by Borg, utterer's meaning delivers "the semantic content of a sentence where there is a convention among a community of speakers to use an expression of type x in the way specified by the given instance of utterer's meaning."[9] Given the Gricean project to the effect that its sentence has its semantic content via utterer's meaning in a language community and conventional speaker intentions perform an explanatorily indispensable role in explaining utterer's meaning, conventional speaker intentions have a role in determining constitutive semantic contents. Thus, such conventional speaker intentions seems to be the theoretical formulation of the speaker intentions seen as a precondition of meaning for languages in the trivial thought experiment above. Second, there are "current speaker intentions". Borg [9] identifies it in Sperber and Wilson's (hereafter S&W) relevance theory. In relevance theory, "relevance" is a technical term: in a specified communication, an interpretation of a communicative act (e.g., an utterance of a sentence) is relevant only if during the communicative event the cognitive cost of processing the interpretation is outweighed by the cognitive benefits of that processing. And the "interpretation" here means that the addressee succeeds in getting what the speaker intended to communicate by the utterance of a sentence. In addition, for S&W, semantics is a decoding process which is the first step in linguistic comprehension, and it cannot but deliver an incomplete, non-propositional, and non-truth-evaluable logical form. In order to arrive at the propositional or truth-evaluable content for the utterance in every communicative event, speaker intentions are necessarily required in a further step after the semantic decoding. The speaker intentions mentioned here are current speaker intentions, because they should be "always" ongoing in order for the utterance in question to have a propositional content.

Notably, these two kinds of speaker intentions are brought into play with different theoretical motivations. Conventional speaker intentions in the Gricean project are, according to Borg, considered as an intrinsic part of meaning. And they play a necessary role in the philosophical explanation of where meaning comes from. In contrast, current speaker intentions are required as part of a theory about the mechanism of pragmatic interpretation in every communicational event. Additionally, Borg's distinction on speaker intentions is effectively similar to but just terminologically different

---

[9] Borg's analysis of Grice as a conventionalist is however debatable.

from Bach's distinction between the intentions for indexicals to have semantic values and the intentions, in using indexicals, to refer to something. Thus, we could dub their distinctions together as Semantic-Intention (SI)/Pragmatic-Intention (PI) distinction.

Borg [9] considers that only SI (but not PI) is the determinant constitutive in semantic contents of all the indexicals, while C&L ignore the SI/PI distinction and leave the door open for both to play a role in semantics. On Bach's side, speaker intention is distinguished from context, and SI is just involved in semantic contents of automatic indexicals (pure indexicals), PI discretionary indexicals (true demonstratives).

4 Concluding Remarks

The schism within semantic minimalism in terms of the range and intention problems can now be wholly formulated.

In Bach's radical version, context-sensitive expressions are only automatic indexicals whose semantic contents depend on NC and SI. Discretionary indexicals are semantically incomplete and PI determines their references. Hidden indexicals express propositional radicals due to non-propositionalism.

In Borg's strong version, context-sensitive expressions are comprised of pure indexicals and true demonstratives. Given that the semantic contents of true demonstratives are defined as syntactically generated singular concepts and identifying their references is considered as a post-semantic task, the semantic contents of both kinds of indexicals depend on NC and SI. Additionally, PI and WC fall outside the semantic considerations. Contrary to Bach, Borg considers propositionalism as part of her minimalism, and the sentence containing hidden indexicals express a "liberal true condition".

In C&L's weak version, all the expressions in the Basic Set are context-sensitive. Postulating the so-called hidden indexicals and semantic incompleteness is untenable, and thus the sentence, like "John is ready", allegedly containing hidden indexicals, express a proposition: John is ready. Moreover, the semantics/pragmatics, NC/WC, SI/PI distinctions are all ignored and C&L take them to be theoretically unimportant.

As is seen, though all the three versions of semantic minimalism hold that context-sensitivity is exclusively licensed by grammar, their specific answers to the range and intention problems totally diverge, which, on this point, results in the three distinctive pictures of semantic minimalism. Surely, each minimalist can have a distinctive point of view of semantic minimalism, but the specification of these three versions may make us recognize its often neglected diversity.

Acknowledgement. This paper is funded by Chinese Scholarship Council, grant number: 201306140060. Special thanks go to my supervisor Anne Reboul and the autonomous reviewer for helpful comments.

References

1. Bach, K.: Reference, Intention, and Context: Do Demonstratives Really Refer. Unpublished Work
2. Bach, K.: The semantics-pragmatics distinction: what it is and why it matters. In: Turner, K. (ed.) The Semantics/Pragmatics Interface from Different Points of View, pp. 65–84. Elsevier Science Ltd., Amsterdam (1999)
3. Bach, K.: The excluded middle: semantic minimalism without minimal propositions. Philos. Phenomenological Res. **73**(2), 435–442 (2006)
4. Bach, K.: Minimalism for Dummies: Reply to Cappelen and Lepore. http://online.sfsu.edu/~kbach
5. Bach, K.: Why speaker intentions aren't part of context (2009)
6. Bach, K.: Context dependance (such as it is). In: García-Carpintero, M., Kölbel, M. (eds.) The Continuum Companion to the Philosophy of Language, pp. 153–184. Continuum Press, London (2012)
7. Bach, K.: The lure of linguistification. In: Penco, C., Domaneschi, F. (eds.) What Is Said and What Is Not, pp. 87–97. CSLI Publications, Stanford (2013)
8. Borg, E.: Minimal Semantics. Oxford University Press, Oxford (2004)
9. Borg, E.: Intention-based semantics. In: Lepore, E., Smith, B.C. (eds.) The Oxford Handbook of Philosophy of Language, pp. 250–266. Clarendon Press, Oxford (2006)
10. Borg, E.: Minimalism versus contextualism in semantics. In: Preyer, G., Peter, G. (eds.) Context-Sensitivity and Semantic Minimalism: New Essays on Semantics and Pragmatics, pp. 339–359. Oxford University Press, Oxford (2007)
11. Borg, E.: Pursuing Meaning. Oxford University Press, Oxford (2012)
12. Cappelen, H.: Semantics and pragmatics: some central issues. In: Preyer, G., Peter, G. (eds.) Context-Sensitivity and Semantic Minimalism: New Essays on Semantics and Pragmatics, pp. 3–22. Oxford University Press, Oxford (2007)
13. Cappelen, H., Lepore, E.: A tall tale: in defense of semantic minimalism and speech act pluralism. Can. J. Philos. **34**(Suppl.), 2–28 (2004)
14. Cappelen, H., Lepore, E.: Insensitive Semantics: A Defense of Semantic Minimalism and Speech Act Pluralism. Blackwell Publishing Ltd., Hoboken (2005)
15. Cappelen, H.: Reply to bach. In: PPR Symposium on Insensitive Semantics (2006)
16. Kaplan, D.: Demonstratives. In: Almog, J., Perry, J., Wettetein, H. (eds.) Themes from Kaplan, pp. 481–563. Oxford University Press, Oxford (1989)
17. Robbins, P.: Minimalism and modularity. In: Preyer, G., Peter, G. (eds.) Context-Sensitivity and Semantic Minimalism: New Essays on Semantics and Pragmatics, pp. 303–319. Oxford University Press, Oxford (2007)
18. Stokke, A.: Intention-sensitive semantics. Synthese **175**(3), 383–404 (2010)

Security Policy Model for Ubiquitous Social Systems

Vladimir Jovanovikj[1,2(✉)], Dušan Gabrijelčič[1], and Tomaž Klobučar[1]

[1] Laboratory for Open Systems and Networks,
Jožef Stefan Institute, Ljubljana, Slovenia
vladimir@e5.ijs.si
[2] Jožef Stefan International Postgraduate School, Ljubljana, Slovenia

Abstract. Ubiquitous social systems encompass ubiquitous computing, enterprise mobility and consumerization of IT, amplifying the threats associated to these fields. Context-aware security systems have been proposed as solutions for many of these threats. We argue that policy models used by these systems are not suitable for ubiquitous social systems. They lack of sufficient abstractions for specification and analysis of security policies and unnecessarily burden them with context reasoning rules. This can compromise the correctness of security policies and the performance of security systems. To address these issues, we propose a security policy model for ubiquitous social systems. The model defines all possible contextual information as policy abstractions, enabling clear and precise analysis of how they influence access control. Moreover, it takes into account the social related aspect and introduces an object life cycle. As a result, our model provides more intuitive abstractions and facilitates policy specification and context-aware security provisioning.

Keywords: Security · Context · Security policy · Ubiquitous computing · Consumerization of IT · Mobile devices

1 Introduction

Ubiquitous social systems are environments which encompass ubiquitous computing and the trends of enterprise mobility and consumerization of IT [8]. In such environments, a user uses her own mobile device for performing activities within both domains of professional and personal life, usually simultaneously, with the same consumer-oriented applications and in surroundings different than those in which they are natively performed. This blurs the boundaries between these domains, meaning the activities cannot be easily separated and secured. As a result, the threats associated to the encompassed fields are amplified, which makes ubiquitous social systems attractive targets for attacks.

Many researchers have proposed context-aware security systems as possible solutions for ubiquitous social systems (e.g., [1,3–5,9,10,12]). However, they provide limited solutions, as they deal only with targeted use cases (e.g., smart home [4], smart hospital [3,5,9], or mobile workers [1,12]). In particular, they

© Springer International Publishing AG 2017
P. Brézillon et al. (Eds.): CONTEXT 2017, LNAI 10257, pp. 302–314, 2017.
DOI: 10.1007/978-3-319-57837-8_24

lack of appropriate security policy models, which are able to abstract the characteristics details of security policies including security context. The policy models used by these systems are not applicable mainly due to two reasons. First, they do not provide sufficient abstractions and lack of comprehensive analysis about how security context influences access control. Thus, it is unclear how existing security systems adapt their behavior upon context changes. Second, they use an arbitrary level of abstraction of contextual information in security policies. Researchers have pointed out that it is more sophisticated for context-aware systems to adapt to high-level contextual information [2,6], since they meaningfully interpret raw sensor data through the process of context reasoning. Several policy models (e.g., [5,12]) support such contextual information, but they unnecessarily burden policies with reasoning rules. As a result, this can compromise the correctness of security policies and the performance of security systems.

In this paper, we propose a security policy model for ubiquitous social systems. Our model represents a range of applicable security policies and enables their analysis. It gives security context a primary role in decision making and defines all possible contextual information as policy abstractions, based on our conceptual model of security context presented in [8]. This enables more clear and precise analysis of how important contextual information influence access control, as the underlying security service. Our policy model provides intuitive abstractions for ubiquitous social systems, as it takes into account the social related aspect, and introduces a novel state diagram to represent the life cycle of objects. The latter makes provision of context-aware security behaviour easier, in particular detection of context changes and specification of reactions upon these changes. As a whole, our policy model facilitates specification and analysis of security policies applicable for ubiquitous social systems.

The paper is structured as follows. First, we describe the policy models used by existing context-aware security systems in Sect. 2. Next, we shortly present our conceptual model of security context as background in Sect. 3. Afterwards, we describe a motivation scenario to illustrate ubiquitous social systems in Sect. 4. Then, we present our policy model for ubiquitous social systems in Sect. 5. This is followed by an evaluation of the applicability of the model for describing our motivation scenario in Sect. 6. Finally, we conclude the paper in Sect. 7.

2   Related Work

Several works have tried to extend traditional policy models to include security context. Most of them are based on Role-based access control (RBAC) model [7], extending it mainly in two directions. First, RBAC's policy abstractions and assignments are constrained with contextual conditions (e.g., roles in [4], objects in [9], both rights and roles in [3], and subject-role and role-right assignment in [9]), meaning they are active only when these conditions hold, w.r.t. the current security context. Second, RBAC is extended with additional abstractions defined through contextual conditions. For example, [5] introduces *context* to express various security contexts over subjects, objects and actions, which complement RBAC rules, essentially specifying that a subject can perform an action over an object only if the conditions hold w.r.t. the current security context. Usage control (UCON) model [11] has also been extended in [1], with an additional abstraction *context*, similar to the UCON's attribute. Context is used for specification of conditions that are evaluated prior granting rights or during their usage. These constraints denote that a subject can be granted a right, or it can use this right, as long as the specified conditions hold, w.r.t. the current security context. Otherwise, the right is not given, or needs to be revoked.

Few works defined policy models particularly for context-aware security. [12] defines context for an operation performed over an object, also through contextual conditions. If the conditions hold, a context is active and the subject is allowed to perform the operation over the object. As context changes, so does active contexts and allowed operations over objects. Furthermore, [10] represents security policies graphically, as so called contextual graphs. A node in such graph denotes a contextual condition, which needs to be checked w.r.t. the current security context, or a security action, which needs to be performed when reached. Policy evaluation, in this case, is a path through the graph that determines what security actions need to be performed w.r.t. the current security context.

Existing policy models for context-aware security mostly consider security context as an add-on and rarely model reactions upon context change. Moreover, they mainly take low-level contextual information into account, which change frequently, leading to poor performance of security systems and even towards denial of service attacks. Some models (e.g., [5,12]) support high-level contextual information, but place the reasoning rules in security policies. This requires policy makers to be extensively familiar with context reasoning, which can influence the correctness of the policies. It can even compromise the performance of security systems as context reasoning will be performed during each decision.

3   Background

We shortly describe security context according to our conceptual model. For detailed description, we refer the reader to [8].

Security context is any information that can be used to characterize the situation of an entity (person or device, which can be also seen as a composition of its resources), considered relevant for security, regarding a particular task or activity. *Activity* is a process of an entity executing an operation over a resource, while trying to accomplish certain goals. Activities can be performed over three types of resources: data—a persistent storage of information, channel—a pathway for exchanging information, and application—a software component for achieving functionalities over information. More precisely, a security context of an activity a is a tuple, $ctx_a = (a, focus, assoc_a, sett_a, sprop_a)$, consisting of the activity itself, the focus of the user, $focus$, the social concepts that characterize a—association, $assoc_a$, and setting, $sett_a$—and the values of the security properties[1] of resources currently involved in a. We describe focus, association and setting through *social groups*, which are communities where people participate in order to achieve their goals more easily. Within them, people perform different activities, according to their roles. Social groups can be categorized into social domains depending on the goals and roles they support[2]. Focus is a social group, which describes the user's motivation while performing an activity, and whose goals are considered primary for the user at a given moment. Association and setting are social groups common for all participants and observers[3] of an activity, respectively, which describe them appropriately.

4 Motivation

We present a typical ubiquitous social system scenario. It includes use cases encountered in common practice, which represent the characteristics of IT consumerization, and take into account standardized security guidelines. Our use case centers around Alice—a finance manager at ACME1, which is a traditional company, trying to follow modern technological trends, by allowing its employees to use their own mobile devices (e.g., phone or tablet) for work. It is still conservative in this regard, allowing them to use their devices exclusively for work purposes while at work. Thus, employees can install various apps on their devices, but they can use only apps approved by the company policy for work. For example, intelligent assistant apps are forbidden, as they send audio recordings to remote servers and can potentially leak confidential company conversations. But, Alice's favorite word processing app is allowed, as ACME1 approves it.

Scene 1. Alice is in her office, preparing a report on her phone with the *Office* app. The app collects usage statistics and tries to send them to a remote server, but this should not be allowed, as it might also leak the confidential report. Also, Alice should not be able to check a personal document, since ACME1 allows her to open only work documents while using the *Office* app for work purposes.

Scene 2. Alice wants to call home, but ACME1 does not allow her to use her phone for other than work purposes while at the office. So, she decides to leave company premises. As she logs out on the access control device with her phone, all apps she has been using for work are automatically closed.

Scene 3. Alice enters her apartment, after unlocking the door with her phone. She wants to review the report she made earlier, but is not able to open it. According to the company policy, employees can access work documents only inside company premises.

---

[1] Security property is a quality that describes a resource or its usage, with respect to the objectives of security, i.e., confidentiality, integrity and availability.

[2] Examples of social domains are family or research department, whereas examples of social groups are their particular realization.

[3] Participant is an entity involved in an activity by consuming or generating resources, whereas observer is an entity that can monitor an activity which is being performed.

5 Context-Aware Activity Control Model

We propose a security policy model for ubiquitous social systems. Our model enables each social group to protect its own assets by controlling their interactions with other assets during activities[4]. It is based on security context and emphasizes activity instead of access as a single unit of control. (Access is more related with the operation inside an activity and does not leave an impression of a concept from which security context rises. Also, access suggests only a single interaction between the involved assets (i.e., subject vs. object), whereas we advocate several possible ones.) Thus, we refer to our model as context-aware activity control (CA-ACON) model. Below, first we define its policy abstractions in Sect. 5.1, and then we define its policy rules in Sect. 5.2.

5.1 Policy Abstractions

Policy abstractions are placeholders in security policies, which are replaced by particular elements from the system state during their evaluation. Our policy model consists of the following abstractions: activity, subject, object, origin, security context of activity, continuous activities and current security contexts. Figure 1 illustrates these policy abstractions and the relations between them[5].

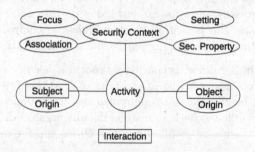

Fig. 1. Policy abstractions of the model

Activity. We define *activity* same as in [8] (see Sect. 3). But, we deal only with simple activities and treat complex activities as sequences of simple ones, which need to be controlled separately. We denote the set of activities as A.

Subject and Object. *Subject* is a resource which performs an activity by carrying out an operation, whereas *object* is a resource over which an activity is performed. A resource can reside in two states: active and passive. A resource in

---

[4] Asset is a resource assigned to a social group, or an entity defined as its member. Entities are assets as they are responsible for achieving the social group goals.

[5] Since continuous activities and current security contexts are activities and security contexts, respectively, they are represented through these abstractions on the figure.

passive state is used for storing information and functionalities in the device's memory for future use. It is kept like a closed container whose contents are not accessible directly. Contrary, a resource in active state is like an open container, whose information can be read and modified, in case of data and channel, or whose functionality can be executed, in case of application. For example, in Linux a passive application is an executable file, a passive data/channel is a regular file, an active application is a process, and an active data/channel is a file descriptor. If we take resource states into account, a subject is an application in active state, whereas an object is data, channel or application, either in passive or active state. It follows any resource is an object and that applications can be both subjects and objects, i.e., subjects are also objects. We denote the set of all subjects and objects as S and O, and we denote the sets of passive and active objects with O_P and $O_A, O = O_P + O_A$.

Object Life Cycle. Seven types of activities can be performed over objects, depending on the operation carried out during the activity. They are: *create, open, execute, read, write, close* and *destroy* activity. Each of them is performed over a particular object state and has a particular effect on the object, which results in state transitions. The possible activity types, together with the possible object states and state transitions, compose the life cycle of an object (Fig. 2).

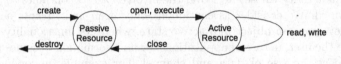

Fig. 2. Object life cycle

We describe object life cycle as follows. Each object o begins its life cycle when certain subject s performs a *create* activity, $(s, create, o)$, which adds a new element in $O_P, O_P = O_P + \{o\}$. In order to be directly used, o must be activated. Data and channels are activated with the *open* activity, whereas applications are activate with the *execute* activity[6]. Both $(s, open, o)$, and $(s, execute, o)$ move o from O_P to $O_A, O_P = O_P - \{o\}, O_A = O_A + \{o\}$. While in active state, a data or channel can be read or written numerous times, without changing its state. During a *read* activity, $(s, read, o)$, information from o is transferred into s, whereas during a *write* activity, $(s, write, o)$, information from s is transferred into o, modifying it. On the other hand, while in active state an application becomes capable of providing its functionality, i.e., it becomes a subject, $S = S + \{o\}$, and can perform activities over other objects. An object o stays in an active state as long as it is not deactivated with a *close* activity, $(s, close, o)$, which moves o back to $O_P, O_A = O_A - \{o\}, O_P = O_P + \{o\}$. It also removes o from $S, S = S - \{o\}$, in case o is an application. The transitions between the

---

[6] Since activating applications has different security implications than activating data and channels, we use two activity types in order to control them separately.

passive and active object states can be performed many times during its life cycle. Finally, a *destroy* activity, $(s, destroy, o)$ destroys the object and removes it from the O_P, $O_P = O_P - \{o\}$.

Security Context of Activity. We define *security context of activity* same as in [8] (see Sect. 3). Security context can change as other activities are performed.

Origin. Subjects and objects can be classified according to their origin. *Origin* is a single social group a resource can be related with, which captures the purpose of its creation. For an application, origin captures the social group whose goals it is used for achieving, whereas for a data or a channel, origin captures the social group whose information it is used to contain. Resources inherit their origin from the subject which created them. We assume there is an application for each social group from which resources related with that social group inherit their origin, either directly or indirectly. We define origin as a function, $org : Res \rightarrow SG$, which maps a resource to a social group. (We denote the set of all social groups as SG.) The origins of all subjects and objects compose the set of all origins, Org, defined as a set of tuples $(o, org(o))$, where $o \in O^7$.

Continuous Activities. Each activity is performed when the subject carries out the operation of the activity over the object, after which, we assume that the effects of that activity over the involved assets are manifested. *Continuous activity* is an activity whose effect over the involved assets continues to last after it is performed. We consider as continuous only *open* and *execute* activities[8], because they move an object into active state, where its functionality becomes available to the user, in case of applications, or its information becomes available to the subject, in case of data and channel. For example, an open activity, $(s, open, o)$, makes a data object o available to the subject s for reading and writing, during number of activities in the future. This is different than a single read activity, $(s, read, o)$, during which the information is exchanged between the subject and the object only when it is performed, and not afterwords.

Current Security Contexts. We consider that the security context of a continuous activity can change after it is performed. As a result, it needs to be controlled after the activity is allowed, at each context change. In order to be able to detect context changes, we keep track of all continuous activities which are currently being performed, and we constantly monitor their security context. We define a function named *current security context*, $cctx : A \rightarrow Ctx$, which maps an activity to its security context at the given moment. We denote the set of all security contexts as Ctx. We define *current continuous activities* $A_C \subset A$, as a set of all continuous activities whose effect still lasts over some object. We further define *current security contexts* $CCtx$ as a set of tuples $(a, cctx(a))$ of the current security context of each continuous activity $a \in A_C$. The elements in $CCtx$ are constantly updated in order to contain relevant values.

---

[7] Since subjects are objects, this implies that Org also includes origins of subjects.

[8] *Destroy* activity as not continuous, because its effect over the involved object does not exist, as the object is destroyed after its execution.

Interaction. We define *interaction* as an ability or a mean for communication between two assets involved in an activity, which can have a security implication. During an activity, parallel interactions occur between all the involved assets. An asset can be involved in an activity as follows: a resource can act as subject or object, whereas an entity can act as user, participant or observer of the activity[9]. All interactions can be easily translated into interactions between social groups, by mapping the involved assets to their relating social groups: (i) the subject and object are related with the social group in their origin, (ii) the user is related with the social group in his focus, i.e., the focus of the activity, (iii) the participants are related with the social group in the association, and (iv) the observers are related with the social group in the setting of the activity. We denote the set of all interactions as *Int*. We consider only interactions involving the subject as relevant for security, that is, subject-object, subject-user, subject-participant and subject-observer interactions (Fig. 3). The reason for this is twofold. First, the subject performs activities and hence it drives each interaction. Any interaction involving the object either: (i) goes through the subject, for example in case of data, since the user/participants/observers cannot access data directly, or (ii) is negligible, for example in case of channel and application, since channels only serve as pathways for communication between subjects and the user/participants/observers, and the purpose of applications is to be used as subjects. Second, the subject is usually the only target over which security policies can be enforced. Any discussion of direct interactions between the user, the participants and the observers is futile, as it cannot be enforced.

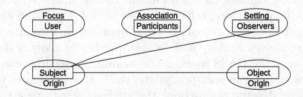

Fig. 3. Security relevant interactions between assets involved in an activity

5.2   Policy Rules

Policy rules are statements specified over policy abstractions, which must hold in order for the desired security objectives of the policy to be achieved. Our policy model recognizes two types of policy rules: group and default policy rules.

Group Policy Rules. These rules apply for assets related with a particular social group. They are specified in form of authorization and express the security requirements of a social group regarding particular interactions during an activity. We refer to a set of group policy rules, specific to a single social group, as

---

[9] One entity acts both as user and participant in an activity. In the former case, it initiates the activity, whereas in the latter it participates in it.

its group policy. A group policy is taken into account for each decision regarding an activity, which involves an asset related with that social group. Since they are specific for each social group, group policy rules need to be specified explicitly, with the help of a policy language.

Default Policy Rules. These rules apply for assets related with any social group. They are constant and can be implemented implicitly by the context-aware security system using our model. We define three default policy rules:

- *Basic rule:* An activity is allowed to be performed only if all interactions during it are allowed by the social groups whose assets are involved.
- *Contextual rule:* If a security context of a continuous activity changes, then the basic rule for this activity must be reevaluated. In case the activity is not allowed according to the basic rule, then the effect of this activity needs to be terminated, according to the termination rule. Otherwise, it remains in the set of continuous activities.
- *Termination rule:* The effects of a continuous activity are terminated by closing the object over which it is performed. In case there are other continuous activities involving the same object, they need to be terminated too.

6 Evaluation

We show the applicability of our policy model by using it to analyze two scenes from our motivation scenario from Sect. 4. We describe how a context-aware security system (CASS), running on Alice's mobile device, makes security decisions, based on the security policies specified with our model. The CASS monitors each resource and intercepts each activity request, upon which, examines the security context of the requested activity and decides whether to allow or deny it. For a continuous activity, the CASS continues to monitor its security contexts. If the context changes and becomes inappropriate, the CASS terminates the activity.

We make several assumptions prior the analysis. First, we assume Alice is a member of three social groups, referred[10] to as: work, home, and public[11]. We assume the CASS keeps information about the structure of these social groups (members and their roles) and has their security policies specified. For example, Alice's work social group, representing the ACME1 company, consists of all employees and equipment, including: Alice as finance manager, Adam as accountant, AP_1 as access point, R_1 as router, P_1 as printer, S_1 as server, etc.

Furthermore, we assume each social group has its own set of applications, which are used by the user while achieving its goals. If the user wants to use the functionality of an application in several social groups, it needs to be installed for each of them. We label applications according to the social group for which they are installed. For example, if Alice wants to use the *Launcher* app for starting

---

[10] Since people are often part of a single social group from a social domain, we refer to social groups by their domains, e.g., work is ACME1 and home is Alice's family.

[11] As explained in [8], the public social group is default and contains all entities.

apps in each work, home and public social group, it needs to be installed three times, as $Launcher_W$, $Launcher_H$, and $Launcher_P$, respectively.

Finally, we assume each social group has its own group policy, which states what contextual conditions need to be satisfied in order particular interactions during activities to be allowed for its assets. For example, one rule from Alice's work policy states that: "*Subject-user* interaction during *execute* activity is allowed, only if subject's origin and user's (activity's) focus are the *work* social group". From the aspect of work social group as subject's origin, this rule allows work subjects to execute objects only in work focus. On the other hand, from the aspect of work social group as user's focus, this rule allows only work subjects to execute objects while focus is work. Table 1 lists Alice's work, home and public policies, in particular, what kind of policy rules they consist of. We refer to a rule which allows only interactions between assets from the same social group, as closed rule. Consequently, we refer to a rule which allows interactions between asset from one social group and asset from any other social groups as open rule.

Table 1. Group policies applicable in our motivation scenario.

Policy	Interaction			
	Sub-obj	Sub-usr	Sub-par	Sub-obs
Work policy	Closed	Closed	Closed	Closed
Home policy	Closed	Closed	Closed	Open
Public policy	Open	Open	Open	Open

Scene 1. Alice is in her office and her focus is her work social group. This can be determined from her previous activity of logging on the electronic access control system installed at the entrance of ACME1 premises. She prepares the report with the $Office_W$ app as follows. First, $Office_W$ app opens the report doc_{W1}, as data object, $a_1 = (Office_W, open, doc_{W1})$. Then, it reads the report's content, $a_2 = (Office_W, read, doc_{W1})$ and shows it on the screen, through a screen channel, $scr_{W1}, a_3 = (Office_W, write, scr_{W1})$. $Office_W$ captures what Alice is typing through a channel to the touch sensor, $tch_{W1}, a_4 = (Office_W, read, tch_{W1})$, and writes that to the report, $a_5 = (Office_W, write, doc_{W1})$. $Office_W$ app submits a request for each of these activities, and the CASS makes a security decision for each request. We assume association and setting of a_1, a_2, and a_5 are empty as they happen inside the mobile device and have no participants and observers. On the other hand, association and setting of a_3 and a_4 are the work social group as there are only work group members around. We assume doc_{W1}, sch_{W1} and sch_{W1} has been created earlier by the $Office_W$, so their origin is the work social group. Since work policy is the only applicable for these decisions, all interactions during these activities are allowed according to it and the *basic rule*. After a_1 is performed, it is added in the set of continuous activities A_C and its security context is added in the set of current contexts, $CCtx$.

Furthermore, the decision making for the activity of opening a network channel, $ch_{W1}, a_6 = (Office_W, open, ch_{W1})$, goes as follows. The CASS obtains the following needed information for the decision. The focus of a_6 is the work social group same as above, whereas its association and setting are the public social group, as the remote server is unknown and by default member only of the public social group. We assume ch_{W1} has been created earlier by the $Office_W$, so its origin is the work social group. Thus, the CASS takes two *group policies* into account: work and public. The evaluation goes as follows: (i) subject-object interaction is allowed because the subject and the object originate from the same social group; (ii) subject-user interaction is allowed because the subject's origin is same as the (user's) focus; (iii) while subject-participants interaction is allowed from the aspect of public social group, because it allows any interaction, this interaction is not allowed from the aspect of work social group, as the association is different than the subject's origin. (iv) while subject-observer interaction is allowed from the aspect of public social group, because it allows any interaction, this interaction is not allowed from the aspect of work social group, as the setting is different than the subject's origin. As a result, the CASS makes a decision that a_6 is not allowed, according to the *basic rule*, i.e., $Office_W$ app cannot open the ch_{W1} channel to communicate with the remote server.

Finally, $Office_W$ app tries to open a home document $doc_{H1}, a_7 = (Office_W, open, doc_{H1})$. For this activity, the CASS takes into account the home policy, in addition to the work policy. According to these group policies, the subject-object interaction is not allowed during this activity, from aspect of both work and home social group, as the subject and object originate from different social groups. Thus, the CASS evaluates that a_7 is not allowed, according to the *basic rule* and prevents the $Office_W$ from opening the data.

Scene 2. Alice is in her office and wants to call home, but is not able to use home applications at work. According to her work policy, subject-observer interactions are not allowed during such activities, as the subject's origin (home social group), is different than the setting of these activities (work social group, as only work group members around). Thus, she leaves the company premises.

On her way out, Alice logs out with her mobile device at the access control system, which changes her focus from work to public social group. This applies for all continuous activities in A_C, and for all future activities. The CASS detects these changes when $CCtx$ is updated with the new values[12], upon which it starts making new security decision for each activity in A_C. This is done according to the *contextual* and the *basic rules*. $CCtx$ consists of the execution activities of all subjects and the opening activities of the channel and data objects they use. One can imagine that, at this moment, this set contains the execution activities of the $Office_W$ and the $Launcher_W$, and the opening activities of the screen and touch channels these apps use for communication with Alice. All these objects originate from the work social group. The CASS takes two *group policies* into account for

---

[12] The values of the association and setting will also change, since there are public group members around.

these decisions: public and work. Since these activities are not allowed according to the *basic rule*, they need to be closed according to the *termination rule*.

As soon as Alice is outside, she starts the *Launcher*$_H$ app, which changes her focus from public to home social group. Now, she is able to operate with home apps, because the setting of these activities is not her work social group anymore, but public. Both public and home policies allow the subject-observer interaction during these activities. Also, all other interactions are allowed according to the home policy, as it is the only one applicable for them.

7 Conclusion and Future Work

In this paper, we defined a security policy model for ubiquitous social systems. Our model centers around security context and defines all possible contextual information as policy abstractions. Since these information are few and of high level of abstraction, our model enables clear and precise analysis of how they influence access control. Furthermore, our policy abstractions are more intuitive for ubiquitous social systems, as they include social concepts and are specifically tailored for providing context-aware security behaviour. In addition, our model combines security policies specified by different policy makers, enabling each social group to specify its own security policy.

As future work, we plan to define a policy language for our model, based on Datalog, which will enable specification of group policies for ubiquitous social systems. We also plan to implement a prototype of context-aware security system, which will use our policy model and language for making security decisions.

References

1. Bai, G., Gu, L., Feng, T., Guo, Y., Chen, X.: Context-aware usage control for Android. In: Jajodia, S., Zhou, J. (eds.) SecureComm 2010. LNICSSITE, vol. 50, pp. 326–343. Springer, Heidelberg (2010). doi:10.1007/978-3-642-16161-2_19
2. Bettini, C., Brdiczka, O., Henricksen, K., Indulska, J., Nicklas, D., Ranganathan, A., Riboni, D.: A survey of context modelling and reasoning techniques. Pervasive Mob. Comput. **6**(2), 161–180 (2010)
3. Bonatti, P., Galdi, C., Torres, D.: ERBAC: Event-driven RBAC. In: Proceedings of the ACM Symposium on Access Control Models and Technologies, pp. 125–136. ACM (2013)
4. Covington, M.J., Long, W., Srinivasan, S., Dev, A.K., Ahamad, M., Abowd, G.D.: Securing context-aware applications using environment roles. In: Proceedings of the ACM Symposium on Access Control Models and Technologies, SACMAT 2001, pp. 10–20. ACM (2001)
5. Cuppens, F., Cuppens-Boulahia, N.: Modeling contextual security policies. Int. J. Inf. Secur. **7**(4), 285–305 (2008)
6. Dey, A.K.: Understanding and using context. Pers. Ubiquit. Comput. **5**(1), 4–7 (2001)
7. Ferraiolo, D.F., Sandhu, R., Gavrila, S., Kuhn, D.R., Chandramouli, R.: Proposed NIST standard for role-based access control. ACM Trans. Inf. Syst. Secur. (TISSEC) **4**(3), 224–274 (2001)

8. Jovanovikj, V., Gabrijelčič, D., Klobučar, T.: A conceptual model of security context. Int. J. Inf. Secur. **13**(6), 571–581 (2014)
9. Kulkarni, D., Tripathi, A.: Context-aware role-based access control in pervasive computing systems. In: Proceedings of the ACM Symposium on Access Control Models and Technologies, SACMAT 2008, pp. 113–122. ACM (2008)
10. Mostefaoui, G.K.: Towards a conceptual and software framework for integrating context-based security in pervasive environments. Ph.D. thesis, University of Fribourg (2004)
11. Park, J., Sandhu, R.: The UCON ABC usage control model. ACM Trans. Inf. Syst. Secur. (TISSEC) **7**(1), 128–174 (2004)
12. Toninelli, A., Montanari, R., Kagal, L., Lassila, O.: Proteus: A semantic context-aware adaptive policy model. In: Proceedings of the IEEE International Symposium on Policies for Distributed Systems and Networks, POLICY 2007, pp. 129–140. IEEE Computer Society (2007)

The Role of the Ostensive Communicative Context in the Childhood Social Learning

Emiliano Loria(✉)

Consortium FINO, Turin/Genoa, Italy
emiliano.loria@edu.unito.it

Abstract. In 2006 Gergely Csibra and György Gergely proposed a new type of social cognitive learning mechanism, called "natural pedagogy", grounded on the ostensive communication. According to their theory human infants show very early sensitivity to communicative and ostensive cues that indicate teaching contexts; they tend to interpret certain actions (e.g. gaze shift or pointing) occurring in these communicative contexts as referential cues to identify the referents about which new information will be provided. Furthermore, they argue, infants can infer that the information revealed about the referents in such ostensive communicative teaching contexts will not only be new and relevant, but will consist of publicly shared and universal cultural knowledge that is, thus, generalizable and shareable with other members of the cultural community. This last crucial point makes rise the question if mindreading capacities are involved in the pedagogical system, insofar infants are able to ascribe to others beliefs in the form of knowledge content transmitted and acquired in ostensive way.

Keywords: Ostensive communication · Referential expectation · Social learning · Natural pedagogy · Infant cognition · Mindreading

1 Premises to the Natural Pedagogy

Human communication is often ostensive: it advertises itself as deliberate communication rather than just providing an information source for others [1]. Beyond specifying that a certain act is meant to carry content for others, the ostensive nature of communication is also important in determining to whom the content is addressed. Indeed, ostensive signals serve both functions at the same time: they specify the addressee and mark the accompanying actions as communicative [2]. Such signals include eye contact, deictic gestures, calling others by name, and adjusting one's actions temporally or spatially to the addressee, such as in turn-taking or blocking someone's path, etc.

The dominant channel of human communication is vocal, and the linguistic content of speech can its self indicate whom it is meant to target. But not always. Indeed, speech does not necessarily reveal to whom it is addressed, especially for young infants who are unable to decode its semantic content. To overcome such difficulty, adults often explicitly mark their communication as infant-directed. For example, they may communicate with the special intonation termed as infant-directed speech (IDS), also

© Springer International Publishing AG 2017
P. Brézillon et al. (Eds.): CONTEXT 2017, LNAI 10257, pp. 315–323, 2017.
DOI: 10.1007/978-3-319-57837-8_25

called "motherese language", that is a spread communicative tendency which seems to be independent of the culture, the language, or the experience of the parents [3].

Infants seem attuned to these signals from an early age. Newborns prefer to look at faces with direct gaze compared to averted gaze, and prefer to listen to IDS compared to adult-directed speech (ADS) [4]; by around five months of age infants can already start to learn new ostensive signals, such as their name [5]. The behavioural responses with which infants respond to these signals are very similar: they smile, the pay enhanced attention to the source, and tend to follow its directional movement following the ostensive signals [6]. One important aspect of the ostensive signals, and eye gaze in particular, is their referential nature. Eyes point to the subject of someone's attention and intention provide a reliable signal to identify and share the topic during communication and social learning [7].

The theory of "natural pedagogy" is grounded on this ostensive form of communication. It is a cognitive social learning system that enables the fast and efficient transmission of cultural knowledge by communication between individuals, in particular adults and infants [8–11].

2 Cultural Transmission to Human Infants

One of the most curious aspect of human culture is the presence, transmission, maintenance, and relative resistance to modification of many cultural forms in spite of (i) their cognitive causal-structural and/or functional 'opacity' to its users, and (ii) their downright lack of locally adaptive value to particular members of the culture. By the term 'opacity' I refer here to the fact that human culture is often characterized by cultural skills, habits and procedures whose underlying causal mechanism is not (or not fully) understood by the members of the community (such as switching on the tv, hanging garlic in the window to keep vampirs away, starting a car-engine by turning on the ignition key, etc.). Note that such cultural forms are often preserved and transmitted even when their causal efficacy or adaptive effect is only assumed (believed), but not directly perceived.

Gergely and Csibra argued that the property of cognitive 'opacity', that first emerged in hominid cultural environments, represented evolutionary pressure for the selection of the type of social cognitive learning mechanism that they call "natural pedagogy" [8]. They hypothesize that in human infancy, initially, imitative learning is triggered, and certainly strongly facilitated, by the presence of ostensive-communicative cues that accompany the behavioural manifestations of cultural information by others. Furthermore, they argue that the infant interprets the ostensive-communicative cues addressed to her as indicating that the other (the adult) is about to manifest for the infant some significant aspect of cultural knowledge that will be new and relevant for her and that, therefore, should be fast learned[1].

---

[1] These assumptions are directly analogous to the Gricean pragmatic assumptions of ostensive communication as spelled out in Sperber and Wilson's relevance theory [1]. However, in Csibra' and Gergely's view, the pedagogical stance is a primary adaptation for cultural learning and not a specialized module dedicated to the recovery of speaker's intent in linguistic communication.

In particular, they suggest that human individuals, who possess cultural knowledge, are naturally inclined not only to use, but also to ostensively manifest their knowledge to (and for the benefit of) naïve conspecifics, while the latter by actively seeking out, attending to, and being specially receptive to such communicative manifestations of knowledgeable others.

Pedagogical knowledge transfer is triggered by specific communicative cues (such as eye-contact, contingent reactivity, the prosodic pattern of 'motherese', and being addressed by one's own name). In pedagogy, on the one hand, it is the very fact that a knowledgeable conspecific (a 'teacher') ostensively communicates her cultural knowledge by manifesting it for the novice (the 'learner') is what ensures the cultural relevance of the knowledge content transmitted. On other hand, infants are equipped with specialized cognitive resources that enable them to learn from infant-direct teaching.

1 Infants show very early sensitivity to communicative and ostensive cues that indicate teaching contexts (including eye-contact, contingent reactivity, IDS, and hearing one's name).
2 They tend to interpret certain actions (e.g. gaze shift or pointing) occurring in these communicative contexts as referential cues to identify the referents about which new information will be provided.
3 They expect the adult/teacher to ostensively manifest by her behaviour the relevant and the new information about the referent identified.
4 Information revealed about the referents in such ostensive communicative teaching contexts will not only be new and relevant, but will consist of publicly shared and universal cultural knowledge that is, thus, generalizable and shareable with other members of the cultural community [8, 12].

Experimental evidences suggest that ostensive communicative context allows that (a) infants do not encode the perspectives of other agents as person-specific sources of knowledge, and (b) infants learn about the object, rather than the agent's disposition towards that object [12–14].

Egyed and her colleagues [15], indeed, argued that the referential expectation triggered by pedagogical condition characterizes infant's attention in object-centered way. In other terms, in the pedagogical context the infants would learn new information about the referent, I mean, about the particular object that is referenced in the ostensive communication, and not about the agent (her preferences, desires and other mental states) according to the person-centered perspective assumed by the standard mindreading account.

When another person's object-directed behavioural manifestations are observed in an ostensive cuing context, natural pedagogy predicts that infants will *not* interpret the content of such manifestations as expressing the specific subjective mental states that the other holds about the referent, but rather they will use such communicative displays as the basis to infer the new information about the relevant properties of the referent object that they are being taught about. Furthermore, it is very important to underline that natural pedagogy theory assumes that ostensive cues trigger in-built assumptions about the *universality* of the epistemic information that the other's communicative manifestations convey about the referent [8, 9]. In other words, the knowledge that infants acquire in this way is ascribed to everybody, because they assume the equivalence of others' mind. The assumption that allows this general ascription of informative contents is called by Gergely e Csibra the assumption of universality [8–12].

I propose that this knowledge attribution competence is the proof of a cognitive functional cooperation between a primary form of mindreading and the natural pedagogy mechanism. Until now Gergely and Csibra have refused such a involvement, and in order to be clear about any commitment about natural pedagogy and mindreading I need to specify in what a primary form of mindreading consists.

3 Mindreading and Natural Pedagogy

3.1 Mindreading's Marker

Mindreading, or Theory of Mind, is an agent's capability of representing another individual's mental states, so as to be able to understand, predict, and explain her behavior. According to simulation accounts, human beings ground their capacity to mindread in the introspective awareness that they have of their own mental states [16]. To understand and predict another individual's actions, we would imagine to be placed in her situation and doing what she is doing. We would then observe what is going on inside ourselves, and attribute to the other agent the mental states that we would have if we were her. This "like-me" perspective [17] generates hard problems about infants' mind. One of these consists in the assumption that inner introspection is an innate capacity. Instead, it's more reasonable to presume that introspective abilities are gained during the development [18, 19].

In other respects, according to theory–theory accounts, our knowledge about the mind makes up an everyday framework theory [20]. A mindreader would employ mental states as theoretical constructs in the prediction and the explanation of behavior. On this view, learning and experience are crucial In the acquisition of mindreading: the child, like a scientist, would conjure up several successive theories of mind, always discarding the current one whenever it is falsified by new data collected. Also in this case, we would have several problems with early reasoning abilities ascribed to toddlers. Indeed, it is hard to conceive of infants' need to devote their efforts of understanding the world in terms of building a theory like a scientist in the lab. Therefore, by the notion of mindreading I suggest to take a constructivist perspective that may reveal how during the ontogenetic development the slow maturation of several competences occurs and builds the full system. However, some of these competences start to emerge very early in infancy, primarily under the form of ascription of false beliefs to others [19, 21, 22].

In the last decade, a number of studies have offered new evidence that before the end of their second year, human infants are able not only to ascribe motivations to others but also to represent the contents of others' false beliefs and to ascribe to others false beliefs that they do not share. False Belief (FB) tasks require the child to ascribe to a protagonist a belief that diverges both from reality and the child's own belief and to explain or predict the subjectively rational action of the protagonist on this basis[2].

Most of the controversy in ToM research was inspired by developmental findings suggesting that implicit and explicit ToM processes may have different developmental paths. It is common to identify explicit tasks as those that employ some form of verbal or other communicative performance as the dependent measure, whereas implicit tasks are those that use other kinds of measure, such as reaction times [19].

Important studies using the nonverbal violation-of-expectation looking paradigm provided ToM processes are in place in early infancy, around the first birthday [23–25] and also before [26], contrary to explicit tasks that show that only after the age of 4 years children answer correctly. The different results reveal a developmental gap. However, what we can figure out from explicit or implicit experimental tasks is that the simplest marker of mindreading is the faculty to ascribe (false) beliefs to others. It is still very hard to establish when and how such a faculty starts to play, but we can claim that where we can register false-belief ascription, there we have mindreading.

Recently, the developmental gap question on FB tasks has arisen whether there could be a social cognitive mechanism that is in the *middle-ground*. Such a middle-ground stage is called *minimal* mindreading by Apperly and Butterfill [27, 28], who are advocates of the two-systems model and take full-blown mindreading to be a uniquely human meta-representational cognitive capacity. Apperly and Butterfill call explicit-ToM system "the *normative* account of mindreading", and only this is considered the 'proper' ToM, whereas the implicit system is considered only a precursor of the full-fledged ToM, which may not involve understanding beliefs at all. The two systems are separate and do not speak to each other: the early developing, fast and efficient system is supposed to persist throughout development into adulthood along side the later-developing system.

Jacob [29] and Carruthers [30] criticized this approach under several points of view, and they suggest that there is just a single mindreading system that exists throughout, but which undergoes gradual conceptual enrichment through infancy and childhood. In this sense, gaze monitoring and joint attention, imitation, infant's emotional reaction to others and belief-ascriptions should not be viewed as precursors of later mindreading abilities, rather than as manifestations of true mindreading. As Tirassa and colleagues argue, the ontogeny of an organ or function (whether mental or otherwise) should be understood and described in terms of an initial state, a developmental dynamic, and possibly a mature state [21].

3.2   Universality Without Natural Pedagogy

Under the same constructivist perspective also Kovács [22] invites to give up to treat ToM abilities as a monolithic construct. She suggests to analyze separately five potential building blocks of belief-attribution ability, identified in (i) opening a

---

[2] In a typical change-of-location FB task, the child sees the following scenario: a performer A puts an object O into box 1 and leaves, meanwhile in her absence, performer B moves O to box 2. Upon the performer A's return, the test question to child is then "where A will look for O"?

'belief file'; (ii) computing the content of such beliefs; (iii) linking belief representations to the corresponding agents; (iv) belief evaluations: pondering true and false beliefs; and (v) performing inferences upon others' (false) beliefs for behavioral predictions. A separate analysis of these ToM subcomponents could allow a careful examination of their developmental emergence and integration. For my purpose the third component pointed by Kovács is the crucial one.

In this regard, the researchers Kampis, Somogyi, Itakura and Király [31] proposed that early theory of mind processes lack the binding of belief content to the belief holder. They tested whether 10-month-old infants would encode knowledge conveyed in a social situation as person-specific, or if these situations trigger the acquisition of more general knowledge in a non person-specific way. Their aim was to see whether infants who look at an agent expressing his or her attitude towards an object would expect a newly introduced agent to have the same attitude.

Following Luo [32], they showed infants a scenario in which Agent A expressed a particular attitude (a preferential choice) towards an object. They introduced the scenario with two objects present. In the next step they manipulated the perspectives of the infant and the agent such that the infant, but not the agent, saw that one of the two objects had been removed. After this the agent approached the remaining object.

Therefore, in the eyes of the infants, the agent did not make a preferential choice (given the role of contrastive choice mentioned earlier), but according to the agent's knowledge two objects were present when the choice was made. In order for infants to interpret the situation as an expression of preference, they had to view the action from the agent's perspective; moreover, they had to take into account the agent's (false) belief based on what the agent previously perceived (namely, not witnessing the removal of the object). In the test phase they introduced a new agent (Agent B), who once chose consistently with Agent A, once inconsistently. To test the range of agents that the acquired knowledge could be applied to, the researchers varied whether Agent B was an adult or a 2-year-old child. Their crucial condition was the FB condition, where the agent falsely believed that there were two objects and hence she believed she was making a real choice.

Their results confirm that infants can rely on the perspectives and knowledge of other agents, hence, when attributing choice, infants don't rely on their own visual access to the scenario; rather, they take into account the agent's conflicting perspective and epistemic state, which in the experiment's scenario was the reverse of what infants could themselves see. Thus, infants must integrate the attributed beliefs with the preference in order to interpret the agent's actions and have expectation regarding her or another agent's behavior [31]. According to Kampis and colleagues infants use the knowledge of another agent to predict not only the actions of this agent exclusively, but also the behavior of other agents[3].

---

[3] Their striking results invite to refine the interpretation of early mindreading competencies of infants provided by Lou [32], who argues that 10-month-olds encode the attributed mental states as belonging to that specific person only. On the contrary, it seems that infants do not handle the emergent information based on someone's visual access in a person-specific way. They can use the acquired information to predict the actions of other agents accordingly.

The very important point that I want to underline is that the experimental conditions and procedures were not settled in a pedagogical-ostensive manner. This is not specified by the authors, but it represents a crucial interpretative point. Indeed, as predicted by the natural pedagogy theory, and in particular by the assumption of universality [12, 13], infants do not interpret the inferred preferential choice of an agent as related to that person; rather, they seem to infer that the content of the preferential choice could also be appropriate for other agents. Thus, belief computation and preference attribution can be used not only to learn about others but also to learn about the world through the lenses of others. These are the same conclusions advanced by Kampis and colleagues [31], but they refer to another kind of contextual condition, that do not engage the features of ostensive communicative relations.

Therefore, I argue that natural pedagogy mechanism incorporates, as its component, the ToM competence already available in the infant's cognitive architecture even if it is limited to simple domains like for example ascription of true or false belief about the location of an object. Then, the natural pedagogy mechanism applies this competence in the ostensive communicative context in order to ascribe to others knowledge content for the benefit of a social learning as fast, frugal and efficient as possible.

However, such a cooperation between early mindreading system and natural pedagogy has to be balanced little by little during child development with the maturation of mindreading abilities and domains. Children will learn that others' minds are not equal, so I suggest that the degree of epistemic trust, triggered by ostensive communication and grounding natural pedagogy account, changes through the individual growth, and therefore also the weight of universality-bias changes. I wish this will be the matter of further research.

4 Conclusion

In Gergely' and Csibra's view the complex cognitive system that they call "natural pedagogy" is a primary species-specific cognitive adaptation to ensure fast, efficient, and "relevance-proof" learning of cultural knowledge in humans. The natural pedagogy allows the acquisition of reliable, shared and generalizable cultural knowledge without the extended acquisition process that trial-and-error learning and statistical observational learning necessitate.

The pedagogical relationship is grounded on a particular communicative context characterized by ostensive cues manifested by adults and correctly interpreted by infants in terms of referential signals. The ostensive communication creates the referential expectation in infants and it allows to shift the attention from the specific person who produces the manifest communicative act, to the referent object of the communicative context. I suggest that the knowledge acquired, in virtue of ostensive communicative context, is ascribed by infants to other members of the community, in accordance with the early mindreading system, that emerges in the ontogenetic development of individuals under the form of a cognitive skill able to ascribe epistemic states to others without the binding of belief contents to the belief holders.

Comparing the fundamentals of natural pedagogy mechanism and the results of Kampis and collegues' experiments on infants' ToM capacities, I suggest to draw an early developmental path that allows infants to acquire cultural knowledge through the perspective of others, in virtue of an epistemic cooperation of these two autonomous but not independent cognitive systems. In this way, from a particular learning communicative context, infants are able very early (around or before the first birthday) to generalize their informative acquisitions outside the episodic bounds of the particular situation.

References

1. Sperber, D., Wilson, D.: Relevance: Communication and Cognition, 2nd edn. Blackwell, Oxford (1995)
2. Csibra, G.: Recognizing communicative intentions in infancy. Mind Lang. **25**(2), 141–168 (2010). doi:10.1111/j.1468-0017.2009.01384.x
3. Lloyd-Fox, S., Széplaki-Köllőd, B., Yin, J., Csibra, G.: Are you talking to me? Neural activations in 6-month-old infants in response to being addressed during natural interactions. Cortex **70**, 35–48 (2015). doi:10.1016/j.cortex.2015.02.005
4. Farroni, T., Csibra, G., Simion, F., Johnson, M.H.: Eye contact detection in humans from birth. Proc. Natl. Acad. Sci. U.S.A. **99**(14), 9602–9605 (2002). doi:10.1073/pnas.152159999
5. Mandel, D.R., Jusczyk, P.W., Pisoni, D.B.: Infants' recognition of the sound patterns of their own names. Psychol. Sci. **6**, 314–317 (1995). doi:10.1111/j.1467-9280.1995.tb00517.x
6. Deligianni, F., Senju, A., Gergely, G., Csibra, G.: Automated gaze-contingent object elicit orientation following in 8-months-old infants. Develop. Psychol. **47**, 1499–1503 (2011). doi:10.1037/a0025659
7. Senju, A., Csibra, G., Johnson, M.H.: Understanding the referential nature of looking: infants' preference for object-directed gaze. Cognition **108**, 303–319 (2008). doi:10.1016/j.cognition.2008.02.009
8. Csibra, G., Gergely, G.: Social learning and social cognition: the case for pedagogy. In: Munakata, Y., Johnson, M.H. (eds.) Processes of Change in Brain and Cognitive Development. Attention and Performance, vol. XXI, pp. 249–274. Oxford UP, Oxford (2006)
9. Csibra, G., Gergely, G.: Natural pedagogy. Trends Cogn. Sci. **13**, 148–153 (2009). doi:10.1016/j.tics.2009.01.005
10. Csibra, G., Gergely, G.: Natural pedagogy as evolutionary adaptation. Philos. Trans. Roy. Soc. B **366**, 1149–1157 (2011). doi:10.1098/rstb.2010.0319
11. Csibra, G., Gergely, G.: Natural pedagogy. In: Banaji, M.R., Gelman, S.A. (eds.) Navigating the Social World: What Infants, Children and Other Species Can Teach Us. Oxford UP, Oxford (2013). doi:10.1093/acprof:oso/9780199890712.003.0023
12. Gergely, G., Egyed, K., Király, I.: On pedagogy. Develop. Sci. **10**(1), 139–146 (2007). doi:10.1111/j.1467-7687.2007.00576.x
13. Gergely, G.: Learning about versus learning from other minds: natural pedagogy and its implications. In: Carruthers, P., Laurence, S., Stich, S. (eds.) The Innate Mind: Foundations and the Future, vol. 3. Oxford UP, Oxford (2007)
14. Jacob, P., Gergely, G.: Reasoning about instrumental and communicative agency in human infancy. In: Benson, J., Xu, F., Kushnir, T. (eds.) Rational Constructivism in Cognitive Development, pp. 59–94. Elsevier Inc., Academic Press, Cambridge (2012)
15. Egyed, K., Király, I., Gergely, G.: Communicating shared knowledge in infancy. Psychol. Sci. **24**(7), 1348–1353 (2013). doi:10.1177/0956797612471952

16. Goldman, A.: Simulating Minds: The Philosophy, Psychology, and Neuroscience of Mindreading. Oxford UP, Oxford (2006). doi:10.1093/0195138929.001.0001
17. Meltzoff, A.N.: Imitation and other minds: the like-me hypothesis. In: Hurley, S., Chater, N. (eds.) Perspectives on Imitation: From Neuroscience to Social Science, pp. 55–77. MIT Press, Cambridge (2005)
18. Carruthers, P.: Opacity of Mind: An Integrative Theory of Self-Knowledge. Oxford UP, Oxford (2011)
19. Carruthers, P.: Mindreading in infancy. Mind Lang. **28**, 141–172 (2013). doi:10.1111/mila. 12014
20. Carey, S.: On the origin of causal understanding. In: Premack, A.J., Premack, D., Sperber, D. (eds.) Causal Cognition: A Multi Disciplinary Debate, pp. 268–308 Oxford, New York (1995)
21. Tirassa, M., Bosco, F.M., Colle, L.: Rethinking the ontogeny of mindreading. Conscious. Cogn. **15**, 197–217 (2006). doi:10.1016/j.concog.2005.06.005
22. Kovács, A.M.: Belief files in theory of mind reasoning. Rev. Philos. Psychol. **7**(2), 509–527 (2016). doi:10.1007/s13164-015-0236-5
23. Onishi, K.H., Baillargeon, R.: Do 15-month-old infants understand false beliefs? Science **308**, 255–258 (2005). doi:10.1126/science.1107621
24. Surian, L., Caldi, S., Sperber, D.: Attribution of beliefs by 13 month-old infants. Psychol. Sci. **18**, 550–586 (2007). doi:10.1111/j.1467-9280.2007.01943.x
25. Southgate, V., Senju, A., Csibra, G.: Action anticipation through attribution of false belief by 2-year-olds. Psychol. Sci. **18**, 587–592 (2007)
26. Kovács, A.M., Téglás, E., Endress, A.D.: The social sense: susceptibly to others' beliefs in human infants and adults. Science **330**, 1830–1834 (2010). doi:10.1126/science.1190792
27. Apperly, I., Butterfill, S.: Do humans have two systems to track beliefs and belief-like states? Psychol. Rev. **116**(4), 953–970 (2009). doi:10.1037/a0016923
28. Butterfill, S., Apperly, I.: How to construct a minimal theory of mind. Mind Lang. **28**, 606–637 (2013). doi:10.1111/mila.12036
29. Jacob, P.: Challenging the two-systems model of mindreading (in press). https://iscinauguration.sciencesconf.org/data/program/Re_sumePierreJacob_1.docx
30. Carruthers, P.: Two systems for mindreading? Rev. Philos. Psychol. **7**(1), 141–162 (2016). doi:10.1007/s13164-015-0259-y
31. Kampis, D., Somogyi, E., Itakura, S., Király, I.: Do infants bind mental states to agents? Cognition **129**, 232–240 (2013). doi:10.1016/j.cognition.2013.07.004
32. Luo, Y.: Do 10-month-old infants understand others' false beliefs? Cognition **121**(3), 289–298 (2011). doi:10.1016/j.cognition.2011.07.011

Towards Contextualizing Community Detection in Dynamic Social Networks

Wala Rebhi[1]([⊠]), Nesrine Ben Yahia[1], Narjès Bellamine Ben Saoud[1],
and Chihab Hanachi[2]

[1] RIADI Laboratory, National School of Computer Sciences,
University of Manouba, Manouba, Tunisia
Wala.rebhi@gmail.com, {Nesrine.benyahia,Narjes.Bellamine}@ensi.rnu.tn
[2] Institut de Recherche En Informatique de Toulouse (IRIT), Toulouse, France
Chihab.Hanachi@irit.fr

Abstract. With the growing number of users and the huge amount of information in dynamic social networks, contextualizing community detection has been a challenging task. Thus, modeling these social networks is a key issue for the process of contextualized community detection. In this work, we propose a temporal multiplex information graph-based model to represent dynamic social networks: we consider simultaneously the social network dynamicity, its structure (different social connections) and various members' profiles so as to calculate similarities between "nodes" in each specific context. Finally a comparative study on a real social network shows the efficiency of our approach and illustrates practical uses.

Keywords: Temporal multiplex information graph · Dynamic social networks · Contextualized community detection · Modularity · Inertia · Similarity

1 Introduction

With the widespread use of online social networks in recent years, a huge number of users have become highly dynamic and continually seeking for new collaborators to form communities [1]. Yet, contextualizing community detection has been a challenging task. In fact, using context to find relevant communities and highly-connected-modules is crucial and hard mainly with dynamic networks of context-dependent individuals.

Therefore, as dynamic social network is a complex system [2], modeling it is a key issue for the process of contextualized community detection. In this setting, most widespread community detection approaches consider the social network as a graph and then analyze its structure with graph properties and algorithms built around its structure [3]. Even more, in some very influential works in the literature such as [4], the terms "graph" and "network" are used interchangeably [5]. In fact, graph is a powerful mathematical abstraction for representing

© Springer International Publishing AG 2017
P. Brézillon et al. (Eds.): CONTEXT 2017, LNAI 10257, pp. 324–336, 2017.
DOI: 10.1007/978-3-319-57837-8_26

entities (i.e., actors in social network) and their relationships [6]. However, each proposed graph-based model until recently is used to detect community in social network taking into account just one aspect: either the network structure or the similarity between nodes or network dynamicity. Furthermore, none of these existing models is including social context in its community construction.

Thus, in this work we propose a temporal multiplex information graph-based model for contextualized community detection in dynamic social networks. This model considers simultaneously the social network dynamicity, its structure (different social connections) and various members' profiles so as to calculate similarities between "nodes" in each specific context. In addition, a combined metric is defined in order to find relevant communities in the proposed graph.

The outline of this paper is as follows: in Section two, we present the definition of dynamic social networks and their characteristics. In Section three, we present an overview of different graph-based models used to deal with community detection in social networks. Then, we propose our graph-based model designed to be better suited for representing social networks. Finally, we report on an experiment designed to test how well different graphs allow community detection in particular contexts.

2   Communities and Contexts in Dynamic Social Networks

Social network can be generally defined as a group of individuals who are connected by a set of relationships [7]. For example, we can consider a research laboratory, illustrated by Fig. 1, as a social network. Within this network, there are different types of relationships between researchers. Indeed, the same members can be connected by a co-publication relationship on DBLP[1], a friendship on Facebook[2], or a professional relationship on Linkedin[3]. In addition, each member has a specific profile describing him in each social network: DBLP profile, Facebook profile and Linkedin profile.

Furthermore, a key characteristic of social networks is their continual change [7]. Real-world social networks such as the research laboratory are not always static. New nodes or new links could appear (new researchers could join the laboratory), and existing nodes or existing links could disappear (former members may leave the laboratory) [8]. Thus, dynamic social network can be defined as a succession of static social networks [9].

Besides, a common feature of dynamic social networks is community structure [10]. However, defining a community is quite a challenging task [3]. The most commonly used definition is that of [11]: "network communities are groups of vertices within a network that have a high density of within-group connections but a lower density of between-group connection".

---

[1] http://dblp.uni-trier.de/.

[2] https://fr-fr.facebook.com/.

[3] https://www.linkedin.com/uas/login.

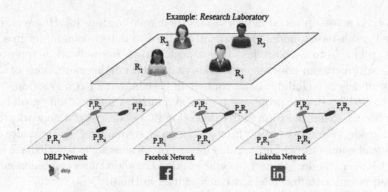

Fig. 1. Research laboratory as a social network

Despite its widespread use [3], this definition considers only the structural aspect of the community. This is why others community definitions based on vertex similarity are proposed. Indeed, [12] defines communities, calling them also clusters or modules, as groups of vertices that probably share common properties and/or play similar roles within the graph.

Inspired from these definitions, in this paper we propose to consider a community as a group of actors strongly connected and more weakly connected to the rest of the network and who have similar contexts. For example, spatial and temporal contexts can be treated to detect communities based on the availability of members.

As the notion of context is very large [13], several definitions of context have been proposed. From the diverse definitions of context, we adopt one of the most widely accepted and more formal [14] as proposed by [15]: "Context is any information that can be used to characterize the situation of an entity. An entity is a person, place, or object that is considered relevant to the interaction between a user and an application, including the user and applications themselves". In the case of community detection, a situation is defined as the image at a given time of the social network. Thus, community detection context is any information referring to this situation which is relevant to the community detection process. As illustrated in Fig. 2, and in order to design our community detection context model, we reuse the generic context model proposed by [14]. Therefore, we consider three context categories: Extrinsic Context, Interface Context and Intrinsic context. These correspond to the following interrelated elements in the triggering of the community detection process: the **who** question: user's profile attributes (Intrinsic Context) such as temporal context (time-bound), spatial context (related to the geographical location), emotional context (related to mood), user's activity, user's personality (collaboration degree), user's technical skills, or user's interests, etc., the **why** question: community detection need (Interface Context) and the **where** question: the environment itself (Extrinsic Context) [14].

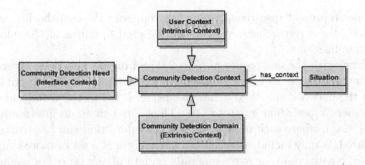

Fig. 2. Community detection context model

For example, a situation can be a member in the research laboratory who is seeking for collaborators to resolve a problem for a scientific research. For this situation, Table 1 shows different elements of community detection context.

Table 1. Community detection context example

Context categories	Information	Context element
Intrinsic context	Member in the research laboratory	User context
Interface context	Resolve a problem	Community detection need
Extrinsic context	Scientific research	Community detection domain

In the next section we will present a brief survey of graph-based models used for community detection in social networks.

3   Graph-Based Models for Community Detection in Social Networks

Community detection is presented by [16] as a partitioning networks technique into communities. In this context, a growing number of community detection methods have recently been published.

Most community detection algorithms lie in *monoplex graph* such as [11] and [17]. A monoplex graph, named also single layer graph [18], is defined as a tuple G = (V, E) where V is the set of vertices or nodes representing individuals and E is the set of edges that connect pairs of nodes. In Fig. 3(a), for example, we have represented a monoplex graph with four nodes and three edges (without specifying the weights). This may correspond to a portion of a research laboratory, where nodes represent researchers and edges represent the coauthoring relationships among these researchers. Weights can be used to represent the number of common publications.

However, with the emergence of Web 2.0 and digital networks, the concept of social networks has to be generalized to account for features describing the actors of the network and their relationships. This led to the definition of new concepts such *information graph* by [19]. Thus, [20] defines an information network as a graph where each node is described by data that can be structured or unstructured. It may include digital data in the form of a set or more commonly of a vector, textual data, or more generally of data of any type. For example, as showed in Fig. 3(b), a research laboratory can be considered as an information network where each researcher is described through a vector enumerating his name, his age and his job.

In some recent works of community detection, another issue arises around the *multiplexes graphs* in order to deal with the multiple aspects of relationships within social network. In this context, [21] defines a multiplex graph, named also multi-slice graph or multi-relational graph or multilayer graph [22], as a graph composed of a set of nodes of the same type, connected by different types of relations. Each layer contains the same set of nodes. But each layer corresponds to a different type of relationship. For example, as illustrated by Fig. 3(c), in the case of bibliographic networks, [23] defines it as a multiplex graph where nodes are authors and each layer corresponds to a different relationship: co-publication, co-citation, co-cited and co-participation in a conference.

All works cited above are interested in the community detection in static networks. However, real-world social networks are not always static. In this context, others graph-based models are proposed in order to consider social network dynamicity. For example, [24] and [9] consider that a *temporal graph* is a succession of static graphs (Fig. 3(d)), each of them representing the state of the complex network at a given time. As result, the temporal graph G on a set of snapshots $S = \{1, 2, \ldots, n\}$ is $G = \{G_1, G_2, \ldots, G_n\}$ with $G_i = (V_i; E_i)$ the snapshot i with nodes V_i and edges E_i.

Figure 3 shows an example of each type of graph.

Each graph-based model is used to detect community in social network taking into account just one aspect: either the network structure or the similarity between nodes or network dynamicity.

Thus, inspiring from these graph-based models and in order to contextualize community detection in dynamic social network, we need a new graph-based model which considers simultaneously the social network dynamicity, its structure (different social connections) and various members' profiles so as to calculate similarities between "nodes" in each specific context. This graph-based model will be described in the next section.

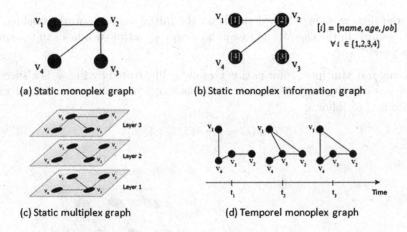

Fig. 3. Examples of graph-based models for community detection

4   Graph-Based Model for Contextualized Community Detection in Dynamic Social Networks

4.1   Temporal Multiplex Information Graph-Based Model Description

In this paper, our aim is to propose a graph-based model to represent dynamic social networks. This model aims to facilitate the contextualization of community detection within dynamic social networks.

Therefore, we propose firstly to reuse a *multiplex graph* in order to represent different types of relationships. Then, as community detection is contextualized, we propose to reuse *information graph*. In fact, due to this type of graph we can represent various members' profiles so as to calculate similarities between "nodes" in each specific context. Finally, to represent dynamicity, we propose simply to add a time parameter. Indeed, we consider a dynamic multiplex social network as a succession of *static multiplex social networks* (where at each time step considered we have a constant number of nodes and edges).

To present the proposed graph-model in a formal way, we use the following notations:

- TMIG : Temporal Multiplex Information Graph
- MIG_i : a static Multiplex Information Graph at time t_i
- $N^{(i)}$: the set of Nodes of MIG_i
- $E_j^{(i)}$: The set of edges of MIG_i which represents edges between nodes of MIG_i linked by the same type of relationship j
- $IG_j^{(i)}$: Monoplex Information Graph which represents the layer j of MIG_i
- $P_j^{(i)}$: the set of Nodes of $IG_j^{(i)}$
- t_i : time

– w : the time window which depends on the initial social network considered. For example in the case of the research laboratory a time window can be equal to a year.

The Temporal Multiplex Information Graph, as illustrated by Fig. 4, is a succession of static multiplex information networks. So, a possible mathematical way to write it is as follows:

$$TMIG = \bigcup_i (MIG_i, t_i). \tag{1}$$

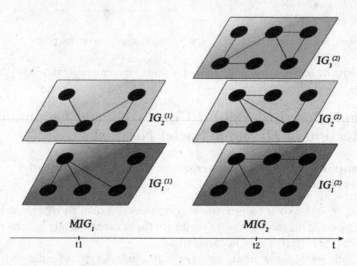

Fig. 4. Example of temporal multiplex information graph-based model

Each static Multiplex Information graph MIG_i at time t_i is characterized by a fixed number Nbr_i of nodes and a fixed number K_i of slices. Indeed, Nbr_i is the number of the social network members at time t_i; and K_i is the number of relationships types between them at time t_i.

$$MIG_i = \left\langle N^{(i)}, E_1^{(i)}, E_2^{(i)}, \ldots, E_{K_i}^{(i)} \right\rangle. \tag{2}$$

$$N^{(i)} = \left\langle N_1^{(i)}, N_2^{(i)}, N_3^{(i)}, \ldots, N_{Nbr_i}^{(i)} \right\rangle. \tag{3}$$

Each node $N_j^{(i)}$ is associated at the most K_i profiles $P_{j,l}^{(i)}$, $l \in \{1 \ldots K_i\}$ (we propose to use ontology to define and to model conceptually each user profile) and it is characterized by K_i weights $p_{j,l}^{(i)}(C)$, $l \in \{1 \ldots Ki\}$. Each weight depends on the community detection context denoted by C, and it represents similarities between profiles. If the node isn't associated at a profile (for example, if a member of the laboratory hasn't a Facebook account) its weight will be zero.

$$N_j^{(i)} = \left\{ (P_{j,l}^{(i)}, p_{j,l}^{(i)}(C)); l \in \{1 \ldots K_i\} \right\}; \forall j \in \{1 \ldots Nbr_i\}. \tag{4}$$

Each set of edges $E_j^{(i)}$ can be written as follows:

$$E_j^{(i)} = \left\{ (P_{x,j}^{(i)}, P_{y,j}^{(i)}, v_{x,y}^{(i,j)}); x, y \in \{1 \dots Nbr_i\} \right\}; \forall j \in \{1 \dots k_i\}. \tag{5}$$

$v_{x,y}^{(i,j)}$ is the weight of the edge between $P_{x,j}^{(i)}$ and $P_{y,j}^{(i)}$. This weight represents the structural similarity between the two nodes. For example, for a co-publishing relationship, structural similarity may be the number of published papers.

Each monoplex information graph $IG_j^{(i)}$, can be written in the form given by (6).

$$IG_j^{(i)} = \left\langle P_j^{(i)}, E_j^{(i)} \right\rangle. \tag{6}$$

With $P_j^{(i)}$ is:

$$P_j^{(i)} = \left\{ P_{l,j}^{(i)}; l \in \{1 \dots Nbr_i\} \right\}; \forall j \in \{1 \dots K_i\}. \tag{7}$$

4.2   Contextualized Community Detection Algorithm

In order to contextualize community detection at a given time t_i, we propose to define a new combined metric Q_{TMIG}. This metric given by (8) is a function of two parameters: the context noted C and the time t_i. Inspired from [25], the proposed metric Q_{TMIG} is based on a weighted combination of two components that must be maximized simultaneously:

$$Q_{TMIG}(C, t_i) = \alpha(C)M_{MIG_i}(C) + (1 - \alpha(C))I_{MIG_i}(C). \tag{8}$$

The first component concerns the degree of social interactions between individuals based on the assumption that people who frequently socialize (have interactions between them) are more likely to collaborate together. It relies on the structural quality, thus we propose to define a new contextualized modularity noted $M_{MIG_i}(C)$ and given by (9). This contextualized modularity is based on the modularity M of Newman for weighted graphs.

$$M_{MIG_i}(C) = \sum_{j=1}^{K_i} \beta_j(C)M_{IG_{i,j}}. \tag{9}$$

The second component concerns the attribute similarity. Thus, we propose to reuse the notion of inertia $I_{MIG_i}(C)$ [26]. Inertia is a metric that permits to measure the dispersion of a weighted cloud (a set of nodes where each node has a weight). In order to calculate this inertia, we propose to define for each node $N_l^{(i)}$ a global weight $p_l^{(i)}(C)$ as:

$$p_l^{(i)}(C) = \sum_{j=1}^{K_i} \gamma_j(C)p_{l,j}^{(i)}(C). \tag{10}$$

$\alpha(C)$ is a dynamic weighting factor where $0 < \alpha(C) < 1$ that can be changed. This factor is related to the community detection context C. If we want for example to obtain equitability between modularity proportion and inter-classes inertia proportion, we can set $\alpha(C)$ to 0.5.

The coefficients $\beta_j(C)$ and $\gamma_j(C)$ are related to the community detection context C too. And they must be chosen so that:

$$\sum_{j=1}^{K_i} \beta_j(C) = 1. \tag{11}$$

$$\sum_{j=1}^{K_i} \gamma_j(C) = 1. \tag{12}$$

Finally, in order to maximize this contextualized combined quality, which is a NP-hard (non-deterministic polynomialtime hard) optimization, we use a computational optimization technique (i.e. Particle Swarm Optimization) as proposed in the community detection approach of [25].

5   Experimentation: Research Laboratory Case Study

To experiment the temporal multiplex information graph-based model, we choose part of the computer sciences research laboratory RIADI[4] as a dynamic social network that contains 155 members. As the example in Sect. 2, we consider three relationships: co-publication relationship on DBLP(represented by 3582 edges), friendship on Facebook (represented by 1253 edges), and professional relationship on Linkedin (represented by 261 edges). Thus, this social network will be represented by the proposed temporal multiplex information graph-based model. Each node represents a researcher, and it is associated at three profiles: DBLP profile, Facebook profile and Linkedin profile. All these data are collected manually. Then, to calculate the weight of each node, we define two different situations:

Situation 1. The first situation is: a researcher has a problem in the Java development. He is looking for help to resolve his problem. For this situation, we will assign the context C1 : we choose to set $\beta_1(C1)$ to 0.5, $\beta_2(C1)$ to 0(as we will not consider Facebook Graph for professional problem), $\beta_3(C1)$ to 0.5, $\gamma_1(C1)$ to 0.5, $\gamma_2(C1)$ to 0 and $\gamma_3(C1)$ to 0.5. For similarities, we will consider only technical skills and the availability of each researcher (spatial and temporal context).

Situation 2. The second situation is: a researcher is looking for car sharing to go home. For this situation, we will assign the context C2 : we choose to set $\beta_1(C2)$ to 0.25, $\beta_2(C2)$ to 0.5, $\beta_3(C2)$ to 0.25, $\gamma_1(C2)$ to 0, $\gamma_2(C2)$ to 1 and $\gamma_3(C2)$ to 0. For similarities, we will consider the spatial context of the participants (current location) and home address.

---

[4] www.riadi.rnu.tn.

For the two contexts, we choose to set $\alpha(C)$ to 0.5 so as to obtain equitability between modularity proportion and inter-classes inertia proportion and we apply the contextualized community detection approach using this graph-based model in each specific context.

Then, in order to evaluate the proposed model, we propose to compare its results with the results of other graph-based models for community detection. Thus, we choose to represent the research laboratory as a monoplex graph (nodes represent researchers and edges represent collaborative relationship) in order to apply the well-known Louvain community algorithm proposed in [17].

Then, we represent the considered social network as a monoplex information graph (nodes represent researchers and each one has a weight which represents the similarity between this node profile and the problem holder profile; and edges represent collaborative relationship) in order to apply the combined community detection approach of [25]. Finally, the research laboratory is represented by a multiplex graph in order to apply the Generalized-modularity optimization approach of [27].

The comparison between these approaches, given in Table 2, is based on the detected community size, the number of jointly detected members in order to know if the model will take into account the context, and the modularity and the inter-classes inertia proportion of the detected community given separately in each context.

Table 2. Comparison between qualities of the detected community

Graph-based model type	Community detection algorithm	Detected community modularity M		Detected community Inertia I		Detected community Size S		Number of jointly detected member
		M(C1)	M(C2)	I(C1)	I(C2)	S(C1)	S(C2)	
Monoplex graph	Louvain algorithm [17]	0.15	0.10	0.41	0.20	11	11	11
Monoplex Information graph	Combined community detection algorithm [25]	0.19	0.14	0.86	0.56	33	33	33
Multiplex graph	Generalized modularity optimization [27]	0.22	0.19	0.65	0.48	18	18	18
Temporal multiplex information graph	Contextualized community detection algorithm	0.27	0.23	0.96	0.98	26	8	3

For the selected example and as illustrated by Table 2, using the temporal multiplex information graph-based model gives better results than the three other models. Indeed, the three models detect the same community in both cases (Context 1 and Context 2). However, thanks to the proposed graph-based model, it is possible to contextualize community detection in dynamic social network as we obtain different and better results for each specific context. These results may suggest that the monoplex graph and the monoplex information graph lead to a great loss of information about the heterogeneous nature of links in social network. For the multiplex graph model, it gives important results for modularity but it does not deal with similarities between users. Furthermore, none of these models take into account the community detection context.

At this stage of work, we just detect community at instant t_i. Nonetheless, the temporal aspect in this model will be used to study community resilience using its productivity and its maturity during the evolution of the social network.

6   Conclusion and Further Research

This paper has proposed a temporal multiplex information graph-based model for contextualized community detection in dynamic social networks. To do so, we have considered simultaneously the social network dynamicity, the network structure (different social connections) and various members' profiles so as to calculate similarities between "nodes" in each specific context. Then, to contextualize community detection, we have proposed a new combined metric adapted for multiplex graph which combines the network structure (social connections) and profiles homophily (similarities). Finally, we have tested the proposed graph-based model with other models. The experimentation showed that using temporal multiplex information graph-based model gives better results for contextualized community detection in dynamic social networks.

In future works, we aim to test the performance and the scalability of the proposed graph-based model for community detection in other contexts using real large-scale dynamic social networks or benchmarks.

References

1. Milioris, D.: Trend Detection and Information Propagation in Dynamic Social Networks. Doctoral dissertation, École Polytechnique (2015)
2. Barabâsi, A.L., Jeong, H., Néda, Z., Ravasz, E., Schubert, A., Vicsek, T.: Evolution of the social network of scientific collaborations. Phys. A: Stat. Mech. Appl. **311**(3), 590–614 (2002)
3. Plantié, M., Crampes, M.: Survey on social community detection. In: Ramzan, N., van Zwol, R., Lee, J.-S., Clüver, K., Hua, X.-S. (eds.) Social Media Retrieval, pp. 65–85. Springer, Heidelberg (2013)
4. Newman, M.E.J.: Networks: An Introduction, 1st edn. Oxford University Press, Oxford (2010)

5. Psorakis, I., Roberts, S.J., Rezek, I., Sheldon, B.C.: Inferring social network structure in ecological systems from spatio-temporal data streams. J. R. Soc. Interface **9**, 1–10 (2012). rsif2012022

6. Ford, D.A., Kaufman, J.H., Mesika, Y.: Modeling in space and time. In: Castillo-Chavez, C., Chen, H., Lober, W.B., Thurmond, M., Zeng, D. (eds.) Infectious Disease Informatics and Biosurveillance, vol. 27, pp. 191–206. Springer, Berlin (2011)

7. Xu, A., Zheng, X.: Dynamic social network analysis using latent space model and an integrated clustering algorithm. In: Eighth IEEE International Conference on Dependable, Autonomic and Secure Computing, DASC 2009, pp. 620–625. IEEE (2009)

8. Ngonmang, B., Viennet, E.: Dynamique des communautés par prédiction d'interactions dans les réseaux sociaux. EGC, 553–556 (2014)

9. Aynaud, T., Guillaume, J.-L.: Multi-step community detection and hierarchical time segmentation in evolving networks. In: Fifth SNA-KDD Workshop Social Network Mining and Analysis, in Conjunction with the 17th ACM SIGKDD International Conference on Knowledge Discovery and Data Mining, KDD (2011)

10. Lancichinetti, A., Fortunato, S., Kertész, J.: Detecting the overlapping and hierarchical community structure in complex networks. New J. Phys. **11**(3), 033015 (2009)

11. Girvan, M., Newman, M.E.J.: Community structure in social and biological networks. Proc. Nat. Acad. Sci. U.S.A. **99**(12), 7821–7826 (2002)

12. Fortunato, S.: Community detection in graphs. Phys. Rep. **486**(3–5), 103 (2009)

13. Zimmermann, A., Lorenz, A., Oppermann, R.: An operational definition of context. In: Kokinov, B., Richardson, D.C., Roth-Berghofer, T.R., Vieu, L. (eds.) CONTEXT 2007. LNCS (LNAI), vol. 4635, pp. 558–571. Springer, Heidelberg (2007). doi:10.1007/978-3-540-74255-5_42

14. Zainol, Z., Nakata, K.: Generic context ontology modelling: a review and framework. In: 2nd International Conference on Computer Technology and Development (ICCTD), pp. 126–130. IEEE (2010)

15. Dey, A.K.: Understanding and using context. Pers. Ubiquit. Comput. **5**(1), 4–7 (2001)

16. Newman, M.E.J., Girvan, M.: Finding and evaluating community structure in networks. J. Phys. Rev. **69**(2), 026113 (2004)

17. Blondel, V., Guillaume, J.-L., Lambiotte, R., Lefebvre, E.: Fast unfolding of communities in large networks. J. Stat. Mech.: Theory Exp. **2008**(10), P10008 (2008)

18. Kim, J., Lee, J.G.: Community detection in multi-layer graphs: a survey. ACM SIGMOD Rec. **44**(3), 37–48 (2015)

19. Moser, F., Ge, R., Ester, M.: Joint cluster analysis of attribute and relationship data without a-priori specification of the number of clusters. In: Dans Proceedings of the 13th ACM SIGKDD International Conference on Knowledge Discovery and Data Mining, pp. 510–519 (2007)

20. Combe, D.: Détection de communautés dans les réseaux d'information utilisant liens et attributs (2013)

21. Kanawati, R.: Détection de communautés dans les grands graphes d'interactions (multiplexes): état de l'art (2013)

22. Boccaletti, S., Bianconi, G., Criado, R., Del Genio, C.I., Gómez-Gardeñes, J., Romance, M., Sendiña-Nadal, I., Wang, Z., Zanin, M.: The structure and dynamics of multilayer networks. Phys. Rep. **544**(1), 1–122 (2014)

23. Kanawati, R.: Co-authorship link prediction in multiplex bibliographical networks. In: Multiplex Network Workshop - European Conference on Complex Systems (ECCS 2013) (2013)
24. Nguyen, N., Dinh, T., Xuan, Y., Thai, M.: Adaptive algorithms for detecting community structure in dynamic social networks. In: 2011 Proceedings of IEEE INFOCOM, pp. 2282–2290 (2011)
25. Ben Yahia, N., Bellamine, N., Ben Ghezala, H.: Community-based collaboration recommendation to support mixed decision making support. J. Decis. Syst. **23**(3), 350–371 (2014)
26. Lebart, L., Maurineau, A., Piron, M.: Traitement des données statistiques. Dunod, Paris (1982)
27. Mucha, P.J., Richardson, T., Macon, K., Porter, M.A., Onnela, J.P.: Community structure in time-dependent, multiscale, and multiplex networks. science **328**(5980), 876–878 (2010)

Influence of Lexical Markers on the Production of Contextual Factors Inducing Irony

Elora Rivière[✉] and Maud Champagne-Lavau

Aix Marseille Univ., CNRS, LPL, Aix-en-Provence, France
elora.riviere@lpl-aix.fr,
maud.champagne-lavau@univ-amu.fr

Abstract. Previous research has suggested that contextual factors are required to lead to an ironic interpretation of an utterance. The aim of the present study was to assess—in French—whether the presence of lexical markers influences the production of these contextual factors: allusion to a failed expectancy, negative attitude and presence of a victim.

1 Introduction

Previous research has suggested that contextual factors are required to lead to an ironic interpretation of an utterance. The highlighted contextual factors have been: the allusion to a failed expectancy, which is the fact to allude to a difference between previous expectations and the actual reality (Kumon-Nakamura et al. 1995; Utsumi 2000); view by others as the presence of an echo, the fact to mention a previous speech or events, thoughts, social norms or shared expectancies (Kreuz and Glucksberg 1989; Sperber and Wilson 1986). Another highlighted contextual factor is pragmatic insincerity, which is the violation of one or more felicity conditions in order to call the attention on the failed expectancy and express the speaker attitude towards this failure (Kumon-Nakamura et al. 1995; Utsumi 2000). The two last factors are the expression of negative attitude, which can be described as the indirect expression of negative feelings about the failure of the expectancy (Utsumi 2000) and specific to sarcasm, the presence of a victim (Utsumi 2000). The victim of irony is an identifiable person or group of persons targeted by a negative comment. Campbell and Katz (2012) were the first to experimentally test the necessity of these factors in the sarcastic interpretation of an utterance. They worked with the Constraints Satisfaction approach that allows the study of all these factors at the same time and the interaction between them. Indeed this approach suggests that the non-literal interpretation of an utterance would be preco-ciously accessible only if the context (i.e., contextual factors) promoting this inter-pretation is substantial enough. The Constraints Satisfaction approach supposes that the several factors (i.e., called constraints in this approach) give a probabilistic base for a competitive interpretation in parallel and throughout the time. Some constraints then may be more likely to play a role early in the understanding process while others would play a later role. Within this framework, Campbell and Katz (2012) reported that pragmatic insincerity is neither necessary nor sufficient, confirming the results of Colston (2000) about the non-necessity of the pragmatic insincerity. They also showed

© Springer International Publishing AG 2017
P. Brézillon et al. (Eds.): CONTEXT 2017, LNAI 10257, pp. 337–342, 2017.
DOI: 10.1007/978-3-319-57837-8_27

that none of these other contextual factors is necessary but each is sufficient in the comprehension of sarcasm.[1]

However Campbell and Katz (2012) did not manipulate features of the target utterances such as ironic markers or type of irony. There is a distinction between factors (i.e., constraints) and markers of irony. Indeed, factors have to be present for an utterance to be qualify as ironic, without their presence an utterance is no longer ironic (Attardo et al. 2003). On the other hand, ironic markers (e.g., lexical markers) are defined as meta-communicative clues, helping but non essential in the comprehension of irony (Attardo 2000). Burgers et al. (2012) showed that ironic markers such as lexical markers increase irony comprehension and reduce perceived complexity. In addition, the Implicit Display Theory (Utsumi 2000) suggests that for an utterance to be understood as ironic, this utterance has to be embedded in an ironic environment and it implicitly displays this ironic environment. The lexical markers may contribute to implicitly display the ironic environment. Thus the role of lexical marker in the comprehension of an utterance as ironic seems to be sizeable.

The aim of the present study was to assess—in French—whether the presence of lexical markers influences the production of constraints inducing irony. According to this short literature review, the constraints tested were allusion to a failed expectancy, negative attitude and presence of a victim.

Our hypothesis was that if lexical markers influence the production of the factors, then the production of these factors should be more important when the ironic target utterance includes a lexical marker.

2 Material and Method

2.1 Production Task

Twenty participants, 11 women and 9 men (mean age = 21.2 years ± 2.3; mean level of education = 15.1 years ± 2.0) were asked to complete 20 minimal contexts to induce an ironic interpretation of a target utterance (e.g., *What beautiful weather*) (Fig. 1).

Target utterances were manipulated according to the type of verbal irony: with a victim, directed against someone (e.g., *You are so fast*) versus about a situation (e.g., *What beautiful weather*) and according to the presence (e.g., ***What** beautiful weather*) vs. absence (e.g., *It is useful*) of a lexical marker leading to the 4 following conditions: irony with a victim and presence of a lexical marker; irony with a victim without the presence of a lexical marker; irony about situation with presence of a lexical marker; and irony about a situation without the presence of a lexical marker. There were five target utterances for each of the four conditions.

[1] Sarcasm is a variable of verbal irony (Colston 2000). Sarcasm is characterized by the factors characterizing verbal irony and added to them by the presence of a negative comment about an identifiable victim or a group of identifiable victims (Kumon-Nakamura et al. 1995).

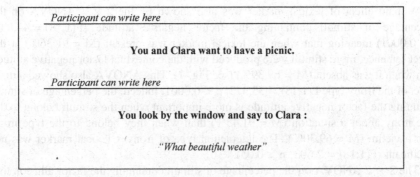

Participant can write here
_____

You and Clara want to have a picnic.

Participant can write here
_____

You look by the window and say to Clara :

"What beautiful weather"

Fig. 1. Example of minimal context and target utterance as presented to participants

2.2   Target Utterances Validation

Before the task of context production, the target utterances were validated by another group of participants containing 22 women and 22 men (mean age = 24.9 ± 2.4; mean level of education = 15.9 ± 1.4). The purpose of this validation, done on 35 utterances, was to select 20 utterances that can be' equally understood as sincere and as ironic to ensure that if a target utterance was judged as ironic after the step of context completion, it was due to the constraints added by the participants and not due to the target utterances themselves. To achieve this validation, the participants were asked to evaluate, on a seven points Likert scale, the use frequency of each utterance as sarcastic. The utterances that obtained a middle score between 2.5 and 4.5 were selected.

3   Results

The 400 contexts were produced and then judged as ironic or not. In a second step, the 300 stimuli recognized as ironic were analyzed for the presence of each contextual factor (i.e., allusion to a failed expectancy, negative attitude and presence of a victim). Two types of irony (with victim or about a situation) × 2 lexical markers (presence or absence) repeated-measure ANOVAs were performed on the percentage of stimuli containing each pragmatic constraint (presence of a victim, negative tension and allusion to a failed expectancy).

The 2 × 2 ANOVA on the percentage of stimuli containing the factor presence of a victim results showed a main effect of the lexical marker on the percentage of stimuli containing the contextual factor presence of a victim (F(1,18) = 12.426; p = 0.002) meaning that when the lexical marker was present (M = 41.83%), less stimuli were produced with the contextual factor presence of a victim than when it was absent (M = 53.03%). It also showed a main effect of the type of irony (F(1,18) = 253.349; p < 0.0001) meaning that the irony with a victim (M = 85.66%) contains a percentage more important of stimuli including this factor than irony about a situation (M = 9.20%). The interaction type of irony x lexical marker was no significant: F(1,18) = 3.906; p = 0.064.

A main effect of lexical marker was also shown by the 2×2 ANOVA on the percentage of stimuli containing the factor negative attitude ($F(1,18) = 44.032$; $p < 0.0001$) meaning that when the lexical marker was present ($M = 91.36\%$) in the target sentence, more stimuli were produced with the contextual factor negative attitude than when it was absent ($M = 69.39\%$) (see Fig. 2). This ANOVA also showed a main effect of the irony type $F(1,18) = 33.312$; $p < 0.0001$. Indeed, the percentage of stimuli including the factor negative attitude is more important when the stimuli belong to the type irony about a situation ($M = 91.45\%$) than when they belong to the type irony with a victim ($M = 69.30\%$). The interaction type of irony x lexical marker was not significant ($F(1,18) = 2.602$; $p > 0.05$).

The 2×2 ANOVA on the percentage of stimuli containing the factor allusion to a failed expectancy showed no significant effect of the lexical marker $F(1,18) = 3.588$; $p = 0.074$. It did not show any significant effect of the type of irony ($F(1,18) = 1.613$; $p > 0.05$). The interaction type of irony x lexical marker didn't reach significance: $F(1,18) = 1.124$; $p > 0.05$.

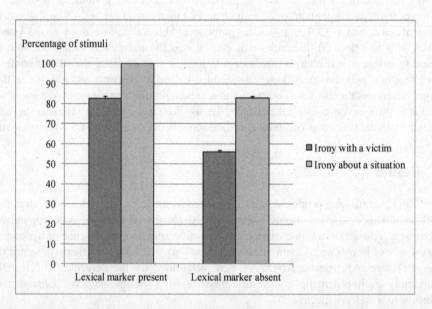

Fig. 2. Percentage of stimuli containing the factor negative attitude in function of the presence or absence of the lexical marker in the target utterances and of the type of irony.

4 Discussion

The results showed that the presence of a lexical marker in the target utterance influences the production of factors presence of a victim and negative attitude but does not influence the production of the factor allusion to a failed expectancy.

The fact that lexical markers are often hyperbolic and thus invite to an increase of the negative feeling most likely explains the results obtained for the factor negative attitude. Indeed our results showed that the factor negative attitude was more present when the ironic target utterance includes a lexical marker than when the lexical marker is absent of the target utterance. These results are in agreement with the Implicit Display Theory (Utsumi 2000). The linked made by Utsumi (2000) between negative attitude and the presence of lexical marker in the ironic target utterance can effectively be confirmed by our results.

By contrast, the pragmatic constraint presence of a victim was more present when the ironic target utterance did not include a lexical marker than when it included a lexical marker. There is no literature about the influence of lexical marker on the presence of a victim but maybe these results could be explained by the Constraints Satisfaction approach. Indeed, this approach considers that no constraint is necessary but that they are sufficient to reach a stable state, in this case the comprehension of the utterance as ironic or as sincere. Due to the influence of the presence of a lexical marker on the production of the factor negative attitude, this factor would be stronger and may play a precocious role. In consequence, the role played by the factor presence of a victim would be undermined in the presence of a lexical marker. More research should be necessary to confirm this hypothesis.

No effect of the lexical marker has been found on the factor allusion to a failed expectancy. These results could be explained by the fact that the constraint allusion to a failed expectancy is the most present constraint in the ironic utterances. It could be possible that its role in context to the comprehension of irony is so strong that its production is not influenced by linguistic constraint specific to the ironic target utterance. Allusion to failed expectancy (Kumon-Nakamura et al. 1995; Utsumi 2000), or view by others as the presence of an echo (Kreuz and Glucksberg 1989; Sperber and Wilson 1986), seems to be the constraint whose role, played in the comprehension of an utterance as ironic, makes the most consensus in the literature. The sizeable role of this factor is reflected by the authors' agreement and is probably the reason why the presence or absence of a lexical marker did not influence the production of this factor.

Our results seemed to show that the different features as factors and ironic markers as lexical markers play intermingled roles in irony processing.

As a conclusion, features of the ironic utterances such as the presence of a lexical marker could have an influence on the production of the factors present in the context and whose role is to induce an ironic interpretation of the utterance. Until now, the various features (i.e., factors and ironic markers as lexical markers) playing a role in irony processing have been studied separately but our results highlighted the need to study all types of features at the same time and in interactions. It will be very interesting, using the Satisfaction Constraint approach to evaluate the weight of each factor and to see if some ironic markers as the presence of a lexical marker have an influence on this weight. Moreover, the influence, on the production of factors, of other types of features such as the sociological ones, whose role on irony processing have been shown (Gibbs 2000; Ivanko et al. 2004) should also be taken into account.

References

Attardo, S.: Irony markers and functions: towards a goal-oriented theory of irony and its processing. Rask **12**, 3–20 (2000)

Attardo, S., Eisterhold, J., Hay, J., Poggi, I.: Multimodal markers of irony and sarcasm. Humor – Int. J. Humor Res. **16**(2), 243–260 (2003)

Burgers, C., van Mulken, M., Schellens, P.J.: Type of evaluation and marking of irony: the role of perceived complexity and comprehension. J. Pragmat. **44**(3), 231–242 (2012)

Campbell, J.D., Katz, A.N.: Are there necessary conditions for inducing a sense of sarcastic irony? Discourse Process. **49**(6), 459–480 (2012)

Colston, H.L.: On necessary conditions for verbal irony comprehension. Pragmat. Cogn. **8**, 277–324 (2000)

Gibbs Jr., R.W.: Irony in talk among friends. Metaphor Symbol **15**, 5–27 (2000)

Ivanko, S.L., Pexman, P.M., Olineck, K.M.: How sarcastic are you? Individual differences and verbal irony. J. Lang. Soc. Psychol. **23**(3), 244–271 (2004)

Kreuz, R.J., Glucksberg, S.: How to be sarcastic: the echoic reminder theory of verbal irony. J. Exp. Psychol. Gen. **118**(4), 374–386 (1989)

Kumon-Nakamura, S., Glucksberg, S., Brown, M.: How about another piece of pie: the allusional pretense theory of discourse irony. J. Exp. Psychol. Gen. **124**(1), 3–21 (1995)

Sperber, D., Wilson, D.: Relevance: Communication and Cognition (1986)

Utsumi, A.: Verbal irony as implicit display of ironic environment: distinguishing ironic utterances from nonirony. J. Pragmat. **32**, 1777–1806 (2000)

Context and Natural Language in Formal Concept Analysis

Tim Wray and Peter Eklund[(⊠)]

IT University of Copenhagen, Rued Langgaards Vej 7,
2300 Copenhagen S., Denmark
{tiwr,petw}@itu.dk

Abstract. COLLECTIONWEB is a framework that uses Formal Concept Analysis (FCA) to link contextually related objects within museum collections. These connections are used to drive a number of user interactions that are intended to promote exploration and discovery. The idea is based on museological perspectives that emphasise the importance of the human, social and cultural contexts that are associated with objects. This paper presents an application of these museological concepts as related to the principles of Formal Concept Analysis along with a description of how the COLLECTIONWEB framework generates narratives based on conceptual pathways. The framework has been applied to a number of user facing applications and provides insights on how FCA and natural language pipelines can be used to provide contextual, linked navigation within museum collections.

Keywords: Formal Concept Analysis · Museums · Context

1 Introduction

The trend of providing open, contextual access to online museum collections follows an ongoing movement from the 1980s known as the *New Museology* movement [1,5,7,11,12]. Given the museum's role in collecting, creating and shaping knowledge, the *context* of an object has become an increasingly important part of its analysis, interpretation and communication. In the 1990s, technologists realised the computational capability of digitised online museum collections in the ability to provide increased access to the collection and connect otherwise disparate objects together [10].

Within a museological setting, context can refer to an object's materials, construction, design, ornamentation, provenance, history, environment, connection to people and human society [5,6]. This focus towards context reflects a shift from a *classical* worldview, where objects were classed in terms of order, hierarchy and taxonomy, to a modern perspective where objects are analysed in terms of links to other objects, people, social and cultural histories [5]. Integral to the study of the artefact is its typological groupings among similar artefacts: for example, Pearce [6] describes how the process of contextualisation with other

© Springer International Publishing AG 2017
P. Brézillon et al. (Eds.): CONTEXT 2017, LNAI 10257, pp. 343–355, 2017.
DOI: 10.1007/978-3-319-57837-8_28

objects – such as comparing a newly acquired silver spoon to other spoons of similar material and construction, or a newly discovered portrait that shares similar lines and brush work with other portraits – remains fundamental to the process of dating, provenancing and interpretation. In recognition of this, Skov [11, p. 39] describes the following characteristics of museum collections:

– All artefacts, including copies or replicas of existing artefacts, are inherently unique. They are often described in relation to, or as influenced by, the collection.
– The human, social and cultural contexts of their artefacts are just as important, or more important, than the artefact itself [5].

These characteristics highlight the implicitly contextual nature of museum collections. COLLECTIONWEB is a framework that was developed to harvest existing museum meta-data in an attempt to provide contextual links among the objects and in doing so provide user experiences that promote user exploration and discovery. The framework consists of two parts: a Formal Concept Analysis-based engine that groups objects of similar characteristics and a natural language expression engine that provides *concept narratives* based on a series of similar – yet diverging – groups of objects. Formal Concept Analysis is closely tied to the philosophical logic of human thought – particularly in terms of how objects are grouped within a specific context or domain, such as a museum collection. Hence, the paper is structured as follows: in Sect. 2, we present an overview of Formal Concept Analysis, and in particular introduce the notions of *formal concepts* and *formal contexts* that respectively describe typological groups of objects and the collections that they occur in. In Sect. 3, a demonstration of how these constructs can be used to provide *natural language narratives* of linked objects is also demonstrated.

2   Formal Concept Analysis – Concepts and Context

Formal Concept Analysis is based on the cognitive constructs of *concepts* and *contexts* [14]. *Concepts* can be understood as basic units of thought formed by observations of existing phenomena "formed in dynamic processes within social and cultural environments" [13, p. 2]. According to this definition [13], a *concept* consists of a set of objects as its *extension*, and all attributes, properties and meanings that apply to those objects as its *intension*. As an example, if one considers the descriptor of "abstract paintings with geometric patterns" (its intension) and the actual 7 paintings that fit that description (its extension), then a concept is defined as the simultaneous perception of that intension and extension – i.e., the qualities of those paintings as *attributes* (or *formal attributes*) and the actual paintings as *objects* (or *formal objects*) defined by those attributes.

In Formal Concept Analysis, concepts are mathematized as *formal concepts* defined as a pair (G, M) with a set of objects G (its extension) and a set of attributes M that describe those objects (its intension). Within a museum collection, a formal concept (G, M) can be used to circumscribe a set of objects G

that possess attributes or meta-data M. For example, the following is a formal concept (A, B) that describes a set of works from an art collection, where A represents a set of titles of 3 works from the collection, and B represents a set of attributes that describe those works:

$A = \{$'Bush Rocks After the Rain', 'Solar Boat', 'Port Kembla Landscape'$\}$

$B = \{$'abstract', 'painting'$\}$

Formal Concept Analysis typically works within a *context* with a fixed set of attributes and objects. In this way, a context could be thought of as the entire set of objects within a museum data-set, and the meta-data and attribute values that apply to those objects. In FCA, the context is mathematized as a *formal context* as $K(G, M, I)$ where G and M respectively describe its set of objects and attributes and I describes the associations between them. Formally, each $g \in G$ is interpreted as an object of that context and each $m \in M$ is interpreted as an attribute of that context, and $I \subseteq G \times M$ is a binary relation where $(g, m) \in I$ is read "object g has attribute m" or gIm. Table 1 shows a formal context as a cross-table, with rows representing objects and columns representing attributes. The presence of $\times$ in row i and column j indicates that the object i has attribute j, or conversely that the attribute in j describes the object in i.

Table 1. The cross-table of formal context $K(G, M, I)$ containing information about the objects (G) and their attributes (M).

$K(G, M, I)$	Painting	Abstract	Coarse brush strokes	Geometric patterns	Print	Sculpture
Waiting, Port Kembla	$\times$		$\times$			
Bush Rocks after the Rain	$\times$	$\times$	$\times$			
Port Kembla Landscape	$\times$	$\times$		$\times$		
Large Jug		$\times$		$\times$	$\times$	
Gateway to Mt. Keira		$\times$		$\times$		$\times$
Solar Boat	$\times$	$\times$	$\times$	$\times$		

For a formal concept (A, B), A' is the set of attributes common to all objects in A, and B' is the set of objects common to all attributes in B. Hence, a formal concept (A, B) of context $K(G, M, I)$ is a pair where $A \subseteq G$, $B \subseteq M$, $A' = B$, $B' = A$, where A is its *concept extent* (or just *extent*) and B is its *concept intent* (or just *intent*). As such, a formal concept of a formal context can be formed by taking an attribute and collecting all objects that it describes, and then again collecting all common attributes shared by those objects. The construction of formal concepts in this manner provides an inferencing mechanism, as one could assert that "attribute m implies attribute n".

Using the context in Table 1 as an example, let m be attribute 'coarse brush strokes' and C be the objects described by m:

$C = \{$'Bush Rocks After the Rain', 'Waiting, Port Kembla', 'Solar Boat'$\}$

Now let D be the attributes common to C:

$D = \{$'painting', 'coarse brush strokes'$\}$

This forms the formal concept (C, D) from the objects described by $m = \{$'coarse brush strokes'$\}$, induces the additional attribute $n = \{$'painting'$\}$. Via this process, one could assert that "all works with coarse brush strokes are paintings":

$C = \{$'Bush Rocks After the Rain', 'Waiting, Port Kembla', 'Solar Boat'$\}$

$D = \{$'painting', 'coarse brush strokes'$\}$

2.1   Concept Ordering and Similarity

Formal concepts of a context have an ordering, where formal concepts can be more specific or general than other formal concepts. A formal concept (A_1, B_1) is more specific than another concept (A_2, B_2) if the objects of the first formal concept are a sub-set of the second formal concept, and the attributes of the first formal concept are a super-set of the second formal concept. Hence, an order relation over formal concepts can be defined as:

$$(A_1, B_1) \leq (A_2, B_2) \iff A_1 \subseteq A_2$$

which is equivalent to:

$$(A_1, B_1) \leq (A_2, B_2) \iff B_1 \supseteq B_2$$

For example, as a comparison to the previous formal concept (C, D) consider the following formal concept (E, F):

$$E = \{$$'Bush Rocks After the Rain', 'Solar Boat'$$\}$$

$$F = \{$$'painting', 'abstract', 'coarse brush strokes'$$\}$$

Given that $E \subset C$ and $F \supset D$, $(E, F) < (C, D)$ – i.e., formal concept (E, F) represents a more 'specific' concept than formal concept (C, D). Likewise, (E, F) is a subconcept of (C, D), and (C, D) is a superconcept of (E, F).

Formal concepts do not necessarily group objects into exclusive categories, and any formal concept can contain objects from another formal concept. Dually, any objects, or group of objects represented by a formal concept can share attributes from other formal concepts. For example, within the context of the collection, the formal concept (C, D) shares objects 'Bush Rocks after the Rain' and 'Solar Boat' and the attribute 'painting' with (A, B). To this end, the two concepts (A, B) and (C, D) are different formal concepts, but share a degree of *concept similarity* [9], a metric used within the COLLECTIONWEB framework to rank similarity and relevance among formal concepts within the context of a museum collection.

3   Natural Language Narratives

CollectionWeb uses Formal Concept Analysis to provide interfaces and Web Services for importing, extracting and navigating museum collection metadata in natural language. It also provides the ability to generate structures of conceptually linked content expressed as a series of natural language *concept narratives*. These structures are used are used to provide the navigation and interface for the *Brooklyn Museum Canvas* (Fig. 1) – a data visualisation that allows users to navigate and explore collection of conceptually related content via artist, theme and visual imagery.

The framework interfaces with existing museum databases to provide a *formal context* based on a selected and configured set of data-fields from the museum's data store. As an example, consider the following object record that shows the metadata associated with a work by photographer Consuelo Kanaga shown in Fig. 2.

```
{
  "id": "157697",
  "title": "[Untitled] (Mother with Children, New York)",
  "objectDate": "1922-1924",
  "objectDateBegin": "1922",
  "objectDateEnd": "1924",
  "medium": "Gelatin silver photograph (from glass plate negative)",
  "description": "Portrait-group Condition: good",
  "attributeIDs": [8, 10, 107, 333, 974, 2808, ... ]
}
```

The attribute identifiers from the `attributeIDs` field can be dereferenced to yield the following values:

20th century	children
American	photograph
child	New York
1920s	mother
mother and child	Consuelo Kanaga
melancholy	poverty

As described in Sect. 2, a single *formal concept* can be formed from an object and its attributes. The attribute values can be used to describe the object in natural language:

An object associated with 20th Century, American, children, 1920s, photograph, New York, mother, Consuelo Kanaga, melancholy, poverty, mother and child

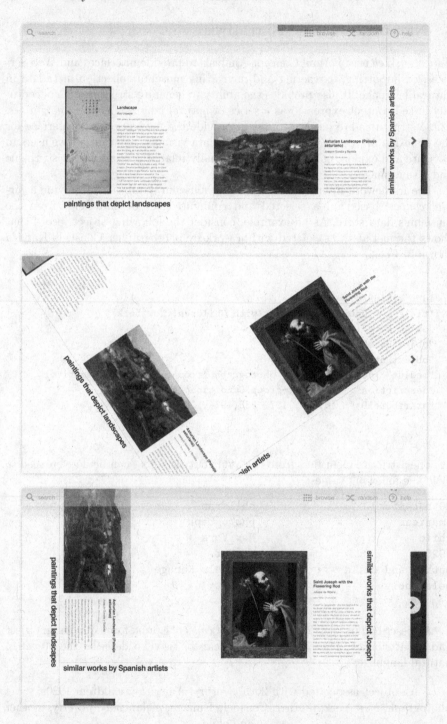

Fig. 1. The *Brooklyn Museum Canvas* uses *concept narratives* to link pathways of conceptually related objects from the Brooklyn Museum's online collection.

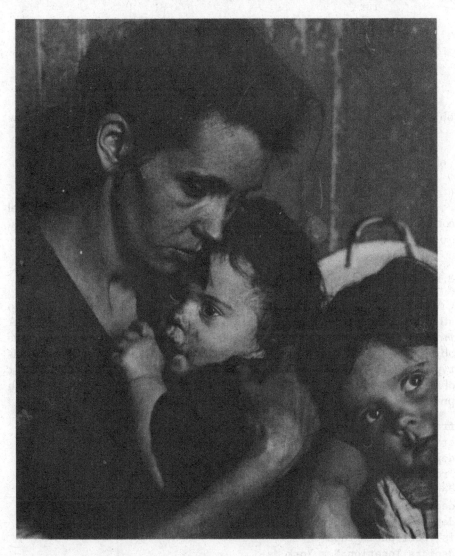

Fig. 2. *Untitled (Mother with Children, New York)* by American photographer Consuelo Kanaga, the image associated with a single record from the Brooklyn Museum's online collection.

Given that the object concept does not exist in isolation, but in fact exists within a *formal context*, COLLECTIONWEB uses Formal Concept Analysis to compute similar [9] and neighbouring [2] formal concepts. These formal concepts contain objects from the collection that are conceptually related to *Untitled (Mother with Children, New York)*:

objects associated with 20th century, 1920s, photograph, mother objects associated with 20th century, American, child, 1920s, children, photograph, Consuelo Kanaga

objects associated with 20th century, American, child, children, 1920s, photograph, New York, Consuelo Kanaga, melancholy, poverty

objects associated with 20th century, American, child, 1920s, photograph, New York, Consuelo Kanaga, melancholy, poverty

objects associated with 20th century, American, child, children, photograph, Consuelo Kanaga, mother and child

These natural language statements only list the attribute values of the formal concept. While accurate in their descriptions, they offer relatively little expression in terms of how the objects are grouped and related to one another.

3.1 Predicates and Parsers

COLLECTIONWEB uses *predicates* to add an additional semantic layer to attributes and *parsers* to express these semantics in natural language. A *predicate* is a qualifier that characterises how the attribute is related to the object. For example, the work in Fig. 2 is byArtist:Consuelo Kanaga and is typeOf:photograph that depicts:location:New York. The following is a list of all attributes of the *Untitled* work by Consuelo Kanaga, as supplemented with predicates:

```
fromTimePeriod:20th century
artistNationality:American
depicts:person-subject:child
fromTimePeriod:1920s
depicts:person-subject:mother and child
depicts:emotional-subject:melancholy
depicts:person-subject:children
isTypeOf:photograph
depicts:location:New York
depicts:person-subject:mother
byArtist:Consuelo Kanaga
depicts:emotional-subject:poverty
```

Predicates exist independently of attributes: an attribute may be assigned to one predicate but a predicate may be assigned to multiple attributes. COLLECTIONWEB does not map explicit relationships between predicates, nor does it allow more than one predicate to be assigned to a single attribute instance. In such cases, if a single attribute is assigned to the same object, but with two different predicates – for example, an object may be associatedWithAgent:Consuelo Kanaga and/or created byArtist:Consuelo Kanaga – COLLECTIONWEB treats both occurrences as two separate attributes, each being potentially assignable to the object.

Predicates can be used to determine how an attribute – or set of attributes – share a common root predicate. For example, the following attributes:

```
fromTimePeriod:20th century
fromTimePeriod:1920s
fromTimePeriod:1930s
fromTimePeriod:1940s
```

If assigned as attributes to a formal concept, will produce a formal concept with the following natural language expression:

works from the 1920s to the 1940s

This is because the above attributes were assigned to the fromTimePeriod predicate, one of COLLECTIONWEB's built-in predicates that can be used to express common metadata fields found within museum collections. Each built-in *predicate* is linked to a *parser*. The *predicate* describes the semantic relationship between an object and an attribute and contains simple natural language processing rules and templates, whereas its *parser* contains *procedural* functionality on how a certain class of attributes should be mined from its free text field and subsequently expressed in natural language.

The COLLECTIONWEB framework contains several built-in predicates – each with their own *parser* – that allow natural language extraction and expression of common metadata found in museum collections – date ranges, artwork series, mediums, keywords and titles. The parsers use the Illinois Part of Speech Tagger[1] [8] to recognise nouns and noun phrases, and the Stanford Named-Entity Recogniser[2] [4] to identify people, places and organisations. Predicates and parsers can be used to build complete natural language descriptions of any formal concept. They are designed to be customised and configurable to work with any museum collection either by using the existing built-in predicates or by creating custom predicates. COLLECTIONWEB uses a *predicate map*, which is a two-dimensional array of predicates where each predicate describes a natural language phrase fragment, such as made with steel and wood or depicts farmhouses and animals. The predicate map can be used to:

- Map associations between NL phrase fragments and predicates that in turn map to the metadata fields within the museum collection.
- Describe the order that phrase fragments occur, and prioritize which fragments should be displayed at a given position within the phrase.
- Describe, in a declarative manner, how each phrase fragment is displayed for a given set of attribute values.

---

[1] http://cogcomp.cs.illinois.edu/page/download_view/POS.
[2] http://nlp.stanford.edu/software/CRF-NER.shtml.

Figure 3 shows how a predicate map generates the natural language phrase *photographs by Consuelo Kanaga from the 1920s made with gelatin silver that depict poverty in New York* from the attributes of its formal concept. The predicate map is shown in the centre of the figure, where the horizontal ordering of its columns corresponds with the ordering of the phrase fragments within the natural language statement, and the ordering of each row item corresponds to the priority of predicates displayed. For example, as the first column lists the predicates is and isTypeOf, COLLECTIONWEB will first search for any attributes within the formal concept with the predicate is, and if it finds none, it then searches for any attributes with the predicate isTypeOf. The algorithm then produces a phrase fragment for the attribute isTypeOf:photograph using the isTypeOf predicate, which then forms the first part of the phrase.

The algorithm then moves to the second column as it searches for any attributes with the byArtist predicate. As there is such an attribute present – byArtist:Consuelo Kanaga – it renders its phrase fragment and subsequently ignores any attributes with the artistNationality or fromLocation predicates. Such ordering could be used to denote an implicit hierarchy of concepts as expressed in natural language without producing excessively long natural language descriptions. As an example, if the attribute byArtist:Consuelo Kanaga and depicts:emotional-subject:poverty were to be 'removed' from the concept by means of navigating to its upper neighbour, the generated natural language statement would instead read as *photographs by American artists from the 1920s made with gelatin silver that depict New York.*

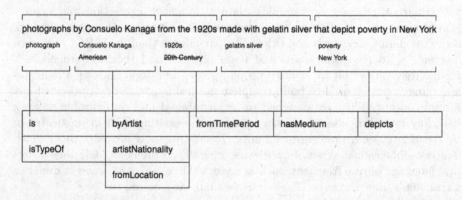

Source Attributes

isTypeOf:photograph   fromTimePeriod:20th century
byArtist:Consuelo Kanaga   hasMedium:gelatin silver
artistNationality:American   depicts:location:New York
fromTimePeriod:1920s   depicts:emotional-subject:poverty

Fig. 3. An example of how a formal concept can be expressed in natural language from its source attributes using a predicate map.

The predicates `is`, `isTypeOf`, `fromTimePeriod` and `depicts` are built in to the COLLECTIONWEB framework, each with a *parser* that dictates how a phrase fragment should be expressed for a given set of attribute values. However, the predicates `byArtist`, `artistNationality`, `fromLocation` and `hasMedium` are not built-in – instead, they are provided in this example as custom predicates. Custom predicates can be defined to express any metadata field on an object within a museum collection. They use an additional field that dictates how that predicate is displayed as a phrase fragment, prepending any necessary prepositions, suffixes or prefixes so that its attribute values are inserted into the phrase. For example, the custom predicate `hasMedium` uses `made with {attribute}` so that the attribute `hasMaterial:gelatin silver` appears as `made with gelatin silver`. Likewise, custom predicate `artistNationality` uses `by {attribute} artists` so that attribute `artistNationality:American` appears as `by American artists`.

Using predicates and parsers – including some that are already built into the framework – the following example shows the list of concepts that are similar to Kanaga's *Untitled* work, but with the natural language expression rules applied:

other photographs from the 1920s that depict mothers

other photographs by Consuelo Kanaga from the 1920s that depict children

other photographs by Consuelo Kanaga from the 20th century that depict mothers and children in poverty and melancholy

other photographs by Consuelo Kanaga from the 1920s that depict children in poverty and melancholy in New York

other photographs by Consuelo Kanaga from the 20th century that depict children

...

The above listing shows concepts that appear more nuanced and expressive than a list of attribute values. In this case, these concepts – as related to Kanaga's *Untitled* work in Fig. 2 – link to other works that depict mothers, children and poverty from a similar time period.

Formal concepts are inherently spatial and relational. As generated from a formal context, formal concepts can be related to one another in terms of their ordering or similarity. In addition to describing concepts individually, *Collection-Web* also expresses *relations* between two formal concepts in natural language. Expressing the conceptual relationships among formal concepts – as well as their content – allows *CollectionWeb* to describe not only concepts or groups of objects in their isolation, but also describe a chain of concepts as they would appear as part of user's navigation pathway as they would navigate among and across formal concepts.

In the following example, each label represents the generated natural language fragment from the attributes of a formal concept: each one having a super-set of objects and a subset of attributes than the formal concept that proceeds it. COLLECTIONWEB uses attributes and predicates to describe, in natural language, how each formal concept is related to the one before it. This allows the creation of a *concept narrative*, as demonstrated as follows:

photographs by Consuelo Kanaga from the 1920s

⇓

more photographs by American artists from the 20th century

⇓

other works by American artists from the 20th century

The above *concept narrative* follows a generalisation trajectory, as it begins with a specific formal concept and moves to more, general formal concepts. *Concept narratives* can also be used to describe a series of formal concepts that are presented based on their *concept similarity* – i.e., each concept may be related to one another in terms of sharing common attributes or objects, but may not be more specific or more general than the one that proceeds it:

photographs by Consuelo Kanaga that depict poverty

⇓

similar photographs that depict mothers in melancholy

⇓

more works by Consuelo Kanaga that also depict mothers

These *concept narratives* are used to generate a tree like structure of intercon-nected pathways as demonstrated within the *Brooklyn Museum Canvas* (Fig. 1) visualisation – its primary interface element is a single, contiguous, linked path-way structure that highlights the connections that objects have with one another and allow users to visualise their navigation history through works related by artist, theme and visual imagery.

4   Conclusion

In this paper, we have shown how an effective and simple ontology of predicates can be organised into a predicate map with accompanying parsers to generate rich and contextual natural language descriptions of formal concepts. It fol-lows the design goal of a more narrative-like expression of the rich connections that objects have with one another within museum collections. The techniques described have been used in several museum-based system described in *Virtual Museum of the Pacific* [3], the *Brooklyn Museum Canvas* [15] and the *A Place for Art* [16] iPad app. The innovation here is the application of natural language processing to formal concept analysis, in particular the systematic treatment of formal concepts as natural language fragments.

References

1. Anderson, G.: Reinventing the Museum: Historical and Contemporary Perspectives on the Paradigm Shift. Rowman Altamira, Lanham (2004)
2. Carpineto, C., Romano, G.: Concept Data Analysis: Theory and Applications. Wiley, Hoboken (2004)
3. Eklund, P., Goodall, P., Wray, T.: Cluster-based navigation for a virtual museum. In: 9th RIAO Conference - Adaptivity, Personalization and Fusion - of Heterogeneous Information. ACM Press, Paris, April 2010
4. Finkel, J., Grenager, T., Manning, C.: Incorporating non-local information into information extraction systems by Gibbs sampling. In: Proceedings of the 43rd Annual Meeting of the Association for Computational Linguistics (ACL 2005), pp. 363–370 (2005)
5. Hooper-Greenhill, E.: Museums and the Shaping of Knowledge. Routledge, Abingdon (1992)
6. Pearce, S.: Thinking about things. In: Pearce, S. (ed.) Interpreting Objects and Collections. Routledge, London (1994)
7. Ross, M.: Interpreting the new museology. Mus. Soc. **2**(2), 84–103 (2004)
8. Roth, D., Zelenko, D.: Part of speech tagging using a network of linear separators. In: Proceedings of the 17th International Conference on Computational Linguistics, pp. 1136–1142 (1998)
9. Saquer, J., Deogun, J.: Concept aproximations based on rough sets and similarity measures. Int. J. Appl. Math. Comput. Sci. **11**, 655–674 (2001)
10. Schweibenz, W.: The "Virtual Museum": new perspectives for museums to present objects and information using the internet as a knowledge base and communication system. In: Zimmermann, H., Schramm, B. (eds.) Knowledge Management und Kommunikationssysteme, Workflow Management, Multimedia, Knowledge Transfer. Proceedings des 6. Internationalen Symposiums für Informationswissenschaft (ISI 1998), pp. 3–7 (1998)
11. Skov, M.: The reinvented museum: exploring information seeking behaviour in a digital museum context. Ph.D. thesis, Royal School of Library and Information Science (2009)
12. Styliani, S., Fotis, L., Kostas, K., Petros, P.: Virtual museums, a survey and some issues for consideration. J. Cult. Herit. **10**(4), 520–528 (2009). http://linkinghub.elsevier.com/retrieve/pii/S1296207409000880
13. Wille, R.: Formal concept analysis as mathematical theory of concepts and concept hierarchies. In: Ganter, B., Stumme, G., Wille, R. (eds.) Formal Concept Analysis. LNCS (LNAI), vol. 3626, pp. 1–33. Springer, Heidelberg (2005). doi:10.1007/11528784_1
14. Wille, R., Ganter, B.: Formal Concept Analysis: Mathematical Foundations. Springer, Berlin (1999)
15. Wray, T., Eklund, P.: Concepts and collections: a case study using objects from the brooklyn museum. In: Predoiu, L., Hennicke, S., Nurnberger, A., Mitschick, A., Ross, S. (eds.) Proceedings of the 1st International Workshop on Semantic Digital Archives, pp. 109–120 (2011)
16. Wray, T., Eklund, P., Kautz, K.: Pathways through information landscapes: alternative design criteria for digital art collections. In: ICIS 2013 Proceedings, Milan, Italy (2013)

Context Awareness

Context-Aware User Interfaces for Intelligent Emergency Applications

Feras A. Batarseh[1(✉)] and Jash Pithadia[2]

[1] College of Science, George Mason University, Fairfax, VA 22030, USA
fbatarse@gmu.edu
[2] Department of Computer Science, George Mason University,
Fairfax, VA 22030, USA
jpithadi@gmu.edu

Abstract. The importance of context in many recent software engineering research studies has been rising significantly. Injecting context awareness into software systems has facilitated multiple facets of modelling, increasing user satisfaction, and increased the level of User Interface (UI) intelligence. Context has been a major part of traditional Artificial Intelligence (AI), lately however, it is being deployed to a wider spectrum of research topics such as human cognition, the internet of things, software usability and many others. In this paper, a new context-aware method for emergency applications is introduced. An emergency is a situation that poses an immediate risk to life, health, property or environment. There is an obvious gap in applying context to such critical cases; this paper shows that context awareness in user interfaces can play an important role with notifications and improving human reactions during such unfortunate and unforeseen incidents. The proposed method is evaluated through live emergency drills and simulations, the experimental results are presented.

Keywords: Context awareness · Emergency applications · Mobile apps · User interfaces design and development

1 Introduction and State-of-the-Art

For Artificial Intelligence (AI) to reach its intended goals, it must be studied from both the theoretical and practical perspectives. It is believed [1–5] that context applications are able to amplify the *goodness* of AI. Such applications are gateways to reducing challenges and fears of machines intelligence. The main goal of this paper is to demonstrate that by injecting context into software, it can eventually save lives. Also, the work presented shows that context is needed in cases where human beings lose some percentage of their good judgement skills under pressure.

1.1 The Importance of Emergency Notifications

Emergencies are faced by every living being on the planet. While there are many **reactive** notification systems available [5–9], no proactive and personalized emergency notification system is found. Very few systems (that report suspicious activities) are

© Springer International Publishing AG 2017
P. Brézillon et al. (Eds.): CONTEXT 2017, LNAI 10257, pp. 359–369, 2017.
DOI: 10.1007/978-3-319-57837-8_29

obtainable for first responders, let alone for normal citizens. A real-time notification system can be a way of alerting or notifying people about a current emergency. Alerting people during an emergency is very crucial. People have the right to know what is happening in their surroundings, simply because they will be able to take a decision that might save their lives. There are several different kinds of emergencies such as: medical issues, natural disaster, and robbery/theft. Such emergencies can take place in different environments; at home, in public, at college, isolated locations, and many other places [8, 9]. In many countries, help during emergencies is provided solely by the police, fire service or medical service. That is not sufficient though, there is a need for a system which could is more intelligent and swift.

The context-aware system should include the following features: firstly, providing real-time notification to the public based on their demographics and location. Secondly, receiving emergency updates about surroundings. Thirdly, providing the user with first responders contact information based on their demographics and location. Using location information for cases where for example a person is in need of blood, nearby users in radius can help based on their blood-type and location. Fourthly, communication with the outside world is very important during emergencies, therefore, the system should be used to communicate with the public and provide services via audio, text messages and potentially video. People with disabilities such as the hearing and visually impaired should also be taken into consideration and the system needs to be customized to cater to all their needs in cases of emergency. Citizens should be provided with notifications of situational knowledge during emergency and activities around the neighborhood. In terms of context awareness, there are two major parts: The *user's context*, and the *environment/emergency's context*. The work in this paper is concerned with one environment: **a university campus,** therefore, the majority of focus is on the context of the user. We aim to explore to many other environments and emergencies as part of future work.

1.2   State-of-the-Art in Emergency Notification Systems

During an emergency, the most important things humans need are: getting the fastest help possible, notifying friends and family, getting help from first responders, and receiving knowledge of the emergency's status. Most persons call 911 during an emergency and over 70% of such calls come from mobile phones. This introduces an important question: how can a mobile device be used to notify people during an emergency? Some suggest using *push notification* and intelligent UIs. After performing a search on Google Play [10] or Apple's App Store [10] for the word "Emergency", search results are mostly for emergency games or other non-relevant apps. Therefore, most users still call 911 for emergency because they have few other choices. The national emergency system's average response time is 10 min or more [6, 7, 11]. That is deemed to be too long, given that-for example- every two seconds someone in the U.S. needs blood [12]. Unfortunately, very few methods besides calling the cops (police) are available to humans these days; other prominent existing tools include: **1. Code-Red:** Sends user alerts which are initially authorized by public safety officials. These alerts are then sent to users based on their location. The types of alerts sent by Code-Red are mostly weather emergencies, community emergencies and not personal or relevant emergencies. However, if public safety in a particular area is not subscribed to Code-Red, that location will not receive any alerts [11]. **2. American Red Cross:** There are several apps provided by the Red Cross, for example, one for tornado and another for earthquake emergencies, these applications provide alerts and user can let others know they are safe by sending their location (similar to Facebook's mark your safety feature, *which only helps the safe!* [5, 7, 8]). However, as it is evident, the Red Cross is very specific to certain types of emergencies, and not all [12]. **3. ICE Standard ER with Smart911™:** ICE Standard ER is an app available on the Apple store. It provides functions such as emergency data for health information and medical contacts. It provides information automatically to 911 operators via Smart911 [13]. **4. Smart911:** When a user calls 911, the 911 respondent and the first responders both will know the exact location of the person under emergency. The user can also add house information, medical history, and vehicle information. All this data will be available to Police and Emergency Medical Services. However, again, this is merely a 911 service, and it is also reactive and not proactive [14].

NENA (National Emergency Number Association) published a study showing that in the US, each year, there are approximately 240 million calls made to 911; which congests the system all the time [15] (remember that the population of the US in 2017 is about 320 million). Moreover, 70% or more of the calls are made using wireless devices. When a user dials 911 on their cell phone or wireless device, the Public Safety Answering Point (PSPA) is responsible for routing calls during emergencies, this system has been known to be very slow, centralized and had no improvements done to it in a very long time [7–9, 15]. We strongly believe that the PSAP system needs to notify the users in areas undergoing emergencies using the GPS location service and by making people in a certain physical radius aware of a situation.

Depending on the location, time, and nature of the emergency, a large variety of limitations could present themselves when it comes to communicating details of an emergency and that can influence actions taken to protect life and property. For example, an audio public address system might be rendered ineffective if the emergency happens to be a terrorist attack. The broadcast would disregard most or all of those who have a hearing impairment (would also cause panic). Another common example might be the limitation of a fire alarm's siren component in a school that has deaf students. Emergency examples can vary, their contexts are different, and so the mentioned list of existing systems is not sufficient. For instance, observe these three examples, and how different emergencies can be: **Example 1:** There is a chemical spill in an area and a user reports the spill to PSPA. People around the radius need to be notified. **Example 2:** A child is lost at an event. The image is sent to all the people in nearby radius which will speed up the process. And after the child is found all the users are notified of the outcome. **Example 3:** There is a sexual harassment case on campus and the university police needs to be notified and students needs to protect themselves.

Not only those three cases are distinct, but who reacts to them, the type of victim, the type of attacker, and many other aspects are different. Therefore, a generic, intelligent and *context-aware* system is required. One thing though that most emergencies share is using cell phones to react to them. It seems to be the first thing that anyone does in an emergency is using their cellphone. Even using the cell phone in a centralized system may lead to overloading of public services (such as cellular phone networks). That can result in the delay of vital SMS messages. An effective emergency communication system should arguably be able to overcome as many of these potential limitations as possible. The next section discusses emergency systems on university campuses around the US.

1.3   Current University Notification Systems

Major public universities in the US have a big number of students, for example George Mason University has over 30,000 students; the University of Central Florida has over 50,000 students and so on (not considering faculty and staff). Therefore, university campuses are easy targets for criminals, sexual abusers, thieves, and other types of offenders. Most universities are open to the public, and so although security is most times enforced, it is very important to use technology and intelligent software to maximize security and safety. University emergency notification systems are no different. The major issues that a university emergency system might face include: 1. Bulk on-campus messages cannot be sent during emergencies due to network traffic, downtime or a system crash. 2. Users having received notification for an emergency are unlikely to maintain normal usage patterns. In particular, users are likely to attempt to contact their friends and/or family soon after learning about such conditions and lead to a bit of chaos on campus (2006 Virginia Tech massacre where 32 individuals were killed) [16]. 3. Cellular networks are increasingly becoming the primary means of communication during emergencies. Riding the widely held perception that text messaging is a reliable method of rapidly distributing messages, a large number of colleges, universities, and municipalities have spent tens of millions of dollars to deploy third-party cellular systems (although they have so many limitations). 4. TAM (Technology Acceptance Model) posits that technology usage is determined by a person's behavioral intentions, so while being flooded by the crime alert emails, students either consciously or unconsciously are trying to avoid getting another alert service from the university, (Northern Illinois University shooting incident). Most systems don't allow the users to provide feedback and push data upstream, whilst all systems push data downstream towards the users, and leave them with no answers if they have questions. In the method presented in this paper, *context allows for upstream and downstream messages and notifications.*

Therefore, and based on the listed discussion points, in this paper, the following hypothesis is being studied: **IF** *users have access to a Context-Aware User Interfaces for Intelligent Emergency Applications,* **THEN** *that would reduce the response time and increase on-campus safety.* The following sections aim to answer the mentioned limitations and test the hypothesis.

2   Context-Aware Emergency Application (CEA)

This section introduces the main contribution of this paper, the context aware notification emergency system and its associated university mobile app.

2.1   The CEA Method

The amount of time spent trying to remember important contact information during an emergency situation is time that can be saved and spent reacting to the situation. To be able to deal with the situation however, it is important to understand its context. This section introduces the Context-driven Emergency Application (CEA) method. In CEA, context is based on the following six main pillars: **1. Emergency Situation, 2. Personality Type, 3. Age, 4. Gender, 5. Language, and 6. Role at the University (staff, faculty, student residing at dorms, non-resident).**

To identify these contextual pillars, and as the user starts using the emergency system, they need to enter data and answer a number of questions. The questions in the app will be based on the personality divisions of the Myers-Briggs type indication. The Myers-Briggs type indicator is used to 'know' whom the user is and what aspects identify their personality, and based on that the app may be able to provide an interface with which he/she may interact with in a user friendly way. Different personality types and age groups have varied reactions to the same situation, hence it becomes a necessity to accurately gauge how the user will react to a wide variety of situations. Once the personality type is determined, the second part of the questioning will be for collecting ethnographic data (Age, Gender, Language and Role at the university). Every country has a different culture along with specific rules and limitations that people within that culture generally abide to. Once the ethnographic observations are collected (including languages), they will be used to determine how the user will react to a given emergency situation with context to the culture he/she belongs to. When an emergency occurs, the user's preferred language is used to minimize any translation or comprehension delays. The user's role at the university is also important in how they would react to an emergency, for example, a student residing at the dorms might run to the dorms in case of a theft or a shooting rampage, however the non-resident student would want to run to their car or out of campus. All of the mentioned items will be used to present the best possible interface to the user during an emergency. The flexibility of the interface is constituted in the following technologies: 1. The application reorders the user entered emergency contacts information to best suit the user's need according to the emergency status, current geographic location, and the 6 context elements. 2. The application changes colors based on the time of the day (brighter colors at night). 3. The application updates the language based on the users' preference 4. The application allows for upstreaming and down-streaming of media with a single click. 5. The application modifies the font sizes based on the age of the user. The experimental work illustrates detailed examples of the changes in context that CEA manages. Please refer to Fig. 1 for a visual of the CEA method. All of the mentioned settings could be modified and the user has full control over how the UI would look in case of emergency. The application provides the user with two modes: Normal Mode and Emergency Mode, they can different or they can be setup to be the same, which is the user's choice. In any case, the CEA process is the core of the emergency app; that is presented next.

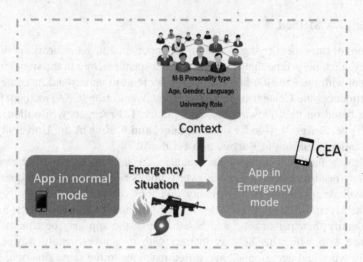

Fig. 1. The CEA method

2.2 The CEA Process

The steps of Context-aware emergency method are discussed next. This algorithm is built into the CEA mobile app that is presented as well. CEA's 6 step algorithm includes: 1. The user installs the app and enters their personal information; (manual). 2. The CEA app evaluates the MB personality group of the user; (manual). 3. The app defines the 'normal mode', and instantly creates the app with the colors, shapes, roles and language preferences; (automatic). 4. The app defines 'after hours' mode, and sets up colors and brightness based on the time of the day; (automatic). 5. While the app is running, it is creating the version of the app in 'emergency mode'; (automatic). 6. In case of an emergency, using the 6 context aspects, the app switches to the emergency mode; (automatic but initiated by the user's entering the nature of the emergency with one click). Emergencies are suggested in the app based on the time of day. As it is evident in the steps, only the first two steps are performed by the user manually. Figure 2 below illustrates the first two manual steps inside the CEA app.

All other four automated steps are done in the background through the code. The next section focuses on step 6 (*during an emergency*) and the different ways that the app may look in different contexts for different users.

3 Experimental Evaluation of CEA

The experiments include two main parts: 1. Present a study with comparisons to existing emergency systems. That includes user feedback and a detailed electronic survey that was answered by more than 40 users (mostly students). 2. A simulation of an emergency use case; results are shown based on 6 types of users.

Fig. 2. The CEA app (context collection phase)

3.1 Experimental Study #1: CEA vs. Existing Apps and Services

A survey was conducted across campus to evaluate the quality of the existing university system vs. CEA. An electronic survey was created with these questions: 1. Do you use the university emergency app? 2. Rate the university app from 1–10. 3. Do you use any emergency application? 4. If yes to Q3, then name the emergency app. 5. Would you feel safer if you have a personalized emergency app? 6. What are the features/improvements that you would like to see in the new app?

Questions 4 and 5 are deemed to be the most important questions, simply because the main goal of this research is to increase safety. However, before introducing the results, it is important to discuss the existing university system. The current system is not only found at our university (GMU), it was found that many other universities provide the same quality app as our university, no app was found that is intelligent or context-aware. The existing app merely lists numbers that are randomly considered to be the most important ones. The user is required to call the appropriate number during emergencies. The most common survey answers to what the student would do because they don't like the existing app are: *no action* or *call 911*. It is very unsafe to call 911 with all emergency situations. 911 can't help with all events on campus, calling them would lead to wasting valuable time. Additionally, most students answered with a Not Applicable (NA), which means that they wouldn't know what to do. The current app has non-emergency information, which is a waste of crucial screen real estate that could be used for other more important functions. The results of the survey are show in Fig. 3. Only **15%** of students use the existing emergency app, **5%** use another emergency apps, and **92.5%** of users would like a personalized smart app. Additionally, in the survey, the students provided some feedback on their preferences on what needs to be in the contextual app, here are some example responses: 1. "Tracking the

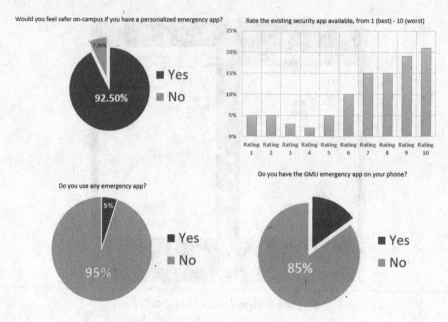

Fig. 3. Experimental results for study #1 of CEA

GPS Location of the incident and forward to other people for help/immediate action/sharing information". 2. "App that works when the network is weak". 3. "An app which can have a community of people who can connect and help the person in emergency". 4. "One click implementation". 5. "Location services to be enabled in the app". 6. "Report incident to support media exchange". All of these features are included in the CEA system. It can be deduced from the results of experimental study 1 above that students are reluctant to use emergency apps because there is a lack of user interaction, usability and also lack in functionalities like reporting incidences, sharing location with friends and family, and emergency notifications based on location. Additionally, they would like a personalized app as they think that will increase their safety, but will it? That is evaluated in the next experimental section. In the next section, use cases for different test subjects are deployed in a live experiment and simulations to evaluate the value of CEA's contextual model.

3.2 Experimental Study #2: The CEA Live Study

The CEA app starts with default settings, for example, a default color: blue. Blue is artistically associated with truth and clarity - making it acceptable to most age groups and genders. However, a big percentage of female students said purple was their favorite color (0% of men said purple was their favorite color). Moreover, CEA uses icons for young adults and larger textual icons for older adults.

Additionally, users feel more confident when reading a text message in their native language during an emergency situation. CEA has multiple built-in languages.

As for the Myers Briggs personality types. For example, the user can be either a **Perceiver** or a **Judger**. Perceivers like to keep their options open and they are playful and casual. They have difficulty in making decisions and like to keep their plans flexible. Judgers take responsibilities seriously and they like to stick with plans; they like rules and pay attention to time. We provide Judgers with a more structured format for the app, and allow the CEA algorithm to be more 'dynamic' if the user is a Perceiver. This experiment **was performed during a serious traffic jam on campus, and also through a simulated snow storm**, with the following 6 test subjects using the app: **Tester 1**: Male, Student, 18 years, Working, Residing off campus. **Tester 2**: Female, Student, 20 years, Residing at dorm (sends emergency notification to fellow neighbors in dorm, and suggest hiding in certain places). **Tester 3** Female, International Student, 22 years. **Tester 4** Female, 50 years, Non-resident, Working on campus. **Tester 5** Male, 70 years, not working on campus. **Tester 6** Male, 40 years, Faculty. In case of an emergency during/before/after class, faculty members can send notification to students in that class regarding the emergency. Like in a case of a snowstorm, students are unaware if the college is operational or if classes are cancelled. The college officials usually send email notification to students, but students prefer to check with their professor. The snow storm drill and live traffic jam were executed for a sufficient amount of time, and the 6 users used their apps for emergency functions, screen shots

Fig. 4. Experimental results for the live study #2 of CEA

were captured during the experiment. The results of CEA in the app are shown in Fig. 4. When the traffic jam occurred, a report incident feature shows, as it is displayed in **part b** of Fig. 4.

Additionally, when it is a snow storm, the environmental office was listed first on top before anything else, along with facilities management (for quicker access). The user just clicks on the name and it connects them to the desired party. In snow storms, students probably care less about sexual assault and they want access to a phone number in case they got stuck in snow (now they just call 911, which is absurd, but with CEA they get the environmental office or facilities management). That is shown in **part a** (Fig. 4). Our test subject #3 doesn't prefer to use English in case of emergency. Rather, the student wants to use her native language, and that is shown in her app when the emergency occurred in **part d**. **Part c** illustrates a color change for male users (test subjects #1, 5 and 6). **Part e** of Fig. 4 is shown for test subject #2, a female (purple) that lives in the dorm and needs to hide in case of emergency. Females can see the option for calling the university police and the sexual assault officers much higher than males in the list of numbers. **Part f** of Fig. 4 is for test subject #6, the professor. The professor is a male that gets access to the university police, and also can send messages and share notifications with his students easily. This (upstream) feature is more readily available for professors and staff than the students. This experiment is deemed a successful one due to the successful nature of the outcomes of the CEA app interface.

4 Conclusions and Future Work

This paper introduces a context-based method that aims to increase safety and provide intelligent procedures during emergencies. The 6-steps method is called CEA. No existing system is as intelligent and proactive as CEA. CEA was developed into a mobile app, and distributed to students at George Mason University for testing and evaluation. The results were very positive, especially given the current state of the art in emergency apps. A survey was conducted and the students are very anxious to see an updated app that is personalized and context-aware. The CEA app was tested with 6 different types of users, and yielded big differences in the interface based on the personality, role, age, gender, nationality, and the nature of the emergency (simulated during a snow storm and also tested during an unusual traffic incident on campus).

Our future work includes (but not limited to) the following next steps: 1. Test the CEA app with more users, more simulations and emergency incidents. 2. Evaluate other types of systems and emergency apps – compare them to CEA. 3. Perform a deeper study of context in emergencies from a wider point of view, such as: creating more contextual models, introduce more environment factors into the model, and perform extra evaluations. 4. Start distributing the system on campus through the university store to officially endorse it as the main emergency app on campus. This way more feedback will be received; more analytics will be collected to evaluate and improve the app. 5. More aspects will be included to help identify what is included in context (such as body types, degree, and major/minor). Additionally, explore other existing emergency studies [17, 18]. 6. Communicate with other universities and make the app readily available for them as well. 7. Expand the idea to more work places outside universities, such as hospitals, companies and other public places. 8. Lastly, provide video recording for upstream and downstream, and not be limited to messages & texts. For AI and context to reach their intended goals and widespread usage, they need to be deployed for righteous causes. We believe that nothing is more important than the safety of innocent individuals; therefore, we hope that this field can be used for the general good of humans (through applications such as the one presented in this paper). If our contextual system will one day be able to save one life; that will be the ultimate success milestone that we aim to accomplish.

References

1. Batarseh, F.A., Gonzalez, A.J., Knauf, R.: Context-assisted test cases reduction for cloud validation. In: Brézillon, P., Blackburn, P., Dapoigny, R. (eds.) CONTEXT 2013. LNCS (LNAI), vol. 8175, pp. 288–301. Springer, Heidelberg (2013). doi:10.1007/978-3-642-40972-1_22
2. Brézillon, P.: Context in problem solving: a survey. Knowl. Eng. Rev. **14**(1), 1–34 (1999)
3. Brézillon, P.: Modeling and using context: past, present and future. Rapport de Recherche du LIP6 2002/010, Université Paris 6, France (2002)
4. Batarseh, F.A.: Incremental Lifecycle Validation of Knowledge-Based Systems through CommonKADS, A Doctoral Dissertation published at the University of Central Florida, May 2011
5. Brézillon, P., Gonzalez, A.J.: Context in Computing: A Cross Disciplinary Approach for Modelling the Real World. Springer, Heidelberg (2014). ISBN 978-1-4939-1886-7
6. Ogata, K., Ifukube, T.: Effects of communication on continued use of an emergency notification system. In: World Automation Congress (WAC), Mexico, pp. 1–5 (2012)
7. Beltran, J., Leon, M., Martınez A., Hipolito, J.: Health emergency event notification system, towards to the seamless service mobility. In: IEEE 3rd International Conference on Serious Games and Applications for Health (SeGAH), Brazil, pp. 1–7 (2014)
8. Ada, S., Sharman, R., Han, W., Brennan, J.: Factors impacting the intention to use emergency notification services in campus emergencies: an empirical investigation. IEEE's Trans. Prof. Commun. **59**(2), 89–109 (2016)
9. Loreti, P., Mazzenga, F., Giuliano, R.: Proximity emergency wireless networks: the PEN for CEC EU Project. Euro Med Telco Conference (EMTC), Italy, pp. 1–6 (2014)
10. Apple & Google Stores. https://itunes.apple.com/ and https://play.google.come/
11. EC Network. http://ecnetwork.com/community-notification/
12. The Red Cross Web. http://www.redcrossblood.org/learn-about-blood/
13. ICE Standard Tech. http://www.icestandardtech.com/smart911
14. Smart 911 Software. https://www.smart911.com/
15. National Emergency Number Association, Web. https://www.nena.org/
16. Kaminskia, R., Koons-Witta, B., Thompsonb, N., Weiss, D.: The impacts of the Virginia Tech and Northern Illinois University shootings on fear of crime on campus. Elsevier's J. Crim. Justice **38**(1), 88–98 (2010)
17. Diniz, V., et al.: Decision Making Support in Emergency Response. Encyclopedia Decis. Making Decis. Support Technol. **1**, 184–191 (2008)
18. Canós, J.H., Penadés, M.C., Solís, C., Borges, M., Llavador, M.: Using spatial hypertext to visualize composite knowledge in emergency responses. In: Proceedings of the 7th International Conference on Information Systems for Crisis Response and Management (ISCRAM 2010), Seattle, USA, May 2010

Unified Modeling of Quality of Context and Quality of Situation for Context-Aware Applications in the Internet of Things

Sophie Chabridon[1]([✉]), Amel Bouzeghoub[1], Anis Ahmed-Nacer[1],
Pierrick Marie[2], and Thierry Desprats[2]

[1] SAMOVAR, Télécom SudParis, CNRS Université Paris-Saclay, Évry, France
Sophie.Chabridon@telecom-sudparis.eu
[2] Université of Toulouse, IRIT UMR 5505, Toulouse, France

Abstract. This paper discusses the requirements of situation identification in the Internet of Things and the necessity to consider the quality of the input context data during the inference process for deriving a situation and evaluating its resulting quality. We propose to extend previous works by integrating the QoCIM meta-model within the muSIC framework dedicated to situation identification. Situation identification is derived using an ontological approach and Quality criteria are aggregated using the fuzzy Choquet operator for computing the quality of a situation. This paper shows that QoCIM allows to model quality of context (QoC) as well as quality of situation in a unified approach.

1 Introduction

Multiple and heterogeneous sources of information such as open data, social networks, clouds, wireless sensor networks, and the Internet of the Things are now able to provide context data and contribute to the development of new mobile and context-aware applications. However, context data are known to be inherently uncertain [7] and an evaluation of their quality is essential in order to take relevant decisions based on these context data. We distinguish context data from context information in that raw data are unprocessed and retrieved directly from a data source, such as a sensor, and context information is obtained by processing raw context data.

The IoT is characterized by the extreme heterogeneity and large quantity of objects it can interconnect, as well as the spontaneous nature of their interactions. To deal with the enormous amount of context data collected from the IoT, new solutions are thus necessary to add value to these context data and identify contextual situations of high level of abstraction relevant to the applications. This paper focuses on solutions for measuring the quality of the identified situation resulting from the analysis and agregation of multiple context data of diverse quality. Quality of context (QoC) must therefore be integrated during the whole processing chain from the acquisition of raw context data to the identification of high level context situation.

© Springer International Publishing AG 2017
P. Brézillon et al. (Eds.): CONTEXT 2017, LNAI 10257, pp. 370–374, 2017.
DOI: 10.1007/978-3-319-57837-8_30

2 Related Works

Situation identification calls for reasoning techniques for deriving high level and meaningful information from raw context data. Moreover, one way to integrate quality in the reasoning process is to use methods to aggregate the various quality indicators attached as meta-data to context data, as can be done with QoCIM [9], into a unique indicator measuring the quality of the identified situation. We review below, firstly, some reasoning techniques and, secondly, aggregation techniques and discuss their relevancy to the case of the IoT where a high amount of data come from heterogeneous and dynamic context sources.

[11] classifies context reasoning techniques into six broad categories, namely supervised learning, unsupervised learning, rules, fuzzy logic, ontological reasoning and probabilistic reasoning.

This analysis shows that for the IoT, the most promising methods are fuzzy logic and ontological reasoning. Fuzzy logic enables approximate reasoning using confidence values representing degrees of membership to a given interval. Truth values may be defined in natural language allowing to deal with uncertainty. Ontological reasoning is based on description logic and is supported by semantic web languages such as RDF or OWL. Ontologies allow complex reasoning and can manipulate both numerical and textual data.

For aggregating multiple QoC criteria, constraints are given by the IoT. Weights may be attributed to QoC criteria but cannot be static and should be determined dynamically as runtime conditions change. Context data as well as QoC criteria are heterogeneous and cannot be restricted in type. Additionally, aggregation should consider QoC criteria of various types to be aggregated in a new criteria of potentially a different type. Therefore a generic solution is required to aggregate primitive criteria into a composite criterion deduced in an automatic manner. Classical linear combination operators are limited to static weights. Fuzzy operators such as OWA (Ordered Weighted Averaging) are more promising. OWA allows to select the criteria to be aggregated and cannot represent any interaction among criteria. The Choquet integral [4] can be seen as a generalization of OWA and can be used in cases [5] where dependencies exist among criteria as it gives a weight to each criterion as well as to the series of values of the alternative combining the remaining criteria.

3 Integrating QoC in the Process of Situation Identification

We present in this section how we take into account QoC in the reasoning process for identifying situations. QoC is modeled using the QoCIM meta-model [9], and situation identification is performed by the muSIC framework.

3.1 QoCIM: A Meta-Model for Managing Quality of Context

Context data are known to be inherently uncertain due to the imperfection of physical sensors and the difficulty to model the real world [1,7]. Therefore, taking into account the knowledge of the quality of context (QoC) [3] becomes essential for the system to suggest relevant decisions to applications. Several works have proposed their own vision of QoC with a list of criteria. We have proposed the Quality of Context Information Model (QoCIM) [9] in an effort to leverage previous works addressing QoC in order to represent any QoC criterion and indicator. It results from an analysis of context-aware management systems proposed over the last 15 years [8] as well as the QoC criteria proposed in the literature. This study enabled us to identify relevant design elements and the required properties of the solution: (1) Expressivity to manipulate context information according to its QoC level. (2) Genericity to ensure interoperability of QoC metadata exchanged among all the entities of the context manager. (3) Calculability to allow information sources to evaluate the quality of the context information they produce and consumer entities to interpret or transform the QoC values they receive. QoCIM[1] allows to manipulate any type of QoC criterion during context lifecycle and comes with a tool suite for generating Java source code for manipulating QoC and a library of computing functions such as aggregation, inference, filtering, etc. [10].

3.2   muSIC: Detecting Situations of Interest

With the increasing amount of context data available in the IoT, detecting situations of interest in pervasive systems is a crucial feature. This helps such systems to focus on meaningful situations in which relevant actions should be performed. In the INCOME project, we combined an Ontological Context Manager (OCM) with an Adaptive Multi-Agent System (AMAS) for providing the muSIC (multi-scale Situation Identification from Context) framework for an adaptive solution for situation identification [6]. The OCM module enables to represent a situation with an ontology and a set of static rules. It receives raw context data and derives context information of a higher abstraction level. The AMAS module then analyses these abstracted context data relying on agents that consider rules provided by OCM in order to identify situation types at runtime.

We define a situation as "a set of semantic relations between concepts (in one context dimension or between several context dimensions) which are valid and stable during an interval of time", where the term dimension means a context type such as location, time, activity, etc. [2]. This definition distinguishes context and situation. In a situation, meanings are assigned to context data, a set of sensor data may be considered as a context dimension, and temporal aspects are involved. A *situation* is represented by all the numerical or semantical values of the characteristics of a set of information. A *situation type* is a semantic value (modelled as a string) that can be associated with several situations. A situation type is defined by a set of conditions. Each condition relates to the possible values of a characteristic of a data (but a situation type does not have necessarily a condition for every characteristic). For example, the situation type "AtWork" is

---

[1] https://fusionforge.int-evry.fr/www/qocim/.

associated with the situations: "I am at Lab on monday at 8:05 AM", "I am at Lab on monday at 9:38 AM", etc.

3.3 Contribution

Figure 1 illustrates the integration of muSIC and QoCIM within a Distributed Context Manager. MuDEBS[2] and muContext[3] constitute the core of the Distributed Context Manager developed in the INCOME project. Based on these frameworks, QoCIM is able to qualify both context data acquired from context producers and high level context information delivered to end-user applications through meta-data.

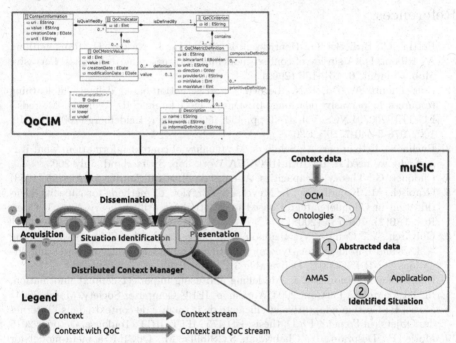

Fig. 1. QoCIM integration with muSIC

MuSIC is deployed within software entities that consume and produce qualified context information. The purpose of these entities is to identify qualified situations based on context data as described in Sect. 3.2. The qualified situations are then used by end-user applications to offer more advanced services and suggest different recommendations. To identify high level situations, the muSIC process is divided into two steps. OCM first extracts abstracted data from qualified context information coming from the acquisition layer of the Distributed Context Manager. An AMAS then derives qualified high level situations for

---

[2] https://fusionforge.int-evry.fr/www/mudebs/.

[3] https://fusionforge.int-evry.fr/www/mucontext/.

end-users applications. The situations are finally delivered in the presentation layer of the Distributed Context Manager.

The abstraction level of the criteria used to qualify context data and situations follows the abstraction level of the information. As a consequence, low level criteria, "precision", "accuracy", "freshness" for example, are associated to context data while high level criteria, for example "trustworthiness", are used to qualify identified situations. As discussed in Sect. 2, a Choquet fuzzy operator is relevant for aggregating multiple quality criteria of different types and has been implemented. In our solution, all of these criteria are modelled and manipulated using the computing operators provided by the QoCIM framework.

References

1. Bettini, C., Brdiczka, O., Henricksen, K., Indulska, J., Nicklas, D., Ranganathan, A., Riboni, D.: A survey of context modelling and reasoning techniques. Pervasive Mob. Comput. **6**, 161–180 (2009)
2. Bouzeghoub, A., Do, K.N., Lecocq, C.: A situation-based delivery of learning resources in pervasive learning. In: Duval, E., Klamma, R., Wolpers, M. (eds.) EC-TEL 2007. LNCS, vol. 4753, pp. 450–456. Springer, Heidelberg (2007). doi:10.1007/978-3-540-75195-3_36
3. Buchholz, T., Kupper, A., Schiffers, M.: Quality of context information: what it is and why we need it. In: 10th HPOVUA Workshop, Switzerland, July 2003
4. Choquet, G.: Theory of capacities. Annales de l'Institut Fourier **5**, 131–295 (1953)
5. Grabisch, M., Kojadinovic, I., Meyer, P.: A review of methods for capacity identification in Choquet integral based multi-attribute utility theory. Eur. J. Oper. Res. **186**(2), 766–785 (2008)
6. Guivarch, V., Camps, V., Péninou, A., Bouzeghoub, A.: Software integrating AMAS and ontologies for dynamic identification and learning of contextual situations. ANR INCOME, Deliverable 3.2, July 2015
7. Henricksen, K., Indulska, J.: Modelling and using imperfect context information. In: 1st CoMoRea PerCom 2004 Workshop. IEEE Computer Society, March 2004
8. Marie, P.: Gestion adaptative et efficiente de la qualité de contexte dans l'Internet des Objets (in French). Ph.D. thesis, ED 475 MITT, IRIT, Toulouse, October 2015
9. Marie, P., Desprats, T., Chabridon, S., Sibilla, M.: QoCIM: a meta-model for quality of context. In: Brézillon, P., Blackburn, P., Dapoigny, R. (eds.) CONTEXT 2013. LNCS (LNAI), vol. 8175, pp. 302–315. Springer, Heidelberg (2013). doi:10.1007/978-3-642-40972-1_23
10. Marie, P., Desprats, T., Chabridon, S., Sibilla, M., Taconet, C.: From ambient sensing to IoT-based context computing: an open framework for end to end QoC management. Sensors **15**(6), 14180–14206 (2015)
11. Perera, C., Zaslavsky, A., Christen, P., Georgakopoulos, D.: Context aware computing for the internet of things: a survey. IEEE Commun. Surv. Tutor. **16**(1), 414–454 (2014)

Requirements Elicitation and Complex Systems Modeling: An Interdisciplinary Approach to Emergency Situations

Elaine Alves de Carvalho[(✉)], Alessandro Jatobá,
and Paulo Victor Rodrigues de Carvalho

Post-Graduate Program in Informatics, Núcleo de Computação Eletrônica,
Universidade Federal do Rio de Janeiro,
PO Box 2324 CEP 20001-970, Rio de Janeiro, RJ, Brazil
nane.alves@gmail.com, paulov195617@gmail.com,
ajatoba@gmail.com

Abstract. Information systems are important technological allies on the organization context. In emergency situations, they can be even more necessary. Classical information system specification approaches do not focus in relevant aspects of sociotechnical relations. They adopt simplified ways to represent reality and do not consider functional interactions between equipment, procedures and human resources of sociotechnical systems. In consequence, technological devices become insufficient in the capacity to respond to disaster situations.

The focus of this work is to propose a discussion that contributes to create a heuristic approach to better define system requirements. The goal is to combine context modeling methods and human factors to model complex interactions in emergency situations.

Keywords: Information system · Emergency situation · Complex system modeling · Requirement elicitation

1 Introduction

In general, emergency situations are challenges for classical engineering approaches because their deterministic techniques are sometimes incapable to respond all adverse events [2]. An emergency situation deals with scenarios that has adverse consequences. It requires swift action, mobilization of massive resources and recomposition of actor's networks [2].

Engineering is an activity that tries to design structured processes and products to meet a specific necessity, using information about known context. Classical engineering methods, in general, allow people to make the best changes with the available resources [4].

It is recognized that modern sociotechnical systems provide dynamic and integrated management services through collaboration of humans. However, information and technology methods normally used in classical Engineering are not able to describe and model systems. It happens because they not totally consider functional interactions

© Springer International Publishing AG 2017
P. Brézillon et al. (Eds.): CONTEXT 2017, LNAI 10257, pp. 375–380, 2017.
DOI: 10.1007/978-3-319-57837-8_31

between equipment, procedures and human resources [4]. It is especially true for disaster and emergency management settings. They use models focused on technical functions and describe the system usage via a small number of imagined operational scenarios.

Then, another approach is necessary to think about Systemic Engineering modeling methods [7]. It can be applied in emergency management to grasp the complexity of the system in terms of dependencies, functional interactions, variability (endogenous and exogenous), system dynamics and eventual migration to a different state of risk over time.

1.1   Research Problem

This work leads to the following research problem:

- How to define a heuristic approach to specify information systems requirements in the context of emergency situations?

The objective is to define a manner to better understand common characteristics of emergency situations addressing guidelines in order to predict behaviors and functionalities for information systems. Cognitive and Resilience Engineering concepts, methods and techniques for modeling complex systems will be applied in such approach.

This research entails better understanding over application of Ergonomics, Human Factors, Context Modeling and Requirements Engineering concepts in an interdisciplinary way. Thus, the expected result is to generate guidelines for complex systems specification activity in emergency situations.

In this way, the proposed research intends to minimize some problem consequences of traditional Engineering approaches that seek to decompose systems into parts loosing relevant information [13]. Thus, the conventional science methods will be replaced by General System Theory and Cybernetic concepts. Such theories consider how parts are interconnected and interact with the environment and other social aspects [13].

1.2   Research Context

The research could be applied to several emergency contexts. Hospitals, Fire Departments and Regulation Systems are examples of fields that involve different interfaces and need to deal with emergency responses, especially agent and resources coordination and integration. Regulatory systems are also promising research fields because they are in a complex emergency context that deal with rational decisions based on a supposedly known environment [9].

In Health Care, a system can be an integrated delivery system, a centrally owned multihospital system, or a virtual system comprised of many different partners over a wide geographic area. Moreover, an emergency room or an obstetrical unit is also a system, and any element in the health care system might belong to multiple subsystems [5]. Given such emergency contexts, Health Care is the chosen field to apply the interdisciplinary approach proposed in this research.

2   Methodologies Summary

Classical workflow management systems and their supported languages as BPMN are better for structured processes rather than complex, dynamic, and unpredictable systems, which require much flexibility [11]. Complex systems, in general, are irreducible and they cannot be decomposed in a simplified model without losing relevant information [10]. Therefore, other methods should be applied and combined to properly represent these systems and its aspects.

2.1   Contextual Design

The Contextual Design has a basic principle: project focused on the user to design information systems that reflect the way people develop the work involved. This approach tries to understand customer needs by collecting and interpreting data to generate requirements that meet user needs satisfactorily.

This approach has three phases:

1. Contextualization phase that involves visits for data collection and modeling to interpret and understand user's needs;
2. Analysis and modeling phase that consolidates concepts of the product to be developed from data collected and modeled;
3. Identification of need phase that involves the concepts projection to develop interfaces and system requirements to be validated and tested by users [1].

That is a method that incorporates socio-technical aspects and typical complex systems characteristics in emergency situations. Context Design will be applied to address human aspects and explore the information flows generated during the execution of work "as done" in emergency situations. The information analysis points out some important characteristics to discover informational requirements for technological devices in disaster contexts. Thus, Contextual Design contributes to the research approach because it substantially helps to understand the complexity in actor's interactions and their information flows improving FRAM method that will be discussed below.

2.2   Cognitive Work Analysis (CWA)

The complex cognitive system method proposed by Hoffman and Woods [6] considers that people's networks constantly interact through technology. Therefore, technology is supposed to support this network, not only its actions, but rather seeks understanding what actors are thinking while performing tasks.

The cognitive work analysis is a systematic manner to evaluate workers behavioral constraints and competencies, domain models, strategies, socio-organizational factors and control tasks. Such aspects are crucial to support technologies. That approach is considered ecological, as actors will acquire a mental model compatible with a specific context behavior to perform their tasks [12].

Cognitive work analysis will contribute to this study by providing the means to understand the constraints in the emergency contexts and improving the system modeling in complex socio-technical environments. This method will complement the results expected by the application of Contextual Design methodology in order to extend FRAM method. The restrictions identified during the tasks execution will be considered and analyzed to create some guidelines that better represent system requirements constraints. The strategy is to extend the benefits of such method aggregating value to the others mentioned previously.

2.3   Functional Resonance Analysis Method (FRAM)

Functional Resonance Analysis Method (FRAM) is a systematic method for modeling that tries to identify the accidents causes. It is an approach to model complex systems and its origin is the Resilience Engineering [9]. The main goal is to identify how a system should have worked to achieve success considering functions variability aspects. The model instances allow to evaluate functions and conditions in which they occurred [9].

In the FRAM method, functions are described by means of six aspects [8]:

1. Input: activates the function and/or is used or transformed to produce the output;
2. Output: is the result of the function. Constitutes the links to downstream functions;
3. Precondition: system conditions that must be fulfilled before a function can be carried out;
4. Resources (execution conditions): is needed or consumed by the function when it is active (matter, energy, competence, software, manpower);
5. Control: supervises or regulates the function (e.g. plans, procedures, guidelines or other functions);
6. Time: temporal aspects that affect how the function is carried out (constraint, resource).

The aspects presented above (mainly input, output and preconditions) will be explored in the research field. The purpose is to address heuristics to improve variability aspects in complex system requirements specification.

The FRAM method is applied here to model the work "as done" and the variable aspects not completely represented by linear models. The instances and system complex detailed descriptions address important "pattern" characteristics. Those aspects can generate system requirements information guidelines for technological devices in emergency contexts.

Therefore, applying the FRAM approach, the intention is to represent the instances of a situation and evaluate them in emergency contexts. The analysis results identify some common characteristics of emergency contexts and enable the creation of guidelines to better understand required functionalities for information systems in emergency situations.

3   Expected Results

The methods presented above combine different aspects to aggregate understanding abstraction levels and to produce some expected results in complex systems analysis for emergency situations as follows (Table 1):

Table 1. Expected Results

Method	Application	Expected results
Contextual design	Process applied to identify the main information about performance and actor's interests in emergency situations	Models elaboration to allow information flows applied to emergency contexts
Cognitive work analysis - CWA	Procedures to identify mental models and constraints in disaster context	Information flows pattern detection aligned to constraints identified in emergency situations
Functional resonance analysis method – FRAM	Method to model functions, instances and their variability in emergency situations	Functions and instances patterns detection in disaster situation

The framework above presents a strategy to aggregate value to FRAM modeling. The idea is to systematically aggregate more information by applying Cognitive Work Analysis and Contextual Design concepts together. The proposal is to create a FRAM extension to model complex systems in emergency situations.

This extended FRAM is supposed to detail socio-technical aspects, highlighting information flows and environment constraints. The goal is to point out heuristics to describe system requirements more suitable to emergency contexts.

4   Discussion

The classical way to define information system requirements is no longer valid, especially when dealing with complex systems [3]. So, the proposed study deals with methods combination to improve the accuracy of FRAM models in emergency scenarios. The final expected result is a set of heuristics to guide complex system requirements specification. Thus, the research question is justified by the contribution to elicitation phase in Requirements Engineering in disaster contexts.

However, throughout this research some questions are not completely solved when the emergency context is Health care, as follows:

1. Are the selected methods enough to accomplish the expected result?
2. What are the remaining gaps in this approach?
3. Are there any other methods that should be incorporated in the approach? How they can minimize identified gaps to improve FRAM? Are there other concepts and methods necessary to generate heuristics for information systems requirements?
4. Which other emergency context does the proposed approach suit better?

These questions indicate further opportunities for research addressing issues related to the complexity levels and robustness of system requirements in emergency situations. An exhaustive bibliographic search will be necessary to discover relevant related works and to guarantee satisfactory results.

5 Conclusion

The proposed work applies an interdisciplinary strategy to aggregate different concepts and to explore the contributions of Cognitive and Resilience Engineering. The Health Care as intended fieldwork deals with many questions to achieve the main purpose.

The major goal combines sociotechnical concepts and Requirements Engineering tools to generate heuristics and to improve complex system requirements specification in emergency scenarios.

References

1. Beyer, H., Holtzblatt, K.: Contextual Design. Morgan Kaufmann, San Francisco (1998)
2. Guarnieri, F., Travadel, S.: Engineering thinking in emergency situations: a new nuclear safety concept. Bull. At. Sci. **70**(6), 79–86 (2014)
3. Katina, P., Keating, C.B., Jaradat, R.M.: System requirements engineering in complex situations. Requirements Eng. **19**, 45–62 (2014)
4. Koen, B.V.: Definition of the Engineering Method. American Society for Engineering Education, Washington, DC (1985)
5. Kohn, L.T., Corrigan, J., Donaldson, M.S.: To Err Is Human: Building a Safer Health System. National Academy Press, Washington, DC (2000)
6. Hoffman, R.R., Woods, D.D.: Studying cognitive systems in context: preface to the special section. Hum. Factors **42**(1), 1–7 (2000)
7. Hollnagel, E.: Barriers and Accident Prevention. Ashgate, Aldershot (2004)
8. Hollnagel, E., Hounsgaard, J., Colligan, L.: FRAM – The Functional Resonance Analysis Method – A Handbook for the Practical Use of the Method. Centre for Quality, Southern Region of Denmark (2014)
9. Hollnagel, E., Woods, D.: Joint Cognitive Systems: Foundations of Cognitive Systems Engineering. CRC Press, Boca Ratón (2005)
10. Pavard, B., Dugdale, J.: The contribution of complexity theory to the study of sociotechnical cooperative systems. In: Minai, A.A., Bar-Yam, Y. (eds.) Proceedings of the Third International Conference on Unifying Themes in Complex Systems, pp. 39–48. Springer, Heidelberg (2006)
11. Van Der Aalst, W.M.P., Pesic, M., Schonenberg, H.: Declarative workflows: balancing between flexibility and support. Comput. Sci. - Res. Dev. **23**(2), 99–113 (2009)
12. Vicente, K.J.: Cognitive Work Analysis: Toward Safe, Productive, and Healthy Computer-Based Work, 1st edn. Lawrence Erlbaum, Mahwah (1999)
13. Vieira, F.K.: O Uso da Teoria Geral dos Sistemas para Análise e Investigação de Acidentes Aeronáuticos. Ph.D. thesis. Universidade Federal do Rio de Janeiro- COPPE/UFRJ, Rio de Janeiro, Brasil (2016)

Modeling Situations in an Intelligent Connected Furniture Environment

Cedric Deffo Sikounmo$^{(\boxtimes)}$, Eric Benoit, and Stephane Perrin

Laboratoire d'Informatique, Systèmes,
Traitement de l'Information et de la Connaissance (LISTIC),
Université Savoie Mont Blanc, 74944 Annecy-Le-Vieux, France
{cedric.deffo-sikounmo,eric.benoit,stephane.perrin}@univ-smb.fr

Abstract. The Internet of Thing allows objects and services to interact with each other. The goal of this study is to recognize high level states of the rooms and more generally of the home. We want to be able to obtain intermediate states like "someone is in the kitchen" or "night mode". In the specific case of home activity and state measurement, we consider that a set of furniture units is especially suitable for providing low level information. Recognizing and identifying house states or other high level information can be done using several methods. In this paper, we present an ontology based method. In the following, a situation is considered to be realized when the hypothesis which represents it are fulfilled. Using this approach, we show that multiple instances of situation context are distinguishable.

Keywords: Indentification of situation · Ontology · Internet of Things · Context · Furniture

1 Introduction

The Internet of Thing is perceived as a pervasive presence around us of a variety of things or objects interacting between each other. The given things are physical objects or virtual ones. The physical objects are mainly connected objects. Virtual objects have no existence in the concrete world but they are also able to propose services. The goal of our study is to recognize high level states of the rooms and more generally of the home i.e. normal state, abnormal state or alarm. In addition, we want to be able to obtain intermediate states like "someone is in the kitchen" or "night mode". In the specific case of home activity and state measurement, we consider that furniture units are especially suitable to provide low level information. This is particularly due to their presence around the house and because they are non-intrusive nature. Recognizing and identifying house states or other high level information can be done using several methods. In this paper, we propose to use an ontology-based approach to represent a context made of an aggregation of realized situations. The used ontologies can be supplied and updated directly by sensors. As suggested by [4], we apply inference

© Springer International Publishing AG 2017
P. Brézillon et al. (Eds.): CONTEXT 2017, LNAI 10257, pp. 381–394, 2017.
DOI: 10.1007/978-3-319-57837-8_32

rules on the graph that represents the concept ontology i.e. the ontology of physical entities. This thus provides high level information. However, inference rules are applied on the graph representing the ontology of realized situations. The latter allows the designer to take into consideration dynamic modification of the measured scene without adding new rules. However, if a situation has multiple instances, the problem turns out to distinguish each instance of the others. In this paper, we propose to attach rules on the situation. Using this approach, we show that multiple instances of context within a situation are distinguishable. In the next section on this paper, we discuss about several approaches to model and to represent information of context. In the Sect. 3, we present the ontology based representation of a furniture community. Section 4 presents the representation of situations in a furniture community. Section 5 explains the recognition process, illustrated with an example.

2   State of the Art

In the literature, several studies were realized on the various situations that can be observed in an intelligent environment. Several studies do not consider the distinction between a situation and a context [3,16,17]. The information of context is generally defined as any information being used to characterize the situation of an entity. Such entity can be a person, a place or an object that is considered as relevant for the interaction between a user and an application, including the user and the application themselves [12]. In this paper, which relates to a community of intelligent connected furniture units, we distinguish three types of context information as proposed in [3]:

Raw context: Context whose related information is directly acquired through sensors. For example, the localization, the current time or any environmental parameters.

Interpreted context: Information of context derived from the raw contexts. For example: Sat on a chair; day periods like the morning, the afternoon or the evening; activities such as sleeping, working.

Live context: Information obtained by recurring combination of the raw contexts and the interpreted contexts which makes sense for a human. For example: working at the office, looking at the TV within the living room.

Several approaches propose to model context information. Gu et al. [16] classified these approaches into three categories:

Application oriented approach: This approach produces models of context for specific applications. These models are generally proprietary models and don't have a formal basis. They don't support the knowledge sharing between the various systems [21].

Model oriented approach: This category of models usually uses conceptual modeling approaches to represent the context. We can quote studies in [18,24] which uses the entity-relation model, studies in [19] which uses at the same time the entity-relation model and UML diagrams. Finally, studies in [20] reformulate this model with the extension of "the object-Role Modeling" (ORM) [20]. Although this approach takes into account the temporal aspect of context information, it badly supports the generalization of knowledge and the reasoning. In [13], Gonzalez and Ahlers offers an intelligent, context-based behavior representation from the different perceptions of a submarine for training simulations. They use a hierarchical representation of contexts and they add rules to determine the best tactics to adopt depending on the situations that arise.

Ontology oriented approach: The context can be regarded as a kind of specific knowledge. It can be modeled like an ontology. Indeed, the use of ontologies allows not only the context modeling, but also the inference engine based reasoning on the collected data [17].

We will use this latter approach in the following section in order to represent different information from contexts in a community of connected and intelligent furniture units.

3   Representation of a Furnitures Community

3.1   Presentation

A community of furniture units is a set of furniture pieces of various species like table, chair, bed, or mirror. These furniture units lead to a given environment. An environment must be understood as any place within where furniture pieces may exist. It can be for example a house, the parts of a house or an office. In this paper, we define a community of intelligent connected furniture units as a set of furniture units, objects and humans interconnected within an environment. In this community, the furniture pieces and the other objects can be intelligent ones i.e. be able to acquire, to handle and to exchange knowledge. In such environment, the furniture pieces, the objects and the humans are considered as the actors of the system. In the case of a house, several furniture units communities related to the different rooms can be identified. A house is generally divided into multiple rooms: living room, room, kitchen, shower, balcony, garden, hollow, garage, etc. A furniture unit can be dedicated to a given room or not, for example a bed or a chair. In the same way, a category of furniture unit can have several variations which are specific to a given room. Moreover, the ontology also includes objects that are not furniture units but that interact with them. For example, a TV interacts with a TV cabinet, so it must be considered into the ontology. In addition, it must be putted forward that human activities related to furniture are part of the most raised activities in a house. As the data acquisition requires sensors, the intelligent connected furniture units found naturally their place in the smart home. The chosen tool for the classification of the data given by sensors is an ontology based one. Such kind of tool already shows its popularity in the field of the engineering of knowledge due to its portability, its evolutionary and its flexibility [16].

3.2   Representation

Let us first describe the list of concepts and relations used to build the ontology. The Fig. 1 presents an ontology of a community of smart connected furniture pieces. We can raise:

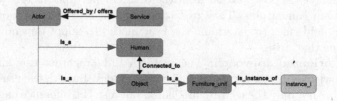

Fig. 1. Ontology of a community of furniture

Concepts

– **Actor** is the basic concept used to represent the objects, the furniture units and the living beings in a community of connected entities.
– **Service** is concept representing the various features or capabilities which an actor can offer.
– **Human** is the concept that represents the human beings in the community.
– **Object** represents the non-human actors.
– **Furniture_unit** represents a piece of furniture. A furniture piece is described by its style, its category, its functions and by the whole of the parts which compose it. The style is a set of aesthetic criteria and of materials, which helps to recognize the furniture period and its design. The category of a furniture unit refers to its species: tables, chairs, beds, mirrors. A function of a furniture unit leads to the various services it can offer to its user. The construction of a furniture requires various parts which can depend on its category, such as a mounting in the case of a chair or a table, a plate in the case of a table, a back and a seat in the case of a chair. As a result, the ontology of a furniture unit includes the following properties: "Style", "category", "features" and "parts".
– **Instance_i** represents the individuals i.e. the entities resulting from the instantiation of the various concepts. Except for services, each instance leads to a physical entity.

Relations

– **Is_a: concept** $\longrightarrow$ **concept** is the subsomption relation (hierarchisation). It is a transitive relation.
– **Type: individual** $\longrightarrow$ **concept** binds concrete entities to an abstract concept.
– **Part_of: Actor** $\longrightarrow$ **Actor** and **Has_part: Actor** $\longrightarrow$ **Actor** are the part-to-whole mereological relations between Actor concepts.
– **Offered_by: Service** $\longrightarrow$ **Actor** and **offers: Actor** $\longrightarrow$ **Service** are relations establishing a link between an actor and the various services it offers.

- **Connected_to: Actor** $\longrightarrow$ **Actor** is a topological relation used to formalize the interaction between actors.
- **Part_of: Actor individual** $\longrightarrow$ **Actor individual** and **Has_part: Actor individual** $\longrightarrow$ **Actor individual** are the part-to-whole mereological relations between Actor instances. They are inferred from the **Is_instance_of** and the mereological relations between Actor concepts.
- **Connected_to: Actor individual** $\longrightarrow$ **Actor individual** is a topological relation used to translate the interaction between actor individuals. The instances of this relation are given by the observation of the individuals, i.e. the physical entities.

This ontology aggregates the various concepts of an environment made of a community of intelligent connected furniture units, connected objects and beings humans. Into the following section, we introduce the representation of the various situations which rise from the interpretation of the contexts of the concept instances.

4   Representation of the Situations in Furniture Community

4.1   Presentation

We define a situation as follow. A situation is define on a set of actors. Each actor produces sensor data, the raw context, and interprets them to produce its interpreted context. The situation aggregates the raw contexts and the interpreted contexts issued from these actors. Its then appear as an ontology. We distinguish the definition and the realization of situation: The definition is a concept ontology, and the realization is an instance ontology. Actually, the definition of a situation is also called a reference situation and leads to the concept of infon as proposed by Devlin in [11].

In this section we provide a representation of the various situations that can be found in an environment holding a community of connected and intelligent furniture units. Given an environment we seek to represent the various actors and the relations between them as described in Sect. 3. After this classification stage, the resulting ontology is instantiated and initialized according to the facts of the actor instances. The facts of a furniture unit instance comes from the measured values acquired by its sensors. From this ontology instantiated, we try to recognize the various situations of the environment and the relations which exist between them. Several definitions were proposed in the literature.

In [26], Ye et al. define a situation as an external semantic interpretation of the data sensor.

- The *interpretation* term explains the fact that the situations allot significances to the measured values.
- The *external* term reflects the fact that interpretation is the applications point of view rather than the sensors one.
- The term *semantic* reflects the fact that an interpretation gives a significance to a set of relations between objects. The concerned sets are themselves defined by data given by sensors.

They alternatively define a situation by the collection of the relevant contexts, by discovering the significant correlations between them, and by the assignment of labels with a descriptive name.

An ontology in the artificial intelligence domain can be defined as the "explicit specifications of a conceptualization"; who is a means of representation, of knowledge sharing and of knowledge reasoning [14]. Several papers gives an outline of the approaches of reasoning on ontology based contexts [4, 8, 26]. As example we can quote SOUPA [6] (Standard Ontology for Ubiquitous and Pervasive Applications) which is based on Cobra-HAVE (Ontology for Context Broker Structures). SOUPA defines a vocabulary to describe the situational conditions such as: "in meeting" or "out of town". Dapoigny and Barlatier [9] formalize the context by using calculations of inductive constructions for the lower layer and ontologies for the upper layer. CONON (CONtext ONtology) is developed by Wang et al. [23]. CONON bases on the concept "context entities", which is a general term from which rises the concepts like "hiring", "person", or "activity". Here, the situations are defined in term of rules.

Example 1. (?u locatedIn Bedroom) & (Bedroom lightLevel LOW) & (Bedroom drapeStatus CLOSED) $\longrightarrow$ (?u situation SLEEPING)

Gu et al. [15] develop the SOCAM system (Service Oriented Context Aware Middelware) where the concept of situation is similar to the CONON one. Anagnostopoulos et al. [2] proposes a "technical situation awareness" based on the combination of ontology and fuzzy logic where the situations are concepts and relations.

Example 2. $\bigwedge_{i=1}^{N}$ context(x_i,user) $\longrightarrow$ IsInvolvedIn(situation,user), N > 1

The Example 1 is similar to the Example 2 in both cases a situation is represented by rules. Boytsov et al. [5] bases work which precedes to define a generator of situations. Moreover, they present two concepts of situations: a potential situation is an entity; A potential situation is a relation. Gu et al. [15] develop system SOCAM (Service Oriented Context Aware Middelware) or the concept of situation is similar to that of CONON.

4.2   Representation

Concepts. In the proposed approach, we distinguish the definition of a situation from its realization. The realization of a situation is materialized by the

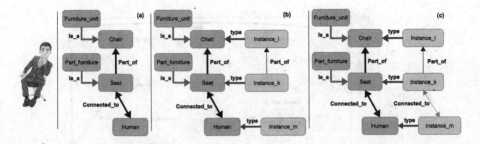

Fig. 2. Sitting situation: (a) graph of the reference situation (b) instantiation of two individuals of types Chair and Human (c) observation of the connected_to relation between individuals

existence of a sub-graph on individuals linked by the relations Has_part, Part_of and Connected_to. A situation is then defined by a set of rules on concepts.

Thus, the mathematical representation of a situation can be written as follows: let N, the set of the nodes, V the set of the relations and R the set of the rules then the situation S can be defined as: $S = G(N, V, R)$.

Example 3.

– **Sitting situation** is the graph where:
$N = \{Chair, Seat, Human\}$,
$V = \{Part\_of, Has\_part, Is\_instance\_of, connected\_to\}$
and
$R = [r_1 = \{(Part\_of(Seat, Chair) \vee Has\_part(Chair, Seat)) \wedge Connected\_to$
$(Human, Seat)\}]$.
Let *Sitting_situation* denoting the result of this inference. It represents the fact that the Sitting situation is realized.
A graph of the situation "position seat" is given in Fig. 2. One can note the various steps of the realization of a situation which will be detailed in the Sect. 5.2. First of all, the step (a) in the Fig. 2 represents the graph of the situation which refers to sitting. The step (b) shows us a instantiation of this graph with different instances from the concepts "Seat", "Chair" and "Human". The step (c) of the Fig. 2 established the relations between the instances while basing itself on the observation; an example we can quote the study of the data sensors.
– **Working situation** is a graph where:
$N = \{Sitting\_situation, Computer, Human, Table, Support\}$,
$V = \{Part\_of, Has\_part, Is\_instance\_of, connected\_to, Close\_to\}$
and
$R = [r_1 = \{Sitting\_situation \wedge Connected\_to(Computer, Support) \wedge$
$Connected\_to(Human, Computer) \wedge Close\_to(Chair, Table)\}$,
$r_2 = \{Connected\_to(Computer, Support) \wedge Connected\_to(Human, Compu$-
$ter)\}]$.
A graph representation of the situation "work" is given by the Fig. 3 and the relation *"Close_to"* is describing in [10].

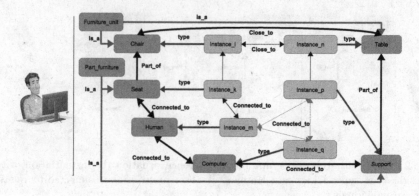

Fig. 3. Graph of the reference situation labeled "work"

Relations

- **The generalization:** a situation generalizes another situation, if the realization of the second one implies the realization of the first one. For example the situation "to listen to the music" is a specialization of the situation "entertainment" [25].
- **The composition:** a situation can result from the composition of other smaller situations; for example the situation "barbecue" breaks up into these two situations "uses a barbecue with gas" and "uses food". In [22] McCowan et al., define a situation of group (for example 'discussion' or 'presentation') like a composition of situations of individual users (for example 'to speak', 'to write').
- **of dependence:** a situation depends on another situation, if an occurrence of first is determined by an occurrence of the second. The dependence can be one limited time or unlimited, as proposed by [7]. Sometimes, in the long run the dependence can be more useful while deducing from the high level situations. For example, a situation "of going to work" to perhaps better infer a situation "to return to the house of work" than of other situations dependent on short ranges.
- **temporal sequence** a situation can occur before or after another situation, or interlace with another situation; for example, the situation "taken of the pill" must be realized after the situation "dinner" [1].

5   Situations Discovery in Furniture Units Community

Several techniques for the situation discovery were already proposed. Ye et al. [26] class them in two categories which are:

Specifications based technics. These approaches generally build a model of
situation with an a priori expert knowledge, and reasons on it with measured values as inputs. As example of technique we can quote Space "Logic
programming" "spacial and temporal logic", "ontology" and "Fuzzy logic".

Training based techniques. The large variability of the specifications and
identifications of the situations, that come from factors like time or the place
or the individual, returns inconvenient the specifications based techniques.
Training techniques were largely applied to the training of complex associations between the situations and the measured values. In [26] Ye et al.
characterizes this training based techniques.

Our contribution in this area consists of a complete situation discovery
process based on specifications techniques. In addition, it provides all situation
instances in our instantiated concept ontology.

In the literature, the studies on the situation recognition in an pervasive
computing environment assume that several basic situations are known without
worrying about the way they are obtained. Moreover, a separation between the
concept ontology of the sensors and the situations ontology is noticed. In this
paper, the representation we propose makes it possible to describe furniture
units and the various entities found in their environment. Thus, starting from an
instantiation ontology presented in Sect. 3, the situation references as described
in Sect. 4 is used for the situation discovery process. This last process provides
the desired realized situations. The complete process is detailed bellow. In this
paper, the instance of a concept ontology is an ontology where each constitutive
entity is associated with a set of facts. Each fact is a measured value of an entity
property.

5.1   Situation Recognition

The situation recognition technique proposed here assumes the existence of an
instance of concept ontology and a set of reference situations. The recognition
of situations is first processed from the entities of the instance of our concept
ontology and then performed from the situations deduced from this first stage.

Recognition of Situations Starting from the Context Instances
Recognition of situations starting from the raw and interpreted context instances
is the first way to recognize the various situations of an environment. Knowing
a instantiated ontology, the contexts of the various instances are collected. The
interpreted contexts also called basic situations are deduced from this collected
information.

Example 4. We want to know if a person sat on a chair. For that, the chair is
instrumented with sensors located on his base and back. A person is sitting on
a chair if he is in contact with the chair on its seat points. Moreover, there are
several types of sitting attitudes which depend of the contact between the human
and the back of the chair. The Fig. 2 gives a representation of a basic situation
reference.

Recognition of Situations Starting from the Basic Situations

High level situations are raised from the basic situations. They are combinations of the basic situations and/or of the entities of our instantiated ontology.

Example 5. The recognition of a working situation is performs throw the recognition of the basic situations like **a person sitting on a chair, a computer on a table, a running computer, a person in contact with the table and the chair near the table**. The Fig. 3 gives a situation reference.

In a general way a situation is known as potentially realizable or recognizable in an instance of our concept ontology O^i if for any item of the set of the whole nodes situation N there exists an instance in O^i.

Proposition 1. $S = G(N, V, R)$ *is a potential situation (a situation definition) if:* $\forall c \in N, \exists i; i$ *instance_of* c *and* $i \in O^i$.

The recognition of situations makes it possible to present the various potential situations of the system, without being certain of their realization.

5.2   Realization Situations

Given a instance ontology and a set of potential recognized situations, a situation is said to be realized if there exists at least a subgraph of the instance ontology graph that respects at least one of the rules of our reference situation.

Proposition 2. *A situation* $S = G(N, V, R)$ *is realized if:* $\exists G_i(N_i, V, r_i); r_i$ *is verified, with* $N_i = \{i/(i \ is\_instance\_of \ c) \wedge (c \in N)\}$ *and* $r_i \in R$. G_i *is also called instance of the reference situation* S.

To discover situation in an environment of intelligent connected furniture our system must carry out two stages which are:

Step 1. Recognition of all potential situations based on a list of reference situations.

Step 2. Discovering the situations realized starting from the potential situations extracted in step 1.

   Thus, this approach enables us to list all the situations of an intelligent connected furniture environment. Moreover, for each new entity, the same process is reiterated. That makes this approach dynamic in time.

5.3   Application

In a first time, let an ontology instance describing an environment made up of three humans and two chairs and a table as described in the Fig. 4. In a second time the same instance of concept ontology with new relations as shown in the Fig. 5 is given. We seek to recognize the various situations in which the actors of our environment are concerned. For that, we define the following situations references:

Input: O^i an ontology instance
Input: L_RS a list of the reference situations
Output: L_PS a list of the potential situations

foreach $s \in L_RS$ **do**
  if $(\forall c \in N(s), \exists i; i \; instance\_of \; c \; and \; i \in O^i)$ **then**
    | $L_PS \leftarrow L_PS + s$
  end
end
return L_PS;

Algorithm 1: Discovered potential situations

Input: O^i an ontology instance
Input: L_PS a list of the potential situations
Output: LS a list of the situations carried

foreach $s \in L_PS$ **do**
  if $(\exists r \in R(s); r \; is \; verified)$ **then**
    | $LS \leftarrow LS + s$
  end
end
return LS;

Algorithm 2: Discovered situations realized.

- **Working situation** is a graph or: $N = \{Sitting\_situation, Human, Table\}$, $V = \{Part\_of, Is\_instance\_of, connected\_to, Close\_to\}$ and $R = [r_1 = \{sitting\_situation \; \land \; Connected\_to(Human, Table) \; \land \; Close\_to(Chair, Table)\}, r_2 = \{Connected\_to(Human, Table)\}]$.
- **Sitting situation** is a graph or:
  $N = \{Chair, Seat, Human\}$, $V = \{Part\_of, Is\_instance\_of, connected\_to\}$ and $R = [r_1 = \{(Part\_of(Seat, Chair) \lor Has\_part(Chair, Seat)) \land Connected\_to(Human, Seat)\}]$.
- **Close to situation** is a graph or: $N = \{Chair, Table\}$, $V = \{Close\_to\}$ and $R = [r_1 = \{(Close\_to(Seat, Chair)\}]$.

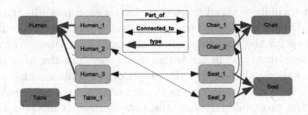

Fig. 4. Example of instance of an ontology representing an environment made up of chairs and humans

By applying the steps presented in Sect. 5.2 we have the following results:

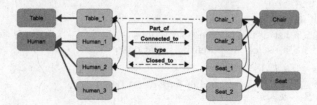

Fig. 5. Example of instance of an ontology representing an environment made up of chairs, the table and humans

– case of the Fig. 4
  Step 1 (discovery of all potential situations) result of Algorithm 1:
  {Close to situation, Sitting situation, Working situation}
  Step 2 (discovered of realized situations) result of Algorithm 2:
  {Sitting situation(Human_1, Chair_2), Sitting situation(Human_2, Chair_1)}
– case of the Fig. 5
  Step 1 (discovery of all potential situations) result of Algorithm 1:
  {Close to situation, Sitting situation, Working situation}
  Step 2 (discovered of realized situations) result of Algorithm 2:
  {Sitting situation(Human_1, Chair_2), Sitting situation (Human_2, Chair_1),
  Close to situation(Table_1, Chair_1), working situation(Human_1)}.

6   Conclusion and Perspectives

In this paper we propose a generic representation of the situations of a community of intelligent connected furniture units. For that, we chose a representation of the physical entities by using ontologies. This representation enables us to emphasize the various parts of a furniture and another entities which can collaborate or interact with furniture units. From the description of community of furniture units, we seek to recognize the various states of our community. Thus, to recognize such states, reference situations are modeled by graphs made of nodes and relations and by rules. From this representation of situations references, we define algorithms which make it possible to find potentially realizable situations and actually realized situations. Given examples illustrate the use of the proposed algorithms in order to provide desired actually realized situations. The future work for the improvement of the presented study will concern the discovery of new situations in an autonomous way and the association of the masses to the various elements of the graph of a situation. This last point of improvement will make possible to perform uncertainty based reasoning using theories like: the probability theory, the fuzzy sub-set theory or the evidence theory.

Acknowledgments. This research is supported by the Universite Savoie Mont Blanc, the Association des Pays de Savoie and Miliboo Corporation.

References

1. Workshops Proceedings of the 7th IEEE International Conference on Data Mining (ICDM 2007), Omaha, Nebraska, USA, 28–31 October 2007. IEEE Computer Society (2007)
2. Anagnostopoulos, C., Ntarladimas, Y., Hadjiefthymiades, S.: Situational computing: an innovative architecture with imprecise reasoning. J. Syst. Softw. **80**(12), 1993–2014 (2007)
3. Attard, J., Scerri, S., Rivera, I., Handschuh, S.: Ontology-based situation recognition for context-aware systems. In: I-SEMANTICS 2013–9th International Conference on Semantic Systems, ISEM 2013, Graz, Austria, 4–6 September 2013, pp. 113–120 (2013)
4. Bettini, C., Brdiczka, O., Henricksen, K., Indulska, J., Nicklas, D., Ranganathan, A., Riboni, D.: A survey of context modelling and reasoning techniques. Pervasive Mob. Comput. **6**(2), 161–180 (2010)
5. Boytsov, A., Zaslavsky, A., Eryilmaz, E., Albayrak, S.: Situation awareness meets ontologies: a context spaces case study. In: Christiansen, H., Stojanovic, I., Papadopoulos, G.A. (eds.) CONTEXT 2015. LNCS (LNAI), vol. 9405, pp. 3–17. Springer, Cham (2015). doi:10.1007/978-3-319-25591-0_1
6. Chen, H., Perich, F., Finin, T.W., Joshi, A.: SOUPA: standard ontology for ubiquitous and pervasive applications. In: 1st Annual International Conference on Mobile and Ubiquitous Systems (MobiQuitous 2004), Networking and Services, Cambridge, MA, USA, pp. 258–267, 22–25 August 2004
7. Choudhury, T., Quigley, A.J., Strang, T., Suginuma, K. (eds.): LoCA 2009. LNCS, vol. 5561. Springer, Heidelberg (2009)
8. Compton, M., Henson, C.A., Neuhaus, H., Lefort, L., Sheth, A.P.: A survey of the semantic specification of sensors. In: Proceedings of the 2nd International Workshop on Semantic Sensor Networks (SSN 2009), Collocated with the 8th International Semantic Web Conference (ISWC-2009), Washington DC, USA, 26 October 2009, pp. 17–32 (2009)
9. Dapoigny, R., Barlatier, P.: Formalizing context for domain ontologies in Coq. In: Brézillon, P., Gonzalez, A.J. (eds.) Context in Computing - A Cross-Disciplinary Approach for Modeling the Real World, pp. 437–454. Springer, New York (2014)
10. Sikounmo, C.D., Benoit, E., Perrin, S.: States measurement in a context of intelligent connected furnitures. In: 2016 Joint IMEKO TC1-TC7-TC13 Symposium "Metrology Across the Sciences: Wishful Thinking?". To be Published in IoP Science, Berkeley Evaluation and Assessment Research Center, Berkeley, USA, August 2016
11. Devlin, K.: Situation theory and situation semantics. In: Logic and the Modalities in the Twentieth Century, pp. 601–664 (2006)
12. Dey, A.K.: Understanding and using context. Pers. Ubiquit. Comput. **5**(1), 4–7 (2001)
13. Gonzalez, A.J., Ahlers, R.: Context-based representation of intelligent behavior in training simulations. Trans. Soc. Comput. Simul. **15**(4), 153–166 (1998)
14. Gruber, T.: Ontology. In: Liu, L., Tamer Özsu, M. (eds.) Encyclopedia of Database Systems, pp. 1963–1965. Springer, New York (2009)
15. Gu, T., Pung, H.K., Zhang, D.: A service-oriented middleware for building context-aware services. J. Netw. Comput. Appl. **28**(1), 1–18 (2005)
16. Gu, T., Wang, X.H., Pung, H.K., Zhang, D.Q.: An ontology-based context model in intelligent environments. In: Proceedings of Communication Networks and Distributed Systems Modeling and Simulation Conference, pp. 270–275 (2004)

17. Guermah, H., Fissaa, T., Hafiddi, H., Nassar, M., Kriouile, A.: An ontology oriented architecture for context aware services adaptation (2014). CoRR abs/1404.3280

18. Harter, A., Hopper, A., Steggles, P., Ward, A., Webster, P.: The anatomy of a context-aware application. Wirel. Netw. **8**(2–3), 187–197 (2002)

19. Henricksen, K., Indulska, J., Rakotonirainy, A.: Modeling context information in pervasive computing systems. In: Mattern, F., Naghshineh, M. (eds.) Pervasive 2002. LNCS, vol. 2414, pp. 167–180. Springer, Heidelberg (2002). doi:10.1007/3-540-45866-2_14

20. Henricksen, K., Indulska, J., Rakotonirainy, A.: Generating context management infrastructure from high-level context models. In: 4th International Conference on Mobile Data Management (MDM) - Industrial Track, pp. 1–6 (2003)

21. Kindberg, T., Barton, J.: A web-based nomadic computing system. Comput. Netw. **35**(4), 443–456 (2001)

22. McCowan, I., Gatica-Perez, D., Bengio, S., Lathoud, G., Barnard, M., Zhang, D.: Automatic analysis of multimodal group actions in meetings. IEEE Trans. Pattern Anal. Mach. Intell. **27**(3), 305–317 (2005)

23. Wang, X., Zhang, D., Gu, T., Pung, H.K.: Ontology based context modeling and reasoning using OWL. In: 2nd IEEE Conference on Pervasive Computing and Communications Workshops (PerCom 2004 Workshops), Orlando, FL, USA, pp. 18–22, 14–17 March 2004

24. Wu, H., Siegel, M., Ablay, S.: Sensor fusion for context understanding. In: Proceedings of the 19th IEEE Instrumentation and Measurement Technology Conference, IMTC/2002, vol. 1, pp. 13–17 (2002)

25. Ye, J., Coyle, L., Dobson, S.A., Nixon, P.: Representing and manipulating situation hierarchies using situation lattices. Rev. d'Intell. Artif. **22**(5), 647–667 (2008)

26. Ye, J., Dobson, S., McKeever, S.: Situation identification techniques in pervasive computing: a review. Pervasive Mob. Comput. **8**(1), 36–66 (2012)

Context-Aware Big Data Analytics and Visualization for City-Wide Traffic Accidents

Xiaoliang Fan[1,2](✉), Baoqin He[3], and Patrick Brézillon[4]

[1] School of Information Science and Engineering,
Lanzhou University, Lanzhou, China
fanxiaoliang@lzu.edu.cn
[2] Fujian Key Laboratory of Sensing and Computing for Smart City,
Xiamen University, Xiamen, China
[3] Information Department, Xiamen Airlines, Xiamen, China
hebaoqin@xiamenair.com
[4] LIP6, University Pierre and Marie Curie, Paris, France
Patrick.brezillon@lip6.fr

Abstract. Various traffic big data has been emerging in cities, such as road networks, GPS trajectories of buses and taxicabs, traffic flows, accidents, etc. Based on the massive traffic accident data from January to December 2015 in Xiamen, China, we propose a novel accident 0analytics and visualization method in both spatial and temporal dimensions to predict when and where an accident with a specific crash type will occur consequentially by whom. First, we analyze and visualize accident occurrences and key features in both temporal and spatial view. Second, we propose our context-aware methodology. Finally, we illustrate spatio-temporal visualization results through two case studies. These findings would not only help traffic police department implement instant personnel assignments among simultaneous accidents, but also inform individual drivers about accident-prone sections and most dangerous time spans, which would require their most attention.

Keywords: Big data analytics · Context awareness · Crash-type analysis · Visualization

1 Introduction

Big Data analytics and visualization have been driving nearly every aspect of society, including intelligent transportation, manufacturing, financial services, etc. [1]. Despite significant development and advancement in vehicle technology and transportation engineering over the last 50 years, traffic accidents are still one of the major accidental causes of deaths and injuries worldwide. For example, there are around 600–700 traffic accidents daily in Xiamen, a city with over 3.8 million populations in China. Accident data seems not to be a big data scenario due to its "small" volume. However, accident data analyses face typical big data challenges as well: (1) it is necessary to analyze accidents data very rapidly ("velocity" feature of big data). For example, even a very

© Springer International Publishing AG 2017
P. Brézillon et al. (Eds.): CONTEXT 2017, LNAI 10257, pp. 395–405, 2017.
DOI: 10.1007/978-3-319-57837-8_33

small accident may cause big traffic congestion in rush hours at crowded segments; and (2) it is quite difficult to mine the value of accident data ("value" feature of big data), especially in the spatio-temporal view precisely. For example, it is nearly impossible to predict when and where occur which type of accidents.

The analysis and prediction of accident occurrences are research areas of considerable interest for a long time [2]. Comprehensive works have been investigated to find the most important risks and variables that might contribute to accident occurrences [9]. However, the limitations of previous works are [3]: (1) they considered temporal and spatial view separately. Thus, the analysis of accident occurrences with spatio-temporal correlations has not been fully explored; and (2) they pay inadequate attentions on the feature extraction of crash types analysis.

In this paper, we propose a novel context-aware accident analytics and visualization method in spatio-temporal dimension to foresee when and where an accident with a certain crash type will happen consequentially by whom. We first analyze and visualize accident occurrences and key features in both temporal and spatial view. Second, we illustrate spatio-temporal visualization results through two case studies. The abundant sources of 200,678 accident records come from Xiamen City in China from January 2015 to December 2015.

The reminder of this paper is organized as follows. Section 2 discusses the related works. Section 3 introduces datasets and our observations. Section 4 presents the context-aware methodology. In Sect. 5, we illustrate our results through two case studies. Finally, Sect. 6 concludes this paper.

2 Related Works

2.1 Accident Occurrences Analysis

Comprehensive surveys could be found to explore the most important risks and variables that might contribute to accident occurrences [4, 5, 7, 10]. Later, several models focus on the impact of temporal and spatial patterns on accident occurrences separately. Lord and Geedipally [6] discussed the effects of modeling single-/multi- vehicle crashes, separately and jointly. Park and Harghani [14] studies the impact of the primary incident on the secondary incidents.

Furthermore, many crash type models were designed to reveal the features of crash occurrences to minimize the severity of crashes. Qin et al. [8] proposed a Bayesian framework to predict crash occurrences in relation to the hourly exposure by crash types. In addition, four features were considered as main factors that cause accidents in crash types [10]:

- Geometric factors, such as number of lanes, grade, road segments, road crossings, etc. For example, sideswipe crashes are more likely to occur in Multiple-lane, and rear-end crashes are more likely to occur in steep grade;
- Weather, such as typhoon, rains, heavy rains, and snow;
- Traffic, such as speed, volume, and travel time;
- Driver characteristics, such as age, sex, and driving years.

However, existing works mainly discussed the features in a qualitative dimension, while paying inadequate attentions on the feature extraction of crash types analysis. Instead, in this paper, we exploit the impact of features, such as weather and driver characteristics, on various crash types to uncover the spatio-temporal correlations in accident occurrences.

2.2 Traffic Big Data Analytics and Visualization

There are three major types of traffic data: (1) event based traffic data are usually log data collected manually; (2) location based traffic data are collected by detectors, inductive loops, and video cameras, which records a few statistical quantities, e.g. flow volume, occupancy or speed; and (3) movement based traffic data are directly collected from GPS devices as trajectories.

Wang et al. [11] designed an interactive system for visual analysis of urban traffic congestion based on GPS trajectories. Pack et al. [12] conducted incidents visualization from sensors data. Specifically, they designed a linked view interface to visualize the spatial, temporal and multi-dimensional aspects of accidents. Piringer et al. [13] presented an automatic method to detect and prioritize different types of events by surveillance videos in a tunnel.

Compared with previous works, in this paper, we explore accident occurrences and crash types analysis, combining the significant impact of both weather and driver characteristics. It is a combination of event-based and location-based traffic data analytics and visualization.

3 Heterogeneous Datasets and Observations

3.1 Datasets and Preprocessing

In this paper, we use the following four datasets for accident occurrences and crash-type analysis, provided by the Xiamen ITCC:

- *Dataset_1* consists 12 months of **accident data** from January 2015 to December 2015 in Xiamen, totally 200,678 records. Each record has 112 fields, indicating when, where and how the crash occurred.
- *Dataset_2* describes information on **accident vehicles and drivers**. Each record includes fields, such as who were involved in accidents as well as information on driver characteristics (e.g., age, sex, driving years). The timespan of this dataset is also from January 2015 to December 2015.
- *Dataset_3* is the **weather forecasting data** in Xiamen from January 2015 to December 2015, crawled from the website[1].
- *Dataset_4* is the **road networks** of Xiamen. It contains administrative region, expressway, urban main roads, branch roads, etc.

---

[1] Weather forecasting website, http://lishi.tianqi.com/xiamen/index.html.

Data Pre-processing. Three raw datasets (Dataset_1, Dataset_2 and Dataset_3) are fused that fields with little correlations to accident occurrences are deleted. Therefore, we extracted 15 fields from three datasets. Other pre-processing methods include data integration, data conversion and data reduction.

3.2   Observations

First, we investigated the temporal pattern in accident occurrences in. Figure 1 demonstrates the temporal view of accident occurrences in a periodical pattern which is corresponding to the common sense. As shown in Fig. 1(a), weekdays have obvious morning and evening peak, while such peaks are not repeatable in the weekend (Fig. 1 (b)) which indicates less accidents happened during the weekend. In addition, Fig. 1(c) is the overlay chart of the periodical pattern, which indicates is that the early peak in the weekend is both smaller and more postponed than those in the weekdays. In summary, the early and evening peak of accidents is closely correlated to the peak hours in urban roads.

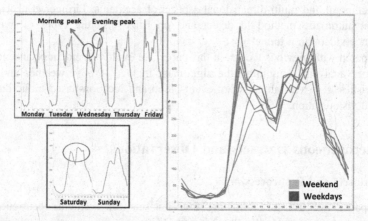

Fig. 1. Temporal view of accident occurrences: the periodical pattern in six months: (a, top left) separate charts by weekdays; (b, down left) separate charts by weekend; and (c, right) the overlay chart.

Second, we exploit the spatial pattern in accident occurrences with different granularities. Figure 2(a) shows the latitude and longitude coordinates of each accident, and totally 5682 accident occurred in January. Figure 2(b) describes the spatial view of accident occurrences by administration region of the traffic police (the deeper the color, the more the accident in the region). Figure 2(c) shows where accidents occurred on the totally 144 road segments in Xiamen Island, including the four bridges and one tunnel which are connected with the Island. Finally, Fig. 2(d) illustrates the accident occurrences in the totally 99 road crossings in Xiamen Island.

There is an indication that the spatial view of accident occurrences meets the condition of long-tail distribution. For instance, a few road segments and crossings have many accidents while most of others have few accidents spatially.

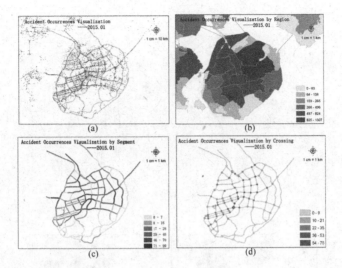

Fig. 2. Spatial view and visualization of accident occurrences for one month with different granularities: (a) coordinates of each accident; (b) by region; (c) by road segment; and (d) by crossing.

Third, we aim to make the observation of distinguished spatio-temporal patterns on six selected road segments in Xiamen Island. Through road segments classification, Fig. 3 shows the distinguished spatio-temporal patterns on six selected road segments in Xiamen Island. As shown in Fig. 3(a), each segment represents its distinguished temporal pattern in accident occurrences visualization.

We believe that such differences are mainly due to the following factors correlated to the segment:

- *Commuting hours*: Figure 3(b) shows a main bridge which links the Xiamen Island to outsides on weekdays, with both a morning peak when people go to work from home, and an evening peak when people go back home after work.
- *Tourist attractions*: Figure 3(c) shows on segments next to two biggest tourist attractions in Xiamen (i.e., "Gulangyu Island" and "ZhongShan Road", accidents often happen at weekends. In fact, Xiamen is one of the famous tourist destinations nationwide on weekends and holiday.
- *Peak change*: Figure 3(d) and (f) show two road segments with very different behaviors: as shown in Fig. 3(d), morning accident peaks often come earlier near primary schools, because parents bring children to school before they drive to work on weekdays; while as described in Fig. 3(f), evening accident peaks were always postponed close to shopping malls, because people are likely to go shopping or have a dinner after work.
- *Accident-prone segments*: Figure 3(e) shows that on arterial roads in the city downtown, which are also accident-prone segments, accidents could occur at almost any time span. This finding is coherent to the traffic flows at congestion-prone segments.
- *Expressways*: as shown in Fig. 3(g), accidents occurred very occasionally on expressways such as "Chenggong expressway". Because expressways usually have smooth traffic condition.

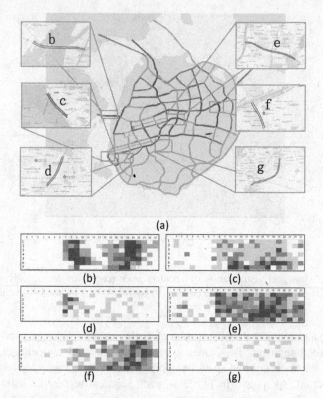

Fig. 3. Distinguished spatio-temporal patterns on six selected road segments in Xiamen

4 Context-Aware Methodology

Figure 4 describes the context-aware methodology of accident occurrences analytics and visualization. Our visual analysis work consists of two phases. The first phase is data collection and fusion (left in Fig. 4). Second, in the preprocessing phase (center in Fig. 4), we start from the input data, and extract data that fits our model. Finally, in the third phase of visual exploration and analysis (right in Fig. 4), we explore the pre-processed data in analysis and visualization. The methodology will be implemented in Sect. 4 as three case studies. In addition, we employ the Tableau Desktop V9.0[2] for the visualization.

5 Case Studies and Results

We have proposed a novel accident occurrences analytics method for accident big data in multiple views. The following two cases will demonstrate the visualization results.

---

[2] Tableau Desktop 8.3, www.tableau.com.

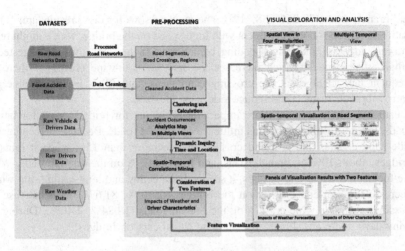

Fig. 4. The context-aware methodology of accident analytics and visualization.

5.1 Crash Types Analysis on Weather

Figure 5 presents visualization results of crash-type analysis with the feature of weather. We first select three types of road segments: (1) four bridges in the top left of Fig. 5(a); (2) an arterial road in top center of Fig. 5(a); and (3) several branch roads in the top right of Fig. 5(a). We notice that there is no intersection or ramp on the bridges, while there are zebra crossings and crossings on arterial roads. It seems that there is hardly any connection between weather and accident occurrences, but it is interesting to combine two features with the temporal feature.

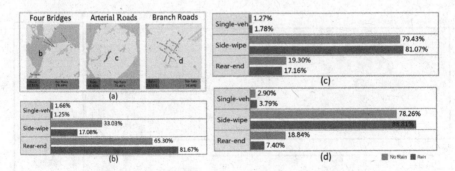

Fig. 5. The impact of weather on crash types, which has different influence on crash types: (a) three selected typical types of road segments; (b) the influence of weather on bridges; (c) the influence of weather on arterial roads; (d) the influence of weather on branch roads.

As a result, the visualization results have the following indications:

- Most accidents are rear-end crashes on the bridges (65.30%, 81.67%). On the contrary, most accidents are side-wipe crashes on arterial roads (79.43%, 81.07%)

and branch roads (78.26%, 88.81%). The main reasons for these results are: (1) the traffic condition is normally fluent with high speed on the bridge, which might result in rear-end crashes due to speeding behaviors; (2) they are always congested in urban arterial roads, which increases the risk for side-wipe crashes if there are frequent lane changes at the crossings and turns; and (3) it is unavoidable that narrow branch roads could induce side-wipe crashes.

- Weather is likely to have more impact on accidents for bridges, next for branch roads, but doesn't have obvious influence on arterial roads. Because percentages of side-wipe crashes and rear-end crashes change more than 15% when it rains on bridges, about 10% on branch roads, and less than 3% on the arterial roads. When we focus on the rear-end crashes, it seems that a heavy and long-lasting rain would decrease the rear-end crashes on the bridges (65.30%, 81.67%), but increase the possibility of side-wipe crashes on the branch roads (18.84%, 7.40%). During the rainy days, there are slippery ground and speed cars on bridges.

5.2 Crash-Type Analysis on Driver Characteristics

Figure 6 shows the impact of driver characteristics on spatio-temporal analysis in the global view. The panel contains: map view (Fig. 6(a)), temporal view (Fig. 6(b)), and driver view (Fig. 6(c)). Figure 6(d) shows interactions on data filter. Location, time stamp, age, driving years and sex could filter accidents. From the map view, we can select road segments, crossings and regions through shape filters. In Fig. 6(b), bar plots show the histograms of accidents occurrences every day. There are three group of bar plots in Fig. 6(c), sex view (left), age view (center) and the view of driving years (right) respectively, as shown in legends of Fig. 6(d). To each group, four columns represent

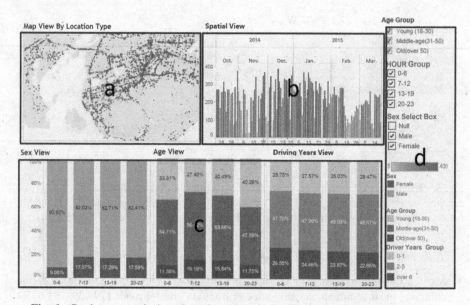

Fig. 6. Crash types analysis and spatio-temporal visualization on driver characteristics.

four periods in a day (0–7, 7–12, 12–19, and 19–24). And each bar shows the percentage distribution of accident occurrences for specific characteristic in specific periods. For example, in the sex view, 90.92% accidents are attributed to male driver from 0:00am to 7:00am, and 9.08% accidents come from female driver in the same time span.

By temporal and spatial filters, we can explore how driver characteristics affect accident occurrences in different urban functional regions with our visual interface in Fig. 7. In this context, our work chooses nightlife region (Fig. 7(a)), airport region (Fig. 7(b)), commercial region (Fig. 7(c)), and hospital region (Fig. 7(d)) as objects of study to explore the spatiotemporal distribution by driver characteristics. The four mini-map on the left of Fig. 7 shows the selected regions, and the detailed distributions can be examined in the bar plots right next to the mini-maps.

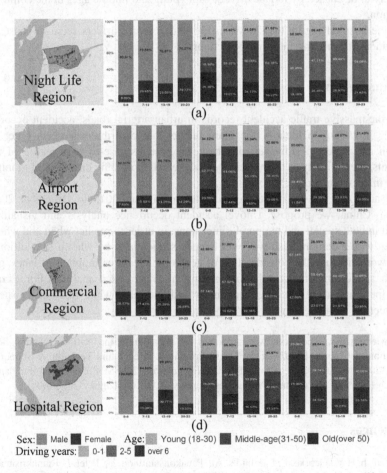

Fig. 7. The impact of driver characteristic in four types of region: (a) night life region; (b) airport region; (c) commercial region; (d) hospital region.

The visualization results have the following indications:

- In the nightlife region (as shown in Fig. 7(a)), we first find that more senior people are responsible for accidents than those in other regions. Second, accidents are relatively rare caused by female due to the more activeness of male in the nightlife. Third, more middle-age drivers are responsible for accidents in the morning and at noon. Finally, nearly half of midnight accident caused by novice drivers (less than a year), and they are likely to practice driving at airport region in the midnight.
- During the midnight, accidents are more likely to occur by male drivers than female drivers in the commercial region (as shown in Fig. 7(c)), due to high frequency of shopping for female. In addition, compared with other regions, accidents are more likely to be caused by female drivers with young and middle ages in the commercial region.
- In the hospital region (as shown in Fig. 7(d)), senior drivers seem to cause more accidents during the morning peak hours.

6 Conclusion

Given the massive traffic accident records in urban arterial roads, accident occurrence analysis is known to identify the main factors that contribute to crash type, crash position and severity. However, due to heterogeneous case-by-case nature of traffic accidents, the difficulty to quantitatively analyze massive traffic data has led to minimal effects in previous works.

By analyzing the traffic accident data from January 2015 to December 2015 in Xiamen, China, we propose a novel accident occurrence analysis and visualization method in both spatial and temporal dimensions, in order to predict when and where an accident with a certain crash type will happen sequentially by whom. In addition, our future works include the consideration of geometrics features (number of lanes, grade, etc.) in spatio-temporal correlations mining in crash types analysis. For example, sideswipe crashes are likely to happen on multiple lane, while rear-end crashes are often seen in road segments with steep grade.

Acknowledgments. The work was supported by grants from the National Natural Science Foundation of China (61300232); the Gansu Provincial Science and Technology Support Program (1504WKCA087); the China Postdoc Foundation (2015M580564); and Fundamental Research Funds for the Central Universities (lzujbky-2015-100, lzujbky-2016-br04).

References

1. Jagadish, H.V., Gehrke, J.: Labrinidis, Al., Papakonstantinou, Y., Patel, J., Ramakrishnan, R.: Big data and its technical challenges. Commun. ACM 57(7), 86–94 (2004). doi:10.1145/2611567
2. Ma, J., Kockelman, K.M., Damien, P.: A multivariate Poisson-lognormal regression model for prediction of crash counts by severity, using Bayesian methods. Accid. Anal. Prev. 40(3), 964–975 (2008)

3. Lin, L., Wang, Q., Sadek, A.W.: A novel variable selection method based on frequent pattern tree for real-time traffic accident risk prediction. Transp. Res. Part C **55**, 444–459 (2015). doi:10.1016/j.trc.2015.03.015

4. Hauer, E.: Speed and safety. Transp. Res. Rec. **2103**, 10–17 (2009). doi:10.3141/2103-02

5. Zhang, G., Yau, K.W., Zhang, X.: Analyzing fault and severity in pedestrian–motor vehicle accidents in China. Accid. Anal. Prev. **73**, 141–150 (2014). doi:10.1016/j.aap.2014.08.018

6. Lord, D., Geedipally, S.: Investigating the effect of modeling single-vehicle and multi-vehicle crashes separately on confidence intervals of Poisson–Gamma models. Accid. Anal. Prev. **42**(4), 1273–1282 (2010)

7. Yu, R., Abdel-Aty, M.: Utilizing support vector machine in real-time crash risk evaluation. Accid. Anal. Prev. **51**, 252–259 (2013)

8. Qin, X., Ivan, J., Ravishanker, N., Liu, J., Tepas, D.: Bayesian estimation of hourly exposure functions by crash type and time of day. Accid. Anal. Prev. **38**(6), 1071–1080 (2006). doi:10.1016/j.aap.2006.04.012

9. Yu, R., Abdel-Aty, M.A., Ahmed, M.M., Wang, X.: Utilizing microscopic traffic and weather data to analyze real-time crash patterns in the context of active traffic management. IEEE Trans. Intell. Transp. Syst. **15**(1), 205–213 (2014). doi:10.1109/TITS.2013.2276089

10. Zhang, G., Yau, K.W., Zhang, X.: Risk factors associated with traffic violations and accident severity in China. Accid. Anal. Prev. **59**, 18–25 (2013). doi:10.1016/j.aap.2013.05.004

11. Wang, Z., Lu, M., Yuan, X., Zhang, J., de Wetering, H.: Visual traffic jam analysis based on trajectory data. IEEE Trans. Vis. Comput. Graph. **19**(12), 2159–2168 (2013). doi:10.1109/TVCG.2013.228

12. Pack, M., Wongsuphasawat, K., VanDaniker, M., Filippova, D.: Ice–visual analytics for transportation incident datasets. In: Proceedings of IEEE International Conference on Information Reuse and Integration, pp. 200–205 (2009)

13. Piringer, H., Buchetics, M., Benedik, R.: AlVis: situation awareness in the surveillance of road tunnels. In: Proceedings of IEEE VAST, pp. 153–162 (2012)

14. Park, H., Haghani, A.: Real-time prediction of secondary incident occurrences using vehicle probe data. Transportation Research Part C: Emerging Technologies (in press)

Context Aware Data Synchronisation During Emergencies

Alireza Hassani[1(✉)], Pari Delir Haghighi[1], Frada Burstein[1],
and Scott Davey[2]

[1] Faculty of Information Technology, Monash University, Melbourne, Australia
{ali.hassani,pari.delirhaghighi,
frada.burstein}@monash.edu.au
[2] Datalink Internet Systems Pty Ltd, Melbourne, Australia
sdavey@datalink.com.au

Abstract. Today emergency management teams highly use internet-connected devices to improve the accuracy and immediacy of data collection and sharing. However, most cloud-based data synchronisation models rely on centralised components to share their data between users and do not support situations where the internet connection is unreliable or unavailable. This becomes particularly important when working in disaster-affected areas, where the internet infrastructure itself may be damaged but multiple, offline users are within close range of each other. Peer-to-peer data synchronisation can provide a great opportunity for performing data synchronisation locally between the mobile peers in an offline mode. However, it introduces new challenges in terms of conflict resolution, security and data consistency and integrity. In this paper, we propose a context-aware peer to peer data synchronisation framework for mobile environments when the internet becomes unavailable. The proposed approach introduces novel methods for peer discovery, user authentication and authorisation, as well as managing data versioning.

Keywords: Context model · Context-aware computing · Data synchronisation

1 Introduction

Most collaboration software products are based on a client-server architecture and heavily rely on a central server and the internet access. However, there might be situations where the internet connection can be interrupted and temporarily unavailable due to possible heavy congestion or damages to the infrastructure e.g. during emergencies.

Emergency operations centres are usually located away from the disaster area and typically have access to the internet, but field workers must work within the disaster area to collect data electronically, often in conditions where internet connections are unavailable. Internet disruption during and after disasters is common and expected: in 2009, Victoria's Black Saturday fires destroyed entire townships, and vital telecommunications and power infrastructure were destroyed and others heavily congested to the point of being unusable [1]; in 2014 and 2015 separate bushfires in Victoria's Halls

© Springer International Publishing AG 2017
P. Brézillon et al. (Eds.): CONTEXT 2017, LNAI 10257, pp. 406–417, 2017.
DOI: 10.1007/978-3-319-57837-8_34

Gap and Separation Creek townships burned in areas with no 3G reception hampering recovery activity; and parts of Victoria were left without communications for 20 days due to large-scale communications infrastructure failure in 2012 [2, 3]. According to Emergency Management Australia [4], best practice post-disaster data collection includes four aims: it must be accurate (e.g. GPS, structured data), timely (e.g. collected and shared quickly), and available to those who need it (e.g. security and authentication), and collected and sorted into appropriate categories and forms (e.g. data integrity and structure).

Peer-to-peer data synchronisation enables performing data synchronisation locally between the mobile peers in an offline mode. However, it introduces new challenges in terms of conflict resolution, security and data consistency and integrity. For instance, consider two field workers collect different pieces of information about the same object (e.g. a property on fire) which leads to conflict during the data synchronization. The most common approach to resolve such a conflict is to choose the most recent data. However, this approach does not always guarantee to choose the most accurate information. To clarify, assume one of the workers is an experienced firefighter and the other one is a red cross volunteer. Therefore, the information provided by the firefighter can be considered more accurate and reliable compared to the information provided by the other worker. To mitigate this problem and improve the quality of data, we enhanced our data synchronisation approach with context-awareness. Context-awareness can bring significant benefits to the data synchronisation problem. Usually, portable devices (e.g. smartphones, PDA, and tablets) with limited resources and battery are used during the data collection in emergency situations. Therefore, it is essential to choose the frequency and level of data synchronization (which consume considerable amount of battery) wisely through using a context-aware approach.

This paper proposes a context-aware peer to peer data synchronisation approach for emergency situations. The framework introduces a context model that is specific to peer to peer data synchronisation. The framework aims to synchronise client data between multiple nearby clients when there is no internet access. To achieve this goal, it includes various methods to deal with connectivity and peer discovery, authentication and authorisation, data synchronisation, and conflict resolution according to the context of user, data, environment and location. While there are some promising approaches [5, 6] for peer to peer data synchronization, to the best of our knowledge, none of them applied context-awareness as an overarching solution to the data synchronisation and conflict resolution problems.

2 Related Work

Data synchronisation techniques can be categorised into four sub-classes: slow-sync synchronisation, fast-sync synchronisation, timestamp synchronisation, and log synchronisation. Slow-sync [2] is a naïve approach where one of the devices involved in the synchronisation procedure sends its whole data to the other device. Then, the receiver device uses this data for local comparison [3]. This approach is highly inefficient particularly when the size of data is very large and/or when only minor changes are needed. In these cases, the communication overheads and synchronisation time will increase linearly with the data size, independent of the number of modifications [7]. However, slow-sync is easy to implement.

Fast-sync [7] is a more efficient approach compared to slow-sync. In this approach, each client stores information regarding its records in the form of status flags. These flags indicate what changes have been made since the last sync. During the sync devices only transmit the records assigned with flags and after the sync is done, all the flags are reset [8]. This approach is an ideal solution for the hub-and-spoke model [9]. While fast-sync improves the efficiency considerably, it is difficult to apply it when multiple clients are involved because it is unable to keep track of changes made by those devices. However, SyncML [10] which is an enhanced fast-sync approach overcomes this shortcoming by requiring each device to keep a set of status flags for each of its records with respect to every other device on the network. Modifying a record in one device updates the status flag of that device and is propagated to other devices. The Palm synchronisation protocol [11], also known as HotSync, is a combination of fast-sync and slow-sync. It uses the fast-sync method whenever it is applicable (i.e. in the hub-and-spoke model); otherwise, it switches to slow-sync.

In timestamp synchronisation [9], clients not only maintain information about the status (i.e. inserted, modified, or deleted) of the modified records, but also about when the modification happened using timestamps. During synchronisation, devices only send the items that have been changed since the last sync, therefore, it is more efficient compared to the status flag method. Yet, it can become inefficient when the number of clients is more than two. Log synchronisation is a common approach used in databases. Every change is executed as a transaction and also saved in a log. These logs are then synchronised with other clients. When the log is synchronised, each operation is replayed on the other client. The only issue is that the size of the log can significantly grow. Endo et al. [12] propose an approach to synchronise data and manage ownership of the data for peer-to-peer applications by saving the changes in the shared data (using a log approach) in multiple lists but this results in redundancy.

In order to enable the peer-to-peer synchronisation among multiple devices, each device in the network need to keep track of the changes it makes and those made by other devices [13]. This allows each device to know about all types of changes. In our proposed approach, we propose a solution that aims to address this point.

Conflicts in data synchronisation can be classified into three key operations: insert, delete and update. There are numerous studies about data conflict and consistency models [14–16]. Balasubramaniam and Pierce [14] and Ramsey and Csirmaz [15] studied about file synchronisation in a replicated file system. In Balasubramaniam et al. work [14], conflict resolution rules are applied based on a condition change of a file system before and after synchronisation. Alternatively, Ramsey and Csirmaz [15] presents rules based on the operations applied to each replica. Shamim Hossain et al. [16] proposed three approaches for conflict resolution: (i) auto synchronisation, (ii) semi-auto synchronisation, and (iii) user-involved synchronisation. In auto synchronisation the sources resolve conflict between updates using absorption resolution rule [17]. The absorption rule gives higher priority to the update that has the higher execution level. Therefore, initiators can resolve a conflict automatically. Meanwhile, in semi-auto synchronisation, a user's involvement is necessary to decide the update order. This approach is used when conflicting updates have the same execution level.

However, sources can resolve the conflict automatically if any intermediate source has information about the update execution order. In user-involved synchronisation, the users with higher authority mainly decide the update order. Several general conflicts resolution policies are introduced such as the recent-data-wins approach [18]. There are also application-based policies including: originator wins, recipient wins, client wins, server wins, and duplication apply where the modification is applied on a duplicated data item.

The literature shows that there are limited studies that incorporate context-awareness into data synchronisation. To address this, the next section introduces an overarching context model to optimise P2P data synchronisation in mobile environments.

3 Context Model

Context is a broad term that entails many aspects. It provides more useful and meaningful information about an entity. According to Dey [19], "Context is any information that can be used to characterize the situation of an entity". In order to capture the required context in P2P data synchronisation domain, we consider four key context entities including User, Data, Environment and Location.

User Context. According to Dey [19], "context information is only relevant if it influences a user's task". This is why a user plays a vital role in the context-aware computing environments. The User Context Model consists of a collection of contextual information, which defines both the characteristics of a user and his/her device. These include three context attributes of User Profile, User Situation and User Device. The User Profile context represents the user's characteristics such as role (e.g. admin) and expertise (e.g. emergency service workers, and field assessors). The User Situation context describes the current state of the user such as the activity in which the user is currently involved. The Device profile context represents the details of the device owned by each user such as its type (e.g. a tablet), its memory, storage and processing capabilities, and its operating system (e.g. Android or iOS).

Data Context. Figure 1 shows our proposed context model for representing data. It provides metadata to describe the semantic of each record, and consists of five contexts described here. *Type* defines the data format. Each record could be an image, text, video, or audio. *Description* represents extra information such as file size, equivalent vocabulary (synonyms) and domain of the data (e.g. medical, or fire). *Priority* shows the importance of each record. Regarding data sync, some information might be critical and other types of information can be considered less relevant or trivial and could be overlooked for optimization purposes. *Conflict properties* defines the required metadata for conflict resolution and includes two context elements of conflict rules and conflict methods. The usage and importance of these elements are discussed in Sect. 4.2. *Level of Access* is defined for each data item by the system administrator to set up a hierarchy of users. Thus, the users with the low-level access can access only a limited set of information whereas the highest-level users can access the most sensitive data on the system.

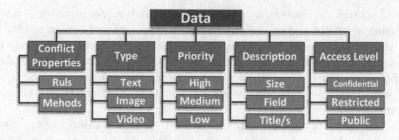

Fig. 1. Data Context Model

Environment Context Model is used to describe the variables that can influence a user's decision-making and behaviour. The environment model (see Fig. 2) includes physical conditions, the weather, and the type of the situation. The situation can have three criticality levels to represent the criticality of the emergency or disaster.

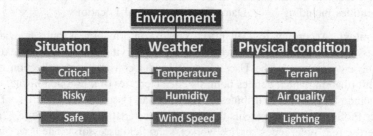

Fig. 2. Environment Context Model

Location Context Model describes location information in terms of geographical location and semantic location. The geographical location provides information about the absolute location of users (i.e. latitude and longitude). The semantic location describes the characteristic of a given location which can be expressed using proximity or the name of the places (e.g. near Camden in Sydney's southwest).

4 A Context Aware P2P Data Synchronisation Framework

In this section, we propose a generic and comprehensive Context-Aware Peer-to-Peer Data Synchronisation (CA- P2P-DS) framework for distributed environments where the internet access is unavailable (see Fig. 3). The proposed framework comprises of seven main components, namely User Interface, Context Manger, Sync Manager, Handshake Manager, Messaging, Connectivity Manager, and Data Manager.

User interface enables users to retrieve and manipulate the data, see available peers, and send a sync request to a selected peer.

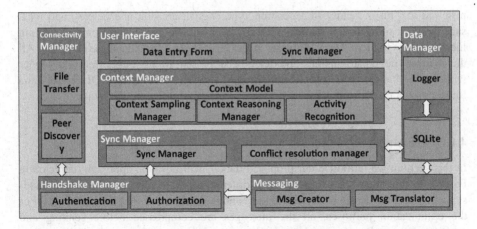

Fig. 3. An overview of CA-P2P-DS architecture

Context Manager consists of four sub-components: Context Model, Context Sampling Manager, Context Reasoning Manager, and Activity Recognition. The Context model is responsible for modelling and representing all the required contextual information in the domain (discussed in Sect. 3). The Context Sampling Manager is responsible for sampling the participants' context in an efficient manner to minimize the sampling overhead. Context Reasoning Manager and Activity Recognition Manager analyse the raw data to infer users' high-level contextual information and identify their current level of activity (e.g. running, walking, and stationary) respectively. The output of Context Manager is then used by Conflict Resolution Manager. **Sync Manager** maintains data consistency among all devices and consists of Sync Manager (see Sect. 4.1) and Conflict Resolution Manager (see Sect. 4.2). **Handshake Manager** is responsible for managing connections that a peer establishes with another peer. The handshake includes the steps for verifying the connection and the authorization of the peer making a connection. During this procedure, peers will exchange their signed tokens with each other. This helps to have peers with different roles and different level of access. For authentication, a digital signature scheme is considered that consists of three algorithms: (i) a key generation algorithm that selects a private key uniformly at random from a set of possible private keys. The algorithm outputs the private key and a corresponding public key; (ii) a signing algorithm that, given a message and a private key, produces a signature; and (iii) a signature verifying algorithm that, given the message, public key and signature, either accepts or rejects the message. In our proposed P2P-DS framework, all devices are expected to have already had one handshake with the server before being used. During this handshake, the server will generate and share a signed token (with the use of private key) for each peer that contains the user's role and expiration date. It also shares the corresponding public key with all peers. In the next step, during peers' handshake, they will exchange their tokens. Then each device will decrypt the received token with the use of shared public key to obtain the role of the other peer.

Messaging is responsible for message creation and parsing. Each message has several fields such as msg _No (A unique id to identify messages), msg_type (e.g. sync msg and log_msg), sender Id, operation_type (e.g. insert, edit and delete), and message_body. **Connectivity manager** discovers available peers and enables sending files/messages to them. **Data Manager** stores changes in a local database (SQLite). All the changes (i.e. create, update, and delete) will be sent to the logger first. The logger will log the changes (with a logical timestamp) and store them in the SQLite DB. Data Manager also enables the user to roll back to the version before the sync.

4.1 Sync Manager

In this section, we introduce our proposed data synchronisation approach (depicted in Fig. 4). In this approach, we define five different types of messages including handshake Request and Response, sync Request and Response, and sync End messages. For the optimization purposes, all the messages are compressed before sending and exchanged through a secure channel. Further, a logical clock is used to time-stamp messages. To explain our sync mode, here we present a scenario where device A is interested to sync its data with device B:

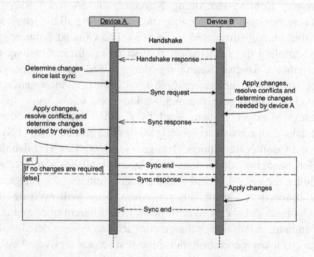

Fig. 4. The proposed sync approach

- *handshakeRequest* **message** - to start the procedure, peer A sends a handshake message to Peer B. This message contains a token of Device A which has been issued by the main server when the A logged in for the first time. The token will be used by the receiver peer for authentication purposes.
- *handshakeResponse* has the same structure as handshake message (token and last log ID). This message will be issued by Device B after it receives the handshake message from A. However, Device B will authenticate Device A (based on the token) first and send the handshakeResponse message only if the authentication succeeds, otherwise, a syncEnd message with an error code will be sent to Device A.

- *syncRequest* will be issued by Device A after it receives the handshakeResponse message form Device B and successfully authenticates it. This message contains all the changes in the shared data since the last sync between Device A and B. To determine the changes to be sent to Device B, Device A will use the context model. First, it retrieves B's role from its token and only includes the data that Device B has a right to access. Further, A also checks the environmental situation (e.g. situation is critical) and based on that, considers the required changes (e.g. high priority data). *syncResponse* is issued by Device B and contains the changes needed by Device A. To find the required changes by Device A, Device B will generate two lists: *request* and *response*. The *request* list contains those changes that need to be done by Device B since the last sync and are unchanged in Device A. To generate this list, like *syncRequest*, the context (role) of device A and environmental situation context will be considered. The response list contains the conflicted data (those data which has been changed by both devices since the last sync) where Device B is the winner of conflict resolution. In another word, all the shared data will be included in the *response* if it meets these two conditions: (1) the value of the shared data is changed by both devices since last sync, and (2) Device B wins the conflict. Further, when Device A receives *syncRequest* from Device B, it will apply the required changes and resolve possible conflicts. In the case of the response list, all the changes will be applied by Device A without checking the conflicts because Device B has already resolved them. In the case of request list, Device A will check for the possible conflicts and resolve them. During the conflict resolution, a new response list will be generated which contains the shared data where Device A is the winner. If this list is not empty, a new syncRequest message will be sent to Device B.
- *syncEnd* message will be issued when the sync procedure is finished successfully. However, this message can also be issued if an error occurs and the sync fails.

The above explanation shows the workflow of the proposed data synchronisation approach. As it is mentioned, contextual intelligence is used in several parts of this approach to improve the data synchronisation. For instance, in critical situation, only those data will be synced that has higher priority to improve the speed of data synchronisation and minimize the battery consumption of devices involved in data sync.

4.2 Conflict Resolution Manager

Data synchronisation between multiple replicated data inevitably encounters conflicts. These conflicts need to be detected and resolved properly. As discussed in Sect. 3, this procedure can be performed using three approaches including automatic, user-involved, and semi-automatic conflict resolution methods [16]. Our proposed Conflict Resolution Manager will choose the appropriate approach for each record based on its context (Data Context Model). By default, it applies user-involved conflict resolution for critical data, semi auto-sync for the data with medium priority and automatic conflict resolution for less critical data. However, the appropriate conflict resolution approach for each data can be defined in its context. In the case of automatic and semi-automatic conflict resolution, we apply a rule-based conflict resolution. Based on the proposed context model, it is possible to define a specific set of rules for each type of data. However, if the context model does not have any rules defined, a default rule (i.e. Recent Data Wins) is applied. Some examples of possible rules include: (1) Higher-Authority User Wins; (2) Expert User Wins (here a user with more relevant experience has the higher priority); (3) Recent Data Wins; and (4) Most Reliable/Accurate Device Wins. The flowchart of conflict resolution is shown in Fig. 5.

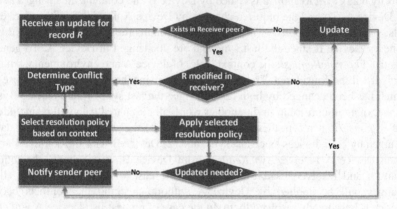

Fig. 5. Conflict resolution flowchart

5   Implementation and Experiments

To validate the proposed context-aware P2P data synchronisation approach, an Android application was implemented. In this section, we provide the details of the implemented prototype and results of data synchronisation experiments.

Peer Discovery and Connectivity. For peer discovery and connectivity, we used the Wi-Fi P2P API1. Wi-Fi P2P allows Android devices to connect directly to each other via Wi-Fi without an intermediate access point. These APIs can discover and connect to other devices when each device supports Wi-Fi P2P, then communicate over a speedy connection across distances longer than a Bluetooth connection. A user interface is designed for peer discover that can list all the available peers and allows users to choose the peer they are interested for data sync. After a user presses the connect button, a notification is sent to the selected peer, and if the peer accepts the sync request, data synchronisation will start.

Security. To achieve security, we implemented a RESTful web-service using J2EE technologies. This server is responsible for registering and authenticating users. Furthermore, it is also responsible for generating public/private key, and authentication token for each user when they login. In this research, an RSA algorithm was used for encryption and decryption of data.

Context Manager. To implement context manager module, Google Awareness API is used. The Awareness API exposes seven different types of context, including location, weather, user activity, and nearby beacons, enabling the app to get information about the user's current situation and environment. Based on the proposed context model, we combine these context signals to make inferences about the user's current context.

- Data Sync and Conflict Resolution: The application is tested on two android devices (Samsung Galaxy S III and Samsung GALAXY Note). We designed a set of test cases to evaluate our application under various circumstances by considering all the possible situations. The following parameters were considered during the conducted evaluation:
- Defining users with different roles (e.g. public user, admin user, registered user) and expertise (e.g. firefighter, emergency service workers, and ...)
- Defining environments with different Situations (i.e. Critical, Risky, and Safe)
- Defining various data items with different access level (e.g. public, confidential, or restricted), conflict resolution policy (e.g. expert user wins, higher-authority user wins, recent data wins, etc.)
- Conflict resolution method (e.g. replace, merge, add, average)
- Priority (i.e. High, medium, low)

During our experiments, all the test cases were passed successfully. The proposed framework handled offline data synchronization and resolved the possible conflicts.

Performance Evaluation. We evaluate the performance of the proposed data synchronisation framework by running the developed application on two android devices. We conducted 20 experiments by increasing the number of changes on the shared data from 0 to 1000 (with the increment step set to 100), and logged the number of exchanged messages, the volume of the exchanged messages, the volume of changed data, and synchronisation time. Figure 6 shows the results of the experiments. In the first experiment, we ran the sync algorithm without making any changes to the shared data to observe the possible overheads that could be incurred by the proposed framework.

The outcome of this experiment showed that syncing overhead is minor and can be neglected. In the rest of the experiments, it can be observed that increasing the number of changes has a slight impact on the volume of total exchanged messages and synchronisation time (see Fig. 6).

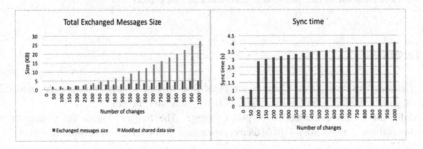

Fig. 6. Experimental results

More interestingly, it can be observed in the first graph of Fig. 6 that the volume of exchanged messages remained almost unchanged (increased from 1.7b kb to 4.7 kb), while the volume of changed shared data increased almost 60 times (from 0.47 kb to 26.9 kb). The reason behind this fact is that the messages are compressed before exchanging.

6 Conclusion and Future Work

Data Synchronisation is a well-studied area in a wide range of domains. Several solutions have been developed to deal with this problem. The applicability of these solutions depends on the chosen distributed model. Most of these solutions are designed for a hub-and-spoke model where the data is synchronised through a hub, a central server, but most solutions cannot be directly applied to a peer-to-peer model because the changes need to be synchronised with multiple clients. Synchronisation between multiple replicated data versions inevitably encounters conflicts. The main types of conflict involve the operations that must be performed on the same data record and occur when synchronisation is performed on multiple client devices. In this paper, we described a novel context-aware P2P data synchronisation framework for emergency situationswhich utilises user context to optimise data exchange and resolve conflicts between potential mobile hosts. The privacy and security of data can also be dealt with appropriately by including client credentials into the context model consisting meta-data about User, Data, Environment and Location. The implementation and evaluation demonstrated the use of this approach for synchronising data in the emergency management applications like Crisisworks tool for emergency managers. This approach would allow the users on the move to exchange updated information and receive new assignments without the need to look for a stable internet connection to the main server.

We presented the evaluation of our approach by running the developed application on two android devices. In our future work we are planning to evaluate the credibility of the proposed data sync approach by conduction a real-world experiment where hundreds of devices are involved.

Acknowledgements. This research was funded by the State Government Technology Development Voucher program and Datalink Internet Systems Pty Ltd. We acknowledge Peter Kakris's contribution to the initiation and conduct of this project.

References

1. Victorian Bushfires Royal Commission Final Report (2009). http://www.royalcommission.vic.gov.au/finaldocuments/summary/PF/VBRC_Summary_PF.pdf
2. Halls Gap: CFA concerned over phone outage, The Stawell Times-News. http://www.stawelltimes.com.au/story/4101016/emergency-concerns-over-grampians-phone-outage/?cs=12

3. Warrnambool Exchange Fire, Consumer and Social Impact Analysis, ACCAN (2014). https://accan.org.au/files/Grants/2014%20RMIT%20Warrnambool%20report_final.pdf
4. Manual 14 - Post-Disaster Survey And Assessment, Emergency Management Australia, Australian Emergency Manuals Series, Part III, Volume 2 (2001). https://www.aidr.org.au/media/1447/manual-14-post-disaster-survey-and-assessment.pdf
5. Chen, K., Shen, H., Zhang, H.: Leveraging social networks for P2P content-based file sharing in disconnected MANETs. IEEE Trans. Mob. Comput. 13, 235–249 (2014)
6. Raj, M., Kant, K., Das, S.K.: Energy adaptive mechanism for P2P file sharing protocols. In: Caragiannis, I., et al. (eds.) Euro-Par 2012. LNCS, vol. 7640, pp. 89–99. Springer, Heidelberg (2013). doi:10.1007/978-3-642-36949-0_11
7. Agarwal, S., Starobinski, D., Trachtenberg, A.: On the scalability of data synchronization protocols for PDAs and mobile devices. IEEE Netw. 16, 22–28 (2002)
8. Shial, G., Majhi, S.K.: Techniques for file synchronisation: a survey. J. Glob. Res. Comput. Sci. 5(11), 1–4 (2014)
9. Starobinski, D., Trachtenberg, A., Agarwal, S.: Efficient PDA synchronization. IEEE Trans. Mob. Comput. 2(1), 40–51 (2003)
10. SyncML. http://www.syncml.org
11. Palm developer knowledgebase manuals. http://palmos.com/dev/support/docs/palmos/ReferenceTOC.htm
12. Endo, S., Miyamoto, T., Kumagai, S., Fujii, T.: A data synchronization method for peer-to-peer collaboration systems. In: IEEE International Symposium on Communications and Information Technology 2004 ISCIT 2004, vol. 1, pp. 368–373 (2004)
13. Judge, F., Kalra, G.S.: Peer-to-peer data synchronization architecture (2010)
14. Balasubramaniam, S., Pierce, B.C.: What is a file synchronizer? In: MOBICOM 1998 (1998)
15. Ramsey, N., Csirmaz, E.: An algebraic approach to file synchronization. ACM SIGSOFT Softw. Eng. Notes 26(5), 175 (2001)
16. Shamim Hossain, M., Masud, M., Muhammad, G., Rawashdeh, M., Hassan, M.M.: Automated and user involved data synchronization in collaborative e-health environments. Comput. Hum. Behav. 30, 485–490 (2014)
17. Santoro, N.: Design and Analysis of Distributed Algorithms. Wiley-Interscience, Hoboken (2006)
18. Lee, Y., Kim, Y., Choi, H.: Conflict resolution of data synchronization in mobile environment. In: Laganá, A., Gavrilova, M.L., Kumar, V., Mun, Y., Tan, C.J.K., Gervasi, O. (eds.) ICCSA 2004. LNCS, vol. 3044, pp. 196–205. Springer, Heidelberg (2004). doi:10.1007/978-3-540-24709-8_21
19. Dey, A.K.: Understanding and using context. Pers. Ubiquit. Comput. 5(1), 4–7 (2001)

Is 'Context-Aware Reasoning = Case-Based Reasoning'?

Nawaz Khan[✉], Unai Alegre, Dean Kramer, and Juan Carlos Augusto

R.G. on Development of Intelligent Environments,
Department of Computer Science, Middlesex University, London, UK
{N.x.Khan,U.Alegre,D.Kramer,J.Augusto}@mdx.ac.uk

Abstract. The purpose of this paper is to explore the similarities and differences and then argue for the potential synergies between two methodologies, namely Context-aware Reasoning and Case-based Reasoning, that are amongst the tools which can be used for intelligent environment (IE) system development. Through a case study supported by a review of the literature, we argue that context awareness and case based reasoning are not equal and are complementary methodologies to solve a domain specific problem, rather, the IE development paradigm must build a cooperation between these two approaches to overcome the individual drawbacks and to maximise the success of the IE systems.

1 Introduction

Todays complex systems generate vast amounts of data from the external environment in order to provide an informed decision to the user. This data is collected through sensors, cameras, computers and by many other input devices, thus, equipping us with intelligent services. However, this sheer amount of data may cause the system effectiveness to be lost in hyper-space if not classified into useful and meaningful preference based set of choices [33]. In the domain of ubiquitous computing, developers are faced with plethora of techniques [6]. Some of these are well-established, others are reasonably new. Some researchers even combined multiple approaches as an integrated process [32]. This article looks at commonly used approaches, an established technique like case-based reasoning (CBR) and a newly more ad-hoc development like context-awareness reasoning (C-AR). The question we want to examine in this paper is whether context-awareness brought something truly new to ubiquitous computing in terms of knowledge presentation and reasoning. More specifically we are exploring how the synergies between C-AR and CBR can improve the quality of users' interaction with IE system.

Ubiquitous computing may use context-awareness or a case-based reasoning to develop a personalised recommendation, may be looking at the past history of the user, or may be by understanding his attempt to search and find a product [36]. To illustrate this: we may say, a user can visit Amazon to find a book for himself, in this case the recommendation set for the user will be those books that

© Springer International Publishing AG 2017
P. Brézillon et al. (Eds.): CONTEXT 2017, LNAI 10257, pp. 418–431, 2017.
DOI: 10.1007/978-3-319-57837-8_35

the user has bought in the past. However, if the user is willing to purchase book as a gift for his wife, then the choice set of recommendation will be different than the books he buys for himself. So, we would see these two disjoint events as an application of case base reasoning or may be an application of context awareness. This article presents first a brief description of C-AR and CBR in Sects. 2 and 3, we compare them conceptually in Sects. 4 and 5 and we illustrate the conceptual comparison in Sect. 6 with a case study.

2 Concept of Context Awareness (C-AR)

Contextual awareness stemmed from the desire of Ubiquitous Computing to increase the usability of computerised systems through the implicit interpretation of what the user wants. The concept of Context-awareness was introduced by Schilit and Theimer [34] when they proposed information mapping for a network system. Context-awareness deploys an environmental information set that is available for a given circumstances in order to perform an act that assists a user to make a decision [15]. The ambition is to embed human-like contextual awareness into systems, to make the interaction with them more natural. It has to be mentioned that there is a lack of agreement on the definition of context [3]. The theory of context varies as it has been defined in different research areas, for example, Schilit and Theimer identified a context by means of location, identities, neighbourhood objects and people and any variations on the objects [34]. It presents the multifarious dimensionality towards identifying a context and these are: physical factors dimension, human factors dimension and time dimension [35]. Whereas Benerecetti et al. [11] classified context into two subsets, namely, 'physical context' and 'cultural context'. The cultural context includes the users personal data, social and belief information.

Dey and Abowd [14] defined the context as any information that can be used to characterise the situation of an entity, where an entity can be a person, place, physical or computational object that is considered relevant to the interaction between a user and an application, including the user and the application themselves. Dey extends his work by proposing a framework where context values will be obtained from four types of context [16,17], i.e., location, identity, time and activity. Abowd et al. [2] considered these as primary context. Furthermore, they considered secondary context any context that can be found using primary context. Perera et al. [31] classified the context into operational and conceptual. In the operational view, context is considered either primary if the information is retrieved without using other existing context information or secondary, if it can be computed using existing context. In the conceptual perspective, context is classified into activity, time, identity and location [14]. The rest of the contexts in this perspective can be obtained combining the elements between themselves. He proposed the context aware application as 'a system is context-aware if it uses context to provide relevant information and/or services to the user, where relevancy depends on the users task'.

Dey [15] suggested that the three main activities that context aware applications should perform are: (i) the presentation of information and services to a user, (ii) automatic execution of a service, and (iii) tagging of context to information for later retrieval. C-AR have been closely related to human interaction since its inception. Alegre et al. [4] studied the way the system can interact with the users, classifying it intothe Execution and Configuration phases. The first one refers to the actions/behaviours of the system when a specific situation arises. The second one is related to the adjustment of actions/behaviours that a system will be exhibiting in the future. These two independent modalities of interaction can have a degree of active/passiveness. By 'active', they refer to the interactions in which the system changes its content autonomously. By 'passive', they mean those where the user has explicit involvement in the actions taken by the system. By observing the interaction modalities of users with context-aware systems, they extended Dey and Abowds [15] classification of the features of a C-AR as: (a) Presentation of information to the stakeholders; (b) Active or passive execution of a service; (c) Active or passive configuration of a service; (d) Tagging context to information [3].

Typically, the information of a context-aware system has four stages [31]. They are:

1. Acquisition: where the data considered as context is retrieved from the sources. These sources can be very disparate, including any type of physical, logical or virtual sensors [20].
2. Modelling: after the data is acquired, it needs to be Modelled, formatting the values from the sensors into something that can be used by an application (e.g., from coordinates to the name of a city).
3. Reasoning: this data can also be used to create higher level information by Reasoning.
4. Dissemination: Low and high level context information has to be available to the different applications, through a process known as Dissemination.

The next two sections focus on the techniques available for context modelling and reasoning.

2.1   Context Modelling

One important aspect of a C-AR, is how the information will be processed and stored. Typically, these kind of applications use a context model, which identifies a concrete subset of the context that is realistically attainable from sensors, applications and from users and then subsequently are exploited in the execution of the task [19]. The most popular context modelling techniques are [14,18,31]:

- Key-value Modelling: key-value pairs are used for context information.
- Markup Scheme Modelling: Models data using tags such as XML.
- Graphical Modelling: demonstrates relationships of context data using graphical notations.
- Object Based Modelling: Object oriented concepts are used to model data using class hierarchies and relationships.

– Logic Based Modelling: Facts, expressions and rules are used to represent context information.
– Ontology Based Modelling: The context is organized into ontologies, using semantic technologies.

2.2 Context Reasoning

Abowd et al. [2] suggest classifying reasoning in C-AR as: i. Pre-processing: where the aim is to make later processing easier by recognizing the relevant context attributes, handling missing ones and clearing the data, ii. Sensor data fusion: where the data is integrated from multiple resources and iii. Context inference: that creates high-level information from low-level information.

Further to this, numerous works [8,19,31], surveyed the approaches deployed for context-reasoning in Ubiquitous computing. They are summarised as:

– Supervised learning: Training examples are collected, labelled according to the expected results and then a function is derived to generate the expected results by using the training example data.
– Unsupervised learning: This category of techniques can find hidden structures in unlabelled data.
– Rules: It defines what has to be done in a simple way, typically in IF-THEN-ELSE format.
– Probabilistic logic: Allows decisions to be made based on probabilities attached to the facts related to the problem.
– Fuzzy-logic: In traditional logic acceptable truth values are as 0 and 1, in fuzzy logic partial values in between are acceptable. This method is similar to probabilistic reasoning, but membership set represents degree of confidence rather than probability.
– Ontology based: Its foundations are on description logic, a family of logic based knowledge representation formalisms.

3 Concept of Case-Based Reasoning (CBR)

CBR is an artificial intelligence approach to determine a similarity amongst a set of cases [25]. CBR method of similarity indexing is foundation of many intelligent systems. This method entails, indexing cases, retrieving the best past case from memory, adapting the old solution to conform to the new situation, testing whether the proposed solution is successful, and learning to prohibit solution fails. CBR has been viewed as a technology for automated, intelligent problem solving based on cases that present a circumstance [24].

CBR is based on the notion that the similar cases will have similar solutions. Hence, this method looks into the previous cases, analyse the similarity of cases, analyse the previous solutions of those cases and then propose a new solution based on the similarity of the previous cases and solutions [38]. The knowledge base contains the general domain knowledge, which is the set of rules needed for reasoning in this domain and sometimes some general facts (i.e., which are known to be always true). In a rule-based system, these IF-THEN rules and general facts represent the knowledge of the system. However, one of the important advantages of CBR is its ability to evolve by accumulating cases and each time a new solution set is emerged from the evolving case base. The nearest neighbour algorithm determines the similarity or dissimilarity of a new case with the case base and follows a cyclical process of Retrieve-Reuse-Revise-Retain [1].

However, the overall objective of this case based reasoning is to build up context reasoning, in other words, representing knowledge. Therefore, the concept of context awareness underpins the context reasoning for knowledge representation. Context reasoning system development paradigm uses two types of symbolic knowledge as a context: Facts and Rules. The facts and rules are then used for reasoning within the domain of a given problem. The reasoning process is based on logic, and allows the rule-based system to search through the problem space and arrive to a conclusion or a solution of a given problem based on the initial conditions (initial facts). The initial condition can be, for example, a set of facts describing a fault in a system, and the conclusion may be another fact stating the reason of that fault. Unlike conventional programs in which the precise steps are defined in clear algorithmic terms, rule-based systems are largely declarative and parallel in nature.

Perera et al. [31] describes the knowledge reasoning as a process of giving high-level context deductions from a set of contexts. The most fundamental aspects of building up reasoning involves: i. propositions: description of facts, ii. Logical operators: negate, conjunction and disjunction and iii. Inference: deriving conclusion about one fact based on a set of rules, in other words, fact is the implication of rules which are derived from context data. However, one crucial aspect of reasoning inference is conflict resolution [7], therefore, there should be a strategy to select one fact from the conflict set. There are different strategies for conflict resolution, for example, i. Refraction: once the rule has fired it will not be used, ii. Recency: use the fact that has been used recently in such a situation, iii. Specificity: use the fact with the more specific contexts, iv. Priority: ranking the factors and selection of priority with the highest rank, and and v. Parallel: all facts are contributed as a different set of reasoning.

4   CBR and C-AR in IE Development

In the Intelligent Environment development paradigm, sensors are utilised to capture contexts to produce cases. Therefore, capturing all these contexts for reasoning is not feasible [31]. The case based system implementation relies on decision making based on three parameters: pattern recognition-conflict resolution-action. The Recognition-action cycle is repeated until the solution is reached or no applicable rule can be found in the knowledge base. The reasoning build up by the environment is very similar to those of human experts. Basically, there are two ways to carry out the reasoning process: forward chaining (or data-driven) and backward chaining (or goal-driven). In both reasoning processes, we need to use the search strategies to guide the reasoning. Because a practical rule-based system normally contains a high volume context information which creates a large searching space.

There is much evidence where we see CBR is applied to the development of context aware applications and vice-versa [32]. It is demonstrated in Leakes work [27] that CBR can benefit developing a context aware system in designing smart homes where users can customise the requirements by building a case and system can gain knowledge from the context of the environment and then match a case. Kofod and Aamondt [21,22] developed a mobile context aware system where context information is embedded into cases for a situations assessment. Kumar et al. [26] developed an interesting system for e-commerce applications where two distinctive cases are created, i.e., user cases and product cases. These two cases are built upon the context of users and products to incorporate multiple context dimensions to the cases. Lee and Lee [28] developed a music recommendation system where users behaviour, demographics and context details are used for a case base recommendation. However, it can be argued that incorporating CBR into C-AR depends on the availability of contextual knowledge of an action, if the requisite contextual data is not available CBR can support C-AR by recalling previous case. This integration can improve quality of IE sytem when domain knowledge is limited.

5   CBR and C-AR Distinctions and Dynamic Relationship

This section focuses on the synergies and differences between the aspects of CBR and C-AR. Some of the techniques for CBR could also be used in C-AR and vice versa. On one hand, the origins of context-awareness stemmed from the need of different areas such as Ubiquitous Computing, Ambient Intelligence or Intelligent environments of having an enhanced human-computer interaction. On the other hand, the CBR method is used to solve problems that are based on similar solutions applied before. Applied to context-aware systems, this could help its configuration, enabling the evolution of the system after its implementation. At a first sight, it looks like CBR could be used to develop the configuration of context-aware systems in both its active and passive modalities [29,37].

Also, the information in CBR and C-AR is treated in a different way. C-AR need to acquire the information from distributed and heterogeneous sources. All this data needs to be modelled and translated in a meaningful way, so that it can be reasoned to obtain higher level information [13]. Finally, the data needs to be ready for different applications on demand. On the contrary, CBR follows a different process. The first step is similar to the acquisition of context, but instead of using different distributed sources, it retrieves the information from a memory of existing cases. Then, this process is followed by the reuse stage, where the solution is mapped from the previous case to the target problem. This stage can also involve an adaptation to the solution according to the circumstantial needs. Once the solution is mapped to the target situation, it is tested and revised until it has been successfully adapted to the target problem. At this point the solution is stored in the case memory. As it can be observed, these two process are quite different.

The context modelling stage is related to the knowledge representation of the system. These techniques are currently used to assign a meaning to the information that comes from the sensors but it could also be used to store the different cases in the memory. Case based reasoning supported by a rich knowledge model could be a promising approach to assess situations by being context aware [22,23]. Markup scheme and Ontology based modelling seem the most promising ones for CBR. Reasoning techniques in context-aware systems, are used for pre-processing, sensor data fusion and context inference. On the other hand, CBR takes an alternative view. Rather than seeing reasoning as primarily a composition process, it looks at it as remembering one or concrete set of concrete instances or cases and basing decisions on comparisons between the new situation and the old instance [25]. Nevertheless, most of the reasoning techniques used in context-awareness have been also used in CBR approaches [10].

Kofod-Petersen [21] identified the main challenges for using CBR in Ambient Intelligence are: i. Acquiring the initial cases, ii. Coping with the vast number of case being constructed during run time, iii. Knowing when to initiate a case-based reasoning cycle and iv. Knowing whether a case was classified correctly.

In Table 1, we summarise the pros and cons of both the C-AR and CBR methods of problem solving. We also attempt to identify the synergies between these two methods and derived a distinction between C-AR and CBR (Table 2). Table 2 points out how these two reasoning development methodologies are complementary to each other.

6   Case Study

In an effort to understand the differences and synergies between both C-AR and CBR, let us consider a case study based on an EU Project named POSEIDON [5]. The project is aimed at increasing the social independence and integration of people with Downs Syndrome through the use of IE technologies. An approach taken in POSEIDON to help better integrate our user group in society is through the improvement of individual effectiveness at navigating their environment, for example from home to work. In Table 3, we summarize the user driven situations within our case study where C-AR and CBR can be applied as a solution.

6.1   Uses of Context-Awareness in POSEIDON

Services developed in the POSEIDON project include a mobile element. This mobile element is composed of multiple services, including an app for navigation and calendaring, and a mobile context reasoner. The context reasoning for the mobile is designed to be a centralized entity for providing context-awareness services to multiple mobile applications on a single device. This reasoner can infer contexts using data from mobile sensors, data from web services, and data

Table 1. A comparison study of CBR and CAR in IE development

Attributes	Context aware reasoning	Case based reasoning
Generic feature	Improve the HCI using implicit information from situation Process involves: acquisition, modelling, reasoning and dissemination	Solve problems based on solutions to similar problem Process involves: retrieve, reuse, revise and retain
Merging challenge	CBR in C-AR: acquiring the initial cases Coping with high amount of cases constructed at runtime Knowing when to initiate a case-based reasoning cycle Knowing whether a case was classified correctly	CAR in CBR: inferring facts from cases Storing the inferences in a meaningful way in the context model
Merging advantages in IE	Evolution: C-AR can benefit from the possibility of retrieving similar cases and adapting them according to the circumstances Expert system like solutions: it can enable C-AR to solve problems in contextual situations that are partially understood since it creates a better understanding of the situation for each case High level context awareness can be generated from database	Pattern recognition: context validation through data semantics Conflict resolution: semantics matching from context database Knowledge representation: allow edit, search and debugging knowledge Knowledge base: reasoning process accumulates new facts and add them to the searching space
Merging challenge in IE	Evolution: CBR can adapt solutions that are better match for the current situation. Nevertheless, this introduces some loss of control over what the system is executing and why Heavy-weight operations: CBR requires to compare all the possible cases at runtime, which can be computationally expensive	Pattern recognition: depends on the reliability of the context acquisition. Semantic conflicts may arise C-AR typically operates with devices that do not have plentiful resources Conflict resolution: validity of the resolution depends on real data sets New set of data are generated without the context facts

Table 2. Synergies between C-AR and CBR methods for IE development

Synergies	Configuration interaction modality of C-AR could be based on the solutions to similar cases
	Internal and external contexts can be added in an intelligent environment system to derive reasoning for a case in order to represent knowledge
	Context reasoning enables to build up a case for a fact and can represent knowledge
	Cases are modelled by deploying context mapping based knowledge representation
	Data storage for C-AR and CBR is domain specific and establishes a relationship amongst the facts
	It is supported by meta logic and follows the same principles of data acquisition
	Context modelling involves knowledge acquisition knowledge representation and knowledge extraction; thus, build a case for a problem
	Context distribution is achieved when a reasoning is generated from a set of contextual facts, thus, represent the knowledge
	Goal driven case based reasoning can be supported by multi-dimensional context acquisition and by supplying personalised and localised context reasoning

from other applications on the device. Context information is inferred over by the use of stream reasoning, using C-SPARQL [9] for atomic level contexts, and forward reasoning [4] for context aggregations. These rules enable the reasoner to infer contexts, which are then broadcasted to each of the requiring applications.

In POSEIDON, context-awareness is used predominantly to provide information that can benefit the user, and also detect and provide options if the system suspects the user requires assistance. Different examples of the use of context include:

- Clothing advice based on weather conditions at planned destination. This can include to wear a coat if it is particularly cold, or take an umbrella if rain is expected. Lastly, we suggest to apply sunblock if the day is especially hot and sunny.
- Offering to call their carer if the system finds they deviate from the route, or are standstill for too long. Deviations requiring the offering of help include large single deviations where rerouting is required, or when the primary user makes small deviations too often. Being standstill for too long can be sign that their connection service e.g. a bus has not arrived, and may require further assistance.
- Determining when to begin giving navigational instructions based if they are indoors or outdoors. Instructions should be given when they are required. If the user is not outside ready to begin, it is of little benefit informing them make a particular turn.

6.2   Possible Uses of Case Based Reasoning

When considering possible uses of CBR within our project, we can foresee both isolated uses, and uses in conjunction with the context-awareness technologies already adopted. Firstly, in our project part of improving the independence of our user group is through navigation assistance. A second way that we can assist is helping our user group in daily tasks. This can include job related tasks, and leisure/home related tasks e.g. making lunch, cleaning. For our user group, they can have difficulty with abstraction, which can make learning tasks difficult, even if similar to each other. Often, minor differences in the context can render a task as a completely different one. Already, video based instructions are used for different tasks including making a coffee. One problem that arises is that new videos are required for different coffee machines and equipment they might use. A user friendly expert system could be useful for these situations assist the users by applying the knowledge of other similar tasks. This will be helpful in situations such as the ones described as only differing fragments of the task will be needed to be added to the system. In terms of supporting the creation/maintenance of cases, this will need to be an ongoing task of the primary user, and their carers.

Researchers have in the past used CBR in context-aware systems [22,23]. These approaches tend to have strengths on the ability to deal with new situations at runtime, where approaches based on predefined adaptation paths can struggle. In terms of context-aware development, CBR can be more useful in the adaptation/result phase, after context inference. The reason for this is that when adding additional contexts will often require developer intervention. This can include implantation of components to acquire new raw data from a sensor/data source, and specific rules on what situations that raw data represents, including aggregations with others. How the system behaves and/or adapts when in that collection of context situations can however change. For example, when considering navigational assistance, it is possible as the individual becomes more independent, other conditions in conjunction with the system determining the user needs assistance could determine a different action is taken. This could include not providing them the ability to call their carer, if they know the way home. Using CBR for adaptation strategies could also help prevent the issues with too many cases caused by arbitrary raw data including time.

7   Discussion

This article aims to initiate the further study of two different approaches that could potentially be used for strengthen each other. On one hand, C-AR aims to improve HCI by using of context, on the other hand, CBR tries to solve problems by using similar solutions used before to solve alike problems. C-AR can benefit from retrieving similar cases to provide different services or information. This could enable this kind of systems to solve problems that are partially understood since it can enable the creation of a better understanding in each case. On the other hand CBR could benefit from the pattern recognition, conflict resolution knowledge representation and knowledge bases of C-AR. The foremost challenges

Table 3. Challenges that can be met by C-AR/CBR or combination of both

Problem domain	Solution domain and reasons
Context raw data highly variable	Rule based context awareness, as does not require too many cases to be created
Dealing with evolving context adaptation	CBR based adaptation, as follows new adaptations strategies to be applied and evolve
Knowledge based system to assist users in tasks	CBR only, as it can assist the user in new situations where a particular task guide does not currently exist

we identified are: i. Lack of methodical description of why context awareness or case based reasoning is adopted for the implementation of intelligent systems, ii. Can we perform the same task by deploying either of these two methods, and iii. If there is a set of synergy in between these two approaches where they can supplement each other to derive reasoning.

There are challenges when trying to use CBR in C-AR. The first one will be to acquire the initial cases and coping with a high amount of cases constructed. Also, knowing when to initiate a case-based reasoning cycle and if it was correctly classified. Involvement from the users could be required for this purpose, such as feedback. On the other hand, when using C-AR in CBR, the challenge will be to infer facts from cases and storing the inferences in a meaningful way. The term context mainly used when contexts are derived when sensors perceive an environment and when there are complex method of acquiring data that can add more semantics to the data set in order to perceive an environment, i.e., cameras, move around sensing devices. The heterogeneous sources of information that elicit physical contexts as well as cultural contexts, an intelligent environment can build and use a contextual picture of the situation to perceive the environmental change [5]. Whereas, 'context reasoning' terms are used when high degree of meaningful information is extracted from the context data and provide a fact for an action to be taken [30]. This context awareness is middleware that supplies necessary feedback to the interface to adapt a situation for better services. Interestingly, contextual information can be used to derive a set of higher level contexts to deal with domain specific cases, which has then be termed as case based reasoning in several applications. The approach of higher degree of context awareness to build up a fact are evident in many intelligent systems, i.e., CARISMA [12], SOCAM [18] etc. Context-aware systems can be configured in order to evolve for adapting the changing needs of the users. We acknowledge that the adaptation of a context-aware system can be supported by CBR.

The challenge of building IE systems is to know exactly what reasoning method to use, however, it is still not very clear if context awareness and case base reasoning performs the same services or the concepts can be used interchangeably depending on the problem solution that we sought for. However, we can reach to a consensus that context awareness deals with continuous environment adaptation when contextual data are captured in real time, case based reasoning is the knowledge representation from a set of the facts. In our case study, context awareness predominantly assists the users by capturing atomic level context and then aggregating them to enable users to adapt specific situations. We can see that the use of CBR can help improve systems like POSEIDON by use of features in isolation, e.g., to assist task learning, but also in the current context-awareness system through use in each application on selecting the correction adaptation path for that set of context situations it is in. This solution can improve how the system deals in particular situations by allowing the adaptation strategy to change, but also helps keep the number of cases smaller than using it in the context inference itself.

8 Conclusion

In this paper we attempted to compare context-aware reasoning and case-based reasoning in order to build an argument how their dynamic relationship can assist scientists developing intelligent environment system. The applicability of these approaches is used in problem solving, but, it is not clear their range of applicability in the area of IEs. We have studied the main points where context-aware computing can benefit of case-based reasoning. We have provided a first insight on the distinction between when to use of context-awareness or case based reasoning and the key synergies for merging these approaches. In this review, with the use of literature and a case study, we made a case that expectation on intelligent system usability influence the selection of the methodologies. However, it is evident from our discussion that the fundamental development paradigm for such an intelligent system must consider multi-dimensional context data capture and then making these context data available to middleware in order to build up the context awareness and this context awareness gradually develops the cases and facts for knowledge representation. In other words, we can say the synergies between case based reasoning and context awareness are the fundamentals for the success of an intelligent system where contextual data is acquired for immediate situation adaptation.

References

1. Aamodt, A., Plaza, E.: Case-based reasoning: fundamental issues, methodological variations, and system approaches. Artif. Intell. Commun. **7**, 39–59 (1994)
2. Abowd, G.D., Dey, A.K., Brown, P.J., Davies, N., Smith, M., Steggles, P.: Towards a better understanding of context and context-awareness. In: Gellersen, H.-W. (ed.) HUC 1999. LNCS, vol. 1707, pp. 304–307. Springer, Heidelberg (1999). doi:10.1007/3-540-48157-5_29

3. Alegre, U., Augusto, J.C., Aztiria, A.: Temporal reasoning for intuitive specification of context-awareness. In: Proceedings of the 2014 International Conference on Intelligent Environments (IE), pp. 234–241. IEEE (2014)

4. Alegre, U., Augusto, J.C., Clark, T.: Engineering context-aware systems and applications: a survey. J. Syst. Softw. **117**, 55–83 (2016). Elsevier, ISSN 0164-1212

5. Augusto, J.C., Grimstad, T., Wichert, R., Schulze, E., Braun, A., Rødevand, G.M., Ridley, V.: Personalized smart environments to increase inclusion of people with downs syndrome. In: Augusto, J.C., Wichert, R., Collier, R., Keyson, D., Salah, A.A., Tan, A.-H. (eds.) AmI 2013. LNCS, vol. 8309, pp. 223–228. Springer, Cham (2013). doi:10.1007/978-3-319-03647-2_16

6. Augusto, J.C., Callaghan, V., Cook, D., Kameas, A., Satoh, I.: Intelligent environments: a manifesto. Hum.-Centric Comput. Inf. Sci. **3**, 12 (2013). doi:10.1186/2192-1962-3-12

7. Aztiria, A., Augusto, J.C., Basagoiti, R., Izaguirre, A., Cook, D.J.: Learning frequent behaviours of the users in intelligent environments. IEEE Trans. Syst. Man Cybern. Syst. **43**(6), 1265–1278 (2013)

8. Baldauf, M., Dustdar, S., Rosenberg, F.: A survey on context-aware systems. Int. J. Ad Hoc Ubiquitous Comput. **2**(4), 263–277 (2007)

9. Barbieri, D., Braga, D., Ceri, S., Valle, E.D., Grossniklaus, M.: Querying RDF streams with C-SPARQL. SIGMOD Rec. **39**(1), 20–26 (2010). doi:10.1145/1860702.1860705

10. Begum, S., et al.: Case-based reasoning systems in the health sciences: a survey of recent trends and developments. IEEE Trans. Syst. Man Cybern. Part C Appl. Rev. **41**(4), 421–434 (2011)

11. Benerecetti, M., Bouquet, P., Bonifacio, M.: Distributed context-aware system. Hum.-Comput. Interact. **16**, 213–228 (2000)

12. Capra, L., Emmerich, W., Mascolo, C.: Carisma: context-aware reflective middleware system for mobile applications. IEEE Trans. Softw. Eng. **29**(10), 929–945 (2003)

13. Cuddy, S., Katchabaw, M., Lutfiyya, H.: Context-aware service selection based on dynamic, static service attributes. In: IEEE International Conference on Wireless and Mobile Computing, Networking and Communications (2005)

14. Dey, A.K.: Understanding and using context. Pers. Ubiquit. Comput. **5**, 4–7 (2001)

15. Dey, A.K., Abowd, G.D.: Towards a better understanding of context and context-awareness. In: CHI 2000 Workshop on the What, Who, Where, When, Why, and How of Context-Awareness, The Hague, Netherlands, pp. 1–6 (2000)

16. Dey, A.K., Futakawa, M., Salber, D., Abowd, G.D.: Combining context-awareness with wearable computing. In: Proceedings Symposium on Wearable Computers, pp. 21–28 (1999)

17. Dey, A.K., Salber, D., Abowd, G.: A conceptual framework and a toolkit for supporting the rapid prototyping of context-aware applications. Hum.-Comput. Interact. **16**, 97–166 (2001)

18. Gu, T., Pung, H.K., Zhang, D.Q.: A service-oriented middleware for building context-aware services. J. Netw. Comput. Appl. **28**(1), 1–18 (2005)

19. Henricksen, K.: A Framework for Context-Aware Pervasive Computing Applications. Computer Science, School of Information Technology and Electrical Engineering, The University of Queensland (2003)

20. Indulska, J., Sutton, P.: Location management in pervasive systems. In: Australasian Information Security Workshop Conference on ACSW Frontiers 2003, vol. 21, pp. 143–151. Australian Computer Society Inc. (2003)

21. Kofod-Petersen, A.: Challenges in case-based reasoning for context awareness in ambient intelligent systems. In: 1st Workshop on Case-Based Reasoning and Context Awareness (CACOA 2006) (2006)

22. Kofod-Petersen, A., Aamodt, A.: Contextualised ambient intelligence through case-based reasoning. In: Roth-Berghofer, T.R., Göker, M.H., Güvenir, H.A. (eds.) ECCBR 2006. LNCS (LNAI), vol. 4106, pp. 211–225. Springer, Heidelberg (2006). doi:10.1007/11805816_17

23. Kofod-Petersen, A., Aamodt, A.: Case-based situation assessment in a mobile context-aware systems. In: Workshop on Artificial Intelligence for Mobile Systems, Seattle, AIMS 2003 (2003)

24. Kolodner, J.L.: Case-Based Reasoning. Morgan Kaufman, San Mateo (1993)

25. Kolodner, J.: Case-Based Reasoning. Morgan Kaufmann, San Mateo (2014)

26. Kumar, P., Gopalan, S., Sridhar, V.: Context enabled multi-CBR based recommendation engine for e-commerce. In: Proceedings of IEEE International Conference on e-Business Engineering, ICEBE 2005, pp. 237–244. IEEE Computer Society Press, Los Alamitos (2005)

27. Leake, D., Maguitman, A., Reichherzer, T.: Cases, context, and comfort: opportunities for case-based reasoning in smart homes. In: Augusto, J.C., Nugent, C.D. (eds.) Designing Smart Homes. LNCS (LNAI), vol. 4008, pp. 109–131. Springer, Heidelberg (2006). doi:10.1007/11788485_7

28. Lee, J.S., Lee, J.C.: Context awareness by case-based reasoning in a music recommendation system. In: Ichikawa, H., Cho, W.-D., Satoh, I., Youn, H.Y. (eds.) UCS 2007. LNCS, vol. 4836, pp. 45–58. Springer, Heidelberg (2007). doi:10.1007/978-3-540-76772-5_4

29. Ma, T., et al.: Context-aware implementation based on CBR for smart home. In: IEEE International Conference on Wireless and Mobile Computing, Networking and Communications, (WiMob 2005), vol. 4. IEEE (2005)

30. Mishra, N., Petrovic, S., Sundar, S.: A self-adaptive case-based reasoning system for dose planning in prostate cancer radiotherapy. Med. Phys. **38**(12), 6528–6538 (2011)

31. Perera, C., Zaslavsky, A., Christen, P., Georgakopoulos, D.: Context aware computing for the internet of things: a survey. IEEE Commun. Surv. Tutor. **16**(1), 414–454 (2014)

32. Pla, A., Coll, J., Mordvaniuk, N., López, B.: Context-aware case-based reasoning. In: Prasath, R., O'Reilly, P., Kathirvalavakumar, T. (eds.) MIKE 2014. LNCS (LNAI), vol. 8891, pp. 229–238. Springer, Cham (2014). doi:10.1007/978-3-319-13817-6_23

33. Resnick, P., Varian, H.R.: Recommender systems. Commun. ACM **40**, 56–58 (1997)

34. Schilit, B., Theimer, M.: Disseminating active map information to mobile hosts. IEEE Netw. **8**, 22–32 (1994)

35. Schmidt, A., Beigl, M., Gellersen, H.W.: There is more to context than location. Comput. Graph. **23**, 893–901 (1999)

36. Tsatsoulis, C., Cheng, Q., Wei, H.Y.: Integrating cased-based reasoning and decision theory. IEEE Expert **12**(4), 46–55 (1997)

37. Ur, B., McManus, E., Ho, M.P.Y., Littman, M.L.: Practical trigger-action programming in the smart home. In: Proceedings of CHI 2014, pp. 803–812. ACM (2014)

38. Watson, I.: Applying Case-Based Reasoning: Techniques for Enterprise System. Morgan Kaufmann, San Francisco (1997)

Quality on Context Engineering

Manuele Kirsch Pinheiro[(⊠)] and Carine Souveyet

Centre de Recherche en Informatique,
Université Paris 1 Panthéon Sorbonne, Paris, France
{Manuele.Kirsch-Pinheiro,
Carine.Souveyet}@univ-parisl.fr

Abstract. Engineering context-aware applications is a complex task. Not only the notion of context correspond to a large and complex notion, but its support on software applications involves multiple technical challenges and issues. Among these, the notion of Quality of Context (QoC) appears as a transversal concern affecting all the aspects of supporting context on such applications. Indeed, with the growing development of context-aware applications, it becomes essential to start considering quality of context on every step of the application development. The goal of this paper is to incite discussion on the issues related to supporting QoC on context-aware applications. Staring by considering the need of a context engineering process, we discuss the impact of considering quality during all steps of this process. Our goal is to promote quality concerns on a global context engineering approach.

Keywords: Context engineering · Context-aware application development · QoC

1 Introduction

Quality of Context (QoC) is an important issue on context-aware applications. With the growing development of such applications on multiple domains (health care, smart homes, transport, etc.), the importance of managing QoC is also growing, since the consequences of a low quality observation on the application behavior might be dramatic, or at least, may seriously affect the application reliably. Indeed, quality of observed context information may heavily influence the behavior of such applications, leading to possible undesired or unexpected results. Yet, context information is intrinsically uncertain. According to [11], context information is naturally dynamic and uncertain: it may contain errors, be out-of-date or even incomplete. For instance, the quality of the information collected by a given sensor may vary according to several different and possible unpredictable factors, leading to erroneous, incomplete or missing information. Uncertainty being indissociable from context information, handling quality of context becomes a central concern for reaching the reliability that is mandatory for the development of context-aware applications in the near future.

Unfortunately, supporting the notion of context on a software application is a complex task. Context information corresponds to a large and ambiguous concept, whose support implies several challenges. Understanding such a complex notion and

© Springer International Publishing AG 2017
P. Brézillon et al. (Eds.): CONTEXT 2017, LNAI 10257, pp. 432–439, 2017.
DOI: 10.1007/978-3-319-57837-8_36

identifying these challenges represent a hard task for software developers, making the development of context-aware applications particularly challenging. In order to tackle this issue, we have proposed in [9] a requirement analysis process intend to help non-expert designers on this application design process. This requirement analysis process is based on a context management roadmap, in which we have identified several dimensions highlighting on each one multiple challenges for context management.

Even if this roadmap [9] offers a global view of context management issues, it lacks a deeper analysis on the effects of considering QoC on context management. Indeed, it did not consider the management of QoC in deep, limiting its analysis to only some dimensions. We believe that QoC may influence each dimension of the roadmap, and not only some aspects, as the representation of context information as considered by [7]. Thus, in this poster, we intend to tackle this question, considering quality as a transversal concern, affecting all aspects of context management.

Based on the proposed roadmap, we propose in this poster a transversal analysis of challenges raise by considering quality of context on different aspects of context management. Our main goal is not necessarily to give solutions to these challenges, but mainly rising the necessary discussion about supporting quality on context-aware application development. We advocate that this discussion is essential for the development and expansion of future context-aware applications.

This poster is organized as follows: Sect. 2 introduces the original context management roadmap, while Sect. 3 considers effect of quality concerns on every dimension of the roadmap. Section 4 presents our conclusions.

2   Context Management Roadmap

Supporting the notion of context on software application represents a challenging task. First of all, the notion of context itself corresponds to a large and ambiguous notion that has been analyzed on several different ways on Computer Science and on other domains [3–5]. Supporting this notion on a software application involves different challenges, from acquiring and modeling this information till its interpretation and exploitation for different purposes [1–3, 9]. Acquiring the necessary knowledge for developing software application exploring this notion represents then a challenge for non-expert users.

In [9], we have tackled this question, by proposing a requirement analysis process and a context management roadmap, which consider multiple dimensions of supporting context on software applications. Indeed, there are several kinds of software applications that use the notion of context, not only context-aware applications. Adaptation of the application behavior, as proposed by context-aware applications, is not the only possible purpose of using context on a software. This notion may be explored on several ways, with different implications on the application design and behavior. We believe that considering context information on such applications, whatever its purposes is, demands a global approach, allowing to better apprehend the different aspects involved on the management of context information. The proposed roadmap [9] intents to be a first step towards such a global context engineering approach.

This roadmap, illustrated on Fig. 1, considers different aspects of managing the notion of context on a software application [9]. It considers different challenges related to the context management, organized on multiples dimensions. Each dimension focuses on different aspects and tackles different issues necessary to context management. For instance, *Purpose* dimension focuses on the purpose of using such information on a given application and the meanings and mechanisms of reaching it. The *Subject* dimension focuses on what information could be considered as context and how to identify relevant elements. The *Model* dimension considers context modeling issues. *Acquisition* highlights the challenges of acquiring context information from the environment, which implies considering the capture devices, the observation process and the management of context sources. The *Interpretation* dimension considers the challenges related to the interpretation of context information on its different forms (interpretation rules, context mining, etc.), while the *Diffusion* dimension explores the issues related to the transmission of context information among multiple nodes.

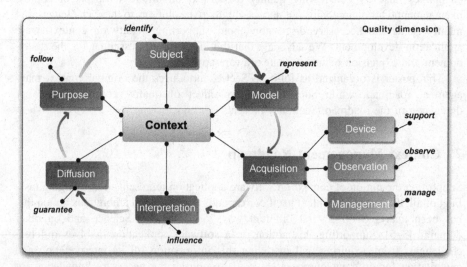

Fig. 1. Quality as a transversal plan affecting all the roadmap dimensions (modified from [9]).

As one may observe, roadmap proposed in [9] do not consider the influence of quality, limiting its analysis to some dimensions, as the acquisition and the subject dimensions. Nevertheless, several works pointed out the notion of Quality of Context [6, 7, 12]. These works illustrated quite well the variety of aspects related to QoC: [12] tackles the influence of QoC on context prediction and interpretation; [6] handles QoC on the software development through a MDE approach; while [7] proposes dealing with QoC on the context modeling. In our opinion, managing quality of context is not only a matter of representing correctly the context information or its meta-data. It demands a deeper reflection on the influence on QoC on all aspects of context management. For us, quality should be a transversal concern affecting all dimensions and steps of a context engineering process.

Based on the roadmap presented on [9], we discuss in the next section the influence of QoC concerns on each dimension of the roadmap.

3 The Quality Concern

Quality of context is a transversal concern that influences all aspects of the context management. This concern is represented in Fig. 1 as a transversal plan, affecting all other dimensions represented in the roadmap. On every dimension, particular challenges are considered and somehow influenced by the notion of quality. Indeed, when considering each dimension, we should consider the influence of taking QoC into account on supporting the dimension challenges. Thus, for each dimension, we tried to identify questions that should be considered when thinking about the influence of QoC. The main goal here is not necessarily to give solutions to these questions, but mainly to raise discussion on the impact of QoC on context management.

First dimension, *Purpose*, considers the purposes for which the notion of context is used in an application. According its purpose (*e.g.* adaption, decision making, etc.), an application can be more or less sensitive to errors or low quality context information. For example, a context-aware application explores context data for adaptation purposes. Errors on the context information may lead to erroneous decisions, which accordingly to the application domain, may be more or less important. The management of QoC should then start by considering what are the consequences of a poor quality context information and the consequences of having no information about it. For instance, let us consider a health care application which proposes to automatically adapt insulin levels according to patient's glycaemia or call emergency whenever the patient falls down. Reliability of this kind of application depends on the quality of observed context, since erroneous information may lead to a wrong decision with important consequences. These consequences should be considered but also the costs of managing QoC. Reaching application purposes implies several mechanisms that are potentially affect by QoC. Including QoC on those may represent a cost that should be considered. Will the cost of observing QoC be more or less important than the risk of non-observing it? For instance, in a heath care application, considering QoC on the adaptation process implies using different algorithms for detecting and eliminating suspicious measures. Such algorithms will consume processing and battery of hosting device. These represent an execution cost, in addition to design and development costs. Even if those can be significant compare to overall application costs, the risks and the possible consequences of not considering QoC justify these costs. Application developer should consider *the risks and the costs that will follow QoC* observation on the application purpose. However, one question raises from this dimension: how to measure such risks and costs?

Analyzing remaining dimensions may give us some insights about costs and risks of observing (or not) QoC. The dimension *Subject* considers what kind of information can be observed as context information. When identifying relevant context information, we may also identify possible QoC indicators that can be associated to it. Often, QoC consists of several elements like precision, up-to-dateness, freshness or probability of correctness [12]. Identifying what context information will be observed allow application developers to *identify either what quality information is relevant* to be associated with it for reaching application purpose. For instance, when considering location information, different quality indicators can be considered, such as estimated error or precision, freshness (which can be obtained regarding production time) or even the number of available satellites, when considering GPS data. Indeed, several QoC criteria are possible, as illustrated by Marie et al. [10]. These authors have identified and compared different QoC indicators proposed in the literature, highlighting the variation in terms and in meaning of these criteria.

All identified information should be represented in an appropriate context model. Considering QoC on the *Model* dimension implies considering *how to represent QoC information*, how it will be associated with observed context. Several researches have been done about context models [3–5], and multiple proposes have already considered the question of QoC [6, 7, 12], often through meta-data representing QoC indicators. For instance, Marie et al. [10] have proposed a QoC meta-model in which quality indicators are associated with context information. Each QoC indicator has also a set of associated values and it is defined by a QoC criterion containing a set of defined metrics. As summarized by Bettini et al. [3], a good context modeling approach must include modeling of context information quality to support reasoning about context.

It is impossible to consider context information without considering its acquisition. *Acquisition* dimension has three main focus: *device, observation* and *management*. When considering the necessary acquiring devices for context information, it is also important to consider if these *devices are able to support acquiring QoC indicators*. Similar to context information, QoC indicators are calculated based on information supplied by acquiring devices. The possibility to obtain a given QoC indicator depends on the capability of these devices offering basis information. For example, when considering GPS data, the number of satellites can be used for supposing data precision. If this information cannot be obtained for any reason, this criterion will be unavailable. Similarly, data confidence can also be considered as a quality indicator. Considering, for example, a team application that constantly informs users about project context (and progress), information about task progression might heavily depend on the information supplied by the users themselves. In this case, it seems difficult to estimate data confidence and then trustworthiness of this information. Besides, assuring quality of context information leads to choosing appropriate acquisition devices,, and consequently, to the costs associated with such devices. For instance, on a smart home application, one may consider using ground sensors for detecting a resident's fall, since these devices may offer a better accuracy for falling detection than simple accelerometers. The cost associated with these devices cab be justified according the application purposes (e.g. if application is designed for supporting medical care or special needs residents).

Similarly, context observing policies are directly influenced by QoC considerations. For instance, considering if a given context information needs a very frequent observation probably implies that freshness is a relevant QoC indicator for this information. It is often the case of location information on transport applications: when considering moving vehicles, the freshness of location information will indicate if this information can be still used or if new measures are necessary. Application developers must then consider *how to observe QoC indicators* during context observation process and how often this observation process should be realized. Finally, the management of acquiring infrastructure is also influenced by QoC. Observed environment being more and more dynamic, it is necessary to manage acquiring devices on this environment. This management can be influenced by QoC indicators (for example, deactivating a given device if precision offered by it is too low or reactivating it in order to increase overall system precision). In [9], we have considered a scenario in which flood and depth sensors distributed in a river are turned off in order to save battery and on again in order to guarantee that every portion of the river has enough sensors observing it, improving the quality of overall observation system. It is then important to consider not only *how to manage QoC information*, but also *how to manage acquisition environment according to QoC information?*

In order to contribute to application purpose, context information should often be interpreted using different reasoning mechanisms [3, 11], which is the focus of *Interpretation* dimension. Quality of context information may affect such mechanisms and influence the reliability of target application. An illustration of this influence is given by Vanrompay et al. [12]. In this work, authors discuss a set of metrics evaluating QoC and propose using such metrics on context prediction, in order to prevent low quality information affecting prediction mechanism. Works such as [12] demonstrate the importance of considering *how QoC influence context reasoning and interpretation*, and how can these reasoning mechanisms can explore QoC information for better results?

Finally, more and more context information is used on distributed software application needing the transmission of such information over multiple nodes. The *Diffusion* dimension considers challenges related to the distribution of context information [2]. When considering QoC on such distributed environments is then important to consider whether this transmission may affect quality of transmitted context information. For instance, real time context information may be affected by network latency and become out-of-date. When considering, for example, an application such as [8] that deploys its components on remote nodes according to available resources, if information about these resources is outdated because of network latency, deployment decision may lead to user's dissatisfaction and performance lost. It is then necessary, for application developers, to consider not only *how to guarantee QoC information transfer*, but also *how to guarantee that this diffusion of context information will not affect QoC?*

As illustrated on Fig. 1, quality concerns affect all aspects of context management, and consequently, all kind of software applications using this notion. It is worth noting that, as the variety of examples given in this section let us suppose, every dimension proposed in the roadmap on Fig. 1 will not equally influence all kind of applications. The relevance of each dimension depends on the purpose of the application itself and on the considered context information. It is then essential to consider and discuss on each dimension, considering its possible relevance for an application and the influence of the quality concern on it. In this section, we raise questions about the influence of quality concerns on every aspect. More than solutions, the main goal here is to initiate discussion and point out this influence and the importance of considering QoC on every aspect of context management.

4   Conclusion

A lot of research has been done around context and quality of context [3, 6, 7, 9], proposing interesting solutions for different issues. The main challenge now is not only dealing with remaining unsolved issues, but maybe is about acquiring necessary knowledge for developing new application. Non-expert software developers, when developing context-aware applications, are face to a very complex concept, whose understanding and management is far from simple. With the development of IoT and connected devices, and their integration in our everyday life, it becomes essential to form a new generation of software developers that are able to reason about context support and its challenges, including QoC. More than only technical solutions (that remain necessary), we need also to go further towards context engineering approaches, offering a global approach for apprehend the context notion on software development. Rising questions and discussion about the impact of QoC on context management is, for us, an important step towards a true context engineering approach.

References

1. Baldauf, M., Dustdar, S., Rosenberg, F.: A survey on context-aware systems. Int. J. Ad Hoc Ubiquit. Comput. **2**(4), 263–277 (2007)
2. Bellavista, P., Corradi, A., Fanelli, M., Foschini, L.: A survey of context data distribution for mobile ubiquitous systems. ACM Comput. Surv. **45**, 1–49 (2013)
3. Bettini, C., Brdiczka, O., Henricksen, K., Indulska, J., Nicklas, D., Ranganathan, A., Riboni, D.: A survey of context modelling and reasoning techniques. Pervasive Mob. Comput. **6**(2), 161–180 (2010). Elsevier
4. Brézillon, J., Brézillon, P.: Context modeling: context as a dressing of a focus. In: Kokinov, B., Richardson, D.C., Roth-Berghofer, T.R., Vieu, L. (eds.) CONTEXT 2007. LNCS (LNAI), vol. 4635, pp. 136–149. Springer, Heidelberg (2007). doi:10.1007/978-3-540-74255-5_11
5. Brézillon, P.: Context-based development of experience bases. In: Brézillon, P., Blackburn, P., Dapoigny, R. (eds.) CONTEXT 2013. LNCS (LNAI), vol. 8175, pp. 87–100. Springer, Heidelberg (2013). doi:10.1007/978-3-642-40972-1_7
6. Chabridon, S., Conan, C., Abid, Z., Taconet, C.: Building ubiquitous QoC-aware applications through model-driven software engineering. Sci. Comput. Program. **78**(10), 1912–1929 (2013). Elsevier
7. Chalmers, D., Dulay, N., Sloman, M.: Towards reasoning about context in the presence of uncertainty. In: 1st International Workshop on Advanced Context Modelling, Reasoning and Management (2004)
8. Da, K., Roose, P., Dalmau, M., Nevado, J., Karchoud, R.: Kali2Much: a context middleware for autonomic adaptation-driven platform. In: 1st ACM Workshop on Middleware for Context-Aware Applications in the IoT (M4IoT@Middleware 2014), pp. 25–30 (2014)
9. Kirsch-Pinheiro, M., Mazo, R., Souveyet, C., Sprovieri, D.: Requirements analysis for context-oriented systems. Procedia Comput. Sci. **83**, 253–261 (2016). 7th International Conference on Ambient Systems, Networks and Technologies (ANT 2016). Elsevier

10. Marie, P., Desprats, T., Chabridon, S., Sibilla, M.: The QoCIM framework: concepts and tools for quality of context management. In: Brézillon, P., Gonzalez, A.J. (eds.) Context in Computing: A Cross-Disciplinary Approach for Modeling the Real World, pp. 155–172. Springer New York, New York (2014)

11. Vanrompay, Y., Kirsch-Pinheiro, M., Berbers, Y.: Service selection with uncertain context information. Reiff-Marganiec, S., Tilly, M. (eds.) Handbook of Research on Service-Oriented Systems and Non-Functional Properties: Future Directions, pp. 192–215 (2011)

12. Vanrompay, Y., Mehlhase, S., Berbers, Y.: An effective quality measure for prediction of context information. In: 8th IEEE International Conference on Pervasive Computing and Communications Workshops (PERCOM Workshops), pp. 13–17 (2010)

Supporting Context-Aware Engineering Based on Stream Reasoning

Dean Kramer and Juan Carlos Augusto[✉]

R.G on Development of Intelligent Environments, Department of Computer Science,
Middlesex University London, London, UK
j.augusto@mdx.ac.uk

Abstract. In a world of increasing dynamism, context-awareness gives promise through the ability to detect changes in the context of devices, environment, and people. Equally, with stream reasoning using languages including C-SPARQL, continuous streams of raw data in RDF can be reasoned over for context-awareness. Writing many context queries and rules this way can however be error prone, and often contains boilerplate. In this paper, we present a context modelling notation designed to support the creation of context-awareness based on stream reasoning systems. In validating our language there is tool support which, amongst other benefits, can generate context queries in C-SPARQL and context aggregation rules for higher level context knowledge processing. An Android-compatible mobile platform context reasoner was developed which can handle these deployable context rules. This methodology and associated tools has been validated as part of an EU funded project.

Keywords: Context-awareness · Stream reasoning · Context modelling

1 Introduction

Context-awareness is becoming an increasingly core feature of mobile services. Most services so far make use one single atomic context, for example if location services are enabled in a mobile phone an app can suggest eating places nearby. However, contexts of interest can involve a wide range of contextual features e.g. temperature, luminosity, spatio-temporal coordinates, type of activity a user is performing, level of surrounding noise, and others. In combination, different situations of interest for providing useful service can be identified. These services can be created as a group of rules where we specify that given certain contextual conditions are satisfied we want the system to reach in a particular way. However the accumulation of rules and the aggregation of more than one rule to create higher level rules can easily lead to hidden indirect interactions within that set of rules which may go unnoticed to developers and be the cause of undesirable system behaviour.

Hence developers in the area have rightly resorted to different ways to understand contexts and their inter-relationships. For example, the use of ontologies

© Springer International Publishing AG 2017
P. Brézillon et al. (Eds.): CONTEXT 2017, LNAI 10257, pp. 440–453, 2017.
DOI: 10.1007/978-3-319-57837-8_37

for context-aware systems has been a popular approach for modelling context, and for context reasoning. These ontologies are often modelled using the Web Ontology Language (OWL), which allows for an explicit specification of the different contextual information in the system. The drawbacks to using static queries over ontologies that change frequently, and unsuccessful practical consideration of temporal features have been discussed by Valle et al. [24]. Mobile applications are becoming increasingly based on streams of high frequency real time data, hence there is a need for reasoners to have the ability to reason over temporal elements of the information. As a result, recent developments have started to get increasingly involved with *stream reasoning*. One such stream reasoning language includes C-SPARQL [5]. C-SPARQL extends the SPARQL query language to express and handle continuous queries, and allow for temporal based queries and reasoning through the use of RDF quadruples. By using stream reasoning, RDF tuples from different sensors and services can be queried in real-time.

To generate some form of stream reasoning based on languages like C-SPARQL, different queries often need to be created by hand. Creating these queries however can often be error prone, and also include a lot of boilerplate which could be present in many queries. This is particularly the case when contexts can contain many different states. Understanding a context tree hierarchy can be made more difficult if all rules and queries are based purely in text. In this paper, we propose the use of stream reasoning in mobile context-awareness system. To support developers in using stream reasoning, we propose a new modelling notation developed to assist in model abstraction. This notation can then generate the appropriate queries to be deployable on a mobile context reasoner developed to harness stream reasoning. This contribution is actually very consistent with recent surveys highlighting the lack of methodological support available to the community of context-aware systems developers [1].

The remainder of this paper is structured as following: In Sect. 2 we introduce a real life scenario which we use to illustrate our contribution. Section 3 presents the state of art regarding context modelling. Then in Sect. 4, we present our graphical notation used to model context. Next in Sect. 5, we describe how our context models are transformed to C-SPARQL rules, which are deployable on a running system. In Sect. 6 we validate our approach, and finally conclude and describe future work in Sect. 7.

2 Motivation

The research and innovation we report in this paper have been influenced by practical needs and informed by our experience and related research. Our practical needs come from a European project with a varied mix of stakeholders, which include end user organizations and commercial companies from several countries. Each of these add requirements in terms of usability, efficiency, affordability and dependability. Our innovation balances these. To illustrate the type of situations our modelling notation and reasoning software can support, we introduce a context scenario which is extracted from the real life situation we support within the European research project where the method and tool we report in this paper are being used.

As a practical scenario, people with different cognitive disabilities, particularly Down's Syndrome can face challenges integrating with society due to difficulties navigating their environment. Many young individuals with these disabilities often still want to retain or gain independence, much like other young people without cognitive disabilities. One way context-awareness can assist those users is by allowing them to navigate safely, giving them the ability to travel alone, however prompting the user if it perceives a problem. One of these problems can relate to following the route on their mobile device. In terms of deviating a route in mobile navigation systems, often the user either makes a small deviation (requiring a short return to their journey) or make a large deviation (where a completely new route needs calculating). To give people with cognitive disabilities independence, yet provide support when in need, we could suggest that those users should get support (asked if they wish to call their carer) if they have made a large deviation, and likely lost. Continuing this, to give some independence, and to prevent frustrating the user, we can allow the user to make a certain number of small mistakes without asking if they need assistance. This can allow them to make some corrections by themselves without interference, but still help them if they continue to make many small route mistakes. We can consider this a navigation assistance context, which can have both states "needed" and "not-needed". These contexts will need to handle temporal elements, as several of the opportunities for assistance will relate to helping them achieve goals at specific times (e.g., reaching school by 8AM or being reminded to pack Gym clothing on Wednesday), time can also be an indicator of certain desirable/undesirable situations (e.g., standing still for a long time in the way to a place, taking too long to reach a place, or being off the expected route for too long).

3   Related Work

In order for a system to be context-aware it must deal with a number of important issues, some of them are internal (system own awareness of current internal status and capabilities) and some are external and relates to the real world (for example, place, time, user preferences and needs). To achieve these, a context-aware system needs to model the context information. Context models and languages have predominantly been either *key-value models, markup scheme models, graphical models, object-oriented models, logic based models,* or *ontology based models* [23].

Key-value models are the simplest form of context models, involving a name and context value pairs, which have been used directly (without the use of AI techniques applied) in context-aware systems and frameworks [17]. Markup models are hierarchical data structures which consist of markup tags, attributes, and content, with an example being the Comprehensive Structured Context Profiles (CSCP) [11]. CSCP is based in RDF, and expresses context information

using service profiles, describing context information relevant to different sessions. Graphical models can use different graphical notations including UML,
Object-Role Modelling (ORM), and other domain specific modelling languages.
ORM based context models include the Context Modelling Language (CML)
[12]. Included in CML are constructs for describing information types, type classifications, metadata for quality, and type dependencies. UML based models
include ContextUML [21], and the MUSIC context model [19]. These models can
also be viewed as object-oriented models, as they use different object-orientation
concepts including inheritance, and encapsulation. Other domain specific languages (DSL) for context modelling include PervML [18,20] and MLContext
[13]. Different logic based modelling languages also exist, including the Calculus
of Context-Aware Ambients (CCA) [22], CONAWA [15], SCAFOS [14], and an
algebra of contextualised ontologies [7]. The CCA proposes a logical language
for expressing context properties using context expressions. Context expressions
can be composed to form complex expressions and formulas using first order
operators. The CONAWA calculus was inspired by the ambient calculus [8], and
extends it in a number of ways including syntax extensions, and aims for uniform
representation of entities and context.

All these approaches are useful to some extent, however they have not been
adopted extensively so far and part of the reason is in their complexity, either
conceptually or in terms of their computational requirements. The project which
triggered our research in this area requires of a process which combines development support, with real-time efficiency and correctness. After extensive literature
review and tests in our labs we identified a stream based query processing language which gave us reasonable efficiency in a mobile platform. Programming a
long list of inter-related queries however is not the most pleasurable experience
and it is also error prone not only at individual rule level but also in terms
of understanding the 'big picture' of how the collection of rules relate to each
other. Our context rule modelling language described in the next section facilitates that high level decision making of which contexts to consider and how they
inter-relate. The support we provide offers the following: we abstract from the
specific query language syntactic complications, and secondly force the team to
reflect and judge if the information sources needed for an inference are obtainable. Later on in this paper we explain how once this is determined an automatic
translation into a target query language can be obtained and how we used this
support to help developing a real-life system.

4 Modelling Notation

To alleviate the need for writing all context rules by hand, we introduce a context
modelling notation, illustrated in Fig. 1. In these models, we have three main
context model constructs: *context source, inference rule,* and *context state*.

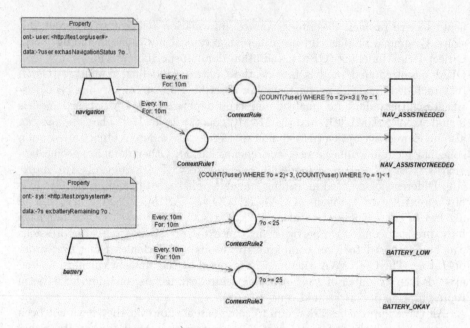

Fig. 1. An example model using our notation

4.1   Context Source

What separates context-aware systems with regular is the ability to infer the context of the device, user, and environment. For the developer to express rules to carry this out, there needs to be raw data for which can be reasoned over. This raw data can come from a variety of sources include sensors, and other off device services including web services. In the modelling notation, a context source object denotes a particular source of raw context data. This raw data is expected to be received in RDF triples. In the model, context sources are denoted with trapezium objects. Each context source can interact with more than a single inference rule. For each context source, there are different properties that can be added. The first includes an *Information Source*, which is used to define specific SPARQL ontological prefixes. The next property is *Data*, which relates to the RDF triples that context source provides. Just as in SPARQL, we denote variable names with a question mark (?) prefix. These variables can then be used in the Inference rules. A single context source can have a relationship between many different inference rules.

4.2   Inference Rule

Raw data alone is not always ideal for creating context-aware applications. For example, when considering remaining battery life in a mobile device, often people are interested to know when it is low, not if it is 67% charged. Having defined the raw data expected to be received by the device, to create more meaningful atomic context information, this raw data needs to be used in a context inference. This object denotes different inference rules that are used to infer a particular context state. Inference rules in our modelling notation can contain a mix of both simple *logical evaluations*, and more complex *functions*. Logical evaluations in the inference rules allow the developer to create rules based on a particular logical conditions, for example "if battery level is greater than 25%". To use logical expressions, the developer can reference particular variables from the context source. Only variables from a context source related to that particular context rule can be used. For multiple logical expressions, these can be separated with a comma allowing a conjuncture of different expressions.

Function usage within an inference rule are related to the different functions built-in to C-SPARQL/SPARQL. These functions can allow the developer to do far more computations over the raw data to assist inference. An example from our project includes calculating the total sum that a person has walked in a particular interval. In the inference rule, these functions can be used whereby the developer states the function signature, any variables required in the parameter parentheses. If the developer wants a particular set of RDF triples being used with the functions, they can be stated. By default, these functions are called with all RDF triples known the inference rule itself. Lastly, the developer can also apply logical evaluations to the returned result of those functions.

4.3   Context State

Having defined the particular inferences the system needs to make on the raw context data, the developer can use context states to be applied if the inference rule evaluates as expressed. Context states can be used for both single atomic contexts, and higher level aggregation contexts.

4.4   Relationships

In addition to these context constructs, there are relationships that exist between them. These construct relationships include:

- **Source - Rule:** This type of relationships defines what raw data the inference rule queries over. Included in this relationship is temporal operators regarding the raw RDF, including *data window size*, and *execution frequency*. Data window size relates primarily to how much RDF data can be included within the rule, and is noted by For. As featured in C-SPARQL, the data window can be either *physical* (a given number of RDF triples) or *logical* (a triples occurring with a given time inteval). Execution frequency relates to how often the inference rule is run in the reasoner, and is noted by Every. This frequency corresponds to sliding logical windows [9] in C-SPARQL, and in essence refers to the possibility of RDF triples being present in more than a single logical window. In practice this will equate to how often that query is updated. If the data window size is physical with exact triples being set, this field is not required.

- **Rule - State:** Inference rules themselves do not include the specific context states the rule equates to. This separation allows the developer to connect more than a single rule to a context state, which can encourage reuse.
- **State - State:** So far, we have considered the modelling of lower level, atomic contexts. These contexts deal with singular situations of an element, based on raw data from sensors. When developing context-aware systems, the ability to aggregate, and reason over a collection of different contexts gives the ability to consider higher level knowledge on a situation. For this, we allow the user to aggregate contexts together in our notation. To aggregate context values, we join the different context states together, and add a logical operator (AND, OR, XOR). If no logical operator is given explicitly, the default value is a conjunction.

4.5   Scenario Context Model

Continuing with the motivating scenario context, we model it using our notation, which can be seen in Fig. 1. We need two specific states, one when navigation assistance is needed, and one when it is not needed. We can name these states NAV_ASSISTNEEDED and NAV_ASSISTNOTNEEDED. Next, we model the context source, which we name "navigation" for ease. In this context source, we expect single RDF triples including the user identifier and its navigationStatus. We assign two variables, one to the user identifier ?user and one to the RDF value ?o. This will allow us to use them in the inference rules, two of which we need to create. For the rule we intend on binding to the NAV_ASSISTNEEDED state, we wish to express that if within the specified time interval, there needs to be 3 or more occurrences where the value in ?o is 2, or there is ever a value of 1. To find out the number of occurrences where ?o has the value of 2, we use the Count function passing the ?user variable. The rule intended for use by the NAV_ASSISTNOTNEEDED context state is more complex. We need to check that both the number of occurances of ?o being 2 is less than 3 times, and also check there are no occurrences of ?o having the value 1. Each of these two Count function uses is separated by a comma, defining the rule as a conjunction of the two.

5   Rule Generation

Following the construction of the overall context model, we need to generate the C-SPARQL queries and aggregation rules to be deployed on the mobile device. First, we get a list of all atomic and aggregate contexts in the model based on object relationships in the model. For atomic rules, context states will need to contain relationships with inference rules. In comparison, aggregation rules will purely have relationships with just other context states.

A C-SPARQL query is created for every atomic context. To do this, first the tree of objects that relate to that atomic context is retrieved. This includes inference rules, and context sources that are linked to those inference rules.

Queries names are generated using a concatenation of both the context state and
_query. Therefore a context state such as NAV_ASSISTNOTNEEDED will create a
query named NAV_ASSISTNOTNEEDED_query. Next, query prefixes are generated,
by using ont properties of the related context sources objects. Following this,
the type of C-SPARQL query is declared, in our case we use Construct queries,
which return an RDF graph based on the result of the query. Next, we set
the temporal operators of the C-SPARQL rules getting the execution frequency
and data window size from the source-rule relationship. In the event there are
multiple context sources with different temporal settings, we set the frequency
to be same as the most frequent using a data window size as the same as the
largest. Using these two temporal settings, we use the data window size value
for the Range, and execution frequency for the Step parameters. Next, Where
clause of the query are generated. Firstly, we copy all the data values from the
related context sources in the rule object tree including all declared variables
in RDF. Following this, we generate any subqueries that might be required
in the context query. Subqueries within our modelling notation are generated
only for handling functions within C-SPARQL. This generation is explained in
the following subsection. Finally, we generate SPARQL Filter clauses for any
inference rule logical evaluations. If multiple logical evaluations have been used,
each comma separated, a filter is created for each one.

5.1 Handling Functions

As introduced earlier, we allow the use of SPARQL aggregate functions in inference rules. When generating C-SPARQL rules, these are handled through the
generation of subqueries. For every function used in the inference rule, a Select
subquery is generated. These generated subqueries are places within the Where
clause block in the main context query. In this generated select query, we first
get the function name and any passed parameters. Next we have to give the
function return variable a name which is added after the AS keyword, which for
this generate a name subqres_ with a incremented number. An example can be
COUNT(?user) As ?subqres_1, which would counts the number of occurrences
of the value held in variable ?user, placing the resulting number in the ?sub-
qres_. Following this, we create the Where clause copying the raw data RDF from
the context sources, the same as the main query. Finally, where functions usage
have a logical evaluations to be used over the resultant variables, we generate
Filter clauses for each evaluation using the variable generated automatically
earlier.

5.2 Aggregate Contexts

As described earlier, we do not use C-SPARQL for context aggregation. We
instead, we generate propositional formulas to represent our aggregation rules.
These rules are evaluated on the deployed mobile device by means of boolean
satisfiability. For satisfiability tests, we generate propositional rules that use

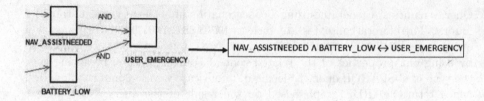

Fig. 2. Aggregation context generation

equality as a method of determining if the aggregate context is true. To generate these aggregation rules, we check the model for Context State-to-Context State relationships. These relationships occur when two context states are joined together, which also have a particular logical connective including AND, NOT, OR. In Fig. 2, we illustrate a context aggregation, and the aggregation rule that is created.

5.3   Mobile Context Reasoner

Complementing the modelling notation, generation of the C-SPARQL queries and aggregate contexts, we designed a mobile context reasoner which uses the C-SPARQL queries and aggregations rules for reasoning. This reasoner is designed to be extensible by different applications which want to reasoner over new contexts. This is carried out by separating raw data retrieval and acquisition from reasoning. Each application can add new raw data observers that get data from sensors, device broadcasts, and cloud services, and add new C-SPARQL and aggregation rules to extend the reasoner in new directions and purposes. Further details of the reasoner can be found in [3].

6   Validation

Currently, we are validating this approach in an FP7 European project aimed to assist project with Down's Syndrome (DS). The core aim of this project is to increase the inclusion of such citizens through the assistance of travelling and navigation. This project is using a combination of home learning, through the use of mix reality to assist users in creating and learning routes with their carers', and context-aware navigational services. An output of the project is to also assist other developers to develop context-aware services for people with DS, and other user with cognitive disabilities to assist them with daily tasks. Within POSEIDON, validation of our approach has been carried out both by implementation, and use with real end users.

6.1   CoMo Tool

Firstly, part of the validation is to help support developers in creating context models and rules using the described approach. To validate our modelling notation, tool support was implemented on top of the modelling tool, *Modelio* which we named *CoMo*[1]. Modelio is an opensource modelling environment that supports notations including UML2, and BPNM2. Modelio supports additional notations through the use of extensions which can be added to Modelio projects. Our tool has been implemented as an extension module which can be added by developer end users to their Modelio installations. As described in this paper, we include the ability to generate C-SPARQL queries and aggregation rules using propositional formula. The Long term goal for our tool is to generate context models for multiple languages. To do so, developers can use and extend our `AbstractModelWriter` class to create language printers for different runtime context systems. Using the modelling tool, each of the constructs are drag and drop objects, and includes tabs for inputting the construct properties. When the user is satisfied with their model, they can select to export the model to C-SPARQL queries and our aggregation rules (Fig. 3).

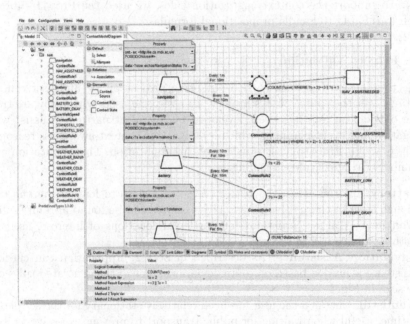

Fig. 3. Context Modeller Modelio extension

6.2   Android Middleware

To validate the mobile reasoner, we have developed a working prototype on the Android platform. This reasoner has been developed to be deployable in following scenarios:

---

[1] Source code available at: https://github.com/deankramer/ContextModeller.

- **Centralised Application:** The reasoner is a completely separate application which can be installed and used independently. Using this approach, the end user can download the reasoner, which is currently available from the Google Play Store.
- **Integrated into an Existing Application:** The reasoner is integrated as a software library into an existing application during compilation.

C-SPARQL has been implemented through the extension of Apache Jena. To include C-SPARQL in Android, we had to make a number of modifications. Firstly C-SPARQL uses Esper, an event processing library by EsperTech, which is not fully compatible with Android. We found an Android compatible version of Esper named Asper, which we used. Secondly, Apache Jena uses the Simple Logging Fascade for Java (SLF4J) library for logging. This as well was changed for the Android equivalent. Other modifications included package renaming in Apache Jena component libraries due to namespace conflicts in the Android SDK. To support the context aggregation rules, we used the Prop4J[2] library, which uses Sat4J to handle propositional formulas.

6.3   Project Validation

Project validation has been carried out using project pilots, and user centred meetings over the course of this project. To assist the users when they are travelling outside, an app has been developed by a project partner to assist with navigation and event planning, which leverages our context-awareness reasoner. In Fig. 5, we illustrate some screenshots of this application. This application uses a number of context rules including:

- **Battery**: Informs when the battery is getting close to low, giving the user enough time to charge the phone. This example can be found also in Fig. 1.
- **Weather**: Weather conditions for particular locations of interest, used for clothing advice before leaving.
- **Navigation Assistence**: As described in Sect. 2. Application can check if assistence is needed based on route deviations. One of the generated rules can be seen in Fig. 4.
- **Standstill**: Checks if the user has been relatively stationary for the set period of time, useful when waiting for public transport to prevent excessive waiting in poor conditions.

Use in the Field. Over the course of this project, a number of opportunities for testing between end-users have taken place. These include single and multi-day user centred meetings, and month long pilots. We have co-operated with people with DS from different countries including UK, Germany, Norway, Luxembourg, Portugal, and Ukraine. For the month long pilots, these were carried out on 3 families in the UK, Germany, and Norway. In these pilots, the primary users

---

[2] http://spl2go.cs.ovgu.de/projects/1.

```
REGISTER QUERY NAV_ASSISTNOTNEEDED_query AS
PREFIX ex: <http://test.org/project/user#>
CONSTRUCT { ex:navigation <http://test.org/context/is> "NAV_ASSISTNOTNEEDED"}
FROM STREAM <http://test.org/context-stream> [RANGE 10m STEP 1m]
WHERE { ?user ex:hasNavigationStatus ?o .
     { SELECT   (COUNT(?user) AS subqres_1)
     WHERE { ?user ex:hasNavigationStatus ?o .
            FILTER( ?o = 2 )
            }
     }
     { SELECT   (COUNT(?user) AS subqres_2)
     WHERE { ?user ex:hasNavigationStatus ?o .
            FILTER( ?o = 1 )
            }
     }
     FILTER ( subqres_2 < 1 && subqres_1 < 3 )  } }
```

Fig. 4. Generated navigation assistance rule

and their carers' were given a smart phone with the context-aware services and navigation application, and mixed reality application to practice their navigation skills. Other works which looked at the effectiveness of services developed on the project includes Kramer et al. [16]. This work found important issues which need to be considered when developing navigational services for people with DS, including safety and directional assistance. For a more detailed description of the validation activities, the reader is recommended to read [2].

Fig. 5. End user navigation and calendar application

7   Conclusion and Future Work

We presented a new context modelling notation that can leverage the use of stream reasoning for context-awareness, with a mobile reasoner that leverages stream reasoning. Using our modelling notation, developers can handle context-awareness from RDF streams, originated from sensors, and other internet services. This modelling notation reduces boilerplate, and facilitates reuse of different elements of the context rule. To facilitate practical benefits of the new methodology we have implemented both a tool for context modelling. Methodology and tool support have been validated by companies developing an FP7 EU project which assists people with Down's Syndrome in various daily life practical situations. The context reasoner using C-SPARQL rules has been used over months of testing by people with Down's Syndrome and their carers'. Although a visual design tool helps thinking of the overall contextual logic of the system it does not guarantee correctness. Hidden combinations may lead to undesirable system behaviour. The need and benefits of using some of the available tools created in Software Engineering to create products which users can trust more have been already proposed in the past [4]. Consequently, our current work is focused on using model checkers, for example UPPAAL [6] for rule verification. UPPAAL is a toolkit for verification of real-time systems, and has been used before for correctness analysis in smart homes [10]. We are investigating the use of model checkers as an approach to increase the correctness of models created in our notation.

References

1. Alegre, U., Augusto, J.C., Clark, T.: Engineering context-aware systems and applications: a survey. J. Syst. Softw. **117**, 55–83 (2016)
2. Augusto, J., Kramer, D., Alegre, U., Covaci, A., Santokhee, A.: The User-centred Intelligent Environments Development Process as a Guide to Co-create Smart Technology for People with Special Needs. Universal Access in the Information Society, January 2017
3. Augusto, J., Kramer, D.: Poseidon deliverable d3.2: reasoning and learning module. Technical report, POSEIDON Project (2015)
4. Augusto, J.C.: Increasing reliability in the development of intelligent environments. In: 5th International Conference on Intelligent Environments (IE-09), pp. 20–21, July 2009
5. Barbieri, D.F., Braga, D., Ceri, S., Valle, E.D., Grossniklaus, M.: C-SPARQL: a continuous query language for RDF data streams. Int. J. Semant. Comput. **04**(01), 3–25 (2010)
6. Behrmann, G., David, A., Larsen, K.G., Hakansson, J., Petterson, P., Wang, Y., Hendriks, M.: Uppaal 4.0. In: Third International Conference on the Quantitative Evaluation of Systems, QEST 2006. pp. 125–126 (2006)
7. Cafezeiro, I., Viterbo, J., Rademaker, A., Haeusler, E.H., Endler, M.: A formal framework for modeling context-aware behavior in ubiquitous computing. In: Margaria, T., Steffen, B. (eds.) ISoLA 2008. CCIS, vol. 17, pp. 519–533. Springer, Heidelberg (2008). doi:10.1007/978-3-540-88479-8_37
8. Cardelli, L.: Mobility and security. In: Lecture Notes for the Marktoberdorf Summer School 1999 (1999)
9. Golab, L., Ozsu, M.T.: Processing sliding window multi-joins in continuous queries over data streams. In: VLDB, pp. 500–511, February 2003
10. Guilly, T.L., Smedegard, J.H., Pedersen, T., Skou, A.: To do and not to do: constrained scenarios for safe smart house. In: 2015 International Conference on Intelligent Environments, pp. 17–24. IEEE, July 2015
11. Held, A., Buchholz, S., Schill, A.: Modeling of context information for pervasive computing applications. In: Proceedings of the 6th World Multiconference on Systemics, Cybernetics and Informatics (SCI2002), p. 6 (2002)
12. Henricksen, K., Indulska, J.: Developing context-aware pervasive computing applications: models and approach. Pervasive Mob. Comput. **2**(1), 37–64 (2006)
13. Hoyos, J.R., García-Molina, J., Botía, J.A.: A domain-specific language for context modeling in context-aware systems. J. Syst. Softw. **86**(11), 2890–2905 (2013)

14. Katsiri, E., Seranno, J.M., Serrat, J.: Application of logic models for pervasive computing environments and context-aware services support. In: Tsihrintzis, G.A., Virvou, M., Jain, L.C. (eds.) Multimedia Services in Intelligent Environments, vol. 2, pp. 105–117. Springer, Berlin (2010)

15. Kjærgaard, M.B., Bunde-pedersen, J.: Towards a formal model of context awareness. In: Proceedings of the International Workshop of Combining Theory and Systems Building in Pervasive Computing-Pervasive 2006, pp. 667–674 (2006)

16. Kramer, D., Covaci, A., Augusto, J.C.: Developing navigational services for people with down's syndrome. In: 2015 International Conference on Intelligent Environments, pp. 128–131 (2015)

17. Kramer, D., Kocurova, A., Oussena, S., Clark, T., Komisarczuk, P.: An extensible, self contained, layered approach to context acquisition. In: Proceedings of the Third International Workshop on Middleware for Pervasive Mobile and Embedded Computing - M-MPAC 2011, pp. 1–7. ACM Press, New York, December 2011

18. Muñoz, J., Pelechano, V., Fons, J.: Model driven development of pervasive systems. In: Proceedings of the 1st International Workshop on Model-Based Methodologies for Pervasive and Embedded Software (MOMPES), pp. 2–14 (2004)

19. Reichle, R., et al.: A comprehensive context modeling framework for pervasive computing systems. In: Meier, R., Terzis, S. (eds.) DAIS 2008. LNCS, vol. 5053, pp. 281–295. Springer, Heidelberg (2008). doi:10.1007/978-3-540-68642-2_23

20. Serral, E., Valderas, P., Muñoz, J., Pelechano, V.: Towards a model driven development of context-aware systems for AmI environments. In: Rudolph, C. (ed.) Developing Ambient Intelligence, pp. 114–124. Springer, Paris (2008)

21. Sheng, Q.Z., Benatallah, B.: ContextUML: A UML-based modeling language for model-driven development of context-aware web services development. In: Proceedings of the International Conference on Mobile Business, pp. 206–212. IEEE Computer Society, Washington, DC (2005)

22. Siewe, F., Zedan, H., Cau, A.: The calculus of context-aware ambients. J. Comput. Syst. Sci. **77**(4), 597–620 (2011)

23. Strang, T., Linnhoff-Popien, C.: A context modeling survey. In: Proceedings of the Workshop on Advanced Context Modelling, Reasoning and Management, Workshop, pp. 1–8 (2004)

24. Valle, E.D., Ceri, S., van Harmelen, F., Fensel, D.: It's a streaming world! Reasoning upon rapidly changing information. IEEE Intell. Syst. **24**(6), 83–89 (2009)

Can an Affect-Sensitive System Afford to Be Context Independent?

Andreas Marpaung[✉] and Avelino Gonzalez

Intelligent System Lab, Department of Computer Science,
University of Central Florida, Orlando, FL, USA
amarpaung@knights.ucf.edu, gonzalez@ucf.edu

Abstract. There has been a wave of interest in affect recognition among researchers in the field of affective computing. Most of these research use a context independent approach. Since humans may misunderstand other's observed facial, vocal, or body behavior without any contextual knowledge, we question whether any of these human-centric affect-sensitive systems can be robust enough without any contextual knowledge. To answer this question, we conducted a study using previously studied audio files in three different settings; these include: no contextual indication, one level of contextual knowledge (either action or relationship/environment), and two levels of contextual knowledge (both action and relationship/environment). Our work confirms that indeed the contextual knowledge can improve recognition of human emotion.

Keywords: Affect recognition · Affective computing · Speech · Paralinguistic · Context-centric · Contextual knowledge

1 Introduction

Affect recognition has attracted many researchers working in various fields ranging from psychology to engineering. Many notable emotion psychologists such as Ekman [1], Frijda [2], and Scherer [3] have proposed different affect theories and have explored the capacity of different modalities in carrying signals of emotion. Sociologists [4] have studied the effect of social interaction (e.g., the environment, the observed subject, or the current tasks), the events, and the objects that not only have influenced the appraisal processes but also the expression of emotion. Markus and Kitayama [5] have provided a model of cultural construction of psychological reality that gave an overview on how societal features shaped behavior and experience. Linguists have studied the role of affective pragmatic information in language production and perception [6]. Recently, computer scientists and engineers have been attempting to build affect recognition systems through different modalities, including facial expressions, speech and language, and body language and gesture [7–9].

Even though there are no known signals that can be read directly from a human's body to tell a computer how one is feeling, emotional information can be conveyed from a broad range of indirect modalities. Inspired by the universality of facial expressions, many researchers have utilized Ekman's Facial Action Coding Systems (FACS) [2] to capture the subtlety of human emotion through 71 different Action Units

© Springer International Publishing AG 2017
P. Brézillon et al. (Eds.): CONTEXT 2017, LNAI 10257, pp. 454–467, 2017.
DOI: 10.1007/978-3-319-57837-8_38

(AUs). A myriad of research work has been produced using facial expressions; some of these include: (1) basic affective states recognition [10], and (2) non-basic affective states detection (e.g., fatigue [11], depression [12], and pain [13]) and some complex mental states such as agreement [14], concentration [15], contemplation [16], confusion [17], and frustration [18].

Speech is another commonly used modality. Not only it is an indispensable means for sharing opinions, ideas, observations, and feelings in human-to-human interaction, but it also conveys emotional content through the linguistic aspect of speech (what it is said) and the paralinguistic aspect of speech (how it is said). Some of these work include the combination of acoustic-prosodic (various features of the utterances which cover the rhythm, stress, and intonation), lexical, and discourse features [19–21]. To overcome the long distance problem confronted by facial expression and speech, some have proposed using body posture and gestures. Laban and Ullman [22], one of the pioneering works, proposed Body Action Coding System (BACS) to identify the AUs correlated to each emotion. Further in-depth interdisciplinary review of the latest research work of affect recognition can be found in [8, 9].

Our work focuses mainly on the paralinguistic aspect of affect recognition through speech. This paper is organized in the following way. Section 2 explains the modified Brunswick model [23] to show the importance of contextual knowledge in interpreting affect expression. Section 3 describes our research questions that have motivated us to conduct this study. Section 4 focuses on the Appraisal Theories of Emotion that have inspired us to work on the context-centric affect recognition domain. Section 5 explains our human participant study that covers the speech corpus and the data collection method. Section 6 discusses our results. Finally, Sect. 7 concludes our work and discusses our future work.

2 Modified Brunswick Model

The modified Brunswick model developed by Scherer [23] shows the importance of contextual knowledge in interpreting affect expression; this knowledge includes situational context, social relationships, and cultural context.

Hess and Hareli [24] define situational context as any knowledge related to the emotion elicitor that covers both factual information and real world knowledge. The factual information indicates anything that happens to the elicitor while the real world knowledge captures any additional information that allows people to deduce further information. For example, my co-worker receiving an increase in his/her salary is factual information while the real world knowledge can associate the salary increase with a happy or surprise emotion, or evidence of an excellent job performance in the past several months. Both factual information and real world knowledge are not only viewed from the elicitor's point-of-view (known as the passive decoding approach), but also from the perceiver's side (known as the active decoding approach). Many traditional affect recognition methods, including in the field of computer science and engineering, implicitly assumes a pattern matching process by associating specific features of an expression to a certain emotion. For example, a high pitch tone with a fast tempo is often associated with joy, surprise or anger. But in Hess and Hareli's model [24], the meaning of emotion expressions in context (MEEC), the affect recognition from nonverbal cues utilizes a two path-model approach where the perceiver adopts an active role in the affect recognition process. With this role, the knowledge of the event/situation and the emotion elicitor can help the perceiver identify emotion more accurately. For example, when the high pitch tone with a fast tempo was expressed after the elicitor found out that his/her car was vandalized, the perceiver can assume that the elicitor is angry. But if the high pitch tone with a fast tempo was expressed after the elicitor received something that he/she had wanted for a long time, the perceiver can assume that the elicitor is either happy or surprised.

Social relationships describe some prescriptive stereotypes that imply certain behavioral norms that may require some level of situational knowledge. For example, if the perceiver holds the stereotype belief that women tend to be more irrational than men, his/her affect recognition ability may be affected by this belief [25]. The social status (high vs. low) affects perceivers ability to recognize affect. One study found out that the observers perceived the same facial expressions as different emotions when the elicitors had different social status [26]. In this study, the fear expression was recognized as anger and contempt by the perceivers when they were told that the elicitor was the boss (with a high status); the same expression was recognized as fear when they were told that the elicitor was the employee with a low status. Gender and age differences also affect the perceivers' judgement in recognizing emotion. Women appear to recognize facial emotions better than men, in particular under conditions of minimal stimulus information, i.e., when facial expression is shown for less than a second [27, 28].

Cultural context is defined as the specific case of norms and differences in cultural values that guide an individual or a group of people to display emotion expressions appropriately. Markus and Kitayama [5] had provided the model of cultural construction of psychological reality that gave an overview on how societal features shaped behavior and experience. This model showed several different entities (*societal features, institutional practices, interpersonal episodes,* and *individual tendencies*) implicitly influenced the other entities and emotion. As social beings, the content of the *societal features, institutional practices,* and *interpersonal episodes* have formed explicit rules and representations, which have regulated and indirectly influenced how humans appraise events and express emotion. Many social psychologists refer to the societal, institutional, and interpersonal influences as rules and representations or cultural factors [4]. These contents of the *societal features,* which includes cultural ideas and values and different structural factors (e.g., factors related to ecology, economy, and the political system), *institutional practices,* and *interpersonal episodes* have internalized and confined in individual minds through the course of socialization. Since emotional events are interpreted and evaluated according to certain cultural models, certain patterns of emotion occur more frequent in one culture than another. For example, Kitayama et al. [29] found out that people in the majority of Asian countries, such as Japan, had the tendency to express the socially engaged emotions, such as shame and respect, more frequently than the United States; on the contrary, the socially disengaged emotions, such as pride and anger, had higher prominence in the United States and the European countries. Through a cross-culture study in four cultures (Germany, Israel, Greece, and the US), Hareli et al. [30] found out that anger was a stronger norm violation signal than sadness or neutral expressions. They also found out that people in Germany and Israel tend to express anger and sadness more intensely than in Greece and the US.

3 Research Questions

The knowledge of context (environment, observed subject, or the current task) is critical in social interaction in order to structure activities, to navigate the world around us, to organize information, to adapt to conditions, to convey ideas to each other and to react appropriately to situations. For example, when we are at a theme park, we tend to walk around with a faster pace and talk louder so that our companions can hear over the ambient noise. However, when we are at a school or a public library, we tend to walk around at a slower pace and whisper when we talk so that we do not disturb other people. In the same way, we tend to laugh at a wedding party but cry at a funeral service.

The scope of contextual cues are not only limited to the environment situation, observed subject, or the current task, but it also goes beyond the linguistic contexts [31]. Since humans have difficulty recognizing isolated words taken out of context, combining these isolated words with one or two preceding words may increase the recognition performance. For example, we know that the word four signifies the number that comes after three and before five. When we don't know the previous or the following words, this word four may have a vague meaning. But when we combine this word four with books to make the phrase four books, the recognition performance can increase. These words will become clearer and more meaningful if spoken in the context of a library.

Humans also have difficulty interpreting expressed emotions of other people in a non face-to-face interaction, but it can be alleviated when the context of conversation is known. As an example, one may find it hard to understand an emotionally-charged person with a thick accent through a phone line. However, when we know that the conversation occurs in a call-in center context, we may be able to associate the high-pitch tone with anger or with a complaint. A misinterpretation may also occur when person A hears a foreigner speaking in a completely unknown language to A. Since A cannot understand any words semantically, A can interpret a high-pitch tone as a happy expression when it is expressed in a theme park environment.

Despite an increasing level of research in human affect recognition through different modalities in the past 20 years, the state-of-the-art of affect recognition research uses datasets collected in varieties of context-free environments [9]. However, since 2012, the context-based affect recognition workshops have emerged within affective computing [7] and intelligent interaction. Through these workshops, many researchers have explored the effect of contextual information that can provide different nuances and complexities in developing human-centric systems for affect recognition [32]. Nevertheless, the state of context-based affect recognition is still in its infancy.

We want to answer two questions that have been of interest to us. First, can adding contextual knowledge improve a human's affect recognition ability when only the paralinguistic aspect of speech is otherwise available? and second, if indeed contextual knowledge helps, what kind of contextual knowledge can more effectively improve a human's affect perception capability?

4 Appraisal Theories of Emotion

Our study was inspired by the Appraisal Theories of Emotion, one of the three major models of emotion which emerged out of different schools of thought. This section briefly describes the relationship between this theory and our context-based affect recognition approach.

The fundamental premise of the appraisal theories of emotion is that emotions are elicited and differentiated based on a person's subjective evaluation or appraisal of the personal significance of the environment based on a number of dimensions or criteria [3, 33, 34]. Scherer, who has been in the forefront of systemizing appraisal theories among all appraisal theorists, postulated several criteria, known as the Stimulus Evaluation (appraisal) Checks (SECs), to differentiate emotional states. These criteria include: goal relevance and goal congruence (which refer to the relevance and congruence of events to reach certain goals), certainty, coping potential or control, and agency (an event caused by oneself, others, or by impersonal circumstances). An example of a person's subjective evaluation that triggers fear is when a person who is walking in a jungle sees a big bear (agency) who has the capability to hurt him (goal congruence) and does not know (certainty) whether he can run away without disturbing the animal (control).

Despite the broad agreement among appraisal theorists on the role of cognitive subjective evaluations in emotions elicitation, many of them disagree on how these evaluations lead to some emotional responses. Some predictions on how the appraisals affected different modalities were made; they include: (1) relationship between the appraisals and vocal expression [35], (2) relationship between the appraisals and facial expression [36], and (3) relationship between the appraisals and psychophysiological activity [37].

Multiple physiological and behavioral response systems are activated in the human's body during an emotional episode; these are controlled by a small region of brain known as the limbic system. Despite the basic similarity in the parts of the brain that control affect expressions in both humans and non-human primates, a humans' ecological constraints, which involve both the physical and social environments, allow humans to have more control over their vocalization [38]. For example, humans tend to speak softer in the public libraries but louder in the theme parks due to the physical constraints; they also express anger to friends differently than expressing anger to their bosses due to the social relationship constraints. Because of human's vocalization complexity, Scherer had emphasized the distinction between the push and pull factors as the determinants that can differentiate a human's affect vocalization [4].

Push factors are defined as the biological action subsystems and the internal support which diverge the voice acoustics features to various different ways without a predetermined direction. Due to their biologically innate features, humans have no control over these internal organs. For example, increased muscle tension caused by the arousal can affect the shape of the vocal tract, breathing patterns, and other paralinguistic behavior. On the contrary, the external pull factors (also called display rules) are defined as the norms or social expectations imposed by external physical and social environment which are controllable by humans. Five different pull factors include: (1) the transmission distance, characteristics and the locality of a sender, (2) self-presentation, (3) the attraction or repelling of others, (4) the conventionalized social signals, and (5) the vocal accommodation to a receiver. Transmission distance, char-acteristics, and the locality affects the sender's style of communication. For example, the face-to-face conversation between the sender and the receiver in the public library is characterized by soft and low-pitched voices while they would converse in loud and high-pitched voices in a crowded and noisy restaurant. Self presentation signifies the impression the sender wants to create in the receiver; it is also known as the vocal mimicry. The attraction or repelling of others shows the social relationship and action tendencies between the sender and the receiver, which is either to approach or to avoid. The conventionalized social signal signifies the stereotyped acoustic sounds that have common meaning for certain groups of people.

The novelty of our approach lies within the treatment of the pull factors as various different contextual knowledge. Dey [39] defines context as "any information that can be used to characterize the situation of an entity. An entity is a person, place, or object that is considered relevant to the interaction between a user and an application, including the user and applications themselves." To humans, building a context model that includes gender, age, social relationship, and conversation topic, may help two people have better conversation. For example, if person A does not know the gender and age of person B, A won't know whether to address person B as either Mr. B or Ms. B. Furthermore, A won't be able to decide whether to speak formally (if B is much older than A) or casually (if B is much younger than A). Thus, either person A or B (or both) may find this social interaction to be awkward. The social relationship can change the interaction when A and B have different social status, e.g., manager and her subordinate, best friends, enemies, etc.

5 Approach

Inspired by other researchers on the benefit of contextual knowledge in disambiguating different emotion categories [40–43], we conducted a study described below. The results of this study serve as evidence on the benefit of contextual cues in affect recognition. The study involved providing audio recordings of an actor uttering words in French in a way that its paralinguistic qualities expressed an emotion. The test subjects (all of whom did not understand French) were asked to indicate the emotion conveyed by the audio files strictly from the paralinguistic qualities. Then, two con-textual cues about the situation that provoked the words were given separately to the subjects, and they were asked to once again determine the emotion being communi-cated in the same recording. The hypothesis is that with the additional contextual cues, the ability of the test subjects to discern the true emotions would improve progressively as the two cues were separately and sequentially provided. We now describe the details of the study as well as the results.

5.1 Speech Material

Audio files from the Geneva Multimodal Emotional Portrayal (GEMEP) database [44] were used for this study. These audio files include 10 (five male and five female) professional French-speaking actors who had previously worked in the artistic productions (mean age of 37.1 years; age range: 25–57 years). These actors portrayed several affective states by saying one of these two pseudo speech sentences (in French): "nekal ibam soud molen!" (equivalent to a declarative statement or an exclamation) or "kouń se mina lod belam" (equivalent to a question) for each affective state. We used this corpus to eliminate some effects attributable to linguistic content.

In this study, we focused on analyzing Ekman's six universal emotions: anger, disgust, fear, joy, sadness, and surprise. Because of the quality of the recordings, with the exception of disgust and surprise, each emotion had audio files spoken by five males and five females; disgust was comprised of two males and two females and surprise was comprised of three males and two females. Readers interested in the emotion elicitation technique, recording procedures and setups, and the statistical analysis of the perceptual accuracy for the believability, authenticity, and plausibility can refer to [44].

5.2 Contextual Knowledge

To induce and elicit certain emotions, the actors used the *felt enacting technique*. This technique is typically used in the theatrical settings where the actors recall or have mental imagery of their relevant personal experiences to enact certain emotions based on the written script given to them prior to the recordings. For our study, we translated these original scripts from French to English using Google Translate [45].

From these translated scripts, we manually extracted two pieces contextual knowledge:

1. Action context. The action context is defined as any information about what happens to a person or a group of people involved in the conversation. An example of the action context for the happy emotion is "A won a great amount of money in the lottery." while "A failed the exam and must resign from A's dream career." is the action context for the sad emotion.
2. Relationship/Environment (R/E) context. The R/E context is defined as any information that relates an object to a person or relates a person to another person (or a group of people). For example, the R/E context for the happy emotion is "A had a lottery ticket." while "A had a final exam." is the R/E context for the sad emotion.

In our study, test subjects were asked to listen to the audio recording without any contextual information and asked to estimate the emotion felt by the speaker. Then, they were given a piece of contextual knowledge (action or R/E) to reconsider their prior choice. Lastly, they were provided with a second piece of contextual knowledge (R/E or action) and were asked to again reconsider their choice. These choices were then compared to the grand truth. The contextual knowledge were presented in a computer-generated randomized order but all emotions had two sequences: (1) no context→action→R/E, and (2) no context→R/E→action.

5.3 Data Collection

Figure 1 shows our user interface, written in Microsoft Visual C++ 2010, used to collect the data from our human participants. The user interface was executed in a Dell Latitude D630 laptop operating Windows XP. For audio purposes, a universal 3.5 mm earbud headset was connected to the laptop's audio jack.

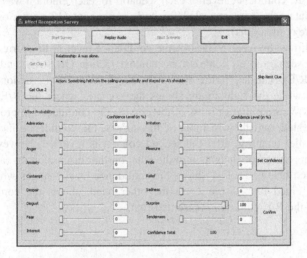

Fig. 1. Our Graphical User Interface (GUI)

Thirty volunteers were recruited for our study – 14 males from 19 to 57 years old (average age of 30 years) and 16 females from 18 to 54 years old (average age of 27.4 years). Each unlimited-time data collection process was conducted in a quiet and comfortable office environment. A short training session on how to operate the GUI was given prior to their participation. The seventeen listed emotions were the ones used in the GEMEP corpus but for this study, we focused on Ekman's six universal emotions.

Each participant was subjected to twelve different randomly generated scenarios; two scenarios for each studied emotion. For each emotion, two different combinations were exposed to each participant; they included: (1) no context→action→R/E and (2) no context→R/E→action. For the first combination, after hearing the audio file and without any further information, the participant selected the emotion (or the emotions) the speaker was trying to convey and set his/her confidence level with his/her choice. Once set, the participant moved on to the next clue. After hearing the same audio file, the action context was revealed. With this contextual knowledge, the participant made any changes (if necessary) to both emotion(s) and confidence level(s) before moving on to the next clue. Once set, the participant heard the same audio file and the second clue, the R/E clue, was revealed. Using the same method, changes could be made to both emotion(s) and confidence level(s) as necessary. Once finalized, the participant could move on to the next scenario. The operational procedures of the second combination was the same as the first one. The only difference between the two combinations was the order the clues were represented to the participants; the second combination displayed the R/E context prior to the action context.

6 Results

For our study, the confidence level of each scenario for each emotion was recorded; the total of 612 data sets were recorded for each participant (12 scenarios × 17 emotions × 3 context situations).

Figure 2 shows the mean values of the confidence level in the correct emotion in three different scenarios: no context, one context (action OR R/E), and two context (action AND R/E). The left figure shows the scenario where the action context was presented first while the right figure shows the scenario where the R/E context was presented first. We note that in most of the curves, the confidence improves after one context is revealed, and then in most of the curves, the confidence increases again, albeit in a smaller quantity, after the second context is revealed. However, there are some exceptions and some insights into the data. Further discussion on each emotion's result is reported below. Table 1 shows the confidence level changes when the action context is presented first. Table 2, on the other hand, shows the confidence level changes when the R/E context is presented first.

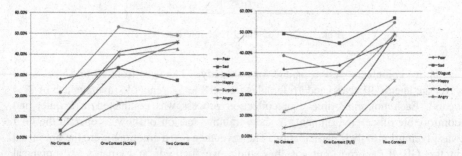

Fig. 2. Mean confidence level for different scenarios Left: No Context→One Context (Action) →Two Contexts (Action+R/E) Right: No Context→One Context (R/E) →Two Contexts (R/E+Action)

Anger
The R/E context for angry includes: (1) had a neighbor I didn't like, (2) had a friendship relation, and (3) had a coworker relationship. The action context includes: (1) vandalized the neighbor's car, (2) abandoned the apartment and owed money, and (3) the coworker seduced his wife. The confidence levels for anger improved from 21.7% to 53.0% and from 30.9% to 54.6% when the action context was given. The test

Table 1. Confidence level changes for No Context→Action→R/E

Emotion	No context	No Context→Action		Action→R/E	
		One context (Action)	Increase/ decrease	Two context (Action+R/E)	Increase/ decrease
Anger	21.7%	53.0%	31.3%	49.0%	−4.0%
Disgust	9.0%	39.5%	30.5%	42.7%	3.2%
Fear	28.1%	33.6%	5.5%	45.8%	12.2%
Happy	9.2%	41.1%	31.9%	46.1%	5.0%
Sad	3.3%	33.3%	30.0%	27.5%	−5.8%
Surprise	1.8%	16.5%	14.7%	20.3%	3.8%

Table 2. Confidence level changes for No Context→R/E→Action

Emotion	No context	No Context→R/E		R/E→Action	
		One context (R/E)	Increase/ decrease	Two context (R/E+Action)	Increase/ decrease
Anger	38.6%	30.9%	−7.7%	54.6%	23.7%
Disgust	12.0%	21.2%	9.2%	49.5%	28.3%
Fear	32.2%	34.3%	2.1%	46.3%	12.0%
Happy	4.2%	9.8%	5.6%	49.0%	39.2%
Sad	49.1%	44.6%	−4.5%	56.7%	12.1%
Surprise	1.4%	1.2%	−0.2%	26.9%	25.7%

subjects were able to rely on the paralinguistic features to identify anger with no prior contextual knowledge, and had better affect recognition accuracy. We found it interesting that the presence of the R/E context reduced the confidence levels by 4% and 7.7%.

Disgust

The R/E context for disgust includes: (1) had a decayed dead fish, (2) had a dead cockroach laid out in the hallway, and (3) had a summer job as a janitor. The action context includes: (1) remembered the previous experience, (2) stepped on the dead cockroach and the sticky substance stuck on one's foot, and (3) remembered the job where one had to clean many dirty and smelly toilets. The confidence levels for disgust improved from 9.0% to 39.5% and from 39.5% to 42.7% for the no context→action→R/E case and from 12.00% to 21.2% and from 21.2% to 49.5% for the no context→R/E→action case. For this emotion, we learned that the presence of the action context in a one-context case and the presence of an action context after the R/E context had a significant improvement in human confidence level (increases of 30.5% and 28.3%).

Fear
The R/E context for fear includes: (1) stood by a stranger, (2) owned a car, and (3) was alone. The action context includes: (1) a stranger pointed a knife, (2) could not stop the car due to the brake failure, and (3) something unexpectedly felt on one's shoulder. The confidence levels for fear improved from 28.1% to 33.6% and from 33.6% to 45.8% for the no context→action→R/E case and from 32.2% to 34.3% and from 34.3% to 46.3% for the no context→R/E→action case. Similar to anger and sadness, humans were able to rely on the paralinguistic features with no prior contextual knowledge and had better affect recognition accuracy. We found out that either one or two additional pieces of contextual knowledge did not significantly improve the confidence level, but the improvements were all positive.

Happiness (Joy)
The R/E context for happy includes: (1) had a lottery ticket, (2) had many friends, and (3) had a long-distance friend. The action context includes: (1) won the lottery, (2) received a beautiful gift, and (3) spent time together. The confidence levels for happy improved from 9.2% to 41.1% and from 41.1% to 46.1% for the no context→action→R/E case and from 4.2% to 9.8% and from 9.8% to 49.0% for the no context→R/E→action case. For this emotion, the data suggests that the action context had a stronger effect on the human subject's affect perception in the presence of a single context. However, when the action context was presented after the R/E context, the confidence level had quadrupled (increased from 5.6% to 39.2%).

Sadness
The R/E context for sadness includes: (1) had final exams to pursue the dream career, (2) was in a marriage relationship, and (3) had a dog. The action context includes: (1) failed test and resigned from a dream job, (2) received divorce paperwork, and (3) had to euthanize the dog. The confidence levels for sadness changed from 3.3% to 33.33% and from 33.3% to 27.50% for the no context → action → R/E case, and from 49.1% to 44.6% and from 44.6% to 56.7% for the no context → R/E → action case. Because the sounds of the voice in the recording were clearly saddened, the test subjects were able to rely on the paralinguistic features with no prior contextual knowledge and had better accuracy in affect recognition. However, the presence of the R/E contextual information did decrease the confidence level by 5.8% and 4.5%.

Surprise
The R/E context for surprise includes: (1) was in an office, (2) was at the waterfall park, and (3) was in the dining room. The action context includes: (1) saw a pigeon fly into the office, (2) the waterfall stopped running, and (3) heard loud noise from next door. The confidence levels for surprise changed from 1.8% to 16.5% and from 16.5% to 20.3% for the no context→action→R/E case, and from 1.4% to 1.2% and from 1.2% to 26.9% for the no context→R/E→action case. Like with the happy emotion, the action context had stronger effect than the R/E context in the single-context case. For the two-context case, the presence of the action context after the R/E context had a stronger effect than the opposite case.

7   Discussion and Future Work

Our study has shown the positive impact of additional contextual knowledge to the human's affect recognition through the paralinguistic features of speech. Between the identified two contexual knowledge elements, we found out that the action context had a more significant impact to the confidence level in human affect recognition ability than did the R/E context. Our finding is also supported by the modified Brunswick model developed by Scherer [33].

In our previous work [46], we used the traditional context-free approach by utilizing several acoustic features of the paralingustic aspect of speech. In our future work, we will take the context-centric approach, inspired by the appraisal theory of emotion, to recognize affect through speech. By framing the appraisal theory in the social context, emotions can be viewed not only as some subjective experiences with some biologically prewired internal processes or bodily states but they are also viewed as the intersubjective experiences and the by-product of self and cultural aspects constructed by different individuals or groups in social contexts.

References

1. Ekman, P., Friesen, W.: Facial Action Coding System: A Technique for the Measurement of Facial Movement. Investigator's Guide 2 Parts. Consulting Psychologists Press, Sunnyvale (1978)
2. Frijda, N.H.: The Emotions. Cambridge University Press, Cambridge (1986)
3. Scherer, K.R.: Vocal correlates of emotional arousal and affective disturbance. In: Wagner, H., Manstead, A. (eds.) Handbook of Social Psychophysiology, pp. 165–197. Wiley, New York (1989)
4. Parkinson, B., Fischer, A., Manstead, A.: Emotion in Social Relations: Cultural, Group, and İnterpersonal Processes. Psychology Press, New York (2005)
5. Kitayama, S., Markus, H.: Emotion and culture: Empirical studies of mutual influence. American Psychological Association, Washington, D.C. (1994). http://dx.doi.org/10.1037/10152-000
6. Chung, C., Pennebaker, J.: Linguistic ınquiry and word count (LIWC): pronounced "Luke,"... and other useful facts: In: McCarthy, P., Boonthum-Denecke, C. (eds.) Applied Natural Language Processing: Identification, Investigation and Resolution, pp. 206–229 (2012)
7. Picard, R.W.: Affective Computing. MIT Press, Cambridge (1997)
8. Zeng, Z., Pantic, M., Roisman, G., Huang, T.: A survey of affect recognition methods: audio, visual, and spontaneous expressions. IEEE Trans. Pattern Anal. Mach. Intell. **31**(1), 39–58 (2009)
9. Calvo, R.A., D'Mello, S.: Affect detection: an ınterdisciplinary review of models, methods, and their applications. IEEE Trans. Affect. Comput. **1**(1), 18–37 (2010)
10. Gunes, H., Hung, H.: Is automatic facial expression recognition of emotions coming to a dead end? The rise of the new kids on the block. Image Vis. Comput. **55**, 6–8 (2016)
11. Cheng, W.C., Liao, H.C., Pan, M.H., Chen, C.C.: A fatigue detection system with eyeglasses removal. In: 15th International Conference on Advanced Communication Technology (ICACT). IEEE (2013)

12. Meng, H., Huang, D., Wang, H., Yang, H., AI-Shuraifi, M., Wang, Y.: Depression recognition based on dynamic facial and vocal expression features using partial least square regression. In: Proceedings of the 3rd ACM International Workshop on Audio/Visual Emotion Challenge (2013)

13. Khan, R.A., Meyer, A., Konik, H., Bouakaz, S.: Pain detection through shape and appearance features. In: 2013 IEEE International Conference on Multimedia and Expo (ICME). IEEE (2013)

14. Bousmalis, K., Marc, M., Maja, P.: Towards the automatic detection of spontaneous agreement and disagreement based on nonverbal behaviour: a survey of related cues, databases, and tools. Image Vis. Comput. **31**(2), 203–221 (2013)

15. Cha, S., Wookhyun, K.: Analyze the learner's concentration using detection of facial feature points (2015)

16. Thepade, S.D., Bidwai, P.V.: Contemplation of image based Iris recognition. Int. J. Eng. Res. Appl. **3**(2), 1056–1066 (2013). ISSN-2248-9622

17. Bosch, N., Chen, Y., D'Mello, S.: It's written on your face: detecting affective states from facial expressions while learning computer programming. In: Trausan-Matu, S., Boyer, K.E., Crosby, M., Panourgia, K. (eds.) ITS 2014. LNCS, vol. 8474, pp. 39–44. Springer, Cham (2014). doi:10.1007/978-3-319-07221-0_5

18. Vasiete, E., Tom, Y.: Multimodal frustration detection on smartphones. In: Proceedings of the 33rd Annual ACM Conference Extended Abstracts on Human Factors in Computing Systems. ACM (2015)

19. Brown, M., Salverda, A.P., Gunlogson, C., Tanenhaus, M.K.: Interpreting prosodic cues in discourse context. Lang. Cogn. Neurosci. **30**(1-2), 149–166 (2015)

20. Sudhakar, R., Manjare, C.A.: Analysis of speech features for emotion detection: a review. In: 2015 International Conference on Computing Communication Control and Automation (ICCUBEA). IEEE (2015)

21. Kakouros, S., Okko, R.: Statistical learning of prosodic patterns and reversal of perceptual cues for sentence prominence. In: Proceedings of the 38th Annual Conference of the Cognitive Science Society, Philadelphia, Pennsylvania (2016)

22. Laban, R., Ullmann, L.: The mastery of movement, 4th edn. Princeton Book Company Publishers, Hightstown (1988)

23. Scherer, K.R.: Personality inference from voice quality: the loud voice of extraversion. Eur. J. Soc. Psychol. **8**, 467–487 (1978)

24. Hess, U., Hareli, S.: The impact of context on the perception of emotions. In: The Expression of Emotion Philosophical, Psychological and Legal Perspectives

25. Shields, S.A.: The Politics of emotion in everyday life appropriate emotion and claims on identity. Rev. Gen. Psychol. **9**(1), 3–15 (2005)

26. Algoe, S.B., Brenda, N., John, D.: Gender and job status as contextual cues for the interpretation of facial expression of emotion. Sex Roles **42**(3–4), 183–208 (2000)

27. Matsumoto, D., Hwang, H.: Judging faces in context. Soc. Pers. Psychol. Compnass **4**(6), 393–402 (2010)

28. Donges, U., Kersting, A., Suslow, T.: Women's greater ability to perceive happy facial emotion automatically: gender differences in affective priming. PLoS ONE **7**(7), e41745 (2012). doi:10.1371/journal.pone.0041745. Zalla, T. (ed.) Ecole Normale Supe'rieure, France

29. Kitayama, S., Markus, H., Kurakawa, M.: Culture, emotion, and well-being: good feelings in Japan and the United States. Cogn. Emot. **14**(1), 93–124 (2000)

30. Hareli, S., Kafetsios, K., Hess, U.: A cross-cultural study on emotion expression and the learning of social norms. Front. Psychol. **6**, 1501 (2015). http://dx.doi.org/10.3389/fpsyg.2015.01501

31. Kitaoka, N., Enami, D., Nakagawa, S.: Effect of acoustic and linguistic contexts on human and machine speech recognition. Comput. Speech Lang. **28**, 769–787 (2014)
32. Hammal, Z., Suarez, M.T.: Towards context based affective computing. In: 2013 Humaine Association Conference on Affective Computing Intelligent Interaction, 2013, p. 802 (2013). ISBN: 9780769550480
33. Lazarus, R.S.: Psychological Stress and the Coping Process. McGraw Hill, New York (1966)
34. Scherer, K., Ellgring, H.: Multimodal expression of emotion: affect programs or componential appraisal patterns? Emotion **7**, 158–171 (2007)
35. Johnstone, T., Reekum, C, and Scherer, K.: Vocal expression correlates of appraisal processes. In: Appraisal Processes in Emotion – Theory, Methods, and Research (2001)
36. Kaiser, S., and Thomas W.: Facial expressions as indicators of appraisal processes. In: Appraisal Processes in Emotion: Theory, Methods, Research, pp. 285–300 (2001)
37. Pecchinenda, A.: The psychophysiology of appraisals (2001)
38. Jürgens, U.: Neural pathways underlying vocal control. Neurosci. Biobehav. Rev. **26**(2), 235–258 (2002)
39. Dey, A.K.: Understanding and using context. Pers. Ubiquit. Comput. Spec. Issue Situated Interact. Ubiquit. Comput. **5**(1), 4–7 (2001)
40. Russell, J.A.: Core affect and the psychological construction of emotion. Psychol. Rev. **110**, 145–172 (2003)
41. Panksepp, J.: Affective Neuroscience: The Foundations of Human and Animal Emotions. Oxford University Press, Cambridge (1998)
42. Keltner, D., Haidt, J.: Social functions of emotions. In: Mayne, T.J., Bonanno, G.A. (eds.) Emotions: Current Issues and Future Directions, pp. 192–213. Guilford Press, New York (2001)
43. Bachorowski, J., Owren, M.: Vocal expression of emotion—acoustic properties of speech are associated with emotional intensity and context. Psychol. Sci. **6**, 219–224 (1995)
44. Bänziger, T., Mortillaro, M., Scherer, K.R.: Introducing the Geneva multimodal expression corpus for experimental research on emotion perception. Emotion (2011). Advance online publication. doi:10.1037/a0025827, http://www.affective-sciences.org/gemep/coreset
45. Google, Inc. https://www.google.com/
46. Marpaung, A., Gonzalez, A.: Toward building automatic affect recognition machine using acoustics features. In: FLAIRS Conference (2014)

Specific Topics: Context in Management

The Role of Context Within the Interactions of Knowledge Intensive Processes

João Carlos de A.R. Gonçalves[(⊠)], Fernanda Araujo Baião, and Flávia Maria Santoro

Federal University of the State of Rio de Janeiro (UNIRIO),
Rio de Janeiro, Brazil
{joao.goncalves, fernanda.baiao,
flavia.santoro}@uniriotec.br

Abstract. With the evolution of the Business Process Management (BPM) research field, many researchers started to perceive a specific type of process as being critical to organizations, the so-called Knowledge-intensive Processes (KiP), characterized by a dynamic and unstable control-flow and complex activities that change frequently at run-time. This research proposes an approach based on the characterization of a KIP in terms of its interactions and the critical role of context during its execution. We argue that a detailed description about their precise conceptualization and how they influence or determine the execution of a KIP is still missing in the literature of this area. The analysis of the interactions that occur during the executions of the activities of a KiP, as well as their associated elements (such as context and speech acts), is vital to its correct understanding, modeling and execution.

1 Introduction

As the Business Process Management (BPM) field of research evolved, many researchers started to perceive a specific type of unstructured process as being critical to most organizations, a.k.a. Knowledge Intensive Processes (KiP). A process is knowledge intensive if its value can only be created through the fulfillment of the knowledge requirements of the process participants. Moreover, they are characterized by a dynamic and unstable control-flow and complex activities that frequently change over time and even at runtime [4].

Marjanovic and Freeze [6] cite customer support, design of new products/services, marketing, management of data quality, IT governance and strategic planning as examples of KiP. They observe that the way organizations deal with this kind of processes has changed over time, e.g. the customer support processes have evolved from highly structured to knowledge-intensive, and personalized, flexible cases.

Based on an extensive literature review, Di Ciccio et al. [3] affirmed that KiP are processes "whose conduct and execution are heavily dependent on knowledge workers performing various interconnected knowledge intensive decision making tasks". According to those authors, the expertise, experience and decision making capabilities of the knowledge workers are essential in this kind of processes. Furthermore, they derived eight key characteristics typical of KiPs namely: knowledge-driven;

© Springer International Publishing AG 2017
P. Brézillon et al. (Eds.): CONTEXT 2017, LNAI 10257, pp. 471–483, 2017.
DOI: 10.1007/978-3-319-57837-8_39

collaboration-oriented; unpredictable; emergent; goal-oriented; event-driven; constraint- and rule-driven; non-repeatable. Additionally, Little and Deokar [5] investigate the relevance of knowledge creation in KiP, and determined that the expansion and use of knowledge across organizations rely on both formal and informal social processes through effective communication.

Focusing on the activity level, we can define a KiP as a collection of activities of a business process, some activities of which can be knowledge intensive (called 'KiA'). The execution of KIAs are optional, depending on information specific for the chosen process instance [11]. The information necessary to decide whether to execute a KiA or not usually come from the context of the process or activity itself, being, for example, application data, process data, functional data, etc. [1].

An important concept within KiP is the context in which it is executed. Context can be defined in terms of executed actions and events being "a complex description of the knowledge shared on physical, social, historical and other circumstances where actions or events happen. Context is not a part of the action or event, but constrains the execution of the action or the interpretation of the event" [2].

Taking this definition to a business process scenario, context is defined as the minimal set of variables that contains all relevant information impacting the design and implementation of a business process [7].

Brezillon and Pomerol [2] also stated that context cannot be isolated, but it must relate to a focus. This focus determines what can be considered relevant within a given context and is represented by a task, a step in problem solving or a decision making, or even the goal of a given process and organization. Within KiPs, we argue that the Knowledge Intensive Activity should be considered as an important (yet, nonexclusive) focus of the context of its associated interactions.

The hindrances to the modeling and management of KiPs come from the knowledge intensity, occurring at either (i) interactions between process participants or (ii) between participants and the external world, during the execution of the process' activities. We argue, however, that the dynamics of interactions of Knowledge Intensive Processes (Context being a main element of it), being a critical part of the knowledge intensity inherent to a KiP, is neither deeply discussed nor precisely understood in the literature.

This work, then, presents a discussion on the role of context at the interactions that occur involving a KiP and its associated concepts. It is structured in 5 Sections. The first section is the introduction that briefly presents the proposal. Section 2 defines the area of Knowledge Intensive Processes in the field of BPM. Section 3 depicts the theoretical definitions of context and its role, especially at the interactions between process participants. Section 4 describes an example scenario that illustrates the proposal and Sect. 5 presents the conclusions and defines future directions of the research.

2 KIP

Traditional approaches for process modeling usually depict a process focusing on the control flow of well-structured activities that an organization performs in order to achieve its goals. However, not all processes present a well-characterized control flow;

Eppler et al. [25] point four attributes to evaluate the degree of complexity of a business process: process steps, stakeholders, process dynamics and interdependencies.

Regarding process structure and the flow of activities, Hagen et al. [26] classify business processes as structured, semi-structured or unstructured. Structured processes are completely pre-defined, easily modeled using a specific language such as Business Process Model and Notation (BPMN), and repetitive, having a fixed sequence of activities. Examples of structured processes are: attendance orders, deliveries, inventory control, and payroll.

Unstructured (or ad hoc) processes comprise a kind of process that changes frequently, with its instances being very different from each other, both in terms of activities performed and flow. Its nature brings additional difficulty to model with a traditional method or notation. Finally, a semi-structured process shares unstructured and structured parts, sharing traits of both process types on different parts of its flow.

Among the diverse definitions of Knowledge Intensive Processes, a concise and brief definition is found on [12], defining KiP as "processes whose conduction and execution are heavily dependent on knowledge workers performing various interconnected knowledge-intensive, decision-making tasks". KiPs are genuinely knowledge-, information- and data-centric and require substantial flexibility at design- and run-time.

Expanding on this brief definition, recent studies [20] point to a set of nine common characteristics for KIPs: (i) Knowledge-Prevalence: Knowledge is of utmost importance for the process. Usually knowledge from different sources and/or tacit knowledge is necessary for process execution; (ii) Collaboration: KIPs include activities often executed by many different process participants and intensive information exchange and coordination between them being a vital part of process execution itself; (iii) Predictability: Due to its unstructured nature, the flow of activities of a KIP can vary at each instance, due to situation specific needs or constraints. (iv) Complexity: The coordination of multiple information success, the variety on its execution flow, the variety of both sub-processes and tasks associated with the process itself and large number of participants makes complexity a key characteristic of a KIP; (v) Structure: It is only possible to define a workflow that depicts a KIP partially, as unpredictable decisions or tasks guided by creativity are an inherent part of the flow of activities, as well as knowledge flows and knowledge transfers between media and persons being necessary to achieve a successful process completion. [4]; (vi) Goal-orientation: Although the unpredictable nature and complexity of KIPs is a hindrance to achieve a consistent structure, a minimum of structure can be achieved by defining milestones or intermediate goals during process execution; (vii) Event-Driven: Internal and external events may affect the quality of information exchanged during a KIP executing or require a participant to react for the successful achievement of the intended KIP process goal; (viii) Repeatability: The exact flow and order of activities, during each instance execution of a KIP, depends on several situational and contextual factors as well as possible external events that affect its participants. KIPs tend to be less repeatable than non-KIP processes, so an exact repetition of an instance, in terms of flow and activities of a previously executed KIP, seems hardly possible, due to the variety of factors affecting each specific execution or instance; (ix) Frequency and Time-Horizon: KIPs tend to have longer run times than non-KIPs and, due to work changing hands over time and the inherent complexity of the process flow itself, no single individual has a full view of the process instance as a whole. Also, KIPs seems to be executed less frequently and are often of an strategic than operational character.

All the above listed characteristics involve the execution of Knowledge Intensive Activities (KiA) during the execution of KiPs. KiA, being also knowledge intensive involve the knowledge necessary for its execution, coming from a variety of sources. the information necessary for KiA execution usually comes from the context of the process or activity itself, being, for example, application data, process data, functional data, etc. When performing a task, a person often consults resources and its selection is based on a number of factors such as her personal skills, experiences or preferences [1].

Our research argues that there is a dependency between the information necessary to execute a KiA and the context involving the activity. The following sections will explore the subject in more detail.

3   Context Within KiP

Vieira et al. [13] expands the definition of context and defines the concepts of contextual element and context. A Contextual Element is any piece of data or information that allows an entity to be characterized within a domain, while Context is the set of instantiated contextual elements that are needed to support a task performed by an agent (human or software) [3]. Moreover, according to Vieira et al. [13], the elements that compose context have a relevant relationship with the task that the agents are performing. A contextual element is stable and can be set at designated time, whereas context is dynamic and must be constructed at runtime, when the interaction occurs.

Therefore, for a Knowledge Intensive Activity of any kind, we have a Context involved, composed of Context Elements necessary to support it. Another element related to its Context is the knowledge exchange related to the Knowledge Intensive Activity itself, being the interactions between participants, in the forms of conversations, usage of social networks and other forms of collaboration and knowledge exchange.

3.1   Interactions and Speech Acts

The knowledge exchange within a KiP will usually take the form of conversations, physical or virtual interactions between agents or any other form of communicative interaction. Searle and Vandeveken [8] describe the minimal unit of human conversation as an illocutionary act, defined as an act that someone performs in producing an utterance such as an act of asserting a proposition, asking someone a question, directing someone to do something, etc. Whenever a speaker utters a sentence in an appropriate context, with certain intentions, he/she performs one or more illocutionary acts. An illocutionary act can be decomposed as three different speech acts: an utterance act (simply uttering an expression), a propositional act (the act of expressing a propositional content) and, if the illocutionary act is successful, a possible perlocutionary act (the effect of the act itself upon the hearer). It is considered as the minimal unit of human conversation, some examples of it are statements, questions and commands [8].

Thus, a generic conversation between participants of a KiP can be defined as an ordered sequence of illocutionary acts, between different speakers and hearers. Each illocutionary act in the sequence creates a limited set of possible replies, in the sense of limited sets of possible speech act to be performed as the next step of the ordered sequence of speech acts at the conversation.

Based on these definitions, Searle and Vandeveken [8] define a taxonomy of illocutionary acts, such as follows:

- Assertive: Speech acts that commit a speaker to believing the expressed proposition (e.g. reciting a creed). For example, "I think it is better for us all to travel by plane", "I believe doing so is necessary."
- Directive: Speech acts that are intended to cause the hearer to perform a particular action (E.g. requests, commands and advice). For example, "George, please finish your work as soon as possible!"
- Commissive: Speech acts that commit a speaker to doing some future action, such as promises and oaths. For example, "I promise to not to break the glass again!" and "I vow to defend our land."
- Expressive: Speech acts that express the speaker's attitudes and emotions towards the proposition, such as congratulations, excuses and thanks. For example, "I thank you so much for your help!" and "I am terribly sorry."
- Declarations: Speech acts that change the social sphere in accord with the proposition of the declaration, such as baptisms or pronouncing someone husband and wife. For example, "I hereby declare you husband and wife." and "We have finished the work."

Thus, during the execution of Knowledge Intensive Activities, the conversations associated with them will happen in the form of one or more illocutionary acts of specific types being performed. Its content, the definition of the roles of "speaker" and "hearer" and its other elements will be called the context of the interaction.

3.2   The Context of an Interaction

The definitions of speech acts requires a following definition of the context of an interaction, representing the context of the utterances (i.e. the propositional content of the illocutionary acts) exchanged between the participants. We start by adopting Searle and Vanderveken's definition of context [8], taking into consideration the elements of an interaction, especially the speakers and their utterances.

At a minimum, the context of the utterance must have a speaker, the one who is performing the utterance, a hearer, the one who hears or receives the utterance, a location, a time, and a set of various other features involving the speaker, hearer, time and location that can be called the world of the utterance.

Therefore, The context of an utterance i has five constituents, called the coordinates of the context: a speaker a; a hearer b; a time t; a location l and a world w. Thus, $i = \{a, b, t, l, w\}$.

Based on the above definition, a number of elements can be described related to the world of an utterance w, that influence directly on the illocutionary acts being performed. Among them, we can cite the beliefs, desires and intention involved at the activity and the process itself, the feelings about the possible courses of action to be taken as examples.

The world of an utterance takes into account the notion of possible worlds. Taking into account the actual world w0 i.e. the present state of affairs, we can think of a possible world as a world in which the objects of the actual world (the actual world) are different and/or as a world which has objects different from the actual ones.

A possible world w1 is accessible from a world w2 when all laws of nature which hold in w2 also hold in w1 i.e. when no state of affairs violate any physical law of w2 [8].

Therefore, a state of affairs can be universally possible (there is at least one possible world where it exists) but not physically possible in a world w (it is not accessible, as it violates a law in world w).

The notion of universally possible and physically possible state of affairs is important, when taking into consideration the utterances involved on a KiP and its activities, as the possible scenarios of a Knowledge Intensive Activity are usually constrained by several laws and contingencies (similar to the physical laws of Searle's definition) thus limiting the possible worlds of utterances during an interaction and the possible illocutionary acts to be performed.

The exchange of speech acts during a conversation not only occurs in an specific context, but also can modify the context as it is happening, as the knowledge being exchanged produces new perceptions at the participants.

This dynamic of the context at an interaction was described by [10] and, based on the analysis of the interactions, an important concept, the Common Ground Context (CG) is defined as: *"Common Ground Context is composed of common or mutual beliefs plus what a speaker presupposes, i.e. what she believes to be common or mutual belief for all participants at a conversation."* [9]

Common Ground includes the notion of pragmatic presupposition, being the knowledge that is implied during an interaction and it includes at its most basic form the preconditions for linguistic interaction (for example, the mutual public knowledge that we are speaking the same language), the norms of turn-taking in dialogue, and more particularized information about conversational plans and goals. It can also be changed or modified by two kinds of event that can change a conversation's CG: speech acts and manifest events, the latter being defined as "an event that, when it occurs, that is mutually recognized to have occurred".

3.3   Definitions and Ontology Representation

Based on the previous work, the Knowledge Intensive Process Ontology (KIPO) [19], we propose an ontology to represent the concepts presented in this paper, the associated concepts of KIPO and the concepts of the Unified Foundational Ontology (UFO). KIPO provides well-founded definitions which enable us to explore the concepts comprised in a KIP and depict how Beliefs, Desires, Intentions and Feelings are inherent to it. As a task ontology, KIPO is an explicit and formal representation of a shared conceptualization [15] and an abstraction that depicts concepts and their relationships of the described process in a domain independent way.

KIPO is composed by five perspectives, each of them a sub-ontology in itself: (i) the Business Process Ontology (BPO): containing common process elements such as Activities, Flows and Data Objects; (ii) the Collaborative Ontology (CO) [22]: depicting concepts common to the knowledge exchange and collaboration between process participants; (iii) the Decision Ontology (DO) [23]: representing the "why" and "how" the decision-making was performed by the people involved in the process; (iv) the Business Rules Ontology (BRO) [24]: representing the rules or constraints that must be observed throughout the execution of a KiP and (v) the Knowledge Intensive Process Core Ontology (KIPCO) [19]: containing concepts and elements that are specific to the Knowledge Intensive Processes, and inter-relate concepts from the other perspectives.

Moreover, KIPO precisely defines the semantics of each concept involved within a KiP by referring to the meta properties of the constructs of a top-level ontology, named Unified Foundational Ontology (UFO) [16]. UFO is a foundational ontology, in the sense that it provides a system of basic categories and relations whose intended meaning is grounded in very general principles inspired by Formal Ontology, Philosophical Logic, Linguistics, and Cognitive Psychology, and formally characterized by means of logical axioms. UFO consists of three main modules: UFO-A [16], an ontology of Endurants (objects); UFO-B [18], an ontology of events (Perdurants); and UFO-C [17], an ontology of social entities built up on UFO-A and UFO-B.

In KIPO, a KiP is typically composed by a set of activities connected by a simple control flow, or even with no control flow at all (as a bag of tasks). At least, some of them (at least one) are Knowledge-Intensive Activities.

An Agent is defined as "the one who intentionally commits to reach a Goal by executing a Knowledge-Intensive Activity. The Agent is motivated by his Desire and acts, according to his Belief. An Agent may experience many Feelings, and each one of those Feelings may be motivated by many of his Beliefs which he is aware of. [21].

Based on a subset of his Beliefs as a rationale, the Desires of the Agent are pondered, in terms of possible courses of action and forms of activity execution. From the pondering task, an Intention is formed, being a type of Desire oriented towards the Activity Goal. The Intentions impel the Agent to execute the Knowledge-Intensive Activity, towards the achievement of the goals of the Knowledge-Intensive Activity.

A key element here is the Belief. Beliefs are defined as Mental Moments (from UFO-C) that are particular to a specific Agent, and generate representation called Externalized Beliefs (defined as Situations at UFO-A) that represent the variety of forms that a Belief can be externalized. Externalized Belief can be either (i) shared between different Agents or (ii) presupposed as common ground (i.e. shared by all Agents) involved in an interaction."

Therefore, the Shared Belief is composed by the Externalized Beliefs that are shared by all Agents participating at a Communicative Interaction. The Common Ground is composed by the Externalized Beliefs that are shared by all Agents participating at a Communicative Interaction plus the Externalized Beliefs that are presupposed to be shared between all Agents participating at a Communicative Interaction.

Agents perform Communicative Interactions in order to exchange knowledge and express Externalized Beliefs, Desires, Intentions, Feelings or Contingencies among them. The Agents' performed speech acts can also modify the Common Ground Context of the Communicative Interaction.

As a result of the analysis of those concepts, Fig. 1 describes the concepts proposed by our research in the form of an Ontology, as depicted below.

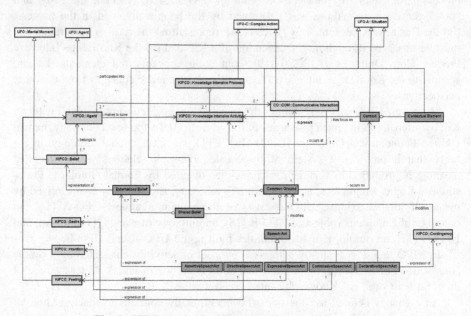

Fig. 1. KIPO ontology with proposed contextual concepts

4 Example Scenario

An example scenario will be depicted below, to illustrate the dynamics of the inter- actions, the usage of speech acts, as well as the contextual elements that compose the context focused on a KiA and the Common Ground of a conversation.

We take for example the KiP "Perform a Marketing Campaign" for an specific product and at an instance of this process, we take an example Activity "Create a new product logo". At the Knowledge Intensive Activity, there are three participants: (i) The contract manager, responsible to manage the creative process and mediate the exchange of ideas between the client and the designer; (ii) The designer, responsible for drawing logo proposals, evaluate elements such as colors, shapes and the impact of each proposals to a prospective client or customer and (iii) The client, that is responsible to provide feedback and decide which logo would be best for his product.

The Context of the Knowledge Intensive Activity is composed of several Con- textual Elements, for example: The logo and the differents ideas about how it should be, the different elements involved on the possible logo, such as shapes, colors and textual messages, the desired effects on the prospective customer, etc. These Contextual

Elements will also be part of the interactions related to the KiA, especially as part of the propositional content of the speech acts performed by the participants.

Now, the initial state of the Common Ground can be considered. It will represent the initial pressupositions that each agent pressuposes every participant believe in. From basic things, such as each participant understands and speaks the same language, that achieving the best possible logo for the product is in everyone's best interests, etc. Starting with this initial state, the Common Ground will be modified by Speech Acts performed (each utterance performed at the meeting) or Contingencies (in the form of events that everyone agree that occurred). An example of a Contingency would be that the scheduled time for the meeting is over.

4.1   Participant Mindset: Beliefs and Externalized Beliefs

The Beliefs of each participant are taken into consideration now: The manager can be described as someone with organizational expertise, focused on the reality of the process and a clear belief of achieving feasible results in time and also believes that the perfect logo does not exist, that the ideal logo is the best possible logo, considering time and manpower constraints.

The designer has a different mindset. His beliefs are focused on the impact of the logo to the public, having a more artistic outlook towards the task involved at the KiA. A logo that is commonplace is not satisfying to his demands, it must be innovative and show the best qualities of the product.

Finally, the client's mindset is focused on the best results and the lowest cost and time. Also, he has already some ideas about how the logo would be like, but he is open to the opinion of the specialists from the hired marketing company.

Further, their Beliefs are Mental Moments (according to UFO and KIPO), each of them being inherent and unique to each participant. For example, Beliefs with similar propositional contents, such as the belief of achieving the best logo for the product, are different in terms of what is considered best for the client, being different from what is considered best for the manager and so on. The Beliefs will generate representations, called Externalized Beliefs, that will be exchanged during the interaction through the Speech Acts performed by the participants.

4.2   Conversations and Speech Acts

The scenario can be analyzed now in terms of its interactions. We have create an example of an excerpt of an interaction, in the form of a meeting between the manager, the client and the designer responsible for the logo.

A conversation can be defined as an ordered sequence of speech acts, between different speakers and hearers. Each illocutionary act in the sequence creates a limited set of possible replies, in the sense of limited sets of possible speech act to be performed as the next step of the ordered sequence of speech acts at the conversation [20].

The excerpt below describe the illocutionary acts of each participants, together with the speech act classification on brackets. It illustrates how a typical interaction involving the contextual elements of a KiA (for example: the logo, the design of it, the color, the values of the product image, etc.). These elements will compose the Context of the interaction, with a focus on the Knowledge Intensive Activity itself.

Manager: "So, please tell us what are your thoughts about your product image." [Directive]

Client: "I firmly believe in a product reaching the customer and presenting him with an idea that improves his life and makes him proud of having purchased it." [Assertive]

Manager: "It's a good starting point, don't you think?" [Expressive]

Manager: "Lifestyle improvement and customer pride.....We can start doing some draft logos reflecting these values, like a brainstorming session. Any ideas?" [Directive]

Designer: "Well, I don't know if it is exactly what you want." [Expressive]

Designer: "But I've made some sketches prior to the meeting" [Declarative]

Designer: "There you go..three logo proposals. Please, tell me what you think." [Directive]

Client: "Of all the three logos, I liked the third the most. It is sober, simple and solid. I'm inclined to pick this one." [Expressive]

Manager: "Well, I beg to differ. I don't think we should invest time in doing the same mistakes of the competition. There are many products with logos with one or two colors." [Assertive]

Manager: "We need something new, that gives people the message in a blink of a second." [Expressive]

Client: "Look, I am all for innovation. I just dont believe in spending the whole month on the design of a logo." [Expressive]

Client: "We have a tight schedule for our product release and we would like to have something to work on as soon as possible." [Declarative]

Manager: "Let me think...perhaps we can start with the simple one and improve on it. What do you think? Is it feasible?" [Directive]

Designer: "Sounds good." [Expressive]

Designer: "I can create different proposals, keeping the simplicity but adding some tweaks." [Commissive]

Designer: "We can evaluate them and pick one of the candidates." [Directive]

Client: "I agree completely." [Expressive]

Client: "It will not be easy, but it will be excellent to merge our viewpoints." [Assertive]

Manager: "Ok, guys. It's lunch time, the meeting is over." [Declarative]

Manager: "We will meet next week to check the logo candidates and decide which one we can start working with." [Directive]

4.3   Common Ground and Shared Belief

At the conversation excerpt of the previous subsection, several elements were exchanged between the participants (all Agents involved at a KiA). All of them will affect the Common Ground and the Shared Belief. There is a difference between them, in the sense that the Common Ground is composed of the Shared Belief plus what is pressuposed as being part of Shared Belief.

The interaction at the excerpt can be divided in three parts for the analysis of the Common Ground dynamics: The first part is the exchange of initial ideas and beliefs for a logo and the best way for the depicting of the values of the organization, by the Manager and the Client. The beliefs presented at the discussion modify the Common Ground and are pressuposed by the participants as the main goals for the second part, where the presentation of the three logo sketches and the discussion of which one is best takes place.

The final part forms the discussion on how the development of the logo proposal is going to happen, as each one of the people involved presents their own feelings and beliefs about how the work should be performed. Again, their general viewpoint is modifying the Common Ground, not only about what is agreed between them, but also about the general presupposition over the specific individual stance of each participant.

A clear example would be the last speech act, that defines the intention of "having another meeting next week". The Externalized Belief that a meeting will occur next week has become part of the Shared Belief (and consequently part of the Common Ground as well). It is different from the case of the different logo proposals, the Designer pressuposes that the Manager and the Client believes that one logo candidate will be chosen at the next meeting. It is a pressuposition, as the Manager has not performed any illocutionary act towards this proposal, simply stating that the meeting was over.

The example shows how the Common Ground and Shared Belief depicts the dynamics of the interaction changing at each step of the conversation and serve as a base concept for further research on this subject.

5 Discussions and Future Directions

Our research highlights the relevance of the context within interactions in a KiP and, more specifically, in the Knowledge Intensive Activities that are part of it. We argue that context is a critical element of it, limiting the course of actions and possible goals by features such as social commitments between agents. Also, an analysis of the dynamics of how the context of an interaction can be modified at run-time and its effects at a KiP is described.

The ontology proposed as a result of the discussions is a previous step towards building a theory on KIP. This conceptual model could be applied to the analysis of interactions regarding a KiP and also on the modeling of a KiP, bringing the perspective of the context of the interactions that occur at a KiA and other elements of a business process.

Future directions of our work will be to investigate the dynamics of interactions and the contextual elements involved at real scenarios and explore the different types of contextual elements such as, for example, each agent's role at an organization, the specific capabilities for the execution of a task.

References

1. Brander, S., Hinkelmann, K., Martin, A., Thönssen, B.: Mining of agile business processes. In: Proceedings of the AAAI Spring Symposium on AI for Business Agility (2011)
2. Brezillon, P., Pomerol, J.C.: Contextual knowledge sharing and cooperation in intelligent assistant systems. Le Trav. Hum. **62**, 223–246 (1999)
3. Di Ciccio, C., Marrella, A., Russo, A.: Knowledge-intensive processes: characteristics, requirements and analysis of contemporary approaches. J. Data Semant. **4**, 29–57 (2014)
4. Gronau, N., Weber, E.: Management of knowledge intensive business processes. In: Desel, J., Pernici, B., Weske, M. (eds.) BPM 2004. LNCS, vol. 3080, pp. 163–178. Springer, Heidelberg (2004). doi:10.1007/978-3-540-25970-1_11
5. Little, T.A., Deokar, A.V.: Understanding knowledge creation in the context of knowledge-intensive business processes. J. Knowl. Manag. **20**(5), 858–879 (2016)
6. Marjanovic, O., Freeze, R.D.: Knowledge intensive business processes: theoretical foundations and research challenges. In: Proceedings of 44th Hawaii International Conference on Systems Science (HICSS-44 2011), Koloa, Kauai, HI, USA, pp. 1–10. IEEE Computer Society (2011)
7. Rosemann, M., Recker, J., Flender, C.: Contextualization of business processes. Int. J. Bus. Process Integr. Manag. **3**(1), 47–60 (2008)
8. Searle, J.R., Vanderveken, D.: Foundations of Illocutionary Logic. Cambridge University Press, Cambridge (1985)
9. Stalnaker, R.: Context. Oxford University Press, Cambridge (2014)
10. Stalnaker, R.: Common ground. Linguist. Philos. **25**(5–6), 701–721 (2002)
11. Witschel, H.F., Hu, B., Riss, U.V., Thönssen, B., Brun, R., Martin, A., Hinkelmann, K.: A collaborative approach to maturing process-related knowledge. In: Hull, R., Mendling, J., Tai, S. (eds.) BPM 2010. LNCS, vol. 6336, pp. 343–358. Springer, Heidelberg (2010). doi:10.1007/978-3-642-15618-2_24
12. Vaculin, R., Hull, R., Heath, T., Cochran, C., Nigam, A., Sukaviriya, P.: Declarative business artifact centric modeling of decision and knowledge intensive business processes. In: The Fifteenth IEEE International Enterprise Computing Conference (EDOC 2011), pp. 151–160 (2011)
13. Vieira, V., Tedesco, P., Salgado, A.C.: Designing context-sensitive systems: an integrated approach. Expert Syst. Appl. **38**(2), 1119–1138 (2011)
14. Searle, J.: Indirect speech acts. In: Syntax and Semantics. 3: Speech Acts, pp. 59–82 (1975)
15. Guarino, N.: Formal ontology, conceptual analysis and knowledge representation. Int. J. Hum. Comput. Stud. **43**(5/6), 625–640 (1995)
16. Guizzardi, G.: Ontological Foundations for Structural Conceptual Models. University of Twente, Enschede (2005)
17. Guizzardi, G., Falbo, R.A., Guizzardi, R.S.S.: Grounding software domain ontologies in the unified foundational ontology (UFO): the case of the ode software process ontology. In: Proceedings of the XI Iberoamerican Workshop on Requirements Engineering and Software Environments, (IDEAS 2008), pp. 244–251 (2008)
18. Guizzardi, G., Wagner, G., Almeida Falbo, R., Guizzardi, R.S.S., Almeida, J.P.A.: Towards ontological foundations for the conceptual modeling of events. In: Ng, W., Storey, V.C., Trujillo, J.C. (eds.) ER 2013. LNCS, vol. 8217, pp. 327–341. Springer, Heidelberg (2013). doi:10.1007/978-3-642-41924-9_27
19. França, J., Netto, J., Carvalho, J., Santoro, F., Baião, F., Pimentel, M.: KIPO: the knowledge intensive process ontology. Softw. Syst. Model. **14**, 1127–1157 (2014). Springer

20. Unger, M., Leopold, H., Mendling, J.: How much flexibility is good for knowledge intensive business processes: a study of the effects of informal work practices. In: HICSS 2015, pp. 4990–4999 (2015)
21. França, J.B.S., Santoro, F.M., Baião, F.A.: Towards characterizing knowledge intensive processes. In: Proceedings of the IEEE 16th International Conference on Computer Supported Cooperative Work in Design, pp. 23–25 (2012)
22. Oliveira, F.F.: Ontology collaboration and its applications. M.Sc. dissertation, Programa de Pós-Graduação em Informática Universidade Federal do Espírito Santo, Vitória, Brazil (2009). (in Portuguese)
23. Pereira, A., Santoro, F.: Cognitive decision making process as context information. In: The 15th IFIP WG8.3 International Conference on Decision Support Systems (DSS 2010), Lisboa, Portugal (2010)
24. Lopes, M., Baião, F., Siqueira, S.: Expressing business rules in a foundational-based domain ontology: towards higher-quality conceptual models. In: International Conference on Information Integration and Web-Based Applications and Services, Paris (2010)
25. Eppler, M.J., Seifried, P.M., Ropnack, A.: Improving knowledge intensive processes through an enterprise knowledge medium. In: ACM Special Interest Group on Computer Personnel Research (1999)
26. Hagen, C.R., Ratz, D., Povalej, R.: Towards self-organizing knowledge intensive processes. J. Univ. Knowl. Manag. 2, 148–169 (2005)

Contextual Support for Emergency Management Training: Challenges for Simulation and Serious Games

Ilona Heldal[(✉)]

Western Norway University of Applied Sciences, 5020 Bergen, Norway
ilona.heldal@hvl.no

Abstract. Training collaboration and work in various Emergency Management (EM) can be supported by different technologies, in particular simulations and serious games (SSGs). This paper is based on an investigation of why the promising SSG technologies can be difficult to use, even a long time after their procurement by the user organizations. The focus is on firefighter training. It is based on interviews and observations with major stakeholders from procuring organizations, SSG developers and researchers from seven countries. The results confirm the possible benefits of SSGs, but also highlight an urgent need for new approaches to better integrate these technologies into educational practices in local organizations. To experience meaningful training, there is a need to determine relevant training situations, define recognizable contexts, learning goals and user values. Only when this is done they might successfully be illustrated via the available SSGs.

Keywords: Emergency management · Simulation · Serious games · Training · Representations · Context

1 Introduction

The use of simulations and serious games (SSG) is increasing in emergency management (EM) training and education. SSGs are technologies that provide features that can support learning, and are often built on existing game technologies on which digital reality-like, visual scenarios can be constructed. Using game technologies can mean keeping pace with rapid technical updates. Various game elements such as tasks to accomplish, role-playing, challenges or goals to reach can be included. Promises from SSGs to support everyday training activities are many, e.g. increased motivation, better insight into new situations, accessible training [1] with greater safety [2–4], or better support for decision making [5]. These benefits and promises often overshadow possible problems related to how implementation can be accomplished and how successful use can be achieved in user organizations.

This paper aims to provide a better insight of SSG technology use and non-use, by describing values SSG can produce for organizations having it, in the view of resources needed to manage it, and current technical development. Procuring SSGs and not using them indicates recognizing the strategic importance at a top level, but not prioritizing it

© Springer International Publishing AG 2017
P. Brézillon et al. (Eds.): CONTEXT 2017, LNAI 10257, pp. 484–497, 2017.
DOI: 10.1007/978-3-319-57837-8_40

at the operational level. To better understand the mismatch between procuring managers and instructors responsible for training within the same organization is another purpose of this study. By identifying potential key benefits and limitations, the focus is on user organizations and their opinions.

The analysis is based on data from 33 interviews from seven countries with managers and instructors from user organizations, and with developers and researchers involved in current technical development. The paper discusses the benefits of contextualization for communicating training values with users.

The motivation for this study comes from the fact that there are organizations that invested in the rather costly SSG technology several years ago, but their utilization of it is very limited. For example, utilization may be restricted to showing informative pictures or films. Such examples can be created without expensive resources or licenses to SSG technologies and applications [6].

A well-known benefit of using SSG is to facilitate greater user experiences. Here we need to distinguish eventual confusions due the use of terminologies associated to user experiences. Presence, i.e. the sense of believing that you are in a computer-generated place instead of a real-life setting often indicates user experiences in research from computer science or psychology [7]. In the same field immersion often relates to the properties of providing surrounding experiences by technologies, and can be measured objectively [8]. However, studies from the field of game research use the same word immersive to indicate high experience, also high presence and not necessarily the technical properties. The EM referred to in this paper concern handling accidents and incidents in the first instance, incident commanders on scene. The technologies are - in a broader sense – simulation and serious games, but may also include elements of gamification; so the SSG abbreviation is used in a broad sense. In our study we focus on the main SSGs known to the user organizations, that are the following technologies: XVR[1], RescueSim[2], Fire Studio[3] (mainly pictures on fire and smoke), and Vector Command[4].

2   Background

This study is initiated by actors from the Swedish Civil Contingencies Agency[5] (MSB), which is responsible for the training of firefighters and incident commanders in Sweden. Firefighting is a physically and mentally demanding occupation, besides being potentially dangerous [9]. The agency recognized potential benefits of SSGs, has procured SSGs [10], but still several years later the technology is not used as extensively as expected. MSB has not yet experienced the promised benefits of their

---

[1] http://www.xvrsim.com/?t=gb (retrieved March 1, 2017).

[2] http://vstepsimulation.com/product/rescuesim/ (retrieved March 1, 2017).

[3] http://www.digitalcombustion.com/ (retrieved March 1, 2017).

[4] VectorCommand, and VSTEP, integrated products 2014.

[5] https://www.msb.se/en/?ResetTargetNavigation=true (retrieved March 1, 2017).

investment [11]. Therefore, an investigation of why the seemingly appropriate SSG technology has not been used was initiated.

Technology resistance is not a new phenomenon, and such resistance may even be beneficial for an organization, for example if older technologies are replaced by newer ones without enough advantages to motivate the cost in terms of learning the new technology (see e.g. [12]). However, having a technology without clear reasons for it not being used is confusing [10].

Today, the most common form of training EM is in classroom-like situations and via live training [13]. There are already proven methods at many organizations to develop and assess these training situations, even if this may require extensive resources of training personnel, specialized facilities and well-planned live scenarios. Both training forms are necessary in order to learn rules and regulations; to gain important knowledge and acquire routines and skills. Therefore, one important question when introducing SSGs concerns its role in relation to actual training: that is if SSGs can replace or complement the training methods used today?

Firefighters have to make many time-critical decisions in possibly life-threatening situations where their task is to protect the safety of civilians, themselves as well as buildings and other valuable objects. Due to emergency situations being unpredictable, time-critical and high-risk situations, firefighters have to go through extensive training [6]. Additionally, there are new infrastructures, transportation possibilities, housing, communications, and living habits. There are new materials in our houses, cars, and clothes. Even the magnitude of accidents is changing. Harbors cannot be closed to practice large ship fires [14], and the same fire cannot be repeated hundred times in the same way to allow to prepare or to examine hundred firefighters in the same manner [15].

Many of the new societal changes can result in unexpected situations for rescuing. These are not possible or difficult to consider in classroom training or in training in live settings. An instructor can speak about new situations, but meeting these in simulated environments can offer more realistic experiences [3] or higher awareness for decision making situations [5]. For example; an instructor can prepare to examine a hundred incident commanders in a live simulated scenario like a complicated traffic accident involving vehicles transporting hazardous goods. The scenario can involve fire, smoke, role-players and leaking gas. It is difficult to reproduce the exact same conditions and to conduct the examination in the same manner for all incident commanders.

If incident commanders have to be examined, it is important to be able to follow the same situation and allow commanders to experience their role, several times as similar to a real situation as possible. They will be examined on their problem solving skills which entails rerunning the same situation and discussing how they are thinking is the most important. This would be difficult without computer-based simulations [16]. How to train for 'the unexpected' is far from obvious. Just planning realistic enough training situations requires extensive resources of training personnel, specialized facilities and well-planned even live fire scenarios [3, 9]. Hence, training for preparedness of emergency situations is an extremely challenging task, due to costs, all required equipment and personnel, and the need to collocate and coordinate learners for the training events. Accordingly, these events cannot be arranged [17] frequent as desired and run as many times as desired in an equal manner. For these reasons, SSG is often advocated as a complementary method for emergency service training. However, there are no scientific works arguing how SSG can complement exactly what live training or classroom training can give, in order to gain additional benefits.

Between the many impressive benefits of SSGs, there are also additional ones, e.g. enhancing the motivation to train, providing better insight into new situations, and allowing accessible training with greater safety or less harmful impact on the environment. This is motivated by easier access to information and to expert knowledge anytime and everywhere; by access to naturalistic training situations with safe training conditions [5]; by distributed and group-based training and learning opportunities [4]; and by traceable actions and repeatable scenarios for debriefing and evaluation of a practiced event [18]. The latter provides a learning environment where learning from mistakes is possible, in contrast to real-life settings. Being able to use SSG technology for distance training is particularly attractive for many Scandinavian organizations due to the large number of small rescue services in rural locations.

One of the possible reasons for non-use of SSG can be the confusing message from research: Even though studies argue for additional values with SSGs (see e.g. [14, 19, 20]) there are other, warning studies for possible negative effects of them. Examples for negative effects are: difficulties to provide as accurate and dynamic scenarios as one meets with real accidents [9], people learn wrongly or miss important situations needed to handle real accidents [21], how the instructors' engagement and involvement influences learning outcomes [17] etc. When some research argues for added values while other research warns for negative effects this can be confusing for potential, new users, especially if they already have established methods and evaluations showing actual, required effects with the training.

Using technologies in organizations can be strategically important and methods and models have been developed to assess technology usefulness. One of the most influential models that explain technology adaptations is the technology acceptance model (TAM) developed back in [22]. While the model has several recognized limitations, for this study it can be beneficially the fact that it differentiates two important phases, the preimplementation and the postimplementation phases [23]. Non-use after procurement is an indication of problems with preimplementation and this phase is therefore important for this research. Examining this phase may highlight initial attitudes and beliefs that influence actual routines and habits and a willingness to tackle changes that are needed in relation to technology use [23]. Discussing these properties with users and non-users may highlight motivational factors why SSG is not implemented. By non-users we mean potential beneficiaries having access to the technology.

3   Methodology

In order to better understand reasons behind the non-use of the procured technology in the Swedish Agency, our approach included exploring the opposite situations, that is other organizations where the same type of technology had been successfully implemented and was used in their training programs. To obtain a picture of the use of SSGs for training in civil protection and other similar activities, literature reviews as well as interviews were conducted with relevant stakeholders from organizations in seven

Table 1. Data was collected via 33 interviews from managers (M), instructors or teachers (I), developers (D), and researchers (R). The '+' after the letter indicates that more than one interviews or observations (obs.) were performed from the corresponding group.

Countries	Data collected	From	Overall experiences
Sweden	Interviews and obs.	R+, D+, M+, I+	Non-use
England	Interviews	R, M+	Positive
Eastland	Interviews and obs.	M+, R, I+	Positive
Holland	Interviews	R+, D+, M+	Positive
Norway	Interviews	R+, M+, I+	Non-use
Denmark	Interviews	R, D, M+	Non-use
Singapore	Interview and obs.	M+, I	Positive

different countries: Sweden, Estonia, the Netherlands, Norway, the United Kingdom, Denmark, and Singapore. In total there were 33 interviews divided on the following stakeholder groups: researchers (8), developers (6), managers responsible for procurement from potential user organizations (4) and managers and instructors responsible for training and education (15), see Table 1.

The study started by identifying the main actors involved in SSG research and development during 2014. This was achieved by interviewing researchers active in the field, and conducting a literature review of trends in SSG usage. Search terms for the review were inspired from the work done by Backlund and Hendrix [2] and Crockal [4], and refined after an interview with Per Backlund. Every interview ended by asking the interviewee if s/he knows other actors influencing the state of the art of developing SSGs or organizations, which procured SSGs. This study reports results from 33 interviews. Important patterns begun to emerge when summarizing data from these, but we by no means argue that we did not miss arguments from some representative actors. Furthermore, some individuals had different roles, e.g. we interviewed several managers who were instructors as well, e.g. Andres Mumma from the Estonian Academy of Security Science, researchers who were also involved in SSG development, e.g. Simon Engfeldt-Nielsen from Serious Games Interactive[6].

The interviews were constructed around open-ended questions exploring the respondents' views and experiences regarding SSG's potential to support training and education; benefits and potential risks with using SSGs, and conditions required from eventual others at own organizations for meaningful use of the technology. Each interview lasted between 45 min and 2 h.

4 Introducing SSGs

4.1 Experiences from Educators in Sweden

The study reveals a somewhat hesitant attitude towards integrating SSGs into firefighter training in the Swedish organization. The interviews revealed use of some smaller

---

[6] http://www.seriousgames.dk/.

applications, often available for free or at a low cost that supported specific parts in the training program. Procurement and use were often initiated based on personal interest among the managers or teachers. These limited applications are considered beneficial to learning and the transfer of knowledge to other situations by the organizations. However, the readily available and more complex modern SSG tools are not used and are not integrated into training curricula. The main benefits of using SSGs were recognized by almost all the interviewees, even if certain groups were not familiar with SSG definitions. At some places they used *simulation*, while at some others *virtual reality* or *virtual reality systems*. Managers and teachers from user organizations were not always aware of differences between SSG or e-learning. While the interviews acknowledged the need for more training and self-training for learners, many instructors also felt that they needed more instruction regarding training and education. For part-time firefighters in rural areas in Sweden in particular, the opportunity to train at home or at their home fire station and follow sections of the training on a distance learning basis would be essential. *"Even if the participants come to campus meetings there is little time to do what needs to be done. More training would be needed."* A teacher expressed his wish to provide *"multiplayer"* settings, allowing team training with or without possible teachers present.

4.2   International Experiences

Experiences from the organizations who successfully have implemented SSG for training purposes were that the perceived benefits are considerable. They also recognized that the success was exclusively dependent on a well-planned process and supporting resources for the introduction of the technology. Motivation was gained by formulating concrete improvement needs, by addressing otherwise "impossible" situations and by providing enough resources. An example for handling otherwise impossible situations is from the Port of Rotterdam in the Netherlands. They needed to train large groups in the light of the impossibility of setting up live training at a huge port that could never be shut down. Example for having enough resources available is the Estonian Academy of Security Sciences. They recognized the value of SSGs when they planned to build up an academic program for emergency management that was supported through EU funding.

While the study shows examples and conditions for successful use, it must be recognized that most of the successful use examples involved local organizations rather than nation-wide public safety agencies. The use consisted of integrating SSG in selected training elements and not into complete certified or formal education curricula (except for the example from the Estonian Academy of Security Sciences).

Interviewing users from different countries led to the observation that cost has different meanings for different organizations. The cost of simulation-based training phases at some places are compared to live training (Estonia, Cheshire in the UK, Port of Rotterdam) while in Sweden, for example, the cost also includes travelling costs from faraway places to one of the two training locations in Sweden, with additional costs for part-time learners. Accordingly, being cost effective means something else for the Cheshire Fire and Rescue Service, which in 2013 had 700 occasions for training and assessment with the help of a virtual platform. If compared with the cost of these training sessions live, this number represents a saving of several million pounds. The Oxfordshire Fire and Rescue Service trained all its 200 truck leaders, 25 officers and 15 specialists in hazardous substances on various training levels and in various scenarios for 1½ years. Cost effectiveness in Scandinavia, however, means much fewer 'savings' due the smaller number of people involved in the training situations. Even if there are many training situations at the training centre in the UK, resources for training can be problematic, which also influences developers:

"Budget is the largest concern for Fire Rescue training today. In a troubled economy, many cities and states reduce budget to Fire Rescue making it difficult to get the right equipment needed for training. Fortunately, our software is also helpful in this regard because live training is often more expensive, especially when compared over the long term to what simulation-based training can provide. Additionally, mobile training is becoming more important as it allows a single person or unit to train several departments or station personnel, instead of each unit training on their own."

Similar comments on tight resources allocated for developing serious games is described by a developer from Denmark. He illustrated that reasons for procuring technologies do not take into account resources required for technology introduction. Accordingly, many customers order SSG applications as applications ready to be used, and not as frameworks needed to adjust to own training conditions.

The interviews acknowledged the need for a more coherent technology that not only supports training and learning but also different levels of competence development based on given situations and not taking into account the instructors' competence. The role of the instructors is almost the most important for the introduction of technology, since aligning goals for overall objectives differs from aligning goals for "daily" use [5]. Especially for the latter, the instructor may require additional technical support. Furthermore, teachers need to receive continuous information about the person responsible for gathering information, for current updates and for accessing new opportunities.

4.3 Experiences with Technologies

There are too many different technologies available at the different organizations. At the MSB one can find, for example, XVR (see Fig. 1), FireStudio, Vector Command and several smaller SSGs. Too many and too different technologies can result in confusion.

When interviewing participants from emergency management (prehospital education) from Norway, for example, they expressed worries about handling too many different technologies or versions of technologies. Accordingly, their opinion on utilizing many technologies can take up more time and resources and can cause communication problems internally between the instructors. They believe that: (1) Instructors needed to help each other out, need help with teaching and need to have roughly the same skills in managing technologies, (2) SSGs should not be too diverse since different technologies need to be handled differently and sometimes there is not enough time for this, and (3) technologies from different vendors should be avoided if

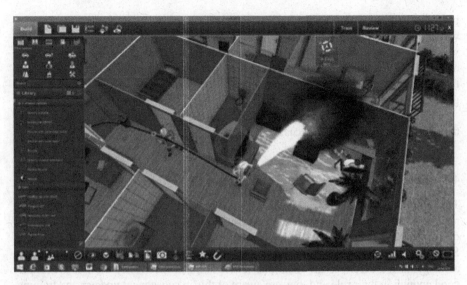

Fig. 1. Using XVR to simulate a fire scenario in a building. Making this interactive simulation after a realistic description takes 10–15 min for an instructor familiar with XVR, but is impossible for an instructor not familiar with simulation technologies.

possible, since potential problems and errors entail risks that service technicians from several vendors need to be on site and cooperate, which can result in delays due to coordination. This information from the users based on their experience contradicts the information from the vendors of the patient simulators.

Manufacturers claim the importance of acquiring various types of simulation solutions, since users do not necessarily need expensive patient simulators when sandbags are enough. Although manufacturers claim that various forms of higher-order simulation are needed to support the various elements, the users have difficulties learning these. They do not wish to obtain more technical skills than necessary to handle the simulators. However, they admit that it is difficult to determine where this level is, and how it varies over time. There were a few instructors with limited or no practical experience who expressed their fear of using SSGs. They considered games to be too complicated and too costly (see the examples from the next section). One person from the group of user organizations expresses a fear of building up a false sense of security by using SSGs:

[I can imagine there are…] *"…possibly false security experiences based on simulations. Like training chemical spills. There is a risk that the learner does not really appreciate the seriousness when later he is standing there in a real-life situation."*

Five of 16 instructors in the study believed that the greatest risk occurs when the instructor is not sufficiently trained to master the technology or the scenario training and assessment.

Cadets from the National Defence University studied use of commercial entertainment games in education Frank [21]. His findings show a phenomenon, as the author chooses to call *gamer mode* that needs to be considered by instructors for planning training and debriefing. This resulted in some students playing the game to win and they no longer maintained the same professional attitude to the game as they would in a real training session. The author defines gamer mode as a conscious attitude of the player to accept and not question the game rules and objectives and not accept the educational goals. The author emphasizes the importance of debriefing after the game as a learning opportunity.

Also this part illustrates the SSG introduction depends on the digital competence of the instructors which is not necessarily know by the managers at the organizations.

4.4   SSG Training for Longer Term

To continuously develop illustrative examples, scenarios, for training while also receiving technical updates needs to be taken in consideration when using SSGs. One of the interviewees from a user organization in Estónia recognized the added value of SSGs and he has used it for the past four years with benefits in both training and assessment. He describes the risks that instructors can face. They are not necessarily good enough in their role and they are aware of this in subsequent updates and training. To provide training situations with increased user experiences requires the instructor to provide good counter play, injects, and present appropriate consequences for decisions and actions. He illustrated a few negative aspects of not working with professionals from the various areas.

"One, for example is that if you do not have a good team of instructors the games do not work together. They [the instructors] need to be very competent in their professions and know the learning methods and technologies. The wrong approach sticks in a student's mind very easily. The development of those products is resource-intensive."

Many instructors mention that learners do not accept new forms of training:

"Some people may be skeptical about simulation or use it as an excuse if they fail to pass an assessment. Frequently the term "I would have done this in the real world" is heard from candidates by our instructors. However, we are four years into using virtual training and candidates should be used to our organization's training and assessment methods."

As mentioned earlier, some of the respondents were not aware of the possibilities of SSG. These technologies are often treated as e-learning technologies. Since e-learning technologies are used by almost all organizations and the added value of SSGs is not known, there is an unwillingness to change to something that is unclear. This is an opinion described in Sweden, Estonia and Denmark.

5   Obstacles and Challenges of Use

5.1   Believes About Instructor Roles and Computer Games

This section discusses possible answers for the motivating questions: How do instructors involved in the introduction of SSGs experience SSGs? How is their understanding affected after direct exposure to using SSGs? Can these experiences be transferred to training situations they are responsible for?

There are already discontinuities between the SSG pre-implementation phase, after procurement, and before it is used. The way pre-implementation is planned influences experiencing SSG effectiveness. Sometimes, non use can be explained by the different attitudes of the procuring managers and instructors [17, 24]. The instructors sensemaking activities regarding these technologies have a great influence [23]. In order to make changes in educational activities which are already working, instructors have to understand the potential and plan for change. They need to know how to initiate activities for matching needs and possibilities via using SSG.

While the interviews acknowledged the need for more training and self-training for firefighters, many educators also felt that they needed more instruction regarding training and education with SSG. Obstacles and challenges that were identified during the interviews from the behalf of the educators, seem to origin from one of the following reasons: a skeptical attitude towards the technology, a mismatch of expectations, or insufficient competence affecting the willingness to incorporate the new technology into the teaching practice.

The attitude towards SSG was sometimes rather skeptical. It was expressed by the opinion that SSG is not an appropriate technology at all: "Games *and learning do not usually belong together. Maybe it's a generational issue. From my perspective I may have a hard time to convince some people to use it...*". Another respondent expressed the fear that SSG would give a false and possibly dangerous impression:

"*[I can imagine there are] possibly false security experiences based on simulations. Like training chemical spills. There is a risk that the learner does not really appreciate the seriousness when later he is standing there in a real-life situation.*"

There were also concerns regarding instructors' competence and mismatch of expectations. There were a few instructors with limited or no practical experience that expressed their fear of using SSGs. They considered games to be too complicated and too costly. SSG software for training can be considered as an empty framework with a large number of available elements from which own, organization-specific training scenarios can be defined. This feature allows for local customization of training scenarios, in order to create highly meaningful learning situations. However, instructors did not consider scenario development as part of their job, due to lack of skills and time.

Another concern was raised which address the reliance of content as well as the competence of instructors: "[The scenario is] *lifelike, but also not. It can easily be used in the wrong way. If you do not have knowledge about how it works, there is a risk that they will reject it after testing it a little. Not having a trained instructor is a risk.*" The instructors' competences were a main concern. Five of 16 instructors believed that the greatest risk occurs when the teacher is not sufficiently trained to master the technology or the scenario training and assessment.

5.2   Enabling Tools Means Enabling Contextual Understanding

It is well known that SSGs are not only enabling tools, but require an underlying methodology for effective utilization. This methodology is not necessarily defined at the same time as, or right after, procurement, but it is essential and needs to contribute to relevant training and in the participating environments.

Environments which formulate their problems and translate these to clear requirements for SSG consider the use of SSG more valuable. For example, there was no other way than by using SSGs to plan training and evaluation in examining a large number of incident commanders in Oxforshire, UK [19]. At Port of Rotteram, very complex cases with huge objects in the large harbor environment [14] could not be handled in live training; harbors cannot be closed and changed to figure as training places [6]. Therefore, corresponding methodologies were defined quickly both in Oxfordshire and Port of Rotterdam.

Having older working methodologies that show training values, e.g. in Sweden and Norway, may result in much longer waiting periods to implement changes to new methods, in this case for SSGs. Also a blocking factor can be long-term experience with methods which already work. If these produce concrete benefits with live training in realistic conditions, the expectation for the new methods will be higher. This is true for the properties of SSGs. For example, sensing and experiencing live training, and being used to modern computer games with film-like graphics, raises the expectation for the fidelity of SSG applications. Low resolutions, less responsive environments, including difficulties in understanding their use, may influence willingness to trust and begin to use SSGs.

Today, there are too many games, e.g. Call of Duty or World of Warcraft with realistic, high fidelity, graphics and smooth interaction around us. This set too high expectations on the SSGs for EM education, which often are quite simplistic. To accept these lower fidelity, or non-realistic aspects means simplifications and compromise. How simplifications can be made and if compromises need to be made, can be questioned. Therefore, to plan with these SSG elements may cause confusion and influence users' willingness to form the SSGs to be usable in own environments. In general, when a successful, modern environment with different methods and evaluations for training is already available, and the benefits of the new system cannot easily be shown, planning for changes can be more difficult.

An answer to the question: Why are the environments procuring SSGs and obviously having the procuring managers support are non-enabling SSGs? showed via the interviews is: The currently working and good enough evaluation methodologies are hard to change, even if these are measuring training outcomes but they are not measuring the real benefits with SSG use.

Without concrete examples from the practitioners, and formulating accurate challenges from the management, the developers cannot develop valuable training situations. If the instructors cannot understand their role and responsibility to describe appropriately requirements to the developers can result a catch 22 situation, an inter-organizational knowledge barrier between practitioners and developers and can result in long-term waiting periods (effect described in e.g. [25]). This locked situation can be solved by better understanding training needs as processes. To begin with describing smaller, but important training needs and to gradually develop more complex situations was the wish list of one of the interviewed instructor. This way of gradually developing more proper training for own situations shows already benefits, according to a follow up study of [6] e.g. for planning training for roof race, or training extrication in Singapore.

6 Early Lessons and Future Work

According to the interview responses regarding experiences from some countries (Estonia, the Netherlands and UK), it is possible to experience higher effectiveness for training firefighters by utilizing SSG. The responses also show reasons why certain organizations do not succeed. There are still hinders to overcome. To handle technology introduction as a process and not as a step at user organizations may resolve unconscious lockups and barriers to development. The pre-implementation phase is not only an important part of this process, but necessary. Instructors play a vital role, and should be involved from the start to support engagement and reduce the risk for mismatching expectations. This concern of instructors' competence is aligned with several previous studies examining the role of SSGs for training and learning, for example [17]. It should be acknowledged, however, that SSG competence is different from general digital literacy since it also involves setting requirements for simulations, and may include scenario development and modification as well.

Prior to procurement, organizations need to realize that they must take an active part in adopting the SSG training technology to their own circumstances and current and future needs, in order to achieve appropriate learning material and by this potential learning benefits. The developers cannot be aware of all requirements from organizations at the beginning. Some of the effects of using technologies cannot appear before actual usage. This may result in failure of SSG utilization. Overcoming this deadlock is essential, since it limits both use and further development and thereby impeding a potential beneficial utilization of available SSGs.

Today SSG is not a "magic bullet" solution which per se contributes to learning after procurement. The result of using serious gaming for training purposes depends on the educational approach that forms the setting for the game and the actual gaming process. Information on the successful introduction of technologies differs between the different stakeholders. Common agreements regarding the benefits of what a technology promises overshadow possible problems related to how implementation can be accomplished and how successful use can be achieved at user organizations.

The low fidelity of the SSG technology expressed in this study as revealed by the obstacles with attitude, expectation and competence, could be overcome if the training scenarios were perceived as more authentic and trustworthy. One way to achieve this, we propose, is to base the SSG scenarios on real, authentic data from previous incident. Defining more believable and valuable scenarios means designing better contexts for SSGs. These should represent training values. For such scenarios there are information, documents, descriptions, narratives that can be used. As an example: rescue services are required to document every incident in standardized event reports. These previous event reports can be digitally analyzed and used for generating scenarios which is not only realistic but based on events that evidently have happened. Merely the knowledge that these scenarios are "based on true stories", a type of "documentary simulations", ought to affect the fidelity issue. In this way, the simulations can be seen as an illustrated true narrative, rather than an attempt to simulate complex unlikely situations. These scenarios can then be used for discussing how the incidents progressed, decisions that were taken, and alternative ways of action. The idea is to spread previous firefighter experiences to many learners and raise a scenarios-awareness among less experienced firefighters. This approach would directly address the challenge to be prepared for what could happen (or has happened in the past), by illustrative examples from the authentic reports or via techniques from serious games, e.g. considering sureties that always need to be represented, shocks or surprises that a firefighter could meet during the everyday work [26]. It will also address the problem that gaming technology is not yet capable of providing a real world scenario that is completely and faithfully accurate in a dynamic virtual environment [9], since the fidelity comes from the narrative behind the scenario, and not from the simulation per se.

Acknowledgments. The author would like to thank the Swedish Civil Contingencies Agency for making it possible to carry out this study, Cecilia Hammar Wijkmark, Lena Pareto for much help and comments, and the responders who allocated time and attention for the interviews or helped with the observations.

References

1. Ott, M., Freina, L.: A literature review on immersive virtual reality in education: state-of-the-art and perspectives. In: Conference Proceedings of eLearning and Software for Education (eLSE), pp 133–141. Universitatea Nationala de Aparare Carol I (2015)
2. Backlund, P., Hendrix, M.: Educational games - are they worth the effort? A literature survey of the effectiveness of serious games. In: 5th International Conference on Games and Virtual Worlds for Serious Applications (VS-GAMES). IEEE Press (2013)
3. Chittaro, L., Sioni, R.: Serious games for emergency preparedness: evaluation of an interactive vs. a non-interactive simulation of a terror attack. Comput. Hum. Behav. **50**, 508–519 (2015)
4. Crookall, D.: Serious games, debriefing, and simulation/gaming as a discipline. Simul. Gaming **41**(6), 898–920 (2015)
5. Molka-Danielsen, J., et al.: Creating safe and effective learning environment for emergency management training using virtual reality. In: Norsk konferanse for organisasjoners bruk av IT (2015)
6. Wijkmark, C.H., Heldal, I.: Kartläggning av State-of-the-art inom Simulering och Serious Games för Utbildning för Räddningstjänsten (in Swedish, Eng.: State-of-the-art within Simulation and Serious Games for Educating Firefighters). Report at University of Skövde School of Informatics, 80 p. (2015)
7. Slater, M., Wilbur, S.: A framework for immersive virtual environments (five): speculations on the role of presence in virtual environments. Presence Teleop. Virt. Environ. **6**(6), 603–616 (1997)
8. Heldal, I.: The usability of collaborative virtual environments: towards an evaluation framework. Ph.D. thesis, Chalmers, Department of Technology Management and Economics, Gothenburg (2004)
9. Williams-Bell, F.M., et al.: Using serious games and virtual simulation for training in the fire service: a review. Fire Technol. **51**(3), 553–584 (2015)

10. Toftedahl, M., et al.: Pedagogiska IT-verktyg för Ledningsträning (in Swedish, Eng.: Pedagogical IT tools for Training for Management). Report at University of Skövde, Gothia Science Park (2012)
11. Heldal, I., Pareto, L., Wijkmark, C.H.: Simulation and serious games for firefighter training: obstacles and challenges for effective use in collaboration and decision making in crisis situations. In: Workshop at ACM CSCW, San-Francisco, USA (2016)
12. Adner, R., Snow, D.C.: 'Old' technology responses to 'New' technology threats: demand heterogeneity and graceful technology retreats. Ind. Corp. Change **19**(5), 1655–1675 (2010)
13. Heldal, I.: Simulation and serious games in emergency management: experiences from two case studies. In: Proceedings of the 22nd International Conference on Virtual Systems and Multimedia (VSMM), Kuala Lumpur, Maleysia. IEEE Press (2016)
14. Jansen, R.: Determining the cost savings for the participants in a joint inter-terminal transport system at the port of rotterdam. J. Supply Chain Manag. 74 (2014). Delft University of Technology
15. Lamb, S., Kwok, K.C.S., Walton, D.: A longitudinal field study of the effects of wind-induced building motion on occupant wellbeing and work performance. J. Wind Eng. Ind. Aerodyn. **133**, 39–51 (2014)
16. Mumma, A.: Why are we playing computer games? The practice of the Estonian Academy of Security Sciences (EASS). In: Pres. at the Nat. RAKEL Seminar (MSB) (2016)
17. Alklind Taylor, A.-S.: Facilitation matters: a framework for instructor-led serious gaming. Ph.D. thesis at the University of Skövde, School of Informatics (2014)
18. Girard, C., Ecalle, J., Magnan, A.: Serious games as new educational tools: how effective are they? A meta-analysis of recent studies. J. Comput. Assist. Learn. **29**(3), 207–219 (2013)
19. Lamb, J.K., et al.: Incident command training: the introspect model. Int. J. Emerg. Serv. **3**(2), 131–143 (2014)
20. Schaafstal, A.M., Johnston, J.H., Oser, R.L.: Training teams for emergency management. Comput. Hum. Behav. **17**(5–6), 615–626 (2001)
21. Frank, A.: Gamer mode - identifying and managing unwanted behaviour in military educational wargaming. Ph.D. thesis at Stockholm, KTH, Department of Military Educational (2014)
22. Davis Jr., F.D.: A technology acceptance model for empirically testing new end-user information systems: theory and results. Ph.D. thesis at Massachusetts Institute of Technology (1986)
23. Venkatesh, V., Bala, H.: Technology acceptance model 3 and a research agenda on interventions. Decis. Sci. **39**(2), 273–315 (2008)
24. Heldal, I., Wijkmark, C.H.: Facilitators and obstacles in the introduction and use of technology: simulation and serious games as support in firefighter training. In: 9th International Conference on Researching Work and Learning, Proceedings of the International Conference of Researching Work and Learning (RWL9), Singapore (2015)
25. Suneson, K., Heldal, I.: Knowledge barriers in launching new telecommunications for public safety. In: International Conference of Intellectual Capital and Knowledge Management (ICICKM), Hong-Kong, pp. 429–439 (2010)
26. Fencott, C., et al.: Game Invaders: The Theory and Understanding of Computer Games. Wiley, Hoboken (2012)

Improving Defect Tracking Using Shared Context

Hassane Tahir[✉] and Patrick Brézillon[iD]

LIP6, University Pierre and Marie Curie (UPMC),
4 Place Jussieu, 75005 Paris, France
hassanetahir@hotmail.com, Patrick.Brezillon@lip6.fr

Abstract. Test engineers log bugs in a defect tracking system to different actors. For instance, in the case of database defects, after the first cycle of bug tracking is completed, the system will notify the Database Administrator (DBA). The DBA can log in to the system and get the bug list with priority. He can then solve the bug and change its status in the system. There are many ways of applying defect tracking by different actors because they do not have the same viewpoints about the contexts related to the management of the defects. Actors need to devote their efforts to develop new practices and use past expert experience in order to create an effective strategy to maintain applications. The paper presents how to contextualize defect tracking based on different expert viewpoints. We show how making shared context explicit can help to improve resolving defects and avoid conflicts between experts having distinct viewpoints.

1 Introduction

Anything that is wrong with a software application is considered as a defect. Defects are not always coding mistakes done by the developers. They can come from any stage in the software development cycle, because every stage involves different actors. Hence it is imperative that all defects get tracked so that experts can be alerted of any issues and they can properly validate and address them. Most times when defects are detected they are not found by the same actor who caused them or will be fixing them. In large teams, with a complex software development process, defects have to go through many actors to ensure they get properly resolved. When these defects are entered into a tracking system, or when they are handed over to other actors, the people involved need to know about it right away so they can address them in a timely manner. The defect tracking system should be able to automatically notify the appropriate actors, and should allow the people entering the defects into the system to notify anyone they deem necessary to know about those defects. A good communication and shared context between different actors is required to quickly resolve incidents and bugs.

Test Engineers, Developers, database and System Administrators use Bug Tracking Systems to record and track the progress of bugs (defects). Specific features should be understood to evaluate the tracking system. In a data integration project, as development of ETL (Extraction, Transformation and Loading) processes is completed, the testing phase will be started. If bugs are found, test engineers can load log of such bugs

© Springer International Publishing AG 2017
P. Brézillon et al. (Eds.): CONTEXT 2017, LNAI 10257, pp. 498–509, 2017.
DOI: 10.1007/978-3-319-57837-8_41

in a bug tracking system to the different actors: Developers, Database Administrator (DBA), etc. For instance, in the case of database bugs, after the first cycle of bug tracking is completed, the system will notify the DBA. The DBA can log in to the system and get the bug list with priority. He can then solve the bug and change the status of that bug in the system. The problem is that most of the time, only technical factors are taken into account. Contextual elements about human and social factors are not considered.

Contextual elements are relevant at a given time (e.g. memory size, hard drives), and the values taken by these contextual elements at that moment: (memory size: 70%, full, hard drives: HP-1, IBM-23). The DBA often developed practices to manage these contextual elements in order to solve the problem at hand. Practices encompass what the users do with procedures. We can point two categories of problems: technical and social. Technical problems can impact the performance of the entire information system of the company. This includes problems due to the database, the server, the network and/or the application. For instance, one of the most important database problems is when users are unable to connect to the database because of a locked account, slow time response or bad performance, and sometimes because the database is down. Social problems are mainly due to bad communications and collaboration with other users. Another example that we can give concerns some collaboration problems due to the bad collaboration between DBA and other actors. In some cases, developers do not cooperate with a DBA to solve database errors due to a bad application coding. The reason for this is that developers may not feel comfortable while their code is being reviewed if their managers are invited.

Defect tracking and processing must be integrated in the data migration project life cycle and the testing process. A defect management process is used to decide what is to become of software defects, or bugs, found in the development cycle for migrating data into the target system. Figure 1 illustrates the process of defect tracking. In this example, the prevalent defect, or bug process can have three basic states:

1. Submitted/Open
2. Resolved
3. Closed

This work relies on the Contextual-Graphs formalism [11] for improving bug tracking process in a data migration process. The main advantage of Contextual Graphs is the possibility to enrich incrementally the system with new knowledge and practice learning capability when needed. Moreover, a Contextual Graph is a good communication tool for helping the different actors of the project to exchange their experiences and viewpoints when solving defects.

The paper begins by the description of a case study about the data migration project: actors involved in the defect tracking and contextual elements. After, we present related works in the literature. Then we present how Contextual Graphs are used to represent shared context in defect tracking. Finally we conclude and evaluate our work.

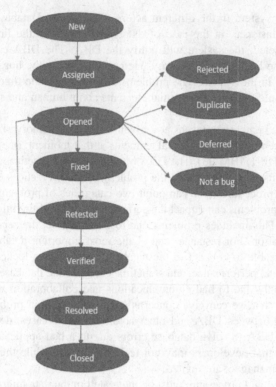

Fig. 1. Example of defect tracking process.

2 A Case Study

This case study presents the data migration project where defects are processed. Data has been processed using ETL (Extraction, Transformation and Loading). The ETL functionality includes the following steps (a) Identifying relevant data in the source systems, (b) Extracting the required relevant data, (c) Customizing and integrating data coming from multiple sources into a common format, (d) Cleaning the resulting data set according to the database and business rules, and (e) Propagating and loading of the data into a target system.

The ETL process (Fig. 2) can involve a great complexity, and critical operational problems that can appear with bad and improperly design. Each ETL system depends on a Database Management System (DBMS), which is composed of a set of subsystems executing specific tasks and compete for system resources allocated by the DBMS.

Actors that might be involved in the defect tracking of the data migration project are: Project Manager of Data Migration (Main Actor), Developers, DBAs and Business Analysts. In this case study, we focus on DBA problems. Many questions may be asked by actors involved in the ETL process. They concern some of the different contextual elements that intervene in the different phases of the ETL process (with their

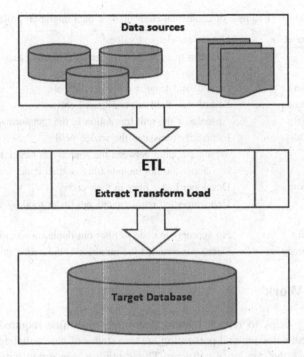

Fig. 2. ETL process used in a data migration.

known values). When any actor (i.e. Developer or a DBA) presents a bug report, most probably, he is asked many questions. Some of them are what is the name of the product? What is the defect? In which component is the defect? In which module is the defect? In which method the defect is? In which environment the defect arises? In which platform the application is created? In which OS (Operating System) the application runs? The information given by the DBA who reports defect might be incomplete initially.

The following are examples of defects contextual elements:

- What is the complexity of the defect causing bad response time? (Low, Medium, High)
- Are ETL workflow jobs updated after detecting an important defect in a mapping?
- Should indexes be dropped and recreated, respectively before and after defects are fixed?
- To fix database defects, is the DBA aware of the new ETL process constraints?

Other contextual elements are shown in Table 1. The following section discusses some of the commonly used approaches to defect tracking.

Table 1. Example of contextual elements in a data migration project

Contextual element	Contextual element values
Missing data	Bad data from the source database (needs cleansing) invalid joins
Truncation of data	Invalid field lengths on target database
Data type mismatch	Source data field not configured correctly
Null translation	Absence of the null translation in the transformation
Wrong translation	Incorrectly translated the source field
Misplaced data	Wrong mapping between the source and target data
Extra records	Developer did not include filter in their code
Not enough records	Developer had a filter in their code
Undocumented requirements	Undocumented requirements not understood by actors
Duplicate records	No appropriate code to filter out duplicate records
Numeric field precision	Developer rounded the numbers to the wrong precision

3   Related Work

Defect tracking helps to reduce the cost, resources and time required for rework. Therefore, defect detection and prevention are two stages of defect management which helps to improve the quality of software. This section is concerned with some of the related work in software engineering, database management and data integration. Many solutions have been proposed to deal with database incidents as in [5, 7].

Gopalakrishnanm presented in his paper [8] an Effective Defect Prevention Approach in Software Process for Achieving Better Quality Levels. He has made analysis of defect detection and prevention techniques which are employed in Agile development. For this analysis data has been gathered from five projects of leading software development companies. Don presented a study of how agile development environment involves defect detection and its prevention once a defect is detected [6]. He has discussed two wide categories of defect management: requirements defects and implementation defects. He concluded that Agile practices lack effective defect management but actually agile developments reduce defects in first place. These categories include finding defects in all types of requirements and technical implementation of a project. However context about social factors are not taken into account. JÖRG discussed the repeated and sustainable discovery process, handling, and treatment of quality defects in software systems [9]. Information about quality defects found in source code has been stored using an automation language. Automation language also represents the defect and treatment history of small parts of the software products. Abhiraja et al. discussed in the paper [1] that quality defects have been detected using test case and preventive actions to improve the quality of software process. If the software process is not working correctly then defect is found. Some preventive actions have been employed to avoid the defects like defects classification and discovering the root causes of the defects. Suma presented a paper [14] about Defect Management Strategies in Software Development. He described in his research that inspection is significant to discover the static defect close to the origin. Rajni presented a study to use defect tracking and defect prevention for the improvement of the quality [12]. Testing is performed when the software is developed and defects found are removed using defect prevention. According to Rajni, 2013, Defect Tracking System still needs improvement and a lot of research is required to mature the Defect Tracking Systems. Sydney et al. used a different technique that is The Defect Management Meeting [15]. In this meeting team members communicate face to face. The meeting is time-boxed to review and prioritize all new defects found. Time-boxing is particularly very helpful when request for change arises late in project and risk of defects increases due to changing requirement. The main goal of this meeting is to review existing defects.

Ansar proposes defect detection and analysis to discover the root causes of potential defects and prevention technique to remove defects [2]. He proposed a defect management process model to produce quality products. This model has been proved very valuable to handle harmful defects. Macros and Guilherme presented a unique concept of Defect causal analysis (DCA) to recover software development process and to reduce the amount of potential defects [10].

Zheng et al. introduced Automated Static Analysis (ASA) to correct failures before inspections or clients reports or doing some tests lead to their discovery [19]. He has demonstrated that static analytical tools account for as a complement for other defect detection techniques and lead to the development of software product with a high quality.

The above solutions cannot always successfully handle all defect tracking tasks in multitude of specific new situations and contexts that differ from the set procedures because of the following:

- Only physical parameters and sensors are considered;
- Not Human-Centered Context (i.e. Social Context: DBA Profile, experience, Knowledge, Conflict with DEVELOPERS, degree of collaboration between DBA and other shareholders...);
- Bad Context Sharing (i.e. Context is implicit). Defects are not always understood by all actors because contextual elements are not explicit.

For these reasons, we are interested to take context into consideration and incorporate it in the defect tracking procedures. Evidence has shown that human experts are very poor at identifying fault-prone software modules [18]. The following section presents how the Contextual Graphs Formalism can help in the contextualization of defect tracking especially when many actors are interacting with each other (i.e. sharing context)

4 Contextual-Graphs for Defect Tracking

4.1 Brief Description of Contextual Graphs

A contextual graph (CxG) allows the representation of the different ways to solve a problem. It is a directed graph, acyclic with one input and one output and a general structure of spindle [3]. Each path in a CxG corresponds to a practice, a way to fix the problem. Figure 3 provides the definition of the four elements in a contextual graph. A more detailed presentation of this formalism and its implementation can be found in [3, 4, 11].

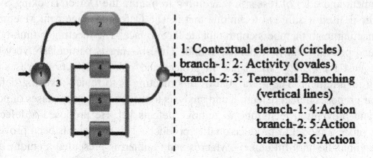

1: Contextual element (circles)
branch-1: 2: Activity (ovales)
branch-2: 3: Temporal Branching
      (vertical lines)
      branch-1: 4: Action
      branch-2: 5: Action
      branch-3: 6: Action

Fig. 3. Elements of a contextual graph

A contextual graph is composed of the following elements: actions, contextual elements, activities and temporal branching.

An **action** is the building block of contextual graphs at the chosen granularity. An action can appear on several paths but it will be in different contexts.

A **contextual element** is a couple of nodes, a contextual node and a recombination node. A contextual node has one input and N branches [1, N] corresponding to the N instantiations of the contextual element already encountered. The recombination node is [N, 1] and shows that, once items on the branch between the contextual and recombination nodes has been processed, it does not matter to know which branch was followed. Contextual elements are used to represent and implement context about the different events occurring in a given situation.

An **activity** is a contextual graph by itself that is identified by participants because it appears on different paths and/or in several contextual graphs. This recurring sub-structure is generally considered as a complex action. An activity is a kind of a contextualized task that can be aggregated in a unit or expanded in a sub graph according to the needs [13].

A **temporal branching** expresses the fact (and reduces the complexity of the representation) that several groups of actions must be accomplished but that the order in which action groups must be considered is not important, or even could be done in parallel, but all actions must be accomplished before continuing the practice development. The temporal branching is the expression of a complex contextual element at a lower granularity of representation.

Contextual graphs represent the set of known practices (strategies) in order to solve a given problem. They also allow incremental acquisition of practices and provide an understandable way to model context-based reasoning. A practice is the path from input to the output of a contextual graph. The problem solving process is guided throw a specific path by the evolution of context over time. Adopting a given practice or strategy among the others is dictated by the values of the different contextual elements forming the situation. However, it is not always obvious for a user to select one of these values. For example, in the area of database administration, to solve a serious performance problem within a given critical situation and context, a DBA may have different options when asking this question: what causes the slow response time of the system? Is it a network problem? Is it a bad database configuration? Is it a bad query in the application programs? Etc.

User practices are added and stored in an experience database. They may differ from each other because of their contexts that are slightly different where users used different actions at a step of the problem solving. The process of practice acquisition by the CxG system concerns the new action to integrate and the contextual element that discriminates that action with the previous one. The integration of the new practice requires either adding a new branch on an existing contextual node, or introducing of a new contextual node to distinguish the alternatives. The phase of incremental acquisition of practices relies on interaction between the CxG system and the users in order to acquire their expertise, which consists of a context-based strategy and its evolution along the process of the problem solving.

4.2 Contextual Graph Representing Collaborative Defect Tracking

4.2.1 Actors Viewpoints in the Context of Defect Tracking

Collaborative defect tracking is a team effort that requires cooperation between the different actors via task allocation, coordination of actions, and if necessary avoidance and/or management of conflicts among members of the organization. Defect tracking can be improved by an efficient collaboration between experts and key individuals: Test Engineers, Developers, System Engineers, Project managers and Business users. Each actor has his own viewpoint of what is the best course of actions and the wished effects. If a view is what someone can see, a viewpoint is from where someone is looking. Viewpoints are used to specify contextual views of actors on a particular problem. They can be used to view certain individual or shared contextual aspects.

One of the greatest challenges is to find a common means to define and reach a target goal (fixed by one individual or an actor) because the increasing number of actors from different backgrounds and domains affects the number of practices used for defect tracking. In addition, when cooperation implies a large number of actors, some compromises are required to facilitate the cooperation. One way is to offer actors the opportunity to understand each other's needs and use their capabilities to make their viewpoints closer to each other with respect to the target goal.

The actor's focus is guided by the mental representation that the actor has of the task in its current step, the situation in which he is and the local environment in which resources are available. The mental representation expresses what the individual context is. In our application, the shared context is built from elements coming from the mental representations of actors intervening directly or indirectly in the task realization. A contextual element provided by an actor must be: (1) extracted from the actor's mental representation, (2) transformed in information to share, and (3) integrated in other experts' mental representation, i.e. transformed in a piece of knowledge coherent in the new mental representation. This is the way to make the different viewpoints compatible among the participants in the collaboration and not necessarily identical because all mental representations are different.

4.2.2 Shared Context

If many software architecture definition and description techniques focus on collaboration and cooperation from the viewpoint of stakeholder team, our approach to collaboration is to focus on context from the viewpoint of one of the actors (i.e. the Project Manager). The reason for this is that the Project Manager is the main actor who needs support to accomplish defect tracking tasks. Therefore the other shareholders have to share Manager Context to assist him reaching his defined goal.

Sharing context in defect tracking means that actor's contexts have a non-empty intersection. The shared context corresponds to the validity context of the design focus. It is built from contextual elements coming from the different members. The shared-context building results from an incremental enrichment of contextual elements coming from individual contexts. Thus, a contextual element proposed by an actor will enter the shared context if accepted (validated) by other actors. Individual contexts are mental representations of the design focus and of its validity context (the shared context). A contextual element provided by an actor must be integrated in other experts' mental representation, i.e. each expert must find a translation of this shared contextual element in his mental representation.

The following are examples of shared context for the specification of viewpoints:

- End user: For example, what are the consequences of an unavailability of a database for his work and workplace?
- Business analysts: What is the consequence of detected defects with respect to business rules?
- System Administration: What is the impact of defects to the system configuration?
- Project manager: What is the impact of detected defects on the database to be maintained? Are defects reproduced on test environment? What is their expected performance? Is there any impact on the planning and resource allocation? How much is the cost of operations? Can the database operations be rescheduled or cancelled?
- Developer: What are the modifications (i.e. sql scripts) with respect to the current situation that need to be done?

A Project Manager is confronted with many different types of stakeholders and concerns. To help him in selecting the right viewpoint for the task at hand, we introduce contextual graphs formalism for the definition and classification of stakeholder's viewpoints. Viewpoints can be used by the project manager to help him inform any stakeholders about defect tracking, in order to achieve understanding, obtain commitment, and convince adversaries. With the help of contextual graph formalism, it is easier to find typical viewpoints that might be useful in a given situation. Figure 4 illustrates defect tracking from the viewpoint of Project Manager.

The Cooperation from the Project Manager viewpoint focuses on the relations of actors with each other and their environment on what is relevant to the concerns of the manager. Interaction between a Project Manager and another actor (i.e. DBA) is visible through their behaviours, and appears in contextual graphs actions. Another

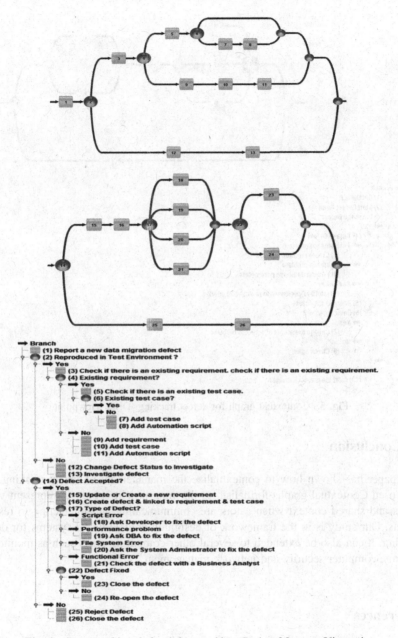

Branch
- (1) Report a new data migration defect
- (2) Reproduced in Test Environment ?
  - **Yes**
    - (3) Check if there is an existing requirement. check if there is an existing requirement.
    - (4) Existing requirement?
      - **Yes**
        - (5) Check if there is an existing test case.
        - (6) Existing test case?
          - **Yes**
          - **No**
            - (7) Add test case
            - (8) Add Automation script
      - **No**
        - (9) Add requirement
        - (10) Add test case
        - (11) Add Automation script
  - **No**
    - (12) Change Defect Status to Investigate
    - (13) Investigate defect
- (14) Defect Accepted?
  - **Yes**
    - (15) Update or Create a new requirement
    - (16) Create defect & linked to requirement & test case
    - (17) Type of Defect?
      - **Script Error**
        - (18) Ask Developer to fix the defect
      - **Performance problem**
        - (19) Ask DBA to fix the defect
      - **File System Error**
        - (20) Ask the System Adminstrator to fix the defect
      - **Functional Error**
        - (21) Check the defect with a Business Analyst
    - (22) Defect Fixed
      - **Yes**
        - (23) Close the defect
      - **No**
        - (24) Re-open the defect
  - **No**
    - (25) Reject Defect
    - (26) Close the defect

Fig. 4. Contextual graph for defect tracking: Project Manager Viewpoint

representation (Fig. 5) is that extracted from the viewpoint of a database administrator and how the defect is processed. This can be helpful for sharing context. Other examples using contextual are graphs can be found in our research papers [16, 17].

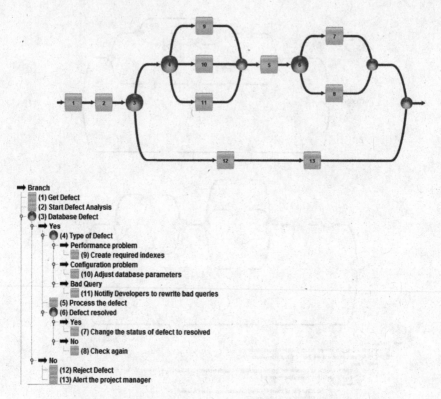

Fig. 5. Contextual graph for defect tracking: DBA Viewpoint.

5   Conclusion

This paper has shown how to contextualize the management of defect tracking. We have used Contextual graphs formalism to illustrate how it is easy to represent viewpoints and shared context when actors are communicating and interacting to resolve defects. Our study is in the framework of designing context-based systems for defect tracking. It can also be extended to several other computing areas such as monitoring systems, computer security and network management.

References

1. Abhiraja, S., et al.: Defect prevention technique in test case of software process for quality improvement. Int. J. Comput. Technol. Appl. 3(1), 56–61 (2012)
2. Ansar, K.: Establishing a defect management process model for software quality improvement. Int. J. Future Comput. Commun. 2(6) (2013)
3. Brézillon, P.: Task-realization models in contextual graphs. In: Dey, A., Kokinov, B., Leake, D., Turner, R. (eds.) CONTEXT 2005. LNCS (LNAI), vol. 3554, pp. 55–68. Springer, Heidelberg (2005). doi:10.1007/11508373_5

4. Brézillon, P., Pomerol, J.-C.: Contextual knowledge and proceduralized context. In: Proceedings of the AAAI 1999 Workshop on Modeling Context in AI Applications, Orlando, Florida, USA. AAAI Technical report, July 1999
5. Carneiro, A., Passos, R., Belian, R., Costa, T., Tedesco, P., Salgado, A.C.: DBSitter: an intelligent tool for database administration. In: Galindo, F., Takizawa, M., Traunmüller, R. (eds.) DEXA 2004. LNCS, vol. 3180, pp. 171–180. Springer, Heidelberg (2004). doi:10. 1007/978-3-540-30075-5_17
6. Don, O.: Defect management in an agile development environment. J. Def. Softw. Eng. (2003). Elissa, K.: Title of paper if known (unpublished)
7. Elfayoumy, S., Patel, J.: Database performance monitoring and tuning using intelligent agent assistants. In: Arabnia, H.R., Deligiannidis, L., Hashemi, R.R. (eds.) Proceedings of the 2012 International Conference on Information & Knowledge Engineering, IKE 2012, WORLDCOMP 2012, Las Vegas Nevada, USA, 16–19 July, CSREA Press (2012)
8. Gopalakrishnanm, N.: Effective defect prevention approach in software process for achieving better quality levels. World Acad. Sci. Eng. Technol. **42** (2008)
9. JÖRG, R.: Handling of software quality defects in agile software development. In: Fraunhofer Institute for Experimental Software Engineering (IESE) (2005)
10. Macros, K., Guilherme, T.: Towards a defect prevention based process improvement approach. In: 34th Euromicro Conference Software Engineering and Advanced Applications. IEEE (2008). doi:10.1109/SEAA.2008.47
11. Pomerol, J.-C., Brézillon, P.: Context proceduralization in decision making. In: Blackburn, P., Ghidini, C., Turner, R.M., Giunchiglia, F. (eds.) CONTEXT 2003. LNCS (LNAI), vol. 2680, pp. 491–498. Springer, Heidelberg (2003). doi:10.1007/3-540-44958-2_42
12. Rajni, et al.: Defect analysis and prevention techniques for improving software quality. Int. J. Adv. Res. Comput. Sci. Softw. Eng. (2013)
13. Sowa, J.F.: Knowledge Representation: Logical, Philosophical, and Computational Foundations. Brooks Cole Publishing Co., Pacific Grove (2000)
14. Suma, V.: Defect management strategies in software development. Wseas Trans. Comput. (2011)
15. Sydney, et al.: Agile-Why the fear. Planit Software Testing (2009)
16. Tahir, H., Brézillon, P.: Contextual graphs platform as a basis for designing a context-based intelligent assistant system. In: Brézillon, P., Blackburn, P., Dapoigny, R. (eds.) CONTEXT 2013. LNCS (LNAI), vol. 8175, pp. 259–273. Springer, Heidelberg (2013). doi:10.1007/ 978-3-642-40972-1_20
17. Tahir, H., Brézillon, P.: Individual decision making based on a shared context. In: International Conference on Decision Support Systems: Fusing DSS into the Fabric of the Context, Anávissos, Greece. Frontiers in Artificial Intelligence and Applications, June 2012. doi:10.3233/978-1-61499-073-4-63
18. Tomaszewski, P., et al.: Statistical models vs. expert estimation for fault prediction in modified code - an industrial case study. J. Syst. Softw. **80**, 1227–1238 (2007)
19. Zheng, J., et al.: On the value of static analysis for fault detection in software. IEEE Trans. Softw. Eng. **32**(4), 240–253 (2006). doi:10.1109/TSE.2006.38

Specific Topics: Context in Learning

Elaborating the Context Calculator: A Design Experiment in Geothermy

Claire Anjou[1(✉)], Thomas Forissier[1], Jacqueline Bourdeau[2],
Yves Mazabraud[1], Roger Nkambou[3], and Frédéric Fournier[3]

[1] Université des Antilles, Guadeloupe, France
{claire.anjou,tforissi,yves.mazabraud}
@espe-guadeloupe.fr
[2] Télé-Université du Québec, Montreal, QC, Canada
jacqueline.bourdeau@licef.ca
[3] UQAM, Montreal, QC, Canada
{nkambou.roger,fournier.frederic}@uqam.ca

Abstract. This paper presents a research project in science education that is positioned at the intersection of computer science and context in learning. The main objective is to improve learning process by creating a software tool that participates, from the inception to the achievement, in the design of leaning scenarios, based on context effects, and, to show that context effects' learning is an efficient method in the development of student's knowledge regarding a concept. The software will compute differences between two – or more – external contexts based on specific parameters, related to the phenomenon or object that students are expected to study. The elaboration of the calculator ("the MazCalc") is conducted using the design based research theory, meaning that several iterations of learning field experiments are conducted in order to collect relevant data which are used for the tool creation. In this paper, the design of the scenario involves students from North America and from the French West Indies and the concept studied is about geothermal energy. The instantiation of the context calculator is made with the geothermal object of study, and the differences are computed in the calculator between the two contexts mentioned. This example makes possible to validate the link between context effects predicted and observed, and also to study the impact of external context on the learning process. This study has been conducted thanks to the GEOTREF project support.

Keywords: Modelling · Context · Science education · Learning · Context effects · Geothermy

1 Introduction

Our study focuses on the contextualization of science education involving fieldwork [1]. In general, context is defined as everything that surround an entity and that have connections with it [2]. A more operational definition is given and discussed in Sect. 2.1.

© Springer International Publishing AG 2017
P. Brézillon et al. (Eds.): CONTEXT 2017, LNAI 10257, pp. 513–526, 2017.
DOI: 10.1007/978-3-319-57837-8_42

One objective is to create a software tool, in order to support the design and development of context-sensitive tasks inside the learning scenario, by considering Context Effects [3]. This software will be able to provide several external context instantiations [4, 5], in relation with the scientific object of study, and to compare them to predict the emergence of Context Effects.

The other objective is to validate the hypotheses that scientific learning will occur thanks to the Context Effects predicted by this software tool. For that, an innovative learning project has been set up.

The project is built using the Design Based Research approach [6], meaning that we are developing theoretical methodology for the tool creation while experimenting it *insitu*. The design experiments are iterative, meaning that the results of one experiment are used to improve the design of the next one.

In this paper, the DBR iteration we are talking about is in the domain of geothermy. The software tool compares two geothermal learning contexts modelling, to highlight the points or concepts about geothermy that shows differences. After this comparison, the objective is to bring to light significant differences and take advantage of them to build a context-sensitive learning scenario about geothermy with the collaboration of two groups of students from those two contexts. The learning is expected to happen thanks to the gaps between contexts that may enrich learners' interactions within and between the two contexts.

Our position is that context gaps during student's collaboration are what create Context Effects [7]. The Context Effect learning is an innovative approach in science education, allowing authentic leaning where students will develop rich and complete conceptions, and will open their mind to very different world contexts.

2   Theoretical Framework

The complex subject area in which is involved this study makes necessary the explanation of all scales of theories that we are dealing with, from the science education one to the context effects one, including the DBR. The MazCalc is also introduced in this section as well as the concept of geothermy.

2.1   Context and Education

We adopted the operational definition of context by Bazire and Brézillon [8], who considers that «context acts like a set of constraints that influence the behaviour of a system embedded in a given task.» In the teaching field, these constraints can be of different nature: epistemological, socio-economical or didactical [9].

The spectrum of relations between context and education consist in inputs derived from several academic disciplines. The context is in most cases defined as an external factor to learning. In educational sociology, this factor shapes the relations between contextual and individual parameters in the pursuing of academic success [10]; in science education [11], it corresponds to institutional constraints weighting on the relationship between student and teacher; in language education [12], it is coupled with the command of language for learners and with the teacher's ability to adapt their teaching. In science education, context-based approach [13] deals with the natural context of student acting as a stimulating factor to providing authentic teaching [1]. Here we use those ideas of authentic external context in view of the fact that they take part in the construction of the internal context thanks to Context Effects.

In the teaching situation studied, the internal context is situated at the level of students' conceptions. Like Giordan [14], we define conceptions as coherent mental images. These conceptions are related to conjunctures and can be considered as situated conception [15]. In this text, the dimension related to the contexts of these conceptions is denominated as internal context.

2.2 Context Effects

In this research work, we aim to explain that student conceptions about geothermy and geothermal context are connected. To this end, an experiment centred on a pedagogical project about geothermy has been set up between students from Canada and Guadeloupe.

Our purpose is to develop a tool that will predict the emergence of Context Effects. In the psychology field, Context Effects have been defined as the influence of an environmental factor on someone's perception [16]. In sciences education the approach is not the same, Context Effects are pedagogical events occurring when there is a clash between student's conceptions, coming from distinct environmental contexts, and about a shared topic being studied [17]. To study context effects, working collaborations on geothermy have been established between Canada and Guadeloupe students, so that they can formulate their conceptions and build together a more accurate understanding idea of geothermy.

In order to maximize the emergence of context effects, two key factors must be taken into account [18] the amount of interactions between students, and the external context gap. The geothermal context in the Caribbean and North America shows many differences (see Sect. 2.5) making it a good topic for the research.

2.3 Design Based Research (DBR)

Design-Based Research (DBR) is a recent research method that is used in educational research and more specifically in education science. It combines theoretical concerns and field considerations to develop solutions to produce successful learning [6].

The first specificity of DBR is the double purpose intended: the progress of theoretical knowledge related to the practical reality and the development of new practical solutions linked with the theory.

The second specificity is the "in situ" mode uses as much for the field actors collaboration than for the micro-experimental tests conducted during the different phases. The DBR engine is the different iterations that provide a wondering about the early or intermediate results and a testing of new ideas (theoretical and experimental) during the next iteration.

DBR distinguish itself from action research that studies problem coming from field actors, and solved jointly by researchers and practioners, and from developmental research, which has no theoretical claim, and can be perform in a laboratory setting [19, 20].

The iteration we are talking about in this paper deals with geothermy and follows two other, the first one in biology was about frogs [21] and the second one in the environmental field was about water.

2.4   The Mazcalc: A Context Calculator

To better understand the context effects and their applications in DBR experiments, and to predict the probability of their occurrence, we have developed a computational model of a context-gap calculator. The idea is to propose a system able to capture and evaluate differences amongst contexts. Our hypothesis is that the more different the contexts under study are, the stronger the context effect is likely to be in the experiment. The very first step of our study was to characterize at best each context. To do so, one may have to study it at different scales (geographical, temporal, and political). The integration of the observations at each relevant scale will allow the modelling of the context (see CLASH model [18]). The two, or more, contexts used in the experiment being well defined, it is then possible to study context effects.

Obviously, two contexts may appear significantly different in one aspect (weather, educational system, geography, economy, politics) and similar in another (language, content of teachings, economy). The context-gap, being the difference between both contexts, is then defined by the summation of all aspects, some very different, some not. Contexts effects may therefore also be studied at different scales. To undergo precise analyses of the context effects, we need to quantify the context gaps. Using a specific calculator [3], we identify parameters, and then assign a numerical value to each context-defining parameter, then we measure the difference between the parameters and so, the overall difference between both contexts. It is then possible to study the link between the context-gaps and to predict the context effects. In the following section, we describe the prototype of this calculator and its testing in geothermy.

2.5   Geothermal Context

Geothermal energy is thermal energy generated and stored in the Earth. Geothermal context is something very complex. It can be define by all sorts of other concepts. For example, it depends on the geology, the industry, the climate, the environment, the resources and many others concepts.

In North America, the bedrock mainly consists of ancient Precambrian rocks from the Canadian Shield. The rocks are cold and the soil temperature in Quebec is constant: 12 °C. The geothermal heat is used to regulate the temperature in buildings, to create spars, to grow crops and other purposes. It is called low temperature geothermy.

The Caribbean Islands are located in a subduction zone between the Atlantic plate and the Caribbean one. Those recent geological formations are creating a great potential for high temperature geothermal energy. In Guadeloupe, this potential has been harnessed and a geothermal power plant produces about 5% of the local demand for electricity.

3 Materials and Methods

In this section, the Materials and methods selected and used for the research is described in two distinct parts: on the one hand for the context calculator; one the other, for the pedagogical experiment.

3.1 The Mazcalc

Mazcalc Ontology
The context, as we hear for the modelling, is something very complex to describe. There are many definitions and theories about this concept and it is choosey to select only one and to stick to it. Not all of the project participants have the same conceptions about how to describe and characterize context. This chapter suggests an ontology that we have clarified in order to formalize the concept of context and to facilitate its usage in the software creation and implementation.

Creation

- A context, in the context modelling tool, is always defined with respect to the object of study hereof: geothermy.
- The object of study is specified by a set of Contextual Parameters to which a variable is assigned, and with a corresponding numerical value defined in natural numbers.
- The parameters have Properties, which define the rules that will be applied for the calculation.
- They can be composite, dependant or independent (if they are composite, the parameter variable choice gives rise to a new parameter depending on the first one, and that can give rise to another composite parameter, forming a tree where values by level are weighted).
- They can be empirical (from the literature), estimated (by experts), calculated (from data) or measured (by learners).
- They can have a qualitative or a quantitative nature.
- They can have a scale of continuous or discrete variables.
- They can have a list of unordered or ordered variables.
- A measuring device (or for monitoring) can be associated to a parameter, providing an explanation for how to collect the appropriate data.
- A parameter is part of one or several families.
- A family is used to split the context: it can be assigned and used:
  - For a investigative domains by student,
  - For an observation scale,
  - For a field of study...

Use

The software has to provide a calculation of context gap for each parameter (for the instructional designer).

- It can compute the global context gap for each family (for the teacher).
- It must contain several pedagogical tools such as:
  - Communication tools.
  - Activities book.
  - Follow-up booklet.
  - Support for test establishment
  - Tools for the identification of context effects.
  - Sensors to capture the observation data.
  - Tools for video analysis (emotion sensor).

Software Elaboration

Different scales of creation and use have been identified and specific actors participate to the software elaboration.

Level 1.

Actors: computer analyst.

Software framework construction regardless from the object studied. The blank frame of the ontology was aforementioned.

As illustrated by the Fig. 1, in this step, only the software skeleton is created and none of the parameters is mentioned. The designer creates the possibility to add the specific parameter and plans the selection for the parameters properties implementation. Figure 1 shows an example for one parameter property.

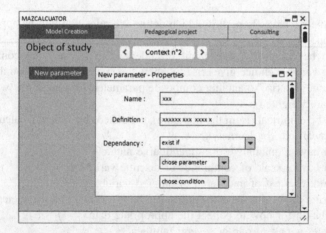

Fig. 1. Wireframe of the first level of creation (add a parameter)

Level 2.

Actors: Domain expert designer and specialists from several contexts.

Modelling for every possible context, regarding the object of study. Specification of all contextual parameters and their properties (Fig. 2).

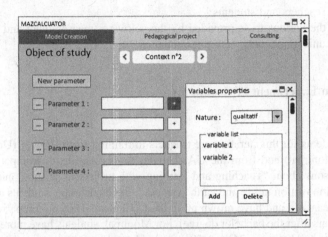

Fig. 2. Wireframe of the second level of creation (specifying the parameter properties)

It is necessary that a number of experts or specialists from various contexts take part in this step, to provide a review of all possible parameters that can represent the domain, in every possible context.

Level 3

Actors: One domain specialist in a particular context.

Final model of a specific context, variable selection for every parameter, implying that the user can add a parameter if necessary (Fig. 3).

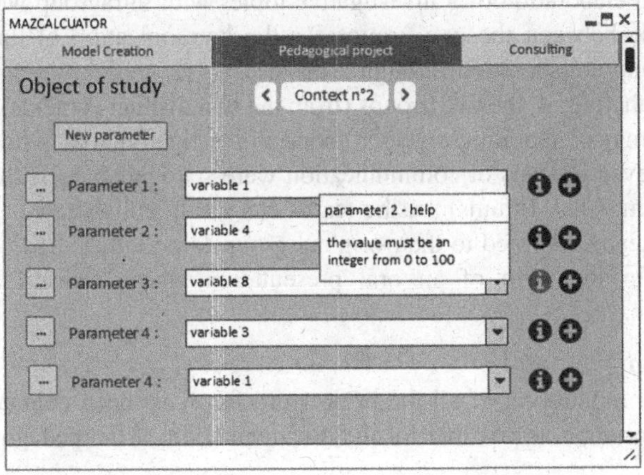

Fig. 3. Wireframe of the third level (implementing variables for the parameters)

Level 4

Actors: Instructional designers

Calculation of context's gaps, and elaboration of learning scenarios involving two or more contexts.

Level 5

Actors: Teachers and students

Uses of the various tools provided by the software (measurement and monitoring tools, communications tools, test questionnaires…)

3.2   Design Experiment in Geothermy

Progression

Selected students for this iteration are teachers in training from UQAM (Université du Québec à Montréal) and from the UA (Université des Antilles) participating respectively in lessons about "Teaching and learning with project in sciences and technologies", and "Innovation in life and earth sciences". In Guadeloupe, students are between 21 and 27 years old and have grown up in the Caribbean. They are preparing a master degree (5 years after the bachelor degree). For Montreal, students have more diversified profiles, they are between 24 and 59 years old, and comes from various countries (Canada, North Africa, Lebanon…), they are also preparing a master degree but some of them already have PhD degree in others fields of study.

Students are committed in a common investigative process focussed on the implantation of a company willing to use geothermal energy as a complement for the cooling of server room and informatics equipments. They have to work together to find the best place in Guadeloupe and in Quebec form the implantation, related to the context characteristics.

The pedagogical experiment lasted four months (from February to May 2016) and is inspired with the Jigsaw method [22]. The first session was organized in two parts: instructions and elaboration of 5 investigative topics with intragroup work, and then a videoconference between the two groups for the harmonization of the investigative topics (intergroup collaboration through a debate).

As explain the Fig. 4, the two groups (from the two distinct contexts) were split in 5 counterpart teams collaborating together about 5 investigative topics (identical ones in each group). Several means of communication were set available for students (Skype, Moodle platform, Chat, forums) so, the teams can easily collaborate.

After that, teams returned to their original group to pool their findings and build a unique result in the form of an oral presentation, shared during a last session videoconference.

Data Collection

A very detailed monitoring of all the project process have been collected in order to get all the information as possible for the documentation of the pedagogical iteration.

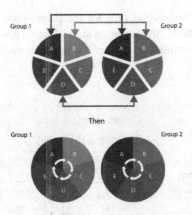

Fig. 4. Teams' organization

- Video recordings of all exchanges
- Audio recordings of some interactions
- Pre-test and post-test questionnaire
- End of session questionnaires regarding students experience
- Follow-up booklet filled by student
- Statement form filled by teachers

For now, only the video recordings of the exchanges and the pre-test and post-test questionnaires are studied and the work is still in progress.

4   Results

4.1   The Mazcalc

The MazCalc preliminary prototype has been elaborated as a brainstorming tool (using Excel) to grasp the potential difficulties that can be encountered in the tool programming and development, in the parameters ontology or in the general operation of the calculator.

In the example shown in the Fig. 5, there are several parameters (B column). Variables are assigned to these parameters, related to the expected context model. Here, two contexts are specified (D and F columns). Specific properties related to each parameter provide the rules that will be applied for the gap calculation. For example, on line 7: "Type of geological formation" gives rise to a pick-list of options. Depending on the chosen variable (cell D7), the pick-list for "Type of rock" (cell D9) will be different. The "Type of geological formation" is so a composite parameter making "Type of rock" a dependent one. The parameter variables "Type of geological formation" are qualitative, discrete, and unordered. The gap calculation between the two contexts for this parameter is 1 or 0 depending on whether the variable is the same or not. For "Type of rock", values are weighted (J9 = 0.5 if the rock's types are different and 0 if they are identical) but only if the variance is zero for the parent parameter. For the parameter "Age of geological formation", the variables are ordered. That means that the gap value will not be the same depending on whether the ages are distant or not.

	B	C	D	E	F	G	H	J
1			Context Modelisation					
2								
3			Geothermal Energy					
5		PARAMETERS	CONTEXT 1		CONTEXT 2		total cho	GAP
7	Type of geological formation		Magmatic	▾	Magmatic	3	2	0,00
8	Age for the geological formation		Tertiary	2	Precambrian	12	11	0,91
9	Type of rock		Volcanic	1	Plutonic	2	-1	0,50
30	Geodynamics		Border of a plate	2	Intra plate	1	1	1,00
42	Climate		Tropical	2	Temperate	1	4	0,25

Fig. 5. Small excel portion of the MazCalculator prototype for geothermy

The contexts gaps' values provided by the calculator are plotted graph (Fig. 6). In this example, we can see that biggest gap is for "geodynamic" and "Type of geological formation" shows no differences. The identification of distant parameters is used to anticipate context's elements that will spearhead the Context Effects. This can give the teacher a line for the elaboration of a teaching, by informing the tasks in the learning scenario and on the themes that will allow the emergence of context effects.

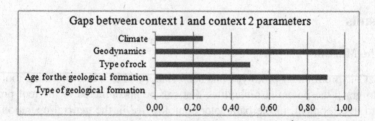

Fig. 6. Graph of the parameter's gaps shown in the MazCalc portion

4.2 The Pedagogical Project

The analysed data for the design experiment allows the identification of students' conceptions and context effects.

Videos

95 min of video recordings between Guadeloupean and Quebec students have been meticulously examined mainly with the argumentative analysis method [24]. Identified Context Effects are linked to different concepts. Here are some examples of context effect explained:

- Climate: the soil is covered with snow in Montreal in winter;
- Environment: there is hot water discharges in the sea in Guadeloupe;
- Energy industry: in Montreal, mainly hydroelectric dams produce electricity;
- Geology: in Guadeloupe the ground is 250 °C at et 1000 m whereas in Montreal it is around 100 °C at 7000 m;
- Hydrology: there is no lake in Guadeloupe;
- Volcanology: there is no active volcano in Quebec;
- Pedagogy: in the light of these differences, the pedagogical approaches are perceived differently by students for Guadeloupe and Montreal;

This allows us to realize the large variety of concepts that can lead to the emergence of context effects, while at the same time being related to the geothermal context of the place. It is so possible to identify them by a video analysis: simultaneously with a content analysis and a gesture analysis.

Pre-test/Post–test
The questionnaire for initial and final conception of geothermy was submitted to the students just before the beginning of the first session and during the last minutes of the last session of the project. The analysis for this questionnaire was performed using statistics methods: Frequency distribution tables, cross-tabulations and Multiple Correspondence Analysis (MCA) with the Statistica software, and with Excel.

Students' conceptions before and after the experiment are synthesised on Fig. 7. The illustration shows the differences between pre-test and post-test for Guadeloupe and Montreal students for 5 questions:

- How do you explain the natural phenomenon of geothermy?
- Draw it.
- What is the product of a geothermal exploitation?
- What deep can we drill for geothermal exploitation?

Answers to those questions have been classified, and three categories have been identified:

- General answer, gathering answers related to the general phenomena of geothermy: ground, soil or Earth heat, power or energy: the answers here describe geothermy in a simple or universal way.
- Contextual answer, related to specific characteristics of geothermy in Quebec (for Canadian) and in the Caribbean (for Guadeloupeans).
- Expert answers, with references to technical or scientific concept of geothermy and, answers describing geothermy in another geothermal context than the one from where the student is.

According to the graph (Fig. 7), students' conceptions have changed between the pre-test and post-test. This analysis reveals that in Guadeloupe the conceptions are mainly contextual before and after the experiment with a small evolution of the expert conceptions, whereas in Montreal, student's conception evolved in a very significantly way, from general (in pre-test) to expert (in post-test).

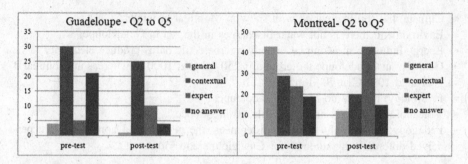

Fig. 7. Graphs of conception's evolution in Guadeloupe and in Montreal between the pre-test and the post-test (population size is on the y-axis).

On the basis of the questionnaire analysis, students' conceptions regarding an object can be various; the local environment plays an important role in the building of those conceptions. In Guadeloupe, the basic understanding of geothermy is very contextual due to the specificities of the geothermal context, (the only French geothermal plant), well known by Guadeloupeans. The conceptions of geothermy are consequently tightly linked to this particular environment.

By contrast, there is no big geothermal plant in Quebec, but low temperature geothermy is something fairly common, it is found in certain buildings (school, museum) or in private homes. The common understanding is therefore linked to this low temperature geothermal context, and the well-known general principle of geothermy is to extract a small amount of degrees from the soil to produce heat.

The video analysis is still in progress and the methodology is being studied to enrich the data treatment. The Rainbow analysis method, [25] for argumentation-based collaborative learning and computer-mediated argumentative interactions can help in understanding how argumentation relates to attempting to solve students' problems of a learning scenario, using support of external representations and knowledge elaboration.

5   Conclusion

The Mazcalc tool has been elaborated and its preliminary prototype implemented and tested on two contexts (Quebec and Guadeloupe) with geothermy as the learning subject. Our context modelling approach and the formal ontology we have designed for it allows us to describe each context and then apply the Mazcalc prototype. The Mazcalc clearly highlighting context gaps between the two distinct geothermal contexts.

The results confirm that the MazCalc was effective in informing the scenario and predicting the probability of context effects. The results of the questionnaire show an improvement of the quality of the of the experts' representations on both sites. By combining the two analyses (Excel and Statistica adapted depending of the question type), we can say that Guadeloupean have evolved from Contextual to Expert-Contextual conceptions, and that Canadian from General-Unclassifiable to

Expert-Contextual conception. This, thanks to context effects created by the social interactions planned in the learning scenario and brought to light by the analysis of the video recordings.

The design experiment showed us that there is a strong link between external context and students' mental models. It is possible to change them for more accurate ones via context effects induced by exchanges between students with different mental models.

The recommendations for the next DBR iteration that we are that the lesson objectives, the project instructions and the speech held by the teachers in both contexts have to be similar or at least completely homogeneous. Students must have the same objectives to maximize collaborations and interactions. It is also important to find a good reason in the pedagogical scenario for interactions, so students can find an interest for the project outcomes in the collaborations with the students from the other environment.

References

1. Schwartz, R.S., Lederman, N.G., Crawford, B.A.: Developing views of nature of science in an authentic context: an explicit approach to bridging the gap between nature of science and scientific inquiry. Sci. Educ. **88**, 610–645 (2004)
2. Abowd, G.D., Dey, A.K., Brown, P.J., Davies, N., Smith, M., Steggles, P.: Towards a better understanding of context and context-awareness. In: Gellersen, Hans-W. (ed.) HUC 1999. LNCS, vol. 1707, pp. 304–307. Springer, Heidelberg (1999). doi:10.1007/3-540-48157-5_29
3. Forissier, T., Bourdeau, J., Mazabraud, Y., Nkambou, R.: Computing the context effect for science learning. In: Brézillon, P., Gonzalez, Avelino J. (eds.) Context in Computing, pp. 255–269. Springer, New York (2014). doi:10.1007/978-1-4939-1887-4_17
4. Van Eijck, M., Roth, W.M.: Towards a chronotopic theory of place in place-based education. Cult. Stud. Sci. Educ. **5**(4), 869–898 (2010)
5. Van Wissen, A., Kamphorst, B., Van Eijk, R.: A constraint-based approach to context. In: Brézillon, P., Blackburn, P., Dapoigny, R. (eds.) CONTEXT 2013. LNCS (LNAI), vol. 8175, pp. 171–184. Springer, Heidelberg (2013). doi:10.1007/978-3-642-40972-1_13
6. Sandoval, W., Bell, P.: Design-based research methods for studying learning in context: introduction. Educ. Psychol. **39**(4), 199–201 (2004)
7. Leurette, S., Forissier, T.: La, Contextualisation dans l'Enseignement des Sciences et Techniques en Guadeloupe. Grand N **83**, 19–26 (2009)
8. Bazire, M., Brézillon, P.: Understanding context before using it. In: Dey, A., Kokinov, B., Leake, D., Turner, R. (eds.) CONTEXT 2005. LNCS (LNAI), vol. 3554, pp. 29–40. Springer, Heidelberg (2005). doi:10.1007/11508373_3
9. Delcroix, A., Forissier, T., Anciaux, F.: Vers un Cadre d'Analyse Opérationnel des Phénomènes de Contextualisation Didactique. In: Anciaux, F., Forissier T., Prudent, L.F. (eds) Contextualisations Didactiques. Approches théoriques, pp. 141–185. L'Harmattancollection Cognition et Formation, Paris (2013)
10. Duru-Bellat, M., Mingat, A.: Le Déroulement de la Scolarité au Collège: le Contexte "Fait des Différences". Rev. Fr. Sociol. **29**(4), 649–666 (1988)
11. Sauvage Luntadi, L., Tupin, F.: La Compétence de Contextualisation au Cœur de la situation d'Enseignement-Apprentissage. Phronesis **1**(1), 102–117 (2012)

12. Blanchet, P., Moore, D., Asselah Rahal, S.: Perspectives pour une Didactique des Langues Contextualisée., Editions des archives contemporaines et en partenariat avec l'Agence universitaire de la Francophonie (2009)
13. King, D.: New perspectives on context-based chemistry education: using a dialectical sociocultural approach to view teaching and learning. Stud. Sci. Educ. **48**(1), 51–87 (2012)
14. Giordan, A., De Vecchi, G.: Les Origines du savoir. Delachaux & Niestlé, Neuchâtel/Paris (1987)
15. Clément, P.: Situated conceptions and obstacles. The example of digestion/excretion. In: Psilos, D., et al. (eds.) Science Education Research in the Knowledge-Based Society, pp. 89–97. Springer, Heidelberg (2003). doi:10.1007/978-94-017-0165-5_10
16. Tourangeau, R., Rasinski, K.A.: Cognitive processes underlying context effects in attitude measurement. Psychol. Bull. **103**(3), 299–314 (1988)
17. Forissier, T.: Eléments de Conceptions des Etudiants de Première Année Scientifique de Guadeloupe sur les Saisons Climatiques et l'Orientation de la Lune. In: A. Delcroix, J.Y. Cariou, H. Ferrière et B. Jeannot-Fourcaud (eds.), Apprentissage, éducation, socialisation et contextualisation didactique: Approches Plurielles. Paris: L'Harmattan, collection «Logiques Sociales» (2015)
18. Forissier, T., Bourdeau, J., Mazabraud, Y., Nkambou, R.: Modeling context effects in science learning: the CLASH model. In: Brézillon, P., Blackburn, P., Dapoigny, R. (eds.) CONTEXT 2013. LNCS (LNAI), vol. 8175, pp. 330–335. Springer, Heidelberg (2013). doi:10.1007/978-3-642-40972-1_25
19. Barrab, S., Kurt, S.: Design-based research: putting stake in the ground. J. Learn. Sci. **13**(1), 1–14 (2004)
20. Bourdeau, J.: The DBR methodology for the study of context in learning. In: Brézillon, P., et al. (eds.) CONTEXT 2017. LNCS (LNAI), vol. 10257, pp. 541–553. Springer, Cham (2017)
21. Fecil, S.: Construire un Enseignement en tenant compte des Effets de Contexte, Mémoire de master, UA, ESPE (2014)
22. Aronson, E.: The Jigsaw Classroom. https://www.jigsaw.org
23. Plantin, C.: Essais sur l'Argumentation. Kimé, Paris (1990)
24. Baker, M., Andriessen, J., Lund, K., Van Amelsvoort, M., Quignard, M.: Rainbow: a framework for analysing computer-mediated pedagogical debates. I J. CSCL **2**(2), 315–357 (2007)

Contextualising Contrastive Discourse Relations: Evidence from Single-Authored and Co-constructed Texts

Anita Fetzer[✉]

University of Augsburg, Augsburg, Germany
anita.fetzer@philhist.uni-augsburg.de

Abstract. This paper compares the linguistic realisation of contrastive discourse relations in single-authored and co-constructed texts produced in an experimental setting in which participants were asked to produce a well-formed argumentative text based on a skeleton text reduced to minimal propositional information while still containing the original argumentative sequential organisation and default configuration of events. The goal was to understand the role of context – linguistic context (or: co-text) and social context - in discourse production, in discourse processing and in the construal of discourse coherence. The study is methodologically compositional across functional approaches to discourse grammar, discourse representation, and discourse pragmatics. The results of the experiment show that co-constructed and single-authored texts utilise a pool of contrastive discourse connectives with the single-authored texts additionally referring to and entextualising linguistic and social context, embedding contrastive contributions accordingly.

Keywords: Contrastive discourse relation · Discourse connective · Coherence strand · Discourse coherence · Linguistic context · Social context · Contextualisation · Entextualisation

1 Introduction

Natural-language communication is a context-dependent endeavour in which language users refer to themselves and their minds, and to each other and each other's minds (Givón 2005), to the immediate and less immediate physical surroundings, including temporal and spatial settings, and to prior and potentially succeeding talk, all of them being constitutive parts of cognitive, social and linguistic context (Fetzer 2012). Discourse – like context – has become more and more indispensible to the analysis of meaning in natural-language communication, and like context, the concept itself is used in diverging frameworks referring to different theoretical constructs. Discourse has been used synonymously with text, i.e. a linguistic-surface and thus linguistic-context phenomenon denoting longer stretches of written and spoken language, it has been used to refer to a sociocognitive construct, i.e. discourse-as-process and discourse-as-product performed and negotiated in social context, and it has been used to refer to both a theoretical construct and to its instantiation in context, i.e. type and token. The claim that discourse contains context, and that context contains discourse is not trivial, but

© Springer International Publishing AG 2017
P. Brézillon et al. (Eds.): CONTEXT 2017, LNAI 10257, pp. 527–540, 2017.
DOI: 10.1007/978-3-319-57837-8_43

rather refers to the relational nature of the two: both are parts-whole configurations in which the whole is more than the sum of its constitutive parts. From a linguistics-based perspective, discourse contains linguistic context (or: co-text), it relies on cognitive context for its production, processing, grounding and construal of discourse coherence, and it contains social context, for instance references to participants and to their temporal, spatial and discursive embeddedness. While discourse is generally conceived of as delimited by communicative formats, e.g. discourse genre, activity type or text-type (cf. discussion in Fetzer 2013), context is generally seen as unbounded, but may be assigned the status of a bounded entity when entextualised[1] in discourse (cf. Fetzer 2011). It needs to be pointed out, however, that the unbounded nature of context does not mean that context is without any structure. If that were the case, natural-language communication would not be rule-governed and could therefore not be felicitous. Rather, context is relational, and "structured context also occurs within a wider context - a metacontext if you will - and that this sequence of contexts is an open, and conceivably infinite, series" (Bateson 1972: 245).

This paper examines the linguistic realisation of the discourse relations Contrast and Corrective Elaboration in argumentative discourse[2]. Contrastive discourse relations are constitutive parts of argumentative sequences in which the relationship between premises and conclusions is negotiated. The paper compares the linguistic context and social context of contrastive discourse relations as well as their linguistic realisation in newspaper editorials from the quality paper *The Guardian* with those in single-authored and co-constructed argumentative texts from editing tasks, considering also excerpts of recorded metadata with the dyad's negotiation about the appropriate linguistic realisation of contrastive discourse relations in context. The single- and co-constructed texts were produced in an experimental setting in which participants were asked to produce a well-formed argumentative text based on a skeleton text reduced to minimal propositional information while still containing the original argumentative sequential organisation and default configuration of events. Contrastive discourse relations are not only of interest because of their linguistic marking with contrastive discourse connectives, e.g. *but, while* or *whereas*, which are functionally equivalent to argumentative operators in the data at hand, with metacommunicative comments, such as *surprisingly*, and with pragmatic word order, that is temporal, spatial and other information positioned at the beginning of a clause (cf. Doherty 2003; Fetzer 2008), but also to internal and external, social-context-anchored negotiation-of-meaning sequences and the administration of discourse common ground (Fetzer 2007).

---

[1] In discourse pragmatics, entextualisation refers to assigning unbounded context the status of a bounded object, for instance by narrowing down the referential domain of an indexical expression (*here*) to a bounded referential domain (*here in Paris*). The use promoted here differs from Park and Bucholtz (2009), who define entextualisation primarily in terms of institutional control and ideology. It shares their stance of approaching entextualisation in terms of "conditions inherent in the transposition of discourse from one context into another" (2009: 489), while considering not only global, but also local context.

[2] Ducrot (1984) and Anscombre and Ducrot (1983) argue for internal and external perspectives on argumentation as internal and external dialogue, as is reflected in argumentative moves, e.g., claim, warrant or backing, and argumentative operators, e.g. *but, since, because, although* and *thus*.

The negotiation of communicative meaning goes hand in hand with the negotiation of the appropriateness of the linguistic realisation of speakers' communicative intentions, considering the participants' information- and face-wants (Brown and Levinson 1987) as well as the social- and linguistic-context constraints of discourse genre.

The paper is based on the premise that discourse is communicative action and thus anchored to rationality, intentionality and consciousness as well as to cooperation and contextualisation. Analogously to the status of relevance in relevance theory, that is communicative action comes in the presumption of being – optimally – relevant, discourse comes in with the presumption of being – more or less – coherent. In natural-language communication the production of discourse as well as its processing is based on this premise, and the premise also holds for discourse-as-a-whole and for its constitutive parts. The parts-whole perspective on discourse does not only imply the truism that the whole is more than the sum of its parts, but also that discourse is both process and product. Being both process and product requires discourse units to be conceptualised relationally and – to employ ethnomethodological terminology – doubly contextual (Heritage 1984), reflecting Bateson's premise that "communication is both context-creating and context-dependent" (1972: 245). By contextualising prior discourse units, the contextualised units pave the ground for the production, processing and grounding of upcoming discourse units, thus indicating how the discourse is intended to proceed, i.e. whether there is some change in the intended direction as is signalled by contrastive discourse connectives or pragmatic word order, for instance, or whether there is no intended change and the discourse is to proceed as originally planned, as is signalled by continuative discourse connectives, such as *additionally* or *moreover*. Another consequence of the premise that discourse comes in with the presumption of being coherent is that discourse processing goes hand in hand with the construal of discourse coherence. While discourse processing is local and bottom-up focussing on individual constitutive parts, the construal of discourse coherence is both bottom-up and top-down, relating individual units with the larger whole.

2   Contrast and Corrective Elaboration

Approaching discourse from a pragmatics-anchored perspective is based on the premise that discourse and its constitutive parts are relational, relating discourse and context, discourse and communicative action, communicative action and language users, and language users with the things they do with words in discourse in context, and the things they do with discourse in context. Only a relational frame of reference can capture the dynamics of discourse, i.e. the unfolding of discourse-as-whole and variation of linearised sequences and variation within linearised sequences, and thus the connectedness between parts and wholes, transcending clearly delimited frames of investigation. Discourse comes in with the presumption of being – more or less – coherent, and language users construe discourse coherence when producing and interpreting discourse. The processing and construal of discourse coherence utilises linguistic and extra-linguistic material, for instance presuppositions, discourse connectives, coherence strands and discourse relations.

Discourse relations have been defined as logical relations holding between two or more discourse units (Asher and Lascarides 2003). For contrastive discourse relations, the relations express semantic dissimilarity manifest in content, illocutionary force and metacommunicative meaning. Coordinating discourse relations keep the discourse on the same level, while subordinating relations introduce a lower level in the discourse hierarchy. This is also reflected in the semantics of coordinating Contrast, which is defined as expressing semantic dissimilarity; subordinating Corrective Elaboration is defined as semantic dissimilarity with the topic of the second discourse unit's proposition specifying the topic of the first discourse unit's proposition mereologically.

To apply the theoretical construct of discourse relations to natural-language communication, logical relations have been operationalised within a pool of defining conditions which are encoded in coherence strands (cf. Givón 1993) and signalled with metacommunicative meaning. Coherence strands are:

- topic continuity and referential continuity
- temporal and aspectual coherence, including modality
- lexical coherence

Metacommunicative meaning is signalled with:

- discourse connectives
- metacommunicative comments
- pragmatic word order

The defining conditions of discourse relations are systematised in Table 1, which is adapted from Maier et al. (2016: 66–67):

Table 1. Discourse relations and their defining conditions

Discourse relation		Defining conditions
Coordinating	Continuation	Common topic
	Narration	Common topic Temporal sequentiality
	Contrast	**Semantic dissimilarity between $\P^2$ and $\P^1$**
	Background	$\P^2$ forms the background of $\P^1$ Common topic
Subordinating/superordinting	Result	$\P^1$ gives reason for (parts of) events in $\P^2$ Connecting two sub-events Temporal precedence of cause
	Comment	$\P^2$ selects $\P^1$ as topic; or: $\P^1$ selects $\P^2$ as topic
	Elaboration	Topic of $\P^2$ specifies topic of $\P^1$ mereologically
	Corrective Elaboration	**Semantic dissimilarity between $\P^2$ and $\P^1$ with topic of $\P^2$ specifying s topic of $\P^1$ mereologically**
	Explanation	$\P^2$ gives reason for (parts of) events in $\P^1$ Temporal consequence

Discourse relations are relational devices par excellence, relating the constitutive parts of discourse. In English, contrastive discourse relations are generally not only encoded in coherence strands but additionally signalled with discourse connectives, metacommunicative comments and pragmatic word order. Frequently they are also supplemented with additionally entextualised temporal, local, social and discursive context, intensifying the degree of discursive glueyness and thereby ensuring speaker-intended interpretation and speaker-intended construal of discourse coherence.

2.1 Data and Method

The linguistic realisation of discourse relations has been examined in written argumentative discourse, that is editorials from the British newspaper *The Guardian*, and in single-authored and co-constructed argumentative texts from an experimental setting. In the professionally produced public media texts Contrast and Corrective Elaboration were signalled with contrastive discourse connectives, primarily *but*, and pragmatic word order, but not generally furnished with further entextualised contextual information (Fetzer and Speyer 2012). To corroborate the results obtained and to shed more light on the assumption that discourse genre is a kind of blueprint in accordance with which language users produce and interpret texts, a case study has been undertaken to find out whether the results for the coding and signalling of discourse relations in an experimental setting based on an editing task, in which participants were asked to produce a well-formed argumentative texts based on a skeleton text with minimal propositional information, were similar to the ones obtained for professional argumentative media discourse. To test this, a study was set up to examine language users' choices of signalling and encoding discourse relations when integrating a given sequence of discourse units with each other. The main interest was not whether or even how a relation between two given discourse units was realised, but rather the variation between different realisations of identical discourse-relation potential. In the study, participants were provided with a text that approximated an underlying representation, and they were asked to "flesh it out" into a fully operational text. Whenever it seemed possible to signal more than one discourse relation connecting two discourse units, participants needed to choose both the discourse relation to employ and whether to encode it in coherence strands only, or whether to encode it in coherence strands and signal it with discourse connectives and/or metacommunicative comments, and/or pragmatic word order (cf. Maier et al. 2016). Participants were provided with the 'bare' text, together with information about medium and genre of the original text (cf. appendix). Their task was to use and edit the 'bare' text and create a coherent and well-formed text of identical discourse genre, with the single constraint that the original sequence of discourse units had to remain unchanged. The data under investigation comprise two sets: 9 single-authored texts and 9 dyadically co-constructed texts, the latter supplemented with recorded metadata – a kind of think-aloud protocol, which documents the dyad's negotiation about well-formed linguistic realisation. As an editing task with 'minimal available text' no new content needed to be generated, while it was still necessary to supplement and integrate additional linguistic material to arrive at an operational text and thus a well-formed, coherent whole. Intrinsic guiding criteria for the selection of additional material were (1) discourse genre as a blueprint, and (2) the sociocognitive construct of discourse common ground with intended readers of the resulting text.

All texts were segmented into discourse units, coded – and inter-rated – for discourse relations and analysed with respect to their linguistic realisations of discourse relations. Discourse relations are encoded in coherence strands and can additionally be signalled with discourse connectives, metacommunicative comments and pragmatic word order. While signalling ensures the activation of relevant defining conditions and thus guides the hearer in their interpretation of discourse relations as intended by the speaker, encoding defining conditions only in coherence strands may carry the risk of the discourse relation not being interpreted as intended by the speaker because the hearer may infer a different discourse relation.

2.2   Results

In the single-authored and co-constructed data, contrastive discourse relations are both encoded and signalled, which corroborates the results obtained from previous research. For the coordinating discourse relation of Contrast, *but* was the most frequently used discourse connective for both single-authored and co-constructed texts with the single-authored texts showing more variation in signalling Contrast, using also the contrastive marker *while*, which may signal both causal and temporal contrast. The subordinating discourse relation of Corrective Elaboration was signalled with various contrastive discourse connectives, showing a preference for *however* in the co-constructed texts and displaying more variation in the single-authored texts using the connectives *yet, despite, instead of, though, although, however, and not just*, and the metacommunicative comments *even better* and *surprisingly*. In coordinating Contrast as well as in subordinating Contrastive Elaboration, semantic dissimilarity was encoded in coherence strands, indexing referential and/or topic continuity, a shift in temporal and aspectual coherence (e.g., 'nowadays' – 'in the past/in the post-war era'; 'London of former days was' – 'London of today is much more'; 'there was a time when NP was' – 'today this NP has changed'; 'last time NP came here' – 'now it's much more exciting!'), and lexical coherence, in particular in scalar or complementary antonymic lexical relations. Frequently the degree of 'contrastiveness' of the linguistic context was intensified by further linguistic material signalling temporal contrast ('but now/today'; 'however now/these days'). Sometimes further fully occupied discourse units were added in the single-authored texts, furnishing Contrast with Background or Explanation thereby not only intensifying the degree of discursive glueyness but also providing subjectified accounts for semantic dissimilarity or contrasting mereological topic specification with the function of accounting for the halt in the flow of discourse and supporting the administration of discourse common ground.

3   Discussion

Discourse relations have been defined by their defining conditions, which are encoded in coherence strands and which can additionally be signalled with discourse connectives, metacommunicative comments and pragmatic word order. The degree of specification of discourse relations in discourse is seen as a structure-based phenomenon depending on the number of coherence strands encoded and signals employed. Underspecification is defined as not fully encoding the defining conditions, thus allowing for multiple assignment of discourse relations, and overspecification is defined as fully encoding the defining conditions and adding discourse-relation-specific signals (discourse connectives, metacommunicative comment, pragmatic word order) to ensure speaker-intended interpretation.

In both single-authored and co-constructed texts, the defining conditions of contrastive discourse relations were encoded in coherence strands and signalled with contrastive discourse connectives, and/or metacommunicative comments, and/or pragmatic word order; sometimes more than one signal was used. The preferred contrastive discourse connective for Contrast was *but*, and the preferred initial constituent for pragmatic word order was a temporal adjunct (e.g., *now, today*). Frequently two signals were employed, intensifying the force of the contrastive discourse connective with pragmatic word order. For Corrective Elaboration, the preferred discourse connective was *however*.

3.1   Contrast

In the following, the encoding and signalling of the coordinating discourse relation of Contrast is analysed. The co-constructed examples are supplemented with extracts from their negotiation-of-production protocols. Examples (1) and (2) are from the co-constructed texts, and (3) and (4) from the single-authored texts. *Temporal* and *aspectual coherence* is printed in *italics*, topic and referential continuity is underlined, **contrastive discourse connectives and metacommunicative comments** are printed in **bold**, and LEXICAL COHERENCE is printed in SMALL CAPS:

(1)   #2/2   *In the past,* London *was* a DOWDY place of tea-houses and STALE rockcakes,

   #2/3   **but** *now* it*'s* MUCH MORE EXCITING

(2)   #1/7a   **While** some Londoners *might find* these foreign tongues THREATENING,

   #1/7b   I *DELIGHT* in hearing them mingled with snatches of French, German, Spanish, Italian, Japanese ...

In (1) and (2), the defining condition of Contrast, semantic dissimilarity between #2/2 and #2/3, and #1/7a and #1/7b, is encoded in topic discontinuity, which may, however, also count as mereological topic specification ('some Londoners' – 'I'), temporal discontinuity (encoded in tense and adjunct), and lexical coherence encoded in antonymic lexical relations, sometimes intensified by comparative constructions ('dowdy' and 'stale/much more exciting'; 'past' – 'now'; 'some' – 'I'; 'threatening' – 'delight'), and it is signalled with the contrastive discourse connectives 'but' and 'while'.

In the metadata, the signalling and encoding of semantic dissimilarity is also an object of talk, the dyads negotiating the kind of linguistic material which needs to be added to turn the bare text into a well-formed whole – with *skeleton-text material* printed in *italics* and **the negotiation of linguistic material to be added** printed in **bold**:

B₁: {05:24} so here it says see also **this is present** | and **then** *London was a dowdy place* **but now and now** *it's much more exciting* so we have put this in the right context so we could start with the british **had seemed** or **in the past** (2s)

B₁: {06:31} erm (2s) erm (3s) i wrote i used now already see **but now** *it's much more exciting* | **but today** how about **today**'s *much more exciting* now how about if we do that but today

A₁: mhm *but today it's*

B₁: *much more exciting* now walking

Participant B₁ does not only mention the contrast to be encoded in tense and temporal adverbials, but also uses them ('this is present'; 'then'; 'had seemed'; 'in the past'; 'but now'; 'but today') when s/he talks about the linguistic material to be filled in to transform the skeleton text into a well-formed argumentative whole. A very similar negotiation takes place between the second dyad, referring to tense ('a jump from the present to the past'). B₂ uses a contrastive discourse connective in their talk ('while'), contextualising 'rock cake', which seems to have caused some processing problems, leading to partial understanding only, and also negotiating the degree of contrast to be added ('it's more exciting' – 'much more exciting'):

B₂: {03:30} **yeah there's a jump from the present to the past** right so there are hm hm case it's true that *london was a dowdy place* **but now** *it's much more exciting* or

A₂: yeah

B₂: **while** it is tr-

A₂: in the past

B₂: *rock cake* is erm like a scone but larger and hard | (2s) buttery

A₂: uh huh {04:00} *and stale rock cakes* **but now** it's more exciting?

B₂: mhm *much more exciting* yeah

A₂: yeah *it's much more exciting*

In the single-authored examples (3) and (4), the defining condition of Contrast, semantic dissimilarity between #D/2 and #D/3, and #M/2 and #M/4 is encoded in topic and referential discontinuity ('The landscape' – 'we') in (3), and in topic discontinuity ('London' – 'this negative perception') and referential discontinuity ('typical view' – 'recent survey') in (4). It is also encoded in aspectual discontinuity (imperfective – perfective aspect) in (3), and temporal and aspectual discontinuity ('was' – 'has changed') in (4). Lexical coherence is encoded in antonymic lexical relations ('look fairly similar – 'changed dramatically''; 'be' – 'change'), and signalled with the contrastive discourse connective 'but' in (3) and with pragmatic word order with a fronted temporal adjunct in (4):

(3)   #D/2   The landscape *may* LOOK FAIRLY SIMILAR
      #D/3   **but** how we *live*, how we *move* around, how we *work* and who we *live* with *has* CHANGED DRAMATICALLY.

(4)   #M/2   ***There was a time*** when THE TYPICAL VIEW OF THE OVERSEAS VISITOR WAS
                that <u>London</u> *was* a dowdy place of tea-houses and stale rock cakes.
      #M/4   ***Today***, according to a recent survey of tourists conducted by the
                London Bureau of Tourism, THIS <u>negative</u> PERCEPTION *HAS CHANGED*

The coordinating discourse relation of Contrast is – structurally speaking – over-specified in the co-constructed and in the single-authored texts, in spite of the fact that Contrast is the discourse relation with the lowest number of overlaps for defining conditions and therefore not very likely not be misinterpreted. There seems to be something special about Contrast, which may – like negation – count as a marked configuration (cf. Doherty 2003; Fetzer 1999; Horn 1989).

3.2   Corrective Elaboration

The defining conditions of the subordinating discourse relation of Corrective Elaboration are (1) sematic dissimilarity between two discourse units, and (2) the topic of the second discourse unit's proposition specifies the topic of the first discourse unit's proposition mereologically. In the co-constructed texts (examples (5) and (6)) and in the single-authored texts (examples (7) and (8)), all Corrective Elaborations are not only encoded in relevant coherence strands, but also signalled with a contrastive discourse connective, generally *however*:

(5)   #2/8   Some would argue that <u>London</u> HAS BECOME the capital of linguistic
                diversity.
      #2/9   **However,** <u>one important group</u> *seems to be LEAVING ITSELF OUT*:
(6)   #3/8   **Surprisingly,** <u>London</u> HAS BECOME the capital of linguistic diversity.
      #3/9   **However,** <u>one important group</u> which *seems to be EXCLUDING* {skeleton
                text: 'leaving'} *ITSELF* {skeleton text: 'out'}

Mereological topic specification is reflected in the parts-whole configuration of 'London' and 'one important group' in (5) and (6), which implies some kind of semantic dissimilarity; this is also made an object of talk in the dyad's negotiation of well-formed realisation ('it is a contrast because this is' – 'it's a bit weird with like in fact and then however'). Semantic dissimilarity is also manifest in a shift in temporal and aspectual coherence ('has become' – 'seems to be leaving itself out'). The degree of semantic dissimilarity is intensified in (5) with the metacommunicative comment 'surprisingly', signifying contrast of expectation, which has also been an object of talk in the negotiation of wellformedness:

A₂: yeah but otherwise how would you link it?
B₂: yeah
A₂: i could just well I mean I'm just thinking |
B₂: well I well ok i can you know or (5s) ok yeah &&& [stuttering] **it is a contrast
      because this is ah**|

A$_2$:   she can do this because she can do that|

B$_2$:   because she can yeah |

A$_2$:   (3s) i'm changing the text &&& [mumbling] **however** *one*

B$_2$:   &&& (mumbling) namely students

A$_2$:   (3s) **it's a bit weird with like in fact and then however**

B$_2$:   yeah

A$_2$:   it's like | a bit too much |

B$_2$:   mhm mhm well just leave it out in fact

A$_2$:   yeah (5 s) it's like overdoing the transition | a bit|

B$_1$:   {08:01}ok and how about *london has become the capital of linguistic diversity* &&& **surprisingly** we need something in there | we need an adverb in there **surprisingly** or i don't know

A$_1$:   yeah yeah let's put in surprisingly

The single-authored data display very similar patterns but provide more social-context information, that is the source of the claim that London has become the capital of linguistic diversity is entextualised in 'her husband', and an additional discourse unit is added supplementing the Corrective Elaboration between #M/8 and #M/9 with the discourse relation of Background signalled with the discourse connective 'while' in (7). In (8) mereological topic specification is reflected in 'an inquiry' and its specification as 'an inquiry into the impact of Tory educational policies' signalled with pragmatic word order introduced by the metacommunicative comment 'even better'. Semantic dissimilarity is also reflected in shifts in tense and modality ('is under way' – 'would be better'):

(7)   #M/8   Her husband interjected, "London HAS BECOME the capital of linguistic diversity".

      #M/9   **However** [#10 **while** linguistic diversity might be a salient feature of the nation's capital,] one important group *seems to be LEAVING ITSELF OUT*:

(8)   #S/13   An inquiry *is underway*—is not bureaucracy wonderful?

      #S/14   **Even better** *would be* an inquiry into the impact of Tory educational policies on closing more and more students out from a university education.

The subordinating discourse relation of Corrective Elaboration is – like coordinating Contrast – overspecified in the co-constructed and single-authored texts, corroborating the results obtained for non-edited argumentative discourse. Structural overspecification thus seems to be the default for contrastive discourse relations in argumentative discourse. But why would language users opt for overspecification for contrastive discourse relations, which share only very few defining conditions with other discourse relations? We assume that the degree of overspecification has several reasons. Firstly, structural overspecification is an attention-guiding device and thus related closely to sociocognitive salience. Secondly, speakers/writers intend to secure the speaker-intended interpretation of contrastive discourse relations, which signal a change in the direction of discursive flow and therefore require particular attention, and thirdly, contrastive discourse relations have a decisive impact on discourse processing as they signal a change and potential restructuring in the administration of the current discourse common ground.

Discourse common ground is a dynamic construct, which is negotiated and updated continuously in natural-language communication, i.e. confirmed, modified or restructured, by storing new information and by updating already stored information. To account for discourse processing and for the construal of discourse coherence, discourse common ground is – analytically – distinguished into an individual's representation of discourse common ground, that individual discourse common ground, and a collective's representation of discourse common ground. Individual discourse common ground administers an individual's administration of discourse processing and construal of discourse coherence, while collective discourse common ground administers negotiated and ratified individual discourse common grounds represented by collective discourse common ground; both may diverge to varying degrees (Fetzer 2007). Contrastive discourse relations may thus not only have a local impact on the administration of discourse common ground, but they may require some restructuring of already stored discursive information in the discourse common ground.

4   Conclusion

Discourse is a multilayered, complex construct, and so is its linearisation. The sequential organisation and linearisation of discourse is not only a linguistic-surface phenomenon, but rather depends on linguistic context, social context and cognitive-context-anchored discourse common ground, which is updated and administered continuously in discourse production and discourse processing. Contrastive discourse relations have an important function in discourse, signalling some change in the flow of discourse, and they have a particularly important function in argumentative discourse where they make manifest that one or more arguments may be controversial.

The structural overspecification of contrastive discourse relations found in the single-authored and co-constructed texts corroborates the results obtained for the linguistic realisation of contrastive discourse relations in media discourse. This provides strong evidence for assigning overspecification the status of default configuration for Contrast and Corrective Elaboration in argumentative discourse, where it is used strategically to contribute to the activation of defining conditions, foregrounding them, making them salient through overt marking and assigning communicative relevance to them. Underspecification, which has not been found for contrastive discourse relations, may reflect cognitive economy.

Context and discourse are dynamic relational constructs with context containing discourse and being contained in discourse. Consequently, context is presupposed in natural-language communication; it is imported into a discourse with indexical expressions or it is entextualised in discursive contributions or in some of its constitutive parts, and it is invoked in a discourse through inferencing. In argumentative discourse, overspecified contrastive discourse relations do not only signal negative contexts and trigger respective inferencing processes, but they also entextualise the kind of 'negativity'.

A dynamic perspective on context entails contextualisation on the one hand, that is retrieving contextual information for discourse processing and discourse production, and grounding and anchoring discursive contributions in sociocognitive discourse common ground. On the other hand, it entails entextualisation, that is encoding and signalling of contextual information, for instance by narrowing down the referential domains of indexical expressions or by signalling contextual frames, as is the case with discourse connectives.

Discourse is interdependent on context, and context is interdependent on discourse. A pragmatic theory of discourse and its premise of indexicality of communicative action does not only offer insights into the multifaceted, multilayered and infinite theoretical construct of context and its instantiation in the production and processing of discourse, but also into the contextual constraints and requirements of discourse in general and of the delimiting frame of discourse genre in particular. By adopting both a bottom-up and top-down – or a micro and macro – approach to context and discourse, and by additionally accounting for interdependencies of their connectedness, it is possible to operationalize discourse with the delimiting frame of discourse genre, which is a structured whole with its genre-specific constraints and requirements. And it is also possible to delimit context as a delimiting frame of embedding context constrained by the contextual constraints and requirements of genre; the delimiting frame of embedding context may, of course, be expanded to a meta-level, should the communicative need arise. Context is thus not a set of propositions excluded from the content of a discursive contribution and construed against the background of the contribution. Rather, context is a constitutive – though not necessarily fully made explicit – part of the contribution. Thus, if context is not given and external to a discursive contribution but rather a constitutive part of it construed and negotiated in the production and processing of discourse, it has the status of an indexical; and if context has the status of an indexical, it can never be saturated. However, it is not only context, which is indexical, but also communicative action realised in the form of discursive contributions, which are carriers and containers of contextualised and entextualised objects as well as constitutive parts of it. Hence, it is not only indexical expressions contained in discursive contributions, which are contextualised in the production and processing of discourse, but rather the discursive contribution and discourse-as-a-whole.

Discourse studies have shown that there is systematic variation in the linguistic realisation of the contextual constraints and requirements of a discourse genre, both for the genre-as-a-whole and for its constitutive parts, as has been demonstrated for the encoding and signalling of contrastive discourse relations. Accounting for systematic variation with respect to the linguistic realisation of discourse and its constitutive parts – in particular with the explicit accommodation of context- and discourse-dependent sociocognitive discourse common ground – may not only lead to a re-assessment of language use, but also support context-dependent instantiations of document design. As for computer science and philosophy of language studies on context and communication, expanding the frame of reference from sentences and propositions to discursive contribution and discourse genre may lead to more refined insights.

Appendix

Argumentative Skeleton Text and Instructions

The following 15 clauses form the backbone of a commentary from the Guardian. You may add or delete any linguistic material which you consider necessary to transform the current text into a well-formed coherent whole, but you may not change the order of the given clauses.

The solitary monoglots

1. the British seem set on isolation from the world
2. London was a dowdy place of tea-houses and stale rock cakes
3. it's much more exciting
4. I can hear people speaking in all the languages of the world
5. was that Pashto or Hindi
6. I can just about differentiate Polish from Lithuanian
7. I delight in hearing them mingled with snatches of French, German, Spanish, Italian, Japanese…
8. London has become the capital of linguistic diversity
9. one important group seems to be leaving itself out
10. students
11. foreign language learning at Britain's schools has been in decline for decades
12. the number of universities offering degrees in modern languages has plummeted
13. an inquiry is under way
14. the number of teenagers taking traditional modern foreign languages at A-level fell to its lowest level since the mid-90 s
15. it's a paradox

References

Anscombre, J.-C., Ducrot, O.: L'Argumentation dans la Langue. Mardaga, Brussels (1983)

Asher, N., Lascarides, A.: Logics of Conversation. Cambridge University Press, Cambridge (2003)

Bateson, G.: Steps to an Ecology of Mind. Chandler Publishing Company, New York (1972)

Brown, P., Levinson, S.: Politeness. Some Universals in Language Usage. Cambridge University Press, Cambridge (1987)

Doherty, M.: Discourse relators and the beginnings of sentences in English and German. Lang. Contrast **3**, 223–251 (2003)

Ducrot, O.: Le Dire et le Dit. Minuit, Paris (1984)

Fetzer, A.: Non-acceptances: re- or un-creating context? In: Bouquet, P., Benerecetti, M., Serafini, L., Brézillon, P., Castellani, F. (eds.) CONTEXT 1999. LNCS (LNAI), vol. 1688, pp. 133–144. Springer, Heidelberg (1999). doi:10.1007/3-540-48315-2_11

Fetzer, A.: Reformulation and common grounds. In: Fetzer, A., Fischer, K. (eds.) Lexical Markers of Common Grounds, pp. 157–179. Elsevier, London (2007)

Fetzer, A.: Theme zones in English media discourse. Forms and functions. J. Pragmat. **40**(9), 1543–1568 (2008)

Fetzer, A.: 'Here is the difference, here is the passion, here is the chance to be part of a great change': strategic context importation in political discourse. In: Fetzer, A., Oishi, E. (eds.) Context and Contexts: Parts Meet Whole?, pp. 115–146. John Benjamins, Amsterdam (2011)

Fetzer, A.: Contexts in interaction: relating pragmatic wastebaskets. In: Finkbeiner, R., Meibauer, J., Schumacher, P. (eds.) What is a Context? Linguistic Approaches and Challenges, pp. 105–127. John Benjamins, Amsterdam (2012)

Fetzer, A.: Structuring of discourse. In: Sbisà, M., Meibauer, J., Turner, K. (eds.) Handbooks of Pragmatics. The Pragmatics of Speech Actions, pp. 685–711. de Gruyter, Berlin (2013)

Fetzer, A., Speyer, A.: Discourse relations in context: local and not-so-local constraints. Intercult. Pragmat. **9**(4), 413–452 (2012)

Givón, T.: English Grammar. A Function-Based Introduction, vol. 2. Benjamins, Amsterdam (1993)

Givòn, T.: Context as Other Minds. John Benjamins, Amsterdam (2005)

Heritage, J.: Garfinkel and Ethnomethodology. Polity Press, Cambridge (1984)

Horn, L.: A Natural History of Negation. Chicago University Press, Chicago (1989)

Maier, R.M., Hofmockel, C., Fetzer, A.: The negotiation of discourse relations in context: co-constructing degrees of overtness. Intercult. Pragmat. **13**(1), 71–105 (2016)

Park, J.S.-Y., Bucholtz, M.: Public transcripts: entextualization and linguistic representation in institutional contexts. Text & Talk **5**, 485–502 (2009)

The DBR Methodology for the Study of Context in Learning

Jacqueline Bourdeau[✉]

TELUQ, Montreal, QC H2S 3L5, Canada
jacqueline.bourdeau@licef.ca

Abstract. In the Design-Based Research (DBR) methodology, the process is as important as the product, and each iteration is considered a sub-result leading to the next one. This methodology is being used in the TEEC project, to both study and elaborate solutions for Learning in Context. This paper describes the origins of the project, as well as the steps taken to conduct it, with a perspective for future work. The DBR methodology is presented as applied in the TEEC project (TEEC = Technologies Educatives et Enseignement en Contexte).

Keywords: Design-based research · DBR · Methodology · Modelling · Context · Learning · Intelligent tutoring systems

1 Introduction

This paper addresses methodological issues in the study of context in learning, involving the design and development of innovative solutions to foster awareness regarding the context in both humans and machines. To start with, the DBR methodology is presented and we explain the reasons for which it has been preferred to others for sustaining a project focussing on context in learning. Second, the project under the acronym TEEC (Technologies Educatives et Enseignement en Contexte, in English Educational technologies and teaching in context) is described, from its inception to the hypotheses and objectives that were set. Following this, we introduce the main elements composing the solution to be designed, developed and tested: the instructional design, the ideas of the context calculator (MazCalc) and of the Context-Aware Intelligent Tutoring System (CAITS), the iterations to test each element of the solution, as well as data collection and trace analysis. As a synthesis of the methodological approach, an overview of the DBR iterations throughout the TEEC project is provided, illustrating the process of making ideas and tools evolve towards a robust solution. Finally, the current status of the project and future work as planned are described.

2 What Is Design-Based Research?

The Design-Based Research methodology (thereafter called DBR) has its roots in the pioneering work by Brown [1], under the name of Design experiments, in an effort to reduce the gap between lab research and *in situ* research, and to allow a process by which both theory and practice can evolve together, based on a design process. It relies

© Springer International Publishing AG 2017
P. Brézillon et al. (Eds.): CONTEXT 2017, LNAI 10257, pp. 541–553, 2017.
DOI: 10.1007/978-3-319-57837-8_44

upon a cybernetic principle where the result of each loop changes the behaviour of a system. DBR then evolved into a full methodology which was claimed by the *DBR Research Collective* and published in the *Educational Researcher Journal* [2] sustained by an article in the *Journal of the Learning Sciences* [3], another one by Wang & Hannafin entitled *Design-based research and technology-enhanced learning environments* [4], another one by Herrington et al. [5], and the book chapter by Reimann [6]. It has been applied in numerous pedagogical innovations [7–12]. DBR can be characterized as a microsystemic methodology, based on system science principles, mainly the feedback loops mechanisms, or iterations, and the goal of comprising the complexity of an authentic situation to study it. In contrast to experimental research, it does not aim to isolate nor control. Unlike participatory design, it promotes the development of theoretical knowledge simultaneously to the design of artefacts.

To our knowledge, DBR has not been applied to study the design of collaborative learning, nor the design of context-aware learning environments.

3   The Inception of the TEEC Project

The TEEC project was born in 2012, and is grounded in previous work both at CRREF (Université des Antilles, French West Indies) on context in learning and at LICEF (TÉLUQ, Canada) on Instructional Design and Intelligent Tutoring Systems. We worked on why and how to reconcile the intellectual traditions of french didactics with instructional design and intelligent tutoring systems.

The first starting point was that science learning tends to happen out of context, or even out of scope that context could be inherent to science learning. The second one was that context modelling was also absent in ITS research, which has sofar mainly concentrated on modelling the domain, the learner and the tutoring [13, 14].

We considered several options to take context into account, among them ignoring context, putting it aside, or putting it on center stage. We then elaborated the hypothesis that learning would be most productive if we can stimulate what we call context effects in a learning scenario. To do so, we need to have: a generic learning scenario capable of producing context effects, a model of context that would allow us to calculate and predict the potential of two contexts to produce the context effect, and several experimentations to test and verify this hypothesis. We called our model the CLASH model, since it aims at fostering learning through a clash between contrasting contexts (similar to the Aha! Effect), as a manifestation of a cognitive clash, leading to a conceptual change in learners [15].

We also soon realized that in order to have a scientific tool to help our design and our predictions, it would be necessary to build a context calculator (later called MazCalc), that would contain the contextual parameters, compute the predicted context effect, and guide the design of the learning scenarios. Finally, we envisioned an intelligent tutoring system that would be context-aware and therefore adaptive and reactive to contextual elements in the learning process, relying on the context analysis performed by the MazCalc software. This system would also contain authoring rules and allow an instructional designer to adapt, improve and edit productive learning scenarios.

The hypotheses that we formulated are the following:

(1) An instructional scenario, designed as to produce a clash between two contrasted contexts, for students working collaboratively on similar topics and shared tasks, that can foster learning while distinguishing basic notions from context-dependent elements, and stimulate the awareness of the gap between their observations and their mental models, which leads to a conceptual change.
(2) Context modelling allows to instantiate and calculate the gaps between contexts using parameters
(3) It is then possible to predict a context effect based on (1) et (2).

The objectives are to:

- Create and test an instructional model based on the emergence of context effects to foster conceptual change (CLASH)
- Elaborate a characterization system to predict context effects using indicators for each domain and topic
- Design and develop a software tool with a meta-model of context, a simulator, and an editing interface to instantiate parameters and equations specific to a domain and to a topic; test it, document it with user guides and release it as an open resource (MazCalc)
- Design learning scenarios and experiments in various domains, topics, and academic levels
- Design and develop a Context-Aware Intelligent Tutoring System (CAITS), with MazCalc as its core, and authoring and tutoring services.

In order to achieve these objectives and test these hypotheses, while working on many fronts at the same time, we needed a methodology that would: (1) allow us to tackle the design of several components at the same time, (2) be concerned both with theory and practice, (3) account for the complexity of the learning situation, (4) respect the authenticity of the learning tasks, (5) allow us to produce results repeatedly along the development of the project, (6) allow us to test not only the hypotheses but also the components.

The DBR methodology proved to be the best candidate for our project, despite the fact that it had not been applied yet to the study of context in learning, nor to telecollaborative learning, nor to the design of a context-aware learning environment. We are fully aware of the challenge related to this innovation, and we expect to live up to this challenge during the project.

To achieve our objectives, we also needed to design several components: an instructional scenario to set the structure of learning activities with their constraints while leaving room for emergent events; a software tool to calculate the contrast between two contexts, to predict the productivity of the scenario, and eventually to modify it; a smart learning environment aware not only of the context itself, but of the context as integrated with the domain and the learner models.

The following three sections introduce the components involved: (1) the instructional design process and its product, the learning scenario; (2) the MazCalc software and the learning environment, (3) the first three design experiments. The last two sections highlight the data collection and trace analysis processes, and the future work as planned for the next three years.

4   The Instructional Design for the CLASH Model

Instructional design is a methodology for designing instruction that pertains to the domain of Educational Technology, and proposes to apply engineering techniques to design instruction [16]. Fundamentally, the design process is composed of: analysis, design, development, implementation, and evaluation. The main instrument is called the learning scenario, which is defined as a structured set of components that specifies objectives, actors, activities, resources, tools, time and space, and which can be applied at different scales (course level, module level). Every specification is justified by its relevance to the objectives, and by the coherence with other elements.

We found out that instructional design would be a cornerstone to designing learning scenarios leading to the awareness of context and of its role in science learning. This is why we envisioned building a generic learning scenario that would allow us to produce and test the eventual context effect, draw conclusions, and improve our model. The scenario is oriented to reach a goal and to meet objectives, which can be either measured or observed. The inspiration for our generic scenario was the Jigsaw scenario [17], known for producing learning though collaboration, and which we adapted to our view. The main idea is to have two teams of learners, in contrasted contexts, working on the same scientific object or phenomenon, performing similar tasks, collecting observation data, exchanging on this object, and discovering the role of context in this learning.

The challenges offered by the TEEC project in terms of instructional design are manifold: negotiation about topics and activities among teachers and (eventually) learners, mechanisms for collaboration, tools for communication and sharing, and for data collection, etc. The main constraints and expectations are listed in Table 1.

Collaborative learning supported by technology (or Computer-Supported Collaborative Learning, CSCL) has been an object of study for more than 10 years[1]. Instructional scenarios or scripts are considered a basic tool for orchestrating and studying CSCL. Fostering discussion among learners experiencing differentiated contexts, cultures or beliefs has been successfully tested in CSCL [18], either inspired by a jigsaw type of scenario [17], or by exploiting international socio-cultural and economical differences [18].

Our approach resonates with Gropper's five recommendations [16] for instructional design research: (1) Reserve the word 'theory' for testable and verified propositions; (2) Translate propositions stated in rationales for a favoured model into testable form; (3) Do the research needed to verify the propositions so translated; (4) Structure or restructure a model based on results from multiple such tests; (5) Evaluate the model as a whole, for reliability and validity of implementation.

---

[1] The International Journal of Computer-Supported Collaborative Learning (ijCSCL) was founded in 2006 by the International Society of the Learning Sciences (ISLS). See http://ijcscl.org/.

Table 1. Constraints and expectations for a TEEC learning scenario

Constraint 1: hypotheses	(1) An instructional scenario, designed for allowing a conceptual change through a clash between two contrasted contexts among learners collaborating on shared topics will foster the learning of the role of context in the domain studied (2) modelling the context makes it possible to calculate parameters of the context as well as the gap between two contexts, (3) It is possible to predict a context effet based on (1) and (2)
Constraint 2: CLASH model:	Experience a context effect allows learners to differentiate the role of context in a domain, and to differentiate what is common to all from what is context-dependent
Constraint 3: collaborative learning scenario	A structured set of learning activities with its calendar; specification of actors, activities, resources, time/space; 2 groups (15-30 participants), 3–6 topics, 3–6 teams per group; pedagogical resources, investigation or inquiry tools; communication and sharing virtual environment
Constraint 4: MAZCALC software	Context calculator, a software tool to enter topics, parameters and their values (quantitative or qualitative) and compute the gap between two contexts, both for predicting and verifying the productivity of a specific scenario
Constraint 5: trace analysis	Analysis of the data collected to inform the study of context in learning; analysis of interactions (among learners, with the learning environment) and of emotions, for detecting and studying the manifestations of context effects
Expectations	Produce results for the testing and the improvement of each component: hypotheses; CLASH model; instructional scenario; MAZCALC software; trace analysis, according the DBR methodology for a series of feedback loops. Inform the overall design and the organisation of the design experiments.

5   Imagining the MazCalc Software and the ITS Architecture

In order to test our hypotheses, we imagined a situation where we would be able to calculate and predict the productivity of a scenario where two teams of learners would work on the same scientific topic, become aware of the differences due to context, exchange about it, and distinguish what is common and what is context-dependent. For this purpose, we conceived a context calculator, called MazCalc, which is a software tool to calculate the contrast between two contexts, to predict the productivity of the scenario, and eventually to modify it for improving the probability of success, that is to obtain accurate learning in and among learners. Starting with the identification of parameters belonging to the domain studied and the topics selected, it is then possible to assign values to these parameters, related to the expected context model. Specific properties related to each parameter provide the rules that can then be applied for the gap calculation. The history as well as the perspectives on the MazCalc are reported by Anjou et al. [19] in this volume.

In our vision, MazCalc would be at the core and would serve the purpose of a Culturally-Aware Intelligent Tutoring System (CAITS). In the tradition of ITS research, the basic architecture is composed of 4 modules: the domain, the learner and the tutoring models, plus the user interface [13, 14]. To our knowledge, there has been no attempt to design an ITS that would contain some modelling of the context and would be capable of changing its behaviour based on its knowledge of context. In order to serve our goals, a conceptual architecture was designed, and the first steps taken towards a meta-model of context for the calculator [20, 21] (Fig. 1).

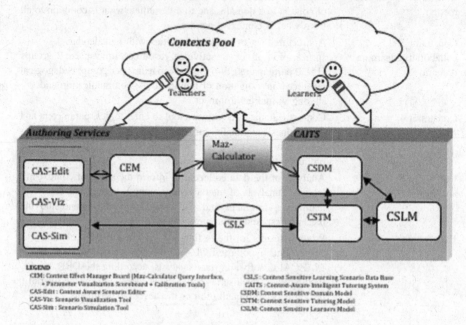

Fig. 1. The CAITS conceptual architecture

Having stated the hypotheses, drawn a model, drafted the tools, and adopted a methodology, we started organizing and preparing the first in *situ* experiments.

6 Three Design Experiments

6.1 The First Experiment in Biology: Gounouj

The first experiment was in Biology in 2013 and was called Gounouj, because it focussed on the frog (gounouj being the term for frog in guadelupean creole), and how it differs between a tropical country (as in Guadelupe) and a nordic one (as in Quebec), although belonging to the same species. We designed the scenario so as the two teams would be focussing on the same object, but would become aware of the context dependencies by making observations and collecting data in their close environment. The frog was chosen for its contrasting potential, since Guadeloupe has the smallest frog, and Quebec the largest one in North America. The six topics for both teams were: calls, nutrition, morphology and taxonomy, sustainable development and relationships with humans, and development. As a first stage of technological integration, the instructional scenario has been implemented in a Learning Management System (LMS, Moodle), in order to interconnect the activities with the sources needed, and to facilitate the recording and the tracing of the data (Fig. 2). The initial scenario can be modified along the experiment to make room for emergent activities or requests from learners.

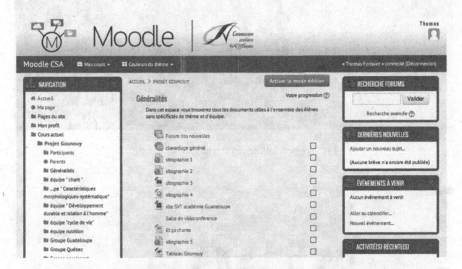

Fig. 2. The Moodle interface for teams working on the frog

Pre-test and post-test were conducted to detect mental representations on frogs (drawing the shape, giving the dimension, singing the call, etc.). As it happened, the two teams, working in and on their own context (Fig. 3), changed their mental representations for more accurate ones, and became aware of the contextual differences (Fig. 4), as was found in the video recordings.

The experiment is well documented (in French) by the Quebec teacher Julie Poulin http://blogues.csaffluents.qc.ca/recit/2014/04/23/apprentissage-des-sciences-en-contexte/, and by the Guadelupean teacher, Sophie Fécil [22].

In general, teachers and learners were happy with the experiment but learners said that they would like to exchange personally with their correspondent learners, as the teachers did.

6.2 The Second Experiment in Environmental Science: Dlo

The second experiment, called Dlo (water in creole), was realized with the same learners and teachers, Fécil and Poulin, and with the scientific support of Lise Parent (TÉLUQ), a water science expert, alias Dr Dlo, whose role was to answer difficult questions, but also ask some to the learners! The two teachers worked in collaboration

Fig. 3. Schoolkids trying to capture a frog.

Fig. 4. The instant of surprise when discovering the foreign context.

to prepare the scenario on water analysis, as well as the resources and the permissions needed On both sides, the kids conducted an investigation on-site and in their science lab, before they exchange their results over videoconferencing (Fig. 5). However, unexpected technical problems happened. Due to the success of the Gounuij experiment, the school in Guadeloupe received a technical upgrade, early during the experiment, although without technical support to implement it. This became a problem that prevented the experiment to happen completely as planned.

Fig. 5. Inter-groups exchange over videoconference

The Dlo experiment will be re-planned after making sure that the technical problems are solved before starting the experiment.

6.3 The Third Experiment in Geothermy

The third design experiment is documented in a detailed way in Anjou et al's paper, 2017 (in this volume) [19]. The topics were: Geology, Geomorphology, Structural, Industry, Environment. The learning scenario included two groups of Teachers in Training from the Université des Antilles (UA) and Université du Québec à Montréal (UQAM), with the support of experts in Geothermy: Yves Mazabraud, (Université des Antilles), and Michel Malo and Jasmin Raymond (INRS-Québec).

This experiment highlighted the challenge of synchronization, since it became a major problem. Although the participants share the same time zone, their respective schedule was different and changing.

7 Data Collection and Trace Analysis

Data collection is performed at each iteration, to test one or more elements of the system: hypotheses, model, instructional design, software design, and data collection tools. Video recordings are the main source of information about the collaboration

Table 2. Overview of the DBR iterations throughout the TEEC project

Iterations	CLASH model	MazCalc,CAITS software	Learning scenarios	Experimentations	Team
1-2012	Hypothesis ObjectivesModel version1	Inception, instantiaton to Biology, CAITS architecture	Biology Gounouij (frog) 6 tasks	Learners: 10–12 yrs Video recordings Pre-test, post test	Bourdeau, Fécil, Forissier, Mazabraud, Stockless, Poulin
2-2013	Refinement adding internal context	Instantiation to Environmental Science	Environmental Science Dlo (water) 6 tasks	Learners: 10–12 years Pre-test post test	Bourdeau, Forissier, Nkambou, Parent, Stockless
3-2014	Refinement: Characterisation of parameters	Development of meta-model, structuration of parameters	Geothermy 6 tasks	Teachers in Training Video recordings Pre-test post test	Anjou, Bourdeau, Forissier, Fournier Mazabraud, Stockless
4- 2015/16	Predictive Analysis	Development of Excel prototype in Geothermy	Geothermy 6 tasks	Learners 12–14 yrs	Anjou, Bourdeau, Forissier, Fournier Mazabraud, Stockless,, experts in Geothermy
Planned: 2017-2019	Validation and improvement	MazCalc development-testing, release; CAITS development-testing,	Socio-economy, Language, Environmental science	Learners 9-11 yrs Learners 15 yrs	Anciaux, Anjou, Bourdeau, Candau, Carignan Forissier, Fournier, Jeannot-Fourcaud, Mazabraud, Nkambou, Odacre Parent, Stockless, Temblay;
	Analysis of epistemic interactions				Baker, Detienne, Bernard
	Automatic Emotion detection				Prevost

process as well as about the individual learning process. At every stage, we extract lessons learned, new ideas, suggestions for improvement or extension for one or more elements of the system. These outputs are then used for the following iteration or development phase.

Between 2013 and 2016, for the tree design experiments described above (Gounouij, Dlo and Geothermy), we collected text-based traces and video recordings.

According to the plans for the following three years, from the beginning of 2017 to the end of 2019, with a similar corpus of data, we will enrich the trace analysis with two methods: analysis of epistemic interactions [23, 24], and automatic detection of emotions in order to validate the visible expressions of the context effect in the video recordings [25].

8. Overview of the DBR Iterations Throughout the TEEC Project

An overview of the DBR iterations throughout the TEEC project is presented in Table 2, with already completed tasks (2012–2016), and the tasks planned for the coming three years (2017–2019), with iterations in three new domains: Socio-economy, Environmental Science, and Language Learning.

9 Current Status and Future Work

Thanks to the results obtained between 2013 and 2016, we have become confident that our approach is valid, despite the logistics problems encountered along the process. It is our plan to test this approach with three new domains: Socio-economy, Environmental Science, and Language Learning. The MazCalc context calculator will be fully developed, tested and documented, with a user guide. The Context-Aware Tutoring System (CAITS) will be developed with two user interfaces: the authoring interface to edit learning scenarios based on the MazCalc, and the tutoring interface to guide the learners through their tasks. In order to test and inform the CLASH model, we intend to add two new dimensions: trace analysis and emotion detection. Trace analysis is going to be performed in the way of the analysis of epistemic interactions among learners to identify the nature of interactions, and validate the manifestations of the context effect. Automatic detection of emotions will also validate the visible expressions of the context effect in the video recordings.

Acknowledgments. For their participation in this project and its experiments, I would like to thank: (1) the team members, Forissier, Delcroix, Anciaux, Mazabraud and Jeannot-Fourcaud, Université des Antilles; Tremblay, Parent, Carignan, and Savard,TÉLUQ; Stockless, Fournier et Nkambou, UQAM; Bernard, Université Paris-Descartes; Baker et Détienne, ParisTech; Prévost, ESIEA, Paris; (2) the experts, the research assistants, the teachers and the students; for English revision, Alexandra Luccioni.

Thanks also to the institutions and the research agencies that support our work: both research centers CRREF, Université des Antilles, and LICEF, Télé-université, 2012–2016; the ANR-FRQSC joint program for France-Québec projects, 2016–2019.

References

1. Brown, A.: Design experiments: theoretical and methodological challenges in creating complex interventions in classroom settings. J. Learn. Sci. **2**(2), 141–178 (1992)
2. Design-Based Research Collective: Design-based research: an emerging paradigm for educational inquiry. Educ. Res. **32**(1), 5–8 (2003)
3. Barab, S., Squire, K.: Design based research: putting a stake in the ground. J. Learn. Sci. **13**(1), 1–14 (2004)
4. Wang, F., Hannafin, M.J.: Design-based research and technology-enhanced learning environments. Educ. Technol. Res. Dev. **53**(4), 5–23 (2005)
5. Herrington, J., McKenney, S., Reeves, T., Oliver, R.: Design-based research and doctoral students: guidelines for preparing a dissertation proposal. Murdoch University (2007). http://researchrepository.murdoch.edu.au/6762/
6. Reimann, P.: Design-based research. In: Markauskaite, L., Freebody, P., Irwin, J. (eds.) Methodological Choice and Design: Scholarship, Policy and Practice in Social and Educational Research, pp. 37–56. Springer, New York (2011)
7. Sandoval, W., Bell, P.: Design-based research methods for studying learning in context: introduction. Educ. Psychol. **39**(4), 199–201 (2004)
8. Anderson, T., Shattuck, J.: Design-based research a decade of progress in education research? Educ. Res. **41**(1), 16–25 (2012)
9. Savard, I.: Modélisation des connaissances pour un design pédagogique intégrant les variables culturelles. Unpublished Ph.D. thesis (2014). http://r-libre.teluq.ca/362/
10. Luccioni, A., Bourdeau, J., Nkambou, R., Coulombe, C., Massardi, J.: STI-DICO: a web-based system for intelligent tutoring of dictionary skills. In: Proceedings of the 25th International Conference Companion on World Wide Web, pp. 923–928. ACM, Geneva (2016)
11. Stockless, A.: Le processus d'adoption d'une innovation pédagogique avec les TIC par les enseignants. Unpublished Ph.D. thesis. Université de Montréal, Montréal (2016)
12. Nkambou, R., Bourdeau, J., Mizoguchi, R.: Advances in Intelligent Tutoring Systems. Studies in Computational Intelligence. Springer, Berlin (2010)
13. Woolf, B.P.: Building Intelligent Interactive Tutors: Student-Centered Strategies For Revolutionizing e-learning. Morgan Kaufmann, Burlington (2010)
14. Forissier, T., Bourdeau, J., Mazabraud, Y., Nkambou, R.: Modeling context effects in science learning: the CLASH model. In: Brézillon, P., Blackburn, P., Dapoigny, R. (eds.) CONTEXT 2013. LNCS (LNAI), vol. 8175, pp. 330–335. Springer, Heidelberg (2013). doi:10.1007/978-3-642-40972-1_25
15. Gropper, G.: Instructional Design. Educ. Technol. **LVII**(1), 40–52 (2017)
16. Aronson, E.: The jigsaw classroom: building cooperation in the classroom. Scott Foresman & Company (1997). https://www.jigsaw.org
17. Erkens, M., Bodemer, D., Hoppe, H.U.: Improving collaborative learning in the classroom text mining based grouping and representing. IJCSCL **11**(4), 4 (2016)

18. Berger, A., Moretti, R., Chastonay, P., Dillenbourg, P., Bchir, A., Baddoura, R.: Teaching community health by exploiting international socio-cultural and economical differences. In: Dillenbourg, P., Eurelings, A., Hakkarainen (eds.) In: Proceedings of the first European Conference on Computer Supported Collaborative Learning, pp. 97–105 (2001). http://www.eculturenet.org/mmi/euro-cscl/Papers/14.pdf
19. Anjou, C., Forissier, T., Bourdeau, J., Mazabraud, Y., Nkambou, R., Fournier, F.: Elaborating the Context Calculator: A Design Experiment in Geothermy, accepted to the Context in Learning 2017 Workshop. (2017)
20. Forissier, T., Bourdeau, J., Mazabraud, Y., Nkambou, R.: Computing the context effect for science learning. In: Brézillon, P., Gonzalez, A.J. (eds.) Context in Computing, pp. 255–269. Springer, New York (2014)
21. Terdjimi, M., Médini, L., Mrissa, M.: Towards a meta-model for context in the web of things. In: Karlsruhe Service Summit Workshop (2016)
22. Fecil, S.: Construire un Enseignement en tenant compte des Effets de Contexte, Unpublished. Master thesis, Université des Antilles (2014)
23. Baker, M., Andriessen, J., Lund, K., Van Amelsvoort, M., Quignard, M.: Rainbow: a framework for analysing computer-mediated Pedagogical debates. I J. CSCL 2(2), 315–357 (2007)
24. Bernard, F.-X., Baker, M.: CoFFEE, un environnement informatique pour l'apprentissage coopératif en co-présence. Actes du colloque «DIDAPRO», Université Paris 5, 21–22 avril 2008. Publications de l'INRP (2009). [http://didapro.mutatice.net/]
25. Nicolle, J., Rapp V., Bailly, K., Prevost, L., Chetouani, M.: Robust continuous prediction of human emotions using multi-scale dynamic cues, Workshop AVEC 2012 (Audio/Visual Emotion Challenge), in conjunction with ICMI2012, pp 501–508 (2012)

Specific Topics: Quality Awareness in Modeling and Using Context in Applications-QAMUCA

A Context Aware Framework for Mobile Crowd-Sensing

Alireza Hassani[1]([⊠]), Pari Delir Haghighi[1], Prem Prakash Jayaraman[2], and Arkady Zaslavsky[3]

[1] Faculty of Information Technology, Monash University, Melbourne, Australia
{Ali.hassani,pari.delirhaghighi}@monash.edu.au
[2] Swinburne University of Technology, Melbourne, Australia
pjayaraman@swin.edu.au
[3] CSIRO, Research Way, Clayton, Melbourne, Australia
arkady.zaslavsky@acm.org

Abstract. Context awareness plays ever increasing role in Mobile Crowd-Sensing (MCS), which relies on sensing capabilities of mobile devices to collect real-time user data and related context. The paper proposes a MCS framework for valuable data collection in order to enable smart applications. The paper also addresses a key challenge in MCS on how to reduce energy consumption in order to encourage user participation. The paper argues that to optimize task allocation costs, it is important for a given query to select the most appropriate participants according to the context of the device, the participant, and the sensing task. Context awareness can significantly reduce the sensing and communication costs. Yet to incorporate context awareness into MCS, there is a need for a standard and overarching context model. This paper proposes a multi-dimensional context model to capture related contextual information in the MCS domain, and incorporate it into a context-aware MCS framework to improve energy efficiency and support task allocation. The paper concludes with discussing implementation and evaluation of the proposed approach.

Keywords: Context model · Context-aware computing · Mobile Crowd-Sensing

1 Introduction

Current advances in mobile technology coupled with the emerging wave of the Internet of Things (IoT) paradigm have led to the development of innovative applications that can collect and query information about people and their environments in real-time. Such applications are referred to as Mobile Crowd Sensing (MCS) applications [1]. The term "crowdsensing" refers to using the power of the crowd to collect data about a phenomenon of interest from a large population of users via the sensors connected to their mobile devices (embedded and external). While the privacy constraints of data collection are important, their discussion goes beyond this paper scope.

MCS applications have two main operations that consume a considerable amount of energy. These operations include sensing which uses the embedded/external sensors

© Springer International Publishing AG 2017
P. Brézillon et al. (Eds.): CONTEXT 2017, LNAI 10257, pp. 557–568, 2017.
DOI: 10.1007/978-3-319-57837-8_45

connected to participants' mobile devices to collect data, and communication that involves sending and receiving data to/from the server. A closely related challenge to energy consumption is efficient task allocation. Generally, in MCS, a set of users from the given population is allocated a crowd sensing tasks by a remote server to meet the needs of the application. A simple strategy (which is used in most MCS systems) is broadcasting this sensing task to all the available participants within a certain geo-location. Obviously, this strategy is expensive because only a small number of users might be able to perform this task, most likely due to their geographical distance to the location of the sensing task or their unsuitability to perform the task [2]. Hence, one of the key challenges in MCS is reducing energy consumption via efficient task allocation in order to encourage user participation [3].

In this paper, we propose a context-aware approach to improve efficiency of task allocation. We demonstrate how context-awareness can be applied in an application like MCS to mitigate the issues around energy consumption. The knowledge about the context of the participant, the device, the task and the location can be used by the MCS applications to optimise task allocation. For example, consider a sensing task for monitoring air pollution in a particular location. If the application incorporates context-awareness, it can use contextual information such as the users' location context to send the sensing task to only those participants who are currently located in the sensing area. If the context of the participant's device is also available, it can be used to select those participants whose mobile phones have sufficient battery remaining to complete the task. Applying such a context-aware approach can significantly improve the efficiency of task allocation.

MCS applications can be categorised into two subclasses based on the level of user's involvement in the task [1]. The first subclass is participatory sensing where users are directly involved in the data collection process. The second is called opportunistic sensing [2] where the sensing task is automatically performed by mobile devices in the background. In this paper, we propose a context-aware approach for opportunistic MCS applications that aims to improve efficiency of task allocation by considering the context of the participant, the device, the task and the location. Most of the works in MCS address the problem of task allocation in participatory MCS, rather than in opportunistic MCS. More importantly, these works only consider spatial context (i.e. location) without taking into consideration multiple dimensions of context. Further, to the best of our knowledge, no study has introduced an overarching context model to optimise task allocation in the field of opportunistic MCS.

2 Related Works

Recently, there has been a great deal of attention given to the energy efficiency problem in crowdsensing. These studies mainly focus on either communication or task allocation costs. Regarding the first category, [3] applies an adaptive positioning mechanism to reduce the sensing energy consumption up to 70%. Another work by Wang et al. [4] introduces a hierarchical framework which relies on less energy consuming sensors (e.g. accelerometer) rather than expensive sensors (e.g. GPS). Their framework uses the most energy consuming sensors if a critical change is detected.

The second category of energy optimisation, which focuses on reducing communication overheads between mobile devices and the server, can be classified further into two subclasses. The works in the first subclass try to adopt low-power communication protocols for uploading sensory data to the server [5]. EffSense [6] reduces the data cost of non-data-plan users by providing other options such as offloading the data to Bluetooth/WiFi gateways and improves energy costs for data-plan users by providing efficient alternatives like uploading the data in parallel with a call. The second group that focuses on optimising energy consumption processes the raw data locally and sends the summarised data to the server. One of the works in this category is proposed by Sherchan et al. [7]. They implement a Context-Aware Real-time Open Mobile Miner (CAROMM) that uses continuous on-device clustering of sensed data to identify changes in clusters and upload the data to the cloud only when a change is detected.

The third category addresses the problem of energy efficiency by allocating the sensing task to a smaller subset of participants based on the similarity between the users' context and the context of the sensing task. This approach can work along with other optimization approaches to optimize the overall energy consumption of MCS systems by reducing the number of exchanged messages. Most approaches in this field mainly rely on location information. Reddy et al. [8] proposed a framework that consists of three main parts namely the qualifier, the assessment, and the progress review. These components are responsible for selecting the participants who meet the minimum requirements for the task, identifying the best subset of users regarding to the corresponding task among all the eligible users and computing the level of trust of users based on their reputation. In a similar approach, Ruan et al. [9] apply movement pattern models that can predict the location of users based on the location historical records. He et al. [10] illustrate that optimal task allocation is an NP-hard problem. They also propose an efficient local ratio based algorithm in order to find an approximate optimal solution. Our proposed framework belongs to the category of optimising task allocation. It aims to improve energy efficiency through context-aware allocation of tasks in opportunistic MCS based on context.

3   A Context Aware Framework for Mobile Crowd Sensing

In this section, we propose a generic MCS framework for Context-Aware Task Allocation (CATA). The framework (depicted in Fig. 1) consists of a client app (running on mobile devices) and a server component.

The components highlighted in lighter colour represent the context-aware task allocation components. Client-side components include:

User Interface enables users to interact with the system and modify their privacy levels.

Task Manager receives sensing tasks from the server and sends them to the CATA after pre-processing. It also registers and monitor the accepted tasks.

Local Context-Aware Task Allocation Manager (L-CATA) consists of two sub-components: a Similarity Model, and a Task Allocation Manager. The first sub-component is used to compute the similarity between the context of the user and

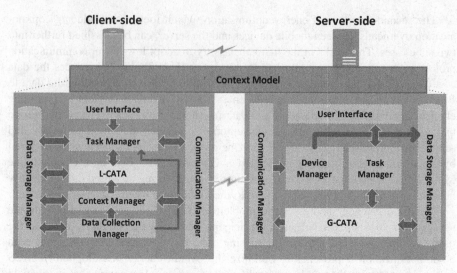

Fig. 1. The architecture of the MCS framework with context-aware task allocation.

the context of received sensing task. Then, the Task Allocation Manager uses this output to decide whether to reject or accept the incoming task.

Context Manager consists of three sub-components. Context Sampling Manager is responsible for sampling the participants' context in an efficient manner to minimise the processing overheads. Context Reasoning Manager and Activity Recognition Manager use the raw data (received from the Data Collection Manager) to infer high-level context about users (e.g. in a meeting) and identify their current level of activity (e.g. running). These sub-components represent context based on our proposed context model for MCS (see Sect. 4).

Data Collection Manager performs data collection. It consists of two sub-components: the Sensor Manager, which collects sensory data, and the Social Media Manager, which retrieves information about the users from social media.

Communication Manager manages all the communications between mobile devices and the server.

Data Storage Manager is responsible for storing different types of information such as the participant's context, received sensing tasks, or sensed data.

The details of the server-side components are as follows.

User Interface provides a graphical interface with a set of tools that helps the administrator of crowdsensing application to create, modify, and monitor sensing tasks.

Task Manager has two sub-components: (1) Task Creation manager, creates sensing tasks and defines the context of each task; and (2) Task Scheduling manager registers the sensing tasks on the server and schedules task allocation jobs.

Device Manager is responsible for updating task assignment jobs and user context, and registering the user.

Global Context-Aware Task Allocation Manager (G-CATA) aims to find an adequate number of participants with high eligibility for each sensing task based on available user contextual information. This component consists of 5 sub-components: Eligibility model, Similarity model, Cost model, Reputation model and Task Allocation Manager. The first four components are used to compute the eligibility of each user for a given sensing task (for details refer to [11]).

Data Storage includes a database that stores the information about each sensing task and all the useful data received from the mobile devices at the server side.

Communications Manager is responsible to initiate and manage communications between mobile devices and the server. It uses a push-based method for sending tasks to mobile devices and employs a RESTful web service for receiving sensory data and context updates from mobile devices.

4 Context Model

According to [12], "Context is any information that can be used to characterize the situation of an entity." Specifically, in this paper, context-awareness delivers the ability to effectively use the context obtained through various sources to further enhance the task allocation efficiency in MCS. In order to capture all the required contextual information in MCS domain, we consider three fundamental context models including participant context, location context and task context.

4.1 Participant Context Model

Dey [12] suggests that "context information is only relevant if it influences a user's task". This emphasises the importance of a participant's context and how it relates to the context of a task in the context-aware computing environments. The Participant Context Model (shown in Fig. 2) consists of a collection of contextual information which define both the characteristics of a user and his/her device.

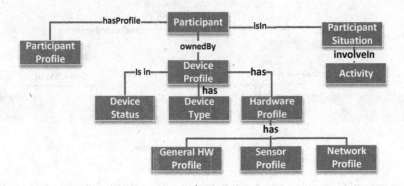

Fig. 2. The participant context model.

Participant Profile represents the general user's characteristics such as age, gender, occupation and so on. Participant Situation describes the current state of the participants such as the activity that the user is currently involved in. Device profile describes the characteristics of the device owned by each participant. It consists of three entities discussed below:

Device Status provides information about the current condition of the device. It has a range of different attributes such as device position (e.g. placed in the pocket, face-down/face-up on the table), device mode (e.g. active call or idle), device battery level, and the available networks (e.g. Wi-Fi, GPRS). It also provides spatial information about the device by linking to the location context model.

Device Type simply determines the category that the device belongs to. A device can be a tablet, a PDA or a smartphone.

Device Hardware Profile describes the specification and capabilities of each device. We classify this Profile into three sub-classes: (i) the Sensor Profile determines the available sensors (built-in or external) and their specifications (e.g. power, maximum range, resolution) for each device, (ii) the Network Profile represents the networks such as Wi-Fi, 4G, GPRS, and Bluetooth that are supported by the device; (iii) and the General Hardware profile illustrates the remaining hardware capabilities of each device such as computation power, display, and memory.

4.2 Task Context

The Task Context Model represents information about a sensing task (see Fig. 3). This model comprises Task Description and Task Preference. Task Description specifies the details of where and when the sensing task will take place, what sensory data needs to be collected, and how many users are needed to accomplish the task. Task Preference provides a description of the ideal participant for a given task.

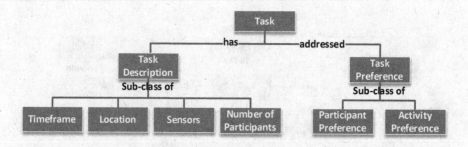

Fig. 3. The task context model.

For example, consider a task for monitoring the activity level of male students between 20 and 25 years of age. For this task, the male participants who are students in the age range between 20 and 25 are considered as the best match. We also assign a weight to each context to indicate its importance (discussed in Sect. 5).

4.3 Location Context

Location is a primary context. As Fig. 4 illustrates Location Context Model describes location based on Geographical and Semantic Location. The Geographical Location provides information about the current location of users. This component consists of the coordinates which represent the exact location of users using latitude and longitude, and the coded location that identifies the area a user is located in. On the other hand, Semantic Location describes the characteristic of a given location. This component divides location into three subclasses based on the nature of the location: Indoors (e.g. classroom, office, home), Outdoors (e.g. park, playground), and Vehicle (e.g. bus, car). The Participant context and the task context relate the Location Model with 'locatedIn' and 'takePlaceIn' properties respectively.

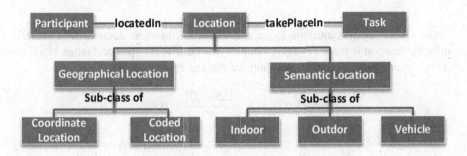

Fig. 4. The location context model.

5 Context-Aware Task Allocation

As discussed in Sect. 3, the proposed MCS framework incorporates context awareness at both the client side and the server side. At the server side, contextual information is used to find an adequate number of participants with high eligibility, which is called a candidate set, for each sensing task. Then, the sensing task will be pushed to their corresponding candidate set. At the client side, the contextual information will be used locally on participants' devices to determine whether to accept or reject the received sensing tasks. A context similarity algorithm [11] is used to calculate the similarity between the context of a sensing task t_j and the context of participant p_i. The context similarity model includes functions to compare a Boolean values, numeric context values, semantic concepts, and vectors [11]. Figure 5 shows an example of a scenario where the context of a sensing task is compared to the participant's context. For simplicity in this example, we consider the same weight of 0.25 for all the attributes.

As the data type of the first context attribute (gender) is Boolean, a simple Boolean comparison function is applied as follow:

$$sim(Male, Male) = 1$$

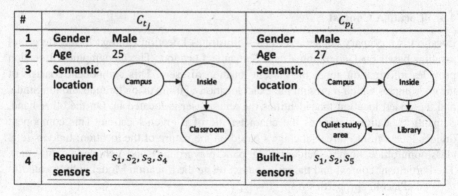

#	C_{t_j}		C_{p_i}	
1	Gender	Male	Gender	Male
2	Age	25	Age	27
3	Semantic location	Campus → Inside ↓ Classroom	Semantic location	Campus → Inside ↓ Quiet study area ← Library
4	Required sensors	s_1, s_2, s_3, s_4	Built-in sensors	s_1, s_2, s_5

Fig. 5. An example of task and participant context.

The second context attribute is the age which is a numeric context, so a numeric similarity function is used. For this example, we consider the span and range of values (i.e. maximum value − minimum value) for the age context as 80.

$$\text{sim}(25, 27) = 1 - \frac{|25 - 27|}{80} = 0.975$$

The third context attribute refers to a semantic concept. A semantic similarity function is used to compare these two contexts. We incorporate a depth variable to represent the number of edges on the path from the given node to the root node. $LC(k_1, k_2)$ denotes the lowest common concept node of both k_1 and k_2. The semantic similarity is then calculated using the following equation:

$$\text{sim}(k_1, k_2) = \frac{\text{depth}(LC(k_1, k_2))}{\text{depth}(k_1)} \tag{1}$$

Based on the given definition, 'Inside' is the lowest common concept node for this example. Therefore, the similarity between these two contexts is calculated as follow:

$$\frac{2 * depth(Inside)}{depth(Quiet\ study\ area) + depth(Classroom)} = \frac{2 * 2}{4 + 3} \approx 0.57$$

The last context attribute in Fig. 5 is a vector of required sensors by the task and a vector of available sensors on the mobile device, so the similarity is computed as shown below (n refers to the number of set elements):

$$\frac{n(\{s_1, s_2, s_3, s_4\} \cap \{s_1, s_2, s_5\})}{n(\{s_1, s_2, s_3, s_4\})} = \frac{n(\{s_1, s_2\})}{n(\{s_1, s_2, s_3, s_4\})} = \frac{2}{4} = 0.5$$

After we calculate the similarity values for all the different types of context we can compute the overall and final similarity value based on the following equation:

$$Similarity\left(C_{t_j}, C_{p_i}\right) = \sum_{k=1}^{n} w_{c_k} * sim\left(C_{t_j}[k], C_{p_i}[k]\right) \qquad (2)$$

w_{c_k} is the weight of context c_k; $c_{t_j}[k]$ and $c_{p_i}[k]$ stands for the k-th contextual element of c_{t_j} and C_{p_i} respectively and $Similarity\left(c_{t_j}, c_{p_i}\right)$ is the similarity between c_{t_j} and c_{p_i}. Based on Eq. 2, the similarity between Ctj and Cpi (as shown Fig. 5) is computed as blow:

$$Similarity\left(C_{t_j}, C_{p_i}\right) = 0.25 * (1 + 0.975 + 0.57 + 0.5) = 0.76125$$

On top of the context similarity, since optimizing the energy consumption of MCS systems is one of the main challenges that we want to address in this paper, we also considered the cost efficiency of a device during calculating the eligibility of a participant. Therefore, our task allocation approach can allocate the sensing task to the adequate number of participants how can execute the sensing task with minimum cost (which leads to optimizing the global energy consumption of such a system).

6 Implementation

In this section, the prototype implementation of the proposed context-aware MCS framework is described.

6.1 Server-Side Implementation

To implement the server-side component we use J2EE including Enterprise JavaBeans (EJBs)[1] and JavaServer Faces (JSFs)[2]. The server-side application is responsible to provide: (i) registering new participants on the server, managing and storing the incoming data (e.g. sensory data, context update) from mobile devices, and (ii) creating and allocating sensing tasks to the right subset of participants using the context.

In the server-side application, two user interfaces were developed to facilitate the interactions between the users and the application. The user interfaces are actually web pages built with JavaServer Faces technology. JavaServer Faces (JSF) is a Java-based web application framework intended to simplify development integration of web-based user interfaces. The first web page provides an interface for task creation. It consists of a form with several of text input as shown on the left-hand side of Fig. 6. The right-hand side of Fig. 6 shows the second web page which is used to visualise sensing tasks, participants, and the result of task assignment on a map for reporting purposes. It has a table of available tasks and their description on top of the page. It displays data on the Google map using markers where each marker represents a participant. Each task has a Select button. When this button is clicked, the participants whose contexts match the context of the sensing task are highlighted in green colour.

---

[1] https://docs.oracle.com/javaee/7/tutorial/ejb-intro.htm.
[2] https://docs.oracle.com/javaee/7/tutorial/jsf-intro.htm.

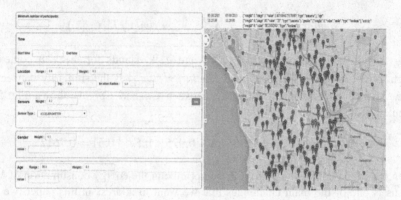

Fig. 6. Task Creation UI and Report UI. (Color figure online)

6.2 Client-Side Implementation

In the client-side implementation, we built a mobile application for Android platform. The client-side application provides three main functionalities. The first functionality is executing sensing task and sending the results back to the server. The second functionality is detecting the context of device and the participant's contexts, storing them locally for future usage, and sharing them with the server when it is needed. The last functionality is receiving sensing tasks from the server, deciding to accept or reject the task, and informing the server of its decision. The client-side mobile application provides an interface to enable users to interact with the system using Android Fragments.

The first fragment presents the current context of users such as location, battery level, available networks, and current activity. The second fragment is designed to show the details of sensing tasks accepted by the device. And the third fragment enables users to modify and control their level of involvement and privacy. The screenshots of these fragments are shown in Fig. 7.

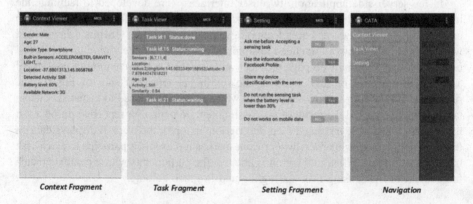

Fig. 7. Client-side user interface

7 Evaluation

We have used our prototype to validate that our proposed context-aware task allocation can improve efficiency. We have considered four main metrics: Task Coverage, Average Eligibility, Allocation Message Overhead [11], and Total Message Overhead. In this paper, we focus only on the last one. The Total Message Overhead for a sensing task is defined as the total number of messages exchanged between the server-side and client-side applications in both allocation and execution phases.

To conduct this evaluation, a big dataset of participants was needed. Since performing real-world experiments are very difficult, we implemented a data simulator for synthesising the required datasets. A random location generator was implemented which generated data points (i.e. latitude/longitude) uniformly, randomly, and independently within a circle of radius r around a specified location c. In the case of numeric contextual attributes such as age and battery level, we defined a range for each attribute and generated a random number in the given range. For the rest of attributes such as gender, activity and network, a set of possible values were considered. For each participant, the context value was randomly selected from the associated set.

In our implementation, the server-side task allocation component (G-CATA) shares all the available sensing tasks with the participants, and the client-side application makes the decision to accept or reject the tasks. We assumed that a participant will accept an incoming task if the similarity between its context and the task's context is higher than 50%. We repeated the experiments for each task by increasing the number of participants from 100 to 1000 and obtained their average as our result. The results of this experiment are shown in Fig. 8. As the figure shows, the number of exchanged messages without context-aware task allocation is significantly high. The reason is that without context-awareness the sensing task will be sent to all the participants and no optimisation is used for distributing the tasks. Thus, as a result a sensing task is performed by more participants than it is required. In contrast, using context-aware task allocation, the sensing task is performed by at most the k participants where k is equal to the minimum number of participants for each task.

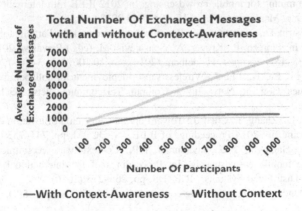

Fig. 8. Total Message Overhead

8 Conclusion

In this paper, we proposed and developed an MCS framework that takes advantage of context-awareness to improve the task allocation process. The proposed framework exemplifies how context-awareness can be effectively incorporated to the advantage of applications such as MCS. To evaluate our approach, we performed experiments to determine the total message overhead during the task allocation process. Experimental outcomes show significant improvements in the efficiency of task allocation. In our future work, we intend to implement a mobility model to predict the future location of participants.

References

1. Ganti, R.K., Ye, F., Lei, H.: Mobile crowdsensing: current state and future challenges. IEEE Commun. Mag. **49**, 32–39 (2011)
2. Lane, N.D., Miluzzo, E., Lu, H., Peebles, D., Choudhury, T., Campbell, A.T.: A survey of mobile phone sensing. IEEE Commun. Mag. **48**(9), 140–150 (2010)
3. Baier, P., Durr, F., Rothermel, K.: Efficient distribution of sensing queries in public sensing systems. In: 2013 IEEE 10th Internaional Conference on Mobile Ad-Hoc Sensor Systems, pp. 272–280, October 2013
4. Wang, Y., Lin, J., Annavaram, M., Jacobson, Q.A., Hong, J., Krishnamachari, B., Sadeh, N.: A framework of energy efficient mobile sensing for automatic user state recognition. In: Proceedings of the 7th International Conference on Mobile Systems, Applications, and Services, MobiSys 2009, pp. 179–192 (2009)
5. Ra, M.-R., Liu, B., La Porta, T.F., Govindan, R.: Medusa: a programming framework for crowd-sensing applications. In: Proceedings of 10th international conference on Mobile Systems, Applications, and Services, MobiSys 2012, pp. 337–350 (2012)
6. Wang, L., Zhang, D., Xiong, H.: EffSense: energy-efficient and cost-effective data uploading in mobile crowdsensing. In: Proceedings of the 2013 ACM Conference on Pervasive and Ubiquitous Computing Adjunct Publication, UbiComp 2013, pp. 1075–1086 (2013)
7. Sherchan, W., Jayaraman, P.P., Krishnaswamy, S., Zaslavsky, A., Loke, S., Sinha, A.: Using on-the-move mining for mobile crowdsensing. In: 2012 IEEE 13th International Conference on Mobile Data Management, pp. 115–124, July 2012
8. Reddy, S., Estrin, D., Srivastava, M.: Recruitment Framework for Participatory Sensing Data Collections. In: Floréen, P., Krüger, A., Spasojevic, M. (eds.) Pervasive 2010. LNCS, vol. 6030, pp. 138–155. Springer, Heidelberg (2010). doi:10.1007/978-3-642-12654-3_9
9. Ruan, Z., Ngai, E.C.H., Liu, J.: Wireless sensor deployment for collaborative sensing with mobile phones. Comput. Netw. Int. J. Comput. Telecommun. Netw. **55**(15), 3224–3245 (2011)
10. He, S., Shin, D., Zhang, J., Chen, J.: Toward optimal allocation of location dependent tasks in crowdsensing. In: 2014 Proceedings of IEEE, INFOCOM, pp. 745–753 (2014)
11. Hassani, A., Haghighi, P.D., Jayaraman, P.P.: Context-aware recruitment scheme for opportunistic mobile crowdsensing. In: Proceedings of the International Conference on Parallel and Distributed Systems - ICPADS, pp. 266–273 (2016)
12. Dey, A.K.: Understanding and using context. Pers. Ubiquit. Comput. **5**(1), 4–7 (2001)

Quality Parameters as Modeling Language Abstractions for Context-Aware Applications: An AAL Case Study

José Ramón Hoyos[1]([⊠]), Davy Preuveneers[2], and Jesús J. García-Molina[1]

[1] Facultad de Informatica, Campus de Espinardo,
Universidad de Murcia, 30100 Murcia, Spain
{jose.hoyos, jmolina}@um.es
[2] Department of Computer Science, imec-DistriNet-KU Leuven,
Celestijnenlaan 200A, 3001 Heverlee, Belgium
davy.preuveneers@cs.kuleuven.be

Abstract. The quality of context information is still one of the most overlooked factors by developers and end-users, and this makes context-aware applications less reliable. While there is recent work in this area that focuses on identifying and modeling relevant quality parameters for context information, software developers still have not yet adopted these solutions at large because they do not offer the right set of abstractions that they are familiar with. This paper presents model and language constructs, as well as software engineering tools to address these quality of context concerns. We demonstrate our overarching solution on a non-trivial Ambient Assisted Living scenario involving assistance services for the elderly supported by indoor localization technologies.

1 Introduction

Recent years have been marked by a growing adoption of intelligent systems and context-aware applications to create Ambient Assisted Living (AAL) environments. These intelligent systems leverage any relevant information about the inhabitants and their surroundings, and adapt accordingly to their needs and desires. However, thus far during the development of such sophisticated applications, little attention is being paid by software engineers to the quality of the information their applications depend on, and the implication of relying on old or inaccurate context information to automate decisions. Indeed, while contemporary middleware frameworks allow these engineers to make abstraction of the basic functionalities and interfaces of sensors and actuators, most frameworks – with a few notable exceptions [2] – hardly offer any means to take the quality of the context into consideration.

Especially for AAL scenarios, location information is key, as the current position of users in the house often drives the smart home automation and the assistance towards the users. Obviously, the accuracy of the in-house positioning system is one of the most straightforward quality parameters, but it is not the only parameter that can be used to eliminate any contextual uncertainty. In this work, we will demonstrate how other

© Springer International Publishing AG 2017
P. Brézillon et al. (Eds.): CONTEXT 2017, LNAI 10257, pp. 569–581, 2017.
DOI: 10.1007/978-3-319-57837-8_46

quality parameters can play a pivotal role to reliably detect and respond to situations of interest in an AAL scenario that focuses on assistance services for elderly people that are supported by indoor localization technologies. To address these concerns, we offer modeling and language abstractions as well as software engineering building blocks and tools to help developers of AAL applications to build more reliable and intelligent systems. The contributions in this paper are threefold:

1) We propose a way to model context situations with quality parameters by using the MLContext DSL [6].
2) We test the influence of quality parameters in detecting relevant situations by means of a case study.
3) We take advantage of the features of MLContext to automatically generate code following an MDE approach. We generate code for a Java framework that lets us represent and simulate the case study scenario.

By simulating the above AAL scenario, we show how user location detection is improved by using both, the accuracy and the relevance factor.

This paper is organized as follows. In Sect. 2, we review relevant quality parameters to characterize the contextual circumstances of a situation of interest. Section 3 presents an AAL motivating use case that will be used in Sect. 4 to demonstrate these quality aspects. In Sect. 5, we briefly discuss the code generation supported by our framework, before evaluating and validating our work in Sect. 6. We conclude in Sect. 7, summarizing our contributions and suggesting topics for further research.

2 Quality Parameters

The notion of quality is not a new concept in a world where one party is delivering a service to another. During the development of complex software applications, quality assurance testing is part of the software engineering cycle to ensure that the application meets not only the functional requirements of an application (i.e. having all the necessary features in place), but also the non-functional requirements (i.e. meeting strict timing constraints, service level agreements about performance, scalability and availability, etc.).

The main goal of quality assurance is to eliminate uncertainty about the behavior of an application. However, for applications that react to the current situation of its users, there is a strong dependency on information to drive the behavior of the context-aware application, and the developer may not be in the position to exhaustively explore likely circumstances to ascertain whether his application recognizes context situations reliably. That is why quality of context [3, 4], or any information describing the quality of the information used as context information, should be a first class citizen in the development of context-aware applications. There are some works related to quality of context which include case studies based on user's location [11], and they use quality of context to filter sources of context (and select the more suitable one), but not to eliminate uncertainty. In the remainder of this paper, we will use *location* as a primitive context concept, and we will discuss the influence of quality parameters to determine if a context situation is occurring. Beyond the *accuracy* of the positioning technology, we also account for *relevance* as a quality parameter [1] to eliminate uncertainty. The challenge that we address, is the fact that it is not always clear how to represent it in a context model or how to compute it. In the next sections, we will show how to indicate that something is important or relevant and how much, by proposing a mechanism to model it with our MLContext DSL. We will show how to include those parameters in the context model, and how they can be used to improve location-awareness of a user in a house.

3   Case Study

The following case study is based on the "Localized and Assisted on the Move" scenario from the AAL Open Association (AALOA) [5]. In this scenario, assistance services for elderly people are supported by indoor localization technologies.

Lina is the main character of this scenario. She is 78-years old and has adult children, but she lives alone. Although they live far from Lina, they can know about her whereabouts at any moment based on the information that comes from an AAL system installed at her home.

Lina's house has five rooms: hall, livingroom, kitchen, bathroom and bedroom, as shown in Fig. 1(a). There is a localization system that can follow the movements of Lina and provides her position to other subsystems. This system uses a WIFI network, with fixed beacons (that can triangulate her position to get its coordinates). The accuracy of the WIFI network is 1.25 m. There are also some motion sensors installed in the house that can detect the presence of someone in a room, but cannot distinguish between people. These sensors have an accuracy of 99.9% because sometimes they can report a false positive (e.g. an open window that causes the movement of a curtain). In this scenario, the motion sensors do not cover an entire room, and not all the rooms, such as the bedroom, have sensors installed (Fig. 1(b)). Therefore, Lina could be in a room and not being detected by the sensors in that room.

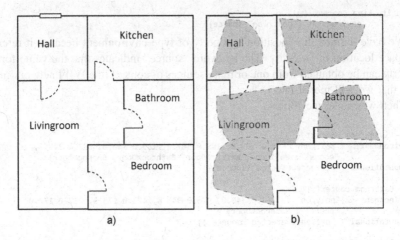

Fig. 1. Lina's house.

If the WIFI localization technique cannot determine exactly what room Lina is in (for example, when the coordinates of Lina are very close to a wall), the motion sensors might help to resolve the uncertainty.

We will create a context model to represent this scenario. Firstly, this context model will include quality parameters related to the sensors and the WIFI network, and we will add later a requirement based in a relevance factor. The next section shall describe the context model we created.

4   Modeling the Scenario Context

We have used our MLContext domain specific language (DSL) for creating the context model. MLContext is a platform-independent language specially designed for modeling context and the quality of context, and it is part of a Model Driven Engineering (MDE) solution to automatically generate code from the context models [6, 7].

MLContext uses two kinds of models: the context model and the application model. The context model represents the context information which includes the entities, their properties and the sources of context that are available for the context-aware application. The application model, meanwhile, represents those aspects related to activities and context situations, along with information related to sensors (including technical details such as precision, resolution, etc.), which are specific for a particular application.

Therefore, we could make changes at the application level (e.g. one of the sensors is changed by another with a higher precision) without having the need to change the context model.

We will follow the modeling method proposed in [7] in order to model the example scenario.

4.1   Context Model

First, we define the user Lina. We are interested in knowing her position.

```
entity Lina context {
        environment {"position" source}}
```

We have defined the "position" property of type environment because it refers to the space location of an entity. The keyword "source" indicates that the value for this property can be obtained from one or more sources of context (the WIFI network in this case, that we will model later).

Then we model the rooms.

```
entity Livingroom context {
   environment   {"polygon" : "2.0 507.0, 189.0 507.0, 189.0 340.0, 287.0 340.0, ...
                   "doors" : HallDoor, KitchenDoor, BathroomDoor, BedroomDoor}
   computational {"presenceDetected" source }}

entity Bathroom context {
   environment   {"polygon" : "287.0 340.0, 473.0 340.0, 473.0 173.0, 287.0 173.0"
                   "doors" : BathroomDoor}
   computational { "presenceDetected" source }}

entity BathroomDoor context { environment{ "polygon" : "287.0 248.0, 287.0 298.0"}}
```

For the sake of space, we only show the definition of two of the rooms, the livingroom and the bathroom. Each room has two properties of type *environment* ("polygon" and "doors") and one of type *computational* ("presenceDetected"). The "polygon" property contains the coordinates of the polygon that delimitates the room, and can be used by our application to draw a blueprint of the house. The "doors" property indicates the doors located in the room. They are used to know how the rooms are connected between them.

The "presenceDetected" property indicates if a person has been detected in the room. It gets its value from the sensors installed in the room. These sensors will be modeled later as sources of context.

Once we have defined the entities of our context model, we can specify a category for each one.

```
categories {
    User: Lina
    Room: Hall, Kitchen, Livingroom, BathroomDoor, Bedroom
    Door: HallDoor, KitchenDoor, BathroomDoor, BedroomDoor, Exit
    Exit: MainDoor
}
```

We have defined four categories: *User*, *Room*, *Door*, and *Exit* as a subcategory of *Door*. MLContext will infer the properties for each category from the properties of its entities.

To complete the context model, we will define the sources of context: the WIFI network and the motion sensors.

```
contextSource WIFI {
        interfaceID : "network"
        methodName : "getWIFIPosition" {
                supply: Lina.position
                returnValue : "coordinatesXY"}}
```

We have specified a "network" identifier for the interface of this context source. It refers to the interface for the controller, which includes a method named "getWIFIPosition" that will be used to get the position of Lina. The return value is in the "coordinatesXY" format. The middleware or the application should be able to know in which room those coordinates are.

Finally, we will define a source of context for the motion sensors "PresenceDetectorSystem".

```
contextSource PresenceDetectorSystem {
        interfaceID : "presenceDetector"
        methodName : "getPresenceHall" {
                supply : Hall.presenceDetected returnValue : "boolean"}
        methodName : "getPresenceKitchen" {
                supply : Kitchen.presenceDetected returnValue : "boolean"}
        methodName : "getPresenceLivingroom" {
                supply : Livingroom.presenceDetected returnValue : "boolean"}
        methodName : "getPresenceBathroom" {
                supply : Bathroom.presenceDetected returnValue : "boolean"}
        methodName : "getPresenceBedroom" {
                supply : Bedroom.presenceDetected returnValue : "boolean"}
}
```

The methods for the *PresenceDetectorSystem* return a boolean value which indicates if a movement has been detected in a room.

MLContext has been defined as a DSL based on an Ecore metamodel [8]. Figure 2 shows an excerpt of the model generated for the textual specification presented above.

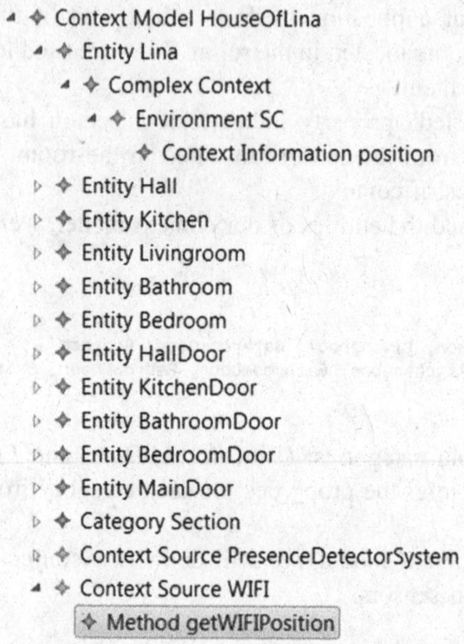

```
⊿ ✦ Context Model HouseOfLina
    ⊿ ✦ Entity Lina
        ⊿ ✦ Complex Context
            ⊿ ✦ Environment SC
                ✦ Context Information position
    ▷ ✦ Entity Hall
    ▷ ✦ Entity Kitchen
    ▷ ✦ Entity Livingroom
    ▷ ✦ Entity Bathroom
    ▷ ✦ Entity Bedroom
    ▷ ✦ Entity HallDoor
    ▷ ✦ Entity KitchenDoor
    ▷ ✦ Entity BathroomDoor
    ▷ ✦ Entity BedroomDoor
    ▷ ✦ Entity MainDoor
    ▷ ✦ Category Section
    ▷ ✦ Context Source PresenceDetectorSystem
    ⊿ ✦ Context Source WIFI
        ✦ Method getWIFIPosition
```

Fig. 2. Generated context model.

4.2 Application Model

As we have previously mentioned the application model represents information related to sensors and those aspects related to context situations, which are specific for a particular application. The elements of the application model will reference elements from the context model.

We will only consider two quality parameters for the context sources in this scenario: *accuracy*, and *units*.

First we will define an information provider for the "network" interface:

```
provider network { name : "WIFIprovider"
                   location : "HouseOfLina"
                   method : getWIFIPosition {
                   accuracy : "1.25"
                   units : "meters"}}
```

The "network" interface links the "WIFIprovider" with the source of context WIFI (note that "network" is the name of the interface defined for the WIFI in the context model). The "location" property specifies where is located this provider. It can be a description or an entity of the context model. We have also specified an accuracy of 1.25 m for this provider. Our accuracy definition has been taken from [9]: "the degree of closeness of a quantity to its actual (true) value".

Next, we will define the providers for the motion sensors. We show only the bathroom and livingroom motion sensor definition as an example because the definition for the others sensors is similar.

```
provider presenceDetector { name : "HallPresenceDetector"
                            location : Hall
                            method : getPresenceHall { accuracy : "0.1%"}        }

provider presenceDetector { name : "LivingroomPresenceDetector1"
                            location : Livingroom
                            method : getPresenceLivingroom {accuracy : "0.1%"}}

provider presenceDetector { name : "LivingroomPresenceDetector2"
                            location : Livingroom
                            method : getPresenceLivingroom {accuracy : "0.1%"}}
```

We have expressed the accuracy as a percentage of error (0.1%). This value means that there is only a 0.1% error when detecting movement.

As we can see in Fig. 1(b) there are two motion sensors in the livingroom, so we need to define two providers for the *getPresenceLivingroom* method of the presenceDetector interface.

4.3   Context Situations

In this scenario, we will define a context situation where quality parameters can be used to determine if the situation is occurring. As an example, we will define a context situation for knowing if Lina is in the bathroom.

Because there are two types of context sources, the context-aware middleware or the application can compute the probability that Lina is in the bathroom in three ways:

- **By only using the WIFI network**. This context situation compares the position of Lina to check if it is in the bathroom. The position of Lina is obtained from the WIFI context source.

```
situation Lina_is_in_Bathroom {
    #Lina.position==#Bathroom
    }
```

Since the WIFI context source has an accuracy of 1.25 m, it is possible to get false positives and negatives. Figure 3(a) shows a situation where the application reports that Lina is in bathroom but she is in a different room. However, the accuracy quality parameter could be used to improve the detection of the position of Lina. In this sense, the application knows that the position reported by the WIFI might not be the actual position, and Lina could be anywhere within 1.25 m from the reported position Fig. 3(b).

Therefore, the middleware can compute the probability that Lina is in the bathroom. This could be obtained, for example, as the percentage of the area of the accuracy circle that is inside the bathroom, Fig. 4(a). The developer of the application could establish a threshold for the probability computed (for example 0.5) below which the position would not be detected in the bathroom.

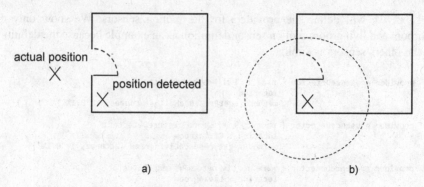

Fig. 3. False positive (a) and accuracy radius (b).

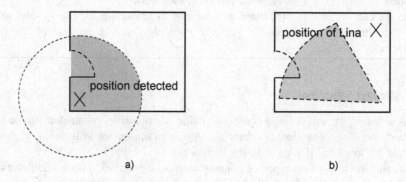

Fig. 4. Probability that Lina is in the bathroom (a), false negative (b)

- **By only using the motion sensor**. In this case, we check if the "presenceDetected" property of the bathroom has a true value. This value is obtained from the presence detector system by using the motion sensor installed in the bathroom.

```
situation Lina_is_in_Bathroom {
    #Bathroom.presenceDetected==true
    }
```

On the one hand, when the motion sensor detects a presence, we are (99.9%) sure that Lina is in the bathroom. On the other hand, the motion sensor not always detects a presence when Lina is in the bathroom, because the focus of the sensor does not cover the entire bathroom (Fig. 4(b)). This situation can also report a false positive when there is more than one person in the room.

- **By using both, the network and motion sensors combined**. This context situation checks the position of Lina as well as the motion sensor installed in the bathroom.

```
situation Lina_is_in_Bathroom {
    #Lina.position==#Bathroom AND
    #Bathroom.presenceDetected==true
    }
```

When the application cannot determine exactly whether Lina is in the bathroom by using the position reported by the WIFI, the information from the motion sensor can help to resolve the uncertainty.

However, this specification will fail when Lina is in the bathroom and the motion sensor does not detect her. The application will report a false negative like in the context situation that we defined by only using the sensor.

Therefore, to achieve better results, we could change the previous specification as follows:

```
situation Lina_is_in_Bathroom {
        #Lina.position==#Bathroom OR
        (#Lina.position==#Bathroom AND
        #Bathroom.presenceDetected==true)
        }
```

This way, if the sensor does not detect a presence in the bathroom the application will use only the information from the WIFI network to check if the position is in the bathroom.

Note that by using the previous specification of context situation, the value of probability reported will be the same independently of whether the motion sensor detects Lina in the bathroom or not. If the value of probability does not pass the threshold defined by the developer (e.g. 0.5) Lina will not be detected in the bathroom.

However, we know intuitively that the probability that Lina is in the bathroom should be higher if both, the WIFI network and the presence detector system, report Lina at that location. Therefore, the language provides the "relevance" quality parameter to specify that. We have defined three levels for this parameter: HIGH, MEDIUM and LOW.

```
situation Lina_is_in_Bathroom {
        #Lina.position==#Bathroom OR
        (#Lina.position==#Bathroom [relevance == "HIGH"] AND
        #Bathroom.presenceDetected==true)
}
```

The "HIGH" value for the relevance parameter indicates that is more likely that Lina is in the bathroom if the position of Lina is in the bathroom and the motion sensor detects her, and also that is less probable that Lina is in the bathroom if only the WIFI reports her at that position but not the sensor. This could help to reduce false positives.

The other two values are "MEDIUM" and "LOW". A "MEDIUM" value will indicate that is more likely that Lina is in the bathroom if both, the WIFI and the sensor report that Lina is in the bathroom, but does not lower the probability that Lina is in the bathroom if only the WIFI detect her. A value of "LOW" will indicate that we know that it is very unlikely that both, the WIFI and the motion sensor will report that Lina is in the bathroom.

By using the relevance parameter, the application can raise (or lower) the value of probability reported by this context situation to pass the threshold.

In the validation section, we will compare the different ways of model this context situation and also the influence of using the quality parameters (accuracy and relevance).

Note that there exist other ways of modeling this context situation. For example, if we have motion sensors in all the rooms, we could also model this context situation by checking the motion sensors of all the rooms but the bathroom. If none of the motion sensors does detect Lina, then it will be highly probable that she is in the bathroom.

5 Generating Code

We can automatically generate code for our Java framework from the context model. By using a model-to-code transformation, a Java class is generated for each of the categories defined in the model, and a builder is created, which initializes all the rooms and connects them by using the defined doors (Fig. 5). The generated code includes the context sources and their interfaces, and they are linked with their corresponding properties. The framework allows us to position and move the users in the house.

```java
public ModelBuilder(){
    model=new House();
    door1 = new Door("HallDoor","64.0 173.0, 114.0 173.0");
    door2=new Door("KitchenDoor","209.0 173.0, 258.0 173.0");
    door3=new Door("BathroomDoor","287.0 248.0, 287.0 298.0");
    door4=new Door("BedroomDoor","189.0 411.0, 189.0 462.0");

    exit1=new Exit("MainDoor","63.0 6.0, 118.0 6.0");
    Hall=new Room("Hall","2.0 173.0, 189.0 173.0, 189.0 6.0, 2.0 6.0");
    Kitchen=new Room("Kitchen","189.0 173.0, 473.0 173.0, 473.0 6.0, 189.0 6.0");
    ...
    Hall.addDoor(door1); Hall.addDoor(exit1);
    Kitchen.addDoor(door2);
    ...
    //providers
    HallPresenceDetector=new PresenceDetector("HallpresenceDetector");
    KitchenPresenceDetector=new PresenceDetector("KitchenPresenceDetector");
```

Fig. 5. Excerpt of the generated code

By writing the code for the methods of the providers (wifi and sensors), we completed the scenario. This will let us to invoke the methods from the context sources for the simulation.

6 Validation

We have followed the approach proposed in [10] to validate our proposal by simulating the scenario. For this, we have generated code for the Java framework described in the previous section and analyzed the quantitative results.

We have compared the results with and without quality parameters for the three context situations defined in Sect. 4, and we have also considered the possibility that there is another person in the house. We have generated 100000 random positions for Lina in her house. Of these, 13317 were located at the bathroom.

Table 1 shows the results of the simulation without using quality parameters. The first column is the number of correct detections (i.e. Lina is in the bathroom and it is

Table 1. Simulation results without using quality.

Without quality (13317 positions generated at the bathroom)			
	Correct detections	False positives	False negatives
WIFI only	11353	1051	1964
Sensor only	7311	94	6006
Sensor only and another person	7739	6333	5578

reported by the context situation). The second is the number of false positives (i.e. Lina is not in the bathroom but the context situation reports that she is there). The third is the number of false negatives (i.e. Lina is in the bathroom but the context situation does not detect her).

First, we used only the WIFI network without using quality parameters. The context situation was able to detect Lina 11353 times (85%). There were also false positives (1%) and false negatives (15%) due to the accuracy of the network. Next we tested the same positions by using only the motion sensor. This way the context situation was able to detect Lina 7311 times (55%), because the motion sensor does not cover the entire area of the bathroom (high number of false negatives). There are also a small number of false positives because the sensor has an accuracy of 0.1%.

When we introduced another person in the house, the number of false positives greatly increased because the motion sensor does not distinguish between two people. The number of correct detections was also slightly increased and the false negatives decreased (this increase was due to the situations where two people were at the bathroom).

Then, we used quality parameters, so the middleware could know the accuracy of the WIFI network and the relevance of the context facts.

Table 2 shows the results of the simulation taking into account quality parameters for the same 13317 positions.

Table 2. Simulation results using quality

With quality parameters (13317 positions generated at the bathroom, umbral 0.5, relevance is considered)			
	Correct detections	False positives	False negatives
WIFI only	13317	5265	0
WIFI and sensor	13305	4789	12
WIFI, sensor and another person	13307	4840	10

When we used the quality parameters information of the WIFI, the application was able to compute the probability that Lina was in the bathroom, as explained in Sect. 4.3. We used a threshold of 0.5 for our application. Therefore, the context situation only detected Lina when the probability was greater than 50%.

By using the WIFI network, the application detected Lina 13317 times (100%), but the false positives slightly increased too (6%). There were no false negatives.

To reduce the number of false positives, we combined the information provided by the WIFI and the motion sensor. When used the WIFI and the sensor, the application detected Lina in the bathroom 13305 times (99.9%) and the false positives were reduced to 4789.

These results were almost the same when we introduced another person in the house because the WIFI only detects Lina.

7 Conclusion and Future Work

In this paper, we have shown that it is possible to model the same context situation in different ways. The designer should carefully consider which way is the best to define a context situation, especially when we have different context sources that can supply related information.

We must take into account that the supplied information is often inaccurate, and the context-aware application could take a wrong decision based on this information. The use of quality parameters can help the application to take the right decision.

On the one hand, from the results of the validation, we can conclude that the use of quality parameters greatly improves the detection of context situations and reduces the number of false negatives, but it can also increase the number of false positives.

Note that in most context-aware applications, especially those where the safety of the user is involved, a false negative is more dangerous than a false positive. For example, not detecting that the user has entered in a dangerous zone, or not detecting that the user has fallen to the floor.

By combining the information from several context sources (e.g. WIFI and motion sensor) we can reduce the number of false positives.

On the other hand, the relevance quality parameter can help us to compute uncertainty context situations. As an example, we have shown in this paper how it can help us to model a context situation where a motion sensor does not cover an entire room and the WIFI network cannot accurately locate the user.

When modeling a context situation with quality parameters, the middleware can compute the probability that the context situation occurs, but it is responsibility of the developer to determine a threshold value. In this sense the application will consider that the context situation is occurring when the probability is greater than the threshold. The threshold value will depend on the concrete application.

Another subjective factor is how much the relevance factor must increase or decrease the probability of a context situation. It depends on the target platform and how the concrete middleware computes it. In our Java framework the relevance factor increases the probability by 4, therefore a probability of 0.2 will be taken into account (for a threshold of 0.5) if it is relevant.

As future work, we are planning to test other scenarios as well as to identify some guidelines, which can help developers to calculate the relevance factor.

References

1. Truong, H.-L., Dustdar, S., Maurino, A., Comerio, M.: Context, quality and relevance: dependencies and impacts on restful web services design. In: Daniel, F., Facca, F.M. (eds.) ICWE 2010. LNCS, vol. 6385, pp. 347–359. Springer, Heidelberg (2010). doi:10.1007/978-3-642-16985-4_31

2. Chabridon, S., Conan, D., Desprats, T., Mbarki, M., Taconet, C., Lim, L., Marie, P., Rottenberg, S.: A framework for multiscale-, qoc- and privacy-aware context dissemination in the internet of things. In: Guo, S., Liao, X., Liu, F., Zhu, Y. (eds.) CollaborateCom 2015. LNICSSITE, vol. 163, pp. 207–218. Springer, Cham (2016). doi:10.1007/978-3-319-28910-6_19

3. Krause, M., Hochstatter, I.: Challenges in modelling and using quality of context (QoC). In: Magedanz, T., Karmouch, A., Pierre, S., Venieris, I. (eds.) MATA 2005. LNCS, vol. 3744, pp. 324–333. Springer, Heidelberg (2005). doi:10.1007/11569510_31

4. Rogova, G., Bosse, E.: Information quality in information fusion. In: Proceedings of FUSION 2010, 13th Conference on Multisource Information Fusion, Edinburgh, Scotland (2010)

5. AAL Open Association (AALOA). http://www.aaloa.org/

6. Hoyos, J.R., García-Molina, J., Botía, J.A.: A domain-specific language for context modeling in context-aware systems. J. Syst. Softw. **86**(11), 2890–2905 (2013)

7. Hoyos, J.R., García-Molina, J., Botía, J.A., Preuveneers, D.: A model-driven approach for quality of context in pervasive systems. Comput. Electr. Eng. **55**, 39–58 (2016)

8. Steinberg, D., Budinsky, F., Paternostro, M., Merks, E.: EMF: Eclipse Modeling Framework 2.0. Pearson Education, Upper Saddle River (2009)

9. Carr, J.J., Brown, J.M.: Introduction to Biomedical Equipment Technology, 3rd edn. Prentice Hall, Upper Saddle River (2010)

10. McKeever, S., Ye, J., Coyle, L., Dobson, S.: A context quality model to support transparent reasoning with uncertain context. In: Rothermel, K., Fritsch, D., Blochinger, W., Dürr, F. (eds.) QuaCon 2009. LNCS, vol. 5786, pp. 65–75. Springer, Heidelberg (2009). doi:10.1007/978-3-642-04559-2_6

11. Chabridon, S., Conan, D., Abid, Z., Taconet, C.: Building ubiquitous QoC-aware applications through model-driven software engineering. Sci. Comput. Program. **78**(10), 1912–1929 (2013)

Focus on the User: A User Relative Coordinate System for Activity Detection

Andreas Jahn[✉], Marek Bachmann, Philipp Wenzel, and Klaus David

Chair for Communication Technology (ComTec), Faculty of Electrical Engineering
and Computer Science, University of Kassel, Kassel, Germany
comtec@comtec.eecs.uni-kassel.de

Abstract. The information about a person's activity, as a special type
of contextual information, can be used for a multitude of applications.
Thus, activity detection is a focus in research. For activity detection, usually measured sensor data are processed and matched to known activities.
Unfortunately, measured sensor data can be inconsistent for the same
activity. Depending on the device orientation and in which direction of
compass the user is heading (while carrying out an activity) the sensor
data changes. As a result, expected values on one sensor axis appear on
another one and it is challenging for a pre-generated activity detection
model to match the sensor data to the activity. However, the intuitive
solution seems to be easy: *focus on the user*. Regardless of the device orientation or the cardinal direction, the activity never change for the user.
In this paper, we present an approach to *focus on the user* in activity
detection. We convert sensor data into a representation relative to the
user. Thus, the sensor data stay consistent regardless of the device orientation or the cardinal direction. We show that by using the *focus on the
user* approach the detection rates increase up to 21.7%. Also, the detection is more reliable (lower standard deviation). We prove the reliable
activity detection for different device orientations, cardinal directions,
types of algorithms, sensor sets, activities, and sensor positions.

Keywords: Context awareness · Activity detection · User oriented ·
Device orientation independence · Coordinate system

1 Introduction

The information about a person's activity, as a special type of contextual information, can be used for a multitude of applications. For example, in energy management, the energy efficiency can be improved by using activity-aware energy
management systems. Lighting, heating, ventilation, and workstations in offices
can automatically be switched to power save mode if the user is away from the
office [8]. In health care, activity awareness can be used to complement and
improve telemedical services. For example, the detection of physical activity can
be used for therapies and treatments [11].

© Springer International Publishing AG 2017
P. Brézillon et al. (Eds.): CONTEXT 2017, LNAI 10257, pp. 582–595, 2017.
DOI: 10.1007/978-3-319-57837-8_47

To enable devices to detect activities autonomously, motion sensors like the smartphones' built-in accelerometer and gyroscope are used. The measured sensor data are processed and matched to activities. As a result, nowadays the detection of activities like standing, sitting, or walking is possible [4]. To improve the detection accuracy or to detect additional activities the use of additional information sources is a common approach. Additional information sources have been investigated as, for instance, multiple sensors attached to multiple body positions [14], or as statistical data, such as time use surveys [3]. To improve the detection accuracy, also novel features have been investigated. For instance, a feature that detects the position of a hand, supports the detection of the smoking activity [13].

All these approaches rely on consistent sensor data. Unfortunately, values of measured sensor data can be inconsistent for several sensors, such as the accelerometer or the gyroscope, even though they represent the same activity. Exemplarily, we consider sensor values given relative to a device such as a smartphone. These sensor values change whenever the smartphone orientation changes. For example, in a device orientation 1 (O1) the gravity force appears on the accelerometer's y-axis, as shown in Figs. 1a and 2. When the same activity is being conducted but the device orientation is changed, for instance, by a sideways rotation of 90° (orientation 2 (O2)), the gravity force appears on the x-axis. Consequently, the measured sensor data on the x- and y-axis change for an unchanged activity. A matching of these changed sensor data to known activities becomes challenging. This problem is known as device-orientation-problem. A possible solution is keeping the smartphone constantly in the same orientation. But it seems to be unrealistic and inconvenient for the user to keep the smartphone in a fixed orientation. To address the device-orientation-problem a representation of sensor values relative to the world was investigated (Fig. 1b) [17]. Here all sensor data are converted into a fixed representation relative to the world's gravity and the magnetic north. Thus, the device orientation becomes irrelevant. Unfortunately, a new problem arises. Since the measured sensor data are given relative to the world, the activity walking - towards north - appears on the y-axis while walking - towards west - appears on the x-axis. The same activity conducted in different directions of the compass appears on different sensor axes. Matching the changing sensor data with known activities is challenging again. We call this the cardinal-direction-problem.

However, for humans it seems to be easy to detect another human's activities. Intuitively we have an understanding of what a person's "front" or "side" is, in which direction an activity is being conducted, and what actual activity is being conducted. This understanding is independent of the device orientation or the cardinal direction. We intuitively *focus on the user*.

In this paper, we investigate the *focus on the user* approach. To do so, we convert measured sensor data into a representation that is defined relative to the user. We name this representation *user coordinate system* (*UCS*), see Fig. 1c. We evaluate the *focus on the user* approach against the representation relative to device (*device coordinate system, DCS*) and the representation relative to the

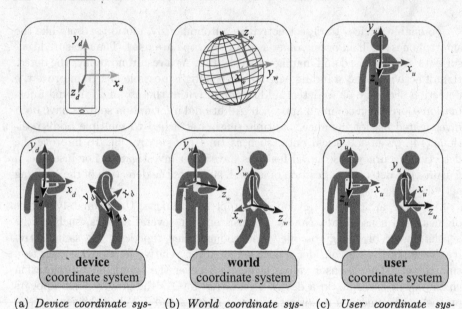

(a) *Device coordinate system (DCS).*   (b) *World coordinate system (WCS).*   (c) *User coordinate system (UCS).*

Fig. 1. Coordinate systems relative to the device (a), relative to the world (b), and relative to the user (c).

world (*world coordinate system, WCS*) in an eight device orientations and four cardinal directions experimental setup. We detail the evaluation results for four types of algorithms, two sensor sets, five activities, and two sensor positions. Using the *UCS* improves the activity detection rates compared to coordinate systems relative to the device or the world.

The remainder of this paper is organized as follows. Section 2 provides an overview about the related work. Section 3 details the methodology of the *focus on the user* approach. Section 4 focuses on the experiment, followed by Sect. 5, where the results are presented and discussed. Last, Sect. 6 summarizes the results.

2   Related Work

Sensor data measured by a smartphone are relative to the device and, thus, based on the *device coordinate system (DCS)*. We subscript the *DCS* with d. The *DCS* is defined relative to the smartphone's screen. The x_d-axis refers to the horizontal component and points to the right. The y_d-axis points to the top of the screen and contains the vertical component. The z_d-axis points outside and is perpendicular to the screen (see Fig. 1a). Due to the definition relative to the smartphone's screen, its orientation changes whenever the device orientation changes - it is (device) orientation dependent. Many authors use the *DCS* for their investigations. Using the DCS the detectability of activities like standing, walking, or running was proven [4,14]. Also, the fixed orientation relative to the screen can be used to differentiate between activities. For instance, the activities standing and sitting can be differentiated by the orientation of a device carried in the pocket. When the device is upright, the user is standing, when the device is rotated sideways, the user is sitting. However, on the same time, the fixed orientation to the screen can be a disadvantage. Detecting an activity like walking with an unknown or changing device orientation is challenging due to the device-orientation-problem, i.e. inconsistent sensor data. The challenge of inconsistent sensor data is mainly addressed in two ways: device orientation independent features and sensor data conversion.

Device orientation independent features counter the device-orientation-problem by representing data features in a consistent, orientation-independent way. For example, features are extracted based on the accelerometer's magnitude instead of the individual and orientation dependent x_d-, y_d- and z_d-axis. These features have the shortcoming of losing the three directional information and, hence, detection accuracy [10].

The second approach to address the challenge of inconsistent sensor data is sensor data conversion. Measured sensor data are converted into a consistent representation that is independent of the device orientation or the directions of the compass. Mizell converts the sensor data by approximating the vertical and horizontal components of the sensor data. The resulting vector p is the vertical component of the dynamic acceleration (activity). The resulting horizontal vector h is calculated by vector subtraction since a 3D vector is the sum of its vertical and both horizontal components [12]. This approach keeps the vertical and horizontal information, but it is impossible to know the direction of h relative to the horizontal axis in the world's 3D coordinate system. Yang addressed this by calculating the magnitude of vector h [18]. Kunze et al. get the direction of the horizontal axis by analyzing where the acceleration has the greatest variation [7]. However, all these approaches lose the information of one dimension of the three-dimensional activities, which might lower the activity detection accuracies. To keep the three-dimensional information, sensor data can be converted into a consistent representation by changing the coordinate system the sensor data are represented in.

Thiemjarus converted the three-dimensional sensor data with respect to the gravity to achieve a consistent data representation [16]. Other approaches used the gravity force and the magnetic north to convert sensor data into a consistent representation relative to the world. The *world coordinate system* (*WCS*) is defined relative to the world, i.e. relative to the world's gravity force and the magnetic north. We subscript the *WCS* with w. The x_w-axis runs west-east. The y_w-axis points out of the center of the earth and contains the gravity force. The z_w-axis points to the magnetic north, see Fig. 1b. The advantage of the *WCS* is the device orientation independence. Investigations show that by using the *WCS* the activity detection accuracy may increase [17]. A drawback of the *WCS* is the loss of the connection to the users. The walking activity, for instance, by the user heading in a northerly direction of the compass appears on the x_w-axis, while the same activity by the same user in a westerly direction of the compass appears on the z_w-axis. Hence, the *WCS* suffers from the cardinal-direction-problem.

To address both, the device-orientation-problem and the cardinal-direction-problem, the *focus on the user* approach relies on data conversion into a coordinate system relative to the user. We name the resulting coordinate system as *user coordinate system (UCS)*. We subscript the *UCS* axes with u. The x_u-axis refers to the horizontal component and points to the left side of the user. The y_u-axis refers to the vertical component and points to the sky. Thus, y_u contains the gravity force. The z_u-axis refers to the second horizontal component and points to the user's front, i.e. the user's heading. Therefore, independently of the device orientation or the direction of the compass the user is heading to a user's forward motion appears on the z_u-axis. A side way motion appears on the x_u-axis, and a vertical motion such as a jump appears on the y_u-axis. The *UCS* is shown in Fig. 1c. Ali et al. converted sensor data into a coordinate system relative to the user. The authors used the converted sensor data for the purpose of indoor localization [2].

The shift from one coordinate system into another is conducted by rotating in the point of origin based on a rotation matrix R. To calculate R the "new coordinate axes" need to be determined first. While for the *WCS* the axes to the magnetic north and the world's gravity vector can be gathered by using appropriate sensors, it is challenging to get the axes for the *UCS*. The vertical axis can be gathered by using the accelerometer's gravity information, too. To gather the forward axis (the direction in which the user is heading) Ali et al. examined patterns in the leveled horizontal and vertical acceleration components [2]. Unfortunately, this approach does not consider different device orientations. Henpraserttae et al. consider different device orientations and estimate the forward axis by computing the principal axis of the data which are orthogonal to the vertical axis, assuming that most of the activity is in forward-backward direction [5]. However, due to the noisy nature of smartphone accelerometer data, both approaches accumulate errors over time. Kusber et al. presented an approach to examine the user's direction that is device orientation independent and less prone to accelerometer measurement errors [9]. The authors identify the device orientation and remap the sensor measurements to the default device orientation (upright, display points to the user). Subsequently, the user's direction is calculated as an offset between user direction and magnetic north. The sideward axis is orthogonal to the vertical axis and the forward axis.

3   Methodology

To convert the sensor data the *focus on the user* approach implements a two-step protocol:

First, we convert the measured sensor data from *DCS* into *WCS* by a 3D rotation. Secondly, we align the z-axis with the user's direction by a 1D rotation over the y-axis. Below the two steps are presented in detail.

First, the *DCS* into *WCS* conversion is conducted. Based on the information of gravity (gathered from the accelerometer) and magnetic north (gathered from the magnetometer) the quaternion vector is calculated and transferred to the rotation matrix R. Using R we conduct the 3D rotation into the *WCS*.

Secondly, we conduct the *WCS* into *UCS* conversion. This 1D rotation aligns the z-axis with the user's forward axis. To gather the forward axis we follow the approach presented by Kusber et al. in [9]. Thus, we identified the smartphone orientation and remapped the sensor data to the default orientation. The forward axis is then given by the magnetometer. However, we extended the proposed approach to handle an infinite number of device orientations. Finally, we implement the rotation. Consequently, the z-axis is aligned with the user's direction and the sensor data are converted into the *UCS*.

The introduced two-step protocol allows us to evaluate the detection accuracy for each of the three coordinate systems *DCS*, *WCS*, and *UCS* separately.

4   Experiment

To evaluate the *focus on the user* approach the considered dataset needs to contain activity data distinguished by two parameters: the device orientation and the cardinal direction. Unfortunately, such a dataset is not publicly available. Thus, we measured these data and made them available to the public: https:// www.comtec.eecs.uni-kassel.de/public_data/.

In the data collection experiment, we collected data for five physical activities. These were standing, walking, running, ascending stairs, and descending stairs. These activities are often used in related studies. It was shown that these activities are well recognizable with a fixed device orientation [4]. Thus, they are appropriate to illustrate the device-orientation-problem, the cardinal-direction-problem, and our proposed solution. Nine participants were involved in the data collection experiment, seven males and two females, aged between 20 and 30 years. Each participant was equipped with two smartphones, positioned on the upper-arm and on the belt. These positions were chosen since they are frequently used in daily life and several device orientations are likely [6]. The smartphones' positions on the participants' bodies are fixed. We measured accelerometer, gyroscope, and magnetometer data. In this work, we use the built-in sensors of the commercially available smartphone Nexus 5. The operating system on the Nexus 5 device was Android Version 5.1.1.

The data were recorded for each activity at a sampling rate of 50 Hz (50 samples per second). This sampling rate is sufficient to detect human physical activities [15]. During the experiment, the collected sensor data were labeled with the according activity by a second person. No further modifications have been made to the measured sensor data.

4.1   Device Orientation

There is an infinite number of possible different device orientations in a real world scenario. For our experiment, we exemplarily consider eight different smartphone orientations. These are defined relative to the user's body. Orientation 1 (O1) represents the smartphone upright, display facing to the body. O2 represents the smartphone upright, display facing away from the body. O3 represents the smartphone top down, display facing to the body. O4 represents the smartphone in a top down orientation, display pointing away from the body. O5 represents the smartphone rotated sideways (90°), top to user direction, display facing to the body. O6 represents the smartphone rotated sideways (90°), top to user direction, display facing away from the body. O7 represents the smartphone rotated sideways (−90°), bottom to user direction, display facing to the body. Finally, O8 represents the smartphone rotated sideways (−90°), bottom to user direction, display facing away from the body. All orientations are shown in Fig. 2 and summarized in Table 1.

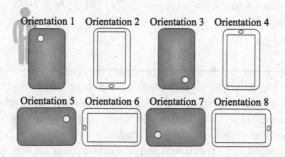

Fig. 2. The eight exemplarily considered device orientations.

4.2   Cardinal Directions

For each device orientation sensor data were measured for all activities in four cardinal directions. The measurements took place in a public park. The park provided pathways in all four main cardinal directions. We choose all of them and measured the activities towards the north (N), towards the east (E), towards the south (S), and towards the west (W) (see Table 1). The participants walked around several marks spaced out by 80 m.

For ascending and descending stairs the 3-floor university building was chosen. The participants ascended and descended stairs between the 1st and the 3rd floor on different staircases towards all four cardinal directions. In total, the test-path was ≈16 km long. Overall, 120 h of sensor data were recorded.

4.3   Data Processing

Subsequently to the data measurements, we pre-processed the sensor data, generated an activity detection model, and evaluated the model.

Table 1. To evaluate the approach eight device orientations and four cardinal directions were considered. Two device orientations were considered in the training set and six in the test set resulting in 28 training set-test set combinations.

device orientations	cardinal directions
Orientation 1 (O1)	North (N)
Orientation 2 (O2)	West (W)
Orientation 3 (O3)	South (S)
Orientation 4 (O4)	East (E)
$\vdots$	
Orientation 8 (O8)	

training set	test set
O1,O2 + N,S	O3-O8 + E,W
O1,O3 + N,S	O2,O4-O8 + E,W
$\vdots$	$\vdots$
O7,O8 + N,S	O1-O6 + E,W

Pre-processing. In pre-processing we first convert each sensor recording into the different representations. Since the sensor data are recorded in the *DCS* we convert the collected accelerometer and gyroscope data into the *WCS* and the *UCS* representation. Subsequently, we extract the features. For feature extraction we used the sliding window approach. Due to current research results we set the window size to 2.0 s and the overlap to 50% of the window size. For every created window, the features of mean, variance, standard deviation, minimum, and maximum were extracted.

Activity Model Generation. To detect the set of activities we use four different types of classification algorithms, namely, a lazy learner, a decision tree, a rule-based, and a Bayesian classifier. More precisely, we used the algorithms IBk, J48, JRip, and Naive Bayes implemented in the WEKA toolkit [1]. Activity detection models were generated for *DCS*, *WCS*, and *UCS* separately.

Evaluation. The evaluation uses a "leave-six-orientations-and-two-cardinal-directions-out" protocol. For model generation (training) we use two device orientations and for evaluation (testing) the remaining six device orientations. In addition, the training sets contain the activities measured in northern and southern direction while the test sets contain the activities measured in eastern and western direction. Thus, for each participant 28 different training set and test set combinations were evaluated (see Table 1). We calculated the activity detection rates mean values and the corresponding standard deviations.

5   Results

In our investigation, we assumed that the computation of the orientation-independent components requires minimal resources (in terms of computing power and time). Hence, the comparisons are made on the detection accuracy and F-Measure, respectively, given in percentages. We used the default evaluation setting as below:

sensor:	accelerometer
algorithms:	IBk, J48, JRip, NaiveBayes
activities:	standing, walking, running, ascending stairs, descending stairs
sensor positions:	belt, upper-arm
evaluation:	leave-six-orientations-and-two-cardinal-directions-out

As shown in Sect. 3 identifying the device orientation is crucial for the sensor data conversion. Consequently, we evaluated whether the proposed methodology identifies the device orientation correctly. Therefore, we set the (known) device orientation manually and generated and evaluated the detection models. Subsequently, we automatically identified the device orientation by using the proposed method and generated and evaluated the detection models again. We expected a lower detection accuracy when identifying the orientation automatically but in fact we obtained a 1.4% higher detection accuracy when using the proposed methodology. The higher detection accuracy is due to possible minor device orientation changes during a measurement (e.g. a device rotation of a few degrees). While the evaluation with manually given device orientations did not consider these changes, the evaluation which follows the proposed methodology did so. Hence, the detection accuracy increases. We conclude that the proposed methodology identifies the device orientation correctly.

Next, we evaluated whether the *focus on the user* approach addresses the device-orientation-problem and the cardinal-direction-problem. We compared the *UCS* evaluation results with results of the *DCS* and the *WCS*. Figure 3 shows the experimental results. With a detection accuracy of 84.3% we obtain the highest detection accuracy by *focusing on the user*, i.e. using the *UCS*. Also, the higher detection rate comes along with a lower standard deviation. The *DCS* (62.6%) and *WCS* (79.6%) suffer from some drawbacks.

The *DCS* suffers from the device-orientation-problem. The experimental results show that an activity detection model trained for one orientation performs well for the trained orientation but struggles with other orientations. This was confirmed for up to four orientations trained at the same time. Unfortunately, the detection model complexity increases with the number of trained orientations. As a result, the detection accuracy eventually decreases the more orientations are trained. While the *DCS* struggles with different device orientations, no problems with different cardinal directions were observed. The reason is intuitive. A certain device orientation stays relative to the user's direction since devices worn on the body of course turn with the user when the user changes direction.

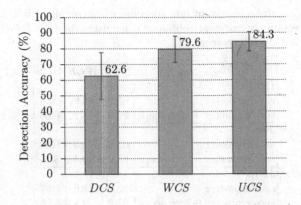

Fig. 3. Detection accuracy for *DCS*, *WCS*, and *UCS*. The highest accuracy is obtained when using the *UCS*.

The *WCS* addresses the device orientation drawbacks of the *DCS*. However, the results also show a decrease in detection accuracy when activities are heading off in different directions of the compass. Activity detection models trained for a cardinal direction struggle to detect the same activity heading off in another direction.

The *UCS* addresses the device-orientation-problem and the cardinal-direction-problem. We obtain the highest detection accuracy when using the *UCS*. This is due to the *focusing on the user* approach. While the other coordinate systems are defined relative to the device or the world, the *UCS* is defined relative to the user. Hence, the measured sensor data are consistent independent of the device orientation and the cardinal direction. The activity detection model is trained and tested with consistent sensor data.

Algorithms. The obtained results are true for all considered algorithms. Figure 4a shows the experimental results for all coordinate systems split into algorithm, i.e. IBk, J48, JRip, and NaiveBayes. For each algorithm the highest detection accuracies are obtained when using the *UCS*. Also, the standard deviation is lowest for the *UCS*.

Sensors. A common approach to increase the activity detection accuracy is the usage of additional sensors. To verify whether this can be confirmed for the *focus on the user* approach we selected two sensor sets: "accelerometer" and "accelerometer + gyroscope". Figure 4a shows the experimental results split into sensor sets. We obtain higher detection accuracies using the sensor set "accelerometer + gyroscope" compared to "accelerometer". For both sensor sets the highest detection accuracy is obtained when using the *UCS*. The experimental results split into coordinate system, algorithm, and sensor set are given in Table 2. We obtain the highest detection accuracies when using the *UCS* (filled cells).

Table 2. Experimental results split into coordinate system, algorithm, and sensor set. The highest detection accuracies are obtained when using the *UCS* (filled cells). Detection accuracies are given in percent (%).

	DCS	*WCS*	*UCS*
IBk			
accelerometer	65.8	81.9	84.4
accelerometer + gyroscope	72.3	83.7	86.8
J48			
accelerometer	62.9	78.5	83.8
accelerometer + gyroscope	66.2	80.4	84.8
JRip			
accelerometer	52.2	77.6	82.7
accelerometer + gyroscope	57.2	79.8	84.0
NaiveBayes			
accelerometer	69.5	80.3	86.1
accelerometer + gyroscope	77.0	82.2	86.8

Activities. In the experimental setup we considered five activities. We evaluate the *focus on the user* approach for each activity. The comparisons are made on the F-Measure. Figure 4c shows the experimental results split into activity, i.e. standing, walking, running, ascending stairs, and descending stairs. For all activities we obtain the highest detection rates when using the *focus on the user* approach, i.e. the *UCS*. Also, the higher detection rates come along with lower standard deviations.

The experimental results show a high detection rate for activity standing. The activity standing is the only static activity within the activity set. Thus, the detection rates are high. Also, we obtain high detection rates for the activity running. Surprisingly, the *DCS* performs well, too. Due to the device-orientation-problem and the cardinal-direction-problem a lower detection rate was expected. However, running is the only highly dynamic activity within the dataset. Thus, the sensor data are unique and enable high detection rates. The evaluation results for activity walking confirm the advantages of the *UCS*. While the *DCS* and *WCS* suffer from the device-orientation-problem and the cardinal-direction-problem, we achieve an F-Measure for activity walking of over 85% considering all eight device orientations and four cardinal directions. For ascending/descending stairs incorrect detections occurred. Ascending and descending stairs were incorrectly detected as walking. This might be due to the limited amount of selected features. However, even though the detection rates are low we obtain the best detection rates by using the *focus on the user* approach.

Sensor Positions. Shoaib et al. showed that the sensor position affects the activity detection results [14]. Thus, we evaluate the *focus on the user*

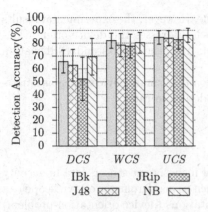

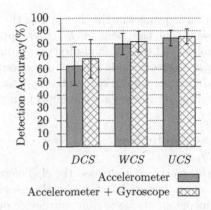

(a) Detection accuracy split into algorithm, i.e. IBk, J48, JRip, and NaiveBayes (NB).

(b) Detection accuracy split into sensor set, i.e. "accelerometer" and "accelerometer + gyroscope".

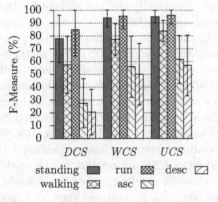

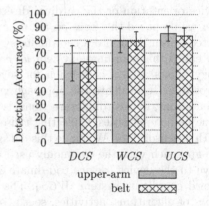

(c) F-Measure split into activity, i.e. standing, walking, running, ascending stairs (asc), and descending stairs (desc).

(d) Detection Accuracy split into sensor position, i.e. upper-arm and belt.

Fig. 4. Detection accuracy for *DCS*, *WCS*, and *UCS*. We obtain the highest detection accuracies by *focusing on the user*, i.e. using the *UCS*. Also, the higher detection rates come along with lower standard deviations.

approach for different sensor positions. The comparisons are made on the detection accuracy. Figure 4d shows the experimental results split into sensor position, i.e. upper-arm and belt. The detection accuracies differ for each position, even though the difference is minor for *WCS* and *UCS*. We obtain for each sensor position the highest detection rates when *focusing on the user*.

The detailed evaluation results are less high compared to other works which consider just one device orientation. We believe this is due to the variety in activity conduction. The participants conducted each activity eight times (once per device orientation). Even though we included breaks during the measurements, motion sequences might change over the time. However, the experimental results showed that the *focus on the user* approach addresses the device-orientation-problem and the cardinal-direction-problem. Also, the lower standard deviation shows a more reliable activity detection.

In future, we will extend the approach to other smart devices such as smart-watches and investigate the impact on the detection rates.

6   Conclusion

In this work, we addressed the challenges of inconsistent sensor data in activity detection. Sensor data for several sensors such as accelerometer or gyroscope can be inconsistent due to different device orientations (device-orientation-problem) or activities head off in different directions of the compass (cardinal-direction-problem). Hence, for a pre-generated activity detection model it is challenging to match (inconsistent) sensor data to the activities. Since regardless of the device orientation or the cardinal direction the activity did not change for the user we proposed the *focus on the user* approach. To *focus on the user* we converted sensor data into a coordinate system that is defined relative to the user. We called this coordinate system *user coordinate system* (*UCS*). The methodology allows a data conversion for several sensors such as accelerometer and gyroscope. To evaluate the approach we collected sensor data for eight device orientations, four cardinal directions, two sensor positions on the body, and five basic human activities. Collecting these data from nine participants resulted in 120 h of sensor data. We made this dataset available to the public. We compared the approach with the commonly used coordinate systems that are defined relative to the device (device coordinate system, *DCS*) and relative to the world (world coordinate system, *WCS*). The evaluation results detailed for different types of algorithms, activities, sensor sets, and sensor positions show in every case increased detection rates when *focusing on the user*, i.e. using the *UCS*. Compared to using the *DCS* activity detection rates increased by up to 21.7%, compared to using the *WCS* the activity detection rates increased by up to 4.7%. Also, the higher detection rates come along with a lower standard deviation what shows a more reliable detection. The evaluation results show that the *focus on the user* approach addresses the challenges of inconsistent sensor data.

Acknowledgments. This work has been [co-]funded by the Social Link Project within the Loewe Program of Excellence in Research, Hesse, Germany.

References

1. Weka 3 - Data Mining with Open Source Machine Learning Software in Java (2016). http://www.cs.waikato.ac.nz/ml/weka/index.html
2. Ali, A.S., Georgy, J., Bruce Wright, D.: Estimation of heading misalignment between a pedestrian and a wearable device. In: International Conference on Localization and GNSS (ICL-GNSS), pp. 1–6, June 2014

3. Borazio, M., Van Laerhoven, K.: Using time use with mobile sensor data: a road to practical mobile activity recognition? In: International Conference on Mobile and Ubiquitous Multimedia, pp. 1–10. ACM, Luleå (2013)
4. Dernbach, S., Das, B., Krishnan, N.C., Thomas, B., Cook, D.: Simple and complex activity recognition through smart phones. In: Intelligent Environments (IE), pp. 214–221, June 2012
5. Henpraserttae, A., Thiemjarus, S., Marukatat, S.: Accurate activity recognition using a mobile phone regardless of device orientation and location. In: International Conference on Body Sensor Networks (BSN), pp. 41–46, May 2011
6. Ichikawa, F., Chipchase, J., Grignani, R.: Where's the phone? A study of mobile phone location in public spaces. In: Mobile Technology, Applications and Systems, pp. 1–8. IEEE (2005)
7. Kunze, K., Lukowicz, P., Partridge, K., Begole, B.: Which way am I facing: inferring horizontal device orientation from an accelerometer signal. In: International Symposium on Wearable Computers (ISWC), pp. 149–150. IEEE, Linz, September 2009
8. Kusber, R., David, K., Klein, B.N.: A novel future internet smart grid application for energy management in offices. In: Future Network and Mobile Summit (FutureNetworkSummit), pp. 1–10, July 2013
9. Kusber, R., Memon, A.Q., Kroll, D., David, K.: Direction detection of users independent of smartphone orientations. In: Vehicular Technology Conference (VTC Fall), pp. 1–6. IEEE, September 2015
10. Lau, S.L.: Comparison of orientation-independent-based-independent-based movement recognition system using classification algorithms. In: IEEE Symposium on Wireless Technology and Applications (ISWTA), pp. 322–326, September 2013
11. Lau, S.L., Konig, I., David, K., Parandian, B., Carius-Dussel, C., Schultz, M.: Supporting patient monitoring using activity recognition with a smartphone. In: International Symposium on Wireless Communication Systems (ISWCS), pp. 810–814 (2010)
12. Mizell, D.: Using gravity to estimate accelerometer orientation. In: International Symposium on Wearable Computers (ISWC), p. 252. IEEE (2003)
13. Scholl, P., van Laerhoven, K.: A feasibility study of wrist-worn accelerometer based detection of smoking habits. In: Innovative Mobile and Internet Services in Ubiquitous Computing (IMIS), pp. 886–891, July 2012
14. Shoaib, M., Bosch, S., Incel, O., Scholten, H., Havinga, P.: A survey of online activity recognition using mobile phones. Sensors 15(1), 2059–2085 (2015)
15. Shoaib, M., Scholten, H., Havinga, P.: Towards physical activity recognition using smartphone sensors. In: IEEE Conference on Ubiquitous Intelligence and Computing and Conference on Autonomic and Trusted Computing (UIC/ATC), pp. 80–87, December 2013
16. Thiemjarus, S.: A device-orientation independent method for activity recognition. In: Body Sensor Networks (BSN), pp. 19–23. IEEE, June 2010
17. Ustev, Y.E., Durmaz Incel, O., Ersoy, C.: User, device and orientation independent human activity recognition on mobile phones: challenges and a proposal. In: Pervasive and Ubiquitous Computing Adjunct Publication, pp. 1427–1436. ACM (2013)
18. Yang, J.: Toward physical activity diary: motion recognition using simple acceleration features with mobile phones. In: Proceedings of 1st International Workshop on Interactive Multimedia for Consumer Electronics. ACM, Beijing (2009)

Specific Topics: Context in the Explanation and Evaluation of Human Reasoning

Contextual Reasoning in Human Cognition and the Implications for Artificial Intelligence Systems

Debra L. Hollister[1]([⊠]), Avelino Gonzalez[2], and James Hollister[2]

[1] Psychological Sciences, Valencia College- Lake Nona Campus,
Orlando, FL, USA
dhollister@valenciacollege.edu
[2] Computer Science Department, University of Central Florida,
Orlando, FL, USA
Avelino.Gonzalez@ucf.edu, JHollister@isl.ucf.edu

Abstract. It has been widely known that reasoning with and about context is an essential aspect of human cognition, permeating language, memory, and reasoning capabilities. This integral process is developed over a lifetime through experiential learning. Given that one goal of artificial intelligence has been to create human-like intelligence in a machine, it is essential to include such contextual considerations in system design and implementation. This paper extends the discussion about contextual reasoning in humans and how modeling it in a computer program can help to get closer to the ultimate intelligent machine.

Keywords: Contextual reasoning · Reasoning with and about context

1 Introduction

It has long been accepted that context plays a critical role in human cognition (see Parker et al. [8] for an extensive discussion of this). The idea of contextual intelligence has been explored and accepted since Sternberg developed his Triarchic Theory of Intelligence and included contextual intelligence as a third component in his theory [1, 2]. Contextual intelligence is often considered one of the most important components in the puzzle to resolve difficulties in everyday interactions with the current environment. This resolution of problems is accomplished through learned associations and ideas in everyday routines that accomplish a desired result. Brezillon [40] equates practical reasoning with contextual reasoning when discussing his Contextual Graphs (CxG). Therefore, we here equate contextual and practical reasoning based on Brezillon's work.

We strongly believe that to create systems that have the full range of human-like intelligence requires imbuing them with the ability to process context – giving the system an idea of when and where the information was previously encountered so that a solution might be found using the situational context. In light of this, this paper seeks to continue and extend the discussion about the many aspects of contextual processing

© Springer International Publishing AG 2017
P. Brézillon et al. (Eds.): CONTEXT 2017, LNAI 10257, pp. 599–608, 2017.
DOI: 10.1007/978-3-319-57837-8_48

in human cognition, how this cognitive ability (or set of cognitive abilities) is developed in humans, and offer insights into what such a system would resemble after being translated into a computing machine.

2 Context in Human Cognition

The ability to analyze the context of a situation and rank the different stimuli is absolutely essential to the ability of the human brain to act and react while embedded in the physical world. Whether we are speaking, encoding, recalling a memory, or using reasoning capabilities, contextual processing plays a vital role in human cognition [3]. It has been shown that without the use of context, it becomes much more problematic to recall specific information regarding an incident [4].

2.1 Context and Language

It is widely accepted that humans utilize contextual processing in linguistic comprehension, whether written or spoken [5]. In order to better define this goal, we take the view that language activates representations within the mind that pertain to definitions and connotations of the words and/or sounds used, and then processing continues. Simply put – the more time one spends recalling and reminiscing about an event, the more likely one is to recall the large as well as small details of that event [6, 7]. We discuss here how individuals mentally process and determine the appropriate context for a situation, and how irrelevant information is kept from activation depending on the context.

One of the most widely accepted models of linguistic processing and representation activation is the semantic network, aka the spreading activation model, proposed by Meyer and Schvaneveldt (1971). As discussed in a previous paper [8], context familiarity is important to process information and this works well in natural language generation (NLG) by humans. NLG is found useful in natural language understanding, response generation, text summarization and machine translation to name only a few applications [9].

Another cognitive theory of linguistic contextual processing is the Attenuation Model outlined by Treisman [36]. This model states that there are different attention channels going into a selective filter in the brain. Being able to distinguish and filter these learned sounds may play a part in the recognition and meaning of language [10].

Treisman's model underscores the idea that we use context in language to highlight relevant information to make the most sense possible out of the myriad of phrases we hear throughout the day [8]. If we were unable to parse and ignore the unnecessary information, there would be an information overload and a loss of understanding in language processing.

Homophones – words that have multiple meanings for the same word sound present a different problem. For example, the car brakes at a stop sign, but one breaks an egg for an omelet for breakfast. There is also a type of dancing called break dancing. Most individuals are able to understand the meaning of a sentence because of the context of the surrounding words. The Treisman model suggests how related contextual information is activated and retrieved in the brain and how phonologically irrelevant information is filtered out. However, it does not seem to explain how contextually irrelevant information is filtered out in a situation such as a homophone, where there would be no phonological cue. Hearing such a word would seemingly highlight two representations simultaneously, resulting in confusion as to which meaning is most appropriate.

In the break vs. brake example, all meanings of the words would be activated until the relevant contextual information was more clearly delineated. For truly successful real time comprehension to occur, it is necessary to keep this extraneous information from affecting the other processes at work. This is accomplished by developing a suppression mechanism as we learn to successfully order schemata. To borrow terminology from Treisman [36], this mechanism would increase the activation threshold for the inappropriate homophone, thus decreasing the likelihood of the activation of its mental representation [11]. This suppression mechanism plays a pivotal role in appropriate real time contextual understanding in human linguistics. Such a context-driven suppression mechanism can play an important role in NLG/NLP. A difficult problem faced by an AI system is that of inefficient contextual information suppression resulting in a myriad of issues [12]. Attending to everything we hear with equal weight would present an impossibly large amount of information to sort through, thus highlighting the need for a contextual parsing system in the brain.

3   Context and Memory

Schemata are cognitive frameworks that help us to retain knowledge about a specific aspect of our worlds [13, 14]. The human memory system is arranged in such a manner as to facilitate the use of contextual processing to augment encoding, storage and retrieval. These greatly affect cognitive behaviors, including perception, attention, learning, and cognition. The associations that we form using context will guide how we remember information and circumstances that will trigger its retrieval.

State dependent memory occurs when we encode new information in a specific context in which it was presented [15]. Because we encode and store not only the information, but also the context in which we learned it, replicating that context when it is time for recall will greatly increase accuracy. The mood congruence during recall also amplifies the state we are in at the time of learning and recalling, according to Drace et al. [16] and explains why we tend to recall pleasant thoughts and memories when we are in a good mood and negative thoughts and memories when our mood is more negative.

Learning is a change in behavior (indirectly linked to context) and can be assimilated and built upon when new information is acquired. The question then becomes how and when these schemata are updated. Long-term memories can be reactivated and then modified and reestablished [17]. This occurs because of the context stored and made available in memory. Although not generally related to research on computational context, extensive work in Case-based and Memory-based Reasoning have used this approach.

In a study involving young children, Hubach et al. [17] found that long term memories were rarely activated when the children were in a familiar setting. However, when the children were in less familiar contexts, the context did trigger the reactivation of the older memories. This indicates that the children were adding new information to their schemata and learning the contextual information for a new situation [17].

4 Reasoning with and About Context

Most problem solving scenarios involve individuals drawing on previous knowledge to help with problem solving. Human reasoning is largely top down, meaning it draws from previous contexts. This is why the elders in a culture are considered to be the wisest individuals; they have the most complex schemata to use in problem solving tasks because they have more experiences/contexts from which to draw. According to Bateson, "older adults are understanding who they are in a newly emerging stage of life and discovering the wisdom they have to offer" [18]. When Lockenhoff et al., did a survey of 26 nations, he found that the majority of surveyed people in those nations believed that wisdom was a characteristic of the elderly [19].

The use of contextual facilitation in learning is highlighted in mathematics education, where there is a view that mathematics is much easier to understand if, instead of being presented in an abstract manner, it is presented in a contextualized format [20]. For example, a student who is having difficulty understanding how to find the area of a surface may be able to understand the formula more easily if it is presented as simply trying to figure out how much paint would be needed to paint a wall. Because the student would have a familiar situation in which to process the information, he/she could focus on the reorganization of the mathematic schemata as facilitated by a previously constructed situational schema. This view coordinates well with the previous assertion that the assimilation of information into long-term memory is affected by context.

Another study involving formal decision making was done by Pennycook and Thompson [21]. Subjects were asked to place fictional individuals in one of two categories after being given base rates for the probability of an individual belonging to a group and a personality profile that was either consistent or at odds with the base rate. The profiles might indicate that the individual was a doctor or a nurse, and the test subjects were asked to specify whether the person was a male or female and whether they lived in apartments or houses. The subjects were much more likely to draw upon the personality profile to make their decision, even when it called for the subject to disregard very strong base rate probability [21]. The subjects made their decisions on these fictional people based on prior knowledge (context) of known people in these positions.

This study provides support for context-driven reasoning over other types of information processing among humans. Statistical modeling can move reasoning, but only so far. We believe that but for more successful navigation within the real world, contextual weighting and real-life experience must be incorporated, as was shown by Pennycook and Thompson [21].

We reiterate here what many previous studies (the literature presented above) have shown: that use of contextual processing is invaluable to human reasoning, indeed inseparable from it. Contexts change, just as people do. The ability to learn and synthesize past experiences and knowledge is essential to the human way of thinking. The importance of involving the synthesis of contextual processing in AI systems seems all the more evident.

5 Development of Human Contextual Reasoning Capability

Human growth and development occur within a setting – that is the context of development. The context includes the family, community, state, culture, and nationality. Each of these settings is influenced by economics, social and historical factors [22, 23]. These researchers found, that this experiential learning view of context does contribute to how humans obtain their contextual processing abilities.

According to Baltes [21] and Kunzmann [24], contexts can be age-graded influences; history-graded influences; or individualized life events that have influenced development for that person. For example, age-graded influences are experienced by many within a similar age range, such as graduation or retirement. History-graded influences are similar to people in the same age bracket because they remember events such as the Great Depression of 1929 or WWII. The highly individualized events influence how one person may be affected by their personal circumstances. Development may be influenced by unusual life situations such as winning the lottery or even the effects of the Zika virus on developing babies [25].

Contextual learning begins at infancy [13, 26, 27]. Infants learn to navigate ambiguous situations by referring to their caregivers. This socio-cultural context in learning was illustrated in a visual cliff study, which presents an infant with a threateningly deep chasm to cross, but that is safely covered by thick clear plastic. The infant is unable to determine if it is safe to cross based on visual cues. However, based on the encouraging affectual displays of his/her mother, the majority of the infants crossed the deep chasm [28].

The power of context learning is evident from the above experiments, and contextual development begins as the child starts to explore his/her world. Contextual learning helps to gather information about the world and how we interact with it. There is also evidence that indicates that recalling a memory for an event reactivates the same brain areas that that became excited during the event itself [29].

Piaget [13, 30] began conceptualizing a goal of learning autonomy as a means of developing children to be able to think for themselves and not have to be told what to do. This is accomplished, according to Piaget and Vygotsky [27], through the exchange of points of view and scaffolding of information and schemata [31, 32].

All information can be affected by the socio-cultural context of culture, economics and gender. Culture affects the behavior of individual members through the context of knowledge that is reinforced in the culture by the other members of the group [33]. Instead of the explicit mimicry of more experienced social agents, children would begin to be able to understand and apply the guidance they receive to decide for themselves what would be appropriate in a given circumstance [13, 27].

For example, once the child learned a particular way of thinking and interacting with the world as a social agent, then she would develop mental schemata, or blueprints, for future decisions. Then, as the child began to experience the world for herself, she could be confronted by discrepancies between these schemata and the events she perceives, and decides on a course of action. New contextual reasoning strategies would develop as a result of discrepancies encountered in the world. The child learns to model and understand contextual cues from the social environment. This behavioral filter provides for more behavioral regularity and maintains the performance of preferred behaviors because of the context association – cognitively and behaviorally [34, 35].

A cycle appears to develop between context and the environment that shapes internal preferences and the agentic action of the child. An agentic action in this case is defined as behavior that is performed with intentionality, forethought, self-reactiveness, and self-reflection [34]. Within these memories, there exist contextual information that assists in our decisions based on how issues and situations have proceeded in the past, allowing us to move forward.

Treisman's [36] dichotic listening project has implications for the application of contextual processing in computer systems. For example, a computer analysis of linguistic scans could greatly benefit from a system that processed the phonological properties of words such as tone, pitch, and timbre. If these properties were deemed to be inappropriate for the type of information it was receiving, then the computer could more quickly reject or ignore the extraneous information based on a preliminary filtering scan.

6 Implementations of Contextual Reasoning in AI Systems

The literature surveyed above points to the conclusion that contextual processing is a necessary and inextricable part of human cognition. This contextual processing is essential and permeates all aspects of life, including linguistic processing, memory encoding, storage and retrieval, thinking, and reasoning capabilities. With this understanding, we recognize that contextual processing is integral in the design of artificial intelligence systems in order to enable them to process information with human-like capabilities.

The AI literature is filled with reports of the implementation of context in AI systems. A full discussion cannot be done in the scope of this paper, but we focus on a few, well-known contextual paradigms that reflect, to a greater or lesser degree, on the cognitive context-based processes discussed above.

We begin with Context-based Reasoning, or CxBR [37, 38]. CxBR has been successfully used to represent tactical knowledge in simulated as well as physical agents. It decomposes the agents' behaviors into major and minor contexts. Each of these contexts contains behavioral information that is relevant to the context of the current situation. This applies the principles of relevancy and exclusion discussed above. CxBR uses environmental cues to adapt an agent being controlled to the situation with the appropriate knowledge. CxBR only concerns itself with a small set of rules by recognizing the current context. Additionally, each context contains environmental information that has to be true for that context to be in control of the agent.

As the situation evolves during a tactical event, another context may become more applicable than the currently active one based on environmental cues and the objectives of the mission. The CxBR system then transitions the control of the agent from the current context to one that better addresses the emerging situation. Within the CxBR model, all of the transitions between contexts are predefined in the model by its creator. CxBR has also been used for machine learning [39], which further addresses the applicability of context to teaching.

CxBR can be related back to Treisman's [36] Attenuation Model as the human/agent both observe the current situation and respond based upon what is currently being observed. In CxBR, as with the Treisman model, each situation is monitored for key factors that help determine when to transition into a new context. It is imperative that the most relevant information/knowledge to solve the problem be retained, while the extraneous information/knowledge be suppressed so that one becomes more competent at intuitively understanding contextual cues in the current situation.

Another contextual paradigm that addresses decision-making is that of Contextual Graphs, or CxG [38, 40]. By representing context at a progressively finer-grained level, the situation can be eventually identified clearly enough so that a decision may be made more efficiently. In Contextual graphs, this decision-making process is streamlined into simple questions and actions. This allows the system to figure out the situations and respond accordingly.

According to Vygotsky [27] and Piaget [13],children learn the schema of decision making through modeling of different behaviors and patterns that would be considered acceptable in a particular culture or context. Instead of the explicit mimicry of more experienced social agents, children would begin to understand and apply the guidance they receive to decide for themselves what would be appropriate in a given circumstance [13, 27]. For example, once the child learned a particular way of thinking and interacting with the world from a social agent view, then she would develop mental schemata, or contexts, much like the contextual graph model.

Turner's Context-Mediated Behaviors (CMB) [41] is somewhat similar to CxBR, but has some critical differences. In CxBR, the transitions between contexts are explicitly defined; however, in CMB, every context is reviewed and analyzed for each situation. In CMB, all contexts are checked to find the appropriate context to transition to. Additionally, CMB allows the merging of contexts when a context by itself cannot successfully be used to address the situation. CMB may use multiple concurrent contexts, all of which could have some element of validity in the complex situation faced by the agent.

Bandura [34] also recognized the similarity of contexts that are considered for Turner's model. In theory, Turner recognized that a variety of contexts must be considered when solving a newly-encountered problem. This cycle appears to develop between context and the environment, shaping internal preferences and the agentic action of the child. This agentic action is based on the context of situation and potential solution of future events based on experiences [34].

7   Conclusion

One of the most important elements in human growth and development is learning. As a child develops physically, emotionally and cognitively, context is an essential component of that learning. As the child gains more experience in the environment, she/he is often able to depend on the context of the situation to help make appropriate decisions.

According to Abowd et al. [42] it has generally been accepted that utilizing context in computing has been a neglected approach in the past in programming. Abowd et al. believes – as do we- that this remains true today. We have seen how understanding the complexity of context allows humans a multitude of behaviors, the ability to learn, and the ability to react and interact intelligently. Likewise, developers who are creating AI systems around the globe have concluded that context is an important component in computing that will allow computers to function as humanlike as possible in a context enriched environment.

References

1. Sternberg, R.J.: Beyond IQ: A Triarchic Theory of Human Intelligence. Cambridge University Press, Cambridge (1985)
2. Sternberg, R.J., Wagner, R.K., Williams, W.M., et al.: Testing common sense. Am. Psychol. **50**, 912–927 (1995)
3. Light, P.E., Butterworth, G.E.: Context and cognition: Ways of learning and knowing. Lawrence Erlbaum Associates, Inc., Mahwah (1992)
4. Smith, S.M., Glenberg, A., Bjork, R.A.: Environmental context and human memory. Mem. Cognit. **6**, 342–353 (1978)
5. Glucksberg, S., Kreuz, R.J., Rho, S.H.: Context can constrain lexical access: implications for models of language comprehension. J. Exp. Psychol. Learn. Mem. Cogn. **12**, 323–335 (1986)
6. Andre, T., Sola, J.: Imagery, verbatim and paraphrased questions and retention of meaningful sentences. J. Educ. Psychol. **68**, 661–669 (1976)
7. Baddeley, A.D.: Domains of recollection. Psychol. Rev. **89**, 708–729 (1982)
8. Parker, J.E., Hollister, D.L., Gonzalez, A.J., Brézillon, P., Parker, S.T.: Looking for a synergy between human and artificial cognition. In: Brézillon, P., Blackburn, P., Dapoigny, R. (eds.) CONTEXT 2013. LNCS (LNAI), vol. 8175, pp. 45–58. Springer, Heidelberg (2013). doi:10.1007/978-3-642-40972-1_4
9. Tang, J., Yang, Y., Carton, S., et al.: Context-Aware Natural Language Generation with Recurrent Neural Networks. arXiv e-prints (2016)
10. Bowers, J.S., Mattys, S.L., Gage, S.H.: Preserved implicit knowledge of a forgotten childhood language. Psychol. Sci. **20**, 1064–1069 (2009)
11. Gernsbacher, M.A.: Less skilled readers have less efficient suppression mechanisms. Psychol. Sci. **4**, 294–298 (1993)
12. Dennett, D.C.: Cognitive wheels: the frame problem of AI. Lang. Thought **3**, 217 (2005)
13. Piaget, J.: The development of thought: equilibration of cognitive structures (Trans A. Rosin). Viking, Greenwood (1977)
14. Wyer, R.S., Srull, T.K.: Handbook of Social Cognition: Applications. Psychology Press, Abingdon (1994)

15. Godden, D.R., Baddeley, A.D.: Context-dependent memory in two natural environments: on land and underwater. Br. J. Psychol. **66**, 325–331 (1975)
16. Drace, S., Ric, F., Desrichard, O.: Affective biases in likelihood perception: a possible role of experimental demand in mood congruence effects. Revue internationale de psychologie sociale **23**, 93–110 (2010)
17. Hupbach, A., Gomez, R., Nadel, L.: Episodic memory updating: the role of context familiarity. Psychon. Bull. Rev. **18**, 787–797 (2011)
18. Bateson, M.C.: Composing a Further Life: The Age of Active Wisdom. Knopf Doubleday Publishing Group, New York City (2011)
19. Löckenhoff, C.E., De Fruyt, F., Terracciano, A., et al.: Perceptions of aging across 26 cultures and their culture-level associates. Psychol. Aging **24**, 941–954 (2009)
20. Van Den Heuvel-Panhuizen, M.: The role of contexts in assessment problems in mathematics. Learn. Math. **25**, 2–23 (2005)
21. Pennycook, G., Thompson, V.A.: Base-rate neglect. Cognitive Illusions Intriguing Phenomena in Judgement Thinking and Memory, pp. 44–61 (2016)
22. Bronfenbrenner, U., Morris, P.A.: The bioecological model of human development. Handbook Child Psychology, pp. 37–43 (2006)
23. Shiraev, E.B., Levy, D.: Cross-Cultural Psychology: Critical Thinking And Contemporary Applications, vol. 3. Pearson Education, Upper Saddle River (2008)
24. Baltes, P.B., Kunzmann, U.: Wisdom. Psychologist **16**, 131–133 (2003)
25. CDC, ZIKA and pregnancy, 18 April 2016. http://www.cdc.gov/zika/pregnancy/question-answers.html
26. Abravanel, E., Ferguson, S.A.: Observational learning and the use of retrieval information during the second and third years. J. Genet. Psychol. **159**, 455–476 (1998)
27. Vygotsky, L.S., Cole, M.: Mind in Society. Harvard University Press, Cambridge (1978)
28. Sorce, J.F., Emde, R.N., Campos, J.J., et al.: Maternal emotional signaling: its effect on the visual cliff behavior of 1-year-olds. Dev. Psychol. **21**, 195 (1985)
29. Danker, J.F., Anderson, J.R.: The ghosts of brain states past: remembering reactivates the brain regions engaged during encoding. Psychol. Bull. **136**, 87–102 (2010)
30. Piaget, J.: The Moral Judgment of the Child. Routledge & Kegan, Abingdon (1932)
31. Bernier, A., Carlson, S.M., Whipple, N.: From external regulation to self-regulation: early parenting precursors of young children's executive functioning. Child Dev. **81**, 326–339 (2010)
32. Hammond, S., Müller, U., Ji, C., et al.: The effects of parental scaffolding on preschoolers' executive function. Dev. Psychol. **48**, 271–281 (2012)
33. Rothbaum, F., Trommsdorff, G.: Do roots and wings complement or oppose one another? The socialization of relatedness and autonomy in cultural context, pp. 461–489 (2007)
34. Bandura, A.: Social cognitive theory: an agentic perspective. Ann. Rev. Psychol. **52**, 1–26 (2001)
35. Raush, H.L., Barry, W.A., Hertel, R.K., et al.: Communication conflict and marriage. Jossey-Bass, San Francisco (1974)
36. Treisman, A.M.: Contextual cues in selective listening. Q. J. Exp. Psychol. **12**, 242–248 (1960)
37. Gonzalez, A.J., Stensrud, B.S., Barrett, G.: Formalizing context-based reasoning: a modeling paradigm for representing tactical human behavior. Int. J. Intell. Syst. **23**, 822–847 (2008)
38. Hollister, J., Parker, S.T., Gonzalez, A.J., DeMara, R.: An extended turing test: a context based approach designed to educate youth in computing. In: Brézillon, P., Blackburn, P., Dapoigny, R. (eds.) CONTEXT 2013. LNCS (LNAI), vol. 8175, pp. 213–221. Springer, Heidelberg (2013). doi:10.1007/978-3-642-40972-1_16

39. Fernlund, H.K., Gonzalez, A.J., Georgiopoulos, M., et al.: Learning tactical human behavior through observation of human performance. IEEE Trans. Syst. Man Cybern. Part B (Cybernetics) **36**, 128–140 (2006)

40. Brézillon, P.: Representation of procedures and practices in contextual graphs. Knowl. Eng. Rev. **18**, 147–174 (2003)

41. Turner, R.M.: Context-mediated behavior for AI applications. In: Mira, J., Pobil, A.P., Ali, M. (eds.) IEA/AIE 1998. LNCS, vol. 1415, pp. 538–545. Springer, Heidelberg (1998). doi:10.1007/3-540-64582-9_785

42. Abowd, G.D., Dey, A.K., Brown, P.J., Davies, N., Smith, M., Steggles, P.: Towards a better understanding of context and context-awareness. In: Gellersen, H.-W. (ed.) HUC 1999. LNCS, vol. 1707, pp. 304–307. Springer, Heidelberg (1999). doi:10.1007/3-540-48157-5_29

Investigating the Causal Link Between Context Triggers and Context: An Adaptive Approach

Thanh Nyan[✉]

University of Manchester, Manchester, UK
t.nyan@manchester.ac.uk

Abstract. This paper focuses on the relation between certain linguistic elements ('context triggers') and the set of assumptions they provide access to, which is necessary to the interpretation of their host utterances. The question it seeks to address is how to go about investigating that relation, which it takes to be causal, but to involve elements pertaining to two levels of description that do not appear to interface, namely, the linguistic level and that of underlying processes and mental representations. Such question can be divided into two sub-questions: one about what might be a suitable approach, the other, about the type of trigger that provides an optimal point of departure. In terms of approach I favor an adaptive one, as it contains the rationale for linking those two levels, and provides the mediating structures and systems to implement that linkage. With regard to the optimal types of trigger, I argue that they are to be found at the discourse level. The ones I will be discussing have contents that bear a strong resemblance to presumed lower-level analogues.

Keywords: Context trigger · Constructed context · Context construction process · Adaptive approach · Discourse constraints · Discourse dynamism

1 Introduction

'Context triggers', as used in this paper, refer to linguistic elements which give rise to a set of assumptions[1] necessary to arrive at an interpretation of their host utterances at the discourse (or text) level. This set of assumptions, which I call 'constructed context' ($context_c$) is the outcome of the process those triggers get under way.

Context studies [12, 14] – as is well known – encompass a wide range of views regarding most (key) issues. One of the very few over which there appears to be consensus –albeit a tacit one – concerns the relation between context triggers[2] and evoked contexts (both in the sense of $context_c$, and context as the source of knowledge being tapped, or $context_k$). This relation is taken to be of a 'causal' nature.

---

[1] The assumption is that within the same linguistic community, with access to the same networks, the connection between triggers and context can be expected to be stable.

[2] Or 'contextual cues' in Gumperz's [15] and Levinson's [20] terminology.

© Springer International Publishing AG 2017
P. Brézillon et al. (Eds.): CONTEXT 2017, LNAI 10257, pp. 609–616, 2017.
DOI: 10.1007/978-3-319-57837-8_49

This paper also takes a causal view of this relation.[3] The way it construes the process under consideration is roughly as follows: this process would access a knowledge source (context$_k$) and import the relevant bits into working memory, where context$_c$ is assembled. (Note that context$_c$ can conceivably draw upon more than one context$_c$).[4]

In terms of goal, it is concerned with the logistics involved in investigating this causal link, at least in those[5] cases that readily lend themselves to such undertaking. More specifically, this amounts to asking (a) what kind of approach is suitable for investigating the process linking trigger and context$_k$, and (b) what kind of trigger constitutes the optimal point of departure for that process, given the nature of the approach.

The decision to examine a link between entities pertaining to both the linguistic and the underlying level (i.e., context triggers and context$_k$) requires an approach which situates both on the same continuum, provides the rationale for the linkage and allows for mediating structures and systems that can implement it. These various criteria appear to be met by an adaptive perspective.

2 Approach and Optimal Type of Trigger

2.1 Adaptive Assumptions

The adaptive perspective I am relying on is the neo-Darwinian theory of evolution,[6] which arises from the Evolutionary Synthesis of the 1930s and 1940s [13, 21], and reconciles Darwin's theory of evolution with facts of genetics. Listed below, are some key assumptions relevant to our purposes:

(a) Language and the brain have co-evolved, with language as the latecomer in the evolutionary process [9]
(b) Evolution tends to recycle existing solutions when faced with the same type of problems [7]
(c) The language system is rooted in our neurobiology and largely depends for its functioning on structures that are already in place and on pre-existing systems – such as the motor, perceptual, action selection, the concept formation one – [6, 8, 11] as well as on their outputs.

What these assumptions entail for the issue at hand is that the link between context$_k$ and the trigger can be construed in terms of an element pertaining to a non-linguistic

---

[3] This question is not about implementation. It takes for granted that there is a pathway between trigger and context, which the triggering process uses, and which becomes established over time [19].

[4] Arising from Ducrot [10] is the idea that the argumentative act and certain particles (e.g., 'au moins' (at least) are conjointly responsible for the same instance of context construction.

[5] Such cases involve linguistic, rather than non-linguistic, triggers, with those triggers contributing to the discourse (or text level).

[6] Also known as the 'synthetic theory'. For further details on this perspective, see Nyan [22].

system making its way into linguistic concepts. Given evolution's recycling tendency, such co-option by the language system of pre-existing solutions would become possible if language is faced with problems of the kind that prompted those solutions to be devised in the first place. These pre-existing solutions can take the form of structures, processing strategies and systems or the outcomes thereof.

2.2 Optimal Type of Trigger

Given the above approach, the optimal type of trigger would be one that provides coding[7] for a content that has a lower-level analogue, or, rather, can be paired with one on grounds of structural and functional similarity.[8] Such contents, can more readily be found at the discourse (or text) level. The ones I will be focusing on take the form of discourse constraints, or constraints that help to promote 'discourse dynamism'.

The remainder of this paper is divided into two sections. Section 3 explains the rationale for construing the functional aspect of the process as just sketched out. It also sets out the grounds for thinking that (linguistic) triggers contributing to context construction at the discourse level constitute an optimal point of departure. Finally, Sect. 4 aims to show in what way the investigation of the causal link in question is facilitated by taking the type of trigger under examination as point of departure in conjunction with an adaptive perspective.

3 Rationale for the Above Construal of the Triggering Process

As a quick reminder, the triggering process, as construed above, is expected to access the knowledge source (context$_k$), assumed to be an open-ended entity, select the relevant portion of knowledge, which, in working memory, serves to construct a bound entity (context$_c$).[9] This constructed context can then be used by the interpretive process.

Support for the idea that knowledge selection occurs can be found in experimental evidence arising (inter alia) from Barsalou's work.[10] According to Barsalou [4], alongside shared concepts stored in long-term memory, which are fairly stable within and across individuals, there are variable concepts (which he calls 'knowledge'). These represent 'different subsets of features from people's knowledge of a category', which subsets are retrieved by the same individual in different situations, or by different individuals in a given situation [4]. Thus, for the concept of piano [4, 5], one would not have in working memory an extended set of features as in long-term memory, but only

---

[7] This means they have to be linguistic, rather than non-linguistic.

[8] In virtue of the complexity argument [13].

[9] If it is the case that we are dealing with 'assemblages' of cues [20] working together, then more than one source of knowledge would have been drawn upon to construct a given context.

[10] See also Barsalou [3] and Kahneman and Miller [18].

a subset, one relevant to the situation at hand: if this situation is a moving situation, the subset would only include information about the weight and the size of pianos.

3.1 Why Privilege Triggers that Contribute[11] to the Discourse Level as Points of Departure?

As mentioned earlier, a preliminary answer is that these triggers provide coding for contents that can be paired with lower-level analogues. What makes those contents amenable to such pairing lies in the structural and/or functional similarity they show to the presumed analogues. Such contents, as was also mentioned, take the form of constraints that support 'discourse dynamism'. Before explaining in what way the fact that these constraints are coded is important for the type of investigation under scrutiny, let us clarify what is meant by 'discourse dynamism'.

3.1.1 Discourse Dynamism

Discourse dynamism may be defined as this property of discourse (or text) that determines the way in which the inferential gap between utterances within a given discourse may be bridged. Alternatively, one can view it as utterances' discursive potential, which potential may or may not be activated. (1) is an illustration of how such potential manifests itself:

(1) Ludwig is in the park.

As an isolated utterance its main communicative content concerns the truthfulness of the representation its propositional content gives of a state of affairs in the world. In other words, the emphasis is on the utterance's word-to-world direction of fit (to use Searle's terminology [23]).

By contrast, as an utterance that constitutes a fragment of discourse, (1) has a different communicative content. Whether its propositional content corresponds to a state of affairs in the world is no longer at issue: the words-to-world direction of fit is taken for granted. What matters at the discourse level is how the utterance links up with the upcoming utterance and the prior co-text (or the context of utterance). Supposing that (1), as a fragment of discourse, serves to convey an argument in support of a conclusion (e.g., to the effect that you can find Ludwig there). If the argument is based on the represented state of affairs, it stands to reason that the speaker takes for granted that the state of affairs is the case. What is at issue is no longer whether the state of affairs actually exists, but whether its existence constitutes a valid reason for reaching the intended conclusion.

---

[11] 'Contribute' is to be preferred to 'occur' as a trigger that occurs at the utterance level and contributes to context construction at that level may also have an impact at the discourse level, in the sense of helping along with 'discourse dynamism' (of which, more below). An example would be an adjective such as 'penniless', which contributes a set of defining features at the utterance level, but gives rise to stances and actions associated with poverty, both on the part of the person thus described and those who respond to his situation.

To account for the discourse potential of utterances such as (1) (i.e. the fact that they can be used as arguments), Ducrot [10] postulates an argumentative component in the structure of utterance meaning.[12] Such component when activated gives rise to constraints on what precedes and what follows.[13] Examples of constraints on continuation that are linked to context triggers are provided by (2) and (3). These constraints manifest themselves by imposing preferred continuations in neutral situations. (a) and (b) are possible continuations for both (2) and (3), but which of them constitutes the preferred option is different in (2) and in (3). The question mark against continuations serves to flag up their non-preferred status.

(2) They have an austere life style.
  (a) You don't want to go and stay with them.
  (b) ? You will find it a nice change, if you go and stay with them.
(3) They have a simple life style.
  (a) ? You don't want to go and stay with them.
  (b) You will find it a nice change, if you go and stay with them.

The constraint that imposes (a) or (b) as the preferred continuation can be associated with the occurrence of a different trigger, 'austere' or 'simple'. Both adjectives, as used in (2) and (3), describe a life style characterised by an absence of luxury. What sets them apart is that the in-built judgement they include as part of their semantic meaning is negative in the case of 'austere' and positive, in that of 'simple'. This difference gives rise to a different constraint on continuation at the discourse level.

What emerges from the above discussion is this: the triggers that are readily amenable to investigation are those that promote discourse dynamism by means of discourse constraints.

Our next concern is to clarify the role such constraints have in facilitating the investigative process. This, I propose to do by discussing the implication of their being coded –in the next sub-section –and by showing –in Sect. 4 – how their resemblance to a presumed analogue can be used as a starting point for further investigation into the nature of the causal link under consideration.

3.1.2   In What Way Do Constraints of the Above Kind Make the Triggers Under Consideration More Amenable to Investigation?

What makes such triggers (or the process they get under way) more amenable to investigation is the fact that the constraints they contain are of the coded kind. This, from an adaptive perspective, presupposes that:

(a) the possibility exists for such constraints to be traced back to lower-level analogues associated with non-linguistic concepts/categories arising from other systems, for instance, in the form of linkages inherent in such categories;

---

[12] We are talking about utterance-type.

[13] Anscombre and Ducrot's argumentation theory (AT), not surprisingly defines utterance meaning primarily in terms of the constraints utterances (as elements of discourse) place on what constitutes an ideal context of utterance and preferred continuations [1, 2].

(b) there is a need at the linguistic level for solutions of the kind these lower-level linkages provide, a need whose level of frequency over time results in the emergence a dedicated process;

(c) there are mediating systems in place for such linkages to enter linguistic concepts.

In other words, the presence of coded constraints can be taken to be an indication that there may be a context$_k$ which is non-linguistic and can be accessed by a given trigger.

The next section takes up a trigger operating at the text level, and sets out to show in what way the investigation of the causal link between trigger and context is facilitated by using the type of trigger under examination as point of departure in conjunction with an adaptive perspective.

4   From Trigger to Context

The sequences listed below all include a trigger –in the form of an adjective denoting a property of an entity to which this property is attributed. This adjective, in turn, contains a constraint on continuation. Of the two possible continuations provided for each example, (a) is the preferred one.

(1) He is a conservative.
  (a) He is likely to be anti-immigration.
  (b) He is likely to be pro-immigration.
(2) He is a historian.
  (a) He will provide you with more background than you know what to do with.
  (b) Don't count on him to provide much background.
(3) This coat is made of cashmere.
  (a) It will keep you warm.
  (b) It will not be warm enough.
(4) John is wealthy.[14]
  (a) He can afford anything he fancies.
  (b) He can't exactly afford anything he fancies.

In all the above examples, the preferred continuation expresses a form of behaviour of the entity under consideration that arises from this entity possessing the property being singled out. In other words, the constraint involved links a specific aspect of the entity and what potential it has in terms of action or effect.

Viewed in this way the constraint bears a strong resemblance to the link found in what is known as the 'pragmatic mode'[15] of representation. Such mode, which involves representing an object under an aspect that highlights its action potential (i.e., what it can be used for), is, according to Jeannerod [16, 17], the way objects are represented in

---

[14] This example is based on Anscombre [2] well known 'Pierre est riche: il peut s'offrir n'importe quoi'. The idea in selecting it is to provide a different take on how it might be analysed.

[15] The semantic mode, by contrast, would list features that need not be related to the object's affordances.

motor intention, when they are goals for action:[16] '...when objects are goals for actions their visual attributes are represented in a specific way (the pragmatic mode) that is used for the selection of appropriate movements and distinct from other possible modalities of representation used for other aspects of object-oriented behaviour (one of them being the semantic mode).'

To return to our constraint, the link it resembles is that between the pragmatic representation of the object and its action potential as based on the aspect under which it is represented. To take example (6), to say of John that he is wealthy would constitute a pragmatic representation, one highlighting his action potential as based on the property denoted by 'wealthy'.

What emerges from this analysis is that the source of knowledge the above triggers tap into may well be a store of concepts involving a pragmatic mode of representation, and possibly arising from the action production system.

The question is: what functional similarity might there be between discourse dynamism (or the implementation thereof) and motor production that would account for the adoption of the pragmatic mode of representation of entity, which mode appears to be activated at the discourse, but not the utterance (or clause) level.

References

1. Anscombre, J.-C. (ed.): Théorie des topoï. Editions Kimé, Paris, Paris (1995)
2. Anscombre, J.-C.: De l'argumentation dans la langue à la théorie des Topoï. In: Anscombre, J.-C. (ed.) Théorie des Topoï, pp. 11–47. Editions Kimé, Paris (1995)
3. Barsalou, L.W.: The instability of graded structure: implications for the nature of concepts. In: Neisser, U. (ed.) Concepts Reconsidered: The Ecological and Intellectual Bases of Categorization, pp. 101–140. Cambridge University Press, New York (1987)
4. Barsalou, L.W.: Flexibility, structure and linguistic vagary in concepts: manifestations of a compositional system of perceptual symbols. In: Collins, A.F., Gathercole, S.E., Conway, M.A., Morris, P.E. (eds.) Theories of Memory, pp. 29–102. Lawrence Erlbaum Associates, Hillsdale, Hove (1993)
5. Barsalou, L.W.: Perceptual symbol systems. Behav. Brain Sci. **22**, 577–660 (1999)
6. Damasio, A.R.: Concepts in the brain. Mind Lang. **4**, 24–28 (1989)
7. Damasio, A.R.: Descartes' Error: Emotion, Reason and the Human Brain. Grosset/Putnam, New York (1994)
8. Damasio, A.R.: The somatic marker hypothesis and the possible function of the prefrontal cortex. Philos. Trans. R. Soc. Lond. B **351**, 1413–1420 (1996)
9. Deacon, T.W.: The Symbolic Species. Norton, New York (1997)
10. Ducrot, O.: Opérateurs argumentatifs et visée argumentative. Cahiers de Linguistique Française **5**, 7–36 (1983)
11. Edelman, G.M.: The Remembered Present. Basic Books, New York (1989)

---

[16] Jeannerod's model for action production include a motor intention or representation which is prior to action execution. This motor representation contains, among other things, a pragmatic representation of objects, when they are goals for the action being considered.

12. Fetzer, A. (ed.): Context and Appropriateness: Micro Meets Macro. John Benjamins, Amsterdam (2007)
13. Futuyma, D.J.: Evolutionary Biology, 3rd edn. Sinaer Associates, Sunderland (1998)
14. Givón, T.: Context as Other Minds: The Pragmatics of Sociality, Cognition and Communication. John Benjamins, Amsterdam (2005)
15. Gumperz, J.: Contextualization and understanding. In: Duranti, A., Goodwin, C. (eds.) Rethinking Context: Language as an Interactive Phenomenon, pp. 229–252. Cambrige University Press, Cambridge (1992)
16. Jeannerod, M.: The representing brain: neural correlates of motor intention and imagery. Behav. Brain Sci. **17**, 187–245 (1994)
17. Jeannerod, M.: Motor Cognition: What Actions Tell the Self. Oxford University Press, Oxford (2006)
18. Kahneman, D., Miller, D.T.: Norm theory: comparing reality and its alternates. Psychol. Rev. **93**(2), 136–153 (1986)
19. Kosslyn, S., Koenig, O.: Wet Mind. The Free Press, New York (1995)
20. Levinson, S.: Contextualizing 'contextuazing cues'. In: Eendmans, S.C., Prevignano, C., Thibault, P. (eds.) Discussing Communication Analysis: John Gumperz, pp. 24–30. Beta Press, Lausanne (1997)
21. Mayr, E.: Some thoughts on the history of the evolutionary synthesis. In: Mayr, E., Provine, W.B. (eds.) The Evolutionary Synthesis, pp. 1–54. Harvard University Press, Cambridge, London (1980)
22. Nyan, T.: Context Construction as Mediated by Discourse Markers: An Adaptive Approach. Brill, Leiden (2016)
23. Searle, J.R.: Expression and Meaning. Cambridge University Press, Cambridge (1979)

Putting Context Dependent Human Logical Reasoning into the Right Context

András Veszelka$^{(\boxtimes)}$

Pellea Human Research and Development Ltd., Kecskemét, Hungary
andras.veszelka@pellea.hu

Abstract. Human logical reasoning has been investigated since the very beginning on erroneous conceptual foundations and in a biased and unsystematic way. With the appropriate approach and with more systematic research, we obtain a fundamentally different picture from that propagated by the literature. It becomes clear that human logical reasoning is not a victim of heuristics, biases, and other distorting effects, but is compatible with logic; what is more, it even becomes clear that this couldn't be otherwise. With the correct interpretation of context and logical necessity many very confusing problems can be approached in a radically new, very simple way. Since the approach presented in this paper is in conflict with an interdisciplinary field that has developed over the course of more than a hundred years, the argument represents a fight that is reminiscent of David and Goliath. My only hope is that common sense can serve as the sling.

Keywords: Conditional · Biconditional · Human reasoning · Fallacies · Biases · Scholastic logic · Wason selection task

1 Introduction

In investigations of the relation between context and logic, irrespective of the specific scientific field, mathematical logic is used as a referential background. It is maintained, as a starting point, that the logical inferences prescribed in mathematical logic are always necessary. In contrast, inferences in everyday life show great variation, and are influenced by many factors. From this perspective, context can be quite simply defined as the totality of the factors causing the possibility that a specific instance (in this case a logical statement) may mean different things due to the variations of these factors. It is assumed that since everyday inferences are consequently unnecessary, they are not logical inferences, but are influenced by various non-logical components. Mathematical logicians had already formulated, at the beginning of the previous century, the basic idea that differences between natural languages and pure, axiomatic logical rules (the perfect artificial language), reveal biases and flaws in human language and reasoning (see e.g. [1]). Even since, in the social sciences, researchers have followed this basic assumption. They direct their research towards revealing the most serious possible flaws and then try to explain these in terms of some strictly non-logical theories.

There are two main problems with this approach. One is that it is conceptually wrong. The other is that in the past hundred years, and particularly in the field of psychology of reasoning in the past fifty years, research has been so unsystematic that

© Springer International Publishing AG 2017
P. Brézillon et al. (Eds.): CONTEXT 2017, LNAI 10257, pp. 617–630, 2017.
DOI: 10.1007/978-3-319-57837-8_50

the prevailing observations are extremely unreliable and in most cases leave us unable to conclude anything with confidence.

With regard to the conceptual error, it is a mistake to rely on mathematical logic when investigating human logical reasoning. Modern, mathematic logic is seen as axiomatic, and as such, as different in nature from natural, everyday languages or reasoning; this, as will be seen in this study, creates a multitude of problems in the investigation of logical reasoning in the human sciences. Using mathematical logic is additionally problematic because there is a plausible alternative.

Before mathematical logic, Aristotelian or scholastic logic was the prevailing form for more than 2,000 years. In this form of logic the logical components that are present in natural languages are not abstracted in an axiomatic way, with the aim of building a coherent system, but are abstracted from experience, from natural language, through natural sample sentences, using everyday human reasoning. This is obviously much closer to the method of the social sciences, where human reasoning and natural language are used and investigated. In addition, all logical components that have been investigated in linguistics and psychology in the past hundred years, that is, that have been determined as relevant in the study of human languages or reasoning (these are principally logical connectives and quantifiers), were previously defined in this ancient, "human" logic, and have remained the same ever since—even in successive mathematical systems of logic.

This means that when researchers have again and again demonstrated the serious differences between logical abstractions and real human inferences over the past hundred years, they did not succeed in showcasing the differences between logic, as a formal language, and natural, non-formal languages, as is generally assumed. Rather, they demonstrated that in scholastic logic these basic components have been extracted erroneously from natural language.

Since in the past hundred years researchers have consistently misinterpreted the starting point itself, namely the observed differences between logic and natural languages, the literature has been developed on the wrong foundations. No one has ever investigated whether the discrepancies between abstractions extracted from everyday sample sentences in antiquity and those observed in comparable sentences today merely show that these logical components were extracted erroneously in antiquity.

In fact, there are only two components that show serious discrepancies between scholastic logic and natural human inferences: the conditional statement and syllogisms. With regard to the conditional statement, mathematical logicians trace back the most general interpretation currently used in mathematical logics—for instance in propositional logic, which causes so many problems in the human sciences—to Philo of Megara, who lived just after Aristotle. Philo can therefore be seen as a historical precursor, but due to the fragmented sources available to us nothing can be known about precisely why Philo interpreted the conditional statement the way he did, and no historical continuity can be observed between Philo and the mathematical logics that appeared in the 19th and 20th centuries. In addition, although before Christ debates about the conditional statement were as heated as today [2], these debates died out shortly after his death and remained that way for many centuries. In Late Antiquity logicians have unified the two main logics of ancient Greek philosophy, Aristotelian and Stoic logic [see e.g. 3]. In the case of the conditional statement, they finally opted for an interpretation which, although it preserved some characteristics from the Stoics, was derived from the work of Aristotle (see [4], 167b1ff), and was predominant until the 19th and 20th centuries, until the appearance of mathematical logics. Unlike Philo's interpretation, mentioned above, for the scholastic interpretation we can precisely reconstruct how and on what grounds it was formulated [5]. Consequently, these arguments can be investigated.

As a matter of fact, despite the differences in display and interpretation, the key abstraction used in mathematical logics, for instance in propositional logic, can be also derived from the previous scholastic interpretation [5]. In the same way, Philo's interpretation can be also derived from the interpretation of Aristotle. As such, when testing the interpretation of propositional logic in the human sciences, researchers were also testing the interpretation of scholastic logic, though they were unaware of this. Consequently, if the agreement between these two separate variants is not merely coincidental, as claimed by mathematical logicians, there is no doubt which interpretation is the basis of the other. Either way, when investigating human logical reasoning, it is by all means reasonable to take the scholastic interpretation into account, and not merely interpretations from mathematical systems of logic—most of which have been interpreted as different in their very nature from human logical inferences.

In the following, it will be shown that there is a trivial abstraction error in the scholastic interpretation of the conditional statement. What is more, it will also be shown that this same abstraction error is responsible for the other characteristic deviation between logic and human inferences, that observed in the interpretation of syllogisms. Fixing these erroneous abstractions sheds a completely different light not merely on human logical reasoning, but also on the relation between logic and context.

2 The Abstraction Error in Logic

Ancient logicians discovered that logical connectives and quantifiers are relational words with which it is possible, to an extent, to map the relations that constitute human philosophical disputes. Today, this idea has transformed into the investigation of human logical reasoning in general. In addition, ancient logicians realized that the linguistic meaning of these connectives and quantifiers can be determined by investigating the relations that they establish between the words they connect. That is, by investigating what inferences they invoke between these connected words. Even today, there is no better way to define the meaning of these words in our everyday language, either in "human" logic or in linguistics or psychology. It is clear that there is nothing mathematical or axiomatic in this approach. Determining the meaning of words used in natural languages is not a mathematical task.

2.1 The Abstraction Error in the Conditional Statement

In scholastic logic, the meaning of the conditional statement, that is, of the if–then connective, which causes the biggest problems today, has been defined by saying that, for instance in case of "if it is a dog, it is happy" (if P antecedent then Q consequent), from "dog" (P) it necessarily follows that "it is happy" (Q), and from "not being happy" (not-Q) it necessarily follows that it is "not a dog" (not-P). These inferences are called *modus ponens* and *modus tollens* inferences. It is also said, however, that from "being happy" (Q) it does not necessarily follow that "it is a dog" (P) and similarly, from "not being a dog" (not-P) it does not necessary follow that "it is not happy" (not-Q) (see e.g. [4]). For this reason, the *affirmation of the consequent* and the *denial of the antecedent* inferences are deemed logically incorrect inferences.

The only available explanation of why these two latter inferences are erroneous— and it is important to emphasize that there is no other explanation available—is that they are incorrect because in the present example other animals, such as cats, can also be happy. Even today, if a logician is asked why these inferences are correct to draw from a conditional statement, if this logician does not simply point out that it is an axiomatic, unquestionable truth, she will use this very same explanation (see e.g. [6]).

However, the explanation is erroneous. In the abstraction, allegedly, the "if P then Q" statement was the focus; however, when describing the relation, a further "R" component was also taken into account, namely "other animals"—for instance "cats"—but this was left undenoted. That is, instead of the "if it is a dog, it is happy" (if P then Q) statement, erroneously the more compound "if it is a dog or a cat, it is happy" (if P or R then Q) statement was used. This more compound statement includes not merely an additional term, but even an additional "or" connective. This is precisely the same as saying in mathematics that 2 = 5 because one can add 3 and 2, even though this 3 and the addition sign are not denoted. It is obvious that no working mathematical system could be built on such rules of addition and subtraction; and the conditional statement has precisely the same significance in logic as addition or subtraction in mathematics. The functioning of logical systems, even the functioning of mathematical logical systems, is highly dependent on the interpretation of the conditional statement.

With everyday sample sentences, and through natural reasoning, it can be demonstrated that the correct abstraction of the "if P then Q" statement, when indeed a relationship between merely "P" and "Q" and one single "if–then" connective is characterized, would include a back and forth connection between the antecedent and the consequent [5]. That is, in addition to the *modus ponens* and *modus tollens*, the aforementioned *denial of the antecedent* and *affirmation of the consequent* are also valid inferences. We see this, for example, in the back and forth relation between the complete left side and the complete right side of the conditional statement, which remains even in the more compound "if it is a dog or a cat, it is happy" statement. From "dog" and "cat" it follows that both are "happy", and from being "happy" it follows that it is "a dog or a cat". So both the *modus ponens* and the *affirmation of the consequent* inferences must be endorsed, only within "dogs or cats", one cannot specifically infer "dog", because we could also be referring to a "cat". This back and forth inference pattern is called an equivalent or biconditional relationship, and it is viewed as one of the most common logical errors both in logic and in the psycho-logical, linguistic, and philosophical literature—not by accident, but precisely because people, in everyday speech and thinking, have always tended to infer in this manner. Logicians have successfully opposed people's intuitions for more than 2,000 years, and have convinced them, by incorrectly referring to an undenoted third term and an undenoted additional "or" connective, as discussed above, that the equivalent interpretation of the conditional statement is erroneous, and that only the *modus ponens* and *modus tollens* inferences are correct.

And what does all of this mean for us? A lot of things. On one hand, it turns out that in many logical fallacies people were actually inferring correctly the whole time. As mentioned, the logical abstractions investigated in the human sciences and people's natural logical inferences mainly deviate in terms of the conditional statement and syllogisms.

Syllogisms have been investigated less intensively in the past hundred years, so in this case there is not such a wide literature to confront. The conditional statement is traditionally equated with one of the four basic statements in syllogisms, the universal affirmative statement. And indeed, in the definition of the universal affirmative statement, precisely the same argumentation is used, and therefore the same abstraction error is committed as in case of the conditional statement (see [7, 8]). This is not a coincidence, because not only can the abstraction error in the conditional statement be traced back to Aristotle ([4], 167b1ff), he is also generally known as the founding father of syllogisms.

It can be also deduced that this erroneous abstraction has influenced the abstraction of the particular statements [5].

Figure 1 shows the traditional interpretation of statements used in syllogisms, expressed in Euler circles. The fixed interpretation can be found in Fig. 2. In the traditional interpretation, one statement can result in several possible diagrams and an X indicates mandatory sections of the diagrams, which must contain an element [9]. Only these sections must be in the diagram; the other sections can be left empty in certain cases, and thus omitted.

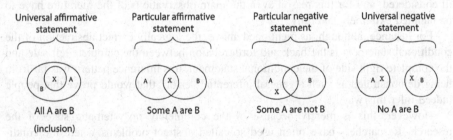

Universal affirmative statement	Particular affirmative statement	Particular negative statement	Universal negative statement

All A are B (inclusion) — Some A are B — Some A are not B — No A are B

Fig. 1. The traditional denotation of statement-types in syllogisms with Euler circles (based on Fig. 5 of [9, 13])

According to this new interpretation, all four statements result in the same diagram in every case, as shown in Fig. 2. Since in this new interpretation all sections must have at least one element, the X marks can be removed. Old data on the syllogistic inferences of people untrained in logic [10–12] reveal that the old representation (Fig. 1) is consistent with people's inferences in only 55% of cases, while in the case of the new representation (Fig. 2), this value is 85% on average.

Moreover, it is very likely that the other 15% is merely the result of the distorting effect of the experimental material [5].

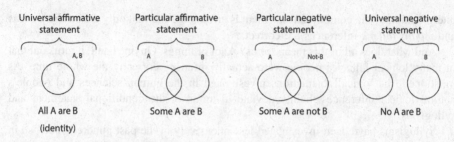

Fig. 2. The updated denotation of statement-types in syllogisms with Euler circles (based on Fig. 3 of [5])

Therefore, although for about a hundred years the literature has claimed that people's everyday syllogistic inferences are heavily distorted by various biases, heuristics, and other effects (see e.g. [14–18]) these assumed distorting effects immediately disappear, and people's logical inferences can be described purely in terms of logic, when the correct basic assumptions and the correct logical abstractions are used.

3 Unreliable Literature

In the case of the conditional statement, the situation is much more complicated, because this connective has been studied much more intensively, and for this reason researchers have buried themselves much more deeply in their erroneous basic assumptions. What is more, the available research is also very unsystematic and ill-considered, and for this reason even the main observations of the literature have to be handled extremely carefully.

For instance, although, as mentioned above, the logically correct abstraction of the conditional statement is the back and forth relation between the complete left side and the complete right side of the conditional statement, this inference pattern was far from being demonstrated as such a general inferential "error" that would prove that people indeed infer this way.

However, this is merely because of the completely unsystematic state of the research. Researchers have often used so-called abstract problems where the conditional statement connects letters and numbers that are independent in everyday life, and for this reason the interpretation of the conditional statement is not influenced by contextual or content-related information from everyday life. Thus, there is a good chance that these tasks indeed show the connection that the if–then statement establishes between the components it connects. For the investigation of these abstract conditional statements four main tasks have been used, the Wason selection task (e.g. [19, 20]), the truth-table evaluation task (e.g. [21]), the inference task (e.g. [22]), and the inference production task (e.g. [23]). In addition, three types of negatives have been used, explicit, implicit, and dichotomous negatives (see e.g. [24]). This makes twelve main experimental layouts altogether (4 × 3); and obviously all twelve need to be tested in order to obtain a good overall picture of the inferences evoked by an abstract conditional statement. This is particularly important when we consider that, from the very beginning, different tasks have produced different results. Despite this, until 2007, when the question had already been under investigation for 40 years, these main tasks and negatives had been tested only in the combinations shown in Table 1.

Table 1. The most frequent responses on the main abstract task-types with the three types of negatives for the abstract conditional statement

	Imp. negatives	Expl. negatives	Dich. negatives
Selection task	P & Q	P & Q	P & Q
Truth table task	Def. truth table*[†]	Def.truth table*/Equivalence?[†]	Equivalence (83%)[‡]
Inference task	?	?	?
Inf production task	?	?	Equivalence (92%)[‡]

[*]In the defective truth-table people evaluate the "P and Q" co-occurrence as verifying, and the "P and not-Q" co-occurrence as falsifying the "if P then Q" conditional statement, and they evaluate the "not-P and Q" and the "not-P and not-Q" co-occurrences as irrelevant.

[†]The authors reporting these results do not report the complete response patterns but only the rate of individual inferences. The defective truth table is still obvious when the task contains implicit negatives, but in case of explicit negatives, the most frequent response could be both the defective truth table and the equivalence [25].

[‡] [26]

All theories in the literature are based on these defective results (see e.g. [18, 27–29]), which equates to several hundred or even thousands of studies discussing these theories, their differences, or the points that they apparently leave unresolved. However, as can be seen in Table 2, it is sufficient to merely test the missing experimental layouts to get a completely different picture from the main data sources used in the literature. Equivalence becomes the predominant response. It is important to stress again that these are not arbitrary experimental tasks; they are recognized as the most important, most significant experimental tasks in the literature.

Table 2. The results obtained on the abstract conditional statement with the main abstract task types and the three types of negatives, [30][*], [31][†]

	Imp. negatives	Expl. negatives	Dich. negatives
Selection task	P & Q[*]	P & Q[*]	P & Q[*]
Truth table task	Def. truth table[‡]	Def. truth table[‡]	Equivalence (50%)[*]
Inference task	Def. truth table[‡]/ Equivalence (48%)[†]	Def. truth table[‡]	Equivalence (42%)[*]/ Equivalence (60%)[†]
Inf production task	Equivalence (73.3%)[*]	Equivalence (52%)[*]	Equivalence (67%)[*]

Note: In the defective truth-table people see the "P and Q" co-occurrence as verifying, and the "P and not-Q" co-occurrence as falsifying the "if P then Q" conditional statement, and they see the "not-P and Q" and the "not-P and not-Q" co-occurrences as irrelevant.

It can be also demonstrated that the tasks that seemingly do not evoke equivalent responses, that is, the Wason selection task and the truth-table task, simply distort the results [5]. For example, the Wason selection task does not evoke the equivalent response of selecting all four cards, even in a thematic task with a clearly equivalent context, but produces the same responses as the abstract selection task [5, 32]. It can be experimentally demonstrated that participants simply avoid the selection of all four cards in the selection task (the P, not-P, Q, and not-Q cards), because they assume that their task is to find a solution by selecting only a few of these four cards [5, 30, 31]. It can be also explained why in truth-table tasks the equivalent responses appear only with dichotomous negatives and why the so-called defective truth table appears with the other two types of negatives [5].

4   Experimentum Crucis

From the abstraction error in the conditional statement discussed above, it follows that the addition of a further antecedent, connected with an "or" to the original antecedent on the left side of the conditional statement, should produce the relationship that logicians erroneously identify as the "if P then Q" conditional statement. So, if this approach is correct, then inserting such a component into the abstract conditional statement should also produce this inference pattern. In a selection task, participants, in order to check the truth of the conditional statement, are asked to select from four schematic cards displaying on their upper sides the four possible logical cases, P, not-P, Q, and not-Q. They need to select the P and not-Q cards, because on the basis of *modus ponens* and *modus tollens*, on the reverse of the P card we should find Q, and on the reverse of the not-Q card we should find not-P. According to the traditional interpretation, on the other side of the not-P card both Q and not-Q, and on the other side of the Q card both P and not-P could figure, so these cards don't need to be checked.

Indirectly, this question has been already investigated in abstract selection tasks where participants were provided with the information that "[c]ards with a P on the front may only have Q on the back, but cards with not-P on the front may have either Q or not-Q on the back" [33] (p. 203), which they were to check in the task. However, in this task very miscellaneous responses were made. On the other hand, when testing this same problem in the inference production task, the rate of correct responses was immediately 82% [5]. In the selection task, participants probably wanted once again to turn over all cards in Hoch and Tschirgi's problem to test whether, for instance, on the other side of the not-P card they would indeed find both Q and not-Q cards. For this reason, in the following abstract selection task the additional alternative antecedent was not explicitly named in the task but came from "outside":

Imagine that four cards are lying in front of you on the table. On one side of the card, there is either the number 4 or the number 6; on the other side, there is either "divisible by two" or "divisible by three". Your task is to check whether each of the four cards on the table conforms with the reality, namely, with the rule that: If the number is 4, then it is divisible by only two. Which card or cards would you turn over to check this?

The cards had the following values: "4", "6", "divisible by two", and "divisible by three", respectively [5] (p. 34).

This task produced the response "P and not-Q" in 41–55% of respondents, officially seen as correct for the conditional statement, instead of the usual "P and Q" responses shown in Tables 1 and 2 [5]. Participants were aware from their everyday experience that the number 6 is also divisible by two, and this altered the original conditional statement in their mind without their being required to check this additional information when solving the task. According to an experiment, no better result can be obtained for the Wason abstract selection task even when participants are explicitly told the correct response and they merely have to select the corresponding cards [34]. This is therefore the maximum result that one can get from the abstract selection task.

In this "easy to resolve" abstract selection task, the component coming from outside, which it is not necessary to check, is the simplest example of context. This task shows that context and logic are not two components different in their very nature, as is assumed in human sciences; context can be described in terms of logic, and its effects can be analysed in the same way as the effects of written-down or verbalised statements.

5   The Problem of Undenoted Context

In the literature investigating human logical inferences, context is customarily left undenoted. The reasons for this again lay in the history of logic. As mentioned, the traditional abstraction of the conditional statement is similar to saying in mathematics that $2 = 5$ because one can add 3 and 2, even though this 3 and the addition sign are not denoted. It is obvious that no working system could be built on such rules of addition and subtraction, because instead of 3, 8 could also be added to 2, and it is likewise possible to expand the right side of the equation. However, if these extra additions and subtractions were not denoted, but $2 = 5$ was always expected to appear, assuming it to be necessarily, always, universally valid, then the only thing that could be seen would be continuously varying results, and so one might conclude that the way people add and subtract numbers in everyday life is not compatible with mathematics. That is, it would be then deduced that people's additions and subtractions do not follow the rules of mathematics.

However absurd this might sound, in the case of logic and context this is exactly what happens. Additional terms with additional connectives can be added to or removed from both sides of the "if P then Q" statement (not merely to the antecedent, and not merely with an "or" connective, as seen previously), and these added terms and connectives would all influence the "result" of the relationship. If these added components are not denoted, as is customary, then of course it appears that the inferences are always different.

For instance let's take a look at confirmation bias, the phenomenon whereby people tend to evaluate things in line with their own beliefs (see e.g. [35]). Is this tendency really so mysterious? Is it really irrational? If the propositions in one's mind were to be described on paper, on their basis some concrete conclusions could very likely be derived; and with the same certainty the thoughts of other people, on the basis of different thoughts, could yield different conclusions. Is this relativism really such a radical discovery? Are researchers really surprised that people do not think the same way about absolutely everything?

Of course, once again, there is an erroneous logical principle behind this phenomenon. In mathematical logic, it is assumed that logical necessity is universal, that it can never change, and that it is always valid. In the human sciences, and within them, for instance in ancient, scholastic logic, necessity should be interpreted in a different way. This does not mean that the given inference is always valid, regardless of the circumstances. It means, instead, that in the context of the available, denoted propositions, there are no alternative inferences. For instance, in case of "if it is a dog, it is happy", it necessarily follows from "dog" that is it "happy"; but if someone arrives at the idea that there are also dogs in a melancholic mood, then from "dog", it no longer necessarily follows that it is "happy", because it can be also "in a melancholic mood". If this additional information is denoted, then the change in the original relationship can be precisely described in terms of logic, without our being required to assume that this is the effect of some another component of a different nature. One might say that if it is true in a domain that "if it is a dog, it is happy", and if it is true in that domain that x is a "dog", then it is also true in that domain that x is "happy", and this is not influenced by the possibility of there being dogs in a "melancholic mood" in some other domain. However, in human inferences, there is only one domain, and all propositions are formulated within this same domain – one's mind. Another problematic, though very common, argument in defence of mathematical logic in the study of human logical reasoning is to say that once it has been stated that "if it is a dog, it is happy", then this is a logical necessity, and if melancholic dogs come to someone's mind, any changes in the inference pattern wouldn't be logical; rather, as assumed in the human sciences, they would be pragmatic.

However, when someone says that $2 + 3 = 5$, this represents a necessity on the basis of the denoted numbers, but no one can prohibit this person or someone else from also adding, for instance, the number 8 to the left side of the equation. In so doing, this person will still remain in the same domain. Naturally, the sum would be then modified to 13, but despite this, it would still remain a mathematical calculation. There seems to be no reason to prohibit allowed additions and subtractions in mathematics from being used in logical inferences. And there is no reason at all to prohibit this in the human sciences.

A number of various non-monotonic logics have been already created with the aim of describing such contextual, defeasible effects, and as such, with the aim of characterizing human inferences (see e.g. [36, 37]). However, the simplest non-monotonic logic emerges when the concept of logical necessity and scholastic logic itself is interpreted correctly, because, by doing so, scholastic logic immediately becomes non-monotonic logic, perfectly tailored to human, everyday inferences.

It couldn't be any other way. As mentioned earlier, scholastic logic is abstracted from natural language, through human reasoning, so naturally, when these abstractions are correct, they should match human language and reasoning. The common incorrect interpretation of logical necessity and all the confusion it generates shows once again that instead of using mathematical logic in the human sciences as the only referential background, it first of all needs to be demonstrated that mathematical logic has some relevance in human fields.

6   A Final Example of Unsystematic Literature

As seen above, mathematical logic has not improved but merely confounded research in human fields. However, in order to happen, this process also required unsystematic, ill-considered research in the human fields, particularly in the field of the psychology of reasoning. To mention a recent example of the latter, there are selection tasks in the literature where the conditional statement is embedded in a context, and where these tasks as a consequence evoke the "P and not-Q" response deemed correct for the conditional statement (but, as seen above, this is in fact incorrect). According to Cosmides [38], in these tasks, the responses seemingly echoing this dictate of logic demonstrate that we possess an in-built cheater-detection module, because most of the tasks include some regulation that has to be observed, and participants were asked to select those cards that could reveal possible violations of these regulations. However, it is likely that in these tasks, from the often very wordy, but nevertheless, according to tradition, completely undenoted and unanalysed context, or from people's everyday background knowledge, the interpretation of the original conditional statement modifies in a similar way as in the "easy to resolve" abstract selection task.

Notably, an obvious characteristic of regulations is that the regulated behaviour is principally independent of the condition by which it is regulated. For instance, the ability to cross the road (P or not-P) and the red/green colour of traffic lights (Q or not-Q) are basically independent of one another ("if P or not-P then Q or not-Q"). This generally known, independent relationship is modified when giving the rule "If you want to cross the road, you have to wait for the light to turn green" ("if P then must be Q"). In all other possible co-occurrences, the P antecedent and the Q consequent remain independent from one another. For instance, if someone doesn't want to cross the road then it doesn't matter whether the traffic light is green (Q) or red (not-Q). When formulating a rule to be obeyed, it therefore creates an inference pattern reminiscent of that traditionally equated with the conditional statement. However, exactly the same phenomenon can be also observed in everyday situations that don't contain any rule to be obeyed, or, in our specific case, any cheater detection. For instance, when someone says "Let's invite Paul and John to the party" and we reply 'Let's invite Paul", this, as a kind of conversational implicature [39], which can be nonetheless described in terms of logic, quite clearly implies "Let's not invite John". It is quite possible that this same phenomenon modifies the logical interpretation of the conditional statement in those thematic Wason selection tasks that include a rule to be obeyed, as discussed above, which could be easily tested in psychological experiments.

It is in itself a conceptual error to postulate cheater detection as the cause of such an inference pattern, in the definition of which no "cheating" component of any kind is included. According to mathematical logicians, the abstraction of the conditional statement is axiomatic, it is not based on sample sentences or on the empirical world, and it can be evaluated merely on the basis of the inner consistency of the created logical system. How, then, can this axiomatic abstraction be triggered by a cheating-detection module? On the other hand, ancient and scholastic logicians define the linguistic meaning of the "if–then" connective by using sample sentences in which, as can be clearly seen in ancient books, or in the "if it is a dog, it is happy" statement used in this paper, no "cheating component" of any kind is present. How then did our cheating-detection module trigger this inference pattern (which has, in addition, even been incorrectly abstracted)?

It could be argued that modifying the logical interpretation of the conditional statement would lead to many system-level dependencies being lost, particularly in mathematical logic. It could be also said that for the purposes of logic, it is not necessary to establish a match with human reasoning. However, the interpretation suggested here also has very interesting system-level dependencies. On the other hand, to be able to investigate the extent to which human logical reasoning could be used as a model for creating an alternative, abstract system of logic, for instance for an artificial agent, first of all human logical reasoning should be interpreted and investigated correctly. For a correct, comprehensive investigation, it's reasonable to take into account scholastic logic, and to consider all its implications.

Acknowledgements. A longer treatment of this work, for instance the experimental results mentioned in this paper, a detailed characterization of the literature of psychology of reasoning, including the current "probabilistic turn", and further arguments in support of the key observations of this paper can be found in the book *Everyday Abstract Conditional Reasoning: in light of a 2,400 Year-Old Mistake in Logic* [5]. The key observations of this paper with different emphases and accompanying arguments have also been submitted for evaluation to the CogSci 2017 conference. I am grateful to the three anonymous reviewers for their valuable comments and to Nicole Standen-Mills for polishing up the language of this paper.

References

1. Frege, G.: Logical investigations. In: McGuinness, B. (ed.) Collected Papers on Mathematics, Logic, and Philosophy, pp. 351–407. Basil Blackwell, Oxford (1918–1919/1984)
2. Kneale, W., Kneale, M.: The Development of Logic. Oxford University Press, Oxford (1962)
3. Bobzien, S.: Ancient logic. In: Zalta, E.N. (ed.) The Stanford Encyclopedia of Philosophy (Winter 2016 Edition). https://plato.stanford.edu/archives/win2016/entries/logic-ancient
4. Aristotle: De sophisticis elenchis. In: Ross, W.D. (ed.) The Works of Aristotle. Oxford University Press, Oxford (1928)
5. Veszelka, A.: Everyday Abstract Conditional Reasoning: In Light of a 2400 Year-Old Mistake in Logic. Pellea Bt., Kecskemét (2014)
6. Tarski, A.: Introduction to Logic and to the Methodology of Deductive Sciences. Dover Publications, Mineola (1946/1995)
7. Jevons, W.S.: Logic. Macmillan, London (1906)
8. Brennan, J.G.: A Handbook of Logic, 2nd edn. Harper and Row, New York (1961)
9. Stenning, K., Oberlander, J.: A cognitive theory of graphical and linguistic reasoning: logic and implementation. Cogn. Sci. **19**(1), 97–140 (1995)
10. Dickstein, L.S.: The effect of figure on syllogistic reasoning. Mem. Cogn. **6**(1), 76–83 (1978)
11. Johnson-Laird, P.N., Bara, B.G.: Syllogistic inference. Cognition **16**, 1–61 (1984)

12. Copeland, D.E.: Theories of categorical reasoning and extended syllogisms. Think. Reason. **12**(4), 379–412 (2006)
13. Stenning, K.: Modelling memory for models. In: Esquerro, J.E., Larrazabal, J.M. (eds.) Cognition, Semantics and Philosophy. Kluwer, Dordrecht (1992)
14. Wilkins, M.C.: The effect of changed material on the ability to do formal syllogistic reasoning. Arch. Psychol. **102**, 1–83 (1928)
15. Woodworth, R.S., Sells, S.B.: An atmosphere effect in formal syllogistic reasoning. J. Exp. Psychol. **18**(4), 451–460 (1935)
16. Woodworth, R.S., Schlosberg, H.: Experimental Psychology, 2nd edn. Holt, Rinehart & Winston, New York (1954)
17. Chater, N., Oaksford, M.: The probability heuristics model of syllogistic reasoning. Cogn. Psychol. **38**, 191–258 (1999)
18. Stenning, K., van Lambalgen, M.: Human Reasoning and Cognitive Science. MIT Press, Cambridge (2008)
19. Wason, P.C.: Reasoning. In: Foss, B.M. (ed.) New Horizons in Psychology, pp. 135–151. Penguin Books, Harmondsworth (1966)
20. Wason, P.C.: Reasoning about a rule. Q. J. Exp. Psychol. **20**, 273–281 (1968)
21. Evans, J.S.B.T.: Interpretation and matching bias in a reasoning task. Q. J. Exp. Psychol. **24**, 193–199 (1972)
22. Rumain, B., Connell, J., Braine, M.D.: Conversational comprehension processes are responsible for reasoning fallacies in children as well as adults: if is not the biconditional. Dev. Psychol. **19**, 471–481 (1983)
23. Byrne, R.M.J.: Suppressing valid inferences with conditionals. Cognition **31**, 61–83 (1989)
24. Johnson-Laird, P.N., Wason, P.C.: A theoretical analysis of insight into a reasoning task. In: Johnson-Laird, P.N., Wason, P.C. (eds.) Thinking: Readings in Cognitive Science, pp. 143–157. Cambridge University Press, Cambridge (1977)
25. Evans, J.S.B.T., Clibbens, J., Rood, B.: The role of implicit and explicit negation in conditional reasoning bias. J. Mem. Lang. **35**(3), 392–409 (1996)
26. George, C.: Rules of inference in the interpretation of the conditional connective. Cahiers de Psychologie Cognitive/Curr. Psychol. Cogn. **12**(2), 115–139 (1992)
27. Johnson-Laird, P.N., Byrne, R.M.J.: Deduction. Lawrence Erlbaum Associates Ltd, Hove (1991)
28. Evans, J.S.B.T., Over, D.E.: If. Oxford University Press, Oxford (2004)
29. Oaksford, M., Chater, N.: Bayesian Rationality: The Probabilistic Approach to Human Reasoning. Oxford University Press, Oxford (2007)
30. Veszelka, A.: A feltételes állítás kísérleti vizsgálata: mégis van benne logika? [The experimental investigation of the conditional statement: Does it have logic?]. Magyar Pszichológiai Szemle **62**(4), 475–488. English version available upon request (2007)
31. Wagner-Egger, P.: Conditional reasoning and the Wason selection task: biconditional interpretation instead of a reasoning bias. Think. Reason. **13**(4), 484–505 (2007)
32. Cheng, P.W., Holyoak, K.J., Nisbett, R.E., Oliver, L.M.: Pragmatic versus syntactic approaches to training deductive reasoning. Cogn. Psychol. **18**, 293–328 (1986)
33. Hoch, S.J., Tschirgi, J.E.: Cue redundancy and extra logical inference in a deductive reasoning task. Mem. Cogn. **11**, 200–209 (1983)
34. Fiddick, L., Erlich, N.: Giving it all away: altruism and answers to the Wason selection task. Evol. Hum. Behav. **31**(2), 131–140 (2010)
35. Mercier, H., Sperber, D.: Why do humans reason? Arguments for an argumentative theory. Behav. Brain Sci. **34**(2), 57–74 (2011). Cambridge University Press (CUP)
36. Reiter, R.: A logic for default reasoning. Artif. Intell. **13**, 81–132 (1980)

37. Nute, D.: Defeasible logic. In: Bartenstein, O., Geske, U., Hannebauer, M., Yoshie, O. (eds.) INAP 2001. LNCS (LNAI), vol. 2543, pp. 151–169. Springer, Heidelberg (2003). doi:10.1007/3-540-36524-9_13
38. Cosmides, L.: The logic of social exchange: has natural selection shaped how humans reason? Studies with Wason selection task. Cognition **31**, 187–316 (1989)
39. Grice, H.P.: Logic and conversation. In: Cole, P., Moran, J.L. (eds.) Syntax and Semantics: Speech Acts, vol. 3, pp. 41–58. Academic, New York (1975)

Specific Topics: Context in Linguistics and Philosophy

Immediate and General Common Ground

Leda Berio[✉], Anja Latrouite, Robert Van Valin, and Gottfried Vosgerau

Heinrich Heine Universität, Universitätstraße 1, 40225 Düsseldorf, Germany
{berio,latrouite,vanvalin,vosgerau}@phil.uni-duesseldorf.de

Abstract. The traditional literalism account of meaning has been challenged by several theories that stress the importance of context and of contextual information in communication, especially for mechanisms of meaning determination and reference fixing. However, the role of lexical meaning in such contextualist accounts often remains only vaguely defined. In this paper, we defend an account of communication that keeps the advantages of contextualist theories, while a new element is introduced that we claim could help to solve some of the remaining issues. By differentiating Immediate and General Common Ground in communication, we draw a distinction between mechanisms related to the situation at hand and those concerned with world and language knowledge. We further argue that such a distinction can help to understand cases of loose use and metaphors of which we provide some examples. Finally, we claim that this distinction has grammatical reality, as it is shown by the examples from Lakhota (North America), Umpithamu (Australia), Kuuk Thaayorre (Australia) and Mongsen Ao (India) discussed in the paper.

1 Common Ground and the Semantics-Pragmatics Interface

1.1 Introduction

Several theories have recently tried to overcome the difficulties that derive from a traditional literalism account of meaning. Two relevant examples we will discuss are Grab Bag Theory (Ray 2011), which embraces a strong form of contextualism, and Relevance Theory (Wilson and Sperber 2012), which tries to extend pragmatics over the boundaries drawn by Grice (1957, 1989). These theories have several advantages as they rightly emphasize the essential role that pragmatics plays in reference fixing and in effective communication in general. From our point of view, however, they fail to provide a solid backbone to verbal communication.

Grab Bag Theory (Rayo 2011), which postulates lexical entries as a collection of conversationally relevant items, only provides a rather vague sketch of how language comprehension works, since it fails to thoroughly explain how the "grab bags" are assembled during learning. Moreover, it does not specify how different mental items pertaining to different domains (e.g. spatial schema, encyclopedic information, mental images) can be grouped together and linked to a lexical

© Springer International Publishing AG 2017
P. Brézillon et al. (Eds.): CONTEXT 2017, LNAI 10257, pp. 633–646, 2017.
DOI: 10.1007/978-3-319-57837-8_51

entry. This poses a serious problem since it is far from being clear how items that work supposedly truth-conditionally can be integrated into a uniformly functioning whole with others that are not. Similarly, Relevance Theory (Wilson and Sperber 2012) modifies the Grecian framework to provide a better understanding of the processes at work during comprehension. However, it seems to deprive lexical meaning of any role, whilst not accounting for what exactly is the starting point from which pragmatic processes can develop.

The idea that will be defended in this paper is that a specific notion of common ground among speakers can help solve the problems that arise from the literature, especially the interface between semantics and pragmatics. The aim is to draw a theoretically sound, cognitively plausible distinction that is also supported by cross-linguistic data.

Instead of taking common ground as a homogeneous and unique factor playing a role in communication, we distinguish between Immediate Common Ground (ICG from now on) and General Common Ground (GCG) as two distinct levels. Although they are constantly interacting, we characterize them according to very specific features that reflect different cognitive aspects of verbal communication. In the remainder of this section, the difference between the two levels will be spelled out. In the following section, the theory will be put to work by showing how it can effectively deal with two examples taken from Wilson and Sperber (2012), by solving some concerns arising from their treatment of the cases. In the third section, the grammatical plausibility of our claim will be demonstrated by providing examples from Lakhota (North America), Umpithamu (Australia), Kuuk Thaayorre (Australia) and Mongsen Ao (India). The last section will summarize the evidence for our theoretical claim.

1.2 Distinguishing Between ICG and GCG

Perception-Attention Mechanisms vs. World-Language-Knowledge. The core of the difference lies in the fact that ICG (Immediate Common Ground) is thought to be related to the knowledge of a given situation that is shared by all communicators (Krifka and Musan 2012): in other words, it is related to the specific situation at hand and the communicative interaction between the two (or more) speakers.

Let us imagine the following everyday situation: two people sitting in an office around a table with two books in front of them. One of them says

(1)   The red ones need to be brought back to the library.

For the utterance to be understood by the other speaker, several factors need to be in play. First of all, the hearer has to perceive the two books, specifically their difference in color. Also, the hearer has to be able to pay attention to the two books and to understand that they are the focus of a joint attention mechanism: so, both the hearer and the speaker are attending to the books and know that their interlocutor is attending to the books as well. Additionally, the property of colour, in this case, is made salient by the speaker by referring to it (and not, for instance, to their size or to their titles). Possibly, several other factors are in play. In general, however, the information gathered by perception of the objects and of the other interlocutor has to be connected to the uttered sentence, in particular to both its meaning and its implications/implicatures. In order to do this, all the relevant information has to be kept in working memory. In this way, the content of communication interacts with the outside world and our ability to perceive it, process it and interact with it. All of this, in our framework, is related to the ICG and constitutes the knowledge related to a communicative situation shared by the speakers.

One might immediately argue, however, that the listed factors are not sufficient for the hearer to understand the utterance: some other pieces of information are needed. Trivially, the word "red" has to be of some significance for the hearer, as "book" and "library" do. Furthermore, in order to fully comprehend what the speaker meant to achieve by uttering sentence (1), the hearer has to know what a library is and, on a deeper level of analysis, that some books are borrowed from libraries and need to be brought back there after a certain period of time. Namely, what is needed is some knowledge about the outside world and some knowledge about the language spoken by the speaker. This level, in our picture, is that of GCG (General Common Ground). And obviously, this kind of knowledge is found in long-term memory, since it is knowledge that is not bound to a specific situation[1].

Note that according to this distinction, on the one hand, reference fixing is determined on the level of ICG: because the speaker and the hearer are in the same place at the same time and because they share perceptual information, the referents of the utterance can be fixed. On the other hand, what pertains to the level of GCG is lexical meaning: lexical entries for "book", "red" and "library", along with word-knowledge, are also required for the utterance to implement an effective communicative act.

The Interaction of the Two Levels. Although our first sketchy clarification might suggest that the two levels of common ground are strictly distinct, we want to defend the view that they are constantly interacting and influencing each other in specific ways. As said, while the ICG pertains to the situation at hand and the context of the communication in process, the GCG is related to knowledge about "the world" (independently of the concrete situation). As such, it includes knowledge about language in general, idiolects that are used in different linguistic groups, conventional implicatures, conventions in general and, ultimately, what is referred to as "stable meaning" or lexical meaning. Information such as encyclopedic entries, for instance, or definitions, are included

---

[1] Note that the distinction is different from the one between narrow context and wide context drawn by Perry (1997). As a matter of fact, he deals with reference fixing only, being concerned with solving the problem of indexicals. Our distinction, on the other hand, tries to capture the more general sentence interpretation problem, of which reference fixing is only a part. We thank Carlo Penco (personal communication) for pointing out the possible confusion.

in the GCG (which makes this distinction fundamentally different from that drawn by Rayo in Grab Bag Theory). This is thought to be the level in which all the information that does not pertain strictly to the situation at hand can be found: however, this kind of knowledge changes constantly. Once a person's use of a particular term, for instance, is noted by other speakers she has often interaction with, this piece of information pertains to the GCG level. The same applies to meaning of lexical entries in general, which are learned during development and "stored" at a level of GCG. Thus, a bottom up relation is present: the ICG-interactions update the GCG.

Hence, communication requires both levels. During communicative interaction, the speaker relies on the knowledge at a GCG level. This level provides— so to say—the basis on which further, context-bound mechanisms (traditionally called pragmatic processes) can operate. Still, all the processes of perception, joint attention, and perspective taking are needed to fix referents and specific meanings that can be said to be understood. Thus, loose use of expressions— which constitutes a case of reference fixing in the wide sense[2]—has to be explained on this level as well, because the meaning of a loosely used expression can only be determined through the information currently available to the speaker in the situation at hand. For instance, the determination of which speeds are referred to when using the expression "too slow" is a matter of ICG. Knowledge about the metaphorical use of lexems, or fixed metaphorical expressions, on the other hand, pertain to the GCG, as they are based on world-language-knowledge. Thus, the "decoding" of the meaning of metaphorically used expressions is heavily based on the GCG, while the ICG is only contributing in the sense that it is necessary to detect the metaphorical use of the expression in the first place (if at all). In the second section, the distinction between loose use and metaphors will be further explained.

Consequences of the Distinction. It is essential to note that the traditional division of semantics and pragmatics is not reflected directly in the division between ICG and GCG: what is traditionally conceived of as semantics and pragmatics is distributed among the two domains. For example: while reference fixing is determined by what is salient and relevant given the ICG, meaning linked to lexical entries does not have to be placed in ICG as well, rather this meaning is part of our knowledge about language (and thus part of the GCG).

Reference fixing is thought to be at a contextual level in accounts like Grab Bag Theory or Relevance Theory, and we are sympathetic with this claim. However, this does not require discarding lexical meaning on the whole. The notion of lexical meaning can be kept on a general level without removing reference fixing from the context at hand. The ability to do so is one of the main advantages of the division of common ground. The meaning of lexical entries is part of knowledge about the world and about language, whereas what a speaker is referring to with a term is determined by the processes that occur during specific

---

[2] "Reference" is used in the wide sense if it includes the determination of meaning of adjectives and verbs, as in "loose use" and related phenomena.

communicative interactions, being linked to perception. In this framework, GCG is to be understood as a level where the linguistic parts are exclusively conventional; lexical meaning and semantic rules, as well as conventional implicatures, pertain to this domain. On the other hand, non-conventional communication is possible on the ICG level.

The distinction between ICG and GCG is clearly cognitively motivated and is rooted in cognitive reality. The GCG correspondes roughly to the commonly shared part of long-term memory, including linguistic "memory" (i.e. the mental lexicon etc.). However, it also includes non-linguistic knowledge and thus is also the basis for the content of thoughts. The ICG, on the other hand, corresponds to the commonly shared part of working memory. It does not contribute to the content of thoughts except for reference-fixing in the narrow sense (i.e. in determining the things that are thought about), and it could not be used to explain thought content without producing a circular argument (or a mystical holism)[3]. However, ICG is the level on which specific shared knowledge of the situation is available, and as such it makes linguistic and non-linguistic communication effective because it allows the communication to be underdetermined and vague at the "semantic" level. In this sense, the ICG is strictly communication-specific.

Ultimately, the GCG/ICG-distinction leads to the following picture: since the ICG allows for effective communication with underdetermined and vague expressions, the "semantics" of lexems is likely to be underdetermined and vague and not expressible in truth-conditional or referential terms. To this extend, Grab Bag Theory and Relevance Theory surely produce relevant arguments. However, it does not vanish altogether: stable meanings remain, although in a vague way, as part of long-term knowledge and thus can serve as a starting point for "pragmatic" operations that take into account the ICG.

2 Theory at Work: Loose Use and Metaphors

2.1 Lexicalized Metaphors

Let us turn to some specific examples that can be elucidated by applying the distinction between the two levels to a real life example. The analysis carried out by Sperber and Wilson in their work related to Relevance Theory (Wilson and Sperber 2012) focuses on several issues concerning the classical understanding of communicative features such as metaphors, tropes, and loose use. One of their main claims is that there is no need of special mechanisms dedicated to the treatment of metaphors, loose use and literal use of language. In a traditional account emphasizing the difference between pragmatics and semantics, loose use and metaphors are considered as exceptions to a rule of meaning determination.

---

[3] The problem would be—in a nutshell—that I would have to interpret my own thoughts in the light of the situation I am in. Since my realization of the situation I am in is part of my "thinking" and of what I am supposed to explain in the first place, the circle arises. Moreover, Wittgenstein's argument against private languages would apply (Wittgenstein 2010).

This means that first the literal meaning is determined and found to be false; in a second step, special pragmatic inferences and/or implicatures are required in order to make sense of the meaning communicated through sentences that are not true in a literal sense.

This is strongly rejected by Relevance Theory. The basic idea is that there is a continuum between tropes, loose use and literal use of language. Accordingly, the pragmatic inferences that are involved in the interpretation of metaphors and loose use are the same as the processes involved in the determination of the literal meaning. While we largely agree that even literal meaning has to be interpreted—in fact, we regard lexical meaning to provide constraints on possible interpretations rather than providing fully detailed literal meanings (cf. Van Valin 1980)—, we think that in accordance with the distinction. Furthermore, distinguishing types of processing helps explain the difference between metaphor and loose use, crosscutting the classical semantics/pragmatics distinction. As said, these levels are not mutually exclusive or working strictly separated, but are interwoven and simultaneously involved in the interpretation of at least most utterances.

To illustrate, let us take the following example adapted from (Wilson and Sperber 2012, p. 85):

(2)   My son is a piglet!

This case is described as metaphorical use of "pig" that clearly reflects a judgment of the mother regarding the dirtiness/the eating habits of the child. The comprehension of the utterance, however, is only possible if we have the background knowledge that makes us understand that "being a pig" is used as an equivalent to "being dirty". In order to understand this, a full-blown lexical entry for "pig", including a complete biological description, is not needed, especially not needed to find out that the child referred to is literally not a pig. It is enough to know that pigs are generally regarded as dirty animals that gladly stay in mud, for instance, that they are stereotypically regarded as eating a lot and not likely to behave at a lunch table, and so on. For the present discussion, it is not important whether this piece of information is part of our semantic knowledge or our world knowledge (or whether such a distinction matters at all). The important point is that this knowledge is found in long term memory, knowledge that we have independently of the situation, and thus knowledge that is part of the GCG. And precisely in this respect, the interpretation of "is a piglet" does not differ in principle from the interpretation of "my son" in the example: in order to understand that "my son" refers to the child, the hearer will rely on general (semantic) knowledge as to what kind of things sons are and how they look, as well as general (world) knowledge that the speaker stands in a certain relation to the child referred to. And, exactly parallel to the "piglet" interpretation, the hearer does not have to take into account all of her (semantic and world) knowledge about sons; e.g., that sons also have fathers, that they typically love eating what mom cooks, etc. Clearly, that does not imply that the entire interpretation of the utterance relies on this piece of information alone:

in our framework, the intermediate and general level are constantly interacting online. For example, the resolution of the indexical "my" relies on the specific ICG that is tied to the situation and that specifies who is speaking. However, what has to be stressed here is the role that the conventional relation between "dirty" and "pig" plays: this is not only related to the stereotypical knowledge about pigs that speakers of English have, but also to the frequent use of the word in this type of context. For similar reasons, in our framework, idiolects are to be placed at the GCG level. Once the use of a word as linked to a particular meaning and intention to convey a content is established, the link itself works as a piece of knowledge that is drawn upon when a sentence is comprehended. To this extent, we are completely on Wilson and Sperber's side when they argue that the literal meaning involved here is only a tool for retrieving the content of communicative acts. At the same time, a metaphor such as this one is not to be considered, in our framework, a departure from a norm, as we are not relying on strict semantic norms that are somehow broken in this case. Thus, there is no commitment to a coding-like framework nor to semantic combinatorial rules. Moreover, the interpretation of non-conventional metaphors clearly relies on world knowledge and thus on information found in the General Common Ground as well. So, the understanding of all metaphors involves the GCG, and there are no special interpretation mechanisms at work for them.

2.2 Loose Use

Let us turn to another case treated by Wilson and Sperber (2012, p. 19), which is loose use. One example that is particularly interesting (pp. 54 and 58–60) is

(3)   I need a Kleenex.

In English, (3) is usually interpreted as a request for a tissue, not necessarily of a specific brand. The very same happens in German, for instance, with "Tempo", so that

(4)   Ich brauche ein Tempo.

is also understood as a request for a tissue of some unspecified brand. Wilson and Sperber list the English version among a series of loose use examples, claiming its use is to be placed along the continuum that, as said, they see between literal use of language, tropes and loose use.

One of the main points of Wilson and Sperber's analysis of the above example is the refusal of the idea of taking contextually determined standards of precision into account. Lewis' idea (1979) is that loose use can be dealt with by assuming that there are different standards of precision in play: in some contexts, the use of a word is constrained by lower standards of precision. Wilson and Sperber's idea is that this is an *ad hoc* assumption that does not work with other examples, such as (3).

In this case, they argue

> ...*there is no continuum on which being similar enough to Kleenex*
> *amounts to actually being Kleenex relative to stricter or looser standards of*
> *precision. "Run", "Kleenex" and many other words have sharp conceptual*
> *boundaries and no ordered series of successively broader extensions which*
> *might be picked out by raising or lowering some standard of precision. Yet*
> *these terms are often loosely used.* (Wilson and Sperber 2012, p. 59)

It is certainly true that there is no continuum between being similar to a Kleenex and being a Kleenex; however, this does not seem to imply that the word "Kleenex" has such a sharp conceptual boundary as assumed here, or at least that the boundary is so relevant for the purpose of understanding the utterance. At least in English (and the same applies to German as far as "Tempo" goes) Kleenex has a meaning related to the brand and a relation, part of the world and language knowledge, with the more general concept of tissue. For this reason, however, we would not classify it as a loose use case, but as a trope/a lexicalized convention. In our account, the relation between "Kleenex" and "generic tissue" has place at the due to the brands' popularity. In common language, the use of this trope (a synecdoche) has been lexicalized, such that there is actually a semantic relation between "tissue" and "Kleenex", or between "Taschentuch" and "Tempo". This convention, which we thus place at the level of the GCG, establishes a relation that we might relate to what is commonly called semantic meaning. No information on the particular situation at hand is actually needed to understand the speaker, as the link between the two words is established at a more general level. To understand why this is not a case of loose use in our picture, let us consider an Italian equivalent:

(5)   Mi serve un Kleenex.

(5) is an utterance that would only be understood by an Italian hearer as a request for a tissue in particular situations, as there is no such a thing as a convention linking the brand Kleenex with tissues in Italian. For instance, if a speaker was sneezing and there was a packet of tissues on the table, she could utter (5) and be understood as asking for one of the tissues lying on the table. In this case, the information related to the ICG is of fundamental importance to understand the sentence: it is only because there is perceptual information available to speaker and hearer that (5) can work as an effective sentence. Here, all the mechanisms like perspective taking, joint attention and so on, that we have placed at the level of the ICG, come into play. This is clearly not the case for (3) and (4), as there is no need to appeal to specific information (i.e. to the ICG) to understand the speaker as wanting a generic tissue. This shows that (3) is actually different from (5): the first can be classified as a lexicalized trope, the use of which rests on a convention that pertains to general knowledge of the spoken language, while the latter is a case of loose use.

The difference between the two cases is actually useful to understand the relation between the ICG and the GCG as we shape it; the probably frequent use of the word "Kleenex" as a synecdoche is what has established the convention that has created a new piece of information regarding the use of these words in

English at the GCG level. Something like that has not happened in Italian, where the use of "Kleenex" in this sense has to be understood in light of specific (immediate) contextual situations.

Note that our interpretation is actually supported by what Wilson and Sperber (2012, pp. 19–20) say:

> ...For instance, the word "Kleenex", originally a brand name, may also have come to mean, more generally, a disposable tissue. However, such ambiguities ultimately derive from repeated instances in which the original brand name is loosely used. If "Kleenex" now has tissue as one of its lexical senses, it is because the word was often loosely used to convey this broader meaning before it became lexicalised.

The additional step needed in this description is that, once the trope has been lexicalized in this way, there is no need to consider it as loose use it is now only a matter of semantics, as the meaning "generic tissue" has now a conventional relation with the lexical entry.

To go back to their treatment of the case, then, appealing to a continuum of standard of precision to explain loose use, as Lewis does, is a wrong move because it is, as they underline, not particularly generalizable. Also, it assumes a clear distinction between a literal, precise interpretation of the lexical entry and a vaguer one. However, nothing like that happens in the description we have given above; the frequent use of Kleenex to indicate generic tissues in a particular language is what feeds the GCG level with additional information regarding the use of the two terms, which is what explains its use.

Note that the ICG can also affect the understanding of "Kleenex" in English sentences in a way that reverses the lexicalized trope: If, for example, a person is standing in front of a shelf in a supermarket full of tissues of different brands and utters (3), the knowledge of this information (contained in the ICG) would lead the hearer to understand "Kleenex" not in the lexicalized trope meaning, but in the precise meaning denoting tissues of a specific brand.

Thus, we claim that true loose use (and the inversion of loose use) are grounded in the ICG. As soon as loose use is lexicalized, this information becomes part of the GCG and thus the use of such words ceases to be a case of loose use proper. In this way, our analysis is able to describe the difference between the use of "Kleenex" in English and in Italian. In contrast, the interpretation of metaphors is always relying on the GCG, as metaphors explore some similarities that we know of independently of the specific situation we are in. Therefore, understanding metaphors always involves GCG, independently of how lexicalized the metaphors are (the lexicalization of a metaphor would be a matter of how much of the knowledge about the similarity is considered to be semantic knowledge as opposed to world knowledge).

However, note that this does not contradict the contextualist that literal use and non-literal use of language are to be dealt with as similar cases, and not in the light of a rule-exception dichotomy. The difference between the GCG and the ICG is made to spell out how lexical entries can interact with the level of perception, attention and working memory mechanisms.

The examples given above should make clear that the interaction between the two levels is definitely dynamic, as frequent loose use, for instance, can cause the creation of a convention at the GCG level. Also, it should make evident that we agree with Relevance Theory's point that it is useless to rest on the assumption that there is a definite distinction in quality between literal use, loose use and metaphorical use of sentences. However, we argue that keeping a level such as the GCG–where knowledge about lexical entries, their relations, and the world interact–does not entail denying the role of context, nor embracing a code-theoretical account.

3   Linguistic Evidence for the Distinction

In many languages of the world, the status of verb arguments as part of the ICG or the GCG plays a role for their grammatical marking. Zero realization is often chosen for immediately prementioned and activated referents, e.g. in Japanese and Kaluli. Other languages choose different kinds of articles or case markers in order to distinguish between referents of arguments that have been prementioned and are part of the ICG and those that have not, but may be part of the GCG. A notion that is related to the concept of common ground is "focus". Focus, according to Lambrecht (1994), is what is left of an assertion after we have subtracted the presupposition, i.e. it is the material not included in the ICG. For some languages this kind of "newness" is decisive for whether or not they case mark an argument. In the following we give examples for all of these phenomena.

3.1   Lakhota Definite Articles

Lakhota, a Siouan language spoken in North America, has two definite articles, $ki(\eta)$ and $k'u\eta$. $Ki(\eta)$ is the general default definite article, analogous to English *the*. It can be used to refer to something in the GCG, as well as something in the ICG, i.e. it can be used to refer to something previously mentioned in the discourse, or it can be used to refer to something in the immediate environment of the interlocutors which has not been explicitly mentioned before. $K'u\eta$, on the other hand, can only be used to refer to something in the ICG which has been explicitly mentioned in the discourse; hence it is usually translated as "the aforementioned" (Ullrich 2011 p. 347). It cannot be used to refer to something in the immediate environment of the interlocutors which has not been explicitly mentioned before.

3.2   Focus-Related Ergative Case Marking

An example of optional ergative marking of focal arguments, i.e. arguments not part of the ICG, comes from Umpithamu (Australia, Verstraete 2010).

(6)   woypu-mpal ayngki-n=ina
        ghost-ERG   throw-PST=3PL.NOM
        'It's the ghosts who threw it.'

For non-focal actor arguments, ergative cannot be chosen.

(7)   amitha athuna   yukurrun kali-n=iluwa
        mother 1SG.GEN gear   carry-PST=3SG.NOM
        'My mother carried the gear.'

The opposite phenomenon is observed in Kaluli, a Papuan language (Schieffelin 1985), which has a complex case system. One of its features is that focal actor arguments are assigned ergative case; when the actor is not focal, the actor and undergoer are both normally assigned "neutral case". A similar case of optional ergative marking is found in Kuuk Thaayorre (Australia, Gaby 2008). Here if the actor is not expected based on the ICG, ergative marking is chosen. In (8) and (9), the narrator talks about his childhood and what he did as a child, when all of a sudden in (9) he switches to his parents.

(8)   thowolnam nganjin   parr_r mant
        play:IMPF 1PLEXC.NOM child   small
        'We small children were playing.'

(9)   ngul nganjin   ... nganip-i nganjan thakarr pul   then
        1PLEXC.NOM father-ERG 1PLEXC.ACC   leave:PF 3DU.NOM
        nganam-u
        mother-ERG
        'Then we ... father and mother left us (to go fishing)' (Gaby 2008)

Apart from languages that switch between a Nom-Acc and an Erg-Abs system based on the information status of the Actor, there are also languages that switch between no case marking and case marking in particular context, usually without affecting the role interpretation (based on Kittilä 2005, McGregor 2010, 2013). Still, the interpretation of the sentence may change on a different level, as the following examples show. In Mongoose A (India) the marker nə signals special focus on the actor argument and changes the reading of the sentence in the sense that the actor is understood as not acting in a way that would be predicted based on our world knowledge (GCG), e.g. in the case of chicken they are expected to eat what they are fed. If the NP *chicken* is case-marked, this results in the reading that they are stealing food (they should not be eating).
        Example: Mongoose A (Tibeto-Burman, Coupe 2007)

(10)   a-hən   a-tʃak   tʃʔ-ər-ù?
        NRL-chicken NRL-paddy consume-PRES-DEC
        'The chickens are eating paddy.'

(11)   a-hən   nə a-tʃak   tʃʔ-ər-ù?
        NRL-chicken AGT NRL-paddy consume-PRES-DEC
        'The chickens are eating paddy'. (implying that they are stealing it).

4   Conclusions

The role of context in communication has been debated for a long time and still represents a controversial topic, despite the many changes that new theories and models introduced since Gricean pragmatics has been proposed. One of the most difficult issues to solve is the role that lexical meaning has and whether relying on contextual information means depriving the study of language of "stable meanings". To this extent, the question regarding the interface between semantics and pragmatics is far from being solved. In the current paper, we have proposed a distinction that cross-cuts the line of what is normally looked at as strictly pertaining to semantics and pragmatics, resting on the assumption that there are several levels that interact in communication. Common Ground is divided into Immediate Common Ground (ICG) – related to the situation at hand, where perception, joint attention and short-term memory mechanisms contribute to reference fixing– and General Common Ground (GCG) where conventions regarding language, as well as knowledge regarding the world and long term memory mechanisms have the leading role. As explained through the discussion of different examples, this distinction is also reflected in the difference between different cases of non-literal use. In this picture, what is traditionally called lexical meaning at the level of GCG is effectively employed and actually interacts constantly with information coming from the ICG, with perception and joint attention mechanisms, among other factors, constantly being a source of comprehension of the verbal interaction.

Both ICG and GCG are thought of as dynamic systems of information constantly interacting with each other and with the external world: thus, the core idea is that, to make communication effective, mechanisms that are quite different from each other play an essential role. Considering the notion of common ground as central (instead of context), we aim at including not only the linguistic context of the utterance and the restricted ongoing situation that characterise the conversation, but also all that pertains to the level of communication skills and conventional knowledge that is required for language to be used efficiently.

As it has been argued in this paper, then, the distinction between ICG and GCG is rooted in cognitive reality, as it tries to incorporate the different cognitive processes that are involved in online use and comprehension of language. Additionally, ICG and GCG can be effectively employed as notions in the analysis of non-literal linguistic use, such as tropes and loose use, that have always been a complex problem for the interface between traditionally defined pragmatics and semantics. As underlined, a qualitative distinction between literal use and metaphorical use is an assumption that is rejected by this framework; the general idea is that information shared by the speakers always plays a role in the determination of the meaning. On the other hand, information can be of very different nature and coming from different sources: in this sense, conventions are thought to play a role that is reflected, for instance, more in the use of metaphors than in loose use. We think one of the greatest advantages of the distinction, as shown in Sect. 2, is the possibility to distinguish between cases of lexicalised metaphors and loose use, that reflect differences between different communicative situations. Moreover, the distinction is reflected in how different languages encode different relations between words.

Finally, the fact that different languages seem to encode the difference between the two levels on a grammatical level is particularly encouraging for the picture, as it shows how relevant it is in specific communicative situations. The fact that this happens in different languages on a level that takes into consideration both whether or not something is expected on a knowledge-of-the-world level, as for instance in Mongoose Ao, and whether or not something was mentioned before or not, as in Lakhota, is one of the factors that lead us to think that world-knowledge and language-knowledge can both have different roles according to the common ground level (ICG or GCG) that is considered.

In conclusion, we think that the distinction can be fruitful on many levels. Firstly, it can be used to implement an account of communication grounded in cognition that takes into consideration relevant mechanisms that are involved in online comprehension and production. Secondly, cases like loose use and metaphors can easily be treated in the framework, providing an effective way to capture the variety of uses present in everyday conversation. Thirdly, it points in the direction of a picture of language that does not discard lexical meaning as a whole but provides a starting point for the contextually-driven mechanisms that play an essential role in communication. Finally, it can be supported by relevant cross-linguistic data, as shown.

References

Coupe, A.: A Grammar of Mongsen Ao Mouton de Gruyter, Berlin and New York (2007)

Gaby, A.: Pragmatically case-marked: non syntactic functions of the Thaayorre ergative suffix. In: Mushin, I., Baker, B. (eds.) Discourse and Grammar in Australian Languages, pp. 111–134. Benjamins, Amsterdam (2008)

Grice, P.: Meaning. Philos. Rev. **66**, 377–388 (1957)

Grice, P.: Studies in the Way of Words. Harvard University Press, Cambridge (1989)

Kittilä, S.: Optional marking of arguments. Lang. Sci. **27**, 111–134 (2005)

Krifka, M., Musan, R.: Information structure: overview and linguistic issues. In: Krifka, M., Musan, R. (eds.) The Expression of Information Structure, pp. 1–44. De Gruyter Mouton, Berlin (2012)

Lambrecht, K.: Information Structure and Sentence Form. Cambridge University Press, Cambridge (1994)

Lewis, D.: Scorekeeping in a language game. J. Philos. Logic, **8**(1) (1979). doi:10.1007/bf00258436

McGregor, W.: Optional ergative case marking systems in a typological-semiotic perspective. Lingua **120**, 1610–1636 (2010)

McGregor, W.: Optionality in grammar and language use. Linguistics **51**, 1147–1204 (2013)

Perry, J.: Indexicals and demonstratives. In: Hale, R., Wright, C. (eds.) Companion to the Philosophy of Language. Blackwells Publishers Inc., Oxford (1997)

Rayo, A.: A Plea for Semantic Localism. Nous **47**(4), 647–679 (2011)

Schieffelin, B.: The acquisition of Kaluli. In: Slobin, D. (ed.) The Cross-Linguistic Study of Language- Acquisition, pp. 525–593. Lawrence Earlbaum, Hillsdale (1985)

Ullrich, J.: New Lakota Dictionary, 2nd edn. Lakota Language Corsotium, Bloomington (2001)

Van Valin, R.D.: Meaning and interpretation. J. Pragmat. 4(3), 213–231 (1980). doi:10.1016/0378-2166(80)90037-5

Verstraete, J.C.: Animacy and information structure in the system of ergative marking in Umpithamu. Lingua **120**, 1637–1651 (2010)

Wilson, D., Sperber, D.: Meaning and Relevance. Cambridge University Press, Cambridge (2012)

Wittgenstein, L.: Philosophical Investigations. Wiley, Hoboken (2010)

Gender Roles in Russian Prohibitive Constructions: A Corpus Study

Olga Blinova[✉] and Ekaterina Troshchenkova

Saint Petersburg State University,
7/9 Universitetskaya nab., St. Petersburg 199034, Russia
{o.blinova, e.troschenkova}@spbu.ru

Abstract. The study is aimed at describing various aspects of the context that influence interpretation of a Russian prohibitive construction Noun-Dat.Pl + *нельзя* 'should not' + Verb-Inf. For this the data of the corpus "Russian Web 2011" (15.8 billion words) were used: the queries for several most frequent nouns encoding gender roles (women, men, girls, boys, mothers, fathers, wives, husbands) are analyzed. The study showed that for different cases different degree of broadness for the context is important. Firstly, it is syntactic features of the construction (the elements it consists of and the word order). Secondly, it is the semantic-syntactic features (the semantic role of the dative argument and the meaning of the infinitive). Thirdly, it is the surrounding elements within the sentence or the neighboring sentences. However, in many cases an even broader cognitive and cultural context plays a significant role, thus, one should also pay attention to the topical domain of prohibitions and how the topics are related to the social role expectations existing as background knowledge shared by the members of a community.

Keywords: Social roles · Speech acts · Gender groups · Gender stereotypes · Prohibitive constructions · Semantic roles · Topics · Frequency lists

1 Introduction

The aim of the study is to analyze a Russian prohibitive construction with *нельзя* 'should not' from a structural and cognitive point of view as it conveys stereotypical gender role expectations relevant for the Russian culture. The main point is to look at the aspects of the context on which the construction's interpretation can be based and that restrict its understanding by the language speakers.

We suppose that this task goes beyond simple syntactic and semantic analysis of the narrow context and requires a broader view that takes into account the functional nature of a prohibition as a communicative means of behavior regulation in the society. This leads to the need to apply an interdisciplinary approach that would transcend the limits of traditional linguistic analysis by employing the achievements of modern cognitive science, sociology and social psychology.

© Springer International Publishing AG 2017
P. Brézillon et al. (Eds.): CONTEXT 2017, LNAI 10257, pp. 647–660, 2017.
DOI: 10.1007/978-3-319-57837-8_52

2 Study Design, Material and Method

2.1 The List of Social Roles

Linguistics has borrowed the term "social role" from sociology and social psychology [1–4] which used it to denote socially approved behavior expected from anyone who has a certain position in the social structure. What is of importance for this study is that, as Parsons emphasized it in his theory, when we deal with social roles there are **mutual** expectations both concerning what is expected from the actor playing the role and from others towards this actor. In sociolinguistics and cognitive linguistics social roles were applied to studying a number of, linguistic phenomena: semantics of words and expressions, structure of the communicative acts of various kinds, discursive behavior with different partners [5–8]. Our study dealing with stereotypical expectations about a number of gender roles is focused on their verbal manifestation in prohibitive constructions.

For a list of nouns, encoding the main gender social roles, we used The Frequency Dictionary of Modern Russian Language [9]. Having checked the Frequency List of Nouns, we picked out the most frequent nouns denoting a person. The results are shown in the Table 1.

Table 1. The most frequent nouns meaning 'person'

Lemma	Freq. (ipm)	Rank	Lemma	Freq. (ipm)	Rank
человек 'human being'	2723.0	39	член 'member'	207.4	522
друг 'friend'	874.2	106	брат 'brother'	203.0	542
ребенок 'child'	658.3	137	гражданин 'citizen'	199.4	553
женщина 'woman'	533.3	171	начальник 'boss'	198.9	557
отец 'father'	484.1	192	гость 'guest'	192.7	579
жена 'wife'	376.8	255	мальчик 'boy'	188.0	597
мать 'mother'	330.1	301	представитель 'representative'	185.7	604
мама 'mother'	322.6	309	девочка 'girl'	185.1	606
сын 'son'	285.1	360	герой 'hero'	184.0	609
муж 'husband'	263.0	397	врач 'doctor'	173.1	653
автор 'author'	262.1	398	хозяин 'owner'	170.6	664
мужчина 'man'	253.2	416	писатель 'writer'	166.3	685
товарищ 'friend, comrade'	230.6	462	руководитель 'leader'	162.0	700
директор 'director'	222.2	484	специалист 'specialist, expert'	161.9	701
девушка 'girl (young woman)'	213.3	509	родитель 'parent'	160.0	717

Then gender-related nouns were chosen from the list, which yielded the following pairs: *man – woman, husband – wife, father – mother, girl – boy*. The nouns that did not have a gender pair in the top-30 of the frequency list (such as *son, brother, young woman*) were excluded from further study.

Thus, there are 8 nouns denoting social roles that encode basic gender difference (*man* and *woman*) and "derivative" ones as they take into account the age (*girl* and *boy*), the family status in the nuclear family (*husband* and *wife*) or parental status (*mother* and *father*).

2.2 Prohibitive in Russian

Prohibition can be viewed from the point of view of grammar, logic and pragmatics. From the first point of view the term "prohibitive" is applied to forms and constructions of negative imperative that express a combination of meanings "imperative" + "not" such as "do not do P" [10: 55–56, 11]. In Russian prohibitive is expressed by imperfect imperatives, while perfect imperatives get preventive interpretation, i.e. they serve as warnings [12]. It is noted that in case of a prohibitive the listener-actor can control the action (the action is controllable), unlike with preventives [13].

Prohibition is also studied in the context of logical concepts of possibility and necessity and while describing linguistic expressions (predicates, modal words, etc.) that convey the corresponding modal meanings. The neoclassical deontic logic studies concepts of 'obligation', 'prohibition', 'permission', 'indifference' [14]. Traditionally there are the following deontic modal meanings – "possibility and necessity the fulfilment of which is stipulated by social, legal, moral norms or volition of a particular person" [15]. Prototypical meanings of deontic modality are those of permission and prohibition. Prohibition in this context is viewed as **negation of permission**.

Special attention to prohibition is paid in the speech acts theory. If one uses the taxonomy of J. Searle, "prohibition" is considered to be a directive speech act, i.e. an imperative utterance aimed at making listener act in a certain way [16]; in our case one should speak of the "caused non-acting". Sometimes more particular meanings of the prohibitive are distinguished. Hence, Allan [17] first singles out "prohibitives" as a type of directives and then speaks of the English performative prohibitive verbs *enjoin, forbid, prohibit, proscribe, restrict*.

We will be following interpretation of prohibition as "causation of non-performing a **controllable** action" [13].

Russian has a broad range of prohibitive constructions, including constructions with the imperative (*не делай X* 'don't do X', *прекрати делать X* 'stop doing X', *перестань делать X* 'stop doing X', *не смей делать X* 'don't you dare do X', etc.) as well as a number of impersonal constructions (*нельзя, не разрешено, не позволено, не следует, не стоит, запрещается, не разрешается, не полагается, не положено, стыдно, грешно, зазорно, позорно* etc. *делать X* 'one should not, is not allowed to do X; It is sinful, shameful to do X').

In this article we study an impersonal construction of the type **Noun-Dat. Pl + predicative *нельзя* 'should not' + Verb-Inf**. This construction can be seen as one the basic ones in Russian to express prohibition. This is a standard, stylistically neutral way of conveying prohibitive meaning. Besides, this construction is easy to search for (the search gives a significant number of relevant results). And finally, it is convenient for further analysis of the contents of prohibition: the construction includes an infinitive, thus before automatic processing of the search results in the corpus one doesn't have to carry out preliminary lemmatization.

2.3   The Source Corpus, Search Queries and Results

Prohibitive constructions with *нельзя* 'should not' are studied on the basis of the search results in the corpus "Russian Web 2011" (Russian TenTen corpus, ruTenTen11) that contains 15.8 billion words [18]. For the search Corpus Query Language was used, namely straightforward queries of the following type [word = "*женщинам*"] [word = "*нельзя*"] '**women-Dat.Pl should not**'. We took into account simple word order change and also used queries of the type [word = "*нельзя*"] [word = " *женщинам*"]. The general results obtained in the research are shown in the Table 2.

Table 2. Search results

Query	Count	ipm
[word = "*женщинам*"] [word = "*нельзя*"] 'women'	584	0.03
[word = "*нельзя*"] [word = "*женщинам*"] 'women'	43	0.00
[word = "*мужчинам*"] [word = "*нельзя*"] 'men'	219	0.00
[word = "*нельзя*"] [word = "*мужчинам*"] 'men'	14	0.00
[word = "*матерям*"] [word = "*нельзя*"] 'mothers'	19	0.00
[word = "*нельзя*"] [word = "*матерям*"] 'mothers'	Empty result	
[word = "*отцам*"] [word = "*нельзя*"] 'fathers'	2	0.00
[word = "*нельзя*"] [word = "*отцам*"] 'fathers'	Empty result	
[word = "*женам*"] [word = "*нельзя*"] 'wives'	5	0.00
[word = "*нельзя*"] [word = "*жёнам*"] 'wives'	2	0.00
[word = "*мужьям*"] [word = "*нельзя*"] 'husbands'	1	0.00
[word = "*нельзя*"] [word = "*мужьям*"] 'husbands'	Empty result	
[word = "*девочкам*"] [word = "*нельзя*"] 'girls'	60	0.00
[word = "*нельзя*"] [word = "*девочкам*"] 'girls'	7	0.00
[word = "*мальчикам*"] [word = "*нельзя*"] 'boys'	40	0.00
[word = "*нельзя*"] [word = "*мальчикам*"] 'boys'	8	0.00

The corpus mainly contains prohibitions concerning the basic gender roles of *women* (62,5%) and *men* (23,2%). As to "derivative" roles, most of the prohibitions are about children (11,5%). It is also interesting that in gender pairs female social roles get significantly bigger number of prohibitive constructions, see Table 3.

Table 3. Frequency of the prohibitive construction with *нельзя* for 8 social roles

Social role	Count	Percent	Social role	Count	Percent
women	627	62,45	*mothers*	19	1,89
men	233	23,21	*wives*	7	0,70
girls	67	6,67	*fathers*	2	0,20
boys	48	4,78	*husbands*	1	0,10

2.4 Meaningful Elements of the Prohibitive Construction, Analysis Scheme

The main issue in analyzing the contents of prohibition, expressed by the impersonal construction **Noun-Dat.Pl + нельзя 'should not' + Verb-Inf**, is to look at the semantics of the infinitive of the notional verb. However, Noun-Dat.Pl can encode various semantic roles for the participants of the situation described in the utterance. Dative case of the noun can express semantic roles of the agent, patient, experiencer, possessor. Information about the semantic role of the dative argument allows to describe the situation and find out about the specifics of the prohibition.

It is also important to take into account the information about the category of the people who are covered by the prohibition. This information can be inferred from the attribute to the noun, as the adjective or participle (e.g. *married*) can narrow the category expressed by the noun to a subcategory, so that the prohibition would only concern some representatives of a social role.

Thus, in the further analysis the following types of information were taken into consideration: (1) subcategories of social roles defined on the basis of attributive adjectives used with the Noun-Dat.Pl (see paragraph 3); (2) semantic roles, assigned to dative arguments, correlated with semantic classes of verbs (see paragraph 4); (3) frequencies of verbs (see paragraph 5); (4) "topics" into which different prohibitive situations can be classified (see paragraph 6).

3 Ad Hoc Categorization Within Social Roles

Attribute in preposition to the noun, expressed by the adjective or participle in the contexts like *большим-A-Dat.Pl мальчикам-N-Dat.Pl нельзя плакать-V-Inf* '**big boys should not cry**', characterizes the members of gender groups and allows discriminating several relevant subgroups. Such attributes are found with *women* (#187), *men* (#23), *mothers* (#19), *girls* (#11) and *boys* (#3) in search results. Frequency lists of the attributes were made and analyzed, showing most of the subcategories are found within the category of *women* (Table 4 shows the results that appear in the search twice and more):

It can be seen in the corpus data that women are mainly subcategorized according to their fertility status (*pregnant, nursing, nulliparous*), appearance (*fat, beautiful*), age (*young, senior*), marital status (*married, single*), nationality and faith. Especially large number of prohibitions is about *pregnant women*. According to the frequency lists for other nouns, one can find the following subgroups towards which the prohibitions are

Table 4. Subcategories for women

Attribute	Count	Attribute	Count
беременная 'pregnant'	112	*еврейская* 'Jewish'	2
полная 'fat'	7	*египетская* 'Egyptian'	2
кормящая 'nursing'	6	*красивая* 'beautiful'	2
замужняя 'married'	5	*мусульманская* 'Muslim'	2
молодая 'young'	5	*незамужняя* 'single'	2
нерожавшая 'nulliparous'	4	*пожилая* 'senior'	2
курящая 'smoking'	3		

formulated: *men – Russian* (#3), *married* (#3); *mothers – nursing* (#11), *pregnant* (#4); *girls – small* (#2).

Hence, we see that prohibitions may reflect stereotypical expectations about a particular subgroup of people playing the social role. Which subgroups are most frequently associated with the limitations in their role behavior is of special interest both in themselves (as culturally and cognitively meaningful role subtypes) and in relation to the topics of prohibition.

4   The Repertoire of Semantic Roles and Ambiguity

By "semantic role" we mean – following [19] – "an invariant of different ways to encode the participant" (at the level of morphosyntax) and "generalization of the participant's functions in a number of situations denoted by a group of predicates" (at the level of semantics).

The scheme suggested in Russian FrameBank [20] was chosen as a model for describing the semantic roles. This allowed us not only to ascribe a semantic role label to the dative arguments of the predicate for the construction in question, but also indirectly describe the semantics of the verbs that are included in the construction.

To mark the semantic roles, we used the inventory of FrameBank, see [19]. Only dative arguments were labeled, thus yielding the **following set of semantic roles**: Addressee, Agent, Beneficiary, Contractor, Causer, Content of Thought, Contractor of Social Relationship, Eventual Possessor, Initial Possessor, Part of Patient Under Affecting, Patient, Patient of Social Relationship, Possessor, Reason, Speaker, Speaker/Sound Source, Stimulus, Subject of Behaviour, Subject of Mental State, Subject of Motion, Subject of Perception, Subject of Physiological Response, Subject of Physiological State, Subject of Social Relationship, Theme. These detailed semantic roles are clustered in larger "domains" of Agent, Patient, Experiencer and also reflect the semantics of the verb used in the construction.

There is a number of examples where the dative argument can be ascribed more than one semantic role label. In some cases the ambiguity is removed by broader context, cf. the narrow context where the argument can be ascribed the role of either the Speaker or the Addressee: **женщинам нельзя грубить** 'Women should not be rude/One should not be rude with women', the broader context "*Нельзя бить — она же девочка! Девочкам и женщинам нельзя грубить! Как вы можете так* *разговаривать с женщиной!"* 'You can't beat her – she's a girl! One should not be rude with girls and women! How dare you speak like that to a woman!' With the help of the broader context of the neighboring sentences one can confidently ascribe the role of the Addressee to the argument.

However, sometimes even such broader textual context does not help with ambiguity removal. One has to turn to a larger cognitive and cultural context of the background knowledge of what behavior is expected from a person and towards a person fulfilling a particular social role. Cf. the following examples:

(1) *Ну так учтите: **есть фразы, прощать которые женщинам нельзя.***
    so, bear it in mind: be-Prs sentence-Nom.Pl forgive-Inf which women-Dat.Pl should not-Pred
    So, bear it in mind: there are words for which women should not be forgiven/that women should not forgive.

(2) *Как утверждают мужчины, **женщинам нельзя говорить правду**, причем для их же пользы.*
    as men say, women-Dat.Pl should not-Pred tell-Inf truth-Acc.Sg., for their own sake
    As men say, one should not tell the truth to women/women should not tell the truth, for their own sake.

(3) *То есть **женщинам нельзя говорить "нет"**, требуется следовать принципу тотального «да».*
    that is women-Dat.Pl should not-Pred tell-Inf "no", it should be the principle of a total "yes".
    That is one should not say "no" to women/women should not say "no", it should be the principle of a total "yes".

In these examples interpretation of the argument with either of the two semantic roles (Subject of Physiological State VS Content of Thought; Speaker VS Addressee) is possible. Nevertheless, the right choice of the semantic role can be made taking into consideration who is saying this. Thus, in example (2) the dative argument seems to "ask for" the Addressee interpretation rather than the Speaker, as we know that utterance is from men's point of view ("As men say" and this is "for their (women's) sake").

It is of interest that the change in word order can also serve in ambiguity removal. In the example the dative argument unequivocally gets the Addressee role:

(4) *Нельзя грубить женщинам.*
    should not-Pred say-Inf rude things women-Dat.Pl
    One should not say rude things to women.

On the whole, nouns that mean gender groups can be mostly interpreted in the following semantic roles in the search (Table 5):

We distinguish six main domains for the semantic roles, those of Agent (A), Patient (P), Experiencer (E), Beneficiary (B), Theme (T), and Reason (R). At first, we came up with a hypothesis that children gender groups in the formal semantic-syntactic sense are "more patient-like", while adults are "more agent-like". However, the hypothesis

Table 5. The most common semantic roles[a]

Women	Men	Girls	Boys	Mothers
AG (A) #267 (42.6%)	AG (A) #73 (31.3%)	AG (A) #22 (32.8%)	AG (A) #22 (45.8%)	AG (A) #11 (57.9%)
SMOT (A) #90 (14.4%)	REAS (R) #38 (16.3%)	SMOT (A) #14 (20.9%)	SPSYRESP (E) #6 (12.5%)	SPEAK (A) #2 (10.5%)
TH (T) #38 (6.1%)	SMOT (A) #27 (11.6%)	TH (T) #5 (7.5%)	PAT (P) #4 (8.3%)	TH (T) #1 (5.3%)
EPOSS (B) #27 (4.3%)	TH (T) #19 (8.2%)	AG-SPERC (E) #3 (4.5%)	AG-SPERC (E) #3 (6.3%)	PAT-SOCREL (P) #1 (5.3%)
REAS (R) #22 (3.5%)	EPOSS (B) #14 (6.0%)	EPOSS (B) #3 (4.5%)	SMOT (A) #3 (6.3%)	SPSYST (E) #1 (5.3%)
PAT (P) #21 (3.3%)	SPERC (E) #10 (4.3%)	ADR (E) #3 (4.5%)	CSOCREL (B) #3 (6.3%)	REAS (R) #1 (5.3%)
PPAT (P) #17 (2.7%)	ADR (E) #9 (3.9%)	SPEAK (A) #2 (3.0%)	TH (T) #1 (2.1%)	SPHYSRESR (E) #1 (5.3%)
ADR (E) #15 (2.4%)	SSOCREL (A) #7 (3.0%)	SSOCREL (A) #2 (3.0%)	SPSYST (E) #1 (2.1%)	AG-SPERC (E) #1 (5.3%)
SPEAK (A) #13 (2.1%)	SPSYRESP (E) #6 (2.6%)	CSOCREL (B) #2 (3.0%)	REAS (R) #1 (2.1%)	
SPSYST (E) #13 (2.1%)	SPSYST (E) #4 (1.7%)	SPSYST (E) #1 (1.5%)	ADR (E) #1 (2.1%)	

[a]List of abbreviations: Addressee - ADR; Agent - AG; Contractor - CONTR; Beneficiary - BEN; Causer - CAUS; Content of thought - CONT; Contractor of Social Relationship - CSOCREL; Eventual Possessor - EPOSS; Initial Possessor - IPOSS; Part of Patient under Affecting - PPAT; Patient - PAT; Patient of Social Relationship - PATSOCREL; Possessor - POSS; Reason - REAS; Speaker - SPEAK; Speaker/Sound Source - SPEAK/SOUND; Stimulus - STIM; Subject of Behaviour - SBEH; Subject of Mental State - SMENT; Subject of Motion - SMOT; Subject of Perception - SPERC; Subject of Physiological Response - SPHYSRESR; Subject of Physiological State - SPHYST; Subject of Psychological Response - SPSYRESP; Subject of Psychological State - SPSYST; Subject of social relationship - SSOCREL; Theme - TH. As the number of results obtained for *wives*, *husbands* and *fathers* was extremely small, we have not included these data into the table for comparison.

was disproved by the data: agent roles is the largest domain for all social roles (*mothers* 68.4%, *girls* 59.7%, *women* 59.1%, *boys* 52.1%, *men* 45.9%). There is rather a gender difference in the degree of agentivity for a social role, as male roles have lower percentage in comparison with female roles. Patient roles can be found with *women* (6%), *boys* (8.3%) and *mothers* (5.3%), so there is hardly any explainable tendency for this semantic role in the data. As to Experiencer semantic roles – with the exception of *mothers* (15.9%) – they are less frequent for female roles such as *women* (4.5%) and *girls* (10.5%) than for male ones such as *men* (12.5%) and *boys* (23%).

5 Frequency Lists of Verbs

In analyzing the prohibition contents, it is useful to look at frequency lists of verbs included in the prohibitive construction.

Before showing the results of the analysis, it should be noted that we took into account not only the contexts where it is explicitly mentioned what should not be done, but also constructions without the infinitive where we proceed from the assumption that there is a null element (Ø). Sometimes the meaning of the construction with Ø can be restored on the basis of adjuncts context, cf.:

(5) *Туда женщинам нельзя!*
there- Adv women-Dat.Pl should not- Pred
Women should not go **there!**

(6) *Одногруппника хоронили на татарском кладбище, а **там** женщинам нельзя.*
groupmate-Acc.Sg bury-Past.Pl at the Tatar cemetery, and in there-Adv
women-Dat.Pl should not-Pred
Our groupmate was buried at the Tatar cemetery, and women are not allowed **in there**.

In example (5) the presence of the adjunct (adverb *туда* 'there') shows that the null element belongs to the lexical-semantic class 'verb of motion', thus ascribing the dative argument a semantic role of the 'subject of motion'.

In example (6) the whole context, especially the adverb *там* 'in there', labels the null element as belonging to lexical-semantic class 'verb of staying in a location' and ascribes the semantic role 'theme' to the dative argument.

The contexts of the following type are of special interest:

(7) *Почему мужчинам **все можно**, а **женщинам нельзя**?*
why men-Dat.Pl everything is allowed, and women-Dat.Pl should not-Pred
Why everything is allowed to men and nothing to women?

In such contexts one can see the null Ø that has the qualities of the verb *делать* 'do' and the dative argument has the Agent role.

In the tables below there are lists of the 10 most frequent verbs for each gender role (Tables 6 and 7).

Speaking of similarities and differences for various gender roles, on the one hand, one can see that adult roles of men and women and their younger counterparts of boys and girls (that yielded most of the search results) are all very much linked with the sociocultural expectations of how a person should be dressed and where a person is allowed to go: the four frequency lists include verbs of *носить* 'wear' and *ходить* 'go'. The verb 'go' can also be connected with the idea of not wearing some types of clothes. However, in its other meaning it is usually associated with prohibitions on going to certain places (e.g. *altar*).

On the other hand, some expectations seem to be more gender specific, such as *плакать* 'cry' found in a significant number of contexts for boys and a smaller number of contexts for men, but absent in the frequency list both for girls and women. Another thing to be noted in not just the difference in the presence of a certain verb in the list but

Table 6. Women should not, men should not

Women verb	Count	% of all usages (627)	Men verb	Count	% of all usages (233)
носить 'wear'	45	7.2	*доверять* 'trust'	26	11.2
Ø	41	6.5	Ø	17	7.3
доверять 'trust'	31	4.9	*носить* 'wear'	15	6.4
есть 'eat'	19	3.0	*верить* 'believe/trust'	15	6.4
делать 'do'	18	2.9	*говорить* 'tell/speak'	7	3
ходить 'go'	18	2.9	*быть* 'be'	6	2.6
работать 'work'	14	2.2	*заниматься* 'do, be engaged in an activity'	5	2.1
заходить 'enter'	14	2.2	*дарить* 'give as presents'	5	2.1
пить 'drink'	11	1.8	*плакать* 'cry'	5	2.1
давать 'give'	10	1.6	*находиться* 'be somewhere'	4	1.7

Table 7. Girls should not, boys should not[a]

Girls verb	Count	% of all usages (67)	Boys verb	Count	% of all usages (48)
ходить 'go'	8	11.9	*носить* 'wear'	8	16.7
Ø	7	10.4	*плакать* 'cry'	7	14.6
носить 'wear'	3	4.5	Ø	6	12.5
сидеть 'sit'	3	4.5	*запрещать* 'forbid'	2	4.2
курить 'smoke'	3	4.5	*показывать* 'show'	2	4.2
целоваться 'kiss'	2	3	*ходить* 'go'	2	4.2
пользоваться 'use'	2	3	*порезвиться* 'go playful'	2	4.2
говорить 'tell/speak'	2	3	*употреблять в пищу* 'eat'	1	2
заходить 'enter'	2	3	*делать* 'do'	1	2
давать 'give'	2	3	*появляться* 'appear'	1	2

[a]As the number of results for *wives, mothers, husbands* and *fathers* was small, the relevant tables are not discussed here as statistically irrelevant.

also the difference in frequency relevant to the total number of prohibitive construction usages. From this point of view, it is interesting to compare the roles of men and women. The frequency for *доверять* 'trust' with the women role is just 4.9% of all usages, while with *men* it is 11.2%, if one also takes into account that 6.4% of prohibitions with *men* also include the verb *верить* 'believe/trust' which is a contextual synonym also related to the idea of trust, it turns out that prohibitive constructions with the male role 3.6 times more oriented at lack of trustworthiness than those with the female role.

6   Topics: Inventory of Indexes, Annotation Scheme and Results of Analysis

As verb semantics and the meaning of the construction do not always allow full description of what the prohibition is about, we carried out topic annotating that will cover the whole "object domain" of gender-oriented prohibitions. The process of topic annotating reminds of manually creating a simplified ontology.

Topic annotating was done a posteriori. At first a preliminary list of indexes for prohibitions for women (the most numerous group of prohibitions) was made, then it was broadened for other gender roles and reviewed for all gender roles for consistency. The system of indexes is unified for all groups, but there are specifications (attributes). For example, the index 'clothes = female' (skirt, ear-rings – something that cannot be worn by men) or the index 'places = male' (Mount Aphos, monastery, altar – places where women should not enter). Cf. the following examples 'food = female' *мальчикам нельзя женские травы (мелисса, мята, ромашка и т.д.)* 'One should not give women's herbs to boys (such as balm, mint, chamomile etc.)' or the index 'presents = female' *Люди, придерживающиеся мнения, что мужчинам нельзя дарить розы, считают, что это ставит под вопрос их мужественность и такой подарок якобы указывает на женственность мужчины* 'People who think that men should not be given roses as presents assume that this questions their masculinity and such a present allegedly points at man's femininity'.

Each utterance was ascribed one or more indexes. If the index duplicates the meaning of the attribute in the syntactic group of the dative argument (see paragraph 3), as in *'беременным женщинам нельзя'* 'Pregnant women should not', pregnancy was not included in the context description index. However, if the context is about pregnancy, but there is no corresponding attribute *беременным* for *женщинам*-Dat.Pl, such index is ascribed to the utterance.

The list of indexes to distinguish the topics in the object domain is given in Table 8. The indexes were sorted for all gender roles according to their frequency with the indication of rank and number of entries.

Analysis of the most frequent indexes from the table shows that very often prohibitions are connected with health issues, here one should also take into consideration that less frequent categories such as reproduction, pregnancy, sexual potency, giving birth, growing up physically are also prohibitions associated with health problems that may arise if something is done wrong in this sphere. It is of note that even food and drink prohibitions sometimes are linked with the fact that some products may be dangerous for health (for a subcategory of pregnant women most prohibitions of this kind are, in fact, about such concerns). Another important index is clothes, it is connected with two main variants of prohibitions: prohibition to wear clothes typical of other gender roles and prohibition to wear too little or too provoking clothes. This second type is often linked with another index – that of sacred things. The third index

Table 8. Annotation indexes

Index	#	Rank	Index	#	Rank	Index	#	Rank
Health	189	1	Alcohol	18	20	Giving birth	5	39
Clothes	156	2	Pregnancy	18	21	Being young	5	40
Alien customs and traditions	145	3	Age	17	22	Homosexual	4	41
Attributes	143	4	Reproduction	16	23	Adults	4	42
Sacred things	103	5	Beauty	12	24	Rights	3	43
Prejudices	86	6	Smoking	11	25	Strength	3	44
Trust	79	7	Presents	10	26	Intellect	2	45
Work	55	8	Make-up	10	27	Being light-minded	2	46
Appearance	54	9	Danger	10	28	Weapons	2	47
Sex	51	10	Accessories	9	29	Upbringing	2	48
Food	51	11	Traditions	9	30	Money	2	49
Nudity	46	12	Etiquette	8	31	Personal belongings	2	50
Medical treatment	41	13	Sexual potency	8	32	Medicines	2	51
Unique contexts	38	14	Growing up physically	8	33	History	2	52
Emotions	36	15	Marriage	8	34	Games	2	53
Work loads	34	16	Cats	6	35	Obscene words	2	54
Places	31	17	Education	6	36	Entertainment and leisure time	2	55
Behavior	29	18	Growing up mentally	6	37	Politics	1	56
Menstruation	18	19	Freedom	5	38	Violence	1	57

of alien customs and traditions is mainly about "weird Others". Others in this case are either representatives of a different faith (e.g. *Muslims*, *Judaists*) or quotes from "funny laws" in various USA states.

7 Conclusions and Further Research

The study of a prohibitive construction with нельзя 'should not' for various gender roles in Russian shows that it can be ambiguous and interpreted differently depending on the context. What should be taken into consideration is the fact that for different cases the context of different degree of broadness is important. Firstly, one should look at syntactic features of the construction such as the elements it consists of and the word order. Secondly, the semantic-syntactic features should be paid attention to, such as the semantic role of the dative argument and the meaning of the infinitive. Thirdly, the surrounding elements within the sentence or the neighboring sentences can influence interpretation of the prohibition. However, in some cases an even broader cognitive and cultural context plays a significant role, thus, one should also pay attention to the topical domain of prohibitions and how the topics are related to the social role expectations existing as background knowledge shared by the members of a lingua-cultural community.

Further development of the research in this area could lie in the combination of the detailed analysis of all the aspects mentioned above with the data of a psycholinguistic experiment where the same ambiguous constructions may be offered for interpretation to the native speakers and checked for interpretation consistency, preference in ambiguity removal as well as for the hierarchy of factors influencing their choice.

Acknowledgements. The research is supported by the Russian Science Foundation (RSF), project # 14-18-02070 «Everyday Russian Language in Different Social Groups».

References

1. Goffman, E.: The Presentation of Self in Everyday Life. University of Edinburgh Social Sciences Research Centre (1959)
2. Parsons, T.: O strukture social'nogo dejstvija [On social action structure]. Akademicheskij proekt, Moscow (2000). (in Russian)
3. Kon, I.S.: Lichnost' kak subjekt obshhestvennyh otnoshenij [Person as a subject of social relations]. Znanie, Moscow (1966). (in Russian)
4. Kon, I.S.: Sociologija lichnosti [Sociology of a person]. Politizdat, Moscow (1967). (in Russian)
5. Krysin, L.P.: Rechevoe obshhenie i social'nye roli govorjashhih [Verbal communication and social roles of the interlocutors]. In: Krysin, L.P., Shmeleva, D.N. (eds.) Social'no-lingvisticheskie issledovanija [Sociolinguistic Studies], pp. 42–52 (1976). (in Russian)
6. Krysin, L.P.: Sociolingvisticheskie aspekty izuchenija sovremennogo russkogo jazyka [Sociolinguistic aspects of modern Russian language]. Nauka, Moscow (1989). (in Russian)
7. Belikov, V.I., Krysin, L.P.: Sociolingvistika [Sociolinguistics]. Rossijskij gumanitarnyj universitet, Moscow (2001). (in Russian)
8. Karasik, V.I.: Jazyk social'nogo statusa [Language of social status]. Gnozis, Moscow (2002). (in Russian)
9. Lyashevskaya, O., Sharov, S: Chastotnyj slovar' sovremennogo russkogo jazyka na materialach Nacional'nogo korpusa russkogo jazyka [The frequency dictionary of modern Russian language], Moscow (2009). (in Russian)
10. Goussev, V.J.: Tipologija specializirovannykh glagol'nykh form imperativa [A typology of specialized imperative verb forms]. Unpublished Ph.D. dissertation, Moscow (2005). (in Russian)
11. Aikhenvald, A.Y.: Imperatives and Commands. Oxford University Press, New York (2010)
12. Khrakovskij, V.S., Volodin, A.P.: Semantika i tipologija imperativa: Russkij imperativ [Semantics and typology of imperative: Russian imperative]. Nauka, Leningrad (1986)
13. Biryulin, L.A., Xrakovskij, V.S.: Povelitel'nye predlozhenija: problemy teorii [Imperative sentences: problems of the theory]. In: Xrakovskij, V.S. (ed.) Tipologiya imperativnykh konstruktsii, pp. 5–50. Nauka, St. Petersburg (1992). (in Russian)
14. Gerasimova, I.A.: Deonticheskaja logika i kognitivnye ustanovki [Deontic logic and cognitive attitude]. In: Logical Analysis of the Language: Ethics languages, pp. 7–16. Jazyki russkoj kul'tury, Moscow (2000)

15. Petrova, M.A.: Tipy nemodal'nyh znachenij modal'nyh predikatov (na materiale slavjanskih i germanskih jazykov) [Types of non-modal meanings of modal predicates (on the material of Slavic and Germanic languages)]. Unpublished Ph.D. dissertation, Moscow (2007). (in Russian)
16. Vanderveken, D.: Meaning and Speech Acts, Volume 2: Formal Semantics of Success and Satisfaction. Cambridge University Press, Cambridge (1991)
17. Allan, K.: Linguistic Meaning, vol. 2. Roultedge and Kegan Paul, London (1986)
18. Russian TenTen corpus. https://www.sketchengine.co.uk/rutenten-corpus/
19. Kashkin, E.V., Lyashevskaya, O.N.: Semanticheskie roli i set' konstrukcij v sisteme FrameBank [Semantic roles and construction net in Russian FrameBank]. In: Proceedings of International Conference "Dialog" on Computational Linguistics and Intellectual Technologies, vol. 12-1, pp. 297–311. RSUH, Moscow (2013). (in Russian)
20. FrameBank. http://marker.framebank.ru/verbs.php

A Contextualist Analysis of Insults

Y. Sandy Berkovski(✉)

Bilkent University, Ankara, Turkey
sandy.berkovski@gmail.com

Abstract. For a predicate expression F contained in a sentence S ('x is F') to count as an insult, it should be used in a situation having a number of contextual elements. There should be an audience to whom the utterance of S is addressed. There should be a target of the insult, an individual who the speaker wishes to be shunned, excluded from certain, more or less salient, forms of social cooperation. The purpose of the utterance of S is to persuade the audience, by appeal to their emotions, to shun the target. Slurs have the canonical occasions of use structurally identical to the occasions of insults.

1 The Initial Picture

I want to begin with a large claim. I will not be able to substantiate it here. But I hope, even if undefended, it would not sound outlandish or incoherent. This is partly because it is almost wholly unoriginal. Indeed, it is not a claim, but rather a picture.

In this picture, language has a role to play in our collection of information about the world and about ourselves. We found a way to classify objects, animate and inanimate, to record observations, to describe our subjective experiences, to make predictions about the future. In this propositional employment of language our statements should be evaluated by how well they represent the world. They should be accepted or rejected on the basis of their truth value. I will not of course try to spell out what notion of truth we should endorse, or what notion of truth is most congenial to this picture. But I do want to say that the semantic properties of statements are what get to be examined—should be examined—within that employment of language. The purpose of a statement, 'Wolves are grey' is to say something about the wolves. Our interest, concern with this statement is with its truth and with the analogous semantic properties of its constituent parts. If what it says is true, if wolves are grey, then the statement is accepted; and if they are not, then rejected.

But human life, in its modest beginnings, is not all about description and enquiry. Not even primarily so. It is in the first place about survival and reproduction. As those happen, necessarily so, in the condition of scarcity, it is thus a great deal about managing relations with others. (Plainly it is also about many other things, such as sensory and semi-sensory pleasures and pains—but those I should put aside.)

Our survival and prosperity, the success of our somatic and reproductive efforts, depend on the success of our cooperation with others. Language has a

© Springer International Publishing AG 2017
P. Brézillon et al. (Eds.): CONTEXT 2017, LNAI 10257, pp. 661–674, 2017.
DOI: 10.1007/978-3-319-57837-8_53

role to play here too. Cooperation depends on communication, and language is an effective instrument of communication. In the course of communication, of course, language may once again be employed in its propositional mode. We can exchange with others information about the world, hence improving or impairing our descriptions and predictions.

Cooperation cannot begin before it is clear who one should cooperate with, who is a worthy candidate for the cooperative task at hand, and who is not. Just as there is a competition for material resources, and in part because of that competition, there is normally a competition for allies. Where more than a few actors are involved, and where material resources are relatively scarce, language comes handy in forging alliances. Potential allies communicate to each other the purpose of the alliance, they gather information about each other's abilities, and they present themselves, their own abilities and worth, to each other. Every inclusion in an alliance, at least in a reasonably large group, is at the same time an exclusion. The possible rewards, once the task is completed, will be enough for everyone. Someone must be left behind, when the allies divide the spoils. Alternatively, an alliance is from the start directed against others.

Once again, language is an essential tool. Alliances can be built with non-linguistic means, by embracing, kissing, pushing, and punching. These methods of communication are costly and unsafe. They have another distinct disadvantage. Once people have gained the ability to represent in language the world and themselves, they have also gained the ability to misrepresent it. Misrepresentation is a potent tool in alliance building. It allows one to misrepresent oneself to potential allies—that is, to present oneself as better than one in fact is (the capacity for self-misrepresentation we encounter throughout the animal world, but there it is rudimentary and inflexible). It similarly allows one to present potential and actual rivals as worse than they in fact are.

2   Rhetorical Adaptations

So language has a unique role to play in alliance building. This, I now wish to point out, is a different mode of its employment. Call it the 'rhetorical mode'. One might think it is not interestingly different from the propositional mode, where the purpose is to gather and convey information about the world. Here too, one uses the language to gather and convey information about particular aspects of the world—namely, allies, rivals, and oneself. Just as one describes the properties of flowers and trees, one can describe properties of people. One then uses these descriptions to improve one's relationships in the cooperative effort and generally one's standing in the group.

This deployment of language in the propositional mode envisages a possibility of a prolonged debate where claims are made and objections are heard out. For the practical purposes of alliance building it is defective. The chances that your reasoning is compelling, and that the rival's reasoning is not, are hard to estimate. And on many occasions there would not be enough time to make your argument to begin with.

Hence language must be adapted to serve the purpose of quick persuasion. Instead of elaborating a complex argument of uncertain prospects, it is more promising to appeal to the interlocutors' emotions. Instead of laboriously showing what properties of this man make him an enemy, or disqualify him from being an ally, it is more efficient to appeal to the shame, fear, disgust, or the desire for revenge of your interlocutors. A classic skirmish between Thersites and Odysseus in the *Iliad* contains this exchange:[1]

> [Thersites:] Weaklings! Cowardly creatures! You women, not men, of
> Achaia,
> let's go back home in our ships, and leave this fellow
> here in Troy to gorge on his prizes [...]
> [Odysseus:] Thersites, wild babbler, sharp stump speaker you may be,
> but shut up! (*Il.* 2.235-246)

The insults hurled in these speeches are designed to rally the support behind the speaker, Thersites and Odysseus respectively. The expressions 'weakling', 'cowardly creature', 'wild babbler' appear as though their use is meant to predicate a property of the given subject (Achaian troops or Thersites). However, Thersites could not care less if the Achaians are indeed cowardly. He may in fact believe they are not, and precisely because they are not, he may hope to agitate them into action.

Language in its rhetorical mode, its grammar and syntax, look exactly the same as they would in the propositional mode. Indeed, the terms used in the example before us could well be used in the propositional mode. Thersites could have conducted a semi-theoretical enquiry, collecting statistical data, interviewing different Achaian soldiers, so as to establish how many of them are weaklings, cowards, and how many are not. Those data carry no relevance for him when he is engaged in a public spat with Odysseus and Agamemnon. On the surface his utterances appear to assert propositions. In reality he is merely trying to build an alliance of fellow soldiers against the aristocratic chiefs. *Mutatis mutandis*, the same goes for Odysseus.

3   The Autonomy of Rhetoric

The first conjecture I am raising now is that, syntactic similarities notwithstanding, the semantic properties of sentences in their rhetorical mode should be evaluated differently from the semantic properties of sentences in their propositional mode. The second conjecture is that the rhetorical mode should contain expressions unused and unusable in propositional mode. I shall try to substantiate this claim below. But here is one intuitive reason why it should hold. With the same expressions used in both modes, the addressee cannot be certain what is expected of him. When Thersites asserts 'Achaians are cowards', the addressees

---

[1] See [4].

(here Achaians themselves) may be misled into examining the truth value of this statement. A lengthy debate may ensue:

> — It seems everyone I know in this army is a coward.
> — Yes, but look at Achilles! And are *you* a coward too?
> — So Thersites' universal generalisation must be false.   (1)

It is in Thersites' interest not to allow such a debate to begin and to obscure the real purpose, which is to nudge the Achaians to rebel against the chiefs. A mechanism must, therefore, be introduced to prevent this misunderstanding. There is a need for expressions appealing to the emotions of the audience directly, avoiding the slide into the propositional mode.

Non-linguistic mechanisms are familiar. Raising one's voice, banging on the table, gesturing wildly—all of these contrivances are in the arsenal of public speakers whose purpose is to prepare the audience for action. They are designed to divert the audience's attention from the propositional syntax of the speaker's utterance, to prevent the audience from searching for the propositional content and from assessing its truth value. An aspiring master persuader would look for a linguistic mechanism serving an analogous function. The mechanism should be some kind of a linguistic expression designed to be employed exclusively in the rhetorical mode. I shall attempt to show that mechanisms of this nature can be found, and that their proper understanding would allow us to resolve some of the thorny issues in the current debate on offensive speech.

4   The Rhetorical Function of Insults

Every regular alliance is an alliance against something and often also someone. Such an alliance will be forged, in great part, by linguistic means. Potential allies should be shown why the cause is worthwhile. If the alliance builder wishes to gather the support for his cause, and if the alliance comes at the expense of another individual—an excluded one, a rival, an enemy—then he will seek to portray that individual in a negative light while at the same time stressing the positive characteristics of the alliance members.

If the picture lately sketched is taken for granted, it seems that this alliance building by linguistic means will be carried out in the rhetorical mode. Yet the expressions and syntactic forms deployed in that mode can also be deployed in the propositional mode. Separating between the two modes on any given occasion, one expects, will not be trivial.

One way this separation can be achieved is by working with a sufficiently rich notion of context. We have seen earlier how insulting expressions can be used in building alliances. But whether a particular expression counts as insulting will, on the present view, be determined by the context of utterance. If I come to the doctor's office, he might utter matter-of-factly the sentence:

> You are an alcoholic.   (2)

He utters the statement in the privacy of his office, in a regular voice, typing my information into the computer. He then proceeds to recommend an appropriate treatment. He states it as a diagnosis, a necessary first step in a treatment. By contrast, if a sneering colleague announces that same fact at a business meeting, uttering (2) in the presence of many people, our collegiate relationship may well be over. What elements are responsible for this divergent interpretation?

The predicate 'ξ is an alcoholic' belongs in the vocabulary normally used in the propositional mode. Semantically, the statement appears to carry factual content. To say that x is an alcoholic is to ascribe a certain property to the individual x, and this ascription can be either true or false. What made the utterance offensive in the second case is the features of the context. We might explain it as follows. The speaker insulted the 'target' (the person targeted by the insult), because with his utterance he represented the target as a person not suitable for a range of social tasks. Moreover, the target would normally be able to understand (to infer or to grasp immediately) what the purpose of the utterance should have been, and how that utterance would have been interpreted by the audience. That understanding could be gleaned from the salient features of the context. If the audience, for instance, consisted of recovering alcoholics who also happen to be business colleagues, the statement might well not have been insulting. In the event, however, there was no salient reason for the speaker to utter (2)—no reason, that is, other than to offend.

'ξ is an alcoholic' is an 'incidental insult'. There are occasions where its literal use can be interpreted as insulting. Some other expressions may be wearing the offensive content on their sleeves. If a colleague casually said:

$$\text{You are a sot,} \tag{3}$$

it would be taken as offensive. It certainly would be offensive in the context of a business meeting. Still, there would be contexts, one may argue, where even that term is not offensive. Perhaps a close friend concludes our intimate private conversation about my addiction with (3) and a suggestion to check into a clinic.

5   Testing Semantic Identity

But does the offensive colleague say anything different from the doctor? Both attribute a quality to the subject, but is it the same quality on both occasions? Perhaps the semantic content of the predicate 'ξ is a sot' should be given as 'ξ is an alcoholic'. When we say that someone is a sot, we say semantically nothing more and nothing less that he is an alcoholic, while registering non-semantically our attitudes towards that individual (or perhaps towards alcoholism generally, or alcoholic drinks, or the class of alcoholics as a whole).

A classic test for this hypothesis of meaning equivalence would be to embed the predicates in oblique contexts. We ask whether:

$$\text{Lenin believes that Mussorgsky is an alcoholic} \tag{4}$$

should entail:

$$\text{Lenin believes that Mussorgsky is a sot.} \tag{5}$$

Now it seems to me that the test is inconclusive. If Mussorgsky happens to be just some unfamiliar person, then an average speaker may concede the entailment. Suppose, though, that Mussorgsky is Lenin's favourite composer. Then, conceivably, Lenin would vehemently deny that Mussorgsky is a sot ('You should not speak like that about my favourite composer!'), while admitting that he is an alcoholic.

This latter feature leads to another test, of denial and negation. Someone who wants to deny that Mussorgsky is an alcoholic, can do so with a straightforward negation:

$$\text{No, Mussorgsky is not an alcoholic.} \tag{6}$$

And now, even Lenin can very well utter:

$$\text{No, Mussorgsky is not a sot, he is merely an alcoholic.} \tag{7}$$

If the two predicates had the same meaning, Lenin would have contradicted himself. Since his statement sounds sensible enough, it seems we have evidence, after all, that the sentences 'x is an alcoholic' and 'x is a sot' attribute different properties to x.

6 Property Ascription

Observe now that the locution 'merely' is not superfluous. If the speaker said:

$$\text{No, Mussorgsky is not a sot, he is an alcoholic,} \tag{8}$$

he would have implied that the predicates stand in no logical relation to each other, as in:

$$\text{No, Mussorgsky is not Polish, he is Russian.} \tag{9}$$

By 'merely' the speaker signals a relation between being an alcoholic and being a sot. A very intuitive idea would be to say that the predicate 'ξ is a sot' is a conjunction of predicates in disguise. When we say that someone is a sot, we say that he is an alcoholic of a pernicious kind, that in addition to being an alcoholic he is stupid, unkempt, smelly. Thus Lenin's utterance (7) should be parsed as:

$$\text{No, Mussorgsky is not a stupid, smelly alcoholic; he is an alcoholic}$$
$$\textit{simpliciter}, \text{neither stupid, nor smelly.} \tag{10}$$

The idea that offensive statements ascribe certain properties to the subject is often advanced in the literature on slurs, though its theoretical representations vary.[2] In the inferentialist treatment propounded by Dummett and Williamson the use of 'x is a Boche' should mandate an inference to 'x is cruel'. In Hom's semantic externalism, a conjunction of repugnant properties is part of the semantic value of a pejorative. According to the related null-extensionality thesis of Hom and May, someone who asserts 'a is a Boche' thereby asserts that Germans are inherently cruel (or inherently possess some other repugnant property).[3]

The material adequacy of these forms of analysis is deficient. They attribute to the user a theoretical commitment to associating with a given class of people (Germans or alcoholics) certain determinate properties. This means that there should be a broad agreement among the competent users of the pejorative predicates as to which properties should be associated with the objects in its extension. It is not sensible to expect any such agreement.

A significantly weakened version of the view, that for each user there must at least be one property associated with the extension, is also not credible. When asked about which property he typically associates with sots, other than the property of being an alcoholic, the speaker may be puzzled. Even if he eventually comes up with an answer, the initial difficulty itself is telling. If taken at face value, it should cast doubt on his competence with the term.

There is also a more general problem here, at least if the picture sketched at the outset is correct. An assumption behind the property ascription thesis is that the user of pejorative expressions, at least when they occur in declarative sentences, makes an assertion about how the world is. The addressees of his statement similarly evaluate it on the basis of its truth value. This assumption can be challenged.

The plausibility of the property ascription thesis in large part rests on the possibility of pairing some pejoratives with descriptive terms:

$$\text{sot} \sim \text{alcoholic}$$
$$\text{faggot} \sim \text{homosexual}$$
$$\text{junkie} \sim \text{drug addict.}$$

There are certain descriptions a person should satisfy for him to be called a 'sot', 'faggot', or 'junkie'. One might hate Tchaikovsky as much as one pleases, but calling him a 'sot' reveals the speaker's insufficient command of the language (if he is aware of relevant historical facts). By contrast, it would not be linguistically incompetent for the speaker knowledgeable about Mussorgsky's life to call that composer a 'sot'.

---

[2] Terminological note: in [5] the class of pejoratives consists of swear words, insults, and slurs. Here I ignore swear words completely. I hope it should become clear by the end of this essay why their analysis should differ in principle from the analysis of the other two kinds of expressions. The use of pejoratives, in the present terminology, is normally taken as being *offensive* against someone, a quality shared by 'insults' and 'slurs'. This is in line with the nominal definition in [6], where, rather oddly, the author still includes swear words under the same heading. For an alternative classification of pejoratives and slurs see [7].

[3] See [5, 7, 10].

But consider the expressions 'bastard' or 'motherfucker'. There are no descriptive terms conventionally correlated with them. Originally, these particular terms may have had transparent descriptive meanings, but these are no longer relevant in the current use. 'Bastard' referring to an illegitimate child and 'bastard' a pejorative word are in the current use two homonyms.

What is then the canonical use of 'bastard'? *Is* there such a use? As we have already agreed that there is a level of semantic content separating insulting expressions from non-insulting ones, the canonical use of 'bastard' must be different from the canonical use of any non-insulting expression. With no neutral correlates available, the person apparently does not have to meet any special conditions, does not have to belong to any distinct group, to be called 'bastard'. Such expressions may be called *pure insults*.

7   Expressivism

Rather than saying that the competent use of the insulting term should purport to associate properties with the target, we can say that it purports to express the attitudes of the speaker. Hence the expressivist proposal:[4]

E1. A term t is *insulting* if it is used to *express* derogatory attitudes of the speaker towards the target.

But this formula is inadequate, so far as it fails to capture the reactions of the target. If the speakers use an expression with the full intention of expressing derogatory attitudes, but the targets routinely fail to take an insult, to be insulted, then the expression is not insulting.

Of course if no target, or very few, took an insult when t is applied to them, one would have to ask why t was supposed to express derogatory attitudes in the first place. For t to function as a vehicle for derogatory attitudes, the canonical occasions of its use—those we cite when explaining the term, and when we say that the term is used literally—these occasions must not be merely the occasions where the speaker wishes to express his beliefs or feelings about the target. There must be some other condition characterising the occasion, beyond the fact that the speaker was in a certain state of mind. Such a condition may be that the target is actually insulted. So we say:

E2. A term t is *insulting* if it is used to *express* derogatory attitudes of the speaker towards the target, and the target tends to *be insulted* by the fact of those attitudes.

This claim is not obviously circular. To be insulted is to have an emotional response to the expression of derogatory attitudes. What it consists in we can hope to clarify further without invoking the notion of insulting expression. The

---

[4] See [9] for a sophisticated generalised version of expressivism. See [8] for incorporating the specific idea about slurs' expressive function into a non-expressivist semantic account.

canonical occasion for using an insulting expression would be one where the speaker means to insult, and the target is indeed insulted.

Still, this is not a satisfying solution: its material adequacy is questionable. Suppose Stalin reads in Lenin's private diary:

$$\text{This Stalin is a real bastard!} \qquad (11)$$

It seems to me that Stalin could be upset or angry. He would not be insulted. To be insulted is an emotional response, but it is not a response to the bare fact of the attitudes itself, to the bare evidence of these attitudes. One imagines that Stalin would be insulted if Lenin uttered (11) face to face, and even more so if in public. *Ceteris paribus*, the bigger the audience, the bigger the insult. For the insult to occur, the derogatory attitudes should be expressed in a public setting.

To show now the weakest spot of expressivism, let me take a step back and ask how we should think of those 'derogatory attitudes' whose central role has been taken for granted by expressivism. Again, in the case of 'bastard' or even 'motherfucker', it is rather difficult to pinpoint the specific attitudes. All the same, let us pretend that on some occasions the speaker would express the belief that the target is unreliable, as in this expanded version of (11):

While I have been ill, Stalin tried to grab more power in the Central

Committee. This Stalin is a real bastard! $\qquad (12)$

Something has gone wrong. If all that Lenin meant to express was Stalin's unreliability, there would again be little reason for Stalin to be insulted. Even if Lenin were to say in public merely that Stalin was unreliable, that would be an occasion for a debate, not for an insult.

I fear we are nearing a dead-end. A derogatory attitude is not merely a belief or a feeling about a person (or possibly an animal or a work of art, but ignore any of that). It is *identified* in part by the way it is expressed. An attitude becomes derogatory when it tends to be manifested in a particular way—in an insulting way. Or perhaps it positively cannot be expressed other than in an insulting way. And this is a vicious circle.

8   Outline of the New Proposal

Expressivism has a sound intuition behind it. The attitudes of the speaker are relevant for understanding the linguistic mechanism of insults. Their role is just not that prominent. The true analysis of insults is as follows. Their very introduction into the language, the layer of content (in addition to others if there are any) that is properly insulting, is designed to represent the target as a relatively unsuitable partner in social cooperation. This representation should be understood as taking place in the rhetorical mode. The speaker, in using insults, directly appeals to the audience to treat the target as a socially unsuitable individual. As his utterance is in the rhetorical mode, he is not solemnly putting forward a description, hoping that the audience would draw its own conclusions. His utterance is a call to action, not to reflection or examination.

I do not mean to say that insults are an exact linguistic equivalent of shouting or slamming the table. The speaker has, after all, to *persuade* the audience to shun the target. If he could command it to do so, there would be no essential role for insults play (or perhaps they would have been embedded solely in imperatives). The best way for the speaker to succeed in his rhetorical gambit is to appeal to the audience's emotions. The purpose is to let the members of the audience emotionally reject the target, to prepare them emotionally to shun and ostracise him. So insults often conveniently carry connotations (in the Millian sense of the term) that appeal to the audience's disgust, contempt, sense of revulsion. The use of 'motherfucker' does not predicate any sexual behaviour of the subject. But to call someone a 'motherfucker', with the connotation of a universally repulsive form of incest, is effective in immediately creating a negative emotional attitude towards the target. The same goes for 'bastard', but with this expression gradually losing its negative connotation, it is also far less effective and less insulting than before.

I should now speak of the emotional states of the target and of the speaker himself, and of the roles these states play in understanding insults. An expression is insulting when the target has a regular emotional response to its utterance. The target, we say, is emotionally insulted by a linguistically insulting expression. Under the present analysis, an insulting utterance has an intended audience. The purpose is to make the audience shun the target of the insult. The semantic stability of insults, i.e. the fact that they have canonical occasions of their use (as opposed to incidental insults such as 'ξ is an alcoholic'), means that the target can easily recognise the ostracising significance of their utterance.

Emotional reactions to the situations of ostracism are hardly a mystery. If human organisms are products of evolution, then being hurt by acts of ostracism should have conferred an evolutionary advantage. In the first place, being hurt alerts the victim that something has gone wrong, that this type of situation should be avoided. It does not, however, inform the individual where exactly the problem is, or how it should be solved. Hurt of the kind we now examine can also produce a shock. The victim can be shocked into silence, may become extremely passive. In this way he can accumulate more reserves, mental or physical, to recover from the psychological injury. Finally, outward manifestations of hurt inform others of the necessity to avoid putting themselves in similar situations.

The features just mentioned are in fact the features characterising physical pain.[5] It thus appears possible to align the hurt inflicted by insults with physical pain. Recent research goes a long way toward defending the alignment.[6]

What of the attitudes of the speaker? Should the speaker, at least on canonical occasions, be present in a heightened emotional state, and should he have cognitive attitudes towards the target congruent with the insulting expressions he is using? I think the significance of this issue has been rather overrated. If an

---

[5] See [2].
[6] See [3].

average speaker does not have those congruent attitudes, if he, for instance, is simply paid to deliver his insults, these insults would not be too effective. The audience would be able to gather the lack of passion and the lack of conviction. The speaker would appear insincere. I suppose it is a general theorem in the art of rhetoric that in order to persuade, one has to appear sincere. And of course one simple way to appear sincere is to be sincere. Thus we normally expect the speaker to possess those congruent attitudes, to really believe that the target is contemptible, disgusting, and deserves to be shunned. But these characteristics of the speaker's condition, to repeat, are not necessitated by semantic analysis; they are contingent facts of human psychology.

9   The Case of Slurs

I have now spoken of pure insults. I wish now to say a few words about slurs. It is well to distinguish the two categories. In the first place, unlike pure insults, slurs have neutral correlates. Secondly, the worst offences, in the linguistic realm, are caused by slurs. Thirdly, the semantic behaviour of slurs appears different from that of pure insults. I will comment on the last point before turning to the other two.

It is argued that slurs remain offensive under negation or when embedded in indirect speech. When Lenin says

$$\text{Stalin is a bastard,} \tag{13}$$

one can straightforwardly deny the statement:

$$\text{No, Stalin is not a bastard} \tag{14}$$

without sounding offensive. But when Stalin says:

$$\text{Tchaikovsky is a faggot,} \tag{15}$$

to merely deny the statement would remain offensive:

$$\text{No, Tchaikovsky is not a faggot.} \tag{16}$$

Even more interestingly, slurs wreak havoc in indirect speech.[7] Suppose Lenin wishes to record what Stalin said about Tchaikovsky and then repudiate his derogatory attitude:

Stalin said yesterday that Tchaikovsky was a faggot, but I do not share his
attitudes to homosexuals. (17)

Evidently, Lenin does not wish his remark to be offensive to Tchaikovsky. It is widely accepted that Lenin should fail. His utterance does not merely convey the other speaker's offence—it is itself offensive.

---

[7] See [9].

What I have to say about these phenomena is somewhat close to the views developed in [1], but I will not try to map out the points of contact.[8] I want to begin by noting that pure insults can similarly remain offensive in indirect speech and under negation. Unfortunately, I can find no clear-cut example in the English language; and in any borderline cases, not being a native speaker, I would not trust my linguistic intuitions.

But there is, I think, a perfect example in Russian (you will have to trust me on this one). The Russian language contains the word 'moudak'. It is part of the Russian 'mat', or argo, the forbidden part of the language. That was the case at least until a few decades ago, before general laxity took root. So I will be describing the situation then, rather than at present. 'Moudak' is similar to 'motherfucker' or 'bastard' in that it is used to insult, having no neutral correlate. It is not meant to identify a stable group characterisable in descriptive terms. Yet it is probably a purer insult: whatever its ancient etymological origins, to the modern user of the word it should carry no Millian connotations.

But in other regards 'moudak' is closer to slurs. For suppose Stalin says:

$$\text{Trotsky is a } moudak. \tag{18}$$

Then, if Lenin denies:

$$\text{No, Trotsky is not a } moudak, \tag{19}$$

he would still sound offensive. And again, if Lenin says:

Stalin said yesterday that Trotsky was a *moudak*, but I do not share his views and attitudes, (20)

he would sound offensive. But ask this: offensive to whom? And I think to any Russian speaker it should be clear that Lenin is not offensive specifically to Trotsky. He is rather offensive to the people gathered around. The word is not supposed to be uttered in a polite society. It is a gross offence against manners. People around recoil from hearing the word not because it offends Trotsky, but because it makes them cringe, as any violation of manners would.

You will now say that in (20) Lenin did not utter the word. He merely quoted the word, hence in effect named the word without uttering it. He might have as well said, 'that word, you know, the M-word', and that would not have been offensive. This observation is correct. But the answer is just around the corner. Quoting the offensive word still reminds the speakers of the word itself. And locating the offensiveness of 'moudak' in the domain of manners completes the explanation. For suppose that Stalin passed gas in Lenin's presence. Lenin promptly leaves the room and goes to the party comrades to inform them what Stalin has accomplished. If now Lenin says:

Imagine what just happened: Stalin passed gas! This is gross, no one should ever do that, (21)

---

[8] However, I do not endorse the general theory of slurs in [1].

arguably he, and certainly not Stalin, is already offensive to the people around him. No-one should even mention such episodes. But if Lenin, instead of merely saying what Stalin did, resolved to demonstrate it symbolically (perhaps by making a similar sound, or even by passing gas himself), he would have been *much more* offensive, and no less offensive than Stalin originally was.

Thus, I wish to suggest, the offensiveness of slurs in embedded constructions should be viewed in a similar light. It came to be that certain slurs, such as 'faggot', 'nigger', 'cunt', have become unacceptable in a civilised society. With regard to their status in a public conversation, they are now on a par with '*moudak*'. In indirect speech, for example, their offence is real, but its nature has changed. They do not offend *as* slurs. They offend as any prohibited segment of language would.[9]

10   Review

For a predicate expression F contained in a sentence S ('x is F') to count as an insult, it should be used in a situation having a number of contextual elements. There should be an audience to whom the utterance of S is addressed. There should be a target of the insult, an individual who the speaker wishes to be shunned, excluded from certain, more or less salient, forms of social cooperation. The purpose of the utterance of S is to persuade the audience, by appeal to their emotions, to shun the target. Slurs have the canonical occasions of use structurally identical to the occasions of insults. The details should vary, so far as slurs possess neutral correlates. This modified treatment of slurs I have not attempted to pursue here.

References

1. Anderson, L., Lepore, E.: Slurring words. Noûs **47**(1), 25–48 (2013)
2. Bateson, P.: Assessment of pain in animals. Anim. Behav. **42**, 827–839 (1991)
3. Eisenberger, N.I.: The neural bases of social pain. Psychosom. Med. **74**(2), 126–135 (2012)
4. Green, P.: The Iliad/Homer. University of California Press, Berkeley (2015). Green, P., translated
5. Hom, C.: Pejoratives. Philos. Compass **5**(2), 164–185 (2010)
6. Hom, C.: A puzzle about pejoratives. Philos. Stud. **159**, 383–405 (2012)
7. Hom, C., May, R.: Moral and semantic innocence. Anal. Philos. **54**(3), 293–313 (2013)
8. Jeshion, R.B.: Slurs, dehumanization, and the expression of contempt. In: Sosa, D. (ed.) Bad Words. Oxford University Press (2016)

---

[9] Another brick in the argument would be the observation that some slurs fail to offend in indirect speech or under negation. Examples should include 'junkie', 'doper', 'sot'. These are all unquestionably slurs, e.g., easily meeting the conditions of Jeshion's semantics in [8]. Hence it is a particular property of some slurs that makes them behave in a strange way in embedded constructions.

9. Potts, C.: The expressive dimension. Theoret. Linguist. **33**(2), 165–198 (2007)
10. Williamson, T.: Reference, inference, and the semantics of pejoratives. In: Almog, J., Leonardi, P. (eds.) The Philosophy of David Kaplan, pp. 137–158. Oxford University Press (2009)

Specific Topics: Context in Psychology and Bias

Context and Interference Effects in the Combinations of Natural Concepts

Diederik Aerts[1], Jonito Aerts[2], Lester Beltran[3], Isaac Distrito[4],
Massimiliano Sassoli de Bianchi[1,5], Sandro Sozzo[6(✉)], and Tomas Veloz[1]

[1] Center Leo Apostel for Interdisciplinary Studies (CLEA),
Brussels Free University (VUB), Pleinlaan 2, 1050 Brussel, Belgium
{diraerts,massimiliano.sassoli.de.bianchi}@vub.ac.be,
autoricerca@gmail.com, tveloz@gmail.com
[2] KASK and Conservatory, Jozef Kluyskensstraat 2, 9000 Ghent, Belgium
jonitoarguelles@gmail.com
[3] 825-C Tayuman Street, Tondo, Manila, The Philippines
lestercc21@gmail.com
[4] 2511 Eloriaga Street, Santa Ana, 1009 Manila, The Philippines
isaacdis3to@yahoo.com
[5] Laboratorio di Autoricerca di Base, 6914 Lugano, Switzerland
[6] School of Business and Research Centre IQSCS, University of Leicester,
University Road LE1 7RH, Leicester, UK
ss831@le.ac.uk

Abstract. The mathematical formalism of quantum theory exhibits significant effectiveness when applied to cognitive phenomena that have resisted traditional (set theoretical) modeling. Relying on a decade of research on the operational foundations of micro-physical and conceptual entities, we present a theoretical framework for the representation of concepts and their conjunctions and disjunctions that uses the quantum formalism. This framework provides a unified solution to the 'conceptual combinations problem' of cognitive psychology, explaining the observed deviations from classical (Boolean, fuzzy set and Kolmogorovian) structures in terms of genuine quantum effects. In particular, natural concepts 'interfere' when they combine to form more complex conceptual entities, and they also exhibit a 'quantum-type context-dependence', which are responsible of the 'over- and under-extension' that are systematically observed in experiments on membership judgments.

Keywords: Cognitive psychology · Concept combination · Context effects · Interference effects · Quantum modeling · Quantum structures

1 Introduction

Philosophers and psychologists have always been interested in the deep nature of human concepts, how they are formed, how they combine to create more complex conceptual structures, as expressed by sentences and texts, and how meaning is

© Springer International Publishing AG 2017
P. Brézillon et al. (Eds.): CONTEXT 2017, LNAI 10257, pp. 677–690, 2017.
DOI: 10.1007/978-3-319-57837-8_54

created in these processes. Unveiling aspects of these mysteries is bound to have a massive impact on a variety of domains, from knowledge representation to natural language processing, machine learning and artificial intelligence.

The original idea of a concept as a 'container of objects', called 'instantiations', which can be traced back to Aristotle, was challenged by the first cognitive tests by Eleanor Rosch, which revealed that concepts exhibit aspects, like 'context-dependence', 'vagueness' and 'graded typicality', that prevent a too naïve definition of a concept as a 'set of defining properties that are either possessed or not possessed by individual exemplars' [1,2]. More, these tests infused the suspicion that concepts do not combine by following the algebraic rules of classical logic. A first attempt to preserve a set theoretical modeling came from the 'fuzzy set approach': concepts would be represented by fuzzy sets, while their conjunction (disjunction) satisfies the 'minimum (maximum) rule of fuzzy set conjunction (disjunction)' [3]. However, also this approach was confuted by a whole set of experiments by cognitive psychologists, including Osherson and Smith, who identified the 'Guppy effect' (or 'Pet-Fish problem') in typicality judgments [4], James Hampton, who discovered 'overextension' and 'underextension' effects in membership judgments [5,6], and Alxatib and Pelletier, who detected 'borderline contradictions' in simple propositions of the form "John is tall and John is not tall" [7]. More recently, some of us proved that these data violate Kolmogorov's axioms of classical probability theory [8], thus revealing that classical structures,[1] like Boolean and fuzzy set logic and Kolmogorovian probability, are intrinsically unable to model the way in which concepts combine [9,10] (Sect. 2).

Interestingly, the deviations from classicality observed in typicality and membership judgments were also identified in other domains of cognitive psychology, and are known as 'fallacies of human reasoning', which include conjunctive and disjunctive fallacies, disjunction effects, question order effects, violations of utility theory, etc. [11]. Moreover, in the last decade a novel research programme has taken off, which successfully applies the mathematical formalism of quantum theory (and its possible natural generalizations) to model these fallacies of human reasoning (see, e.g., [9–16]). Even more interestingly, quantum micro-physical entities (like electrons, protons, atoms, etc.) and conceptual entities do exhibit a very similar behavior with respect to 'potentiality' and 'context-dependence', that is, in both micro-physical and conceptual realms a context is able to change the state of the entity under study, thus actualizing potential properties, rather than just unveiling existing, though unknown, values of them [17].

Taking inspiration from our investigations on the operational and realistic approaches to the foundations of quantum physics (see, e.g., [18,19]), we aim to present in this paper a quantum theoretical framework to represent the

---

[1] In this paper, we refer to set theoretical structures as 'classical structures', because they were originally used to represent systems and interactions in classical physics, and later were extended to psychology, economics, statistics, finance, etc. Analogously, we refer to deviations from set theoretical modeling as 'deviations from classicality'.

conjunction and disjunction of two natural concepts. To this end, we firstly provide an operational-realistic foundation of a theory of concepts, which are defined as 'entities in context-dependent states', rather than mere 'containers of instantiations' (Sect. 3). Secondly, we observe that this operational-realistic foundation is compatible with the operational-realistic foundation that justifies the use of the Hilbert space formalism to represent the micro-physical entities, which suggests that the mathematical formalism of quantum theory in Hilbert space is a possible (and in a sense natural) candidate to represent conceptual entities too.

After a brief review of the essentials of the quantum formalism that are needed to understand our results (Sect. 4), we then introduce the quantum theoretical representation of the conjunction and the disjunction of two natural concepts (Sect. 5). In it, deviations from classicality are explained as due to genuine quantum aspects, namely, 'context-dependence', 'emergence', 'interference' and 'superposition'. The approach also explains how new conceptual structures can emerge when concepts combine. We also show that the quantum theoretical framework is powerful enough to model any type of effect that can be detected in concrete experiments, which, by way of example, we do explicitly with some of Hampton's data for the conjunction and the disjunction of two natural concepts.

We conclude by emphasizing that the quantum theoretical modeling is not 'ad hoc', in the sense that it does not arise from a mere modeling of data, but rather it results from the foundational hypothesis that quantum theory (and its possible natural extensions) provides a unified and possibly universal paradigm to represent conceptual entities and their meaning-driven interactions (Sect. 6).

2   The Combination Problem

That concepts exhibit aspects of 'context-dependence', 'vagueness' and 'graded typicality' was already known in the seventies since the investigations of Rosch [1,2]. Her studies challenged the traditional view that concepts are containers of instantiations, together with the implicit assumption that conceptual combinations follow the set theoretical algebraic rules of classical logic. In particular, conceptual gradeness suggested a fuzzy set representation of concepts: for each item X, a concept A is associated with a graded membership $\mu(A)$, while the conjunction 'A and B', respectively the disjunction 'A or B', of the concepts A and B, should satisfy the 'minimum rule of fuzzy set conjunction' $\mu(A \text{ and } B) = \min[\mu(A), \mu(B)]$, respectively the 'maximum rule of fuzzy set disjunction' $\mu(A \text{ or } B) = \max[\mu(A), \mu(B)]$ [3].

In this way, one could still maintain that 'concepts can be represented as (fuzzy) sets and combine according to set theoretical rules'. However, a whole set of experimental findings revealed that the latter does not hold, even if the combinations are simple conjunctions or disjunctions of two concepts. This raised the so-called 'combination problem', that is, how the combination of two concepts should be expressed in terms of the component concepts.

The first obstacle came from the studies of Osherson and Smith. They observed that, for an item like *Guppy*, people rate its typicality with respect to the conjunction *Pet-Fish* higher than its typicality with respect to *Pet* or *Fish*, taken separately. This is the so-called 'Guppy effect' (or 'Pet-Fish problem') [4]. Thus, the Guppy effect violates the minimum rule of fuzzy set conjunction.

But, the most impressive violation of classicality in concept combination came from the experimental studies of psychologist James Hampton, in the late eighties. In a first experiment, Hampton tested the 'membership weight' of various sets of items, e.g., *Cuckoo, Peacock, Toucan, Parrot, Raven*, etc., with respect to pairs of natural concepts, e.g., *Bird* and *Pet*, taken individually, and their conjunction *Bird and Pet* [5]. In a second experiment, Hampton tested the membership weight of various sets of items, e.g., *Apple, Broccoli, Tomato, Mushrooms, Almonds*, etc., with respect to pairs of natural concepts, e.g., *Fruits* and *Vegetables*, again taken individually, and their disjunction *Fruits or Vegetables* [6]. More explicitly, participants were asked to rate, for each item X, its membership with respect to the concepts A, B and their conjunction 'A and B', or disjunction 'A or B' (depending on the pair of concepts considered). Membership was estimated on a 7-point Likert scale, $\{+3, +2, +1, 0, -1, -2, -3\}$, where the choice $+3$ meant that the item was estimated a 'very strong member of the concept', the choice -3 meant that the item was estimated a 'very strong non-member of the concept', and the choice 0 meant that the participant had not preference of membership or non-membership of the concept. Membership estimations were then converted into relative frequencies and, in the large number limit, into 'normalized membership weights'.

Hampton identified systematic deviations from the minimum rule of fuzzy set conjunction, as well as systematic deviations from the maximum rule of fuzzy set disjunction. Adopting his terminology, if the membership weight of an item X with respect to the conjunction 'A and B' of two concepts A and B is higher than the membership weight of X with respect to one concept (both concepts), we say that X is 'overextended' ('double overextended') with respect to the conjunction. Similarly, if the membership weight of an item X with respect to the disjunction 'A or B' of two concepts A and B is less than the membership weight of X with respect to one concept (both concepts), we say that X is 'underextended' ('double underextended') with respect to the disjunction.

Further experiments confirmed and deepened the findings above. Hampton found overextension in the conjunction 'A and not B', where 'not B' denotes the negation of the natural concept B [20]. Alxatib and Pelletier identified 'borderline contradictions' in sentences involving 'A and not A' [7], and some of us also detected overextension and double overextension by simultaneously testing conceptual conjunctions of the form 'A and not B', 'not A and B' and 'not A and not B' [21,22].

In these latter works, it emerged that the observed deviations from classicality are deeper than initially expected, as they depend on the fact that set theoretical structures are too limited to represent conceptual combinations. Indeed, let us consider the membership weights of items with respect to concepts and their conjunctions/disjunctions measured by Hampton [5,6]. In [9,10], we proved that a large part of Hampton's data on conjunctions of two concepts cannot be modeled in a single probability space satisfying the axioms of Kolmogorov [8]. For example, the item *Mint* scored in [5] the membership weight $\mu(A) = 0.87$, with respect to the concept *Food*, $\mu(B) = 0.81$, with respect to the concept *Plant*, and $\mu(A \text{ and } B) = 0.9$, with respect to their conjunction *Food and Plant*. Hence, the item *Mint* exhibits a 'double overextension' with respect to the conjunction *Food and Plant* of the concepts *Food* and *Plant*, and no Kolmogorovian probability representation exists for these data. More generally, the membership weights $\mu(A), \mu(B)$ and $\mu(A \text{ and } B)$ of the item X with respect to concepts A, B and their conjunction 'A and B', respectively, can be represented in a single Kolmogorovian probability space if and only if they satisfy the following inequalities [9]:

$$\mu(A \text{ and } B) - \min\left[\mu(A), \mu(B)\right] \leq 0 \qquad \mu(A) + \mu(B) - \mu(A \text{ and } B) \leq 1 \quad (1)$$

A violation of the first inequality in (1) entails, in particular, that the minimum rule of fuzzy set conjunction does not hold, as in the case of *Mint*.

Similarly, in [9,10] it was proved that a large part of Hampton's data on disjunctions of two concepts cannot be modeled in a single Kolmogorovian probability space. For example, the item *Sunglasses* scored in [6] the membership weight $\mu(A) = 0.4$ with respect to the concept *Sportswear*, $\mu(B) = 0.2$ with respect to the concept *Sports Equipment*, and $\mu(A \text{ or } B) = 0.1$ with respect to their disjunction *Sportswear or Sports Equipment*. Thus, the item *Sunglasses* exhibits 'double underextension' with respect to the disjunction *Sportswear or Sports Equipment* of the concepts *Sportswear* and *Sports Equipment*, and no Kolmogorovian probability representation exists for these data. More generally, the membership weights $\mu(A), \mu(B)$ and $\mu(A \text{ or } B)$ of the item X with respect to concepts A, B and their disjunction 'A or B', respectively, can be represented in a single Kolmogorovian probability space if and only if they satisfy the following inequalities [9]:

$$\max[\mu(A), \mu(B)] - \mu(A \text{ or } B) \leq 0 \qquad 0 \leq \mu(A) + \mu(B) - \mu(A \text{ or } B) \quad (2)$$

A violation of the first inequality in (2) entails, in particular, that the maximum rule of fuzzy set disjunction does not hold, as in the case of *Sunglasses*.

The difficulties above reveal that the formation and combination rules of human concepts do not obey the restrictions of classical (fuzzy set) logic and Kolmogorovian probability theory. Hence, the combination problem needs to be approached with a novel and more general research programme.

3   An Operational-Realistic Foundation

The investigations of the quantum mechanical representability of concepts by our group in Brussels can be traced back to our previous studies on the axiomatic and operational foundations of quantum physics, the differences between classical and quantum structures and the origins of quantum probability (see, e.g., [19]). We recognized that any decision process, e.g., a typicality measurement, or a membership estimation, involves a 'transition from potential to actual', in which an outcome is actualized within a set of possible outcomes, as a consequence of a contextual interaction (of a cognitive nature) between the decision-maker and the conceptual situation that is the object of the decision. Thus, human decision processes exhibit a deep analogy with what occurs in a quantum measurement process, where the measurement context (of a physical nature) influences the measured quantum particle in a non-deterministic way, actualizing properties that were only potential prior to the measurement. Different form 'classical probability', which can only deal with situations of lack of knowledge about actuality, 'quantum probability' is able to formalize such 'contextually driven actualization of potential'. Thus, it can cope with the intrinsic uncertainty underlying both quantum and conceptual realms [17, 23, 24].

These preliminary analogies led us to systematically inquire into the most plausible mathematical structures formalizing both the micro-physical and conceptual entities. In this respect, the formalism of quantum theory, based on complex Hilbert spaces, has always amazed researchers for its impressive effectiveness and predictive power. This inspired a fruitful investigation of the foundations of quantum theory in Hilbert space from physically justified axioms, resting on well defined empirical notions, more directly connected with the operations that are usually performed in a laboratory. Such an operational justification would indeed make the formalism of quantum theory more firmly founded.

A in Geneva and Brussels developed approach to the foundations of quantum physics is the 'State Context Property' (SCoP), in which any physical entity is expressed in terms of the basic notions of 'state', 'context' and 'property', which arise as a consequence of concrete physical operations on macroscopic apparatuses, like preparations and registrations, performed in spatio-temporal domains, like physical laboratories [19]. State transformations, measurements, outcomes, and probabilities can then be expressed in terms of these basic notions. If suitable axioms are imposed on the mathematical structures underlying the SCoP formalism, then the Hilbert space structure of quantum theory emerges as a unique mathematical representation, up to isomorphisms [18].[2]

This line of research inspired the operational approaches applying the quantum formalism outside the microscopic domain of quantum physics [17, 23, 24]. In particular, a very similar realistic and operational description can be given for the conceptual entities of the cognitive domain, in the sense that the SCoP formalism can be employed to also formalize conceptual entities in terms of states, contexts, properties, measurements and probabilities of outcomes [16].

Let us consider the empirical phenomenology of cognitive psychology. Like in physics, where laboratories define spatio-temporal domains, we can introduce 'psychological laboratories', where cognitive experiments are performed. These experiments are performed on situations that are specifically 'prepared' for the experiments, including experimental devices and, for example, structured questionnaires, human participants that interact with the questionnaires in written

---

[2] Interestingly, the approach allowed to put into evidence an important shortcoming of the standard quantum formalism: the impossibility of describing experimentally separated entities [19].

answers, or with each other, e.g., an interviewer and an interviewed. Whenever empirical data are collected from the responses of several participants, a statistics of the obtained outcomes arises. Starting from these empirical facts, we can identify in our approach entities, states, contexts, measurements, outcomes and probabilities of outcomes, as follows.

The complex of experimental procedures conceived by the experimenter, the experimental design and setting and the cognitive effect that one wants to analyze, define a conceptual entity A, and are usually associated with a preparation procedure of a specific state of A. Hence, like in physics, the preparation procedure sets the initial state p_A of the conceptual entity A under study. Let us consider, for example, a questionnaire where a participant is asked to rank on a 7-point Likert scale the membership of a list of items with respect to the concepts *Fruits*, *Vegetables* and their conjunction *Fruits and Vegetables*. The questionnaire defines the states p_{Fruits}, $p_{Vegetables}$ and $p_{Fruits\ and\ Vegetables}$ of the conceptual entities *Fruits*, *Vegetables* and *Fruits and Vegetables*, respectively. Although in some cognitive situations the preparation procedure of a conceptual entity is hardly controllable, the state of the conceptual entity, defined by means of such a preparation procedure, can always be considered to be a 'state of affairs'. It indeed expresses a 'reality of the conceptual entity', in the sense that, once prepared in a given state, such condition is independent of any measurement procedure, and can be equally confronted with the different participants in an experiment, leading to outcome data and their statistics, exactly like in physics.[3]

A context e is an aspect of the experiment that can provoke a change of state of the conceptual entity. For example, the concept *Juicy* can act as a context for the conceptual entity *Fruits*, leading to combined concept *Juicy Fruits*, which can then be also interpreted as a state of the conceptual entity *Fruits*, and more precisely the state describing the situation where 'the fruit is juicy'. A particular type of context is the one introduced by the measurement itself. Indeed, when the cognitive experiment starts, an interaction of a cognitive nature occurs between the conceptual entity A under study and a participant in the experiment, in which the state p_A of the conceptual entity A generally changes, being transformed into another state p. This cognitive interaction is also formalized by means of a context e. For example, if the participant is asked to choose among a list of items, say, *Olive*, *Almond*, *Apple*, etc., the most typical one with respect to *Fruits*, and the answer is *Apple*, then the initial state p_{Fruits} of the conceptual entity *Fruits* changes to p_{Apple}, i.e. to the state describing the situation 'the fruit is an apple', as a consequence of the contextual interaction with the participant.

Thus, the change of the state of a conceptual entity due to a context may be either 'deterministic', hence in principle predictable under the assumption that the initial state is known, or 'intrinsically probabilistic', in the sense that only the probability $\mu(p, e, p_A)$ that the state p_A of A changes to the state p

---

[3] A difference between psychological and physics laboratories is that in the former each participant works as a distinct measuring apparatus, usually producing a single outcome, whereas in the latter a same apparatus is usually used to produce multiple outcomes; see the discussion in [25].

is given. In the example above on typicality estimations, the typicality of the item *Apple* for the concept *Fruits* is formalized by means of the transition probability $\mu(p_{Apple}, e, p_{Fruits})$, where the context e is the context of the typicality measurement. More generally, suppose that the membership of an item X is estimated by a given sample of participants, with respect to a concept A. The item X acts as a context e_X that changes the state p_A of the conceptual entity A into a new state p_X. The decision measurement can then be described as a further context e that changes the state p_X into a new state p. Hence, the membership weight $\mu(A)$ can be expressed as the product of the transition probabilities $\mu(A) = \mu(p_X, e_X, p_A)\mu(p, e, p_X) = \mu(p, e, p_X)$, where the last equality follows from the fact that the change $p_A \rightarrow p_X$ is deterministic, so that $\mu(p_X, e_X, p_A) = 1$.

We have thus described an approach in which, similarly to the operational-realistic foundation of micro-physical entities, a concept can be understood not a container of instantiations, but as an entity in a well-defined state, which can change under the effects of deterministic and indeterministic contexts. This suggests that the Hilbert-based formalism of quantum theory could be a proper candidate to also represent concepts and their interactions.

4   Essentials of Quantum Mathematics

We present in this section some basic definitions and results of the mathematical formalism of quantum theory that are needed when the quantum formalism is applied to represent concepts and their combinations. We will be rigorous, without however dwelling on technical details.

When the quantum mechanical formalism is applied for modeling purposes, each considered entity – in our case a concept – is associated with a complex Hilbert space $\mathcal{H}$, that is, a vector space over the field $\mathbb{C}$ of complex numbers, equipped with an inner product $\langle \cdot | \cdot \rangle$ that maps two vectors $\langle A|$ and $|B\rangle$ onto a complex number $\langle A|B\rangle$. We denote vectors by using the bra-ket notation introduced by Paul Adrien Dirac, one of the pioneers of quantum theory [27]. Vectors can be 'kets', denoted by $|A\rangle$, $|B\rangle$, or 'bras', denoted by $\langle A|$, $\langle B|$. The inner product between the ket vectors $|A\rangle$ and $|B\rangle$, or the bra-vectors $\langle A|$ and $\langle B|$, is realized by juxtaposing the bra vector $\langle A|$ and the ket vector $|B\rangle$, and $\langle A|B\rangle$ is also called a 'bra-ket', and it satisfies the following properties:

  (i) $\langle A|A\rangle \geq 0$;
 (ii) $\langle A|B\rangle = \langle B|A\rangle^*$, where $\langle B|A\rangle^*$ is the complex conjugate of $\langle B|A\rangle$;
(iii) $\langle A|(z|B\rangle + t|C\rangle) = z\langle A|B\rangle + t\langle A|C\rangle$, for $z, t \in \mathbb{C}$, where the sum vector $z|B\rangle + t|C\rangle$ is called a 'superposition' of vectors $|B\rangle$ and $|C\rangle$ in the quantum jargon.

From (ii) and (iii) follows that the inner product $\langle \cdot | \cdot \rangle$ is linear in the ket and anti-linear in the bra, i.e. $(z\langle A| + t\langle B|)|C\rangle = z^*\langle A|C\rangle + t^*\langle B|C\rangle$.

The 'absolute value' of a complex number is defined as the square root of the product of this complex number times its complex conjugate, that is, $|z| = \sqrt{z^*z}$.

Moreover, a A complex number z can either be decomposed into its Cartesian form $z = x + iy$, or into its polar form $z = |z|e^{i\theta} = |z|(\cos\theta + i\sin\theta)$, where $|z|$ denotes the 'absolute value' of z. Hence, one has $|\langle A|B\rangle| = \sqrt{\langle A|B\rangle\langle B|A\rangle}$. We define the 'length' of a ket vector $|A\rangle$ as $|||A\rangle|| = \sqrt{\langle A|A\rangle}$. A vector of unitary length is called a 'unit vector'. We say that the ket vectors $|A\rangle$ and $|B\rangle$ are 'orthogonal', and write $|A\rangle \perp |B\rangle$, if $\langle A|B\rangle = 0$.

We have now introduced the necessary mathematics to state the first modeling rule of quantum theory.

First Quantum Modeling Rule. A state of an entity modeled by quantum theory (in our case a concept) is represented by a unit vector $|A\rangle$, that is, $\langle A|A\rangle = 1$.

We also need to introduce the notion of an orthogonal projection operator M, which is a linear operator on the Hilbert space, that is, a mapping $M : \mathcal{H} \to \mathcal{H}, |A\rangle \mapsto M|A\rangle$, having the properties of being Hermitian and idempotent. This means that, for every $|A\rangle, |B\rangle \in \mathcal{H}$ and $z, t \in \mathbb{C}$, we have:

(i) $M(z|A\rangle + t|B\rangle) = zM|A\rangle + tM|B\rangle$ (linearity)
(ii) $\langle A|M|B\rangle = \langle B|M|A\rangle^*$ (hermiticity)
(iii) $M^2 = M$ (idempotency)

The identity operator $\mathbb{1}$ maps each vector onto itself and is a trivial orthogonal projection operator. We say that two orthogonal projection operators M_k and M_l are orthogonal operators if each vector contained in the range $M_k(\mathcal{H})$ is orthogonal to each vector contained in the range $M_l(\mathcal{H})$, and we write $M_k \perp M_l$, in this case. The orthogonality of the projection operators M_k and M_l can equivalently be expressed as $M_kM_l = 0$, where 0 is the null operator. A set of orthogonal projection operators $\{M_k \mid k = 1, \ldots, n\}$ is called a 'spectral family' if all projectors are mutually orthogonal, that is, $M_k \perp M_l$ for $k \neq l$, and their sum is the identity operator, that is, $\sum_{k=1}^{n} M_k = \mathbb{1}$.

We are now in a position to state the second and third modeling rules of quantum theory.

Second Quantum Modeling Rule. A measurable quantity Q of an entity modeled by quantum theory (in our case a concept), having a set of possible real values $\{q_k \mid k = 1, \ldots, n\}$, is represented by a spectral family $\{M_k \mid k = 1, \ldots, n\}$ in the following way. If the entity is in a state represented by the unit vector $|A\rangle$, then the probability of obtaining the value q_k, $k \in \{1, \ldots, n\}$, in a measurement of the measurable quantity Q, is

$$\mu_A(q_k) = \langle A|M_k|A\rangle = ||M_k|A\rangle||^2 \tag{3}$$

This formula for probabilistic assignment is called the 'Born rule' in the quantum jargon.

Third Quantum Modeling Rule. If the value q_k, $k \in \{1, \ldots, n\}$, is actually obtained in the measurement of a measurable quantity Q on an entity modeled by quantum theory (in our case a concept), when the entity is in an initial state represented by the unit vector $|A\rangle$, then the initial state is changed into an outcome state represented by the vector

$$|A_k\rangle = \frac{M_k|A\rangle}{||M_k|A\rangle||} = \frac{M_k|A\rangle}{\sqrt{\langle A|M_k|A\rangle}} \qquad (4)$$

This change of state is called 'collapse', or 'reduction', in the quantum jargon.

The quantum modeling above can be generalized in different ways, by introducing rules to model composite entities, or weakening the rules above to represent more complex situations.[4] However, what we have here presented is sufficient for attaining our results in the next sections.

5   Effects of Interference and Context

The quantum theoretical framework for conceptual combinations is obtained by canonically representing the operational notions of state and state changes, (membership and typicality) measurements and (deterministic and indeterministic) contexts, introduced in Sect. 2, by means of the specific Hilbert space mathematics of the quantum formalism, as summarized in Sect. 4. We limit ourselves here to specifying the quantum theoretical framework for the conjunction and the disjunction of two concepts [9, 10, 26].

Let us start with the disjunction of two concepts. Consider, for example, the item *Olive*, whose membership was estimated in [6] with respect to the concepts *Fruits*, *Vegetables* and their disjunction *Fruits or Vegetables*. We make three quantum theoretical hypotheses:

(i) Whenever *Fruits* and *Vegetables* combine, they superpose and interfere. As a consequence of this superposition and interference, a new concept *Fruits or Vegetables* emerges.[5]
(ii) Whenever the item *Olive* is considered, a context effect (specific to the item considered) occurs, which produces a deterministic change of state of the conceptual entities *Fruits*, *Vegetables* and *Fruits or Vegetables*. This context effect is different than the one created when a different item, say *Apple*, is considered, again with respect to *Fruits*, *Vegetables* and *Fruits or Vegetables*.
(iii) The decision of a participant who estimates the membership of *Olive* with respect to *Fruits*, *Vegetables* and *Fruits or Vegetables* is considered as a measurement with two outcomes, 'yes' and 'no', on the conceptual entities *Fruits*, *Vegetables* and *Fruits or Vegetables*, respectively.

---

[4] For instance, more general rules of probabilistic assignment than the Born one seem to be necessary for a complete modeling of question order effects data [25].

[5] This is similar to the prototypical example of the two-slit experiment, where a genuine interference pattern emerges when both slits are open, which cannot be explained in a compositional way, i.e., by assuming that the quantum entities (for example, photons) always pass through one or the other slit.

Coming to the representation, let A and B be two concepts and let the membership of the item X be estimated with respect to A, B and their disjunction 'A or B'. Concepts are operationally described as entities in specific states, thus we represent the states of the concepts A and B by the unit vectors $|A\rangle$ and $|B\rangle$, respectively, of a Hilbert space $\mathcal{H}$, whereas the state of the concept 'A or B' is represented by the normalized superposition $|A \text{ or } B\rangle = \frac{1}{\sqrt{2}}(|A\rangle + |B\rangle)$. For the sake of simplicity, we assume in the following that $|A\rangle$ and $|B\rangle$ are orthogonal, that is, $\langle A|B\rangle = 0$.

To describe the context effect produced by the specific item X, we use an orthogonal projection operator N, over the Hilbert space $\mathcal{H}$. (We can understand N as projecting onto the subspace of states that are also states of the concept X). When applied to the unit vectors $|A\rangle$ and $|B\rangle$ and $\frac{1}{\sqrt{2}}(|A\rangle + |B\rangle)$, the operator N produces the new non-unit vectors $N|A\rangle$ and $N|B\rangle$ and $N|A \text{ or } B\rangle = \frac{1}{\sqrt{2}}(N|A\rangle + N|B\rangle)$. The transformed states of the concepts A, B and 'A or B', resulting from the context effect related to the item X, are then represented by the unit vectors $|A_N\rangle$, $|B_N\rangle$ and $|(A \text{ or } B)_N\rangle$, respectively, obtained by normalizing the projected vectors $N|A\rangle$, $N|B\rangle$ and $N|A \text{ or } B\rangle$, respectively. More precisely, using (4), we get

$$|A_N\rangle = \frac{N|A\rangle}{||N|A\rangle||}, \quad |B_N\rangle = \frac{N|B\rangle}{||N|B\rangle||}, \quad |(A \text{ or } B)_N\rangle = \frac{\frac{1}{\sqrt{2}}(N|A\rangle + N|B\rangle)}{||\frac{1}{\sqrt{2}}(N|A\rangle + N|B\rangle)||}. \quad (5)$$

Let us now come to the representation of the decision measurement of a person estimating whether the item X is a member of the concepts A, B and 'A or B'. This corresponds to a measurable quantity with two values, 'yes' and 'no', and is represented by the spectral family $\{M, \mathbb{1} - M\}$, with M an orthogonal projection operator over $\mathcal{H}$. By using the Born rule (3), the probabilities $\mu(A)$, $\mu(B)$ and $\mu(A \text{ or } B)$ that X is estimated as a member of the concepts A, B and 'A or B', respectively, i.e., its membership weights, are given by the inner products $\mu(A) = \langle A_N|M|A_N\rangle$, $\mu(B) = \langle B_N|M|B_N\rangle$ and $\mu(A \text{ or } B) = \langle (A \text{ or } B)_N|M|(A \text{ or } B)_N\rangle$. By using (3) and (5), we thus obtain

$$\mu(A) = \frac{\langle A|NMN|A\rangle}{\langle A|N|A\rangle}, \quad \mu(B) = \frac{\langle B|NMN|B\rangle}{\langle B|N|B\rangle} \quad (6)$$

$$\mu(A \text{ or } B) = \frac{(\langle A| + \langle B|)NMN(|A\rangle + |B\rangle)}{(\langle A| + \langle B|)N(|A\rangle + |B\rangle)}$$
$$= \frac{\langle A|NMN|A\rangle + \langle B|NMN|B\rangle + 2\Re\langle A|NMN|B\rangle}{\langle A|N|A\rangle + \langle B|N|B\rangle + 2\Re\langle A|N|B\rangle} \quad (7)$$

The real parts $\Re\langle A|NMN|B\rangle$ and $\Re\langle A|N|B\rangle$ are the typical 'interference terms' of quantum theory. We now assume that the context effect consisting of considering the item X and the decision measurement consisting of choosing in favor or against membership of item X are 'compatible'. This is a natural assumption, as both contexts are generated by the same item X, and is formalized in quantum theory by requiring the commutativity of the corresponding orthogonal projection operators, that is, $MN = NM$. This entails that $NMN = MNN = MN$, hence

$$\mu(A \text{ or } B) = \frac{\langle A|MN|A \rangle + \langle B|MN|B \rangle + 2\Re\langle A|MN|B \rangle}{\langle A|N|A \rangle + \langle B|N|B \rangle + 2\Re\langle A|N|B \rangle} \tag{8}$$

Using some simple algebra and trigonometry, one can show that (8) reduces to the following expression [26]:

$$\mu(A \text{ or } B) = \frac{n^2\mu(A) + n'^2\mu(B) + 2nn'\sqrt{\mu(A)\mu(B)}\cos\phi_d}{n^2 + n'^2 + 2nn'\cos\phi_d(\sqrt{\mu(A)\mu(B)} - \sqrt{(1-\mu(A))(1-\mu(B))})} \tag{9}$$

where ϕ_d is the 'interference angle for the disjunction', and n, n' and R are real parameters such that

$$R = \sqrt{(1-\mu(A))(1-\mu(B))} - \sqrt{\mu(A)\mu(B)}, \qquad \sqrt{(1-n^2)(1-n'^2)} = nn'|R| \tag{10}$$

One shows that (9) provides a solution for any type of effect that can be experimentally detected, namely, classical data satisfying (2), overextension and underextension. In addition, one shows that the simplest Hilbert space able to do so is the three-dimensional complex Hilbert space $\mathbb{C}^3$, with a suitable choice of the orthogonal projection operators M and N [26]. For example, consider the item *Refrigerator* with respect to the pair of concepts *House Furnishings* and *Furniture*, and their disjunction *House Furnishings or Furniture*. Hampton found $\mu(A) = 0.9$, $\mu(B) = 0.7$ and $\mu(A \text{ or } B) = 0.575$, which means that we are in the situation of 'double underextension' [6]. Eqs. (9)–(10) can be solved for $R = -0.6205$, $n = 0.7331$, $n' = 0.8312$ and $\phi_d = 119.3535°$. The concepts *House Furnishings* and *Furniture* are instead represented by the unit vectors $|A\rangle = (0.6955, 0.2318, 0.6801)$, $|B\rangle = e^{i119.3535°}(0.6955, -0.4553, -0.5559)$, in the canonical base $\{(1,0,0), (0,1,0), (0,0,1)\}$ of $\mathbb{C}^3$ [26].

Coming now to the conjunction of two concepts, the same modeling can be used, *mutatis mutandis*, with the conjunction 'A and B' still represented by a normalized superposition $|A \text{ and } B\rangle = \frac{1}{\sqrt{2}}(|A\rangle + |B\rangle)$, with the previous 'interference angle for the disjunction' ϕ_d now replaced in (9) by an 'interference angle for the conjunction' ϕ_c.

Again, one shows that (9) provides a solution for any type of effect that can be experimentally detected, namely, classical data satisfying (1), overextension and underextension, with the simplest Hilbert space being again $\mathbb{C}^3$ [26]. For example, consider the item *TV* with respect to the pair of concepts *Furniture* and *Household Appliances*, and their conjunction *Furniture and Household Appliances*. Hampton found $\mu(A) = 0.7$, $\mu(B) = 0.9$, and $\mu(A \text{ and } B) = 0.925$, which means that we are in the situation of 'double overextension' [5]. Eqs. (9)–(10) can be solved for $R = -0.6205$, $n = 0.5370$, $n' = 0.9301$ and $\phi_c = 66.79°$. The concepts *Furniture* and *Household Appliances* are instead represented by the unit vectors $|A\rangle = (0.45, 0.29, 0.84)$, $|B\rangle = e^{i66.79°}(0.88, -0.29, -0.37)$, always in the canonical base of $\mathbb{C}^3$ [26].

This completes the construction of a quantum modeling for the conjunction and the disjunction of two concepts. It shows how new conceptual structures emerge from the component concepts without any need for logical connections between the latter, and explains deviations from classicality in terms of genuine quantum effects, such us context-dependence, interference and superposition.

6   Conclusions

We have presented here a quantum theoretical framework to represent natural concepts and their conjunctions and disjunctions. We have shown that such framework can capture genuine quantum aspects, namely, context-dependence, emergence, interference and superposition, and that these aspects are responsible of the deviations from classical logical and probabilistic structures that are observed in membership judgments on conceptual combinations [5–7,20–22]. Hence, the quantum framework provides a solution of the combination problem and constitutes a faithful model for diverse sets of experimental data.

It is however important to stress that the quantum models arising from the present approach are not 'ad hoc', in the sense that they are not devised to merely fit empirical data. They rather emerge from a 'theory based approach', which looks for the most plausible mathematical structures to represent both micro-physical and conceptual realms [19,25]. Indeed, are the deep analogies between the physical and conceptual domains, in the description of measurement processes, that led us to inquire into the realistic-operational foundations of conceptual entities and their description in terms of states, contexts, measurements, outcomes and probabilities, suggesting that quantum structures are very plausible and natural structures to represent both domains. As such, the quantum models are subject to the technical and epistemological constraints of quantum theory, here meant as a possibly universal, coherent and unified theoretical scheme to represent conceptual entities and their interactions.

To conclude, the quantum theoretical framework can be naturally extended to represent more complex conceptual combinations, like conceptual negation and combinations of several concepts. This extension enables the identification of further quantum aspects in conceptual combinations, e.g., 'entanglement' and 'quantum-type indistinguishability', together with identification of new non-classical patterns of violation, which go beyond over- and under-extension, but capture deep aspects of concept formation [21,22] and context effects [25]. However, the presentation of these results would go beyond the scopes and length limits of the present paper.

References

1. Rosch, E.: Natural categories. Cogn. Psychol. **4**, 328–350 (1973)
2. Rosch, E.: Principles of categorization. In: Rosch, E., Lloyd, B. (eds.) Cognition and Categorization, pp. 133–179. Lawrence Erlbaum, Hillsdale (1978)
3. Zadeh, L.: A note on prototype theory and fuzzy sets. Cognition **12**, 291–297 (1982)
4. Osherson, D., Smith, E.: On the adequacy of prototype theory as a theory of concepts. Cognition **9**, 35–58 (1981)
5. Hampton, J.A.: Overextension of conjunctive concepts: evidence for a unitary model for concept typicality and class inclusion. J. Exp. Psychol.: Learn. Mem. Cogn. **14**, 12–32 (1988a)
6. Hampton, J.A.: Disjunction of natural concepts. Mem. Cogn. **16**, 579–591 (1988b)
7. Alxatib, S., Pelletier, J.: On the psychology of truth-gaps. In: Nouwen, R., Rooij, R., Sauerland, U., Schmitz, H.-C. (eds.) VIC 2009. LNCS, vol. 6517, pp. 13–36. Springer, Heidelberg (2011). doi:10.1007/978-3-642-18446-8_2

8. Kolmogorov, A.N.: Grundbegriffe der Wahrscheinlichkeitrechnung. Ergebnisse Der Mathematik (1933). Translated as Foundations of Probability (1950). Chelsea Publishing Company, New York

9. Aerts, D.: Quantum structure in cognition. J. Math. Psychol. **53**, 314–348 (2009)

10. Aerts, D., Gabora, L.S., Sozzo, S.: Concepts and their dynamics: a quantum-theoretic modeling of human thought. Top. Cogn. Sci. **5**, 737–772 (2013)

11. Busemeyer, J.R., Bruza, P.D.: Quantum Models of Cognition and Decision. Cambridge University Press, Cambridge (2012)

12. Aerts, D., Broekaert, J., Gabora, L., Sozzo, S.: Quantum structure and human thought. Behav. Brain Sci. **36**, 274–276 (2013)

13. Pothos, E.M., Busemeyer, J.R.: Can quantum probability provide a new direction for cognitive modeling? Behav. Brain Sci. **36**, 255–274 (2013)

14. Haven, E., Khrennikov, A.: Quantum Social Science. Cambridge University Press, Cambridge (2013)

15. Wang, Z., Solloway, T., Shiffrin, R.M., Busemeyer, J.R.: Context effects produced by question orders reveal quantum nature of human judgments. Proc. Natl. Acad. Sci. **111**, 9431–9436 (2014)

16. Aerts, D., Sassoli de Bianchi, M., Sozzo, S.: On the foundations of the Brussels operational-realistic approach to cognition. Front. Phys. **4**(17) (2015). doi:10.3389/fphy.2016.00017

17. Aerts, D., Aerts, S.: Applications of quantum statistics in psychological studies of decision processes. Found. Sci. **1**, 85–97 (1995)

18. Beltrametti, E.G., Cassinelli, G.: The Logic of Quantum Mechanics. Addison-Wesley, Reading (1981)

19. Aerts, D.: Foundations of quantum physics: a general realistic and operational approach. Int. J. Theoret. Phys. **38**, 289–358 (1999)

20. Hampton, J.A.: Conceptual combination: conjunction and negation of natural concepts. Mem. Cogn. **25**, 888–909 (1997)

21. Aerts, D., Sozzo, S., Veloz, T.: Quantum structure of negation and conjunction in human thought. Front. Psychol. (2015). doi:10.3389/fpsyg.2015.01447

22. Aerts, D., Sozzo, S., Veloz, T.: New fundamental evidence of non-classical structure in the combination of natural concepts. Philos. Trans. R. Soc. A **374**, 20150095 (2016)

23. Aerts, D., Gabora, L.: A theory of concepts and their combinations I: the structure of the sets of contexts and properties. Kybernetes **34**, 167–191 (2005)

24. Aerts, D., Gabora, L.: A theory of concepts and their combinations II: a hilbert space representation. Kybernetes **34**, 192–221 (2005)

25. Aerts, D., Sassoli de Bianchi, M.: . Beyond-quantum modeling of question order effects and response replicability in psychological measurements. J. Math. Psych. (2015, to appear). arXiv:1508.03686[cs.AI]

26. Aerts, D.: Quantum interference and superposition in cognition: development of a theory for the disjunction of concepts. In: Aerts, D., et al. (eds.) Worldviews, Science and Us, pp. 169–211. World Scientific, Singapore (2011)

27. Dirac, P.A.M.: Quantum Mechanics, 4th edn. Oxford University Press, London (1958)

A Computational Logic Approach to the Belief Bias in Human Syllogistic Reasoning

Emmanuelle-Anna Dietz[(✉)]

International Center for Computational Logic, TU Dresden, Dresden, Germany
emmanuelle.dietz@tu-dresden.de

Abstract. Psychological experiments on syllogistic reasoning have shown that participants did not always deduce the classical logically valid conclusions. In particular, the results show that they had difficulties to reason with syllogistic statements that contradicted their own beliefs. We consider a syllogistic reasoning task carried out by Evans, Barston and Pollard, who investigated the belief-bias effect with respect to syllogisms. We propose a formalization of the belief-bias effect for human syllogistic reasoning under the Weak Completion Semantics, a logic programming approach that aims at adequately modeling human reasoning.

1 Introduction

Evans et al. [15] carried out a psychological study about deductive reasoning, which demonstrated possibly conflicting processes in human reasoning. Participants were presented different syllogisms for which they had to decide whether they accepted these syllogisms as valid. Consider S_{vit}:

PREMISE 1	*No nutritional things are inexpensive.*
PREMISE 2	*Some vitamin tablets are inexpensive.*
CONCLUSION	*Some vitamin tablets are not nutritional.*

The CONCLUSION necessarily follows from the premises under classical logic. However, about half of the participants said that the syllogism was not valid. They were explicitly asked to logically validate or invalidate various syllogisms, but did not seem to have the intellectual capability to do so. Even worse, they were not even aware about their inabilities. Participants reflectively read the instructions and understood well that they were required to reason logically from the premises to the conclusion. However, the results show that their intuitions were stronger and delivered a tendency to say '*yes*' or '*no*' depending on whether the syllogism was believable [14]. The responses of participants for various syllogisms, which differed with respect to their validity and whether they were believable in the contextual setting, were evaluated in [15]. Four of them are depicted in Table 1. The first two premises of all four cases are of the same logical form, namely *No A are B. Some C are B.* The first two cases differ from the last two cases with respect to the conclusions: In the first two cases the conclusions correspond to the logical form *Some C are A* and in the last two

© Springer International Publishing AG 2017
P. Brézillon et al. (Eds.): CONTEXT 2017, LNAI 10257, pp. 691–707, 2017.
DOI: 10.1007/978-3-319-57837-8_55

Table 1. Four types of syllogisms taken from [11]. The percentages of the participants that accepted the syllogism as being valid are shown in the last column.

	Type	Case	%
S_{dog}	Valid and believable	*No police dogs are vicious*	92
		Some highly trained dogs are vicious	
		Some highly trained dogs are not police dogs	
S_{vit}	Valid and unbelievable	*No nutritional things are inexpensive*	46
		Some vitamin tablets are inexpensive	
		Some vitamin tablets are not nutritional	
S_{rich}	Invalid and unbelievable	*No millionaires are hard workers*	8
		Some rich people are hard workers	
		Some millionaires are not rich people	
S_{cig}	Invalid and believable	*No addictive things are inexpensive*	92
		Some cigarettes are inexpensive	
		Some addictive things are not cigarettes	

cases the conclusions correspond to the logical form *Some A are C*. The first two syllogisms are indeed valid under classical logic, whereas the last two are not. However, as the last column shows, the percentage of the participants that validated the syllogism, does not necessarily comply with the results under classical logic. Evans, Barston and Pollard asserted that the participants were influenced by their own beliefs, their so-called belief bias.

Khemlani and Johnson-Laird [24] have compared the predictions of 12 cognitive theories to participants' responses in syllogistic reasoning. The Verbal Model Theory [28] performed best with an accurate prediction of 84%, closely followed by the Mental Model Theory [21], which achieved 83%. Recently, [3] developed a logical form for the representation of syllogisms under the logic programming approach, the Weak Completion Semantics, and predicted even 89% of the participants' responses.

The Weak Completion Semantics is a new cognitive theory, which originates from [30], but is mathematically sound [19], and has been successfully applied – among others – to the suppression task [8], the selection task [9] to reasoning about conditionals [5,7] and to spatial reasoning [6]. As the Weak Completion Semantics aims at modeling human reasoning adequately and predicted well the participants' responses in syllogistic reasoning, a natural question to ask, is whether the belief-bias effect in syllogistic reasoning can be modeled within this approach.

After briefly discussing the belief-bias effect, we introduce the Weak Completion Semantics. Taking [3,4] as starting point, Sects. 4 and 5 present six principles for modeling quantified statements in human reasoning and show their representations in logic programs. Finally, Sect. 6 presents how the belief-bias effect can be modeled under the Weak Completion Semantics by discussing the four cases in Table 1.

2   The Belief-Bias Effect

Evans et al. [13] distinguish between the negative and the positive belief bias: The negative belief bias describes the case when the support for an unbelievable conclusion is suppressed. On the other hand, the positive belief bias describes the case when the acceptance for a believable conclusion is raised. Consider again Table 1: The negative belief bias happens for 46% of the participants in the case of S_{vit} and the positive belief bias happens for 92% of the participants in the case of S_{cig}.

As pointed out in [16], Wilkins [31] already observed that syllogisms which conflict with our beliefs are more difficult to solve. Since then, various theories have tried to explain why humans deviate from the classical logically valid answers. Some conclusions can be explained by converting the premises as proposed in [2] or by assuming that the type of the premises creates an atmosphere which influences the acceptance for the conclusion [16,32]. Johnson-Laird and Byrne [22] proposed the mental model theory [21], which additionally supposes the search for counterexamples when validating the conclusion. Later, Stenning and van Lambalgen [30] explain why certain aspects influence the interpretations made by humans when evaluating syllogisms and discuss this in the context of mental models. Evans et al. [10,15] proposed a theory, which in the literature is sometimes referred to as the selective scrutiny model [1,16]. First, humans heuristically accept any syllogism having a believable conclusion, and only proceed with a logical evaluation if the conclusion contradicts their belief. Adler and Rips [1] claim that this behavior is rational in the sense of efficient belief maintenance. Yet another approach, the selective processing model [12], accounts only for a single preferred model: If the conclusion is neutral or believable, humans attempt to construct a model that supports it. Otherwise, they attempt to construct a model that rejects it.

According to Garnham and Oakhill [16] the belief-bias effect can take place at several stages: First, beliefs can influence our understanding of the premises. Second, in case a statement contradicts our belief, we might search for alternative models and check whether the conclusion is plausible. This seems to comply with Stenning and van Lambalgen's proposal to model human reasoning by a two step procedure [30]. The first step, the representational part, determines how our beliefs influence the understanding of the premises. The second step, the procedural part, determines whether we search for alternative models based on the plausibility of the conclusion.

In this paper we will follow up on this distinction when modeling the belief-bias effect.

694   E.-A. Dietz

Table 2. $\top$, $\bot$, and U denote *true*, *false*, and *unknown*, respectively.

F	$\neg F$	$\wedge$	$\top$	U	$\bot$	$\vee$	$\top$	U	$\bot$	$\leftarrow$	$\top$	U	$\bot$	$\leftrightarrow$	$\top$	U	$\bot$
$\top$	$\bot$	$\top$	$\top$	U	$\bot$	$\top$	$\top$	$\top$	$\top$	$\top$	$\top$	$\top$	$\top$	$\top$	$\top$	U	$\bot$
$\bot$	$\top$	U	U	U	$\bot$	U	$\top$	U	U	U	U	$\top$	$\top$	U	U	$\top$	U
U	U	$\bot$	$\bot$	$\bot$	$\bot$	$\bot$	$\top$	U	$\bot$	$\bot$	$\bot$	U	$\top$	$\bot$	$\bot$	U	$\top$

3   Weak Completion Semantics

The general notation, which we will use in the paper, is based on [18,25].

3.1   Logic Programs

We restrict ourselves to datalog programs, i.e., the set of terms consists only of constants and variables.

$$A \leftarrow L_1 \wedge \ldots \ldots \wedge L_n. \tag{1}$$
$$A \leftarrow \top. \tag{2}$$
$$A \leftarrow \bot. \tag{3}$$

A is an atom and the L_i with $1 \leq i \leq n$ are literals. The atom A is called *head* of the clause and the subformula to the right of the implication symbol is called *body* of the clause. If the clause contains variables, then they are implicitly universally quantified within the scope of the entire clause. A *ground clause* is a clause not containing variables. Clauses of the form (2) and (3) are called *facts* and *assumptions*, respectively. The notion of falsehood appears counterintuitive at first sight, but programs will be interpreted under their (weak) completion where we replace the implication by the equivalence sign. We assume a fixed set of constants, denoted by $\mathcal{C}$, which is nonempty and finite. $\mathsf{constants}(\mathcal{P})$ denotes the set of all constants occurring in $\mathcal{P}$. If not stated otherwise, we assume that $\mathcal{C} = \mathsf{constants}(\mathcal{P})$. $g\mathcal{P}$ denotes ground $\mathcal{P}$, which means that $\mathcal{P}$ contains exactly all the ground clauses with respect to the alphabet. $\mathsf{atoms}(\mathcal{P})$ denotes the set of all atoms occurring in $g\mathcal{P}$. If atom A is not the head of any clause in $\mathcal{P}$, then A is *undefined* in $g\mathcal{P}$. The set of all atoms that are undefined in $g\mathcal{P}$ is $\mathsf{undef}(\mathcal{P})$.

3.2   Three-Valued Łukasiewicz Logic

We consider the three-valued Łukasiewicz logic [26], for which the corresponding truth values are $\top$, $\bot$ and U, which mean *true*, *false* and *unknown*, respectively. A *three-valued interpretation* I is a mapping from formulas to the set of truth values $\{\top, \bot, U\}$. The truth value of a given formula under I is determined according to the truth tables in Table 2. We represent an interpretation as a pair $I = \langle I^{\top}, I^{\bot} \rangle$ of disjoint sets of atoms where $I^{\top}$ is the set of all atoms that are mapped to $\top$ by I, and $I^{\bot}$ is the set of all atoms that are mapped to $\bot$

by I. Atoms, which do not occur in $I^\top \cup I^\bot$, are mapped to U. Let $I = \langle I^\top, I^\bot \rangle$ and $J = \langle J^\top, J^\bot \rangle$ be two interpretations: $I \subseteq J$ iff $I^\top \subseteq J^\top$ and $I^\bot \subseteq J^\bot$. $I(F) = \top$ means that a formula F is mapped to true under I. $\mathcal{M}$ is a *model* of $g\mathcal{P}$ if it is an interpretation, which maps each clause occurring in $g\mathcal{P}$ to $\top$. I is the *least model* of $g\mathcal{P}$ iff for any other model J of $g\mathcal{P}$ it holds that $I \subseteq J$.

3.3   Reasoning with Respect to Least Models

Consider the following transformation for $\mathcal{P}$: 1. Replace all clauses in $g\mathcal{P}$ with the same head $A \leftarrow body_1, A \leftarrow body_2, \ldots$ by the single expression $A \leftarrow body_1 \vee body_2, \vee \ldots$. 2. Replace all occurrences of $\leftarrow$ by $\leftrightarrow$. The resulting set of equivalences is called the *weak completion* of $\mathcal{P}$ (wc $\mathcal{P}$). The model intersection property holds for weakly completed programs, which guarantees the existence of a least model for every $\mathcal{P}$ [20]. Stenning and van Lambalgen [30] devised the following operator, which has been generalized for first-order programs in [19]: Let I be an interpretation in $\Phi_\mathcal{P}(I) = \langle J^\top, J^\bot \rangle$, where

$$J^\top = \{A \mid \text{there exists } A \leftarrow body \in g\mathcal{P} \text{ and } I(body) = \top\},$$
$$J^\bot = \{A \mid A \notin \mathsf{undef}(\mathcal{P}) \text{ and for all } A \leftarrow body \in g\mathcal{P} \text{ we find that } I(body) = \bot\}.$$

As shown in [19] the least fixed point of $\Phi_\mathcal{P}$ is identical to the least model of the weak completion of $g\mathcal{P}$ under three-valued Łukasiewicz logic (lm wc $\mathcal{P}$). Starting with $I = \langle \emptyset, \emptyset \rangle$, lm wc $\mathcal{P}$ is computed by iterating $\Phi_\mathcal{P}$. Given a program $\mathcal{P}$ and a formula F, $\mathcal{P} \models_{wcs} F$ iff lm wc $\mathcal{P}(F) = \top$ for formula F.

3.4   Integrity Constraints

A set of *integrity constraints* $\mathcal{IC}$ comprises clauses of the form U $\leftarrow body$, where $body$ is a conjunction of literals. Given $\mathcal{P}$ and $\mathcal{IC}$, $\mathcal{P}$ *satisfies* $\mathcal{IC}$ iff for all U $\leftarrow body \in \mathcal{IC}$, we find that $\mathcal{P} \models_{wcs}$ U $\leftarrow body$ (i.e. $\mathcal{P} \not\models_{wcs} body$).

3.5   Abduction

We extend two-valued abduction [23] for three-valued semantics. The set of abducibles $\mathcal{A}_\mathcal{P}$ may not only contain facts but can also contain assumptions:

$$\mathcal{A}_\mathcal{P} = \{A \leftarrow \top \mid A \in \mathsf{undef}(\mathcal{P})\} \cup \{A \leftarrow \bot \mid A \in \mathsf{undef}(\mathcal{P})\}.$$

Let $\langle \mathcal{P}, \mathcal{A}_\mathcal{P}, \mathcal{IC}, \models_{wcs} \rangle$ be an abductive framework, $\mathcal{E} \subset \mathcal{A}_\mathcal{P}$ and observation $\mathcal{O}$ a non-empty set of literals.

$\mathcal{O}$ is *explained by* $\mathcal{E}$ *given* $\mathcal{P}$ *and* $\mathcal{IC}$ iff $\mathcal{P} \cup \mathcal{E} \models_{wcs} \mathcal{O}$ and $\mathcal{P} \cup \mathcal{E} \models_{wcs} \mathcal{IC}$.
$\mathcal{O}$ is *explained given* $\mathcal{P}$ *and* $\mathcal{IC}$ iff there exists $\mathcal{E}$ s.t. $\mathcal{O}$ is explained by $\mathcal{E}$ given $\mathcal{P}$ and $\mathcal{IC}$.

We assume that explanations are minimal, i.e. there is no other explanation $\mathcal{E}' \subset \mathcal{E}$ for $\mathcal{O}$. We distinguish between skeptical and credulous reasoning in abduction as follows:

F *follows skeptically from* $\mathcal{P}, \mathcal{IC}$ and $\mathcal{O}$ iff $\mathcal{O}$ can be explained given $\mathcal{P}$ and $\mathcal{IC}$, and for all minimal $\mathcal{E}$ for $\mathcal{O}$ given $\mathcal{P}$ and $\mathcal{IC}$, it holds that $\mathcal{P} \cup \mathcal{E} \models_{wcs} F$.

F *follows credulously from* $\mathcal{P}, \mathcal{IC}$ and $\mathcal{O}$ iff there exists a minimal $\mathcal{E}$ for $\mathcal{O}$ given $\mathcal{P}$ and $\mathcal{IC}$, and it holds that $\mathcal{P} \cup \mathcal{E} \models_{wcs} F$.

In the following, we are interested in deriving skeptically entailed information. The entailment relation $\models_{wcs}^{s}$ is an abbreviation to express that a formula follows skeptically, i.e. $\mathcal{P}, \mathcal{IC}, \mathcal{O} \models_{wcs}^{s} F$ denotes that F follows skeptically from $\mathcal{P}, \mathcal{IC}$ and $\mathcal{O}$.

4   Six Principles on Quantified Statements

We introduce six principles for developing the representation of quantified statements and reasoning with respect to them, originally developed in [3]. Some are motivated by ideas from the area of Logic Programming and others are motivated by findings from Cognitive Science.

4.1   Licenses for Inferences (lice)

Stenning and van Lambalgen [30] propose to formalize conditionals in human reasoning not by inferences straight away, but rather by *licenses for inferences*. For instance, the conditional '*if* $y(X)$ *then* $z(X)$' is represented by the program, which consists of

$$z(X) \leftarrow y(X) \wedge \neg ab_{yz}(X). \qquad ab_{yz}(X) \leftarrow \bot.$$

The first clause states that '$z(X)$ *if* $y(X)$ *and* $\neg ab_{yz}(X)$'. The second clause represents the closed-world assumption with respect to $ab_{yz}(X)$, where $ab_{yz}(X)$ is an abnormality predicate. We call this principle *licenses for inferences* (lice).

4.2   Negation by Transformation (trans)

The logic programs we consider under the Weak Completion Semantics do not allow heads of clauses to be negative literals. In order to represent a negative conclusion $\neg y(X)$, we introduce an auxiliary formula $y'(X)$ together with the clause $y(X) \leftarrow \neg y'(X)$ and the integrity constraint $U \leftarrow y(X) \wedge y'(X)$. This is a widely used technique in logic programming. Together with the principle introduced in Sect. 4.1 (lice), this additional clause is extended by the following two clauses:

$$y(X) \leftarrow \neg y'(X) \wedge \neg ab_{nyy}(X). \qquad ab_{nyy}(X) \leftarrow \bot.$$

Additionally, the integrity constraint $U \leftarrow y(X) \wedge y'(X)$ states that an object cannot belong to both, y and y'. We call this principle *negation by transformation* (trans).

4.3   Existential Import and Gricean Implicature (import)

Normally, we do not quantify over objects that do not exist. Accordingly, '*all y are z*' implies '*some y are z*', which is referred to as *existential import* and implied by *Gricean implicature* [17]. Existential import is assumed by the theory of mental models [21] or mental logic [29]. Likewise, humans require existential import for a conditional to be true [30]. Furthermore, the quantifier '*some y are z*' often implies that '*some y are not z*', which again is implied by the Gricean implicature [24]: Someone would not state '*some y are z*' if that person knew that '*all y are z*'. As the person does not say '*all y are z*' but '*some y are z*', we assume that '*not all y are z*', which in turn implies '*some y are not z*'. We call this principle *existential import and Gricean implicature* (import).

4.4   Unknown Generalization (unkGen)

Humans seem to distinguish between '*some y are z*' and '*some z are y*' [24]. However, if we would represent '*some y are z*' by $\exists X(y(X) \land z(X))$ then this is semantically equivalent to $\exists X(z(X) \land y(X))$ because conjunction is commutative in first-order logic. Likewise, as we have discussed in Sect. 4.3, humans seem to distinguish between '*some y are z*' and '*all y are z*'. Accordingly, if we only observe that an object belongs to y and z then we do not want to conclude both, '*some y are z*' and '*all y are z*'. Therefore we introduce the following principle: If we know that '*some y are z*' then there must not only be an object, which belongs to y and z (by Gricean implicature) but there must be another object, which belongs to y and for which it is unknown whether it belongs to z. We call this principle *unknown generalization* (unkGen).

4.5   No Derivation Through Double Negation (dNeg)

Under the Weak Completion Semantics, a positive conclusion can be derived from double negation within two conditionals. Consider the following two conditionals with each having a negative premise: If not x, then y. If not y then z. Additionally, assume that x is true. Let $\mathcal{P} = \{z \leftarrow \neg y,\ y \leftarrow \neg x,\ x \leftarrow \top\}$ be the program that encodes this information. The lm wc $\mathcal{P}$ is $\langle\{x,z\},\{y\}\rangle$: x is true because it is a fact and y is false because the negation of x is false. z is true by the negation of y. However, considering the results in [24], humans seem not to draw conclusions through double negatives. Accordingly, we block them with the abnormalities introduced by principle (import) in Sect. 4.1. We call this principle *no derivation through double negation* (dNeg).

4.6   Search for Alternative Models (searchAlt)

Consider again S_{rich} and S_{add}: The premises are about things which contradict the conclusion. We assume that in case there seems no conclusion possible, humans might try to search for alternative models by explaining some part of the information that is presented. We call this principle *Search for Alternative Models* (searchAlt).

5   Representation of Quantified Statements as Programs

Based on the first five principles of the previous section, we encode the quantified statements in logic programs, where y and z will later be replaced by the properties of the corresponding objects. Note that, different to the principles in Sects. 4.1 to 4.5, principle (searchAlt) in Sect. 4.6 is not about the representation of the quantified statements but about the reasoning process, which will be discussed later. Note that the capital letters in brackets in the title of each of the following subsections, A, E, I and O are the classical abbreviations for the quantifiers *All*, *No*, *Some* and *Some not*.

5.1   All y are z (Ayz)

'*All y are z*' is represented by the program $\mathcal{P}_{Ayz}$, which consists of the following clauses:

$$z(X) \leftarrow y(X) \wedge \neg ab_{yz}(X). \qquad\qquad \text{(lice)}$$
$$ab_{yz}(X) \leftarrow \bot. \qquad\qquad \text{(lice)}$$
$$y(o) \leftarrow \top. \qquad\qquad \text{(import)}$$

The least model of the weak completion of $\mathcal{P}_{Ayz}$, $\mathsf{Im\,wc}\,\mathcal{P}_{Iyz}$, is $\langle\{y(o), z(o)\}, \{ab_{yz}(o)\}\rangle$.

5.2   No y is z (Eyz)

Under FOL '*No y is z*' is represented as $\forall X(y(X) \rightarrow \neg z(X))$, which is equivalent to $\forall X(z(X) \rightarrow \neg y(X))$. $\mathcal{P}_{Eyz}$ consists of the following clauses:

$$y'(X) \leftarrow z(X) \wedge \neg ab_{zny}(X). \qquad\qquad \text{(trans \& lice)}$$
$$ab_{zny}(X) \leftarrow \bot. \qquad\qquad \text{(lice)}$$
$$y(X) \leftarrow \neg y'(X) \wedge \neg ab_{nyy}(X). \qquad\qquad \text{(trans \& lice)}$$
$$z(o) \leftarrow \top. \qquad\qquad \text{(import)}$$
$$ab_{nyy}(o) \leftarrow \bot. \qquad\qquad \text{(lice \& dNeg)}$$

We have the following integrity constraint: $U \leftarrow y(X) \wedge y'(X).$ (trans)
Note that the last clause in $\mathcal{P}_{Eyz}$ cannot be generalized to all X, because otherwise we allow conclusions by double negatives: principle (dNeg) states that we should block conclusions through double negatives. The least model of the weak completion of $\mathcal{P}_{Eyz}$, $\mathsf{Im\,wc}\,\mathcal{P}_{Eyz}$, is $\langle\{y'(o), z(o)\}, \{ab_{zny}(o), ab_{nyy}(o), y(o)\}\rangle$.

5.3   Some y are z (Iyz)

'*Some y are z*' is represented by the program $\mathcal{P}_{Iyz}$:

$$z(X) \leftarrow y(X) \wedge \neg ab_{yz}(X). \qquad\qquad \text{(lice)}$$
$$ab_{yz}(o_1) \leftarrow \bot. \qquad\qquad \text{(unkGen \& lice)}$$
$$y(o_1) \leftarrow \top. \qquad\qquad \text{(import)}$$
$$y(o_2) \leftarrow \top. \qquad\qquad \text{(unkGen)}$$

Im wc $\mathcal{P}_{Iyz}$ is $\langle\{y(o_1), y(o_2), z(o_1)\}, \{ab_{yz}(o_1)\}\rangle$.
Nothing about $ab_{yz}(o_2)$ is stated in $\mathcal{P}_{Iyz}$. Accordingly, $z(o_2)$ stays unknown in Im wc $\mathcal{P}_{Iyz}$.

5.4   Some y are Not z (Oyz)

'*Some y are not z*' is represented by the program $\mathcal{P}_{Oyz}$:

$$z'(X) \leftarrow y(X) \land \neg ab_{ynz}(X). \qquad\qquad \text{(trans \& lice)}$$
$$ab_{ynz}(o_1) \leftarrow \bot. \qquad\qquad \text{(unkGen \& lice)}$$
$$z(X) \leftarrow \neg z'(X) \land \neg ab_{nzz}(X). \qquad\qquad \text{(trans \& lice)}$$
$$y(o_1) \leftarrow \top. \qquad\qquad \text{(import)}$$
$$y(o_2) \leftarrow \top. \qquad\qquad \text{(unkGen)}$$
$$ab_{nzz}(o_1) \leftarrow \bot. \qquad\qquad \text{(dNeg \& lice)}$$
$$ab_{nzz}(o_2) \leftarrow \bot. \qquad\qquad \text{(dNeg \& lice)}$$

We have the following integrity constraint: $U \leftarrow z(X) \land z'(X).$ (trans)
The first four clauses as well as the integrity constraint are derived as in the program $\mathcal{P}_{Eyz}$ except that object o_1 is used instead of o and ab_{ynz} is restricted to o_1 as in $\mathcal{P}_{Iyz}$. The fifth clause of $\mathcal{P}_{Oyz}$ is obtained by principle (unkGen). The last two clauses are not generalized to all objects for the same reason as discussed in Sect. 5.2: The generalization of ab_{nzz} to all objects would lead to conclusions through double negation in case there would be a second premise. The least model of the weak completion of $\mathcal{P}_{Oyz}$, Im wc $\mathcal{P}_{Oyz}$, is $\langle\{y(o_1), y(o_2), z'(o_1)\}, \{ab_{ynz}(o_1), ab_{nzz}(o_1), ab_{nzz}(o_2), z(o_1)\}\rangle$.

5.5   Entailment of the Quantified Statements

We specify when Ayz, Eyz, Iyz or Oyz are entailed by a model.

- $\mathcal{P} \models$ Ayz iff there exists an object o such that $\mathcal{P} \models_{wcs} y(o)$ and for all objects o we find that if $\mathcal{P} \models_{wcs} y(o)$ then $\mathcal{P} \models_{wcs} z(o)$.
- $\mathcal{P} \models$ Eyz iff there exists an object o such that $\mathcal{P} \models_{wcs} z(o)$ and for all objects o we find that if $\mathcal{P} \models_{wcs} z(o)$ then $\mathcal{P} \models_{wcs} \neg y(o)$.
- $\mathcal{P} \models$ Iyz iff there exists an object o_1 such that $\mathcal{P} \models_{wcs} y(o_1) \land z(o_1)$ and there exists an object o_2 such that $\mathcal{P} \models_{wcs} y(o_2)$ and $\mathcal{P} \not\models_{wcs} z(o_2)$.
- $\mathcal{P} \models$ Oyz iff there exists an object o_1 such that $\mathcal{P} \models_{wcs} y(o_1) \land \neg z(o_1)$ and there exists an object o_2 such that $\mathcal{P} \models_{wcs} y(o_2)$ and $\mathcal{P} \not\models_{wcs} \neg z(o_2)$.

If nothing can be concluded, i.e. if $\mathcal{P} \not\models$ Ayz, $\mathcal{P} \not\models$ Eyz, $\mathcal{P} \not\models$ Iyz and $\mathcal{P} \not\models$ Oyz, then principle (searchAlt) applies and we search for alternative models by trying to explain y. Later, y refers to the first property in the conclusion of the syllogism and z refers to the two properties left. For instance, consider S_{dog}: y refers to *highly trained dogs* (*high_trai*) and z is either *police dogs* (*pol_dog*) or *vicious* (*vic*). If nothing between either *high_trai* and *pol_dog* or between *high_trai* and *vic* can be derived, we try to explain *high_trai*.

6   Modeling the Belief-Bias Effect

According to the observations made in Sect. 2, we model the belief-bias effect in two stages: (1) the belief can influence the representation, i.e. how the given information is understood, or (2) the belief can influence the reasoning, i.e. how new information is gained, if nothing can be derived. In the following, we model (1) with help of abnormalities, motivated by principle (lice). (2) is modeled by means of skeptical abduction, motivated by principle (searchAlt). The following four syllogisms are modeled according to the logic program representations proposed in Sects. 5.2 and 5.4.

6.1   No Belief-Bias Effect

$\mathcal{P}_{dog}$ represents the first two premises of S_{dog} and consists of

$$pol\_dog'(X) \leftarrow vic(X) \wedge \neg ab_{pol\_dog'}(X). \hspace{2cm} \text{(trans \& lice)}$$
$$ab_{pol\_dog'}(X) \leftarrow \bot. \hspace{3cm} \text{(lice)}$$
$$pol\_dog(X) \leftarrow \neg pol\_dog'(X) \wedge \neg ab_{pol\_dog}(X). \hspace{1cm} \text{(trans \& lice)}$$
$$vic(o_1) \leftarrow \top. \hspace{3cm} \text{(import)}$$
$$ab_{pol\_dog}(o_1) \leftarrow \bot. \hspace{2.5cm} \text{(lice \& dNeg)}$$
$$vic(X) \leftarrow high\_trai(X) \wedge \neg ab_{vic}(X). \hspace{1.5cm} \text{(lice)}$$
$$ab_{vic}(o_2) \leftarrow \bot. \hspace{2.5cm} \text{(unkGen \& lice)}$$
$$high\_trai(o_2) \leftarrow \top. \hspace{2.5cm} \text{(import)}$$
$$high\_trai(o_3) \leftarrow \top. \hspace{2.5cm} \text{(unkGen)}$$

We have the following integrity constraint: $U \leftarrow pol\_dog(X) \wedge pol\_dog'(X)$. (trans) lm wc $\mathcal{P}_{dog} = \langle I^\top, I^\perp \rangle$, is as follows:

$$I^\top = \{high\_trai(o_2), high\_trai(o_3), pol\_dog'(o_1), pol\_dog'(o_2), vic(o_1), vic(o_2)\},$$
$$I^\perp = \{pol\_dog(o_2), pol\_dog(o_1), ab_{pol\_dog'}(o_1), ab_{pol\_dog'}(o_2), ab_{pol\_dog'}(o_3),$$
$$ab_{pol\_dog}(o_1), ab_{vic}(o_2)\},$$

Indeed, this model entails the CONCLUSION of S_{dog}, *Some highly trained dogs are not police dogs*: There exists an object, o_2, such that $\mathcal{P}_{dog} \models_{wcs}$ $high\_trai(o_2) \wedge \neg pol\_dog(o_2)$ and there exists another object, o_3, such that $\mathcal{P}_{dog} \models_{wcs} high\_trai(o_3)$ and $\mathcal{P}_{dog} \not\models_{wcs} \neg pol\_dog(o_3)$. According to [15], S_{dog} is logically valid and psychologically believable. No conflict arises either at the psychological or at the logical level. The majority validated the syllogism, which complies with what is entailed by lm wc $\mathcal{P}_{dog}$.

6.2   Belief-Bias Effect in Representation Stage

$\mathcal{P}_{vit}$ represents the first two premises of S_{vit} and consists of

$$nutri'(X) \leftarrow inex(X) \wedge \neg ab_{nutri'}(X). \tag{trans \& lice}$$
$$ab_{nutri'}(X) \leftarrow \bot. \tag{lice}$$
$$nutri(X) \leftarrow \neg nutri'(X) \wedge \neg ab_{nutri}(X). \tag{trans \& lice}$$
$$inex(o_1) \leftarrow \top. \tag{import}$$
$$ab_{nutri}(o_1) \leftarrow \bot. \tag{lice \& dNeg}$$
$$inex(X) \leftarrow vitamin(X), \neg ab_{inex}(X). \tag{lice}$$
$$ab_{inex}(o_2) \leftarrow \bot. \tag{unkGen \& lice}$$
$$vitamin(o_2) \leftarrow \top. \tag{import}$$
$$vitamin(o_3) \leftarrow \top. \tag{unkGen}$$

We have the following integrity constraint: $U \leftarrow nutri'(X) \wedge nutri(X).$ (trans)

The corresponding lm wc $\mathcal{P}_{vit} = \langle I^\top, I^\bot \rangle$, is as follows:

$$I^\top = \{vitamin(o_2), vitamin(o_3), inex(o_1), inex(o_2), nutri'(o_1), nutri'(o_2)\}$$
$$I^\bot = \{nutri(o_1), nutri(o_2), ab_{inex}(o_2), ab_{nutri}(o_1), ab_{nutri'}(o_1), ab_{nutri'}(o_2),$$
$$ab_{nutri'}(o_3)\},$$

Indeed this model entails the CONCLUSION of S_{vit}, that *Some vitamin tablets are not nutritional*: There exists an object, o_2, such that $\mathcal{P}_{vit} \models_{wcs}$ $vitamin(o_2) \wedge \neg nutri(o_2)$ and there exists another object, o_3, such that $\mathcal{P}_{vit} \models_{wcs}$ $vitamin(o_3)$ and $\mathcal{P}_{vit} \not\models_{wcs} \neg nutri(o_3)$. The results of the psychological study in Table 1 indicate that there seemed to be two groups of participants: The group that validated the syllogism was not influenced by the bias with respect to nutritional things. Their understanding of the syllogism is reflected by $\mathcal{P}_{vit}$ and their conclusion complies with what is entailed by lm wc $\mathcal{P}_{vit}$. The participants who chose to invalidate the syllogism belong to the other group that has apparently been influenced by their belief. The belief bias occurred in the representation stage. Accordingly, we model this aspect with help of abnormality predicates as follows: Regarding both premises, it is commonly known that

The purpose of vitamin tablets is to aid nutrition.

This belief in the context of PREMISE 1 leads to

If something is a vitamin tablet, then it is abnormal. (*regarding* PREMISE 1 *of* S_{vit})

We extend $\mathcal{P}_{vit}$ accordingly, which results in

$$\mathcal{P}_{vit}^{bias} = \mathcal{P}_{vit} \cup \{ab_{nutri'}(X) \leftarrow vitamin(X)\}.$$

Observe that $ab_{nutri'}(X) \leftarrow vitamin(X)$ overrides $ab_{nutri'}(X) \leftarrow \bot$ under the weak completion of $\mathcal{P}_{vit}^{bias}$. lm wc $\mathcal{P}_{vit}^{bias} = \langle I^\top, I^\bot \rangle$ is

$$I^\top = \{inex(o_1), inex(o_2), vitamin(o_2), vitamin(o_3), ab_{nutri'}(o_2), ab_{nutri'}(o_3)\},$$
$$I^\bot = \{nutri'(o_2), nutri'(o_3), ab_{nutri}(o_1), ab_{inex}(o_2)\}.$$

In this case, the CONCLUSION of S_{vit}, that *Some vitamin tablets are not nutritional,* is not entailed. Actually, nothing is stated about the relation between vitamin tablets and them (not) being nutritional. However, as trivally *Some vitamin tablets are inexpensive* holds, principle (searchAlt) does not apply and we are done. According to [15], S_{vit} is logically valid but psychologically unbelievable. There arises a conflict at the psychological level because we generally assume that the purpose of vitamin tablets is to aid nutrition. The participants who have been influenced by this belief did not validate the syllogism, which complies to the result above, as the CONCLUSION is not entailed by lm wc $\mathcal{P}_{vit}^{bias}$ either.

6.3   Belief-Bias Effect in Reasoning Stage

$\mathcal{P}_{rich}$ represents the first two premises of S_{rich} and consists of

$$
\begin{array}{lr}
mil'(X) \leftarrow hard\_wor(X) \wedge \neg ab_{mil'}(X). & \text{(trans \& lice)} \\
ab_{mil'}(X) \leftarrow \bot. & \text{(lice)} \\
mil(X) \leftarrow \neg mil'(X) \wedge ab_{mil}(X). & \text{(trans \& lice)} \\
hard\_wor(o_1) \leftarrow \top. & \text{(import)} \\
ab_{mil}(o_1) \leftarrow \bot. & \text{(lice \& dNeg)} \\
hard\_wor(X) \leftarrow rich(X) \wedge \neg ab_{hard\_wor}(X). & \text{(lice)} \\
ab_{hard\_wor}(o_2) \leftarrow \bot. & \text{(unkGen \& lice)} \\
rich(o_2) \leftarrow \top. & \text{(import)} \\
rich(o_3) \leftarrow \top. & \text{(unkGen)}
\end{array}
$$

We have the following integrity constraint: $\quad U \leftarrow mil(X) \wedge mil'(X)$.   (trans)
Its least model of the weak completion, $\langle I^\top, I^\perp \rangle$, is as follows:

$$
\begin{aligned}
I^\top &= \{ hard\_wor(o_1), hard\_wor(o_2), mil'(o_1), mil'(o_2), rich(o_2), rich(o_3) \}, \\
I^\perp &= \{ mil(o_1), mil(o_2), ab_{hard\_wor}(o_2), ab_{mil}(o_1), ab_{mil'}(o_1), ab_{mil'}(o_2), \\
&\qquad ab_{mil'}(o_3) \},
\end{aligned}
$$

and does not confirm the CONCLUSION of S_{rich}, that *some millionaires are not rich people.* Actually, the CONCLUSION in S_{rich} states something which contradicts PREMISE 2, and cannot be about any of the previously introduced constant o_1, o_2 or o_3. As nothing can be derived about the relation between mil and $hard\_wor$ nor between mil and $rich$, principle (searchAlt) applies: According to our background knowledge, we know that 'normal' millionaires exist, i.e. millionaires for whom we do not assume anything abnormal with respect to them being millionaires. Additionally, we cannot be sure that all millionaires are normal, i.e. we know that millionaires exist for whom we simply don't know whether they are normal. We formulate this as an observation about two newly introduced constants, let's say o_4, representing a normal millionaire,[1] and o_5, representing a millionaire for whom it is unknown whether he or she is normal:

$$
\mathcal{O} = \{ mil(o_4), \neg ab_{mil'}(o_4), \neg ab_{mil}(o_4), mil(o_5) \}.
$$

---

[1] This implies that all abnormalities about mil or mil' are false with respect to o_4.

If we want to find an explanation for $\mathcal{O}$ with respect to $\mathcal{P}_{mil}$, we can no longer assume that $\mathcal{C} = \text{constants}(\mathcal{P}_{mil})$, because $\mathcal{A}_{\mathcal{P}_{mil}}$ does not contain any facts or assumptions about o_4 and o_5, as o_4 and o_5 do not occur in $\mathcal{P}_{mil}$. Therefore, we specify that the new set of constants under consideration is $\mathcal{C} = \{o_1, o_2, o_3, o_4, o_5\}$. Given that $\text{lm wc}(\mathcal{P}_{mil}) = \langle I^\top, I^\perp \rangle$ as defined above, $\text{lm wc}(\mathcal{P}_{mil}^{\mathcal{C}}) = \langle I^\top, I^\perp \cup \{ab_{mil'}(o_4), ab_{mil'}(o_5)\} \rangle$. The set of abducibles, $\mathcal{A}_{\mathcal{P}_{mil}^{\mathcal{C}}}$, contains six facts and six assumptions about o_4 and o_5:

$$
\begin{array}{lll}
rich(o_4) \leftarrow \top. & ab_{mil}(o_4) \leftarrow \top. & ab_{hard\_wor}(o_4) \leftarrow \top. \\
rich(o_4) \leftarrow \perp. & ab_{mil}(o_4) \leftarrow \perp. & ab_{hard\_wor}(o_4) \leftarrow \perp. \\
rich(o_5) \leftarrow \top. & ab_{mil}(o_5) \leftarrow \top. & ab_{hard\_wor}(o_5) \leftarrow \top. \\
rich(o_5) \leftarrow \perp. & ab_{mil}(o_5) \leftarrow \perp. & ab_{hard\_wor}(o_5) \leftarrow \perp.
\end{array}
$$

We find six (minimal) explanations for $\mathcal{O} = \{mil(o_4), \neg ab_{mil'}(o_4), \neg ab_{mil}(o_4), mil(o_5)\}$, where there are three from which the CONCLUSION of S_{rich} does not follow. Consider one of them, $\mathcal{E} = \{ab_{hard\_wor}(o_4) \leftarrow \top, ab_{mil}(o_4) \leftarrow \perp, ab_{mil}(o_5) \leftarrow \top\}$: Given that $\text{lm wc}(\mathcal{P}_{mil}) = \langle I^\top, I^\perp \rangle$, $\text{lm wc}(\mathcal{P}_{mil} \cup \mathcal{E})^{\mathcal{C}} = \langle J^\top, J^\perp \rangle$ is

$$
J^\top = I^\top \cup \{ab_{hard\_wor}(o_4), mil(o_4), mil(o_5), ab_{mil}(o_5)\},
$$
$$
J^\perp = I^\perp \cup \{ab_{mil}(o_4), ab_{mil'}(o_4), hard\_wor(o_4), mil'(o_4), ab_{mil'}(o_5)\}.
$$

According to the definition for skeptical abduction in Sect. 3.5, one explanation for which the CONCLUSION of S_{rich}, *Some millionaires are not rich people*, does not follow, is enough to show that the CONCLUSION does not follow skeptically from $\mathcal{P}_{mil}^{\mathcal{C}}$, $\mathcal{IC}$ and $\mathcal{O}$. According to [15] this case is neither logically valid nor believable. Almost no one validated S_{rich}, which complies to the result above, as the CONCLUSION is not skeptically entailed by $\mathcal{P}_{mil}^{\mathcal{C}}$, $\mathcal{IC}$ and $\mathcal{O}$ either.

6.4   Belief-Bias Effect in Representation and Reasoning Stage

$\mathcal{P}_{cig}$ represents the first two premises of S_{cig} and consists of

$$
\begin{array}{lr}
add'(X) \leftarrow inex(X) \wedge \neg ab_{add'}(X). & \text{(trans \& lice)} \\
ab_{add'}(X) \leftarrow \perp. & \text{(lice)} \\
add(X) \leftarrow \neg add'(X) \wedge \neg ab_{add}(X). & \text{(trans \& lice)} \\
inex(o_1) \leftarrow \top. & \text{(import)} \\
ab_{add}(o_1) \leftarrow \perp. & \text{(lice \& dNeg)} \\
inex(X) \leftarrow cig(X) \wedge \neg ab_{inex}(X). & \text{(lice)} \\
ab_{inex}(o_2) \leftarrow \perp. & \text{(unkGen \& lice)} \\
cig(o_2) \leftarrow \top. & \text{(import)} \\
cig(o_3) \leftarrow \top. & \text{(unkGen)}
\end{array}
$$

We have the following integrity constraint: $U \leftarrow add(X) \wedge add'(X)$.   (trans) It is commonly known that *Cigarettes are addictive*. This belief in the context of PREMISE 1 leads to

If something is a cigarette, then it is abnormal. (regarding PREMISE 1 *of* S_{cig})

$\mathcal{P}_{cig}$ is extended accordingly. The new program is

$$\mathcal{P}^{\mathsf{bias}}_{cig} = \mathcal{P}_{cig} \cup \{ab_{add'}(X) \leftarrow cig(X)\}.$$

Observe that $ab_{add'}(X) \leftarrow cig(X)$ overrides $ab_{add'}(X) \leftarrow \bot$ under the weak completion of $\mathcal{P}^{\mathsf{bias}}_{cig}$. The least model of the weak completion of $\mathcal{P}^{\mathsf{bias}}_{cig}$, $\mathsf{lm\,wc}\,\mathcal{P}^{\mathsf{bias}}_{cig}$, is

$$\langle \{cig(o_2), cig(o_3), inex(o_1), inex(o_2)\}, \{ab_{add}(o_1), ab_{inex}(o_2)\} \rangle.$$

Similarly to the previous syllogism, this model does not state anything about the CONCLUSION, that *some addictive things are not cigarettes.* Again, the CONCLUSION of S_{cig} is about something, which cannot be o_1, o_2 or o_3. As nothing can be derived about the relation between *add* and *inex* nor between *add* and *cig*, principle (searchAlt) applies: According to our background knowledge, we know that 'normal' addictive things exist, i.e. addictive things for which we do not assume anything abnormal with respect to them being addictive things. Additionally, we cannot be sure that all addictive things are normal, i.e. we know that addictive things exist for which we simply don't know whether they are normal. We formulate this as an observation about two newly introduced constants, let's say o_4, representing normal addictive things[2] and o_5 representing addictive things for which it is unknown whether they are normal:

$$\mathcal{O} = \{add(o_4), \neg ab_{add'}(o_4), \neg ab_{add}(o_4), add(o_5)\}.$$

Let us define $\mathcal{C} = \{o_1, o_2, o_3, o_4, o_5\}$. $\mathsf{lm\,wc}\,\mathcal{P}^{\mathsf{bias},\mathcal{C}}_{cig}$ does not state anything about o_4 nor o_5: All atoms about o_4 and o_5 are unknown in this least model. Given $\mathcal{P}^{\mathsf{bias},\mathcal{C}}_{cig}$, the set of abducibles, $\mathcal{A}_{\mathcal{P}^{\mathsf{bias},\mathcal{C}}_{cig}}$ contains six facts and six assumptions about o_4 and o_5:

$$
\begin{array}{lll}
cig(o_4) \leftarrow \top. & ab_{add}(o_4) \leftarrow \top. & ab_{inex}(o_4) \leftarrow \top. \\
cig(o_4) \leftarrow \bot. & ab_{add}(o_4) \leftarrow \bot. & ab_{inex}(o_4) \leftarrow \bot. \\
cig(o_5) \leftarrow \top. & ab_{add}(o_5) \leftarrow \top. & ab_{inex}(o_5) \leftarrow \top. \\
cig(o_5) \leftarrow \bot. & ab_{add}(o_5) \leftarrow \bot. & ab_{inex}(o_5) \leftarrow \bot.
\end{array}
$$

The only three (minimal) explanations are

$$\mathcal{E}_1 = \mathcal{E}' \cup \{cig(o_5) \leftarrow \bot\}, \ \mathcal{E}_2 = \mathcal{E}' \cup \{ab_{inex}(o_5) \leftarrow \bot\}, \ \text{and} \ \mathcal{E}_3 = \mathcal{E}' \cup \{cig(o_5) \leftarrow \top\},$$

where $\mathcal{E}' = \{cig(o_4) \leftarrow \bot, \ ab_{add}(o_4) \leftarrow \bot, \ ab_{add}(o_5) \leftarrow \bot\}$. Given that $\mathsf{lm\,wc}\,(\mathcal{P}^{\mathsf{bias}}_{cig}) = \langle I^\top, I^\bot \rangle$ as defined above, the least models of the weak completion of $\mathcal{P}^{\mathsf{bias},\mathcal{C}}_{cig}$ together with the corresponding explanations, are as follows:

---

[2] This implies that all abnormalities about *add* or *add'* are false with respect to o_4.

$$\textsf{lm wc}\,(\mathcal{P}^{\textsf{bias},\mathcal{C}}_{cig} \cup \mathcal{E}_1) = \langle I^\top \cup \{add(o_4), add(o_5)\},$$
$$I^\perp \cup \{cig(o_4), inex(o_4), ab_{add}(o_4), ab_{add'}(o_4), add'(o_4),$$
$$ab_{add}(o_5), cig(o_5), ab_{add'}(o_5), inex(o_5), add'(o_5)\}\rangle,$$

$$\textsf{lm wc}\,(\mathcal{P}^{\textsf{bias},\mathcal{C}}_{cig} \cup \mathcal{E}_2) = \langle I^\top \cup \{add(o_4), add(o_5), ab_{inex}(o_5)\},$$
$$I^\perp \cup \{cig(o_4), inex(o_4), ab_{add}(o_4), ab_{add'}(o_4), add'(o_4),$$
$$ab_{add}(o_5), inex(o_5), add'(o_5)\}\rangle,$$

$$\textsf{lm wc}\,(\mathcal{P}^{\textsf{bias},\mathcal{C}}_{cig} \cup \mathcal{E}_3) = \langle I^\top \cup \{add(o_4), add(o_5), cig(o_5), ab_{add'}(o_5)\},$$
$$I^\perp \cup \{cig(o_4), inex(o_4), ab_{add}(o_4), ab_{add'}(o_4), add'(o_4),$$
$$ab_{add}(o_5), add'(o_5)\}\rangle.$$

The CONCLUSION of S_{add}, *Some addictive things are not cigarettes*, follows skeptically from $\mathcal{P}^{\textsf{bias},\mathcal{C}}_{add}$ and $\mathcal{O}$, as the following derivation follows from all explanations for $\mathcal{O}$: There exists an object, o_4, such that $\mathcal{P}^{\textsf{bias},\mathcal{C}}_{cig}, \mathcal{O} \models^s_{wcs}$ $add(o_4) \wedge \neg cig(o_4)$ and there exists another object, o_5, such that $\mathcal{P}^{\textsf{bias},\mathcal{C}}_{cig}, \mathcal{O} \models^s_{wcs}$ $add(o_5)$ and $\mathcal{P}^{\textsf{bias},\mathcal{C}}_{cig}, \mathcal{O} \not\models^s_{wcs} cig(o_5)$. According to [15], S_{cig} is classical logically invalid but psychologically believable and therefore causes a conflict: People are biased and search for a model that confirms their beliefs. This complies with what is entailed skeptically by $\mathcal{P}^{\textsf{bias},\mathcal{C}}_{cig}$, $\mathcal{IC}$ and $\mathcal{O}$.

Note that in this case we need the restriction that explanations are minimal, otherwise $\mathcal{E}' \cup \{ab_{inex}(o_4) \leftarrow \top,\ cig(o_5) \leftarrow \perp\} \supset \mathcal{E}_1$ would be an explanation for $\mathcal{O}$ as well, and we could not derive that the CONCLUSION of S_{add} follows skeptically anymore.

7 Conclusion

By taking the principles presented in [3] as starting point and extending them with the additional principle *Search for Alternative Models*, we show how the belief-bias effect can be modeled by discussing the four cases of Evans et al.'s [15] syllogistic reasoning task. The belief-bias effect can be modeled in two stages: The first stage is where the belief bias seems to occur in the representational part of the syllogism, for instance in S_{vit}. In this case, the belief bias can be modeled by means of abnormality predicates. The belief bias in S_{cig} seems to occur in the representational and the reasoning part of the syllogism. The reasoning part can be modeled with skeptical abduction. Additionally, as the last case shows, explanations are required to be minimal.

To the best of our knowledge, the syllogistic reasoning tasks discussed in the literature have never accounted for providing the option 'I don't know' to the participants. As has been discussed in [27], participants who say that no valid conclusion follows, might have problems to actually find a conclusion easily, possibly meaning that they do not know the answer. The authors also point to [28], who suggested that if a conclusion is stated as being not valid this can mean that the reasoning process is exhausted. An experimental study, which allows the participants to distinguish between *I don't know* and *not valid*, might give us more insights about their reasoning processes.

Acknowledgements. Many thanks to Steffen Hölldobler and Luís Moniz Pereira for valuable feedback.

References

1. Adler, J., Rips, L.: Reasoning: Studies of Human Inference and Its Foundations. Cambridge University Press, Cambridge (2008)
2. Chapman, L.J., Chapman, J.P.: Atmosphere effect re-examined. J. Exp. Psychol. **58**(3), 220–226 (1959)
3. Costa, A., Dietz, E.A., Hölldobler, S., Ragni, M.: A computational logic approach to human syllogistic reasoning (2017, submitted)
4. Dietz, E.A.: A computational logic approach to syllogisms in human reasoning. In: Furbach, U., Schon, C. (eds.) CEUR WS Proceedings on Bridging the Gap Between Human and Automated Reasoning, pp. 17–31 (2015)
5. Dietz, E.-A., Hölldobler, S.: A new computational logic approach to reason with conditionals. In: Calimeri, F., Ianni, G., Truszczynski, M. (eds.) LPNMR 2015. LNCS (LNAI), vol. 9345, pp. 265–278. Springer, Cham (2015). doi:10.1007/978-3-319-23264-5_23
6. Dietz, E.A., Hölldobler, S., Höps, R.: A computational logic approach to human spatial reasoning. In: IEEE Symposium on Human-Like Intelligence (CIHLI) (2015)
7. Dietz, E.A., Hölldobler, S., Pereira, L.M.: On conditionals. In: Gottlob, G., Sutcliffe, G., Voronkov, A. (eds.) GCAI. Epic Series in Computing. EasyChair (2015)
8. Dietz, E.A., Hölldobler, S., Ragni, M.: A computational logic approach to the suppression task. In: Miyake, N., Peebles, D., Cooper, R.P. (eds.) Proceedings of 34th Conference of Cognitive Science Society, pp. 1500–1505. Cognitive Science Society (2012)
9. Dietz, E.A., Hölldobler, S., Ragni, M.: A computational logic approach to the abstract and the social case of the selection task. In: Proceedings of COMMONSENSE 2013 (2013)
10. Evans, J.S.: Bias in Human Reasoning - Causes and Consequences. Essays in Cognitive Psychology. Lawrence Erlbaum, Hove (1989)
11. Evans, J.S.: In two minds: dual-process accounts of reasoning. Trends Cogn. Sci. **7**(10), 454–459 (2003)
12. Evans, J.: Thinking and believing. In: Mental Models in Reasoning (2000)
13. Evans, J., Handley, S., Harper, C.: Necessity, possibility and belief: a study of syllogistic reasoning. Q. J. Exp. Psychol. **54**(3), 935–958 (2001)
14. Evans, J.: Biases in deductive reasoning. In: Pohl, R. (ed.) Cognitive Illusions: A Handbook on Fallacies and Biases in Thinking, Judgement and Memory. Psychology Press, New York (2012)
15. Evans, J., Barston, J.L., Pollard, P.: On the conflict between logic and belief in syllogistic reasoning. Memory Cogn. **11**(3), 295–306 (1983)
16. Garnham, A., Oakhill, J.: Thinking and Reasoning. Wiley, Hoboken (1994)
17. Grice, H.P.: Logic and conversation. In: Cole, P., Morgan, J.L. (eds.) Syntax and Semantics, vol. 3. Academic Press, New York (1975)
18. Hölldobler, S.: Logik und Logikprogrammierung 1: Grundlagen. Kolleg Synchron, Synchron (2009)
19. Hölldobler, S., Kencana Ramli, C.D.P.: Logic programs under three-valued Lukasiewicz semantics. In: Hill, P.M., Warren, D.S. (eds.) ICLP 2009. LNCS, vol. 5649, pp. 464–478. Springer, Heidelberg (2009). doi:10.1007/978-3-642-02846-5_37

20. Hölldobler, S., Kencana Ramli, C.D.P.: Logics and networks for human reasoning. In: Alippi, C., Polycarpou, M., Panayiotou, C., Ellinas, G. (eds.) ICANN 2009. LNCS, vol. 5769, pp. 85–94. Springer, Heidelberg (2009). doi:10.1007/978-3-642-04277-5_9
21. Johnson-Laird, P.N.: Mental Models: Towards a Cognitive Science of Language, Inference, and Consciousness. Harvard University Press, Cambridge (1983)
22. Johnson-Laird, P.N., Byrne, R.M.: Deduction (1991)
23. Kakas, A.C., Kowalski, R.A., Toni, F.: Abductive logic programming. J. Log. Comput. **2**(6), 719–770 (1993)
24. Khemlani, S., Johnson-Laird, P.N.: Theories of the syllogism: a meta-analysis. Psychol. Bull. **138**, 427–457 (2012)
25. Lloyd, J.W.: Foundations of Logic Programming. Springer, New York (1984)
26. Łukasiewicz, J.: O logice trójwartościowej. In: Ruch Filozoficzny, vol. 5, pp. 169–171 (1920). English translation: On three-valued logic. In: Łukasiewicz, J., Borkowski, L. (eds.) Selected Works, pp. 87–88. North Holland, Amsterdam (1990)
27. Newstead, S., Handley, S., Buck, E.: Falsifying mental models: testing the predictions of theories of syllogistic reasoning. Memory Cogn. **27**(2), 344–354 (1999)
28. Polk, T.A., Newell, A.: Deduction as verbal reasoning. Psychol. Rev. **102**(3), 533–566 (1995)
29. Rips, L.J.: The Psychology of Proof: Deductive Reasoning in Human Thinking. MIT Press, Cambridge (1994)
30. Stenning, K., van Lambalgen, M.: Human Reasoning and Cognitive Science. A Bradford Book. MIT Press, Cambridge (2008)
31. Wilkins, M.: The effect of changed material on the ability to do formal syllogistic reasoning. Arch. Psychol. **16**(102), 1–83 (1928)
32. Woodworth, R.S., Sells, S.B.: An atmosphere effect in formal syllogistic reasoning. J. Exp. Psychol. **18**(4), 451–60 (1935)

Schizophrenic Conversations
and Context Shifting

Manuel Rebuschi[1,2,3](✉)

[1] LHSP – Archives Henri-Poincaré (UMR 7117), Nancy, France
[2] MSH Lorraine (USR 3261), Nancy, France
[3] University of Lorraine, Nancy, France
`manuel.rebuschi@univ-lorraine.fr`

Abstract. The present article deals with pathological conversations involving individuals diagnosed as schizophrenic. An interdisciplinary study accounted for discontinuities occurring in such conversations and prior analyses revealed the importance of underspecification. Conversational interpretation and context thus both play crucial roles in schizophrenic discourse. Building on this premise and inspired by previous analyses of fictional discourse, this work presents an experimental analysis of schizophrenic discourse using *pragmatic context*.

Keywords: Schizophrenia · Pathological conversations · Conversational breaks · Natural language semantics · Formal pragmatics · Segmented Discourse Representation Theory (SDRT) · Fiction · Context gaps

1 Introduction

Does it make sense to try to understand "madness"? In severe cases of delirium or acute psychosis associated with schizophrenia, it seems prima facie impossible. People with schizophrenia often appear to deny reality altogether. Apparently illogical thinking supported by delusional, often contradictory beliefs makes rational comprehension inherently difficult. Researchers, and the general public, therefore often rely on external approaches to understanding the pathology by way of, for example, explanations from a third-person perspective.

Without denying the relevance of third-person approaches, I will reject reductionism (whether neurobiological or genetic) and assume that people diagnosed as schizophrenic are *rational*, which by design makes a first-person perspective viable as a means for understanding how they perceive the world.

The present paper builds on a joint interdisciplinary study of pathological conversations between schizophrenic patients and psychologists [1,19,20,25,26]. Research for this study relied on empirical data and several stages of analyses. In a first stage, written transcriptions of recorded conversations were analyzed to identify relevant discontinuities or inconsistencies. These selected excerpts were then formally categorized referencing the semantic and pragmatic framework of the Segmented Discourse Representation Theory (SDRT) [3].

© Springer International Publishing AG 2017
P. Brézillon et al. (Eds.): CONTEXT 2017, LNAI 10257, pp. 708–721, 2017.
DOI: 10.1007/978-3-319-57837-8_56

Linguistic analysis based on SDRT relies on a narrow notion of context I will label *discursive context*, which is a set of accessible possibilities to allow for the continued interpretation of a conversation. Other notions of contexts include general background, presuppositions and attitudes of the interlocutors, or even larger sets of features of the material and social environments [15]. Individuals with schizophrenia, however, sometimes exhibit a tendency to use the discursive context in a deviant manner. This paper explores the hypothesis that context management for schizophrenics represents a more general challenge and perhaps firmer ground for understanding the pathology. The key issues are both formal and conceptual; how do we build formal models of pathological conversations, and will modeling help to further our understanding schizophrenia considered from a more general standpoint.

The paper is structured in three parts. In the first part (Sect. 2), I present the general approach and the main results of the interdisciplinary study mentioned above on pathological conversations. In the second part (Sect. 3), I propose an informal hierarchy comprised of three levels of contexts that can be used for general conversational analysis. In the third part (Sect. 4), I introduce a fourth level, *pragmatic context*. Applied in parallel with semantics of fictional discourse and its use of contexts, this new level may shed new light on our current understanding of schizophrenia.

2 Breaks in Pathological Conversations

Conversations with people diagnosed as schizophrenic can sometimes seem contradictory. This leads to the question: is non-contradiction a necessary precondition for comprehension? Our approach to answering this question relies on the principle of charity. Our linguistic analyses reveal a dual view: we propose to take into account two viewpoints by building two representations of the same conversation, one for each interlocutor [19]. The next issue is then to locate the apparent inconsistencies of the schizophrenic speaker.[1]

2.1 Interpretation and Charity

Is understanding insanity possible? Applying the canons of classical rationality to pronounced cases of schizophrenic delusions seems far-fetched, if not impossible. Characteristics of the disease including denial of reality and contradictory thoughts stemming from delusional beliefs are daunting factors. We would argue, however, that they are not insurmountable and that we should not be content with relying purely on external third-person approaches to understanding the mental processes of people suffering from severe psychosis. We propose that insanity does not definitively exclude rationality on the part of the subject, even if it is a deviant rationality. Consequently, a first-person perspective on such illnesses is defensible.

---

[1] This section is taken from a joint paper with Amblard and Musiol [26]. Those interested by formal or empirical details should refer to this article.

In order to address the question of rationality (and logicality) in schizophrenics, we suggest to assume the principle of charity. Quine [23], and later Davidson [8], have defended the need for the principle of charity in mutual interpretation. The idea is to maximize the truth of others' beliefs, but above all, to assume their consistency, i.e. their logical non-contradiction. The justification of the principle of charity is not only methodological, which is to say that is not exclusively indispensable for interpretation. It is also a conceptual justification in the sense that rationality is here conceived of as constitutive of (the concepts of) true beliefs as well as subjects other attitudes [5].

The issue at this point is what happens when our interlocutors suffer from severe psychosis? Very often, what individuals exhibiting intense psychotic symptoms convey verbally is dismissed as nonsensical, and consequently, is not considered as a reliable basis for any formal analysis of insanity. Indeed, the dominant view on the subject is *reductionist*. According to this viewpoint, insanity should be *fully* explained either by brain dysfunction (neurobiological or genetic reductionism), or by the subconscious (psychoanalytic reductionism). The decided explanation is then constrained to an external *third-person* perspective on the subject. The intended analysis becomes that of causal explanation. If there is a kind of rationalization of insanity via the analysis, the only rationality at work is that of the psychologist. A psychiatrist and a linguist assumed the same hypothesis in their experimental research conducted in the early 1980's [27].

The American philosopher and psychologist Sass [29,30] challenges these reductionist approaches and defends an analysis that takes into account the internal, *first-person* point of view. The issue is not only to explicate but also to *understand* what motivates the 'insane' in terms of *reasons*. This means acknowledging *the subject's rationality* in contrast to what appears in the standard diagnostic criteria in psychiatry.

This first-person approach was seen by Dilthey [10] as the only appropriate option for the "sciences of the mind" (*Geisteswissenschaften*). Let us emphasize that it is perfectly *compatible* with the explanations offered in the third-person perspective by neurobiology and/or genetics, which are dominant in psychiatry. Our intention is neither to verify the value thereof, nor to discuss the classification of psychiatric diseases summarized in the DSM. What we take issue with is *reductionism*. We dispute the idea that the perception of the illness can be fully supported by third-person explanations.

Understanding people suffering from severe psychosis or mental disorders involves adopting to their rationality, which by nature is deviant. The question then becomes, where do we locate such a deviance? When we consider the *rationality* of these individuals, notably those suffering from schizophrenia, we assume, in part, the principle of charity. What consistently emerges from conversations with schizophrenic people is the *apparent* occurrence of contradictions, which manifest in frequent conversational *breaks* or discontinuities. In some cases, these breaks occur at times when the schizophrenic individual gives the *appearance* of accepting (and generating) contradictory judgments. How can we account for this?

2.2   Locating Failures

Locating conversational breaks depends on perspective. From the ordinary speaker's point of view, failures are spontaneously placed in semantics and seen as mere contradictions in the semantic content of their utterances. However, postulating logicality for schizophrenics leads us to take into account their own viewpoints on conversation, where failures must be grounded elsewhere.

In line with other theorists, Sass [29] denies that the *reality-testing deficit*, usually included among the symptoms of schizophrenia, adequately characterizes the thinking of schizophrenic subjects. The reality-testing deficit can act as an obstacle to reality that would result in the production of false and contradictory beliefs. Sass disputes this notion since it brings the deficit to the *content* of mental states, whereas we should consider that the defect involves the *states* themselves. To put it in other words, what is at stake is the mode of presentation of the content rather than the content itself. According to Sass, where we see *beliefs*, the schizophrenic entertains *states* of a type far less committed vis-à-vis reality. For Bonnay and Cozic [5], these are *framework propositions*, a concept which can be approached through Searle's *background capacities* [13, 31].

According to Sass, the mental attitude of schizophrenics is closed to that underlying philosophical solipsism as per Wittgenstein. Let us call *schizo-beliefs* such belief-like attitudes of schizophrenics. The idea is that, far from objectifying the contents of his or her schizo-beliefs, the subject would tend to subjectivize them, that is to say, deny them any genuine status. This is consistent with widespread questioning of perceptions implied by the radical skepticism of solipsism. The delusional thoughts and states resulting from perceptions are treated in the same fashion, as schizo-beliefs rather than beliefs.

How does playing on the container (the type of mental state) allow us to remove contradictions from the content? This is difficult to describe given that schizo-beliefs are characteristic of schizophrenic thinking. They belong to a type of mental state that non-schizophrenics do not have, which explains the difficulty in understanding (e.g. through empathy) schizophrenic subjects. Our proposal is to account for the first-person perspective using third-person methods, in a way similar to Dennett's *heterophenomenology* [9].

Pragmatic Inconsistencies. The strategy we develop for the analysis of conversations is not based on a new classification of mental states.[2] However, we agree with Sass that the problem of schizophrenic thinking, as expressed in conversation, is not a problem of inconsistency of content. We postulate that schizophrenic speakers conform perfectly to classical logic. But we place the deviance of rationality in the *rules of language use*, i.e. in language conventions of rhetorical and pragmatic types. The way contents are structured (for a particular type of mental state in Sass's approach to delusion, by such pragmatic relations in the analysis of pathological conversations we develop) is an essential component of rationality. In short, rationality is not reducible to logicality.

---

[2] But I will come back to Sass's idea in Sect. 4.

Our empirical analyses focus on transcripts of one-on-one conversations between schizophrenic individuals (extraordinary subjects) and a psychologist (ordinary subject). These conversations lead to breaks which are perceived by the ordinary subjects, but not necessarily by the schizophrenic interlocutor causing them. The analysis involves constructing representations of conversations based on the formalism of SDRT. These representations include two levels: semantic representation (i.e. the content of the conversation), and pragmatic representation (i.e. a tree modeling the hierarchical structure of the speech acts that constitute the conversation).

To analyze pathological conversations, we propose the systematic construction of two simultaneous conversational representations, one for each interlocutor. On the schizophrenic's side, according to the principle of charity, there are no semantic contradictions. If there are failures, they occur at the pragmatic level, via violation of SDRT tree construction rules. The situation is different relative to the other side. In the conversations studied, the ordinary speaker is a psychologist asked to continue the interview. She does so in such a way as to repair the conversational structure after a break that would normally cause the interruption of a conversation. We then assume a corresponding postulate according to which the construction of a representation must respect pragmatic constraints. This option causes the appearance of inconsistencies at the semantic level.

The duality of conversational representations reflects the duality of views of the conversation: the schizophrenic subject seems to contradict ordinary subjects, so the conversation works, but the representation of the co-constructed world is inconsistent (in third-person terms). Conversely, because the schizophrenic person's conversational dysfunction is pragmatic in nature, their representation of the world built through the conversation does not suffer from this defect (first-person point of view).

2.3   Formalizing Empirical Data

SDRT combines two levels of analysis in order to account for the interpretive process at work in conversations: semantic content and conversational pragmatics. The first is analyzed via Segmented Discourse Representation Structures (SDRSs) inspired by the DRSs of Discourse Representation Theory (DRT), which is a syntactic construction updated by conversational flow [14]. Conversation also implies pragmatic relations between speech acts, the complexity of which gives rise to a hierarchical structure first described in linguistics in the 1980s [28]. We formalize this structure with the rhetorical relations in SDRT.

The rhetorical structures of SDRT link the actions of speakers and are represented as hierarchical trees with vertical, horizontal and diagonal relations depending on the type under consideration. The tree structure (hierarchical ordering) encodes properties of the discourse and can be used to resolve semantic effects (e.g. prediction of attachment sites or resolution of anaphora). A discourse relation is viewed as a binary relation between speech acts. A narration is thus typically a horizontal relationship (same hierarchical level), as well as the answer to a question, while an elaboration is a vertical relationship (subordinated to what it elaborates on) and a question an oblique relationship (vertical, and thus subordinated, but also horizontal because requiring an answer).

The tree is updated throughout the discourse. Each subsequent intervention by one of the interlocutors is supposed to be related to the conversational representation already built. The structure offers general constraints affecting the attachment sites. The main constraint is the so-called right-frontier constraint, forcing the connection to the nodes located on the right side of the tree.

In order to formalize pathological conversations, we propose two conjectures:

1. Schizophrenics are logically consistent; therefore, conversational breaks occur in the construction process of the pragmatic structure of conversations (i.e., on the rhetorical relationships between SDRSs); and
2. Underspecification (ambiguity) plays a central role in these failures, which could be summarized by the slogan: *A choice is never definitive!*

The first conjecture is nothing but the implementation of the principle of charity. The second conjecture, which is primarily based on empirical observation, is a heuristic for the location of remedial strategies in action by the ordinary speaker. When there is the appearance of discontinuity, the speaker uses the underspecified relations in order to maintain the pragmatic consistency of the dialogue. In other words, the flexibility of underspecified relations enables one to build a conversational representation under any circumstance.

The formalization of conversations is reduced to the elements relevant to our analysis, which means that we abandon anything that does not seem to play a role in explaining the breaks. The representation of semantic content is thus stripped to a minimum, namely to the conversational topic. Each conversational sequence is indeed built around a *theme*, which is the main contextual element relevant to disambiguating the underspecified terms.[3] In ordinary conversations, the conversational theme usually changes after a conventional signal (e.g., "Well, but..." or "Moreover..."), or another form of closure of the current conversational sequence. Maintaining the ongoing theme enables the continuation of a tree, while a theme shift implies a rise through the tree to relate to a dominant node which corresponds to a sequence preceding the exchange.

In order to analyze pathological conversations, we always offer the simultaneous construction of two representations, one for each speaker. For the schizophrenic, the postulate of logicality means that the representation is devoid of contradictions at the semantic level. If there are breakdowns, they operate at the pragmatic level, with a departure from the rules for constructing the SDRT tree. For the ordinary speaker, we assume that the construction of the SDRT tree complies with the pragmatic rules. This option causes the appearance of inconsistencies on the semantic side. According to the "ordinary" subject, the schizophrenic apparently contradicts the dialogical behavior so that the conversation works, but the representation of the co-constructed world is inconsistent.

---

[3] The fact that many ruptures take place around underspecified expressions reinforces our choice to represent the thematic element in the formalization.

Conversely, when we assume dysfunction in a schizophrenic's management of pragmatic relations, the representation of the world built by the conversation does not suffer from this defect.

Analyses of excerpts led us to highlight two transgressions of the standard SDRT rules: *breaks of the right frontier* and *rises through the structure without any acceptable closing* (inconsistency of representation). For the second phenomenon, it is indeed common in corpora to identify items that are used both to close a part of the exchange and to open a new one. But the schizophrenic sometimes does not respect this dual effect and creates an incomplete representation that is not interpretable in a usual way.

Both kinds of transgressions correspond to a problem of management of the discursive context, which in the SDRT framework is constituted by the sites of attachment. Schizophrenic individuals patently shift the context where ordinary people would not, or where the latter would not do so without warning their interlocutor. This is basically a pragmatic inconsistency for it plays at the level of the whole structure of speech acts. Of course, for an interlocutor who sticks to the standard pragmatic rules, the schizophrenic way of conversing appears as semantically inconsistent.

3   Three Levels of Context

As mentioned in the previous section, empirical data collected from pathological conversations with schizophrenic people most often involve a play on ambiguities. Let us give a few examples:[4]

- the polysemy of "dead", alternating between literal and symbolic meanings;
- the polysemy of "lost", alternating between "x is lost" ("I'm lost") and "x lost y" ("I lost my friends");
- indexicals like "here" (underspecification between "here in the room" and "here in hospital")
- over-ambiguisation, with a play on syntax ("provocation" that became "pro-by-vocation").

This puts underspecification at the core of such pathological conversations. It appears that according to schizophrenic people, an interpretative choice is never definitive. There is always the possibility that it will occur again, without warning, whereas for an ordinary speaker it would usually be considered conclusive. Since underspecification resolution depends on contexts at a general level, we can hypothesize that pathological conversations expose a general problem of context management relative to interaction. Of course, this idea is not new and can be related to many analyses according to which schizophrenia is denoted by deficits in context processing (see e.g. [7, 12, 16, 21]).

In the remainder of this section, I will introduce three kinds or levels of context, each of which are likely to play a role in underspecification resolution:

---

[4] For an analysis of these examples, see [2].

1. Discursive context (narrow)
2. Doxastic context (intermediate)
3. Material and social context (large)

This hierarchy of contexts should be considered as a rough guide to make useful distinctions about what arises in discourse and conversation rather than a clear-cut theoretical proposal. As I will argue, a conversational break or an inconsistency may occur as soon as the context is not fully shared between interlocutors. Schizophrenia would then represent a specific case of this general scheme. In the next section, I will introduce a fourth and final level, which will play a specific role in my proposal.

3.1 Discursive Context (Narrow)

The first level under consideration is the most narrow kind of context, labeled as *discursive context*. This is the basic level taken into account in the dynamic analyses of conversations. It consists of the previous steps of a discourse available for further interpretation. Some of its characteristics can be listed:

– discursive context is internal to discourse, i.e. it is a purely linguistic kind of context;
– it can be applied across all the dimensions of discourse, i.e. syntactic, semantic and pragmatic;
– it includes an interactional aspect: a question requires an answer, speech-turns, etc.;
– it contains judgments: representations have a semantic content, or at least a thematic one.

In the theoretical framework of SDRT, this level of context corresponds exactly to the Segmented Discourse Representation Structure (SDRS) currently in progress, to which subsequent language acts can be attached. As such, it offers a number of attachment sites along the right frontier, which are made available to the speakers. This level of context is used to solve anaphora and, in some cases, polysemy and homonymy.

For polysemy and homonymy, underspecified expressions can be disambiguisated by the discursive context in a straightforward manner when the context provides a general theme like in the following example:

Example 1.
a "Max wanted to see the river. He went to the bank."
b "Max needed money. He went to the bank."

For anaphora resolution, a well-known example by Asher and Lascarides [3] is the short discourse:

Example 2. "Max had a lovely evening. He had a great meal. He ate salmon. He ate a lot of cheese. He found *it* really wonderful."

Here the anaphoric pronoun "it" cannot refer to the salmon, but could refer to the cheese, the meal, or the evening. Due to the right-frontier constraint, the sentence "He ate salmon" is indeed no longer available in the discursive context.

3.2   Doxastic Context (Intermediate)

A broader level or kind of context more or less corresponds to what Lewis [18] labeled as *conversational score*. This is the context that makes a language-game possible:

- doxastic context constitutes a *common ground*, i.e. a set of presuppositions shared by the interlocutors, with the beliefs of the speakers about the world and about their interlocutors, etc.;
- it is made up of implicit propositional contents, either common or distributed;
- it presupposes a common social context, or a common form of life in its background.

Doxastic context is pivotal to mutual understanding between speakers. One of its functions is to constrain the thematic possibilities. It enables the interlocutors to solve some cases of homonymy and polysemy.

Thematic constraints obviously appear in different social contexts; an academic will not share the same doxastic context speaking with her colleagues as she would, for example, conversing with an interior decorator. As such, an utterance like the following:

Example 3. "I found a nice paper this morning"

would take on different meanings depending on the context.

To consider another example, speaking about Max's last holidays, and knowing that Max's vacation home is near a river or a lake, interlocutors would accomodate: "He went to the bank", as in Example (1.a) above, even though no explicit link was introduced in previous discourse, thanks to the doxastic context.

3.3   Material and Social Context (Large)

This is the largest kind or level of context. It corresponds to the general background of the conversation, and it is potentially unlimited [15]:

- material and social context can involve locations, immediate physical environment, interlocutors' mutual positions and postures, etc.;
- it includes the social context of the interaction (medical, professional...), the relationships between interlocutors (parents, patients and nursing staff...), cultural environment, etc.;
- it finally includes interlocutors relevant properties: children/adults, pathologies or not, cognitive skills, memory capacities, etc.

This general background context plays a fundamental role in discourse interpretation, both in indirect and direct manners. It partly determines the doxastic context [32] and thus plays an indirect role in interpretation. For instance, conversations with children will involve a set of presuppositions distinctly different from those characteristic of conversations between adults. However, the material context obviously plays a direct role in that it offers the referents of deictics ("this", "that"...) and pure indexicals ("I", "you", "here"...). And some cases of homonymy or of polysemy can be solved using the same level.

4   Schizophrenia and Context Management

It could seem as though the three levels just presented suffice to account for conversations in general and for pathological conversations in particular. Analysis of empirical data shows us that schizophrenic speakers adhere to their own set of rules regarding the discursive context, effectively enabling them to shift the interpretation by discounting the usual rules. But there seems to be another factor at play at the doxastic context level. Do the interlocutors share all of their presuppositions? Perhaps not. It would appear that this relies instead on a more basic level, a pragmatic one, that determines the doxastic context. This pragmatic level may explain some breaks and gaps occurring in conversations with schizophrenics.

4.1   A Fourth Level: The Pragmatic Context (Intermediate)

Our fourth level dermines which *kind of language-game* is played. As I will argue, two interlocutors need not share the same pragmatic context and this gap can lead to subtle effects. Let us briefly present its characteristics:

- the pragmatic context can depend on the social context: a restaurant, a court, a theater... all these social contexts standardly determine specific language-games;
- it determines the kind of speech acts: assertions, pseudo-assertions, avowals, notifications, etc.;
- it determines the kind of mental attitudes expressed by the speakers: beliefs, make-beliefs, commitments, etc.

This level plays two crucial roles: it can shift the whole doxastic context, and as a consequence, can change the resolution of deictics, indexicals, and some cases of homonymy and polysemy.

Pragmatic contexts are theoretically used by philosophers to account for fiction (see Predelli [22], Voltolini [33]). Indeed, since pure indexicals like "I" or "here" are rigid designators, i.e. they denote the same object in every possible world, one cannot explain their use with a mere fictional modality à la Lewis [17]. The idea is then to conceive fictional discourse as being a *context-shifter*. This shifter makes the interlocutors (or the writer and their readers) switch from a serious pragmatic context to a fictional pragmatic context.

As shown here, severeal features of interpretation change as a result of such a switch:

1. the value of indexicals: the fictional speaker referred to by the first-person pronoun "I" is no longer the actual speaker but is instead a fictional narrator;
2. the doxastic context: the presuppositions are now those shared by the fictional characters, and no longer those of the speaker and listeners;
3. the value of deictics, i.e. the interpretation of elements belonging to the material and social context: in the case of fictional context (like theater), one can stage surrounding objects to assign them with a new function.

Pragmatic contexts roughly correspond to Goffman's *frames*, which can be primary or transformed [11]. Pragmatic contexts need not be shared by the interlocutors for the conversation to continue. Simple examples would be speakers lying to trusting listeners, or some cases of fiction telling, e.g. telling stories about Santa Claus to trusting children. The conversation can continue naturally but the gap at the pragmatic level entails a gap at the doxastic level. In both examples, the speaker can continue without expressing personal beliefs, but he or she is interpreted as doing so. Hence, according to the listeners the speaker's assertions broaden the set of common beliefs, which might not necessarily be shared by the speaker.

4.2   From Fiction to Schizophrenia

Switching from a serious to a fictional context implies several fundamental shifts. Basically, there is a change of *language-game* which entails a shift in both speech acts and mental states:

- *speech acts*: assertions are replaced by pretended assertions, questions by pretended questions, etc. (see Walton's [34] conception of *make-believe*);
- *mental states* expressed by our speech acts: beliefs are replaced by pretended beliefs, or even mere *suppositions* (see Whitt [35]).

A general hypothesis can now be proposed using the notion of pragmatic context. Let us assume that there is a *schizophrenic language-game*. This is a specific language-game, which is neither serious, nor fictional, nor poetic, nor humorous – even if it might share several features with all of them. As with any language-game, it involves specific speech acts and mental states:

- *speech acts*: assertions, or at least a part of them, are replaced by *schizo-assertions*, questions by *schizo-questions*, etc.;
- *mental states* expressed by schizophenic speech acts: beliefs (expressed by assertions) are replaced by *schizo-beliefs* (expressed by schizo-assertions).

We can consider schizophrenic speakers as introducing a specific *schizophrenic pragmatic context*, implying a schizophrenic language-game, and in particular schizo-assertions expressing schizo-beliefs. This new pragmatic context potentially allows for a switch to occur relative not only to the material and social context, but to the doxastic context. In conversation processing, it potentially leads to a reinterpretation of indexicals, deictics, homonyms and polysemic terms.

Pathological conversations between ordinary and extraordinary schizophrenic speakers thus introduce a context gap. This gap is similar to that which might occur between the pragmatic context of an actor and the corresponding context of a passer-by with a hidden camera. This is what Goffman labeled *misframing* [11]. The two interlocutors in this case do not play the same language-game, and conversation breaks can occur as general conversational expectations will be mismatched.

This hypothesis could account for several phenomena linked to schizophrenia,[5] like their deviant phenomenology and possible hallucinations [29]. It seems that delusional states associated with schizophrenia do not systematically result in *beliefs* about what is "perceived" by the subject. In many cases, patients behave as though this part of their internal life were private and relatively independent from their public behavior. For instance, they can appear to assert that a princess has entered the room and maintain consistent behavior as they would with the nurse despite their apparent "belief" that she has been replaced by the princess. This would be inconsistent if we were to postulate that every so-called assertion is a genuine one, expressing the speaker's belief. By applying the *schizophrenic pragmatic context*, such situations can be accounted for without denying the subject's consistency.[6]

5 Conclusion

Psycholinguistic and formal approaches to understanding pathological conversations with schizophrenic people can account for conversational discontinuities. These are perceived as genuine contradictions expressed by ordinary interlocutors, which is the third-person viewpoint. Assuming the principle of charity, i.e. if we presuppose that the extraordinary, schizophrenic interlocutors are semantically consistent, effectively brings us closer to being able to reconstruct a first-person viewpoint.

Linguistic modeling sheds light on the major role underspecified phrases play in the context of such breaks. Schizophrenic speakers have the capacity to change the meaning of the same expression multiple times (at least twice, often more) in conversational situations where ordinary speakers would consider the situational context stabilized. This means that for schizophrenic speakers, the context that enables conversational interpretation is not as firmly grounded as it is for other speakers.

In this work, I introduced a distinction between four levels of context with the objective of gaining a more accurate view of the way schizophrenic interlocutors proceed in conversations. The idea of a schizophrenic pragmatic context provides an explanation of some specificities in terms of a specific language-game, which present several similarities with fictional discourse. Moreover, it explains the occurrence of shifts between interlocutors in terms of context gaps. Finally, in terms of contexts and context gaps, applying this new pragmatic context may

---

[5] It is of course not claimed here that schizophrenia could in some way be *reduced* to an impairment in context processing. However, pragmatic contexts offer an insight into conversation analysis that might be translated to other phenomena.

[6] Other strange cases like depersonalization [6] or Cotard's syndrome [4] could be accommodated with the same kind of analysis. These cases are paradoxical from a semantic point of view since the first-person pronoun is still expected to refer even though the speaker believes he or she does not exist. However, this semantic puzzle is not far from those generated by anti-substantialist accounts of the subject, and can be solved using context shifters [24].

enable us to draw relevant connections between psycholinguistic analyses and phenomenological accounts of schizophrenia.

References

1. Amblard, M., Musiol, M., Rebuschi, M.: Une analyse basée sur la S-DRT pour la modélisation de dialogues pathologiques. In: Actes de la 18e conférence sur le Traitement Automatique des Langues Naturelles - TALN (2011)
2. Amblard, M., Musiol, M., Rebuschi, M.: L'interaction conversationnelle l'épreuve du handicapschizophrénique. Recherches sur la philosophie et le langage **31**, 67–89 (2015)
3. Asher, N., Lascarides, A.: Logics of Conversation. Cambridge University Press, Cambridge (2003)
4. Billon, A.: Why are we certain that we exist? Philos. Phenomenol. Res. **91**(3), 723–759 (2015)
5. Bonnay, D., Cozic, M.: Principe de charité et sciences de l'homme. In: Martin, T. (ed.) Les sciences humaines sont-elles des sciences? Vuibert, Paris (2011)
6. Chauvier, S.: Auto-cognition défaillante ou subjectivation déviante. L'Évolution Psychiatr. **74**, 353–362 (2009)
7. Cohen, J.D., Barch, D.M., Carter, C., Servan-Schreiber, D.: Context-processing deficits in schizophrenia: converging evidence from three theoretically motivated cognitive tasks. J. Abnorm. Psychol. **108**(1), 120–133 (1999)
8. Davidson, D.: Mental events. In: Essays on Actions and Events, chap. 20, pp. 137–149 (1980)
9. Dennett, D.: Consciousness Explained. Little, Brown and Company, Boston, New York (1991)
10. Dilthey, W.: Introduction to the Human Sciences. Selected Works, vol. 1. Princeton University Press, Princeton (1989)
11. Goffman, E.: Frame Analysis: An Essay on the Organization of Experience. Harper and Row, New York (1974)
12. Green, M.J., Uhlhaas, P.J., Coltheart, M.: Context processing and social cognition in schizophrenia. Curr. Psychiatry Rev. **1**(1), 11–22 (2005)
13. Henriksen, M.G.: On incomprehensibility in schizophrenia. Phenomenol. Cogn. Sci. **12**(1), 105–129 (2013)
14. Kamp, H., Reyle, U.: From Discourse to Logic: Introduction to Model Theoretic Semantics of Natural Language, Formal Logic and Discourse Representation Theory. Studies in Linguistics and Philosophy. Kluwer Academic, Dordrecht (1993)
15. Kleiber, G.: D'un contexte à l'autre: aspects et dimensions du contexte. L'Information Gramm. **123**, 17–32 (2009)
16. Leroy, F., Beaune, D.: Langage et schizophrénie: intention, contexte et pseudo-concepts. Bull. de Psychol. **479**, 567–577 (2005)
17. Lewis, D.: Truth in fiction. Am. Philos. Q. **15**(1), 37–46 (1978)
18. Lewis, D.: Scorekeeping in a language game. J. Philos. Logic **8**, 338–359 (1979)
19. Musiol, M., Rebuschi, M.: La rationalité de l'incohérence en conversation schizophrène (analyse pragmatique conversationnelle et sémantique formelle). Psychol. française **52**(2), 137–169 (2007)
20. Musiol, M., Rebuschi, M.: Toward a two-step formalization of verbal interaction in schizophrenia: a case study. In: Trognon, A., Batt, M., Caelen, J., Vernant, D. (eds.) Logical Properties of Dialogue, pp. 187–225. PUN, Nancy (2011)

21. Phillips, W.A., Silverstein, S.M.: Convergence of biological and psychological perspectives on cognitive coordination in schizophrenia. Behav. Brain Sci. **26**(1), 65–138 (2003)
22. Predelli, S.: I am not here now. Analysis **58**, 107–115 (1998)
23. Quine, W.V.O.: Word and Object. The MIT Press, Cambridge (1960)
24. Rebuschi, M.: Le cogito sans engagement. Igitur **3**(2), 1–25 (2011)
25. Rebuschi, M., Amblard, M., Musiol, M.: Schizophrénie, logicité et compréhension en première personne. L'Evolution Psychiatr. **78**(1), 127–141 (2013)
26. Rebuschi, M., Amblard, M., Musiol, M.: Using SDRT to analyze pathological conversations: logicality, rationality and pragmatic deviances. In: Rebuschi, M., Batt, M., Heinzmann, G., Lihoreau, F., Musiol, M., Trognon, A. (eds.) Interdisciplinary Works in Logic, Epistemology, vol. 3, pp. 343–368. Psychology and Linguistics. Springer, Dordrecht (2014). doi:10.1007/978-3-319-03044-9_15
27. Rochester, S., Martin, J.: Crazy Talk. A Study of the Discourse of Schizophrenic Speakers. Plenum Press, London (1979)
28. Roulet, E., Auchlin, A., Schelling, M., Moeschler, J., Rubattel, C.: L'articulation du discours en français contemporain. Peter Lang, Berne (1985)
29. Sass, L.A.: The Paradoxes of Delusion: Wittgenstein, Schreber, and the Schizophrenic Mind. Cornell, New York (1994)
30. Sass, L.A.: Incomprehensibility and understanding: on the interpretation of severe mental illness. Philos. Psychiatry Psychol. **10**(2), 125–132 (2003)
31. Searle, J.R.: The Rediscovery of the Mind. The MIT Press, Cambridge (1992)
32. Van Dijk, T.A.: Discourse, context and cognition. Discourse Stud. **8**(1), 159–177 (2006)
33. Voltolini, A.: Fiction as a base of interpretation contexts. Synthese **153**, 23–47 (2006)
34. Walton, K.L.: Mimesis as Make-Believe. On the Foundations of the Representational Arts. Harvard University Press, Harvard (1990)
35. Whitt, L.A.: Fictional contexts and referential opacity. Can. J. Philos. **15**–**2**, 327–338 (1985)

Author Index